The Jews from Ancient Canaan to a Global Culture

This accessibly written volume examines the major periods of Jewish history around the world, from the Jews' distant origins in antiquity through the beginnings of the modern period and the emergence of secular culture.

Although Jews are a small minority, they have settled in almost every part of the world, developing many different subcultures. They have had an outsized impact on global religion even as they have faced prejudice and persecution, and their history makes for a fascinating story of cultural change, adaptation, and survival that is continuing to unfold in the present. Now in a new edition as a split volume, this first volume of a comprehensive history of the Jews draws on up-to-date research to recount the story of the Jews from their beginnings in the ancient Near East through to the dawn of the modern period and the emergence of secular culture. Enhanced by images, limelight given to various historical mysteries, recommendations for how to learn more, as well as other features, the book moves chapter by chapter through the major periods of Jewish history, balancing introductions for those unfamiliar with that history with discussion of new approaches and recent discoveries that have reshaped understanding of the Jewish past.

The book is useful not just for those interested in the Jews themselves but also for readers open to learning about global history from the vantage point of a people whose experiences attest both to the resilience of human culture and to the impact of hate and violence.

Matthias B. Lehmann is Professor of Jewish History at the University of Cologne, where he directs the Martin Buber Institute for Jewish Studies. His publications include *The Baron: Maurice de Hirsch and the Jewish Nineteenth Century* (2022), *Emissaries from the Holy Land* (2014), and the coedited volume *Jews and the Mediterranean* (2020).

Steven Weitzman is a scholar of ancient Judaism and serves at the University of Pennsylvania as Abraham M. Ellis Professor of Hebrew and Semitic Languages and Literatures and as Ella Darivoff Director of the Herbert D. Katz Center for Advanced Judaic Studies. His publications include *The Origin of the Jews: The Quest for Roots in a Rootless Age* (2017), awarded the National Jewish Book Award, and the soon-to-appear *Disasters of Biblical Proportions: The Ten Plagues Then, Now and at the End of the World* (2026).

The Jews from Ancient Canaan to a Global Culture

Matthias B. Lehmann
University of Cologne

Steven Weitzman
University of Pennsylvania

FOURTH EDITION

Routledge
Taylor & Francis Group
NEW YORK AND LONDON

Designed cover image: Moses presents the Ten Commandments to the Jews. Illustration from the Sarajevo Haggadah. A 14th century Jewish manuscript illustration and a Catalonian masterpiece, created in Barcelona, circa 1350, for a prominent Jewish family. World History Archive/Alamy Stock Photo

Fourth edition published 2025
by Routledge
605 Third Avenue, New York, NY 10158

and by Routledge
4 Park Square, Milton Park, Abingdon, Oxon OX14 4RN

Routledge is an imprint of the Taylor & Francis Group, an informa business

First edition published by Pearson Education Inc, 2009
Third edition published by Routledge, 2019

Library of Congress Cataloging-in-Publication Data
Names: Lehmann, Matthias B., 1970- author. | Efron, John M. Jews. | Weitzman, Steven, 1965– author.
Title: The Jews from ancient Canaan to a global culture / Matthias B. Lehmann and Steven Weitzman.
Description: Fourth edition. | Abingdon, Oxon ; New York, NY : Routledge, 2025. | "This book is part of a two-volume work, "The Jews: a History," first published as a single volume in 2009."—Introduction. | Includes bibliographical references and index.
Identifiers: LCCN 2024058516 (print) | LCCN 2024058517 (ebook) | ISBN 9781041007807 (hbk) | ISBN 9781041008026 (pbk) | ISBN 9781003611592 (ebk)
Subjects: LCSH: Jews—History. | Judaism—History.
Classification: LCC DS117 .L43 2025 (print) | LCC DS117 (ebook) | DDC 909/.04924—dc23/eng/20250219
LC record available at https://lccn.loc.gov/2024058516
LC ebook record available at https://lccn.loc.gov/2024058517

ISBN: 978-1-041-00780-7 (hbk)
ISBN: 978-1-041-00802-6 (pbk)
ISBN: 978-1-003-61159-2 (ebk)

DOI: 10.4324/9781003611592

Typeset in Minion Pro
by Apex CoVantage, LLC

CONTENTS

FIGURES

MAPS

Introduction to Volume 1

From Ancient Canaan to a Global Culture

This book is part of a two-volume work, *The Jews: A History*, first published as a single volume in 2009. Each of the previous three editions reflects our evolving sense as scholars and teachers of Jewish studies of how to convey Jewish history to an audience that we envisioned including students as well as general readers. Beyond distilling the Jewish past into a single readable narrative, we wanted from the beginning to highlight historical scholarship as an open-ended inquiry, and that led us in each edition to incorporate new questions, new approaches to history, and new findings. The volumes, if read carefully, also reflect our personal development as scholars living in a world that has seen profound social, cultural, and political changes ever since the third edition, both globally and within Jewish communities. The process of revision continues in the fourth edition, which was composed in the shadow of the Covid pandemic; a war in Ukraine, once a major center of Jewish life; political and social divisions within Israel over the future direction of its political governance; the trauma and violence unleashed by the Hamas attack of October 7, 2023; anti-Israel protests and counterprotests on campuses in the United States and elsewhere; and a resurgence of antisemitism that is both old and new at that time, picking up on stereotypes from earlier eras even as it spread in new ways by social media.

In this present edition, the most obvious change is that we have decided to divide the history into two volumes, one devoted to the premodern period, written by Steven Weitzman and Matthias B. Lehmann, the other to the modern period, composed by John Efron. The main reason for this was practical. From the beginning, we have had the ambition not just to recount Jewish history but to introduce some of the challenges of retrieving and reconstructing Jewish history, including in our narrative discussion of the sources, written material, and now even genetic data, and the challenges of drawing insight from them. Historical scholarship in recent decades has also gotten more and more capacious in terms of how it defines its subject, expanding its focus beyond male elites to try to gain insight into the lives of people with different genders and from various social and economic backgrounds, and we wanted to expand our narrative accordingly. With this edition, we have finally accepted that it is not possible to encompass it all within a single book and have divided it in two with the aim of making its story more digestible for readers.

The focus of this first volume is premodern Jewish history, a history that begins with the ancient Israelites and the biblical sources that record their experiences and traces the history of their descendants in a period that encompasses what historians refer to as Late Antiquity, the Middle Ages, and the "early modern" era of Jewish history to the end of the seventeenth century. During much of this period, the people that we now refer to in English

DOI: 10.4324/9781003611592-1

as the Jews found themselves living under various foreign powers, including the Roman Empire, before and after its Christianization; the Parthian and Sassanian kingdoms, based in Persia; the Islamic caliphates and empires that ruled over the Middle East, parts of Africa, and southern Europe; and the various Christian kingdoms and states that developed in medieval and early modern Europe. The first volume recounts the history of the Jews throughout this period, beginning with their Israelite ancestors in Iron Age Canaan and tracing the experience of their descendants to around 1700, the beginning of the modern period.

The second volume picks up about 300 years ago and extends to the present, relating a period of dramatic, disruptive change that includes Jewish migration to the Western Hemisphere, the rise of secularized forms of Jewish culture, the emergence of Zionism, the rise of Nazism and the genocidal violence of the Holocaust, and the establishment of the State of Israel, among other developments. We make no pretense to being exhaustive—the field of Jewish studies has generated tens of thousands of volumes of scholarship, and new research is being published all the time—and no doubt, other scholars with different backgrounds and sensibilities would relate history in a different way. Our original ambition, however, was to concentrate into a single narrative a deeper, richer, and more up-to-date account than one could find in earlier histories of the Jews used in college classes, and the two volumes of the fourth edition, each designed to fit more easily within a semester, build on that effort in a way we intend to be newly useful.

The way we have divided the two volumes creates the impression that modernity is the single most important turning point in Jewish history. In many respects, it is. The two most populous centers of Jewish life today—the United States and the State of Israel—are relatively recent societies that emerged in the period covered by the second volume: The United States will be celebrating 250 years of existence in 2026, while modern Israel has its origins in a political movement, Zionism, that goes back to the late nineteenth century. Jewish religious life, even as practiced in secluded communities, has been shaped by the encounter with modern life, though sometimes in conscious reaction against it, and secular Jewish identity—based not on religious belief but on ethnic or cultural affiliation—is also a modern development of recent centuries.

While the division of these volumes reinforces this sense of a sharp divide between premodern and modern Jewish history, we urge the reader to avoid thinking of the two volumes as a before-and-after. For one thing, there are a lot of continuities in Jewish culture and society that transcend the differences between the premodern and the modern: There is still no understanding the history of the Jews in a scholarly sense without understanding the prehistory of Jewish culture in the Israelite society that developed in ancient Canaan or without knowing how Jewish thought and behavior were subsequently impacted by interactions with Greek pagan culture, Roman imperialism, Christianity, Zoroastrianism, and Islam. Modernity is indeed a major turning point in Jewish history, but by reading both volumes, the reader will be in a better position to see that modernization itself followed from—and indeed depended upon—many earlier transformations in Jewish life going back to its very beginnings in distant antiquity.

When we first set out to write this book in the early 2000s, we did so in a world already being reshaped by the internet, but at that early point, we never imagined a world overrun by an "infodemic," the overwhelming flood of false or misleading information that has made it all the more difficult to distinguish the true from the false. This flood is certainly having an impact on how people perceive the Jews, as was the case with Covid, where in Great Britain, for example, a survey found that a fifth of the population agreed with the antisemitic conspiracy theory that Jews had spread the virus to collapse the economy for financial gain.[1] The same technological and social changes have also made available many new resources for understanding Jewish history, including electronic access to digitized versions of primary documents, translations, and reference works, but that kind of progress has not necessarily translated into a better understanding of Jewish history. Another recent survey offers a disturbing example, finding major shortcomings in what Americans know about the Holocaust. Over 40,000 concentration camps and ghettos were established in Europe during World War II, and yet 80 years later, nearly half of the respondents could not name a single one; and the same survey found that among adults under the age of 40, one in ten had not even heard the word "Holocaust" before.[2]

Academic scholars of Jewish studies once had the ambition to counteract antisemitism and to reshape Jewish life for the better. Over the two centuries of its existence, it can count many new discoveries and important insights, but it simply does not have the reach and influence to fact-check and counteract all the misinformation now circulating on the internet—not globally and not even among Jews; and such research can sometimes be very frustrating because it does not always answer people's questions in a clear-cut way. Nevertheless, for those with the time and curiosity to deepen their knowledge, there is much to learn from the academic study of Jewish history, and not just about the Jews, but about humanity in general, because Jews have inhabited so many different parts of the world, have interacted with so many other peoples, and have participated in so many important social and cultural changes. We hope the two volumes of this history will help readers position Jewish experience as part of this larger global story.

Notes

1 Daniel Allington, David Hirsh and Louise Katz, "Correlation between coronavirus conspiracism and antisemitism: a cross-sectional study in the United Kingdom," *Scientific Reports* 13, 21104 (2023). https://doi.org/10.1038/s41598-023-41794-y.

2 Claims Conference, "First-Ever 50-State Survey on Holocaust Knowledge of American Millennials and Gen. Z Reveals Shocking Results." https://www.claimscon.org/millennial<ApexURLHyphen/>study/.

CHAPTER 1

Ancient Israel and Other Ancestors

In contemporary English, the phrase "ancient history" can signify a part of the past that does not feel relevant or important anymore. For many people around the world, however, ancient history feels all too relevant, and a painful case in point is the role of ancient Jewish history in the conflict between Israelis and Palestinians.

There are many factors driving the conflict between Israel and the Palestinians, which we will address in the second volume of this history, but one point of contention in this conflict is worth mentioning now because it involves ancient history: the question of who is more original to the land. Tracing their ancestry to the people of Israel depicted in the Bible, many Jews feel a deep emotional and spiritual attachment to the land of Israel based on the strongly held belief that it was their homeland before they were exiled by foreign oppressors. Jews were not the first inhabitants of the land, even according to Jewish tradition (the Bible acknowledges there were people there before the Israelites arrived), but they have long understood their origin to go back to the Israelites settled there in biblical times thousands of years ago, and they can now support this belief with archaeological evidence of Israelite or Jewish presence in the land going back to antiquity. Some (by no means all) Palestinian scholars have contested this history, however, countering that Jews are modern colonizers who have invented history in order to justify taking the land from its indigenous population. The Israeli–Palestinian conflict is not just about ownership of land, in other words; it is also about what happened in "ancient history."

We begin with this example for two reasons: (1) It demonstrates the continued relevance of ancient Jewish history, how it continues to loom large in how Jews—and Palestinians, for that matter—understand their identity, and (2) because it illustrates what makes it difficult to start a history of the Jews—the origin of the Jews has become such a politically charged topic that not everyone even agrees that their history begins in antiquity, no matter what the evidence shows.

And this is only one way that the ancient history of the Jews feels relevant for people today. Christians don't trace their ancestry directly back to Abraham and Moses in the way that Jews do, but they see them as spiritual ancestors, key figures in the relationship between humanity and God that has led to Jesus. Turning to Islam, the Qur'an, the history of the ancient Israelites, is equally important; Moses alone is mentioned 136 times in the Qur'an, and other figures known from the Bible are prominent there, too, as prophetic predecessors to Muhammad—Abraham, David, Solomon. In a similar way, there is no understanding Jewish religion and culture as these exist today without understanding what Jews have inherited from their ancient Israelite ancestors—the sacred texts included in the Bible itself, the centrality of Jerusalem, the concept of exile, and the importance

DOI: 10.4324/9781003611592-2

of the Hebrew language. The relevance of ancient Jewish history for religious and political identity is the major reason people are motivated to study it to begin with. However, the present-day stakes of ancient Jewish history—of how the Jews came to be—can make it difficult to be open to what scholars have learned about that history, especially if their conclusions are at odds with what one already believes.

Our goal in this chapter is not to challenge or to affirm the reader's identity or personal beliefs; we simply want to offer a sense of what modern scholarship has learned or theorized about ancient Jewish history. We know more about that history than we do for a lot of ancient peoples—99+ percent of the history of the human species over the last 200,000–300,000 years has not been recorded and is lost forever. However, the information we have to work with does not amount to very much: For ancient Israelite history prior to around 300 BCE, we have the Hebrew Bible, some testimonies in other written sources, and archaeological evidence of settlements that have been connected to the ancient Israelites, and that leaves many gaps in our understanding. Still, scholars have gained some insights into the ancient Israelites beyond what we are told about them in the Bible, and we seek to squeeze some of that insight into a single chapter. Like all historians, we have our share of biases and blind spots, but the recommended readings at the end of this (and every chapter) will not only give you more information than we can offer here but also expose you to other perspectives on how to interpret the evidence.

An example of how scholars reconstruct ancient Jewish history in different ways emerges from the question of how and when to begin such a history. Jews have long traced their origin to the Five Books of Moses in the Bible, to the story of Abraham and Sarah and their descendants, the Exodus from Egypt, and the revelation at Mount Sinai. We suspect that this is where many readers would expect a book like this to begin, and one has to admit that stories like those told in Genesis and Exodus make for a very compelling opening, one of the most memorable origin stories ever told. But there are some complications that prevent us from simply beginning in this way, including scholarly skepticism about the Bible as a source of historical information.

Over the last few centuries, as European society began to question long-held religious beliefs, scholars likewise came to question the traditional account that traces the Jews back to the people and events described in the Bible, just as scientists came to question the Bible's explanation of how the world began. In the place of the biblical account in the Bible, scholarship went on to develop alternative reconstructions of ancient Jewish history, some directly at odds with what Jews and Christians had long believed about the world. Since our goal in this book is to share the fruits of modern historical research, should we not begin with these scholarly accounts? Perhaps, but that then leads to another complication: Scholars do not agree among themselves about how the Jews originated. They have been successful in raising doubts about the stories of Abraham, Moses, and David—thanks to modern historical and archaeological research, we can no longer be certain that such figures even existed—but they have not settled on an alternative understanding of how the Jews originated. We have to struggle not only with how little we know about ancient Jewish history but also with how many possible ways there are to understand that history.

Consider how difficult it is to resolve *when* Jewish history starts. Before we can begin recounting the history of the Jewish people, we must obviously decide when exactly to begin it, and it is not easy to commit oneself to a particular date or even a century as a starting point. As we have noted, Jews themselves have long believed their history begins with Abraham's sojourn to the land of Canaan and the Exodus from Egypt, but we do not know when these events occurred, if they occurred at all, and there are other problems as well. The people described in much of the Bible do not call themselves Jews, but Israelites, or the "sons of Israel," to be more precise, and their culture and religion differ from that of later Jews in many ways. Perhaps the beginning of Jewish history should be placed at the point at which the ancient Israelites become the Jews, but when exactly does that transformation take place? Many scholars place it at the end of the period described by the Hebrew Bible, in the wake of the Babylonian Exile in 586 BCE. Some place it even later, after the conquests of Alexander the Great in the fourth century BCE, and some still later, in the age of Roman rule and the ascendancy of Christianity. Depending on which account you happen to read, the story of the Jews begins 4,000 years ago in the Middle Bronze Age, or 2,000 years ago in the same age that produced Christianity, and some would go so far as to argue that we cannot really speak of "the Jews"—as opposed to the Israelites or the ancient Judeans—until medieval or modern times.

Why is it so hard to fix a clear starting point for Jewish history? One reason is that we simply do not have a lot of evidence for the earliest periods of Jewish history, but that is not the only complication. Another is that scholars do not agree about what *Jewish* means exactly and how it relates to or differs from overlapping terms used in the Bible, such as *Israelite* and *Hebrew*. The term *Jew* derives from the name "Judah," or *Yehuda*, but even in the Hebrew Bible, that term has several possible meanings, referring to an Israelite tribe, to a territory in the southern part of Canaan, and also to the kingdom based in this territory and ruled by David and his descendants. After the end of the biblical period, the terms translated as *Judean* and *Jewish* acquired still other connotations, signifying a particular way of life or adherence to particular beliefs. The term's ambiguity continues to this day, with *Jewish* signifying a religion for some, for others a cultural or ethnic identity that may not be religious in orientation, and for still others a national identity, such as French, Turkish, or American. To fix a single starting point for "Jewish" history would commit us to a specific definition of *Jewishness* at the expense of other definitions that also have merit.

Still, we must begin somewhere, and this book has opted to begin where Jews themselves have long looked to understand their origins—with "history" as described in the Hebrew Bible. We put the word *history* in quotes here because it is not clear that the biblical account corresponds to what counts as history for a historian, the past as it actually happened. Modern scholarship has expressed doubts about the Hebrew Bible's value as a historical document, questioning whether the people described in the Bible, such as Moses, really existed and whether key events, such as the Exodus and the revelation at Mount Sinai, really occurred. The skepticism of scholars has alienated some Jews and Christians who believe in the Bible as an accurate account of how reality works, but the reasons for this skepticism cannot be dismissed out of hand if one is willing to approach the evidence with an open mind. Mindful of what modern scholarship has concluded about the Bible, we seek in this chapter to open the question of what really happened, to ask whether the biblical account of Israel's history—its stories of Abraham and his family, the Exodus from Egypt, Joshua's conquest of the land of Canaan, the rule of King David—corresponds to the past as reconstructed by historians and archaeologists.

Even as we question the biblical account, however, we will also try to provide a sense of how it tells the story of ancient Israel because, regardless of whether that story corresponds to what actually happened, it is crucial for understanding the development of Jewish culture. For one thing, Jewish culture did not suddenly appear one day; it evolved out of an earlier Israelite culture from which it inherited beliefs about the nature of reality, ritual practices, language(s), texts, patterns of social organization, and memories of where it came from. Why do Jews worship a God who they believe liberated their ancestors from slavery? Why are Canaan and Jerusalem so central in Jewish culture? What are the origins of Jewish practices such as circumcision, resting on the Sabbath, and keeping kosher? Why is Hebrew such an important language in Jewish culture? These questions cannot be answered without referring to pre-Jewish Israelite culture, and biblical literature is our richest source for understanding that culture.

A second reason for beginning with the Bible is that the *perception* of the Bible as the starting point for Jewish history is a historical fact in its own right and an important one for understanding Jewish identity. For the last 2,000 years at least, Jews have looked to the Hebrew Bible to understand who they are and how they are to behave. To this day, in fact, many Jews trace their lineage back to patriarchs such as Abraham and Jacob; during Passover, they recount the Exodus as if in Egypt themselves, and many look forward to the coming of a messiah from the line of King David. We are speaking here of religious Jews, but even secularized Jews—Jews who are not animated by faith in God and do not see their identity as a religious one—can look to the Bible to understand themselves or draw on it as a source for poetry, art, and other forms of cultural expression. Even if the Bible had no value whatsoever as a historical source (and we will see that it actually has great value as such a source), it is important to know what it says about the past, if only to understand how Jews throughout the centuries have seen themselves.

Keeping these points in mind, we have settled on not one but two starting points for Jewish history. The first is ancient Israelite history prior to the Babylonian Exile in 586 BCE. Where did the Israelites come from, and what is the historical connection between them and later Jews? The present chapter will attempt to answer these questions by drawing on the Hebrew Bible, but its testimony will not be sufficient by itself, since according to modern scholarship, its account is questionable, concealing the true origins of the ancient Israelites. What this chapter introduces, therefore, is ancient Israelite history as *reconstructed* by biblical scholars, their best attempt to explain the genesis of the ancient Israelites within the context of what is known about history from other ancient Near Eastern sources and archaeological excavation.

Our second starting point, and the focus of Chapter 2, is the emergence of the Hebrew Bible itself: Where does biblical literature come from, and how did it become so important to Jewish culture? It is no easier to answer these questions than it is to reconstruct ancient Israelite history, for there remains much uncertainty about who wrote the texts included in the Hebrew Bible and when and why they were written. It is also unclear when these texts acquired the resonance and authority they would enjoy in later Jewish culture. Despite the many gaps in our knowledge, however, there is evidence to suggest that the emergence of the Bible marks a watershed moment in the transition from Israelite to Jewish culture; indeed, we will argue that the formation of Jewishness and the formation of the Hebrew Bible are inextricably intertwined.

Searching for Israel's Origins

For modern secular scholars who approach the Bible as a text composed by humans, there is nothing inherently wrong with challenging its testimony as an historical source, and there can be good reason for doing so. Consider a story that may already be familiar to you—the Bible's account of how David defeated the Philistine Goliath:

> A warrior came out of the Philistines' camp, Goliath by name, from Gath, whose height was six cubits and a span. He had a helmet of bronze on his head, and was armed with a coat of mail; the weight of the coat was five thousand bronze shekels. He had greaves of bronze on his legs and a javelin of bronze slung between his shoulders. The shaft of his spear was like a weaver's beam, and his spear's head weighed six hundred shekels of iron.

BCE AND CE: THE RELIGIOUS BACKGROUND OF HOW WE THINK ABOUT HISTORY

As is true of history books in general, this volume employs the abbreviations BCE and CE to help date events in the past, especially the ancient past, but their use to understand Jewish history in particular raises some issues worth thinking about.

There is something ironic about applying the abbreviations BCE (before the Common Era) and CE (of the Common Era) to the Jews: Both terms are tied to a Christian conception of time. CE is a modern equivalent to AD, *anno domini*—"the year of our Lord," namely, the year of Jesus's birth. The idea of dating history in relation to the year of Jesus's birth was first developed in the sixth century CE by a Christian monk named Dionysius Exiguus, and we do not know how he was able to calculate the year of Jesus's birth, though scholars think he wasn't far off (many scholars think that Jesus was probably born sometime between 6 and 4 BCE). Historians developed the abbreviation BC, "before Christ," more recently, in the seventeenth and eighteenth centuries, counting backward from 1 BC (there is no year 0) in order to encompass their growing understanding of events that took place before the onset of Christianity. AD and BC were later changed to CE and BCE, "of the Common Era" and "before the Common Era," not originally to purge them of their religious association with Jesus, but to indicate dates common to all humanity, Christian and non-Christian. To use dates like 586 BCE or 70 CE to describe Jewish history is thus to frame it in terms of a calendar introduced by another religious community.

For their part, Jews have long used their own calendar, which counts from the creation of the world as dated in Jewish tradition. The origins of this calendar are obscure, but the use of Creation as a starting point seems to have been embraced by Jewish communities by the tenth or eleventh century CE, perhaps as a reaction against the growing influence of the Christian calendar, and is still in use to this day (as I write this sentence, in 2025 it is the year 5785 according to the Jewish calendar). While the application of the abbreviations BCE and CE to Jewish history has scholarly value, allowing historians to situate the history of the Jews within a broader history of humanity, the use of this chronological framework is also a reminder that the way scholars think about the past is shaped by the Christian European context in which the academic field of historical research arose.

> As the Philistine drew near to David, David rushed toward the battle line toward the Philistine. David put his hand in his bag, took from there a stone, slung it, and struck the Philistine on his forehead. The stone sank into his forehead, and he fell face down on the ground. So David triumphed over the Philistine with a sling and a stone.
>
> (1 Samuel 17:4–7, 48–50)

For thousands of years, people have accepted this story as true, but is it true in a historical sense? Did David really fight such a battle? Did he win in the way that this episode suggests? Underdogs do occasionally prevail in real life, so the improbability of David's victory isn't enough reason to reject the story. There is, however, at least one specific reason for skepticism: another reference to the defeat of Goliath tucked away elsewhere in the Bible that attributes the giant's defeat to someone else:

> There was another battle with the Philistines at Gob; and Elhanan son of Jaareoregim, the Bethlehemite, struck Goliath the Gittite, the shaft of whose spear was like a weaver's beam.
>
> (2 Samuel 21:19)

Goliath is still the enemy here, described the same way as in the more famous version of the story (cf. 1 Samuel 17:7: "the shaft of his spear was like a weaver's beam"). The hero who slays Goliath is not the young shepherd David, however, but an otherwise obscure warrior named Elhanan. Interpreters have long recognized this problem and tried to reconcile the discrepancy by suggesting that Elhanan was another name for David, but this solution ignores the Bible's claim that David and Elhanan were two different people, a king and his servant. Yet a third reference to this battle in the Bible—this time in a narrative called Chronicles—tries to solve the problem by claiming that David killed Goliath while Elhanan killed Goliath's brother (1 Chronicles 20:5), but Chronicles was written much later than 1–2 Samuel by an author trying to resolve the contradictions that he found in these earlier sources, and his solution, too, is rather contrived. Scholars have therefore proposed another possibility: Perhaps there is no way to reconcile the discrepancy. One or the other of the two accounts is wrong about who killed Goliath,

Which of these accounts is more reliable is an open question, but it seems more likely, given how the biographies of important political figures often become embellished over time, that it is 2 Samuel 21 that records the name of the real slayer of Goliath—David, but the long-forgotten Elhanan, and that the more famous version of the story in 1 Samuel 17 is a later development, an attempt to boost King David's heroic image by giving him the credit for another man's victory. Based on the evidence we have available to us, in other words, the battle of David and Goliath as depicted in the Bible, while making for a memorable story, likely isn't an accurate reflection of the past as it actually unfolded.

Modern scholars raise such possibilities not because they want to undermine people's religious beliefs but because they are committed to a particular way of knowing reality that bases itself not on faith—on what people have long believed to be true—but on empirical evidence, unfettered questioning, and reasoned explanation. Like judges in a trial, the modern scholar wants to hear from multiple witnesses and to cross-examine them about how they know what they claim to know, before rendering a judgment about what happened. This is how scholars approach history in general, and applying the same basic approach to the Bible has led scholars to challenge much of what the Bible says about history, and not just particular episodes, like David's victory over Goliath, but also sometimes even more basic claims—that David did any of the things attributed to him in 1–2 Samuel, for instance, or even that there was a King David.

From the perspective of modern historical scholarship, what the Hebrew Bible says about the past becomes much more credible when other witnesses can back up its testimony, when one can point to other independent sources that can provide corroboration. Since we are not talking about witnesses in a literal sense, what we mean here is corroboration provided by (1) written testimony composed independently of the Bible and/or (2) the discipline of archaeology, the retrieval and interpretation of physical evidence generated by the activities of earlier humans. The written testimony at our disposal includes inscriptions from Israel itself and texts from other ancient Near Eastern cultures that refer to Israel. The archaeological evidence consists of pottery, the remnants of buildings, tools, weapons, jewelry, and so forth. The written evidence can tell us what people thought and how they expressed themselves and sometimes responds to specific historical events. The archaeological evidence can shed light on what people did—the food they ate, the work they did, the battles they fought, the dead they buried. Sometimes, all this evidence confirms what the Bible says about history, and it certainly links it to the geography, language, and culture of the broader ancient Near East, but frequently, it challenges our sense of what really happened or speaks to aspects of Israel's history simply not reflected in biblical literature.

Secular biblical scholarship today is marked by a lively, sometimes heated debate about what really happened in Israelite history. Some scholars argue that there is much that can be learned from the Bible about ancient Israel, but others have proposed alternative accounts of Israelite history that diverge from or even contradict the biblical account. These alternative reconstructions are invariably hypothetical, and you may not find them persuasive, but we believe the most productive response in that instance is to study the evidence more deeply, honestly wrestle with the questions that it raises, and try to develop a more persuasive understanding of what happened.

Let us begin this particular reconstruction with the question of *where* Israelite history begins. The Hebrew Bible acknowledges that people were living in Canaan well before the Israelites arrived there, and their existence has been confirmed by both literary and archaeological evidence. The region that would come to be known as Canaan, a name that is known in pre-biblical sources and whose original meaning is unclear, has been continuously inhabited by humans since prehistoric times and is the site of some of the earliest known settlements, including the site of the later city of Jericho, which was settled as early as 9000 BCE. The cultures of the peoples living in Canaan, including the Israelites, have always been tied to the area's diverse topography and ecology: a coastal region in the west, fertile valleys and rugged hill country in the interior, desert to the east and south. In the period just before the emergence of the Israelites, a period known now as the Late Bronze Age (c. 1550–1200 BCE), Canaan was dominated by various city-states in places like Hazor, Megiddo, and even Jerusalem, cities ruled by kings who controlled not just the city itself but also the surrounding territory and its villages, while the lower classes consisted of farmers, craftspeople, and some nomads and brigands on the margins of society. There were conflicts among these kings, but they were also connected in various ways and all mutually beholden to the king of Egypt, who ruled the region as part of its empire (see Map 1.1).

This was the geographical context in which Israelite culture would develop, and it is one that is accurately registered in biblical texts. The Bible contains stories situated throughout the land of Canaan: Some stories are set in the southern desert region, in the Negev; others take place in the rugged and mountainous interior, the vicinity of Jerusalem; and still others take place in the north, in the vicinity of the Sea of Galilee or the mountain range known as Mt. Carmel. It is clear that whoever produced the stories preserved in books like Genesis, Judges, and 1–2 Samuel was familiar with the terrain, weather conditions, animals, and plant life of ancient Canaan.

But there is so much else about the Bible's description of ancient Israel's history that is unclear or does not match up neatly with what we know from other sources of information. When did the Israelites first appear in the land of Canaan? Is Genesis correct to describe them as migrants or refugees from other places, or did they develop from within the already-existing population present in Canaan in earlier centuries, as archaeological evidence might suggest? Does their history in the land begin with an act of violent conquest, the destruction of Canaanite cities and the massacre or expulsion of their inhabitants, or is there reason to reject the narrative of that conquest in the book of Joshua, as again many biblical scholars and archaeologists are inclined to do based on evidence which seems to contradict the biblical account? There is so much we do not know about the Israelites, but we can be certain of one point: whatever accurate information the Bible may contain, it does not offer a complete picture of their history.

In our effort to find a starting point for our history, we can latch on to at least one fairly solid fact: We can be fairly confident that a people known as "Israel" was already present in Canaan as early as the thirteenth century BCE. How is it that we can know this? The Bible depicts the Israelites as conquering the Canaanites, but it doesn't tell us when exactly this conquest happened. We can be confident that Israel existed by this point because, in addition to the Hebrew Bible's testimony, a people known as Israel is mentioned in another source that we can date to a specific time, a victory hymn

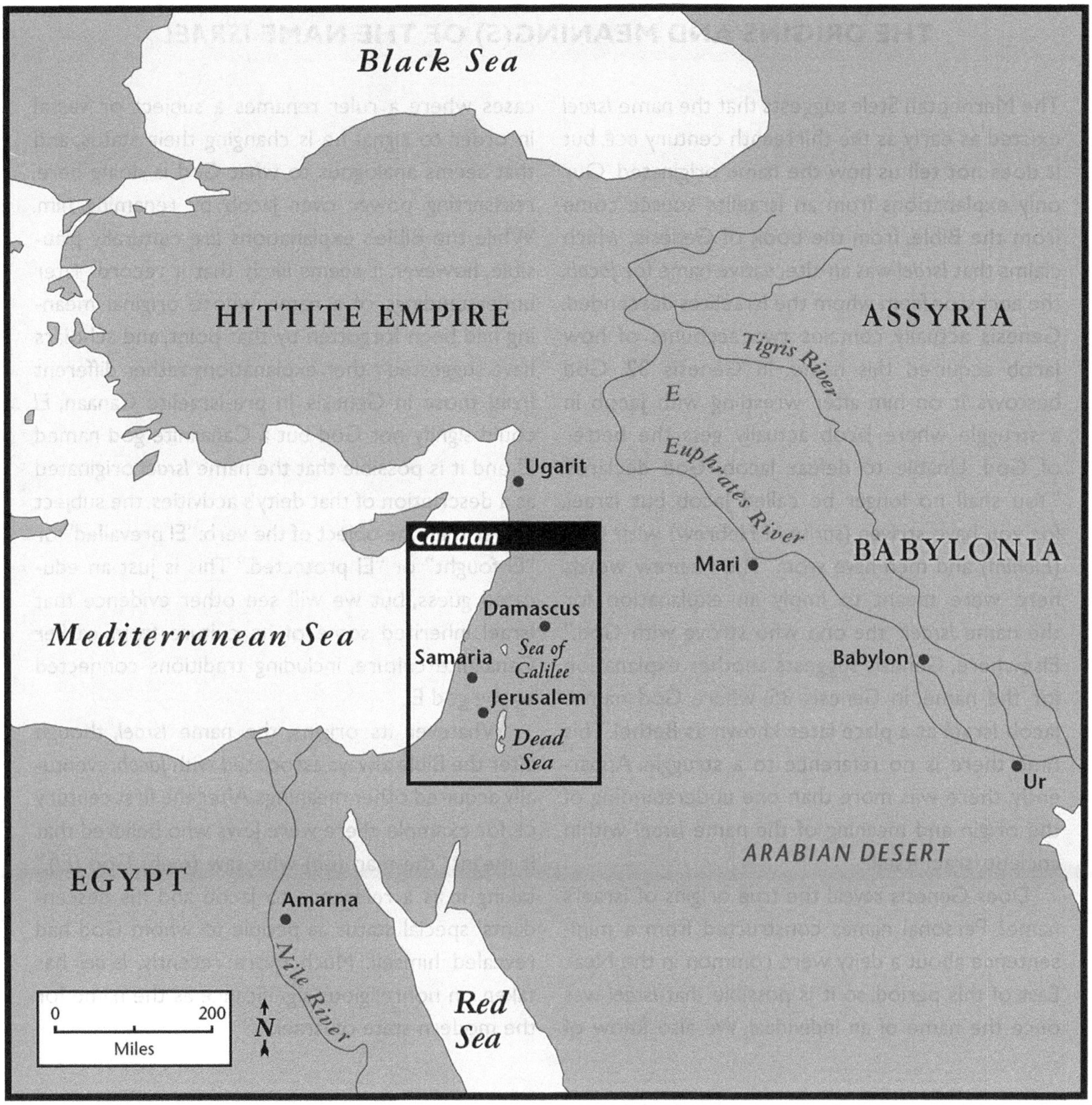

Map 1.1 Canaan in the context of the ancient Near East.

from the reign of the Egyptian king Merneptah (c. 1213–1203 BCE) inscribed on a stele or stone slab. The relevant part of the inscription reads as follows:

Plundered is the Canaan with every evil;
Carried off is Ashkelon;
Seized upon is Gezer;
Yanoam is made as that which does not exist;
Israel is laid waste, his seed is not.

The peoples listed here are various enemies defeated by Merneptah in the land of Canaan, including a people known as Israel, allegedly annihilated by the king (thankfully, that claim was exaggerated, or else this book would have been a very short one). Beyond confirming that Israel lived in Canaan in the time of Merneptah, the inscription may also contain a clue about Israel's social organization at this stage in the development. The Egyptians

THE ORIGINS AND MEANING(S) OF THE NAME *ISRAEL*

The Merneptah Stele suggests that the name *Israel* existed as early as the thirteenth century BCE, but it does not tell us how the name originated. Our only explanations from an Israelite source come from the Bible, from the book of Genesis, which claims that *Israel* was an alternative name for *Jacob*, the ancestor from whom the Israelites descended. Genesis actually contains two accounts of how Jacob acquired this name. In Genesis 32, God bestows it on him after wrestling with Jacob in a struggle where Jacob actually gets the better of God. Unable to defeat Jacob, God declares, "You shall no longer be called Jacob but Israel, for you have striven (*sarita* in Hebrew) with God (*Elohim*) and men have won." The Hebrew words here were meant to imply an explanation for the name *Israel*: "the one who strove with God." Elsewhere, Genesis suggests another explanation for the name, in Genesis 35, where God names Jacob Israel at a place later known as Bethel. This time there is no reference to a struggle. Apparently, there was more than one understanding of the origin and meaning of the name *Israel* within ancient Israel itself.

Does Genesis reveal the true origins of Israel's name? Personal names constructed from a mini-sentence about a deity were common in the Near East of this period, so it is possible that *Israel* was once the name of an individual. We also know of cases where a ruler renames a subject or vassal in order to signal he is changing their status, and that seems analogous to what God is doing here, reasserting power over Jacob by renaming him. While the Bible's explanations are culturally plausible, however, it seems likely that it records later understandings of a name whose original meaning had been forgotten by that point, and scholars have suggested other explanations rather different from those in Genesis. In pre-Israelite Canaan, *El* could signify not God but a Canaanite god named El, and it is possible that the name *Israel* originated as a description of that deity's activities, the subject rather than the object of the verb: "El prevailed" or "El fought" or "El protected." This is just an educated guess, but we will see other evidence that Israel inherited some of its culture from earlier Canaanite culture, including traditions connected to the god El.

Whatever its origins, the name *Israel*, though after the Bible always associated with *Jacob*, eventually acquired other meanings. After the first century CE, for example, there were Jews who believed that it meant "the man (*ish*) who saw (*raah*) God (*El*)," taking it as a reference to Jacob and his descendants' special status as people to whom God had revealed himself. Much more recently, *Israel* has taken on nonreligious significance as the name for the modern state of Israel.

used special signs to indicate what kind of thing a word was, and the names "Ashkelon," "Gezer," and "Yanoam" in the inscription are all written with a sign that indicates they were city-states, whereas "Israel" is written with a sign used to signal a people or an ethnic group.

The difference in signs may indicate that the early Israelites were not associated with a specific city as were other peoples but were a rurally based or nomadic people, which is consistent with how Genesis describes the ancestors of the Israelites—Abraham, Isaac, and Jacob—in the earliest stages of Israelite history as described by the Bible (*see the box* "The Origins and Meaning(s) of the Name *Israel*").

Who is this Israel, and from where did it come? No written sources exist for Israel's history after the Merneptah Stele until the ninth century BCE, leaving a documentary gap in precisely the period when Israelite society was taking shape in the land of Canaan. As the Bible depicts events, the Israelites did not begin as Canaanites but originated as outsiders to the land who migrated to Canaan from abroad. Genesis traces the Israelites' ancestry back to a single person named Abraham, who is said to have traveled with his wife, Sarah, to

Canaan, at God's behest, from a region between the Tigris and the Euphrates Rivers referred to by later Greek authors as *Mesopotamia* (from the Greek for "between the rivers"), a region located in present-day Iraq and Syria. Abraham and his family retain their sense of connection to Mesopotamia even after they settle in Canaan. When it comes time to find a wife for his son Isaac, for example, Abraham shuns the Canaanites and sends his servant back to Mesopotamia, where the servant meets Rebecca, the woman who will marry Isaac. That is also where Abraham's grandson Jacob, or Israel, as he would come to be known after God changes his name, finds his two wives, Leah and Rachel. According to the Bible, in other words, the Israelites did not originate from Canaan itself; they are immigrants from Mesopotamia who retain a sense of connection to their homeland long after they leave it (for more on Mesopotamia, *see the box* "The Biblical World in Brief").

Regardless of whether figures like Abraham existed, the Bible does register an understanding of ancient Near Eastern geography consistent in many ways with what has been learned from other sources. Mesopotamia was host to a succession of civilizations, including the Sumerians, one of the earliest civilizations in the world, and the Assyrians and Babylonians, who play a major role in later biblical history. Mesopotamia was home to some of the earliest cities of the Near East, such as Ur, which was probably the very city mentioned in Genesis 12 as the birthplace of Abraham, and Babylon, the ill-fated Babel described in Genesis 11. Whoever composed this latter story seems to have known something about Babylon. The story's mention of a large tower constructed in the city of Babel, a tower "with its top in the heavens," seems a reference to a large, towering temple that was built in Babylon in honor of its chief god.

Is there evidence to support a Mesopotamian origin for ancient Israel? Scholars have tried to establish the historical plausibility of Abraham and his family by connecting them to a Mesopotamian people known in ancient Near Eastern sources as the Amurru. A related name, translated as *Amorite* in English, is used in the Bible to describe a Canaanite people, but its meaning is different in this context, a much narrower reference to a specific group living in the land of Canaan just before the Israelites' arrival. The Amurru are mentioned in various Mesopotamian sources as a people associated with the West (the word means "western," in fact)—that is, the region of Syria, Phoenicia, and Canaan, which is Western from a Mesopotamian perspective. They seem to have originated as a nomadic or migrant people, growing particularly prominent in the period between 2000 and 1600 BCE. As depicted in the Bible, Abraham and his descendants travel from Mesopotamia to Canaan and back, wandering from camp to camp, never settling in a single place. Their lifestyle fits well with the alleged nomadism of the Amorites, suggesting to some scholars that the stories of Genesis reflect the experiences of real-life Amurru as filtered through the imaginations of later Israelite authors, likely changing or distorting details but nevertheless preserving a kernel of memory from a period between 2000 and 1600 BCE. This scholarly effort to historicize Abraham by connecting his migration to the larger Amurru migration came to be known as the Amorite hypothesis.

There is no way to prove such a hypothesis. Searching for specific individuals like Abraham, Sarah, and their offspring in the scant textual and archaeological remnants that survive from the distant past—a family of sheep- and goat herders that lived in tents and moved from place to place—is much harder than looking for a needle in a haystack, since one at least knows in the latter instance which haystack to look in, whereas for the family of Abraham and Sarah, it is not clear in what historical period one should look. There is thus no way to confirm his existence, much less connect him to a known historical people like the Amurru (in the West Bank city of Hebron, there is a site venerated by religious Jews today as the tomb of Abraham, the Cave of Machpelah, a site that has become embroiled in the conflict between Israel and the Palestinians, but that identification, developing among Jews and Christians in antiquity, isn't based on any actual evidence that it is really Abraham and his descendants buried there).

But on the other hand, one cannot prove that Abraham didn't exist, and scholars looking for something historical in Genesis have pointed to circumstantial evidence. Names resembling *Abram* (Abraham's name before God changed it) and *Jacob* (Abraham's grandson) appear in Mesopotamian sources from the early or mid-second millennium BCE, and the description in Genesis of their behavior—Abraham's adoption of a servant as his heir, the details of how marriages are arranged, the importance of deathbed blessings—also seemed to fit the culture of this period as known from texts discovered at Mesopotamian sites such as the city of Nuzi. When these parallels came to light, they were seen as evidence that Genesis preserves to some degree a memory of Israel's emergence from an earlier nomadic people with links to Mesopotamia.

But this is little more than educated guesswork. No specific event in Genesis can be corroborated, and even the effort to connect Abraham to the Amorites has proven unpersuasive in the end. Maybe there was an Abraham, but such a figure could have as easily lived 1,000 years after the Amurru, since his name and the nomadic lifestyle he led have parallels as well from later periods of Near Eastern history. In fact, indications can be found within Genesis itself that it was composed at a later time. According to Genesis 11, Abraham's family migrated from a place called "Ur of the Chaldeans." As we have noted, Ur is a well-known city in Mesopotamia, but the Chaldeans, a people from south Mesopotamia who are known only from sources dating to the ninth century BCE and later, could not have been living in Ur at the time of Abraham if he came from the period between 2000 and 1600 BCE. Other details in Genesis—its reference to the Philistines, for example—also reflect realities that emerge in Canaan only after about 1200 BCE, complicating attempts to place a historical Abraham in the early centuries of the second millennium BCE. To date, there is no agreed-upon way to distinguish between genuine history and fictionalized invention in the book of Genesis and its account of Israel's origin.

What of the other historical experience that plays such an important role in the Bible's account of Israel's origins: the Exodus from Egypt? In the days of Abraham's grandson Jacob, Genesis relates, Jacob's son Joseph was brought down into Egypt as a slave. Thanks to his skills as a dream interpreter, he eventually arose to a position of power in Egypt, second only to the Egyptian king, and was reunited with his 11 brothers and father, who joined him in Egypt during a famine in Canaan. Their descendants, the 12 tribes of Israel, thrived in Egypt for some time, but at a certain point, a new king came to power who did not remember Joseph and became fearful of the Israelites as they grew more populous, enslaving and oppressing them. It was during this period that Moses, an Israelite but one who grew up in the house of the Egyptian king's daughter, emerged to rescue his people from their plight. Wielding divine power, he inflicted ten plagues on the Egyptians that compelled their king to release the Israelites, and they left for the land of Canaan, though not before crossing the Red Sea, which God parted to allow their passage and then closed in order to drown their Egyptian pursuers. Their escape from Egypt has come to be known in English as the Exodus, from the Greek word meaning "going out" that was used by Christians as a title for the biblical book that tells this story. Can any of the biblical Exodus be confirmed as an actually occurring event? Is there evidence that the Israelites were slaves in Egypt? That there was a Moses who liberated them? That the Israelites had to trek across the Sinai wilderness before settling in the land of Canaan?

Egypt itself was real enough. Like Mesopotamia, Egyptian civilization was a river culture, forming on the banks of the Nile River. Its development is roughly parallel to that of Mesopotamia: A pictographic writing system (hieroglyphics, or their cursive equivalent, *hieratic*) developed there sometime in the fourth millennium BCE, as did the institution of kingship, temples, and other attributes of early Near Eastern civilization. From an early period, even before the invention of writing, Egypt was in contact with Canaan. Egyptians came to Canaan as travelers, soldiers, traders, and—in periods when Egypt controlled Canaan—administrators, while Canaanites traveled to Egypt as migrants, slaves, and traders (in fact, the word *Canaan* might originate from the word for "trader").

The Bible's description of the Israelites as wandering back and forth between Canaan and Egypt, serving as agents of the Egyptian government or becoming its slaves, is certainly historically plausible in a general sense, but establishing that as a possibility is not the same as proving that the Exodus really happened, and the silence of sources outside the Bible lead some to conclude that it did not. While the Merneptah Stele refers to Israel, as we have noted, it is our *only* reference to Israel in ancient Egyptian literature from this early period, and the people to whom the hymn is referring already live in Canaan: There is no hint that they are former slaves, not to mention the ten plagues or the parting of the Red Sea. It is impossible even to determine the period of time to which the Bible refers. Some place the Exodus in the fifteenth century BCE, but others date it to later centuries, and there is no way to decide the matter because what chronological information the Bible supplies fails to match up clearly or consistently with what we know from other sources.

Another reason that scholars doubt that the Exodus actually happened is that the biblical account seems to reflect the influence of ancient Near Eastern storytelling tradition. One of the Exodus story's best-known episodes tells of how Moses's mother saved her son from Pharaoh's lethal decree by putting the baby in a basket and sending him down the Nile River, where he was discovered by Pharaoh's daughter (see Exodus 2). The story is suspiciously similar to a legend told of other ancient Near Eastern leaders, such as Sargon I, founder of the first great Mesopotamian Empire around 2300 BCE. Here is how an inscription describes Sargon's birth:

> Sargon, the mighty king, king of Agade, am I. . . . My mother, the high priestess, conceived me, in secret she bore me. She set me in a basket of rushes, with bitumen she sealed my lid. She cast me into the river which rose not [over] me. The river bore me up and carried me to Akki, the drawer of water. Akki, the drawer of water lifted me out as he dipped his e[w]er. Akki, the drawer of water, appointed me as his gardener.

Just as the portrait of David may have been filled out with material once associated with other heroes, so too does Moses's image reflect a similar fictional expansion. This does not rule out the possibility of a real Moses, but where to draw the line between fact and fiction in the Bible's description of him is unclear—and the same is true for other aspects of the Exodus story that have parallels with stories known from Mesopotamia or Egypt, such as the episode where Moses and Aaron turn the waters of Egypt into blood. Similar episodes of water or other fluids being turned into blood have been found in Mesopotamian and Egyptian storytelling about the gods.

There is one event known from ancient Egyptian history that does bear an intriguing resemblance to the Exodus and may conceivably represent the historical kernel of the story that it tells: the expulsion from Egypt of a group known as the Hyksos. The Hyksos (a Greek transliteration of the Egyptian *heqaw khasut*, "rulers of foreign lands") were a line of Asiatic rulers, quite possibly from Canaan itself, who gained control over part of Egypt in the seventeenth century BCE. Some see Hyksos rule as the background for Joseph's rise to power in Genesis 37–50, for in this period it would be especially plausible for Joseph, a non-Egyptian from Canaan, to rise to a position of power in Egypt. Hyksos rule came to an end in the sixteenth century BCE, when the native Egyptians rebelled against their rule

THE BIBLICAL WORLD IN BRIEF

To better understand the history of ancient Israel, it is extremely helpful to know something about the political, social, and cultural context in which it emerged, including the various peoples with whom it interacted. The following is a brief introduction to some of those peoples and their relationship to the Israelites.

Mesopotamia is a plain between the Tigris and Euphrates Rivers where the first civilization emerged. The rivers flooded in the summer and receded in autumn, leaving behind sediment for growing crops in the winter, to be harvested in spring. The earliest known Mesopotamian civilization is Sumerian. Advanced irrigation systems formed larger settlements, and as the local farm economy grew to include trade, towns emerged, one of the earliest of which is known as Uruk. Towns that grew powerful became city-states with dynastic rulers. Eventually, one ruler called Sargon founded the first empire in history. According to legend, Sargon, like Moses, was sent down the river in a basket, found and raised by a royal gardener or water-drawer, and grew up in the royal house, where he eventually rose to the position of king.

Sometime in the same period as the rise of Mesopotamian civilization, another civilization arose on the Nile River in Egypt. Unlike the Tigris and Euphrates, the Nile flooded regularly and predictably, and there were relatively fewer migrations and invasions into the region as well; thus, Egypt achieved a greater degree of political stability than Mesopotamia did, though it, too, underwent periods of fragmentation. From the beginning of the third millennium until Alexander the Great, ancient Egyptian history is divided into Old, Middle, and New Kingdoms, with three "intermediate periods," when Egypt experienced political division and economic decentralization. Israel emerged at the end of the era dominated by the New Kingdom (at its height under Ramses II, who reigned between 1279 and 1212 BCE) as it gave way to the Third Intermediate Period.

In contrast to the relative stability of Egyptian history, Mesopotamia was dominated by a number of different peoples. Toward the end of the third millennium, the Sumerians were overtaken by the Akkadians, based in the city of Akkad, and they replaced the Sumerian language with a Semitic language now known as Akkadian. From the remnants of that empire developed two major cultural variants of Mesopotamian civilization: a culture based in northern Mesopotamia (what is now northern Iraq) known as Assyria and a southern Mesopotamian culture based in Babylon, in what is now southern Iraq. Empires from Assyria and Babylon, known as the Neo-Assyrian and Neo-Babylonian Empires, respectively, appear prominently in the history described in the Bible as major threats to ancient Israel. The Assyrians exiled 10 of Israel's 12 tribes, the famous 10 lost tribes, while the Babylonians destroyed Jerusalem, and the population that it exiled to Babylonia were the ancestors of the people later known as Jews.

Other peoples also play an important role in the history of ancient Israel.

The Philistines appear to have been part of a larger movement of seafaring raiders known as

and chased them from Egypt, and their expulsion calls to mind the events described in the book of Exodus: the rise of a new king in Egypt who does not remember Joseph and fears the Israelites as enemies, followed by Israel's flight from Egypt. A connection between the Exodus and the Hyksos had already occurred to Manetho, an Egyptian historian who conflates the two stories, more than 2,000 years ago.

As tempting as it is to accept this connection, however, the Hyksos period was not the only time in Egyptian history when people from Canaan settled in Egypt. As we have noted, two-way traffic was frequent between Canaan and Egypt—including the Sea Peoples who originated somewhere in the Aegean world, from a culture similar to that described in the poetry of Homer, and overtook the Eastern Mediterranean at the end of the second millennium BCE. Some of these people threatened Egypt in the age of Ramses II and Merneptah, and the Philistines seem to have emerged from among this people, settling in the southern coast of Canaan in the twelfth century BCE, in the area that bordered what would become the Kingdom of Judah. The Philistines would eventually establish five major city-states on the coast—Gaza, Ashkelon, Ashdod, Ekron, and Gath—and their name is the origin of the word *Palestine*, used by later Greeks and Romans in reference to the area.

The Phoenicians were also settled on the coast of Canaan, in what is now northern Israel and Lebanon, but unlike the Philistines, they were a Canaanite people with a culture that resembled that of the Israelites themselves. At least as known to us from inscriptional and literary sources, they were urbanized peoples, based in cities like Byblos and Tyre. They were known as traders and seafarers in antiquity, establishing colonies throughout the Mediterranean, including Carthage, in present-day Tunisia, which, for a time, rivaled Rome for control over the Mediterranean.

The Arameans, based in Syria, appear to have originated as seminomadic peoples but, by the time of ancient Israel's political consolidation, were developing into various kingdoms in the region between the Assyrian and the Neo-Hittite kingdoms that developed in the wake of the Hittite Empire's collapse in the twelfth century BCE. The Arameans were an occasional threat to the Israelites but were themselves subdued by the Assyrians. The language of the Arameans, Aramaic, would eventually emerge as an international language in the ancient Near East, used for administration and other purposes by many non-Arameans, including Jews.

Along the eastern side of the Jordan River, Israel was neighbored by various peoples that included the Ammonites, Moabites, and Edomites, living in what is now Jordan and southern Israel. The culture of these peoples seems to have been very similar to that of the Israelites, and they are depicted in the book of Genesis as having a close genealogical connection to Israel (the Ammonites and Moabites are traced back to Lot, Abraham's nephew, and the Edomites are traced back to Esau, Jacob's brother), but they are also depicted as hostile rivals. Each developed a kingdom during the period that the Israelites were also developing a monarchy. The ultimate fate of the Moabites and Ammonites is unclear, but at least the Edomites survived into the first century BCE, when their descendants were known as Idumeans. Finally, there are the Canaanites, which, as described in the Bible, means the Canaanite inhabitants of the land inhabited by the Israelites, the territory west of the Jordan River. According to the Five Books of Moses, the Canaanites were supposed to have been driven from the land, and their name blotted from memory, but other biblical sources suggest that they persisted as slaves under Israel's rule. These included peoples like the Jebusites, the inhabitants of Jerusalem before David took over the city, who may have continued there as slaves or a lower class even after his conquest.

slaves imported to Egypt and people fleeing from Egypt into Canaan—all of which makes the idea of Israel's sojourn in Egypt and subsequent Exodus plausible in a general sense but also gives one pause about connecting the Exodus to any specific event, such as the Hyksos expulsion. Egyptian texts from the period between 1500 and 1100 BCE also speak of another troublesome people moving back and forth in this region: tribes of seminomads referred to as the Shasu from the area of Palestine—and they also constitute a possible candidate for the role of proto-Israelite, the pre-Israelite people in the region from whom the Israelites developed. Several such groups seem to have been in the area during the Late Bronze Age, unruly peoples on the fringes of Canaan's urban society who created problems for the authorities (we will be meeting another such people a bit later, the Habiru). While the Israelites may have originated as one of those groups, we lack the evidence to clinch an identification with any of them. On the other hand, it is also possible that the biblical account brings together and conflates memories inherited from or associated with all such groups—the Amorites, the Hyksos, *and* the Shasu.

Unable to verify the biblical account of Israel's origins, many recent scholars have embraced an alternative understanding of Israel's origins that goes beyond, and is even at odds with, how the Bible depicts its past: *The ancient Israelites did not originate as outsiders to the land of Canaan.* They did not migrate there from Mesopotamia or escape there from Egypt. Instead, Israelite culture originated from within Canaan itself as an offshoot of the indigenous culture that had existed there in preceding centuries. According to this hypothesis, the Bible's effort to differentiate Israel from the Canaanites, to assign the Israelites an identity rooted somewhere else, is historically misleading, concealing the true Canaanite origins of Israelite culture.

Several arguments support this proposal, as different as it is from how the Bible depicts Israel's origins. First is the lack of corroborating evidence for the Israelites entering the land of Canaan as invaders. According to the book of Joshua, Israel settled in the land after violently destroying cities such as Jericho and Ai and slaying or displacing their indigenous inhabitants. One might reasonably expect to find evidence of such a destructive military campaign in the archaeological record, evidence of cities violently destroyed in this period, but there is no clear-cut evidence of such a massive conquest. A few Canaanite cities, such as Hazor, show evidence of destruction in this period, but no evidence exists to confirm that this destruction was wrought by the Israelites, and some cities allegedly destroyed at this time, according to the Bible, show no signs of violent destruction at all. What of the famous story of the conquest of Jericho? Again, no evidence of destruction: Jericho in this period did not even have walls to come tumbling down.

Figure 1.1 An image of the ancient Israelites? The scene here, carved into the wall of an Egyptian temple at Karnak and dated to the fourteenth century BCE, shows a group of people known as the Shasu after their defeat by Egyptian forces. The Shasu were a nomadic people that the Egyptians encountered in southern Canaan and elsewhere, and some scholars have identified them as the early Israelites, or the people from whom the Israelites descended.

What archaeology has discovered is evidence of a rapidly growing settlement of Canaan's central highlands during the period associated with Joshua. Prior to this period, Canaan's central highlands, the mountain region between the coastal plain and the eastern desert, were—understandably—sparsely inhabited. The region was difficult to farm, and water was hard to find. The area's new inhabitants found ways to address these problems, however. They cleared the slopes, shaping their steep sides into terraces that made them easier to farm, and they cut cisterns where they could store the water they needed. These settlements appear to be new to the region, rapidly growing in number after around 1200 BCE, but there is no clear evidence that the inhabitants of these settlements were immigrants to Canaan arriving from the Sinai desert or Egypt. If they had just arrived from such places, one might expect their material culture—the houses they lived in, the pots they used—to differ from that of the indigenous population, but it is difficult to recognize such differences in the material evidence that archaeologists have uncovered. If it were not for the biblical story of the Exodus and conquest, there would be no real reason to think these settlements weren't inhabited by "Canaanites," the indigenous people of the region of the Levant pushed by some economic or social pressure to settle in a rugged part of Canaan beyond the control of its city-states.

In addition to this archaeological data, literary evidence connects Israelite culture to the indigenous culture of Canaan. Some of our best sources for Canaanite culture in the period prior to Israel's emergence are the hundreds of texts recovered from the ancient Syrian city-state of Ugarit, a kingdom that was especially prosperous in the fourteenth and thirteenth centuries BCE. The people of Ugarit were not Canaanites themselves—that is, they did not live in the land of Canaan but in what is now Syria to the north—but their culture, religion, and mythology were closely related to those of Canaanites known from later sources. Ugaritic literature tells us much about the gods of Canaan and their misadventures—El, the supreme creator deity; Asherah, his consort and mother of the gods; and Baal, a warrior god associated with fertility (Figure 1.2)—and their description parallels how God is described in the Bible. In fact, the biblical God is given some of the titles bestowed on El or Baal in Ugaritic literature, as in Genesis 14:19, where he is called "El Elyon," El the Most High. There are also striking parallels between Ugaritic and biblical ritual, and between the form of Ugaritic literature and biblical literature (e.g., both Ugaritic and biblical poetry deploy parallelism, in which the two halves of a line parallel each other in some way, as in Exodus 15:2, where the first half of the line "This is my God, and I will praise him" is balanced by the second half, "my father's God and I will exalt him").

Also consistent with the Canaanite origin theory is the language in which most of the Bible is written, now known as Hebrew but sometimes referred to in the Bible as *yehudit*, the language of Judah in southern Canaan (Israelites to the north appear to have spoken a slightly different dialect).

Figure 1.2 A bronze figurine of a male deity, probably the Canaanite storm god Baal, dating from c. 1400 to 1300 BCE. Baal is depicted here as a warrior, poised to throw a spear or lightning strike against his enemies. Compare the description of God in Psalm 18:13–14: "[T]he Lord thundered in the heavens. . . . [H]e sent forth his arrows and scattered (his enemies), great lightning and he overwhelmed them."

Linguists classify this language as an offshoot of a branch of the Semitic family of languages that also includes Arabic, Aramaic, and Ugaritic, and its closest relatives within this branch are other languages that were used in Canaan: Moabite, Ammonite, Edomite, and Phoenician. If Israel's ancestors had originated in Mesopotamia or Egypt, one might expect it to use the languages of those places, or at least for their language to bear a clearer imprint of their influence. Instead, they use the same language that all of Canaan's other indigenous inhabitants used—the same language and the same alphabetic script used to write it down.

The resemblance between Israelite and Canaanite culture becomes all the more striking when contrasted with another people that emerges in Canaan in the same period that the Israelites do: the Philistines. The Philistines came to the coast of Canaan in the early twelfth century BCE as part of a larger migration of peoples identified as the "Sea Peoples" in Egyptian, Ugaritic, and Akkadian sources. They came from the Aegean world of the Mycenaean age, the early Greek world described in Homer's *Iliad* and *Odyssey*, and their Mediterranean background is clearly visible in the archaeological record. Philistine pottery is basically a variant of Mycenaean/Greek pottery; Philistine urban design, craftsmanship, dress, and consumption habits (Philistines liked eating pork and drinking wine mixed with water) all point to the Aegean world as their place of origin. Even what little we know of Philistines' language supports this connection. The Philistine word *seren*, used in the Bible to describe Philistine rulers, is probably related to the Greek *tyrannos*, or "tyrant." In other words, it is possible to clearly demonstrate the Philistines' origins as outsiders to Canaan because the distinctness of their culture is clearly reflected in the archaeological and linguistic record and because it is possible to trace that culture back to its origin in another part of the world beyond the land of Canaan. Not so with the Israelites, whose language, religion, and material culture all connect them to earlier Canaanite culture, as if they developed as an outgrowth of that culture.

But if the Israelites came from within the native population of Canaan, how did they come to see themselves as different from other Canaanites, as outsiders from a region beyond Canaan who had displaced the land's earlier inhabitants? Why is migration so important in how the Israelites remembered their past if they originated from within the indigenous population, the memory of Abraham's sojourn and the memory of the Exodus from Egypt? And why were the authors of the Five Books of Moses so hostile to Canaanites, the peoples that inhabited the land before the Israelites settled there, if they were themselves the descendants of such people?

These are questions under investigation to this day, and to be honest, we do not know the answers. What we can say is that the period when Israel emerged was one of drastic social change throughout the region. The transition from the Late Bronze Age to the early Iron Age in the thirteenth and twelfth centuries BCE is marked by political upheaval, crises, and disruptions in the large empires that dominated the Near East, and there is even evidence that a pandemic might have spread across the region. The New Kingdom of Egypt was in decline in this period, as was the Hittite kingdom in Asia Minor; major urban centers such as Ugarit were destroyed, trade networks broke down, and as the Sea People illustrate, many felt they had to move to survive, displacing those who lived in the territory that they sought for themselves or else expanding into uninhabited territory. Such changes had an impact on life in Canaan, reflected in the destruction or decline of the cities that had dominated Canaan in the Late Bronze Age, the breakdown of ties with Egypt, the arrival of new peoples such as the Philistines, and the proliferation of small settlements and villages in the hinterlands. As major powers like Egypt and the Hittite kingdom withdrew, smaller states emerged to fill the vacuum: These conditions seem to have allowed the Israelites to form a kingdom by the tenth century BCE—the kingdom associated with David and Solomon—as happened among neighboring peoples in the same period, such as the Moabites and the Edomites, who lived in what is now modern-day Jordan.

Some intriguing evidence raises the possibility that the Israelites emerged more specifically out of a Canaanite group that was beginning to assert itself as early as the fourteenth century BCE, though not an ethnic group but a kind of social class of marginal Canaanites. In the centuries prior to the Merneptah Stele, Canaan had

Figure 1.3 Philistine pottery, very similar in its decoration to pottery from the Aegean world.

been under Egyptian control, as we have noted. Important information about what life in Canaan was like in this period comes from a collection of texts discovered in el-Amarna in Egypt in 1887, including a number of letters sent to the Egyptian king by the rulers of Canaanite city-states such as Tyre, Shechem, and Jerusalem. The Amarna Letters indicate that ruling Canaan was a challenge. The Egyptians were represented by a governor in Gaza, but for the most part, they ruled through local kings based in Canaan's city-states, kings who were constantly at odds with one another.

The letters also tell us something about the Canaanite language in this period, the language from which Hebrew evolved. What is most important about these letters for our purposes, however, is their references to a group known as the Habiru (or perhaps *Hapiru*). The meaning of the term is not clear. Some believe it connoted the Habiru's violent character, but it may have originally meant something like "dust maker" (as in someone who left a trail of dust behind) or meant something like *vagabond*. In any case, it is often applied to people who occupy impermanent and socially marginal positions as laborers, mercenaries, runaways, and rebels, as if the term connoted something like *outcast* or *outlaw*. The Habiru groups mentioned in the Amarna Letters, concentrated in parts of Canaan outside the control of its city-states, may have been brigands or fugitives, Canaanites living beyond the control of Canaan's kings or the Egyptians.

Why connect this group to the Israelites? The Habiru have long intrigued scholars because of the name's similarity to *Hebrew*, a word used in the Bible in reference to the Israelites. There are problems with that identification. The term *Hebrew* as used in the Bible always refers to Israel, whereas the Habiru is most likely a designation not of an ethnic group but of a kind of social class, not just in Canaan, but also elsewhere in the ancient Near East. Still, the linguistic similarity between *Hebrew* and *Habiru* is too striking to simply dismiss. Perhaps, some scholars hypothesize, the Israelites/Hebrews originated from a group of unruly Habiru who had taken refuge in the mountains to elude the control of the Canaanite city-states and who, in the wake of the breakdown of Egyptian control and the decline of Canaan's city-states, were eventually able to assert themselves and to become what the Bible refers to as the Hebrews or the Israelites, Canaanite in origin but differentiating themselves from the Canaanite society that they had been resisting. No evidence confirms this reconstruction of the Israelites' origins, but in its favor is the possibility that the term "Hebrew" originated from the word "Habiru."

Taken altogether, the evidence reviewed in this section—the problems with treating biblical books such as Genesis and Exodus as history, and the different picture of Canaanite history that emerges from extrabiblical sources—at least raises the possibility that the Israelites originated in a manner very different from what the Bible asserts. It would be wrong to view this reconstruction as certain fact: It depends on hypotheses that are debatable, and the scholarly consensus, to the extent that there is one, is subject to revision in light of new evidence. What is certain is that we cannot take it for granted that we know the origins of the ancient Israelites (and, by extension, the Jews): The Bible tells us only part of the story of where they came from.

A CONFIRMABLE CHRONOLOGY OF ANCIENT ISRAELITE HISTORY

It is not easy to date the events mentioned in the Hebrew Bible, because the chronological information it provides is implausible (one biblical figure, Methuselah, is said to have lived for 969 years) or too vague to connect to events of a known date. However, a partial chronology can be constructed by correlating biblical chronology with information from extrabiblical sources. We list several of those events here as a way of helping the reader fit what we know about the history of ancient Israel into a larger picture. Events not mentioned here—Abraham's trek from Mesopotamia, the Exodus, Israel's conquest of Canaan—are excluded not because we can prove they did not happen but because they cannot be securely placed within known history or confirmed by other sources.

- **1207 BCE.** The people of Israel appear as inhabitants of Canaan by this point, as corroborated by the reference to "Israel" in the Merneptah Stele.
- **1150 BCE.** Numerous sources document the arrival of the Sea Peoples on the southeast coast of the Mediterranean around 1180 CE, a movement that included the Philistines, who arrived on the southern coast of Canaan at this time. The Philistines' presence is easy to discern archaeologically, and such evidence also shows them expanding into Canaan after the death of the Egyptian king Ramses III in 1153 BCE, the end of Egypt's control over Canaan. It was in this period of expansion, presumably, that the Philistines encountered the Israelites, a confrontation that the Bible associates with the emergence of Israel's monarchy.
- **C. 925 BCE.** King Shishak of Egypt invades Canaan. Mentioned in 1 Kings 14:26 as happening in the fifth year of Rehoboam, Shishak's invasion is the first specific event in the Bible confirmed by an extrabiblical source, an Egyptian text that describes the campaign. If the Bible's chronology is correct, King Solomon would have died five years earlier, in 930 BCE, placing the rise of a monarchy in Israel sometime around 1000 BCE.
- **The ninth century BCE.** The Kingdoms of Israel and Judah exist by this time, as corroborated by an inscription found at Tel Dan that refers to a king of Israel and a king of the House of David. There is, however, no evidence that

FITTING THE BIBLE INTO HISTORY

Even though the biblical account of history can be challenged in many ways, that does not mean that it has no value as a historical source. We have already mentioned an Egyptian inscription that refers to Israel, proving that such a people existed in Canaan as early as the thirteenth century BCE. Whether a Kingdom of David and Solomon existed is a subject of debate, but we have plenty of evidence of monarchic activity in later centuries (*see the box* "A Confirmable Chronology of Ancient Israelite History"). We can likewise confirm the existence of many of the peoples mentioned in the Bible—the Egyptians, the Philistines, the Assyrians, the Moabites, the Edomites, and others—and the Bible's descriptions of Canaan's terrain, weather, and economy are all consistent with what we know about Iron Age Canaan (the Iron Age, succeeding the Bronze Age, is an archaeological era that, in Canaan, runs from around 1200 BCE to the sixth century BCE, more or less the period between the emergence of ancient Israel and the Babylonian Exile). While Israelite history may have been very different from what is depicted in the Bible, at least some of its testimony registers real-life events recorded in other ancient Near Eastern texts or can be substantiated through archaeological finds.

What, then, can we say for sure about Israelite history? The following account of that history these two kingdoms were ever united under David and Solomon, as the Bible claims.

- **853 BCE.** Ahab, king of Israel, participates in a battle against the Assyrians. Ahab is known from the Bible, but this particular battle is reported only by an extrabiblical source, a text from the Assyrian king Shalmaneser III. Assyrian and Babylonian sources also refer to subsequent kings of Israel and Judah from the ninth through the early sixth centuries—among them Jehu, Hezekiah, and Jehoiachin, the last surviving king of Judah. This evidence lines up with how the Bible orders their reigns.
- **722–720 BCE.** Assyria's conquest and destruction of the Northern Kingdom of Israel, reported in 2 Kings 17, are confirmed by Assyrian and Babylonian sources. Fragmentary commemorative inscriptions, Assyrian-style buildings, and imported Assyrian pottery confirm Assyria's rule of the former Kingdom of Israel.
- **701 BCE.** Assyria's conquest of most of Judah, reported in 2 Kings 18–19, is confirmed by Assyrian documentation, including highly detailed reliefs from a palace of Sennacherib that depicts the Assyrian siege of Lachish, a Judahite city.
- **598/97 BCE.** The Babylonians capture of Jerusalem, an event reported in 2 Kings 24, is confirmed by the following report in a Babylonian chronicle:

> In the month of Kislev, the king of Babylonians mobilized his troops and marched to the west. He encamped against the city of Judah (Jerusalem), and on the second of Adar, he captured the city and he seized [its] king. A king of his choice he appointed there; he to[ok] its heavy tribute and carried off to the Babylon.

- From this same period, two seals have been published bearing the name of Baruch, probably the scribe by that name who wrote down the prophecies of Jeremiah, though at least one of these finds is now suspected to be a forgery. Inspiring more confidence are Babylonian texts that confirm the existence of Judahites in Babylonia and even refer to Jehoiachin—the captive king of Judah who was taken off into exile in 598 BCE.

focuses on events and experiences registered in the Bible but also corroborated, at least in part, by extrabiblical sources. This approach yields a different historical picture than the one found in the Bible, beginning Israel's history not with Abraham or the Exodus but with events in Canaan after the thirteenth century BCE, but it is consistent in many ways with what the Bible reports about Israel's history between, roughly, 900 and 500 BCE. It leaves many gaps in our knowledge, but it can help fit the ancient Israelites into what we know of the history of the region, offering insight into their politics, social life, and religion along the way. It can also help us trace lines of continuity that connect the Israelites to Jews of later periods who looked back to the people and events described in biblical literature to understand their origin.

Political Awakenings

Wherever the Israelites came from, we know that by the ninth century BCE, they had developed into what we call today a state—an organized political entity governed from an urban center. The Bible describes the origins and history of this monarchy, a story that involves David, Solomon, and their successors, and we have independent evidence for some of this history. King Hezekiah, for example, who ruled around 700 BCE during an Assyrian attack, is mentioned in an Assyrian inscription that recounts the attack, and archaeologists have uncovered a tunnel that he had constructed during this period to provide Jerusalem with a secure source of water. Given what we can surmise about the origins of Israelite culture, that it emerged from a rural people settled in small villages and towns, how and why did it give rise to an organized state? And to what extent can the Bible's history of this state be confirmed or fleshed out by other sources?

It helps to understand this process to situate it within a broader historical context. As we have noted, a number of major changes occurred in the ancient Near East in the thirteenth and twelfth centuries BCE that help illumine Israel's emergence as a distinct society. One of the most important of these changes was the end of Egypt's control of Canaan in the twelfth century. The Bible nowhere mentions that Canaan had been a colony of Egypt—its authors do not seem to have a memory of Egyptian rule over Canaan, instead remembering their ancestors as having been slaves in Egypt itself—but what history and memory share in common is Egypt's role as a dominant political force from which Israel had to break free before it could form its own independent society. And the Israelites were not the only people in this period and region willing to assert themselves against the Egyptians. An Egyptian tale composed in this period tells of how an Egyptian official named Wenamun traveled to the city of Byblos in what is now Lebanon to purchase timber, only to be told by the ruler there to go away. That a local king would dare show such disrespect to an Egyptian is a hint of the area's emerging independence. Even if we have our doubts about all the miraculous details of the Exodus story—the burning bush, the ten plagues, or a miraculous parting of the Red Sea—there may yet be something historical behind the Bible's claim that Israelite society emerged out of a rejection of Egyptian rule.

As we have also noted, there is also something historical about the biblical description of another confrontation in this period, the struggle between the Israelites and the Philistines. The Philistines, settled on the coast of Canaan, are depicted as a major threat to the Israelites in the period just before the emergence of a monarchy, and the story of David and Goliath—whoever it was who actually killed Goliath—may have it right when it describes them as an intimidating enemy. All around the Eastern Mediterranean, the so-called Sea Peoples, of which the Philistines were one, had a highly disruptive effect. Many important cities, such as Ugarit, were destroyed in this period, and even powerful kingdoms like Egypt had a hard time fending off the Sea Peoples. The Philistines had a similarly disruptive effect on Canaan according to the Bible, and archaeology confirms that they not only established a secure foothold on the coast but also began to expand into Canaan's interior. The Philistines' incursion might have forced many local inhabitants to move inward, which would explain the proliferation of small settlements in Canaan's central highlands in this same period.

Some scholars think that the earliest Israelite state first emerged as a reaction against Philistine domination. In towns like Beth Shemesh, a border town between Israelite and Philistine territory that has been undergoing excavation since the 1990s, archaeologists have found evidence of elaborate fortification efforts that would have required the support of some kind of centralized power—presumably some kind of Israelite state that was seeking to defend its borders against the Philistines. It may not be a coincidence that archaeologists have also found at Beth Shemesh and other sites in the region evidence of cultural practices that distinguish its population, presumably a proto-Israelite population, from that of the nearby Philistines living just a few miles away. The Philistines liked to eat pork, for example, whereas the people of Beth Shemesh did not, as measured by the absence of pig bones at Beth Shemesh versus the frequency of pig bones at nearby Philistine sites. Archaeologists theorize that the taboo against eating pork—a dietary restriction noted in the Bible and practiced by religious Jews to this day—may have originated in this period as a marker of social and cultural difference that helped clarify the identity and allegiance of the people living in the intermediate zone between the Philistines and the local population they were threatening to displace. A similar explanation has been proposed for circumcision, the removal of the foreskin from the penis, another behavior that distinguished the Israelites from the Philistines (in case you are wondering, yes, it is difficult to measure the absence or presence of foreskins in the archaeological record, but the significance of circumcision as a marker of difference between Israelites and Philistines is something that the Bible itself emphasizes). In addition to building walls, in other words, the Canaanite inhabitants of the land began to segregate themselves from the Philistines through social and ritual behavior.

Until the Philistines' arrival, this theory proposes, the Israelites did not actively differentiate themselves from neighboring peoples. We may have an image of the early Israelites in a relief in an Egyptian temple at Karnak, possibly an illustration of the victories described in the Merneptah Stele from 1207 BCE that include that king's conquest of a people named Israel, and if so, they are indistinguishable from other Canaanites. It was only after the arrival of Philistines, true outsiders marked by behavior different from those of the Canaanites, that the Israelites, beginning in the region where they had closest contact with the Philistines, developed a collective self-consciousness fostered through distinct cultural practices of their own. This theory cannot be proven, and it does not account for why the Israelites also came to distinguish themselves from other Canaanites, but it is worth noting for its attempt to explain when and how the ancient Israelites developed a group identity and behavior different from those of other peoples in the area: Israelite identity, like that of Europeans, Americans, and many other national or ethnic groups, may have crystallized as a reaction to the threat, real or perceived, posed by the arrival of another people.

The Philistines' arrival may have been a catalyst for political changes as well. As the Bible depicts events, the Israelites were highly decentralized before this time, a loose confederation of tribes prior to the Philistines' arrival. In theory, they were united by a common ancestry; in practice, they may have felt little allegiance to one another. The book of Judges, named for the temporary leaders that sometimes led the early Israelites into battle against their enemies, records several attempts to establish a more permanent form of leadership in this early period, a form of rule passed down from father to son, but these efforts fail. It is only during their conflict with the Philistines that the Israelites establish permanent, centralized rule. The first king noted by the Bible, Saul, dies during a battle against the Philistines, as does his son and would-be successor Jonathan, but they are replaced by David, who is able to secure his kingdom from the Philistine threat. The Philistines do not disappear; they continued to reside on the coast of Canaan, in places like Ashkelon, and there is evidence of conflict with the Israelites into the eighth century, but at least in the Bible, they appear far less of a threat after David's reign. The securing of a border with the Philistines, together with the withdrawal of Egyptian imperial rule, laid the groundwork for the emergence of an independent Israelite monarchy.

Unfortunately, we do not know as much about the early history of this monarchy as we would like. According to the Bible, David was really the turning point—it was he who established Jerusalem as the capital of his kingdom, and unlike Saul, he successfully passed down power to a son, Solomon, though not without some violent intra-family conflict that led to the deaths of Solomon's older brothers, Amnon, Absalom, and Adonijah. Solomon would go on to become an even more successful king than David, at least in terms of institution-building. The Bible describes him as a ruler of extraordinary wisdom who was able to organize Israel's tribes into a single political unit, acquire a great fortune, exert dominance over surrounding kingdoms, and undertake a number of building projects throughout his kingdom, including a permanent, artfully designed house for God in Jerusalem, the Solomonic Temple.

One might expect evidence of such figures in the archaeological record, and indeed, over the first 50 or 60 years of the twentieth century, archaeologists believed that they had found such evidence—stables in the city of Megiddo where Solomon is supposed to have kept his horses, a Solomonic port on the Red Sea, and Solomonic fortifications at places like Hazor. The Solomonic age seemed to be the first truly historical age in Israel's past—that is, an age that could be confirmed by multiple finds, or at least that is what scholars believed until recently. In the last few decades, however, the scholarly consensus has fractured. Some recent archaeologists maintain that there is something to the biblical description of the kingdoms of David and Solomon, uncovering impressive structures that, in their view, prove the existence of an Israelite state in the tenth century BCE. Other archaeologists have grown skeptical, arguing that archaeological finds once attributed to that period—including all the discoveries noted earlier—have been misinterpreted and belong to other ages. The debate continues, swinging back to the view that David and Solomon may have been real historical figures, significant regional rulers, and all that one can say for now is that it is still not possible to point to clear-cut, incontrovertible evidence of Solomon's reign, not even of his famous temple in Jerusalem. The impressive ruins one can visit at today's Temple Mount in Jerusalem are from the later Second Temple, and there is no trace of an earlier structure at the site (*see the box* "The Search for Solomon's Temple").

Whatever reality might lie behind the biblical account of David and Solomon, even according to the Bible, their kingdom did not remain intact for long. From its inception, we are told, the monarchy was extremely controversial and provoked political and religious dissent. The prophet Samuel had tried to warn the Israelites of the dangers of monarchy when they first demanded a king, and what were perceived as royal abuses, especially Solomon's policy of extracting forced labor from his Israelite subjects to support his ambitious building projects, deepened those reservations among many Israelites. When Solomon's son Rehoboam came to power, a leader named Jeroboam led 10 of the 12 tribes of Israel in a rebellion, leaving the Davidic kingdom in a much-reduced state largely confined to the territory of the tribe of Judah (this kingdom was so closely associated with the territory of Judah, incidentally, that it was also known as the Kingdom of Judah). Jeroboam established a kingdom in the north known as the Kingdom of Israel, and the Kingdoms of Judah and Israel existed side by side for two centuries until the northern kingdom was destroyed by Assyria, which exiled its inhabitants, the ten "lost tribes," to other parts of its empire.

Here, at last, we are beginning to move into a historical period that has some direct corroboration in extrabiblical sources. The inscription from Dan mentioned earlier, from the ninth century BCE, refers to both kingdoms, confirming that they both existed by this point, as do later Mesopotamian sources. Whether there was ever a united Kingdom of Israel, a state that united both Judah and Israel, is an open question, however, and some argue that there were two kingdoms from the very beginning: the Northern Kingdom of Israel, developing first in the ninth century BCE, and the Kingdom of Judah, coming into its own only after the north's destruction at the end of the eighth century BCE. Located in the north, the Kingdom of Israel had close ties with Phoenicia in what is now Lebanon, as when one of its most infamous rulers, Ahab, married a Phoenician named Jezebel, and its economy seems to have benefited from greater agricultural resources and trade relationships. Located in the south and more isolated, Judah was the smaller of the two kingdoms, but it also seems to have been more politically stable. While royal power in the

THE SEARCH FOR SOLOMON'S TEMPLE

Figure 1.4 A reconstruction of Solomon's Temple.

The foregoing reconstruction of Solomon's Temple is based on the biblical account in I Kings 6–7, but we do not really know what this temple looked like, since we have no contemporary images or archaeological evidence to work with (the archaeological remnants of the Temple complex visible in Jerusalem today are from the much later Second Temple, as expanded by Herod in the first century BCE). At the beginning of the twentieth century, in an excavation conducted between 1909 and 1911, a British adventurer named Montagu Parker made an effort to find Solomon's Temple and its treasures beneath the Temple Mount now visible in Jerusalem, but to do so, he had to encroach on a site considered sacred to Muslims, the Dome of the Rock; his efforts sparked rioting, and no archaeologist has been foolish enough to continue the search.

For a time, scholars did think they had one piece of evidence for Solomon's Temple. The object shown in Figure 1.5, a thumb-sized ornament in the shape of a pomegranate and inscribed with Hebrew words that suggested an association with the Temple, was once believed to be a relic from Solomon's Temple, perhaps an ornament from a priestly scepter. That was before 2005; however, in that year, a team of scholars commissioned to investigate the object announced that the inscription appearing on the scepter was probably a modern forgery.

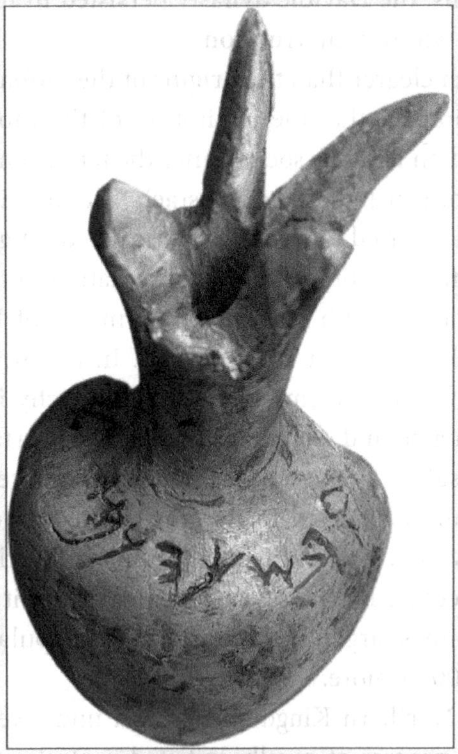

Figure 1.5 An inscribed pomegranate-shaped ornament once thought to be the only known relic of the Temple of Solomon, until its inscription was discovered to be a forgery.

Today, the absence of archaeological evidence for Solomon's Temple has become a charged issue, having been caught up in the Israeli–Palestinian conflict over who should control Jerusalem. Although nothing of the First Temple survives, one cannot simply dismiss the biblical description as a fantasy, because it fits in many ways with what we know about temple architecture from elsewhere in Canaan and Syria in this period, but it is also certainly the case that the search for Solomon's Temple has led many scholars astray. (For more on the controversies generated by biblical archaeology, *see the box* "Biblical Archaeology: A Controversial Quest.")

Northern Kingdom of Israel passed from one ruling family to another through coups and assassinations, the Davidic dynasty persisted in Judah almost without interruption.

Much clearer than the origins of the monarchy is the impact that the institution of the monarchy had on Israelite society after the tenth century BCE, both in Judah and in Israel. The monarchy created, or tried to create, a political and religious center for Israelite culture, consolidating not just power and wealth but also the symbols of Israelite religion under royal control. In Judah, that center was Jerusalem, where the monarchy itself was situated and a temple stood. The importance of Jerusalem as the political and religious center of Judah is reflected in its growth. In the tenth century BCE, it was inhabited by only a few thousand people. By the seventh century BCE, it was many times larger, with an estimated population of 25,000 or more.

Figure 1.6 An ivory plaque from the royal palace in Samaria, capital of the Northern Kingdom of Israel, dating to the ninth or eighth century BCE. The image is of a winged sphinx. This and another 500 or so ivory objects found in the palace complex suggest the wealth and prosperity of Israel's upper class in this period.

The Northern Kingdom of Israel underwent a similar process of royally initiated centralization, perhaps even earlier than the Kingdom of Judah. In 1 Kings 12, it is reported that Jeroboam built two sanctuaries at the borders of his kingdom, one in the south at Bethel, not that far from Jerusalem, and the other in the north at Dan. Each housed a golden calf, identified with the god or gods who led Israel out of Egypt, and their purpose, claimed in 1 Kings, was to dissuade Israelites from continuing to go to the Temple in Jerusalem and thus reverting in their loyalties to the kings who ruled from there. The calves have not been discovered, but a momentous sanctuary has been unearthed at Dan, which includes a large platform area where the calves may conceivably have been displayed. It took longer for the Kingdom of Israel to settle on a permanent site for its royal capital, but it eventually did so at Samaria, where a huge palace also has been excavated.

Even as the emergence of the monarchy centralized society, it also divided it in new ways, setting the stage for the development of two similar but distinct Israelite cultures. The kingdoms of Judah and Israel shared a language and perhaps a reverence for the same god, but according to the Bible, they developed two separate forms of Israelite worship. Judah based its official cult in Jerusalem; the northern kingdom based its shrines at Dan and Bethel. There also emerged within each society new class and social divisions, especially in the wealthier Kingdom of Israel. Prophetic texts like the book of Amos, reflecting the situation in Israel in the mid-eighth century BCE, protest against the self-indulgence of the rich and their exploitation of the poor, or as Amos might have put it, of "buying the needy for a pair of sandals" (Amos 8:6).

By the time the monarchy came to an end in Israel in the eighth century BCE, and in Judah in the sixth century BCE, there may have been subjects happy to see it go. Indeed, the editor who produced the account of the monarchy now found in the Bible, the narrative that runs from the book of Joshua through 2 Kings known by scholars as the Deuteronomistic History, was himself a sharp critic of the monarchy, blaming the misfortunes of his people on the wickedness of its kings and suggesting through his account that Israel should never have sought a king to begin with.

After the demise of the Davidic kingdom during the Babylonian Exile in 586 BCE (to be discussed ahead), the Israelite monarchy came to an end, never to be restored, but its influence persisted well beyond its demise as a functioning institution of governance. Messianism, the expectation that God would send a leader savior, a royal figure, to liberate Israel from its enemies and rebuild the Temple (a belief which we will look at more closely in a coming chapter), was born of the post-exilic hope that God would one day restore the king, and the expectation of such a restoration persists into modern times among religious Jews.

The monarchy also exerted an influence on how Jews conceived of God, referred to as a king in prayers recited to this day, while Jerusalem, the political and religious capital of the Kingdom of Judah, remains important to the spiritual imagination and political aspirations of Jews, as in the word *Zionism*, the modern movement to establish a sovereign homeland for the Jews, which derives from the word *Zion*, a biblical synonym for *Jerusalem*.

Family Ties

The term *history* often calls to mind a sequence of dramatic events and changes—wars, migrations, the rise and fall of leaders, the conception and dissemination of new ideas—that affect large numbers of people. But for most people, life does not unfold on such a grand scale. Think about your own life. Is the most influential person in your life the president of the United States, or is it a parent, a spouse, a sibling, or a friend? Events such as elections, wars, and epidemics certainly shape the world you live in and may even impinge on your personal life in important ways, but so too do events that would not make it into the average history book: the birth of siblings, meeting a future spouse, or losing a loved one. Experience on this more personal level is part of history too, though it may not be as well documented or dramatic as what usually gets recorded in history textbooks. Fortunately, apart from what the evidence reveals about large-scale events such as the end of Egyptian domination and the Philistine incursion, it also tells us something about Israelite life on this more personal scale.

The majority of ancient Israelites lived in villages—one estimate places the figure at 66 percent of the total population of Canaan in the period from 1000 to 500 BCE. The rest lived in larger towns or cities, but these were very small by current standards—Jerusalem in the tenth century BCE was probably home to about 1,000–2,000 people. The center of ancient Israelite/Judahite social life and economic activity was not the palace or the temple but the house, presumably inhabited by the nuclear family, and it was in this setting that life unfolded for the majority of Israelites—birth, marriage, death, and the other events that defined their lives. This is memorably captured in the book of Genesis, which recounts the origins of the Israelites as the history of a single family, focusing on the relationship between husbands and wives, parents, and children, the master of the house and his servants. The family remained the basic organizing unit of ancient Israel throughout the period portrayed by the Bible, which describes the entire people as an extended family, 12 tribes descended from the 12 sons of Jacob: Reuben, Simeon, Levi, Judah, Dan, Naphtali, Gad, Asher, Issachar, Zebulun, Joseph (which was divided into two subtribes, Ephraim and Manasseh, understood as Jacob's grandsons), and Benjamin.

By synthesizing the Bible's testimony with archaeological evidence, scholars have reconstructed a picture of family life in ancient Israel. The most common house plan in ancient Israel is known as a four-roomed house (though it probably had more than four rooms), a house plan that probably predates the Israelites but became widespread in Canaan precisely in the period of Israelite settlement (around 1200 BCE). The family might have lived in the back rooms of the ground floor, but it is also possible that their quarters were on a second story reached by a ladder. Much of the first story was probably used for storage and as a manger for a family's animals, which not only kept the animals safe but also warmed the house when it was cold outside. It is not clear where the bathroom was located. People probably went outside and, in any case, rarely washed themselves.

Some houses shared a courtyard with other houses probably inhabited by members of the same extended family. Indeed, not only immediate neighbors but also members of one's village, and of neighboring villages, were likely kin. The Bible can help fill out what it meant to be part of such an extended kinship unit: Families were united by a responsibility to protect their members. It was the responsibility of the next of kin, a brother or cousin, to avenge the murder of a family member (which could sometimes spark a cycle of revenge and retaliation). According to the Bible, when a married man died without an heir, it was the duty of his next of kin to beget a child with his widow, so as to preserve the deceased's inheritance, a practice known as levirate marriage. We do not know much about what it was like to grow up in such a household. Having children was an important goal of family life, but the Bible reveals very little about what it was like to be a child in such a society. We can tell that boys were favored over girls, and the firstborn male over younger children, but that does not mean that women did not play an important role in family lives and in the household economy. In the families described in the Bible, men like Jacob and David had multiple wives, and it was the relative standing of these wives in relation to one another, which wife was first or which was favored by the husband, that conditioned the social status of their children within the family structure.

Strangely but consistently, in the Bible, younger siblings get the upper hand over their older siblings. This is true, in fact, of most of Israel's most important ancestors: Isaac displaces his older half-brother Ishmael, Jacob prevails over Esau, Joseph overshadows the firstborn Reuben and other older siblings, and both David and Solomon become kings even though each has several older brothers with a greater claim on the throne. Family life in ancient Israel seems to have had its own politics. Male siblings, especially those with different mothers, competed with one another for the father's favor and inheritance; they could even get into lethal conflicts with each other—and that intrafamily struggle was common enough that it left its mark on how the authors of the Bible depicted the history of Israel's early ancestors, a family history fraught with conflict.

Understanding this family structure is important for understanding Israelite society in general. Modern historians often describe Israel as a nation—a community united by a shared territory, language, and common history. The label fits, more or less, but it does not quite capture how Israelites perceived their own identity. Biblical texts such as the book of Genesis suggest that one's family was essential to this identity. Individual Israelites traced their family back at least five generations. Those who did not fit into one's family somehow were considered outsiders, non-Israelites, though groups that lived near the Israelites and shared

Figure 1.7 A reconstructed layout of a typical Israelite house in the period before the sixth century BCE. Most daily activities would have been performed in the central, perhaps unroofed room, while the side rooms are believed to have been used for storage and for keeping animals. Such houses seem to have had a second story, and it may have been there that people slept.

BIBLICAL ARCHAEOLOGY: A CONTROVERSIAL QUEST

Archaeology is the study of past lives through the physical evidence earlier people have left behind of their activities and impact. *Biblical archaeology* is the use of archaeology to illumine biblical literature and the society from which it originated. Some scholars do not think especially highly of biblical archaeology, concluding that it has been misled by a quasireligious impulse to prove the Bible true, but whatever its value for understanding the Bible, the field of biblical archaeology offers a fascinating case study in the challenges of connecting material evidence with literary testimony.

The Bible served as a kind of guidebook for the first archaeological expeditions in nineteenth-century Palestine. The first archaeologists, who were also often theologians, produced maps and topological surveys, through which they sought to connect biblical places to present-day sites and ruins that they encountered during their journeys. However, they overlooked some of the main cities of Canaan because they did not know about the *tell*, a mound formed from layers of human settlement. Archaeologists today have come a long way since the days of Edward Robinson, a Congregationist minister who made the first archaeological survey of Palestine in 1838 but who completely overlooked important sites right under his feet, like Megiddo, because he didn't understand the nature of the tell. Later in the century, however, Flinders Petrie noticed that such mounds were not natural hills but artificial formations created through the piling on of settlements one atop another. It is now known that some tells have 20 or more layers of settlement spanning two or more millennia.

Petrie also realized that since ancient pottery design was standardized according to time and place, potsherds, or broken pieces of pottery, could also be a powerful tool, helping archaeologists distinguish between different cultures and periods of time. Besides potsherds, other finds—architectural remains, glass, metallurgy, and even deposits of refuse—also revealed insights into the origins of particular cultures, their economy, diet, social practices, and other aspects of ancient life not fully illumined by the textual sources. Despite such advances, archaeologists could also go wildly astray in their search for their biblical past. One expedition, led by a German geologist named Karl Mauch, believed that it had discovered evidence of Solomon and the queen of Sheba in southern Africa, not realizing that what seemed like the ruins of the queen's kingdom were actually the work of indigenous Africans. Others traced Solomon's fleet all the way to Brazil, fooled by a forged inscription supposedly left behind by the Phoenician survivors of a shipwreck. Even today, as we noted earlier, it can still be a struggle to distinguish authentic discoveries from sensationalist claims and forged artifacts, especially when an artifact turns up in the antiquities market rather than a controlled excavation.

Over the twentieth century, there emerged a number of important archaeologists who advanced the effort to connect biblical and archaeological evidence. These included figures like William F. Albright (1891–1971), who championed the use of archaeology to illumine the biblical text; Kathleen Kenyon (1906–1979), famous for her excavations in Jericho, who noted certain inconsistencies between archaeological evidence and biblical accounts; and Yigael Yadin (1917–1984), a founding figure in the history of Israeli archaeology, remembered for his excavation of Masada from the Roman period, but also for his work at Hazor and other sites that he connected to Solomon's reign. Such scholars helped establish biblical archaeology as a respectable intellectual enterprise, securing a place for it in academia, but that doesn't mean their interpretations of the evidence were unassailable, and much of what biblical archaeologists have concluded about the material evidence and its connection to the Bible has been challenged.

As Canaanite settlements were unearthed, for instance, inconsistencies emerged between the Bible and the archaeological record. As we have noted, the only major city that shows a layer of

BIBLICAL ARCHAEOLOGY: A CONTROVERSIAL QUEST (CONTINUED)

destruction from the time of the Israelites' conquest of Canaan is Hazor, and it is possible that it was razed not by the Israelites but by the Sea People, who attacked many cities on the Eastern Mediterranean. More recently, based largely on the absence of finds from the relevant period, archaeologists have debated the size, nature, and importance of the Davidic and Solomonic kingdom. Since Egyptian, Assyrian, and Babylonian inscriptions show some correspondence with the biblical account only from the time after Solomon, some archaeologists argue that the biblical description of David and Solomon's kingdom does not correspond to the political reality in the tenth century BCE, rejecting, for example, the link that Yadin drew between fortifications discovered at Megido, Gezer, and Hazor and the biblical verse that mentions that Solomon built walls in those places (1 Kings 9:15). This debate was intensified in light of the claims of an Israeli archaeologist named Eilat Mazar, who claims to have discovered a foundation for a palatial structure in Jerusalem that could have been built in the time of David and Solomon.

This debate among archaeologists is not only about the veracity of the Bible itself, however, but also about how to use archaeology to illumine the past. If archaeology cannot prove that a figure like David existed, does that mean that it has no value for understanding ancient Israelite history? Archaeologists of other regions learn much about the past without the benefit of written evidence. Isn't there much one can learn about the history of Canaan without relying on the Bible to shape what one is looking for? While some archaeologists remain focused on proving particular people or events from the Bible, others now draw on fields like anthropology to broaden their understanding of the past, seeking not to confirm or disprove the Bible's historical claims but to illumine those aspects of Israelite experience not registered in the Bible, including the day-to-day life of the Israelites. To disconnect archaeology from the Bible, some scholars came to describe their subfield as Syro-Palestinian archaeology.

Whatever the relationship between the Bible and the material record, every summer, students can join in the quest to uncover the lives of the Israelites and the many other inhabitants of the region, prehistoric peoples, Canaanites, Philistines, Greek and Roman–era Jews, medieval Crusaders, Ottoman rulers, Palestinians, and a host of others. Several archaeological expeditions in Israel today, including some focused on biblical-era sites, are run as summer field schools designed to train student volunteers in the methods of field archaeology in exchange for their help in the work of excavation. The volunteer model for archaeology in Israel, including enlisting college-age volunteers to help excavate ancient sites, has been disrupted in recent years by the Covid pandemic and violence in the Middle East, but it continues. Two places to look for volunteer opportunities are the "join a dig" page of the website of the Israel Antiquities Authority, at https://www.antiquities.org.il/article_eng.aspx?sec_id=55&subj_id=229, and the website of the Biblical Archaeological Society: https://www.biblicalarchaeology.org/digs/.

certain customs with them and a language—the Edomites, for instance, thought to be the descendants of Jacob's brother Esau, were thought to be closer to Israel on the family tree than less culturally similar peoples, such as the Egyptians. What defined the Israelite community, as implied in the Hebrew Bible—what bound Israelites and Judahites together and tied them to some peoples while distinguishing them from others—were the same ties of kinship that bound together parents, spouses, children, siblings, and cousins into a family.

The kinship-based structure of Israelite/Judahite society left many individuals on the edges of or outside this structure—widows, orphans, and non-Israelites living in Israel's midst—in a highly vulnerable position. In the Bible, God is identified as "the father of orphans and protector of widows" (Psalm 68), showing special concern for those who fell through the cracks of a kinship-based system. Like other ancient Mediterranean societies, Israel had a strong code of hospitality: One was supposed to be welcoming to strangers, offering them a meal if they came to your home. Even so, some Israelites were suspicious and sometimes abusive of strangers, a problem widespread enough that the Bible repeatedly addresses it: "You shall not oppress a resident alien, for you were aliens in the land of Egypt" (Exodus 22:21). Caring for those who fell through the safety net of the family, or stood outside of it, was an issue of great concern to biblical authors.

The most cherished possession that an Israelite family could own was its land, the source of the family's livelihood. When the Israelite king Ahab tried to buy a vineyard next to his palace, offering its owner, an Israelite named Naboth, another plot of land or the equivalent in money, Naboth staunchly refused: "The Lord forbid that I give you my ancestral inheritance" (1 Kings 21:3). If one was fortunate enough to inherit land from one's ancestors, it was vital to keep it in the family. This is why one of the worst punishments the authors of the Hebrew Bible can imagine is exile: the alienation of Israel from its land.

The father, or grandfather, was the ultimate authority in the household, passing that authority to male heirs after his death. In such a system, a woman was usually under the control of men for the duration of her life. As a child, she was under the control of her father; at marriage (brokered between her fiancé and her father), she was subjected to the control of her husband. The household was a place of residence, but also an important site of economic activity—the storage of agricultural produce, the stabling of animals, and the production of pottery and textiles—and the women of the house probably played an important role in all these activities, but their main role was having and caring for children. In the early Israelite society depicted in the book of Genesis, the ultimate blessing that God bestows on Abraham and his descendants, apart from the land, is offspring, especially male offspring. The women of this family—Sarah, Hagar, Rebecca, Rachel, Leah, Bilhah, and Zilpah—are of interest to the storyteller only to the extent that they help realize this blessing (*see the box* "Sex and Death in Ancient Israel").

Not everyone living in the Israelite household was a biological relative; slaves and hired servants lived there as well. Slavery was a universally accepted institution in the ancient Near East, and ancient Israel was no exception. To be sure, the core experience in Israel's collective memory was its escape from slavery, an inspiration for modern-day abolitionists, but actually, the Exodus story does not imply a rejection of slavery as an institution. The Bible implies that the Egyptians were wrong to enslave the Israelites, not because slavery was considered wrong per se, but because the Israelites did not deserve such treatment—they had not been purchased or captured in battle but were the descendants of an ancestor, Joseph, who had once done Egypt a great service and had settled in the land of Egypt along with his father and brothers with the permission of its king. The memory of the Exodus does elicit sympathy for Israelites who have become the slaves of other Israelites, and the Bible limits their servitude and protects them in other ways; but slavery was woven into the fabric of Israelite society, as it was in other ancient Near Eastern societies, and it never occurred to whoever wrote the Bible to abolish it. Slave owners in modern Europe and America used the Bible to justify their own enslavement of people, but there are important differences between modern and ancient slavery: Slavery in nineteenth-century America, for example, was race-based in a way biblical slavery was not.

The family ties that connected ancient Israelites were placed under great stress during experiences like the Babylonian Exile, which displaced many

Israelites, and the social life of their descendants underwent further change in the period of Greek and Roman rule, when there emerged alternatives to family life, such as voluntary communities, like the early Christian and the rabbinic community, which drew some men away from the structure and responsibilities of family life. Still, vestiges of the ancient Israelite family structure persisted well beyond the biblical age, as illustrated by the fate of tribal affiliation, a person's sense of being connected to others in his community as a fellow member of a tribe descended from a common ancestor. We know from the Bible that those who survived the Babylonian Exile still identified as members of tribes—the majority from the tribe of Judah, but some from the tribes of Levi and Benjamin—and evidence from the New Testament and other sources shows that such tribal affiliation continued well into the first century.

Today, the label *Jewish* (derived from the tribal name *Judah*) does not imply a tribal identity in any practical sense—the term took on other geographic, cultural, and religious resonances in the post-biblical period—and Jews today are more likely to think of themselves as members of an ethnic group or a religion than as cousins in a superfamily. Even now, however, tribal identity persists. Note, for example, how some Jews identify themselves as descendants of the Levites, the family charged in the Bible with special duties related to worship (an identity frequently reflected in a person's last name—"Levi," "Levine," and the like—though secularized Jews with such names may not realize or care about their names' original significance). Passed from father to son, Levitical identity is a lingering trace of how tribalism once shaped identity in ancient Israel, a person's place in the community shaped by his position in a family tree.

Surviving Mesopotamian Domination

The political opening created by the end of Egyptian domination at the end of the Bronze Age, during which time the Israelite and Judahite kingdoms developed, began to close in the ninth and eighth centuries BCE as the Assyrian Empire expanded westward from Mesopotamia into Syria and Canaan. As it did with other kingdoms that it encountered, Assyria forced the kings of Israel and Judah to submit to its rule and pay tribute. The Northern Kingdom of Israel, the larger of the two kingdoms, resisted this imposition and was destroyed when the Assyrian king Shalmaneser V and his successor, Sargon II, smashed its rebellion in 722–720 BCE, an event corroborated by Assyrian sources. A people known as the Samaritans claim to this day to descend from the northern tribes of Ephraim and Manasseh (see Chapter 4), but from the vantage point of the Bible's authors and later Jews, the destruction of the northern kingdom marked the end of this part of the Israelite people. The Assyrians exiled the population of the northern kingdom to other parts of their empire, and what happened to these "ten lost tribes" remains a mystery to this day.

The Kingdom of Judah was also conquered by Assyria a few decades later, under the Assyrian ruler Sennacherib, and here, too, the Bible's account (2 Kings 18–19) can be corroborated, at least in part:

> In the fourteenth year of King Hezekiah, Sennacherib king of Assyria came up against all the fortified cities of Judah and captured them. Hezekiah King of Judah sent to the king of Assyria at Lachish saying, "I have sinned. Turn from me and I will bear any penalty you impose on me." So the king of Assyria imposed on Hezekiah a penalty of three hundred silver talents and thirty talents of gold.
>
> (2 Kings 18:13–14)

This is more or less consistent with how events are described by Sennacherib himself in his annals:

> As to Hezekiah, the Judahite, he did not submit to my yoke, I laid siege to 46 of his strong cities, walled forts and to the countless small villages in their vicinity and conquered [them]. . . . I drove out [of them] 200,150 people, young

Figure 1.8 Panel from the black obelisk of King Shalmaneser III, from Nimrud, c. 825 BCE, showing the tribute of King Jehu of Israel, who is on his knees at the feet of the Assyrian king.

and old, male and female, horses, mules, donkeys, camels, big and small cattle beyond counting, and considered [them] booty. [Hezekiah] I made prisoner in Jerusalem, his royal residence, like a bird in the cage.

Sennacherib says that after destroying Judah's other cities and forts, he pinned King Hezekiah in Jerusalem "like a bird in a cage," but he does not destroy Jerusalem itself, as the Assyrians had done with Samaria, the capital of the Northern Kingdom of Israel—perhaps because Hezekiah was willing to pay a fine, as 2 Kings 18:14 reports. On this point, the biblical source seems consistent with the Assyrian account more or less, but then the Bible goes in a different direction, attributing the city's survival to a miraculous defeat of the Assyrian army:

> That night [after Hezekiah prayed to the Lord for help against the Assyrians] an angel of the Lord went out and struck down one hundred and eighty-five thousand in the camp of the Assyrians. When morning dawned—behold, they were all corpses. Then King Sennacherib of Assyria returned home and lived at Nineveh.
> (2 Kings 19:35–36)

According to the Bible, in other words, what ultimately saved Jerusalem was not Hezekiah's submission but an act of divine intervention that destroyed the Assyrian army in Judah and sent Sennacherib packing. Nothing like this is mentioned in the Assyrian account, which depicts what happened as a typical Assyrian victory. We will not try to resolve the discrepancy between the two accounts here, but we do note that each author had reasons for putting his own spin on what happened, with the biblical account serving to underscore the power of God, the Assyrian account underscoring Sennacherib's.

SEX AND DEATH IN ANCIENT ISRAEL

Both sex and death are rooted in human biology, but how people behave sexually and how they respond to death are also shaped by values and norms that can vary from society to society. Most of what we know about sexual behavior and the response to death in ancient Israel comes from the Bible. We cannot treat its testimony as an anthropological report that can tell us what the average Israelite thought about these topics, but it does reveal something of Israelite and Judahite attitudes, anxieties, and practices.

Many people assume that the Bible endorses a prudish attitude toward sex, forbidding it outside of heterosexual marriage. There is and isn't truth to that characterization. Something does seem incompatible between sexuality and God's presence in the Hebrew Bible. Before it can experience God's revelation at Mount Sinai, Israel must abstain from sexual activity (Exodus 19:15), and priests were subject to more sexual restrictions than other Israelites. In contrast to some other ancient Near Eastern deities, God himself never acts in a sexual way, and as far as we know, his worship did not involve any kind of sexual activity. This does not mean that the Bible's authors were opposed to sexual expression in other contexts, however. One of the most erotic texts ever written is the Song of Songs, a collection of love songs attributed to King Solomon but probably written by someone else, perhaps for use in a wedding celebration or for some other erotically charged occasion. The song gives unforgettable expression to the feeling of sexual yearning, the lover's restless desire to be with the beloved:

> In bed at night, I sought the one I love—I sought him but did not find him. I shall rise and go throughout the city, through the streets and through the squares; I will seek the one I love. I sought him but did not find him. The watchmen found me, the ones who patrol the town. "Have you seen the one I love?" Just after I passed them, I found the one I love; I grabbed him, and would not let him go until I brought him to my mother's house, to the room of she who conceived me.
>
> (Song of Songs 3:1–4)

Nowhere in the song is this sexual longing condemned as wrong. To the contrary, it is celebrated as a mighty, irrepressible power: "[V]ast floods cannot quench love, nor rivers drown it" (8:6–7). And we are not dealing here with some kind of spiritual love; the lovers in the song focus on the body of the beloved, described in arousing detail:

> Your rounded thighs are like jewels, a work of art. Your navel is like a round goblet. Let mixed wine not be lacking. Your belly like a heap of wheat hedged with lilies. Your two breasts are like two fawns, twins of a gazelle. . . . [Y]our stature is like a palm, your breasts are like grape clusters. I thought, "I shall climb the palm, I shall take hold of its branches and may your breasts be like grape clusters on a vine, the scent of your breath like apples."
>
> (7:2–9)

But the lovers of the song cannot fully realize their desire for each other. They seem to stand outside society, roaming among beautiful gardens, but society still keeps them apart—"[I]f only it could be as with a brother," says the female lover, "then I could kiss you and no one would despise me" (8:1). The verse presupposes some kind of sanction against sexual intimacy in public; a woman in this society is permitted to kiss a brother in public, but not a lover. The Song of Songs is a remarkably uninhibited celebration of desire, but it also acknowledges social constraints on the physical expression of that desire.

The Hebrew Bible does not treat sex as an inherently sinful activity. To the contrary, Genesis 1 casts sex as the fulfillment of God's first commandment to humanity to be fruitful and multiply. But it does recognize sexual behavior as a potentially destructive act not just for the individuals involved but for the entire community. As related in Leviticus 18, the land had expelled the earlier Canaanites largely because of their sexual behavior, their practice of incest, adultery, homosexuality, and bestiality, acts that confuse the ties that hold a family together, fail to produce children, or blur the boundary between divinely defined categories (male versus female, human versus animal). But lest one think that the Hebrew Bible's sexual ideal is the modern two-parent household, it is worth noting that it also allows for sexual behaviors at odds with contemporary ethical norms: polygamy (men marrying multiple wives, not women marrying multiple husbands) and married men having sex with concubines. It even tolerates rape in a way people today would never accept.

In Israelite culture, a woman's sexual activity was controlled by fathers and husbands, and female sexuality outside that control was considered shameful, even threatening. Seductive and sexually aggressive women were seen as a potentially mortal danger: "[D]o not stray onto her paths, for many are the slain she has struck down" (Proverbs 7:25– 26). Biblical law regulates the sexual life of both men and women, but it imposes more restrictions on the latter. A man could have multiple sexual partners—wives, servants, even prostitutes—and divorce a woman to marry another. By contrast, biblical law does not allow women to engage in polygamy, nor does it sanction female sex before marriage or grant women the right to initiate a divorce. It never explicitly prohibits lesbianism—probably not because it endorsed it but because what women did among themselves, outside their interaction with men or children, was of little interest to biblical lawmakers.

What ancient Israelites actually did behind the (probably not-so-private) walls of their houses is unknown to us, but with the Hebrew Bible's help, one can imagine the darker possibilities. Consider as an example the sexual experience of Jacob's children: His daughter Dinah was raped by a man who subsequently offered to marry her (Genesis 34); his eldest son, Reuben, had sex with Jacob's concubine (Genesis 35:22); Judah, the ancestor of the Judahites, had sex with a woman he thought was a prostitute but was really his daughter-in-law Tamar in disguise (Genesis 38); and Joseph, Jacob's favorite, was propositioned by another man's wife (Genesis 39). Regardless of whether these incidents actually happened, the authors who report them recognize that sexual behavior often involved the exercise of violence and deceit, and beyond restricting sexual activity, biblical law also sought to protect Israelites from being victimized in these ways.

Beyond the biblical account, there is now another kind of evidence that might allow us to gain some understanding of sexual behavior in ancient Israel: the testimony of DNA, the genetic instructions encoded into the cells of an organism that shape its growth and functioning; and it gives us a new way to explore questions like who mated with whom.

How can the cells in a person's body register ancient sexual behavior? To begin with, biologists can take genetic samples from Jews living in a particular place and compare such evidence with the genetic profile of other populations—non-Jews living in the same place, or Jews living in other parts of the world. This kind of analysis reveals that Jewish populations often have a different genetic history than the non-Jews among whom they live, owing in part to the mating customs they followed: Their DNA shows that Jews often mated with the non-Jews among whom they lived, but it also often registers the impact of endogamy—the practice of choosing one's mate from within one's community or tribe. The genetic profiles of many Jews throughout the world show that they have ancestors who originated from the Near East (as shown by genetic connections with contemporary Middle Eastern populations, like Palestinians and Druze), and that they and their descendants often mated with those within their population in ways that kept their profile distinct from that of the non-Jewish populations among whom they lived.

This research is still very new and will no doubt continue to generate many interesting findings, but it should be noted that it is controversial, and some critics question how the evidence is being interpreted. The Nazis used biology—and even genetics itself—to justify their genocidal treatment of the Jews, and some are concerned that contemporary genetics research could be misused in a similar way.

SEX AND DEATH IN ANCIENT ISRAEL (CONTINUED)

Critics also note that, as is the case with textual and archaeological data, the genetic data does not speak for itself: It has to be interpreted and contextualized, and in the course of doing so, genetic historians, like other kinds of historians, can make mistakes in how they make sense of the evidence. An example is a famous study from the late 1990s in which scientists uncovered genetic evidence showing that *Cohanim*, Jewish males who believe themselves to be descendants of the priestly caste established by Moses's brother Aaron, do in fact descend from a common lineage on the paternal side going back an estimated 2,000 or 3,000 years. (The original study, conducted by Karl Skorecki, Michael Hammer, and a team of other scientists, was titled "Y chromosomes in Jewish Priests" and published in the journal *Nature* 385 in 1997.) More recent research, drawing on new data and methods, has called aspects of the original study of the Cohanim into question, and even the authors of the original research have revised their interpretation.

So far, this kind of research has not changed our understanding of ancient Jewish history—or of ancient Jewish sexual history—in a dramatic way, but it does have the potential to expand our understanding of the Jews' mating and reproductive history, not to mention what it can tell us about the impact of events like migration and the history of genetically related medical conditions. Given how difficult it is to recover information about ancient Jewish women in particular, it is especially intriguing that genetic analysis can reveal something about both the male and female ancestors of present-day Jews. Skepticism is warranted, given the criticisms of this kind of research, but so too is openness to what it may yet reveal.

Death and What Comes After

In the pre-Israelite religion of Canaan, or at least in Ugaritic literature, death was imagined as a deity, Mot, not the object of worship in the way other gods were but a powerful, voracious being with an immense mouth and appetite, able not only to consume multitudes of humans but also to overcome the gods. In one of the stories told of him in Ugaritic literature, Mot defeats Baal himself, the god of fertility, and sends him into the underworld. Mot is defeated in turn by the goddess Anat, and Baal is revived, but the victory is only temporary. The struggle against death is an ongoing one.

Biblical literature may allude to the Mot myth, but death is not depicted there as a deity. The power of death is recognized (as in Song of Songs 8:6, "Love is as strong as Death"), but the Hebrew Bible contains no stories of combat between God and death, nor does it record any rituals for fending off death in the way that Ugaritic literature does. In the Bible, death goes the way of other Canaanite deities, such as Baal and Asherah, losing its status as an independent being with a will of its own.

In fact, the Hebrew Bible seems relatively uninterested in addressing the fear of mortality compared with other ancient Near Eastern literature. Much of the *Gilgamesh Epic* from Mesopotamia is a quest to find the secret of immortality. Ancient Egyptian culture seems to have been preoccupied with death and how to make it to a good afterlife. Some part of a person's identity was thought to survive death, going on to an afterlife that could be either very terrible or very pleasant, and various rituals and spells were developed to ensure a happy outcome. The Hebrew Bible does not reflect this kind of preoccupation with death. God does seem to have the power to spare certain special people from death—figures such as Enoch and Elijah—and even to resurrect the dead, as God does through the prophet Elisha in 2 Kings 4, but these are rare exceptions, and for the most part, death is depicted as a divinely ordained part of experience. Those who die do go on to some kind of afterlife in a place called Sheol, but like the Homeric Hades, it seems to be a rather gloomy place, its inhabitants unable to speak: The dead are "cut off" from the Lord (Psalm 88), forsaken and forgotten about. The Israelites believed in ghosts—as shown by 1 Samuel 28, where the ghost of the prophet Samuel rises from the underworld—but the Bible forbids Israel from consulting the dead or making offerings to them. Death and the dead are marginalized in the Hebrew Bible.

None of this is intended to suggest that the death of a loved one was not a traumatic experience for ancient Israelites. Like other ancient Near Eastern peoples, the Israelites expressed their bereavement in an intense and dramatic way, tearing their clothes, putting dust on their heads, beating their breasts, shaving their hair, wearing special mourning garments, and uttering lamentations in honor of the dead. The objects found in tombs—jewelry worn by the deceased and other personal items; possible evidence of food offerings, human- and animal-shaped figurines to protect, or provide company for, the dead; even miniaturized shrines possibly intended to give the dead access to the divine—give further witness to the concern that people had for their dead loved ones.

But in the Hebrew Bible at least, the distress caused by death does not motivate a yearning for immortality in the way that it does in the *Gilgamesh Epic*. Those who wrote Genesis and other books in the Jewish biblical canon do not seem preoccupied with how to overcome death or how to get into heaven—the familiar concepts of heaven and hell simply do not appear in the Hebrew Bible. Instead, what the Israelites described there seem to aspire to is a long, prosperous life and many children, the latter a kind of virtual immortality that sustained a person's memory after death. Abraham's death is the model of a good death: He reached an exceptionally old age (175, according to Genesis 25:8), and by the time he died, he had many descendants. Finally, he was buried in a tomb with his wife, Sarah, on land that he owned. That kind of death—not immortality in heaven, but resting peacefully alongside one's family members in the tomb and a legacy of many children—is what the Hebrew Bible regards as a happy ending to life, and the only kind of immortality it seems to envision is having one's name remembered by one's descendants.

Assyrian domination is well attested in the archaeological record, leaving behind not just a layer of destruction but inscriptions and the remains of buildings that were erected as Assyria sought to integrate Canaan into its westward-expanding empire. It has left a similarly deep imprint on biblical literature. Much of the prophetic literature in the Bible—texts imputed to such prophets as Isaiah, Amos, and Micah—comes from the Assyrian period and records the fear, confusion, and resentment triggered by Assyrian conquest. Why would God allow his chosen people to be subjugated by a foreign people? Was God angry with the people of Judah, and if so, why? Would the enemy's dominance ever come to an end, and what would life be like then? Prophetic literature addresses these questions, interpreting Assyrian conquest as divine punishment, but also holding out hope of God coming to the rescue. Here, for example, is one such note of prophetic consolation, a passage from the book of the prophet Isaiah, who lived in the time of Hezekiah and Sennacherib:

> Therefore thus says the Lord God of hosts: My people that dwell in Zion, don't fear the Assyrians when they beat you with a rod and lift up their staff against you in the way of Egypt, for in a little while my indignation will end, and my anger will be directed to their destruction. . . . On that day his burden will be lifted from your shoulder; his yoke [removed] from your neck and destroyed.
>
> (Isaiah 10:24–27)

Earlier prophets like Samuel, Nathan, and Elijah, figures described in the books of Samuel and Kings, were mostly focused on the king, mediating his relationship with God or protesting against his abuses. In the wake of Assyrian conquest, prophecy took on a new role in Israelite and Judahite society, offering consolation, envisioning a post-conquest future, articulating the desire for revenge at a time when not just their political independence but also their confidence in God's protection were being shaken.

The Kingdom of Judah was able to survive Assyrian conquest because, for whatever reason, the Assyrians left the Kingdom of Judah intact, if only as a rump state, destroying many cities and usurping much territory, but never destroying Jerusalem itself. Babylonian conquest in the period between 598 and 586 BCE was a more devastating experience. The Babylonians in this case were what scholars refer to as the Neo-Babylonians. Whereas the Assyrians were based in northern Mesopotamia, the Babylonians came from the south and were under Assyrian domination themselves, until the Assyrian Empire began to disintegrate in the final decades of the seventh century BCE. In the wake of its collapse, the Neo-Babylonian ruler Nebuchadnezzar II (604–562 BCE) sought to take over Assyrian territory in Syria and Canaan, a link to Egypt and the Mediterranean. This included the Kingdom of Judah, which he initially conquered in 598 BCE, exiling its king, Jehoiachin, and appointing his uncle, who he renamed Zedekiah, to take his place. Judah might have survived as a vassal state but proved restive, with Zedekiah joining a rebellion against the Babylonians that forced Nebuchadnezzar to return, and he effectively destroyed the Kingdom of Judah at this point. In 587 or 586 BCE, he burned down the Jerusalem Temple and looted its contents, killed Zedekiah and his sons, and exiled a substantial portion of Judah's population to Babylonia.

The Kingdom of Judah did not survive these latter events, but many individual Judahites did, and the Bible tells us something of how they adapted to captivity. The book of Jeremiah, the second-longest book of biblical prophecy after Isaiah, suggests that here, too, prophecy helped Judahites come to terms with traumatic social change. Many of the prophecies recorded in Jeremiah are set after Babylon's initial conquest of Jerusalem in 598 BCE, when part of Judah's population had already been exiled to Babylon. One of these prophecies, recorded in Jeremiah 29, is a letter that Jeremiah is said to have written to those exiles. The letter does not encourage the exiles to hope for return but instead urges them to settle down in the cities to which they have been deported:

> Build houses and live; plant gardens and eat their produce. Take wives and have sons and daughters; take women for your sons, and give your daughters to men, that they may bear sons and daughters; multiply there, and do not decrease. Seek the welfare of the city to where I have exiled you, and pray for it to the Lord, for in its welfare will be your welfare.
>
> (Jeremiah 29:5–7)

Faced with the complete devastation of his society, Jeremiah in this passage does not envision or seek an immediate restoration of what has been lost—the land of Canaan, Judah's independence, or the Temple—but instead urges his audience to adapt to their altered circumstances, to submit to foreign rule for the time being and make a life for themselves in exile, the prophet elsewhere predicting a new relationship, a "new covenant," between God and Israel in the future that will eventually restore to them what has been lost, albeit in a newly altered form.

The Babylonian documents known as the Murashu Archive, the records of a banking family compiled in the Mesopotamian city of Nippur, show that Judahites living in Mesopotamia in the fifth century BCE did indeed settle in Babylonia, for the archives include mention of many names identified as Judahite, individuals seemingly integrated into Babylonian social and economic life. In fact, apart from their names, little distinguishes these individuals from the non-Judahites in the Murashu texts; some even gave their children Babylonian names that incorporated the names of Babylonian gods, such as Shamash. If these were the descendants of Judahite exiles, they seem very settled into their new home.

This does not mean, however, that the exiles lost their connection to their former lives in the land of Canaan. Even as the book of Jeremiah counsels its audience to settle down, it also urges them to sustain a long-term hope in the eventual restoration of Israel, envisioning a renewed relationship with God, a revitalized Davidic dynasty, even a newly reunified Israelite people. Such texts as Jeremiah are our best evidence for how it was that Judahite society was able to survive the devastating impact of Mesopotamian conquest despite losing so many central institutions, illustrating a process of creative adjustment that allowed the exiles to sustain their Judahite identity even as they adapted to life in exile under foreign rule.

Learning to adapt in this way proved crucial for the long-term survival of Judahite culture. After the biblical period, its descendants, the Jews, would find themselves ruled by other foreigners: Persians, Greeks, Romans, Muslims, and others. Biblical texts such as Jeremiah proved an important asset in coming to terms with foreign domination, endorsing the decision to submit to foreign rule as a religiously acceptable one and developing ways for Judah to continue its relationship with God outside of Canaan.

The Early History of God

Both the Bible and extrabiblical evidence show that religious life in Israel and Judah, while it had some distinguishing features, resembled that of surrounding cultures. At the center of religious life in the Near East was one's relationship with the gods, beings who were like humans in many respects but were bigger, stronger, harder to see—and perhaps most essentially, lived much longer, either never dying or doing so only if slain by another god. What we call religion in this context was largely about sustaining a relationship with these gods despite the barriers that separated them from humans—seeking their favor and protection, inducing them into revealing themselves, understanding their intentions, caring for their needs, avoiding their anger, seeking their forgiveness. One of the major institutions of ancient Near Eastern culture, the temple was designed as a setting for divine-human interaction, and the stories that we now think of as myths were attempts to understand the gods and their relationship to humans.

Cultivating a relationship with the gods was also the goal of religious practice. Two major objectives of religious practice were (1) to discern the intentions of the gods by reading clues they left in nature, a practice known as divination, and (2) to secure the goodwill of the gods by praising them, tending to their needs, and giving them gifts (prayer and sacrifice). The challenge of sustaining such relationships was that the gods were not so accessible—they were thought to live at a distance, on remote mountaintops or in the heavens, or were simply deemed too large or incomprehensible for humans to experience directly, with the exception of specially favored mortals. Fortunately, the gods sometimes revealed themselves in certain natural settings—mountaintops, caves, trees, by the sides of rivers—or in special buildings constructed for their residence, such as temples. They could also become manifest through the medium of statues or other special objects, like stones and pillars, which they could inhabit if special rituals were performed on them. In these ways, mortals could come into their presence, talk to them, tend to their needs, and interact with them through prayer, sacrifice, and other rites.

All this has a counterpart in Israelite religious life. Archaeologists have uncovered several sanctuaries in Israel and Judah—not the Jerusalem Temple, but the sanctuary at Dan in the north, a temple at Arad in Judah, and other examples. Their design—indeed, even the design of the Jerusalem Temple as described in the Bible—exhibits the conventional characteristics of temples in Syria-Palestine. Some of the sacrifices and rituals prescribed in the Bible resemble rituals known from Ugarit and other ancient Near Eastern culture, and the psalms in the book of Psalms have ancient Near Eastern counterparts too, suggesting the conventions of Judahite prayer were drawn from earlier Near Eastern culture. God himself has many of the characteristics of a typical ancient Near Eastern deity, a creator god, a warrior god, a king, who acts much as his counterparts do in Ugarit, Mesopotamia, or Egypt, convening heavenly councils, crushing his foes, sending dreams and other signs to convey his intentions. There aren't any stories in the Bible that depict God in relationship with other deities, but there are vestiges of such myths here and there. In Genesis 1:26, for example, when God says, "Let us make humankind in our image," scholars explain the use of the plural "us" by comparing the story to other ancient creation stories in which the creator god addresses a divine assembly or council before deciding to create human beings.

In line with these parallels to ancient Near Eastern myth, the worship practices of ancient Israel and Judah were also very similar to those of surrounding cultures. Like other deities, God was attended in the sanctuary by a class of servants, or priests, who oversaw sacrifice and other cultic performances. The Bible condemns some of the divination techniques used in surrounding cultures to discern the will of the gods, but it allows for such others as dream interpretation and the casting of lots. Prophecy is another intriguing point of connection with ancient Near Eastern religion. Prophets are a kind of divine messenger. A deity reveals himself or herself to the prophet in some way, through a vision or a dream, or takes over his body and speaks through the person, and thus delivers a message to some audience, a king, or the community at large. Figures similar to the biblical prophets are known from other ancient Near Eastern literatures. One inscription found at a Jordanian site named Deir 'Alla records the visions of a non-Israelite prophet mentioned in the Bible itself—Balaam, featured in Numbers 22–24. The messages of prophets were delivered orally, in face-to-face encounters, but sometimes they were written down and collected, as is the case with the prophecies recorded in Isaiah and other biblical books. This, too, mirrors what happened in neighboring cultures like Assyria, from which we also have collections of prophetic oracles.

The gods of the ancient Near Eastern cultures surrounding Israel and Judah often manifested themselves to humans in the form of anthropomorphic or zoomorphic statues. The Bible is opposed to the use of human and animal images to represent God, and indeed, no statue of God has been discovered to date, but evidence does exist to show that the Israelites believed their god was actually resident in the sanctuary, manifest in cult symbols that signaled the god's presence indirectly or symbolically rather than representing it in a fully visible form. As described in the Bible, the Ark of the Covenant, a kind of footstool or chariot for God, served such a purpose in the temple, signaling the divine presence but leaving God himself unseen. While other ancient Near Eastern and Mediterranean cultures often used human or animal-like images to visualize their gods, some resembled the biblical cult in using non-representational symbols to suggest rather than represent the deity's presence.

What is most recognizably distinctive about Israelite worship is the deity to whom it was directed. Inscriptions from the period of the Kingdoms of Israel and Judah mention the names of several Canaanite gods—Baal, Asherah, El—but the deity most frequently referred to is a god never mentioned in Ugaritic literature or other sources for Canaanite religion: a god whose name is spelled YHWH. Apart from its appearance in the Bible, YHWH is mentioned in letters, prayers, blessings, and other texts known from inscriptions, and a shortened form, *yahu*, is incorporated into many personal names in Israel and Judah: Uri *yahu* ("YHWH is my light"), Netan *yahu* ("YHWH has given"), and so on. Many of the names we know about from ancient Israelite inscriptions, seals, and other sources are Yahwistic names, suggesting how important the relationship with this deity was to how people defined their identity.

Figure 1.9 Does this photo capture an ancient Israelite representation of God? Some scholars think so. The drawing reproduced here, inscribed on a piece of pottery, was found at a site called Kuntillet Ajrud, an outpost in the southern Negev desert dating to the eighth century BCE. An inscription above the head of the largest standing figure mentions YHWH and "his Asherah"—the latter the name of a goddess known from Ugaritic/Canaanite religion. This has led some scholars to identify the larger standing figure as Yahweh and the seated figure on the right as his companion Asherah. This interpretation is sharply debated, however, and many scholars see reason to identify the figures as Egyptian deities

YHWH (or *Yahweh*, as scholars believe his name was originally pronounced) appears to be a new deity relative to other deities worshipped in Canaan. He does not appear in Ugaritic literature or in any other Canaanite source, though we know of a few place- and personal names that sound similar. While Israel's name, which we know from the Merneptah Stele, goes back to at least the thirteenth century BCE and incorporates a divine name, it is the name "El," a god known from earlier Ugaritic/Canaanite sources, not a form of *Yahweh*, as in later Israelite/Judahite names. *Yahweh* seems to come out of nowhere, appearing for the first time in a clearly datable context in the period of Israel's monarchy, and we can only make educated guesses about its origins (*see the box* "Where Does God Come From?"). Some scholars think he arose under the influence of an iconoclastic Egyptian king named Akhenaten, who ruled Egypt in the fourteenth century BCE and is famous not just for fathering King Tut but also for developing an early form of monotheism centered on the sun god Aten—the sole deity in Akhenaten's newly introduced religious ideology. Especially given the possibility that there might have been Israelites in Egypt at this time, some scholars cannot resist seeing a possible influence on the idea of God as it developed in ancient Israel. Among those who believed in such influence was Sigmund Freud, whose book *Moses and Monotheism* popularized the idea.

Still, it is possible to recognize lines of continuity with Yahweh and earlier Canaanite religion. Judaism as practiced today is monotheistic, acknowledging Yahweh as the only god. The origins of monotheism can certainly be traced back to the Bible, but the Bible also preserves glimpses of an earlier form of Israelite religion much closer to Canaanite polytheism, a religion that identified Yahweh with the Canaanite god El or Baal and allowed for the existence of less-powerful deities alongside him. One such glimpse is preserved in Psalm 89:

> Who among the heavenly beings is like the Lord, a God feared in the council of the holy

WHERE DOES GOD COME FROM?

The early history of God—where and when he was first worshipped—remains a mystery. The earliest reference to God outside the Bible, or YHWH, as his name is spelled, is in a ninth-century Moabite inscription known as the Mesha Stele in a context that associates him with Israel. Whether his history goes back any further is unknown, but scholars have tried to tease out his origins from clues found here and there in the Bible.

One such clue is God's name. The meaning of YHWH is unknown—it is not even clear how to pronounce it, because its vowels have been long forgotten. (In the post-biblical period, Jews began to avoid pronouncing God's name out of respect for its sanctity, at least outside the confines of the Temple, preferring more generic titles instead, and in this way, it seems, its vowels were forgotten. YHWH, as it appears in the Hebrew Bible today, can be written with vowels, but these are taken from the Hebrew word for "My Lord," *Adonay*, pronounced in lieu of God's name.) For its part, though, the Bible suggests a connection to the Hebrew verb "to be." When Moses asks his name, God responds, "I am who I am" (Exodus 3:14)—an answer that puns on the similarity between the consonants of YHWH and the verbal form "I am" (*ehyeh*). While the root of "to be" may be the source of Yahweh's name, the story may misconstrue the precise connection, however, for some scholars think that it arose not from "I am" but from the causative form of "to be"—"the One who *causes* to be," or in other words, "the Creator."

If this reconstruction is correct (and it may not be correct; other etymologies have been proposed), Yahweh's name derives from his role as a creator god. The god El plays this role in Canaanite mythology, and that and other connections to El (e.g., the fact that the Bible assigns Yahweh "El" names, such as *El-Elyon*; the incorporation of *El* in the name *Israel*; Yahweh's association with Asherah, El's consort) all support the idea that Yahweh originated from within the Canaanite pantheon as a version of the god El.

But other clues within the Bible suggest Yahweh originated *outside* Canaan, in the Sinai wilderness between Canaan and Egypt. A few biblical texts describe Yahweh as coming from the south (e.g., Deuteronomy 33:2, Judges 5:4, Habakkuk 3.3–7), and he is called "Yahweh of the South" in inscriptions from Kuntillet Ajrud in the Negev. "South" here seems to be the Sinai wilderness, a territory inhabited by a people known as the Midianites, and some scholars have hypothesized that Yahweh originated as a Midianite god, an idea known as the Midianite hypothesis. Mount Sinai, located in this territory, is where Moses first encounters Yahweh in the burning bush, and where the Israelites establish their covenant with him—stories that may reflect a vague memory of Yahweh as a deity first encountered in this region. How to reconcile Yahweh's Canaanite links with his possible Midianite origins is unclear, but several possibilities arise. Perhaps, for example, Israel adopted Yahweh from the Midianites and subsequently integrated him with more northern traditions connected to the Canaanite god El. Just as there once existed multiple versions of Baal associated with different cities or regions (Baal of Lebanon, Baal of Sidon, etc.), perhaps more than one version of Yahweh may have existed originally—a Yahweh of Samaria *and* a Yahweh of the south—and perhaps the biblical God is a conflation of these different Yahwehs.

> ones, great and dreaded above all around him? Lord God of hosts, who is like You? Your strength and faithfulness surround you. You rule the surge of the sea; when its waves rise, you quiet them. You crushed Rahab like a carcass; with your mighty arm, you scattered your foes.
>
> (Psalm 89:7–10)

The words *heavenly beings* here translate to an expression that literally means "sons of els" and can be taken to mean "gods," and what we know of Canaanite religious tradition supports that interpretation. In Ugaritic literature, the gods, also known as "the holy ones," convene in special assemblies, such as one in which Baal meets with the gods before confronting a god called Yam, the Sea. The psalm seems to be describing a similar divine council, and Yahweh's subjugation of the sea parallels Baal's victory over the sea god known as Yam. Another divine battle story in Ugaritic literature pits Baal against a dragon, Lotan, a rough equivalent to the monster Rahab mentioned in this psalm and an even more precise parallel to another creature defeated by God—Leviathan, a variant of the name *Lotan*, who is alluded to in Psalm 74:13–14: "You divided the sea by your might; you broke the heads of the dragons in the waters. *You crushed the heads of Leviathan.*" The site of Baal's conflict with Yam, and the place where his home is and from which he issues decrees, is the mountain Zaphon in northern Syria, and its description in Ugaritic texts is similar to the Bible's description of the holy mountains of Sinai, and even more so to Zion, the mountain where Yahweh's temple in Jerusalem was located.

Extrabiblical evidence also ties Yahweh to indigenous Canaanite religion. At a site in the Negev known as Kuntillet Ajrud, Hebrew inscriptions were discovered that refer to "Yahweh of Samaria and His Asherah," or "Yahweh of the South and His Asherah." *Asherah* is a goddess known in Ugarit as the female companion of the god El. The inscription may be referring to Asherah herself or to some object associated with her worship. While the meaning of "His Asherah" in these inscriptions is debated, it may indicate that at some stage in Israelite religion, Yahweh, like El in Ugaritic mythology, had a mate.

All this has led to the theory that early Israelite religion was not that different from pre-Israelite Canaanite religion. *Yahweh* was another name for the god El, with a consort named Asherah, or else, he was a variant of the god Baal, defeating the enemies that Baal defeats in Ugaritic myth and taking up residence on a sacred mountain. In this early form of Israelite religion, other, less-important deities seem to have existed, the holy ones alluded to in Psalm 89, though these were overshadowed by Yahweh's superior power. The fact that Yahweh seems to combine the traits of El and Baal may seem strange, but a similar consolidation of the Canaanite divine population has been observed in neighboring cultures in the first millennium, as some of those cultures zeroed in on a single deity as the most important or fused attributes of various deities into a single god. In the second millennium BCE, the single city-state of Ugarit acknowledged the existence of more than 200 gods. By contrast, gods from any given Canaanite state in the first millennium BCE number ten or fewer. Moabite religion coalesced around the god Chemosh, the Edomites around the god Qaws, and the Ammonites around the god Milkom. Perhaps this same trend is reflected in Israelite/Judahite religion, with El and other Canaanite gods consolidated into Yahweh.

How, then, did what we call monotheism emerge, the belief in Yahweh not just as the supreme god but as the only god? While some scholars want to trace it back to the Egyptian reformer Akhenaten in the fourteenth century BCE, the worship of Yahweh as the only god may in fact have emerged later in Israelite history, in the period of Assyrian and Babylonian conquest. The Bible is full of passages that praise God as the most powerful or unique god, but such texts do not necessarily rule out the existence of other deities; similar statements are found in the divine praise of other Near Eastern cultures we know to be polytheistic. Monotheistic statements that unequivocally assert God as the *only* god are surprisingly rare in the Hebrew Bible, surfacing only in texts from the Assyrian–Babylonian–Persian period, such as Isaiah 44:6–8, where God declares, "I am the first and I am the last, *besides me there is no god*." The catalyst for this change might have been the impact of the Mesopotamian imperialism that we described in the last section. Both Assyria and Babylonia were polytheistic cultures, but each flirted with quasi-monotheistic ideas. In one Assyrian text, for example, the body of the god Ninurta is described as a composite of all the other gods: "Lord your face is Shamash (the sun god . . . your head is Adad (a storm god) . . . your neck is Marduk, judge of heaven"—as if all the gods were really only extensions of a single supreme god. The monotheism of such biblical texts as Isaiah 44—the insistence that Yahweh is the one and only god—may reflect the influence of such ideas. Alternatively, monotheism might conceivably have developed as a reaction *against* Mesopotamian dominance, a way to resist efforts to subordinate Yahweh to the conqueror's gods by denying their very existence. The truth is that we do not know how monotheism took root among Israelites, but it emerged in time for it to be one of the inheritances that they passed on to later Jewish culture, becoming the foundational belief for Jewish religious life.

However we understand the origins and history of Yahweh, the point we want to stress here is the importance of this deity in Judahite identity. As in other ancient Near Eastern cultures, a person's identity was defined in ancient Israel and Judah not just by kinship ties, birthplace, or political allegiance but also by a relationship with a deity, a relationship that expressed itself in ritual behavior, myths, and even a person's name. Several deities seem to have been venerated in Israel and Judah—Baal, Asherah, and others—but judging from the prevalence of Yahwistic names and references in the inscriptional record and the Bible, Yahweh was the most popular deity in Canaan of the first millennium, associated with the people of Israel and Judah in a way that the god Chemosh was associated with the Moabites and the god Qaws with the Edomites. How Yahweh was imagined changed in the wake of Assyrian and Babylonian conquest, but Judah's allegiance to him survived, as did many other aspects of ancient Israelite religion—the importance of the Temple (if not the Ark, which was somehow lost by the time of the Babylonian Exile), the use of sacrifice and prayer as the primary acts of worship, the avoidance of divine images, the roles of the priest and the prophet as divine intermediaries, and the use of stories like those in the Bible as a way to understand God's relationship to humans.

From the Historical Israel Back to Biblical Israel

The historical picture we have reconstructed here is very different from the story of Israel that emerges out of the Bible. It is an account without such figures as Abraham, Moses, or King David, without such events as the Exodus or Joshua's conquest. Whereas the Bible sharply distinguishes the Israelites from the Canaanites, locating their origin outside Canaan, we have suggested that Israelite culture may have developed as an offshoot of Canaanite culture, and we have seen reason to identify the Israelites with various precursors in the vicinity—the Amorites, the Hyksos, and the Habiru. We have even complicated God's history, citing evidence that his image and worship may be related to how other peoples in the region conceived and interacted with their gods.

Even as we challenge biblical history in this way, however, we also must acknowledge that the Bible is our single most valuable source for understanding the Israelite culture out of which Jewish culture evolved. Indeed, the Bible captures the beginnings of the process by which Israelite culture evolved into Jewish culture: the emergence of a distinctly Judahite variant of Israelite culture and its evolution under Assyrian and Babylonian conquest.

Still, our understanding of that trajectory is hardly complete. The changes imposed by Babylonian rule—the end of the Davidic dynasty, the destruction of the Temple, and the exile from Judah—play a critical role in the development of Jewish culture out of Judahite culture, but these events alone cannot account for the transformation. It turns out that the Hebrew Bible itself played a catalytic role. Judahites read the Bible, or the texts that would become the Bible, to retrieve the life they had lost through foreign conquest and exile, and through the act of doing so, they created the beginnings of something new: a culture focused on and generated through the interpretation of sacred texts. To understand the rise of Jewish culture, therefore, we must learn more about the Bible itself—how it came to be, what it consists of, and the role that it came to play in Judahite culture as it developed after Babylonian conquest.

For Further Reading

For a more detailed overview of Israelite/Judahite history than can be presented here, see Michael Coogan, *The Oxford History of the Biblical World* (Oxford, England: Oxford University Press, 1998). Although it has grown dated in some respects, we still find the following book useful as an overview of the challenges of reconstructing Israelite history: J. Maxwell Miller and John Hayes, *A History of Ancient Israel and Judah*, 2nd ed. (Philadelphia: Westminster John Knox Press, 1986). For an overview of scholarly efforts to pinpoint the origin of the Jews, see Steven Weitzman, *The Origin of the Jews: The Search for Roots in a Rootless Age* (Princeton, NJ: Princeton University Press, 2017).

On the ancient Near East, see Daniel Snell, *Life in the Ancient Near East 3100–332* BCE (New Haven, CT: Yale University Press, 1997), or more recently, Amanda Podany, *Weavers, Scribes and Kings: A New History of the Ancient Near East* (Oxford: Oxford University Press, 2022). For an English translation of ancient Near Eastern texts, see James B. Pritchard, *Ancient Near Eastern Texts Relating to the Old Testament* (Princeton, NJ: Princeton University Press, 1969), from which this book draws its translations of the Merneptah Stele and other ancient Near Eastern texts; Michael Coogan, *A Reader of Ancient Near Eastern Texts: Sources for the Study of the Old Testament* (Oxford, England: Oxford University Press, 2012). Translations and other online tools for the study of the ancient Near East can also be found at the website ETANA: https://etana.org/home.

On family and daily life in Israel, see Philip King and Lawrence Stager, *Life in Biblical Israel* (Louisville, KY: Westminster John Knox Press, 2001). On Israelite women, see Carol Meyers, *Discovering Eve: Ancient Israelite Women in Context* (New York: Oxford University Press, 1998); and Jennie Ebeling, *Women's Live in Biblical Times* (London: T & T Clark, 2010). On how God relates to Canaanite religion, see Mark Smith, *The Early History of God: Yahweh and Other Deities in Ancient Israel* (San Francisco, CA: Harper Collins, 1990), and on ancient Israelite religion in general, see Susan Niditch, *Ancient Israelite Religion* (New York: Oxford University Press, 1997), and Richard Hess, *Israelite Religions: An Archaeological and Biblical Survey* (Ada, MI: Baker Academic, 2017). For those curious about the new genetic research on the Jews, see David Goldstein, *Jacob's Legacy: A Genetic View of Jewish History* (New Haven, CT: Yale, 2008), and Harry Ostrer, *Legacy: A Genetic History of the Jewish People* (New York: Oxford University Press, 2012). For a critique, see Nadia Abu El-Hajj, *The Genealogical Science: The Search for Jewish Origins and the Politics of Epistemology* (Chicago, IL: University of Chicago Press, 2012).

To find more information about other topics in Israelite history and culture, try D. N. Freedman, ed., *Anchor Bible Dictionary* (New York: Doubleday, 1992). There now also exists a convenient online bibliographical resource for those interested in various subjects in biblical studies and Jewish history: *Oxford Bibliographies*: www.oxfordbibliographies.

com. Much of the bibliography is behind a pay-wall, but some information is freely accessible on the website or can be reached if you have access to the online catalogue of a university library. For a listing of online resources bearing on biblical studies in particular, see *Oxford Biblical Studies Online*: www.oxfordbiblicalstudies.com/resource/InternetResources.xhtml.

CHAPTER 2

BECOMING THE PEOPLE OF THE BOOK

At what point in history did the ancient Israelites recorded in the Bible, the people of the Southern Kingdom of Judah, develop into what we now know as the Jews? How did this change come about, in what circumstances, and what justifies the switch in how we refer to them—why call them "Jews" as opposed to using the biblical "Israelites" or "Hebrews"?

As is often the case when trying to understand the ancient past, it is much easier to explain why we cannot answer these questions than to actually answer them. One reason for the difficulty has to do with the problem that we introduced at the beginning of the last chapter: There is no agreement as to when in history the people later known as the Jews came into being. One reason that we refer to the survivors of the Babylonian Exile as "Jews" is that most of the survivors of that experience were from the tribe of Judah (though some were from the tribes of Levi and Benjamin) or were former inhabitants of the Kingdom of Judah, but scholars' use of the term *Jew* is meant to suggest something else, a kind of cultural and religious transformation that set in after the Exile. The term *Jew* descends from the biblical word *yehudi*, but that label implies a different kind of identity in a biblical context than suggested by the word *Jewish* as used in later periods.

In the Bible, *yehudi* refers to a person from the tribe of Judah, the fourth of Jacob's 12 sons, or to a subject of the Kingdom of David, based in territory that belonged to the tribe of Judah. By the first century CE, the term—and equivalent terms in Aramaic, Greek, and Latin—still had tribal and geographic resonance, but it could also signify something else, a person committed to distinctive laws and customs different from those of other peoples. To be Jewish in this sense did not necessarily require descending from the tribe of Judah or living in the territory of Judah; one needed, rather, to believe and act in certain ways. This kind of identity is what many scholars have in mind by the terms "Jew" and "Judaism"—a kind of religious identity rather than a tribal, ethnic, or geography-based identity—and we do not fully understand how this change came about or even how to distinguish clearly between "Israelite" and "Jew."

An example will help drive home how this definitional issue affects where we place the beginning of Jewish history. Over the course of the nineteenth century, a group of ancient documents came to light that revealed a Judahite (or is it Jewish?) community in the fifth century BCE in a very unexpected place: a small island known as Elephantine, situated in the middle of the Nile River, in what is now southern Egypt. How did Jews (or Judahites) end up in such an out-of-the-way place? Egypt at this point was controlled by the Persian Empire, and these people were stationed there as soldiers working on its behalf, settling on Elephantine with their families to help guard the

DOI: 10.4324/9781003611592-3

frontier zone between southern Egypt and Nubia to the south. The Elephantine Papyri, written in Aramaic (another Semitic language widely used in the ancient Near East under the Persian Empire), provide a remarkable witness to the community that produced them, furnishing scholars with personal and official letters, legal and economic documents, and even a literary text about a wise official named Ahiqar.

The people reflected in these documents refer to themselves as *yehudiyin*, a term often translated by scholars today as "Jews," and there is much to recommend that translation: They worshipped the God known from the Hebrew Bible (Yahweh or Yaho, as he is known in Elephantine texts), bore Yahwistic names, and celebrated such holy days as the Sabbath and the Passover. But they are also different from the Jews we know about from other sources: They did not regard Jerusalem as the only legitimate site of sacrifice—they offered sacrifice to Yaho at a temple situated at Elephantine itself before it was destroyed in 410 BCE—and they seemed to acknowledge other gods alongside Yaho. They might have learned something about biblical law through their contacts with religious authorities in Jerusalem, but the Elephantine Papyri do not include texts that cite or interpret the Bible, much less biblical manuscripts themselves, and there is no evidence that either Abraham, Moses, Joshua, or David was part of the collective memory of the Judean community at Elephantine. If by *Jewish* we mean a person from the land of Judah or descended from Judahites, the Elephantine community can be labeled Jewish, but it would be a mistake to think its members were like the Jews we know from later sources, and it might be less anachronistic to describe them as another, separate offshoot of earlier Judahite culture.

Because the definition of the term *Jewish* is so fuzzy, we will not try to pinpoint a specific date when Judahite culture became Jewish culture. Instead, this chapter will focus on several events that appear in the development of Jewish culture out of Judahite culture. It is not clear that the people involved in these transformative moments saw themselves as different from their ancestors; they probably simply saw themselves as their direct heirs, for what we know of them from late biblical books like Ezra and Nehemiah, composed after the exile, shows that they identified with the Israelites of the pre-exilic period and yearned to preserve or restore the traditions inherited from them. It is only from our later vantage point that we can recognize something new emerging in these sources, a culture distinct enough from earlier Judahite culture to merit a new label. Moving from the term *Judahite* to *Jewish* for this period is a way to signal that difference without obscuring the line of continuity between these cultures.

The present chapter seeks to introduce this transitional period in the formation of Jewish culture, a period that is poorly documented but is nonetheless important for understanding how Jewish culture would develop in subsequent centuries. We will focus on two developments in particular which may be interconnected. The first is the onset of Persian rule in the sixth century BCE, which brought an end to the Neo-Babylonian Empire that had wrought so much destruction on the Kingdom of Judah. Persian governance would go on to shape the political, social, and cultural world in which the ancestors of the Jews developed in the next two centuries. The second event is the emergence of the Bible as a sacred scripture. Some biblical texts were composed before the Babylonian Exile, but many of them were composed or were revised in some way in the Persian age, and it was also in this period that the Bible—or rather, the act of reading the Bible—began to have a major impact on the development of Jewish identity, an influence that continues to this day to the extent that Jews still look to the Bible to understand their origins and how to live their lives. Because of its importance for understanding the Jews, much of this chapter is actually a history of the Bible more than it is a history of the Jews in the Persian period, with sections that explore where biblical literature comes from, what it consists of, why it became so important, and its role in the development of early Jewish culture.

An End and a Beginning

We begin with an event we have already introduced: Babylon's conquest of the Kingdom of Judah in the early sixth century BCE. Although scholars question the Bible's account of this period, most continue to regard it as a watershed moment and with good reason. With the end of the Davidic dynasty, Judah lost its independence, and the political destiny of its inhabitants would henceforth be shaped by foreign rule. The destruction of the Jerusalem Temple disrupted the core of Judahite religious life, forcing Judahites to find new ways to interact with God. Many people may have remained in place in Judah, but a significant portion of the population was exiled to Babylon, and this exiled population seems to be the part of the Judahite society from which we have inherited the texts now collected in the Jewish Bible.

Babylonian conquest had a highly devastating effect on Judahite culture, measurable by the archaeological evidence of destruction during this period, but it also stimulated a considerable amount of creativity, measurable by the literature from this period now preserved in the Bible. We have been mentioning that portions of the Bible were written in the wake of the Babylonian conquest, but one might well argue that most of it was composed, or at least revised, at this time. To be more specific:

1. A number of biblical books were actually composed anew during the period of Babylonian domination or in the following centuries. These include Jeremiah, Ezekiel, and several other prophetic texts that respond directly to Babylonian conquest; Lamentations, which mourns the destruction of Jerusalem; and the narratives Esther, Daniel, Ezra, Nehemiah, and 1 and 2 Chronicles—about 25 percent of the books in the Jewish Bible. Other works, like the book of Ruth, may come from this time too, but that cannot be proven.
2. Additionally, a number of biblical books, though drawing on earlier sources, are believed to have been revised and expanded in the period following Babylonian conquest. These include the narratives in the previously mentioned Deuteronomistic History, the scholarly label for a hypothetical work that included what are now the separate books of Deuteronomy, Joshua, Judges, 1–2 Samuel, and 1–2 Kings. It is believed by many scholars that all these books were originally part of one composition that aimed to tell the history of ancient Israel and how it was led astray by its rulers, and it is certain that it must have been at least supplemented after the Babylonian Exile, since its final two chapters, 2 Kings 24–25, are a report of that event. Many scholars also believe that other sections of the Bible were edited and expanded at this time as well, including the Five Books of Moses.

Whatever destruction the Babylonians imposed on the people of Judah, its survivors were evidently able not just to preserve remnants of their pre-exilic past but also to engage in new forms of intellectual and literary creativity. Unfortunately for our understanding of this period, all that is left of this creativity are the few writings that have been preserved in the Bible, which, as noted, mostly reflect the perspective of those exiled to Babylonia rather than of those left behind in the land of Canaan. Even from the tiny amount of evidence we have, however, it is clear that Judahite culture not only survived in this period but remained creative, thanks in part to the efforts of prophets, historians, psalmists, and unnamed editors.

This apparent outburst of religious and literary creativity, rooted in the impulse to sustain Israelite culture and religion in the face of traumatic disruption, is certainly an important stage in the transition from Judahite to Jewish culture, which

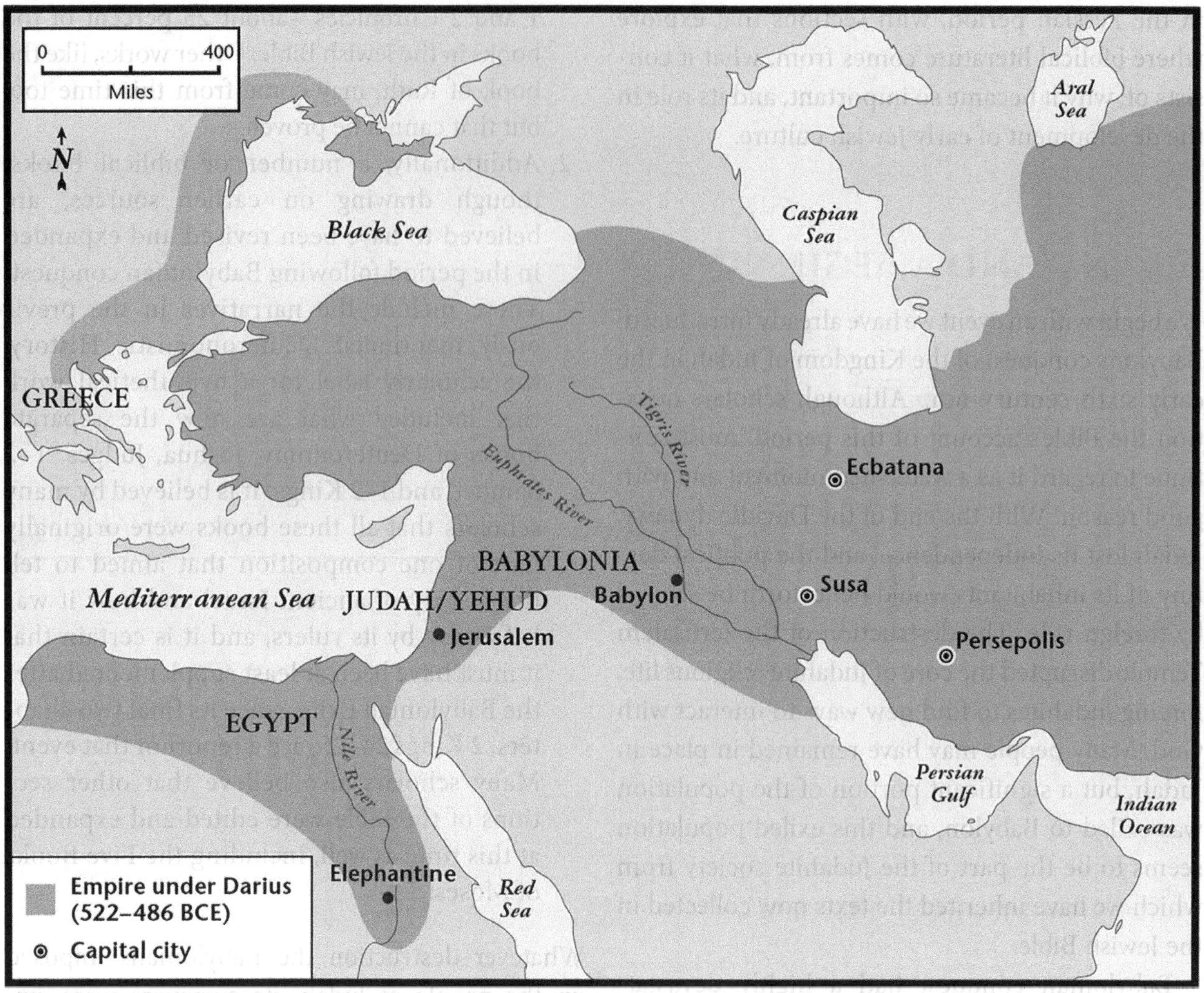

Map 2.1 The Persian Empire ruled by the Achaemenid dynasty (539–332 BCE).

is why many scholars date the beginning of Judaism to 587–586 BCE, the year that Nebuchadnezzar destroyed Jerusalem and its temple. Babylonian rule was relatively brief, however, ending in 539 BCE, when the Neo-Babylonian Empire was itself defeated by the Persian king Cyrus II, founder of the Achaemenid dynasty that would dominate the Near East for the next two centuries (see Map 2.1). The origins of the Persian Empire, emerging around 550 BCE, are mysterious since there are relatively few sources for the empire's earliest history, but we do know that its ruling dynasty was based in present-day Iran and soon developed an empire that reached all the way to Egypt and even encroached into the Greek world, prompting the war between the Persians and the Greeks famously recorded by the Greek historian Herodotus in the fifth century BCE. The latter depicts the kings of Persia as arrogant enemies that the Greeks needed to defeat to preserve their freedom. In biblical sources, Persian rule is depicted as relatively benign compared to the Babylonians, and some cast it as an agent of God, making it possible for the Judeans to return from exile and rebuild the Temple.

Indeed, one of the heroes of this period from the Bible's vantage point is none other than Cyrus himself, the founder of the Persian Empire. We know that Cyrus was a remarkably effective empire builder, consolidating his rule in Iran; conquering

Asia Minor (present-day Turkey), where he sowed the seeds of conflict with the Greeks; and then in 539 BCE, subduing Babylon, which is what gave him control over the Judahites in Babylon itself as well as those settled in the territory of the former Kingdom of Judah. According to the Bible, all this conquest was God's way of restoring his people, God giving Cyrus his empire so that he would return the people of Judah to their home and rebuild their temple in Jerusalem. Greeks remembered the Persians as arrogant barbarians. The Bible remembers the Persians as benign supporters.

In fact, Cyrus himself is cast as something more than a hero in the Bible. Chapters 40–55 of the book of Isaiah—known as Deutero-Isaiah (*deutero* is Greek for "second") because this section seems to have been added to the original core of Isaiah by a later editor—celebrate Cyrus as a divinely appointed savior, commissioned by Yahweh to help restore the Judahites:

> [I the Lord] am the one who says to Cyrus, "my shepherd," and all my desire he shall realize; and who says to Jerusalem, "It shall be rebuilt," and to the temple, "You shall be established." Thus says the Lord to his anointed, to Cyrus, whose right hand I have grasped. . . . I will go before you.
>
> (Isaiah 44:28–45:2)

Why do scholars date this part of Isaiah to the Persian period despite the fact that the prophet Isaiah himself was from the much earlier Assyrian period? This passage contains the answer: Deutero-Isaiah refers explicitly to Cyrus, depicted here as an agent of Jerusalem's restoration. By referring to him as God's "shepherd" and as "his anointed," the text is drawing on language normally applied to Judah's kings to suggest that Cyrus is a ruler similar to David himself, the greatest praise a biblical author could bestow on a political leader. This is such a glowing depiction of Persian rule that some historians have suggested that Deutero-Isaiah is a work of pro-Persian propaganda, a proposal that is not historically implausible, given what we know about how Persian rule presented itself to other communities that it ruled.

Insight into how the biblical portrait of Cyrus served the political ends of Persian rule comes from a Babylonian text from the same period known as the Cyrus Cylinder, discovered in 1879 and now in the British Museum. The Cyrus Cylinder is in the form of a cylinder because it was probably used to roll out multiple copies of its text onto other clay tablets. What it records is an account of how Cyrus was appointed by the Babylonian god Marduk to return the statues of Babylonia's gods to their shrine. Its description of Cyrus as a pious restorer of religious tradition parallels Deutero-Isaiah's claim that God appointed Cyrus to restore the Jerusalem Temple, and some would characterize both compositions as efforts to legitimize Persian conquest as an ally and supporter rather than as merely a conqueror. Realizing that it would be easier to absorb diverse peoples into his empire if he aligned himself with their respective beliefs, Cyrus enlisted the help of native experts to present him in ways that fit him into local religious tradition. We know of an Egyptian official, a doctor and diplomat named Udjahorresnet, who played such a role in Egypt on behalf of the kings of Persia; another figure, an anonymous Babylonian scribe, played a similar role in Mesopotamia by composing a document in the language of Akkadian, the Cyrus Cylinder, to depict Cyrus as a servant of the Babylonian deity Marduk; and yet another scribe, the author of Deutero-Isaiah, did the same thing in relation to Judahite tradition by presenting Cyrus as a servant of God modeled on the Israelite king. These authors wrote in different languages,

Figure 2.1 The Cyrus Cylinder.

appealing to audiences from different cultures and devoted to different gods, but they were using the same strategy, casting Cyrus not as a foreign conqueror but as a divinely appointed restorer of a religious tradition disrupted by their mutual enemy, the Babylonians.

Why would the Judahites have aligned themselves with their Persian rulers in this way, especially given their resistance to earlier foreign conquerors, like the Assyrians and the Babylonians? For one thing, the Judahites might have remembered the disastrous outcome of earlier rebellions. After all, rebellion against the Babylonians had led to Jerusalem's destruction. There might have been other considerations as well. Prophetic sources written in this period—the book of Haggai, for instance, now in the Bible as one of the 12 "minor" prophets—suggest that the returning Judahites had an extremely difficult time farming the land, and famine and poverty might have been one reason that Judahites were willing to accept Persia as a patron.

Another reason might have been the presence in the land of other inhabitants who were not so happy for the Judahites to be there. The Bible refers to this group as "the people of the land," neighboring residents the Judahites encountered upon their return and who sought to frustrate their efforts to rebuild Jerusalem and the Temple. These seem to have included the remnants of the Ammonites, the Moabites, and various Canaanite peoples, along with the inhabitants of the former Kingdom of Israel. The last group, it should be noted, were not actually Israelites themselves according to the Bible, but foreigners who had been settled in the place of the Israelites exiled by the Assyrians, adopted some of the Israelites' ways, and now saw the returning Judahites as rivals (later Jewish sources would describe this community as forebearers of the people known as the Samaritans, to whom we will return in subsequent chapters, but this is not how Samaritans see themselves). Both the returning exiles and their enemies turned to the Persian government for support in their struggle, and the Judahites prevailed in part because they were successful in winning that support. In other words, the Judahites appear to have accepted Persian rule because they saw an alliance with it as a way to address their needs at a time when their position in the former territory of the king of Judah was very precarious.

Despite its role in helping the people of Judah recover what they had lost, however, Persian rule did introduce significant cultural and political changes. The Judahites, both those returning home and those remaining in Babylon or living in Egypt, were now part of a large, multicultural empire that expected their loyalty. They could return to their ancestral land, they were even permitted to rebuild their Temple in Jerusalem, but they were not allowed to restore an independent state in Judah with a king of their own. Instead, this territory was now to be administered as a province known as *Yehud* (Aramaic for *Yehuda*), part of a still larger imperial administrative unit in the Persian Empire, a satrapy known as "Beyond the River" that encompassed the land of Canaan along with other territory west of the Euphrates River.

Not all Judahites may have been willing to accept Persian rule, and biblical texts from this period hint at a certain restiveness among some. Whatever effort such Judahites made to regain their independence failed, however, and Persian control only tightened with time. Cyrus's son Cambyses conquered Egypt, and that gave Persia all the more stake in the area linking Egypt to the rest of its empire, an area that included Yehud. Cambyses did not last long—he died before getting home from Egypt—but the person who emerged as his successor, Darius I (522–486 BCE), greatly consolidated the Persian Empire by restructuring imperial administration, expanding roadways, and even initiating a canal between the Red Sea and the Mediterranean. His decision to allow the completion of the Temple, initiated by Cyrus but halted under

Cambyses, might have been part of this effort, an attempt to tie Yehud more closely together with Persian rule by acting as a sponsor of Jerusalem and its temple.

In addition to changing Judah's political status, Persian rule also fostered significant cultural change, most clearly reflected in a linguistic shift that occurs at this time. We have sometimes referred to the Jewish Bible as the *Hebrew Bible* to reflect the language in which it is written, but that label is slightly misleading because some of the Bible's content—portions of the books of Ezra, Nehemiah, and Daniel—are written in Aramaic, a language that became widespread in the Persian period because of its use as an imperial administrative language. Hebrew was not abandoned—Jews would continue to write in it for many centuries—but Aramaic became so influential at this time that it altered Hebrew grammar and vocabulary and even changed the way its alphabet was written, displacing the script of pre-exilic Hebrew with the Aramaic script in which Hebrew is written to this day. There were even a few Persian loanwords that penetrated Hebrew at this time—most famously, the word *pardes*, from which the word *paradise* is derived, originated as a Persian loanword, meaning "garden" or "park."

Beyond this linguistic change, the integration of the people of Judah into the Persian Empire is also detectable in the stories that the Bible tells about the period. Biblical literature composed in the age of the Achaemenid rulers makes frequent reference to them, often depicting them as good guys, as in Deutero-Isaiah, or at least as willing to support the Jews. Even the biblical book of Esther (probably written in the fourth century BCE), which describes an attempt made during the reign of the Persian king Ahasuerus to destroy the Jews, assigns the blame not to the king himself but to his evil advisor, Haman, who misleads King Ahasuerus into believing that the Jews are disloyal. Fortunately, the king happens to be married to a member of the tribe, a beautiful woman named Esther—and she uses her influence with the king to persuade him to revoke his decree against the Jews and punish Haman instead, an act of deliverance that the Jews are instructed to commemorate by celebrating a holiday known as Purim (named for the lot or *pur* that Haman cast to determine on which day to destroy the Jews). In the Persian Empire, as described in the book of Esther, other subjects seek to harm the Jews, but the Persian king himself is not a hostile power. To the contrary, what saves the Jews is their close connection to the king, exemplified by Esther's marriage to Ahasuerus (for those who might think the Bible prohibits such a marriage between an Israelite and a foreigner, *see the box* "Intermarriage: Biblical Arguments for and Against").

A similar attitude toward Persian rule is reflected in the Elephantine Papyri, mentioned at the beginning of the chapter. The Judahites/Jews there had their own temple, which was threatened by the devotees of an Egyptian deity, Khnum, god of the source of the Nile River—and in fact, their temple dedicated to Yaho was destroyed in 410 BCE. To restore it, the Judahites/Jews of Elephantine also turned to Persian rule for help, petitioning the Persian governor Bagavahya for his support in exchange for using their restored temple to pray to God on his behalf. As is true of the Jews in biblical sources, the Elephantine community sought to preserve itself through an alliance with Persian rule, offering its allegiance in exchange for protection against other hostile local populations (unfortunately, we can't really trace the history of this community much beyond its effort to restore its temple, which may never have been rebuilt).

Even as they were able to restore the forms of temple-centered worship disrupted by Babylonian conquest, however, Judahites had to adapt to a new political environment. Accepting foreign rule meant that Judahites would have to find ways to preserve their indigenous traditions in political contexts ruled by other peoples, and in some

INTERMARRIAGE: BIBLICAL ARGUMENTS FOR AND AGAINST

Although intermarriage between Jews and non-Jews is common in America today, Jews concerned about the future of Jewish culture sometimes express concern about such marriages, believing that they represent a threat to the perpetuation of Jewish traditions and identity. This anxiety can be traced back to the Bible itself, which prohibits marriage between Israelites and neighboring Canaanites. Nehemiah, who played such an important role in rebuilding Jerusalem during the post-exilic period that he has a biblical book named after him, seemed to have been concerned about intermarriage between Israelites and non-Israelite women, cursing and beating Judahites who had married women from Ashdod, Ammon, and Moab. Interestingly, whereas the ban seems to have originated from the fear that Israelites would be led by such marriages to worship the gods of the Canaanites, Nehemiah had another concern: a worry that the children of such marriages were losing their ability to speak the language of Judah.

It is worth noting, however, that other parts of the Hebrew Bible are not as clearly opposed to intermarriage as Nehemiah was. Its ban is focused on non-Israelites who live within the land of Canaan. There is no blanket ban on marrying foreigners in general—to the contrary, Isaac, Jacob, Joseph, and Moses find wives among peoples like the Arameans, the Egyptians, the Midianites, and the Ethiopians, all foreign wives, but women who did not originate from among the Canaanites living in the land. This might be why Esther's marriage with Ahasuerus does not trouble the author of the book of Esther—the Persian king was not a Canaanite. Indeed, not only does the Bible tolerate such relationships, but also some biblical books depict intermarriage in a positive light—most famously, the book of Ruth, believed by many scholars to have been written during the age of Ezra and Nehemiah, which claims that King David himself descended from a marriage between an Israelite named Boaz and a Moabite woman named Ruth. One might counter that Ruth was a convert, adopting the god of her husband, but that argument does not apply to Esther's marriage with Ahasuerus, who shows no signs of adopting his wife's beliefs or Judahite identity.

Although Jews in later periods discouraged marriages with non-Jews, and endogamy (marrying within one's community) was widespread among Jews until the modern period. The Bible itself records a range of attitudes toward marriages between Israelites and non-Israelites, warning against the dangers of such relationships, but only with certain kinds of non-Israelites. As in the books of Esther and Ruth, it even suggests here and there that non-Israelite spouses can play a positive role in the community's survival.

cases, that meant downplaying or reinterpreting their culture to avoid a confrontation. They would have to learn the languages of their rulers, along with other aspects of their rulers' culture, so as to successfully interact with them, and this interaction, together with the new trade contacts opened up under foreign rule, inevitably exposed Judahites to new cultural influences. Their very identity was different now; beyond their sense of themselves as members of a particular family or kingdom, Judahites were now subjects in a vast empire presided over by a ruler who was a remote figure but also, through his officials, a shaper of Judah's political and religious life.

All these changes are part of the story of how Judahite culture evolved into Jewish culture, but by themselves they are not enough to understand the transition. The Persian period is also the age in which Judahites first seem to turn to the Bible, or rather to the texts that would eventually become the Bible, to keep their ancestral culture alive. On the surface, this also seems to be a highly conservative move, a turn back to the past that had been disrupted by Babylonian conquest, but like the acceptance of foreign rule, it, too, represents a new phase in Judahite culture. Indeed, as we will explain, it may well be the single most important development in the Persian period for understanding how Judahite culture gave birth to Jewish culture.

Looking for a specific leader with whom to associate this change, historians often associate it with the scribe Ezra, a priest, scholar, and leader of the Judahite community in the Persian period who may have lived around 450 BCE. In later Jewish tradition, Ezra was remembered as a Moses-like figure, credited with, in effect, re-revealing the laws of Moses in the form that later Jews would know in their own day (e.g., later Jews came to believe that it was Ezra who transcribed the biblical text from Paleo-Hebrew letters into the Aramaic script in which it is now written), along with other religious practices and institutions. That isn't quite his role in the Bible itself, but there he does nonetheless serve an important function, appointed by the Persian king Artaxerxes to lead a contingent of exiles back home and to regulate their life in Judah and Jerusalem "according to the law of [their] God" (Ezra 7). It is not clear what the text means here by "the law of your God," but many scholars believe it is referring to the laws of Moses—that is, the laws in the Five Books of Moses, which Ezra is being asked to enforce in the province of Yehud. Some scholars believe that it was during Ezra's administration that the Five Books of Moses were introduced, not composed (they probably draw on sources from the pre-exilic period), but compiled, edited, and promulgated as a law that the people of Judah were obligated to follow. Together with another official named Nehemiah, a Judahite cupbearer of the Persian king also sent on a mission to Yehud to restore Jerusalem, Ezra is associated with the renewal of Judahite culture as a scripture-based culture, a culture generated through the reading and interpretation of sacred texts.

In all likelihood, the history of what actually happened in this period differs from what we can read in the biblical accounts. We rely for our knowledge of Ezra and Nehemiah on biblical books that bear their name, and these do not provide very much information and suffer from a confused chronology and other historiographical problems that make one doubt that they are telling us a complete or accurate story of what happened. We cannot be certain that Ezra and Nehemiah were really contemporaries as the Bible suggests, and if not, who came first and who came later. Nevertheless, the Persian period does seem to be the age in which what we have been calling the Bible, or at least the core of the Bible—the Five Books of Moses, and

Figure 2.2 Relief sculpture of King Darius the Great.

perhaps other biblical books—achieved the status as a scripture to which Judahites/Jews looked to understand their origins, their obligations to God, and their future.

Because the Bible is so important to Jewish identity, religion, and culture, we feel the need to briefly interrupt our history of the Jews with a brief history of the Bible and how it came to be. By *Bible* we mean the Jewish biblical canon, which did not originate as a single book but, rather, as a collection of scrolls deemed to have a special authority as works revealed or inspired by God (the word *Bible* originates from the Greek words *biblia sacra*, "sacred texts"). Christians also venerate the Bible, of course, but their biblical canon differs from that of the Jews and emerged much later, after the first century CE, and isn't part of our story here. In what follows, we aim to condense the history of the Jewish Bible's formation into two discrete stages. The first, which will require us to go back to the period before Persian rule, encompasses the composition of biblical literature—when and why the texts that would become the Bible were composed in the first place. The second stage is the embrace of these various texts as a scripture, a record of divine revelation that becomes the basis for religious belief and practice. This latter process is often called canonization, the act of declaring something sacred and authoritative, and it may have begun during the Persian period itself. In truth, the processes of the Bible's composition and canonization cannot be neatly distinguished, but dividing our history into these two stages will give some sense of how the Bible came to be and help us see interconnections between its emergence and the emergence of Jewish culture in the same general time period.

Stage 1: The Composition of Biblical Literature

Sometime in the fourth millennium BCE, roughly 5,000–6,000 years ago, writing was invented in the ancient Near East, perhaps originating in Mesopotamia. Writing is something we take for granted now as a part of regular life, but it is a development that transformed the nature of human experience. Speech, communicating by word of mouth, allowed human beings to transmit information and ideas to one another, but its communicative potential was limited. A community without writing had to rely on memory, on oral tradition, a fragile information storage system, to store its collective knowledge. Writing made it possible to store information for longer periods of time, and also to communicate across great distances, and thus enabled many other cultural, social, and economic innovations, allowing for improved accounting, education, and government administration, as well as new forms of storytelling and personal interaction.

Writing also made it possible to communicate with the gods in new ways. The gods sometimes revealed themselves to humans, directly or in the form of a dream, oracle, omen, or vision, but communicating across the human–divine divide was very difficult—the gods lived in faraway places or on mountaintops, and their vast size and radiance made it hard to perceive or interact with them. Writing created a way to cross this barrier and started to play this role in the ancient Near East in the second millennium BCE. In Mesopotamia, for example, certain special texts were thought to come from the mouth of the gods, via human dictation, or else recorded the experiences of those who had experienced divine revelation. People wrote to the gods, and sometimes the gods wrote back, sending written messages directly or revealing the techniques by which their messages, encrypted in the stars and other portents, could be decoded. The idea that writing could bridge the human and the divine realms would prove crucial for the formation of biblical literature, much of it a record of the two-way communication between Israel and Yahweh.

Writing reached Canaan well before it did the ancient Israelites. In fact, it was probably in Canaan or nearby, in places like the Sinai desert, that the

ON WHY THE BIBLE IS NOT A BOOK

Although we are describing the texts collected in the Bible as "books," it is misleading to use that term, and it is certainly anachronistic to think of the Bible itself as a book when situating it in an ancient context. There are several reasons for this.

To begin with, the book as a physical object, as a specific way of preserving and presenting writing, did not emerge until after the events described in the first three or four chapters of this book. The ancient Israelites recorded writing on a number of different media—scrolls formed of animal hides; tablets made of clay, wood, or wax; pottery shards and stones—but the book (sheets of parchment or paper bound together under two covers) was not devised until much later, coming into vogue after the rise of Christianity. Jews transmitted biblical texts as separate scrolls—they still transmit the Five Books of Moses and other biblical books like Esther as scrolls—and these were not published as a single book until long after the age described here.

Another reason not to think of the Bible as a book is that doing so poses the risk that we will project our understanding of books onto the ancient texts included in the Bible. We see books as easy to acquire and handle, but most Jews in antiquity did not have the option of owning a copy of the Five Books of Moses or handling one directly; in the first century CE, for example, there was probably only one copy to be found in an entire village, if that; only a small number of people were able to read it; and the act of reading it was often a public event, something to be performed before an audience. We think of books as the work of individual authors, but this does not apply to many biblical texts either: Many probably reflect the contributions of multiple people over multiple generations, collectively producing something that expanded over the course of its transmission. Few, if any, of these authors put their names to their work, adding content anonymously and transmitting the text in the name of the ancient prophet or sage who originated the words they were supplementing.

It is also worth remembering that the Bible as it exists today is the result of many changes introduced long after antiquity. The biblical texts read by ancient Jews in their original Hebrew did not have the titles that biblical books have today: The titles Genesis, Exodus, and so forth come from the Greek and Latin translations of the Bible read by Christians. English-speaking Jews today use these titles, but the traditional way of referring to them in Jewish culture uses the first word of the Hebrew text as a title (e.g., referring to Genesis as *Bereshit*, Hebrew for "in the beginning"). We speak of "chapters," but the chapters used in English translations of the Bible differ from those that divide the content of the Hebrew text of the Bible, based on chapter divisions introduced during the Middle Ages, and there is much else about the look and content of the Bible today that distinguishes it from the texts read by ancient Judeans/Jews. We think of the Bible as an ancient book, but it wasn't a book in antiquity, and many aspects of it aren't, arising in medieval and modern times.

alphabet was invented sometime in the period between 2000 and 1500 BCE. Using a small number of 20–30 signs to indicate the basic sounds in a language—22 in Hebrew—the *alphabet* (a word derived from the first two letters of this writing system, *aleph* and *bet*) originally followed a pictographic logic: Each letter originally signified some word that began with the sound being represented. Thus, for example, *mem*, the sign that eventually evolved into our letter *M*, derived from a picture of water (*mayim*). Eventually, however, it became unimportant what each sign was visualizing; what was crucial was its association with a particular sound, rather than with an idea or thing.

The alphabet was widely embraced because it was easier to learn and quicker to write than the cumbersome writing systems that existed until that point, writing systems that required remembering hundreds or thousands of signs, and its practical advantages help explain both why it prevailed in Canaan and why it eventually spread to other places, such as Greece and Rome. Inscriptional evidence records various alphabetic experiments in ancient Canaan: It took a while for people to settle on how, and in what direction, to write their letters. By about 1050 BCE, however—not long before our first evidence of the Kingdoms of Israel and Judah, coincidentally—the Canaanite alphabet had settled into a conventional form, from which there then developed more localized scripts—the alphabets used by the Phoenicians, Edomites, Moabites, and Israelites.

Reading and writing were rare skills in antiquity, and as in other Near Eastern societies, there arose in Israel and Judah a class of professional scribes whose job it was to write and read official documents on behalf of the king or the Temple—records, letters, and so forth. Ezra is an example of such scribes, a scholar whose knowledge of how to read and write gave him access to forms of knowledge thought inaccessible to the larger community. Such scribes rarely operated on their own, rather working on behalf of rulers or temples, which generated most of the documents we have from the ancient Near East. But the alphabet was easy enough to learn that professional scribes were not the only ones who used it. We also have examples of non-official writing, texts produced by individuals for their own benefit: pious graffiti, tomb inscriptions, and even a petition for help by someone trying to reclaim a cloak that had been confiscated from him. One of the most remarkable of these inscriptions comes from a tomb at Ketef Hinnom, south of Jerusalem. Two small silver amulets are inscribed with priestly benedictions that are almost identical to a priestly benediction in Numbers 6:24–25: "The Lord bless you and keep you; the Lord make his face to shine upon you, and be gracious to you!" The amulets date to the seventh or sixth century BCE, and as the first known instance of a biblical passage attested outside the Bible, they indicate that its contents were being written down by this time.

Figure 2.3 Fragments of a silver scroll inscribed with portions of the priestly benediction known from Numbers 6.

If we did not have the Hebrew Bible itself, however, nothing in the inscriptional record would ever lead us to guess the existence in ancient Judah of a literature as varied and sophisticated as what is preserved there. Who wrote this literature, when, and why? Trying to answer these questions has kept scholars busy for some three centuries, and it is impossible to describe the countless hypotheses they have generated to explain it. Still, it is worth noting some very basic points of consensus:

1. *The Hebrew Bible reflects the ancient Near Eastern setting in which its contents were composed.* One of the great intellectual accomplishments of the nineteenth century was the decipherment of cuneiform, the writing system developed in Mesopotamia. Scholars were able to understand texts that had not been read for millennia, and among what they discovered were some very precise similarities with a literature people had been reading all along: biblical literature. Especially astonishing was the narrative that has come to be known as the *Gilgamesh Epic*, which, as first announced to the world in 1872 by a scholar named George Smith, includes a flood story strikingly similar to that told in Genesis 6–9. For an example of how this text bears on a biblical work like Genesis, note how this flood story resembles its biblical counterpart (the *Gilgamesh* flood story is told in the first person by the survivor of the flood, a figure named Utnapishtim):

   a. **The Dispatch of Birds**

   At the end of forty days Noah opened the window of the ark that he had made and sent out the raven; and it went back and forth until the waters dried up from the earth. Then he sent the dove from him to see if the waters had subsided from the face of the ground; but the dove found no place to set its foot, and returned to him to the ark, for the waters were still on the face of all the earth, and he put out his hand and took it and brought it into the ark to him. He waited another seven days and again sent out the dove from the ark; and the dove came to him in the evening, and there in its mouth was a freshly plucked olive leaf, and Noah knew that the waters had subsided from the earth.

   (Genesis 8:6–11)

   When the seventh day arrived, I sent forth and set free a dove. The dove went forth, but came back; since no resting place for it was visible, she turned around. Then I sent forth and set free a swallow. The swallow went forth, but came back; since no resting place for it was visible, she turned round. Then I sent forth and set free a raven. The raven went forth and, seeing that the waters had diminished, he eats, circles, caws, and turns not around.

   (*Gilgamesh Epic*, Tablet 11, line 150)

   b. **Pleasing Odors**

   Noah built an altar to the Lord and he took from every clean animal and from every clean bird and offered burnt offerings on the altar. The Lord smelled the pleasing odor.

   (Genesis 8:20–21)

   Then I let out [all] to the four winds and offered a sacrifice. I poured out a libation on the top of the mountain. Seven and seven cult-vessels I set up, upon their potstands I heaped cane, cedarwood, and myrtle. The gods smelled the savor, the gods smelled the sweet savor.

   (*Gilgamesh Epic*, Tablet 11, line 160)

   c. **The Rainbow as Sign**

   God said, "This is the sign of the covenant that I establish between Me and you. . . . [M]y bow I have put in the clouds, and it will be a sign of the covenant between Me and the earth. When I bring clouds over the earth, and the bow appears in the clouds, I will remember my covenant."

   (Genesis 9:12–15)

Figure 2.4 One of the tablets of the *Gilgamesh Epic.*

> When at length as the great goddess [Ishtar] arrived, she lifted up the great jewels which Anu had fashioned to her liking. "Ye gods here, as surely as the lapis upon my neck I shall not forget, I shall be mindful of these days, forgetting [them] never." [The goddess's jeweled necklace is probably to be understood as a rainbow.]
>
> (*Gilgamesh Epic*, Tablet 11, line 165)

The flood story proved to be one of many points of resemblance between biblical and Babylonian literature, though as other ancient sources came to light in the twentieth century, it became clear that the Bible shared much in common with other ancient Near Eastern cultures as well, with Egypt, the Hittites, and the pre-Israelite culture of Canaan itself as known from Ugarit, the Amarna Letters, and Phoenician inscriptions.

And Genesis was not the only biblical text to bear a resemblance to the literature of other ancient Near Eastern peoples. The parallels also included law codes, ritual texts, prophetic oracles, proverbs, psalms, and lamentations—almost every category of literature recorded in the Bible.

One more parallel, this time from the book of Exodus, will help drive home how close the similarity can be.

During the nineteenth or eighteenth century BCE, long before any evidence of Israel, a Babylonian king known as Hammurabi promulgated a series of laws in an effort to establish justice in his kingdom. A copy of those laws inscribed on an 8-foot-tall stela was discovered between 1901 and 1902. The stela features a picture of Hammurabi receiving the symbols of justice from the god Shamash, the Mesopotamian god of justice, and a prologue confirms that the laws have divine authorization, though it is the king who inscribes and enforces them. Some of the laws are strikingly similar to laws recorded in the Five Books of Moses. Compare:

> When a man strikes the eye of a male or the eye of a female slave, and destroys it, he shall free the person to compensate for the eye. If he knocks out the tooth of a male slave or the tooth of a female slave, he shall free him for the tooth.
>
> (Exodus 21:26–27)

> If a man of rank has destroyed the eye of a member of the aristocracy, they shall destroy his eye. If he has broken the bone of another man of rank, they shall break his bone. If he has destroyed the eye of a commoner or broken the bone of a commoner, he shall pay one mina of silver. If he has destroyed the eye of another man's slave or broken the bone of a man's slave, he shall pay one-half his value. If a man of rank has knocked out a tooth of a free-man of his own rank, they shall knock out his tooth. If he has knocked out a commoner's tooth, he shall pay one-third mina of silver.
>
> (*Code of Hammurabi* 196–201)

The Code of Hammurabi and biblical law are not identical. The Babylonian law makes distinctions between different classes (upper-class people and commoners) that biblical law does not, and the two impose different penalties for the same crime. Still, the form, and even the content, of the Babylonian and biblical laws are strikingly similar—clear evidence for scholars that biblical law is rooted in earlier Near Eastern legal tradition. Recently, some fragments of a Mesopotamian law code similar to the Code of Hammurabi were discovered within Canaan itself, coming to light from the Bronze Age city of Hazor, showing that such codes were known in the area and could have plausibly influenced the development of biblical law.

This and the many other parallels between biblical literature and ancient Near Eastern literature that scholars have recognized tell us that the literature now comprising the Hebrew Bible did not come out of a cultural vacuum; its writers drew on storytelling, legal, and other literary traditions shared with scribes from other Near Eastern cultures. Biblical literature does exhibit traits without parallel in other ancient literatures, but its distinctiveness emerges only against a backdrop of pervasive similarity, and the more we learn about ancient Near Eastern literature, the more we learn about how to read biblical literature within the historical and cultural context in which it originated (*see the box* "How Does the Hebrew Bible Differ From Other Ancient Near Eastern Texts?").

2. *In line with the discovery that biblical literature reflects the world in which it was composed, scholars have also come to realize that it is the result not of divine revelation or prophetic inspiration but of human authorship.* A comparative approach to the Bible can help place it in an ancient Near Eastern setting, but it does not tell us who wrote the Bible. Before the onset of the modern age, it scarcely occurred to Jews and Christians to ask this question because they assumed they knew the answer, believing that the Bible was of divine origin, written down by Moses and other prophets transcribing the words of God. In the seventeenth and eighteenth centuries (CE), however—an age when traditional ideas and religious authority were being questioned in Europe—scholars began to doubt the traditional explanation for the Bible's origins, noticing evidence within the Five Books of Moses that seemed to contradict divine or Mosaic authorship.

They noticed, to be more specific, that the Five Books of Moses do not actually describe Moses as the author of the entire narrative. That was an inference by early Jewish and Christian readers of the Bible who were looking to know who wrote these anonymous texts and identified Moses as their author because he is depicted within the narrative as writing down God's words, but these texts never explicitly identify Moses as their author and, in fact, as suggested by hints here and there, seem to be written from someone else's perspective. Not only is Moses himself referred to in the third person, as if it were someone else doing the writing, but also in Deuteronomy 34, the last chapter of the Five Books of Moses, the text even describes his death and burial, events that the real Moses should not have been able to write about.

If Moses did not write the Five Books of Moses, then who did? The Torah itself never discloses its author's identity, but judging from various clues discovered here and there in the text, he lived long after Moses. A famous example of such a clue appears in Genesis 36:31: "These are the kings who reigned in Edom *before any king reigned over the Israelites*." The reference to Israelite monarchy places the verse's author not in the days of Moses but later, after the establishment of the monarchy around 1000 BCE. Whoever wrote the Five Books of Moses, this author was not Moses but someone from a later age.

As they dug deeper, scholars reached an even more surprising conclusion. A close reading of the Five Books of Moses reveals some rather odd features that are hard to explain if the narrative is the work of a single author. In Genesis 6:19, for example, God tells Noah to take two of every kind of animal to store on the ark. Just a few verses later, in 7:2–3, he gives a different version of the same command, instructing Noah to take seven pairs of every clean animal and two of every unclean animal. Why does God seem to repeat the same command twice?

HOW DOES THE HEBREW BIBLE DIFFER FROM OTHER ANCIENT NEAR EASTERN TEXTS?

Although biblical literature resembles the literature of other ancient Near Eastern cultures in many ways, it does have unique characteristics. Part of this distinctiveness is tied to the theological assumptions of the Bible's authors, their belief in Yahweh as the only god that mattered (if not the only god altogether), but it is not just the Bible's theological presuppositions that distinguish it from other ancient Near Eastern mythologies. If modern literary scholarship of the Bible is correct, its authors developed their own distinctive forms of literary communication, developing new ways to convey psychological and moral complexity. For an introduction to the distinctive artistry of biblical literature, see Robert Alter's *The Art of Biblical Narrative* (New York: Basic Books, 1983) or Meir Sternberg's more challenging *The Poetics of Biblical Narrative* (Bloomington: Indiana University Press, 1987).

Ultimately, however, what is most distinctive about the Hebrew Bible is its reception history—the role that it played in later Jewish and Christian history. Some ancient Near Eastern texts, such as the *Gilgamesh Epic*, were also transmitted for long periods of time, and are also considered great works of literature, but no community survived long enough to preserve them beyond antiquity, and it is only in the last two centuries that they have come to light again, retrieved from obscurity through archaeological excavation and the decipherment of such ancient languages as Akkadian and Ugaritic. By contrast, the texts preserved in the Bible were never lost or forgotten—initially preserved by Jews, then by Christians as well—and what distinguishes them from ancient Mesopotamian, Egyptian, or Ugaritic literature is the way they have remained alive for readers. A text like the *Gilgamesh Epic* essentially died and had to be brought back to life by modern scholarship; biblical texts have remained religiously and culturally vital through thousands of years of being read, through Jews and Christians looking to understand these texts as a divine voice speaking to their day and age.

Why is the command different in the two versions, making a distinction between clean and unclean animals in one passage, making no such distinction in another? And why does the text switch from one name for God to another from one passage to the next, using the name *Elohim* in 6:22, then *Yahweh* in 7:1? Genesis—indeed, all of the Five Books of Moses—is full of such inconsistencies.

These books also contain many examples of what biblical scholars refer to as doublets: the same story told twice in slightly varying form—two accounts of how Hagar is driven from Abraham's household (Genesis 16 and 21:9–21), two accounts of how Jacob's name was changed to Israel (Genesis 32:14– 33 and Genesis 35:9–10), and so on. If Moses or any other individual author wrote the Five Books of Moses, why does the text contain so many factual discrepancies, vary its terminology and style, and tell the same basic story in doubled form?

Finding it difficult to answer this question as long as they adhered to the idea that the Five Books of Moses were written by an inspired Moses, scholars came up with another explanation for their authorship, known as the Documentary Hypothesis. This theory proposes that the Five Books of Moses are not actually the work of a single author but a composite of preexisting sources. At some point, an editor wove these sources together into a narrative that is coherent but far from seamless. When this editor's sources contradicted one another, he sometimes let the contradiction stand rather than smoothing it out, perhaps because he wanted to reach different audiences with a stake in different versions of the story he was telling.

The effort to distinguish between and reconstruct these earlier sources is known as source criticism, and using such an approach, scholars have recognized four such sources in the Five Books of Moses, including a source written by an author very interested in ritual matters, known as P, short for the *priestly source*; a source probably from Judah, known as J, from the German spelling of *Yahweh* (hence the *Jahwist* in German), this author's favored word for *God*; a source known as E because of its preference for the word *Elohim* as a name for God; and a source known as D, the core of the book of Deuteronomy, which seems to have been written separately from all the other sources. The Documentary Hypothesis remains a hypothesis—the original sources have not been found—but no one has come up with a more plausible explanation for the puzzling way that the Five Books of Moses tell their tale. It also has the advantage of being consistent with what we know of literary practice in the ancient Near East, for there, too, as illustrated by the evolution of the *Gilgamesh Epic*, texts were often a composite of pre-existing material woven together into a longer document.

The documentary hypothesis does not apply to other books in the Bible, but scholarship has reached similar conclusions about how many of them were composed. We have already noted that part of Isaiah, the section known as Deutero-Isaiah, was written long after the time of the prophet Isaiah in the eighth century BCE. Much of "First Isaiah," Chapters 1–39, do indeed seem to come from the Assyrian period, and it is not impossible that it records the words of the prophet himself, but Chapters 40 and following reflect conditions in the Persian period, even mentioning King Cyrus by name, as we have noted. Jeremiah and Ezekiel also seem to have grown through a long process of supplementation.

This approach to the authorship of the Hebrew Bible not only challenges the traditional view of its authorship but also conflicts with our idea of authorship itself. Like the Five Books of Moses, the Bible's other books were also traditionally ascribed to prophets or divinely inspired kings, such as Solomon. Ascribing a book to a particular person, someone with a name, suits the modern conception of authorship as a fundamentally individual effort. According to biblical scholarship, however, the Five Books of Moses, Isaiah, and other biblical texts in the Hebrew Bible are not individually authored texts; they are more akin to the Web, developing over time, in an unplanned way, through the contributions of multiple people.

While the Documentary Hypothesis is just a hypothesis, we do have other kinds of evidence that biblical books evolved over a long period of time. In Chapter 3, we will introduce the Dead Sea Scrolls. One reason these texts are so important is that they include the earliest known copies of biblical texts that date from as early as the second century BCE. Many of those manuscripts are different from the Hebrew Bible as it is known today, preserving forms of books such as Samuel and Jeremiah at an earlier stage in their literary development. The Dead Sea Scrolls provide us with before-and-after snapshots of the biblical text as it developed, allowing us to see with our own eyes how it grew and changed over the course of its transmission (*see the box* "A Snapshot of the Hebrew Bible in the Making").

3. *The development of biblical literature is tied to the history of the Kingdom of Judah.* Once scholars recognized the Bible as a work of human beings and saw that it reflected the circumstances in which it was composed, they set about trying to contextualize its composition in a more specific way, to place it within the framework of history. The result of this effort was a recognition that the composition of biblical literature spans much of the history of the Kingdom of Judah in particular, and that it reflects a distinctively Judahite (as opposed to northern Israelite) point of view.

A SNAPSHOT OF THE HEBREW BIBLE IN THE MAKING

The biblical manuscripts found among the Dead Sea Scrolls demonstrate that the Hebrew text that constitutes the Jewish Bible today does not always preserve the original form of biblical compositions. A dramatic example is what scholars learned about I Samuel 11 from a version of that text found among the Dead Sea Scrolls. That version contains a passage (marked in italics ahead) that does not appear in the present-day Hebrew text of the Bible. While it is possible that the additional material was inserted into the text secondarily, it is more likely that a scribe accidentally deleted it when he was copying the text that became the version of I Samuel read by Jews today.

I Samuel 11:1–2 as the text appears in the Hebrew Bible today:

> Nahash the Ammonite went up and besieged Jabesh-Gilead. All the men of Jabesh-Gilead said to Nahash, "Make a covenant with us, and we will serve you."

I Samuel 11 as known from the Dead Sea Scrolls (4Q Samuel A):

> *Nahash king of the Ammonites oppressed the Gadites and the Reubenites viciously. He put out the right eye of all of them and brought fear and trembling on Israel. Not one of the Israelites in the region beyond the Jordan remained whose right eye Nahash king of the Ammonites did not put out, except seven thousand men who escaped from the Ammonites and went to Jabesh Gilead. Then, after a month,* Nahash the Ammonite went up and besieged Jabesh-Gilead. So all the men of Jabesh-Gilead said to Nahash, "Make a covenant with us, and we will serve you."

Figure 2.5 A researcher from the Israeli Antiquities Authority examines 2,000-year-old fragments of the Dead Sea Scrolls at the Israel Museum in Jerusalem, Israel, on December 18, 2012. The Israeli Antiquities Authorities and Google are collaborating on a project to put the Dead Sea Scrolls online.

The effort to trace the transmission of the Bible as a text, to reconstruct its earliest form and how it changed over time, involves a kind of scholarship known as *text criticism*, which compares different versions of the Bible in an effort to reconstruct the history of its scribal transmission and the relationship of the versions to each other.

Consider the four sources of the Five Books of Moses that we have just introduced: J, E, P, and D. Two, and possibly three, of those sources are thought to be the work of Judahite authors (J, P, and probably D; E may have come from the north). The historical narratives of Samuel and Kings, focused as they are on the Davidic monarchy and the Jerusalem Temple, also come from Judah, some material perhaps having arisen in the royal court itself, and the book of Ruth, a story about the Moabite woman who became David's great-grandmother, is also Judah-focused. Isaiah, Jeremiah, and the majority of other prophetic texts come from Judah as well or, else, were written by Judahites in exile, as seems the case with Ezekiel. The book of Psalms contains many hymns probably originally composed for use in the Jerusalem Temple, the sayings gathered in Proverbs probably represent the work of Jerusalem intellectuals, and the book of Lamentations preserves the mournful response to Jerusalem's destruction by the Babylonians. Works such as Esther and Ezra-Nehemiah come from Judahites living in exile or, else, recently returned to Judah in the Persian period. In short, most of the Hebrew Bible was composed in Judah or by exiled Judahites, preserving little of the literature and culture of the Northern Kingdom of Israel.

Situating the Bible within Judahite culture explains many things about it. Why does Genesis seem more positively inclined toward Jacob's son Judah, the ancestor of the Judahites, than his older brothers, Reuben, Simeon, and Levi? Why do the best and most important kings in biblical history (Hezekiah and Josiah) come from the House of David in Judah, while many of its worst kings (Jeroboam or Ahab) come from the Northern Kingdom of Israel? Why is the Jerusalem Temple so central while the temples of northern Israel are marginalized or condemned? Why does the Bible seem far more interested in the Judahite survivors of Babylonian conquest and their fate than the Israelite survivors of Assyrian conquest? The answers to these questions emerge when one recognizes the Hebrew Bible as the work of authors coming from the Kingdom of Judah or from the exiles of Judah living in Babylonia.

How is it that so much Judahite literature was preserved compared to what little survives of the literature from the northern kingdom? The Bible itself suggests an answer. When the Kingdom of Israel was destroyed in 722–720 BCE, its inhabitants effectively slipped off the radar screen, deported to other parts of the Assyrian Empire, probably assimilating into the local populations, among whom they settled, or dying out. If we have some of its literature preserved in the Bible, it is probably because some Israelites fled the northern kingdom at the time of its destruction and passed their literary traditions on to the people of Judah. The Kingdom of Judah was eventually destroyed as well, but its population persisted after the Babylonian conquest, preserving their traditions in exile and some eventually returning to Judah. It was almost certainly this community that preserved the texts now collected in the Jewish Bible.

The attempt to reconstruct the origins of biblical literature is an ongoing project, subject to revision in light of new evidence and theories. What scholars have discovered thus far, however, has done much to explain how this literature came to be. Biblical literature is different from other ancient literatures in many ways, but much of it is a variant of the kind of literature produced elsewhere in the ancient Near East in antiquity, reflecting the same compositional and scribal practices that shaped Ugaritic, Babylonian, and Egyptian literature. We can only hypothesize about who wrote the Bible, but it is possible to connect much of its composition to known history—not to events that we are not sure actually happened, such as the Exodus, but certainly to demonstrable historical experiences, such as Assyrian, Babylonian, and Persian conquest. If we were to try to sum up the results of 300 years of biblical scholarship in one sentence, we would say that its most important accomplishment is to reinterpret a text seen as supernatural and timeless as the work of humans from a particular historical period.

What all this does not explain, however, is how biblical literature became *the Bible*, a collection of texts fundamentally different from any other ancient Near Eastern document or library because of its role as a sacred scripture in later Jewish (not to mention Christian) culture. Scholars are probably right that the book of Genesis combines the work of human authors living between 1000 and 500 BCE, that it is basically a variant of ancient Near Eastern literature, and that its composition was influenced by historical events, but all that only deepens the mystery of how such a text came to be seen as divine revelation. To understand that development, we must return to the history of the post-exilic Judahite community in the Persian period, connecting the emergence of the Bible as a sacred scripture to cultural and political changes taking place at this time.

Stage 2: The Canonization of the Bible

What emerged from the period of Babylonian conquest and Persian rule was not the Bible but an assortment of texts—scrolls rather than what we think of today as books. Together, these texts constitute what is now known as the biblical canon, a collection of writings united by the belief among Jews that they have a special religious authority. We do not know why certain books composed in this early period made it into this emerging biblical canon while others did not, but what we do know is that any text composed in pre-exilic Judah, the Babylonian Exile, or during the period of Persian rule that was not included in the canon did not survive, with one possible exception. In our discussion of the Elephantine community, we alluded to a text that preserves the teachings of an Assyrian sage named Ahiqar, an Aramaic composition from the fifth century BCE. We do not know if this text was written by a Judahite—Ahiqar's story was known throughout the ancient world—but we can infer from such evidence that his story was at least known to Judahites in this period, if not a composition they produced themselves. Apart from this chance discovery and a few inscriptions, all the other texts we have from Judah and Jews prior to the second century BCE survived only because they were included in the biblical canon, passed down from one generation to the next because of their sacred status.

But what kind of collection is the Bible, and why did its contents become so important to later Jews? In other ancient Near Eastern texts, scribes developed catalogues of books deemed worthy of a collection in a library or for use as a curriculum in teaching their students. It may be that the first efforts to collect and catalogue Judahite literature had similar motivations, but at some point it became a very different kind of collection, of value not just for ancient scribes but also for the broader community.

Jews came to believe that their connection to the past and their prospects for the future depended on their understanding of these books. They felt an obligation to follow the laws in the Five Books of Moses and looked to other biblical texts for additional guidance about how to live their lives. At stake in their interpretation of biblical literature was their sense of identity, how they differed from other peoples, and their understanding of reality, including their relationship with the god they believed had created that reality. The texts included in the Bible were not necessarily written to serve such purposes. Some, like Genesis, might have originated as stories that parents told their children to answer their questions about where things came from. Others, like some of the hymns in the book of Psalms, may have been intended for recitation during worship in the Jerusalem Temple. The Bible includes prophetic texts written as critiques of contemporary society, but also educational texts probably composed by professional scribes and meant for their students, and one biblical text, the Song of Songs, is so erotic in content that scholars suspect it may have originated as a marriage hymn or even as a kind of pornography. How did such a hodgepodge come to acquire so much significance for Jews?

The earliest stages in the development of the biblical canon may predate the Babylonian Exile. Especially intriguing is the reported discovery of a long-lost Torah of Moses during the reign of King Josiah (640–609 BCE), an incident reported in 2 Kings 22–23. Allegedly rediscovered during repair work on the Temple, the scroll records the commands the people of Judah must follow to keep their covenant with God. The people have been violating those commands, Josiah realizes, and so he initiates a major reform of Judah's religious life, suppressing its idolatrous practices. Modern scholars suspect that the scroll in question was the book of Deuteronomy and that its rediscovery was actually a ruse staged by the king in an effort to pass off a newly composed lawbook as an ancient Mosaic text that people would feel they had to follow. If that hypothesis is correct, what we have in 2 Kings 22–23 is a description of how one of the books of the Five Books of Moses came to be published, which suggests, in turn, that the biblical canon was already developing even before the exile.

This incident happened not long before the Babylonian Exile, however, and from what we can tell, Judahite religion before this was not scripture-centered: Figures like David consult prophets when they want to discern the will of God and are never depicted in the Bible reading the laws of Moses or trying to make sense of its content. Beyond Josiah's reform, what seems to have pushed Judahite culture in this direction was the Babylonian conquest and the disruption that it caused. Judahites seeking to salvage their culture in the wake of that experience turned to these texts to fill in the vacuum left by the destruction of other institutions. God himself was believed to be manifest in the Temple, and for this reason, people visited the Temple to interact with him or take refuge in his presence. The Temple's destruction rendered God inaccessible. For hundreds of years, Judah had been ruled by a single family, the descendants of David, providing a sense of political continuity with the distant past. Nebuchadnezzar put an end to this political tradition when he effectively ended the Davidic line. In response to these abrupt, traumatic changes, Judahites focused on surviving remnants of their culture to connect them to the pre-exilic period, objects like the cultic vessels used in Solomon's Temple that had been deported to Babylon but were potentially retrievable. Texts from ancient Judah were yet another remnant from the pre-exilic past, serving the people of Judah as another link to what they had lost.

Investing these texts with even more important was the fact that so much of it preserved, or seemed to preserve, the words of God to Israel—God's promise to Abraham and his descendants, the divine revelation at Mount Sinai, and the visions and oracles revealed to later prophets, such as Isaiah and Jeremiah. These divine messages had been addressed to earlier Israelites, but some were also intended for future generations; sometimes, in fact, they seemed to address precisely those dire circumstances in which the Judahites found themselves after the Babylonian conquest:

> When Moses finished writing down in a book the words of this teaching [Torah] to the very end, he commanded the Levites who carried the ark of the covenant of the Lord, saying, "Take this book of the teaching [Torah] and put it beside the ark of the covenant of the Lord your God; let it be a witness against you. . . . For I know that after my death you will act corruptly, and you will turn aside from the way that I have commanded you. At the end of days trouble will befall you because you will do what is evil in the sight of the Lord, angering Him with your acts."
>
> (Deuteronomy 31:24–26, 29)

Judahites struggling to survive in a devastated Judah or languishing in Babylonian Exile looked to this and other prophetic passages to find an explanation for their misfortunes. If, as such texts suggested, exile was their punishment for having done evil, there might yet be the opportunity to soften God's anger, to repair Israel's relationship with him, to regain what was lost—but how? In the Five Books of Moses, Jews found a way to learn what God expected of them and a guide for how to move forward, and biblical interpretation—the reading and understanding of texts—thus emerged during this period as a way to re-establish a relationship with God.

Examples of such biblical interpretation can already be found in the Bible itself, in the books of Ezra and Nehemiah. Often treated in biblical manuscripts and by modern scholars as a single composition, Ezra-Nehemiah was probably composed in the fourth century BCE, and as we have noted in passing, it is one of our major sources for the history of the early post-exilic community. Of special relevance to our discussion here is what Ezra-Nehemiah tells us about the emergence of a proto-biblical canon in this period. The Five Books of Moses as we know them today may not have existed by this point, but something like them did, a text Ezra-Nehemiah refers to as "the book of the law" or "the law of Moses." If not referring to the actual Five Books of Moses we have today, this lawbook anticipates many of its characteristics: It contained divine commands that Israel was obligated to obey, it was identified as a "teaching" or "Torah" of Moses, and the public reading of its contents was an important communal experience.

Based on what we can tell from Ezra-Nehemiah, this text was critical to the post-exilic community's efforts to revitalize itself. In its view of things, the first step was the return from exile and the rebuilding of the Temple, but those steps were not sufficient for a full restoration of the community. When Ezra and Nehemiah reached Yehud, they found that things were still terribly awry: Jerusalem was largely unrestored and vulnerable to its enemies. The people were full of complaints, and—of greatest concern to Ezra and Nehemiah—they were on the verge of assimilating into the local population, intermarrying with foreigners, adopting their ways, and even forgetting how to speak their native tongue. The Judahites had returned to the land, but they were still slaves: "Its rich yield goes to the kings whom you have set over us because of our sins; they have power also over our bodies and over our livestock at their pleasure, and we are in great distress" (Nehemiah 9:37). For Ezra-Nehemiah, a full restoration requires the people to recommit to God's law, a process that involves reading and studying Moses's teaching.

From this perspective, the climax of Ezra-Nehemiah occurs in the eighth chapter of Nehemiah, when Ezra summons the people to Jerusalem for a public reading of the law, an opportunity for them to remember what it is that God had commanded them to do. But it takes more than reading the law aloud to understand its contents; it must also be studied and interpreted, a process that begins on the very next day:

> On the first day of the seventh month, Ezra the priest brought the Torah before the congregation, men and women and all who could comprehend what they were hearing. . . . Ezra opened the scroll in the sight of all the people, and as he did so, all the people stood up. Ezra blessed the Lord, the great God, and all the people answered, "Amen, Amen," with hands upraised. Then they bowed their heads and prostrated themselves before the Lord with their faces to the ground. Jeshua, Bani, Sherebiah, Jamin, Akkub, Shebbethai, Hodiah, Maaseiah, Kelita, Azariah, Jozabad, Hanan, Pelaiah, and the Levites explained the Torah to the people while the people stood in their places. They read from the scroll of the Torah of God, translating it and giving the sense, so they understood the reading.
>
> (Nehemiah 8:2–8)

According to the books of Ezra and Nehemiah, neither the Temple's reconstruction nor the appearance of prophets among the people was enough to restore Judah's relationship with God. It was only by reading and understanding the words of the *Torah* (Hebrew for *teaching*, a word eventually applied to the Five Books of Moses) that the Judahites were able to fully restore their relationship with God. According to this narrative, in fact, as Ezra begins to read this Torah, it is as if God himself becomes manifest, with those watching the scribe as he opens the scroll bowing down to acknowledge the sanctity and authority of the words he was reading.

Being able to read the Torah in this early period was not something that came easily to people. Literacy continued to be a rare and hard-won skill, and even for those who knew how to read, biblical literature would have represented a challenge, written in a dialect of Hebrew different from the Aramaic-saturated Hebrew of the post-exilic period and containing many interpretive problems, informational gaps, and linguistic puzzles. To make sense of this text required training and skill that only a few experts possessed, like knowing advanced mathematics in our own day and age, and that is what made figures like Ezra so important for the community: Such figures had the specialized knowledge necessary to read and understand the text.

We would point to Ezra's reading of the Torah as a reflection of an important shift in the transition from Israelite to Jewish culture: the emergence of a sacred text, the Torah of Moses, as the ultimate source of communal and religious norms in Judahite society, and of reading as the act that connected the Judahites to God. We do not know for certain that the Torah referred to in this passage is the Five Books of Moses known today, but it was certainly similar, probably an earlier form of today's Torah, and its role in the early post-exilic community anticipates the Bible's role in later Jewish communities.

This development might have been further encouraged by the Persians, who had a stake in how the communities under their rule were organized. The reader might remember that according to the Bible, Ezra and Nehemiah were actually commissioned by the Persian king himself to govern Judah according to the law of God, and there might be some truth to such a claim. As part of his efforts to consolidate the organization of the Persian Empire, Darius I apparently tried to codify the local laws of the various communities under his rule, or at least this is the implication of a document from Egypt that indicates that he ordered his satrap to form a committee of Egyptian sages to gather in writing all the old laws of Egypt down to the time of Persia's conquest, a collation of public law, temple law, and private law. A similar effort might be reflected in the book of Ezra, where the Persian Empire not only recognizes the law of God but also puts its own authority behind it, ordering it to be taught to those who do not know it and giving Ezra the power to punish those who violate it.

Although their testimony is not very clear, the Elephantine Papyri may preserve a glimpse into Persia's role in disseminating the laws of Moses among Judahites living outside Yehud. One of the Elephantine documents is a letter sent by a certain Hananiah to the Elephantine community instructing it how to keep Passover, a springtime festival. The Elephantine community does not seem to know about the laws of Moses, never citing them in any of its documents, but the following letter, dated to 418 BCE, may be an effort to introduce or impose them:

> Now, this year, the fifth year of King Darius, word was sent from the king to Arsa[mes saying, "Authorize a festival of unleavened bread for the Jew]ish [garrison]" So do you count fou[rteen days of the month of Nisan and] ob[serve the Passover], and from the 15th to the 21st day of [Nisan observe the festival of unleavened bread]. Be (ritually) clean and take heed. [Do n]o work [on the 15th or the 21st day, no]r drink [beer, nor eat] anything [in] which the[re is] leaven [from the 14th at] sundown until the 21st of Nis[an. Br]ing into your closets [anything leavened that you may have on hand] and seal it up between those date[s].

As one can tell from all the words between brackets, the letter is fragmentary and much of its contents must be reconstructed, but what is actually preserved of this document suggests that it was an effort to inform the Elephantine community about how to keep the festival of Passover. Hananiah does not mention the Torah as the source of these laws, but some of his instructions seem to come from it (though not all). What is no less interesting here is that the letter seems to have been commissioned by the Persian government: "Word was sent from the king." How did the laws associated with Moses become so authoritative in Judahite culture? This letter, when read together with the book of Ezra, points to a possible answer: Adopting a policy of respecting local tradition, and recognizing the laws of the Torah as a codification of that tradition for the people of Judah, Persia may have recruited officials like Ezra or the Hananiah of this letter to teach and enforce it as a local law code.

If this is what happened, it apparently had an impact. Not too long after the end of Persian rule, about 120 years after Hananiah wrote his letter, a Greek traveler named Hecataeus, a contemporary of Alexander the Great, wrote a description of Judah, and the society he describes seems governed by the laws of Moses: "The colony was headed by a man named Moses. . . . [H[e established the temple that they hold in chief veneration, instituted their forms of worship and ritual, drew up their laws, and ordered their institutions." If we accept this testimony as authentic, Judah at the end of the Persian period, in the fourth century BCE, was a society governed by the laws of Moses, and that was certainly true of Judah/Jewish culture in the following centuries, when the laws of Moses were not only revered by Jews themselves but also officially recognized by foreign rulers who granted the Jews the right to follow these laws and sometimes backed up their enforcement with their own power—this according to Jewish sources from the first century BCE and later. It is impossible to fill in the gap between the Elephantine Papyri and Hecataeus's description in any detailed way, but the Torah's emergence as a religious and social charter for the people of Judah seems to have taken root in the intervening period, the Persian period, and perhaps with encouragement from the Persian government.

To be clear, we are not trying to suggest that it was Persian rule that created the Five Books of Moses or that it was canonized to serve their political interests. These books were part of the cultural legacy that Jews inherited from ancient Israel, a point of connection to their ancestors, and they read them to learn where they came from and how to sustain their relationship with their god. From a historical perspective, however, it would be a mistake to assume that this commitment to the Five Books of Moses had always been a part of Israelite culture. The books themselves may have existed prior to the Persian period, but there is little evidence to suggest they exerted the authority and influence that they did in the later period—there is no sign of them or their influence, for example, in the texts recovered from the Persian period community of Elephantine. The situation seems different in the centuries following Persian rule, and what little we know about the intervening period helps us understand this transformation by relating it to broader developments in the Persian Empire, including its effort to make subjects more governable by promoting the dissemination and enforcement of local legal tradition.

But all this relates only to the Five Books of Moses. What about the rest of the Jewish Bible? The Jewish biblical canon now has two other parts: (1) the Prophets, the section that includes the historical narratives of Joshua, Judges, 1–2 Samuel, and 1–2 Kings; the large or "major" prophetic texts of Isaiah, Jeremiah, and Ezekiel; and 12 brief or "minor" prophetic books; and (2) the Writings, which include Psalms, Proverbs, Job, Chronicles, Ezra-Nehemiah, and a variety of other writings. (This tripartite structure of the Jewish biblical canon, dividing it into the Torah, Prophets, and Writings, has yielded one of the words that Jews use to this day to refer to the Bible, *Tanak* or *Tanakh*, an acronym constructed from the first letters of *T*orah, *N*evi'im [= the Prophets], and *K*tuvim [= the Writings]). When and how did the books in these sections become a part of the Jewish Bible?

We do not know the answer to this question, but what little we can infer suggests that their canonization was influenced by the earlier canonization of the Five Books of Moses, with these later books considered a kind of supplement or extension of the Torah. Let us begin with the Prophets. The latest books in this section, "minor" prophets like Haggai, Zechariah, and Micah, were composed during the Persian period, and it seems reasonable to suppose that this was when this section of the canon was also settled. What made the content of this section important for early Jews is that it records the words and deeds of the prophets who succeeded Moses—Joshua, Samuel, Elijah, Elisha, Isaiah, Jeremiah, and all the rest—thus sustaining a chain of revelation through the period of the kingship and exile. Moses himself was considered a unique prophet, with more direct access to God than any other human, and these later works of prophecy may have had a lower or second authority compared to his, but they still represented a form of communication with God, a way to learn what he wanted, intended, and expected; and while these prophets rarely add new laws to follow, they do record other kinds of divine messages that reinforce the Torah's authority, including exhortations to remain loyal to God, to avoid worshipping other gods, and to promote social justice by not abusing the poor. They also warn about what will happen if Israel ignores God's commands—the divine punishment that follows disloyalty and disobedience.

The third section of the Jewish Bible, the Writings, consists of a variety of different kinds of writing—hymns to God, didactic texts, and narratives—and is harder to generalize about. It was probably the last section of the Jewish biblical canon to take shape—it still seems to have been somewhat fluid well beyond the Persian period—but it, too, may have begun to take shape in this earlier period. We do not know enough to explain how books like Job or Esther entered the canon, but it may be significant that a number of books in this section are associated with David and Solomon. Many of the psalms in the book of Psalms were ascribed to David; the book of Ruth tells the story of his great-grandmother, a Moabite woman named Ruth; much of 1 and 2 Chronicles is about his reign, while three other books in this section—Proverbs, Ecclesiastes, and the Song of Songs—are said to record the words of Solomon. David and Solomon were obviously important figures in biblical tradition, but as described in Samuel and in Kings, they are flawed figures, great kings but sinful ones who go astray from God. The David and Solomon of the Writings are rather different, pious figures whose writings offer insight into God and guidance for how to behave. It is possible that their writings were included in the Bible because, by the Persian period, David and Solomon were seen as Moses-like figures in their own right, prophets or teachers who offered insight into God and guidance for how to behave.

Scholars believe that the canonization process initially developed in the period between the end of the kingdom of Judah and the centuries of Persian rule, but it's not clear when it ended. Centuries after the Persian period, there was still some debate over whether books like Ecclesiastes should be included in the Jewish biblical canon, and we know of other books that may have been considered canonical by some Jews but rejected by others. Since there was no real way to authenticate a composition as a genuine work of the biblical past, authors sought to pass off certain works as biblical by imitating the style of books like Genesis and by ascribing authorship to biblical figures like Moses and Solomon, yielding a strange and fascinating assortment of texts known in modern times as the Pseudepigrapha (from Greek, meaning "false writing"). We have many such texts that were written in the centuries following Persian rule, books ascribed to Enoch, Moses, and other biblical figures, and it is possible that they became a part of the Bible for some Jews (*see the box* "Biblical Stories the Bible Doesn't Tell"), though they did not make it into the biblical canon venerated by Jews today.

It is not always clear why such text did not make it into the Jewish Bible while other books like Daniel did. In fact, some of these biblical-like works are now a part of certain Christian biblical canons, books like the Wisdom of Solomon that are part of what Catholics refer to as the Deuterocanonical books (Protestants, excluding them from their canon, refer to these texts as the Apocrypha, texts of dubious origin and authority). For the most part, however, such books were probably composed too

BIBLICAL STORIES THE BIBLE DOESN'T TELL

Some pseudepigraphical works were found among the Dead Sea Scrolls, but most were known long before then, from translations into languages such as Greek, Latin, Syriac, Ethiopic, and Armenian that were preserved by various Christian communities. Thanks to these translations, we have all kinds of texts attributed to biblical figures but not preserved in the Bible: "apocalypses" that describe the revelation of divine secrets to biblical figures such as Enoch, Moses, Baruch (Jeremiah's secretary), and Ezra; "testaments" that preserve the last words of Jacob's 12 sons, Moses, and others; and various hymns and prayers attributed to David and Solomon. How do we know these works are not really from the authors to whom they are ascribed? Some Jews and Christians believed that they were, but scholarship has come to recognize that they were actually composed by Jews between 200 BCE and 200 CE (several were also probably reworked by later Christians), in some cases because they were written in Greek as used in this period, in others because they reflect ideas and interpretive traditions, including Christian ideas, known to have arisen in this later time. We do not know why these texts did not become a part of Jewish and Christian Bibles, but chances are that they were simply composed too late to be included, most having been written after the Jewish biblical canon was more or less closed. Written centuries after the age they describe, pseudepigraphical literature cannot help us understand what happened in the age of Abraham and Moses, but it is an extremely useful resource for understanding how the Bible was interpreted in the early Jewish culture that developed in centuries following the period of Babylonian and Persian rule.

Specific examples of such pseudepigraphical works include the following:

I Enoch and other books attributed to the primeval sage Enoch mentioned in Genesis 5:21–24. The biblical text claims that Enoch "walked with God"—something it never explains but that later Jews took to mean that Enoch was taken on a heavenly journey. I Enoch and other words attributed to Enoch describe what he saw and learned in heaven, including secrets of nature and knowledge of the future. Such literature

late to gain mainstream acceptance among Jews. Despite the fluid nature of the canonization process, by the end of the Second Temple period, there does seem to have emerged a consensus among most Jews about the content of scripture as they understood it, a canon that more or less resembles the Jewish Bible as known today.

You might have noticed that over the course of this chapter, we have slipped into using the term *Jewish*, as opposed to *Israelite* or *Judahite*. Why the difference? The Jews we are speaking of here saw themselves as the direct descendants of the Israelites, but their reverence for the Bible and their use of biblical interpretation to understand and connect themselves to God appear to be a major difference from their ancestors in the pre-exilic period. The culture they developed was a good approximation of the Israel described in the Bible—a culture devoted to a god named YHWH, whose worship was centered in Jerusalem, and so forth—but the fact that this reconstituted culture was generated through the reading of the Bible is precisely what distinguishes it from the Israelite religion of earlier centuries. For us, therefore, the emergence of the Bible and biblical interpretation—not an event to be placed in a particular year or even a century but a shift in cultural and religious orientation taking shape over longer period—marks the beginning of Jewish (as distinct from Israelite) history.

seems to first emerge in the third and second centuries BCE.

Jubilees records an alternative revelation to Moses at Mount Sinai delivered by an angel. It tells the history in Genesis and Exodus from an angelic perspective, revealing many details not reported in the corresponding biblical text, including commandments not mentioned there. Interestingly, it operates according to a different kind of calendar than most Jews in this period used, a solar calendar of 364 days different from the lunar calendar that forms the basis of the Jewish calendar to this day. Because they followed the wrong calendar, the author of this work believed, many Israelites had been celebrating the festivals at the wrong time, ruining their relationship with God. Despite its claim to have been revealed at the time of Moses, Jubilees was written in the mid-second century BCE.

The Wisdom of Solomon, probably written in the first century BCE or first century CE, purports to record wisdom that the biblical king tried to share with his fellow kings. The insights it reveals include a description of what happens to people after they die—their judgment by God, the punishment of the wicked, and the immortality granted to the righteous. The Wisdom of Solomon is a deuterocanonical book, included in the Greek Bible and part of the Bible for certain Christian churches today, and it is one of a number of works attributed to Solomon. Another example known from the Pseudepigrapha, perhaps from the fifth or sixth century CE, is the Testament of Solomon, which recounts how the king enlisted various demons to help build the Temple (thus reflecting Solomon's role as a master exorcist and magician).

In addition to works ascribed to biblical figures, we also have preserved in the Apocrypha and Pseudepigrapha a number of biblical-like books clearly written to emulate the Bible and telling stories set in biblical times and modeled on stories in Genesis and other biblical books. Examples from the Apocrypha include Tobit, the story of a righteous man who is among the Israelites deported to Assyria, and Judith, which recounts how a pious widow single-handedly saved her people from Nebuchadnezzar. An example from the Pseudepigrapha is Joseph and Aseneth, an account of Joseph's relationship with his Egyptian wife, here depicted as a convert.

A Crash Course in the Jewish Bible

Because the Bible became so central to Jewish culture after the Persian period, exerting a shaping influence on Jewish life to this day, it is important to have some sense of its contents. We devote the remainder of this chapter to giving you a kind of crash course in the Jewish Bible: an introduction to its contents and meaning as these emerged in early Jewish culture. Readers who feel they are already familiar with the Bible, or who are eager to push on with the narrative of Jewish history, may want to skip ahead to the next chapter. For those who need more of a sense of what we mean by "the Bible" in this book, the following is an attempt to squeeze in some concise introductory information.

By the term *Bible* we mean the Jewish biblical canon, not a single book but a collection of texts deemed sacred and authoritative by Jewish communities. Other religious communities also venerate the Bible, but they define and understand its contents differently. The early Christian Bible relied on a Greek translation of the Bible, which included translations of books found in the Hebrew version used by Jews in the Jewish Bible, but often in a different form and also included deuterocanonical/apocryphal books such as Tobit and Judith not found there. This latter set of books, as noted earlier, is still part of scripture in the Roman Catholic and Eastern Orthodox Churches. For their part, Protestants embraced a canon without the deuterocanonical/Apocryphal books, and Protestant scholars made an effort to go back to the Hebrew text in their translations and commentary, but their Bible, like all Christian Bibles, also includes the New Testament, which is also not part of the Jewish Bible.

Arguably, there are as many conceptions of the Bible as there are religious communities that venerate it (incidentally, biblical figures such as Abraham, Moses, and David are also part of Muslim sacred history, but Muslims believe that God, known in Arabic as *Allah*, also revealed himself to a later prophet, Muhammad, and it is the record of those later revelations, the *Qur'an*, that constitutes the Muslim scriptural canon). Our focus is the Bible as defined and understood by Jews, a text now divided into three sections, as we have mentioned:

Figure 2.6 A page from the "Aleppo Codex," the oldest known manuscript of the complete Hebrew Bible, written around 930 CE. The manuscript was damaged in riots that occurred in Syria in 1947 (note that the bottom right corner of the page has been burned off), but much of it survived. For more on what this fascinating document tells us about the Bible and the effort to find its missing pages, see www.aleppocodex.org.

1. The core of this Bible is the Five Books of Moses: *Bereshit* (Genesis), *Shemot* (Exodus), *Vayikra* (Leviticus), *Bamidbar* (Numbers), and *Devarim* (Deuteronomy), a section identified with the "Torah of Moses" mentioned by such sources as Ezra-Nehemiah. As used in the Bible, the word *Torah* can mean "law"—and so it was translated by the Septuagint, which renders it with the Greek term *nomos*—but it can also mean "teaching." The Torah was read in both ways by early Jews: as a divine law and also as a divine teaching, a source of wisdom and a guide for how to live one's life.
2. The second section of the Jewish biblical canon, the Prophets, contains two kinds of material: (a) The "Former Prophets," texts that record an account of Israelite/Judahite history from the conquest of Canaan to the Babylonian Exile (Joshua, Judges, 1–2 Samuel, and 1–2 Kings; these books are seen as works of prophecy because they were thought to have been written by some of the prophets described within their narrative, like Samuel, a prophet from the time of David), and (b) the "Latter Prophets," texts that record the words of prophets from the period of Assyrian, Babylonian, and Persian rule. The first 3 books in this section, Isaiah, Jeremiah, and Ezekiel, are known as the "Major Prophets" because of their length, while the other 12 books are called the "Minor Prophets" because of their brevity.
3. The third section, the "Writings," includes the Psalms, the Proverbs, the Song of Solomon, Daniel, Ezra-Nehemiah, and other miscellaneous writings. These works were also evidently perceived by early Jews as prophetic, but in contrast to the Torah and the Prophets, which preserve God's efforts to communicate

> with Israel, several of the books in this section record the human side of the divine-human interaction—words addressed to God in gratitude or need (the Psalms) and observations about how God operates (e.g., Proverbs and Ecclesiastes).

Although the Bible read by Jews today shares much in common with the Bible developed in early Jewish culture, they are not the same thing. One way to see this difference is to contrast the Bible in use today with the Greek translation used by ancient Greek-speaking Jews and then by Christians—a translation, but one that captures what the Bible was like more than 2,000 years ago.

The Jewish Bible in use today is known as the Masoretic Bible, named for the group of scribes, the Masoretes, who copied this particular version of the biblical text. Active between the sixth century CE and the tenth century CE, the Masoretes not only copied the Bible but also developed a variety of scribal tools to help Jews read it. In its original form, the Hebrew Bible mainly records the consonants of words, not the vowels (with a few exceptions), and lacks punctuation marks to help readers make sense of the text. Without these guides, the biblical text can be very confusing and ambiguous, hard even to pronounce, much less understand. To facilitate interpretation, the Masoretes developed vowel signs, an accent system, and textual divisions that guided how biblical books were read aloud in the synagogue, and marginal notations that helped with the understanding of particular words.

The Septuagint (a term that originally referred to a Greek translation of the Torah but here is used loosely to describe the Greek translation of the Jewish Bible in its entirety) preserves a form of the biblical canon from a much earlier period than the Masoretic Bible. Not only does this version predate the impact of Masoretic scribal activity, but also it translates a different form of the biblical text. The Greek version of the story of David and Goliath, for example, is some 50 verses shorter than the Masoretic version. While the Masoretic Bible organizes the canon into the three sections that we have been following here—the Torah, the Prophets, and the Writings—the Septuagint is organized in a different way and includes a number of books not found at all in the Masoretic version—deuterocanonical texts/apocryphal texts like Tobit and Judith. The Septuagint may reflect an alternative version of the Bible before its text and ordering were fixed in the form that would become the Jewish Bible venerated by Jews today.

Over time, Jews standardized the version of the biblical text they believed to be authoritative. Many of the textual differences between different manuscripts of the Hebrew text of the Bible were smoothed out by the second century CE, when Jewish religious authorities settled on the particular version of the biblical text that would eventually become the Masoretic Bible. Why did Jews standardize the text in this way? Perhaps because they did not have access to other forms of the Hebrew biblical text, which had been lost by that time—the Temple may have served as a storehouse for biblical manuscripts in their different forms, and its destruction in 70 CE may have entailed their loss—but it is also possible that at a time when there were sharp sectarian divisions among Jews—and an emergent Christian community with its own approach to the Bible—Jewish religious leaders wanted to minimize the differences between biblical versions to reduce the interpretive conflicts that such differences could lead to. In any case, the Masoretic Bible became the authoritative version of the Bible for Jews, transmitted with only small variations through the Middle Ages, and the invention of the printing press around 1440 by Johannes Gutenberg standardized its form and content still more.

The limits of time and space prevent us from summarizing the Bible's contents beyond what we have already done, but some of its most essential claims need to be stressed to understand the development of Jewish culture:

1. *Although God was the creator of the world and all humanity, his relationship with Israel was special, granting it blessings and protection, but also imposing responsibilities that distinguished it from other peoples.* The Bible begins by portraying God as the creator of all the peoples of the world, but it quickly zeroes in on his relationship with Israel, a people especially favored by God as a "treasured possession" (Exodus 19:5). Why God focuses on the Israelites is never made clear. Other peoples are viewed suspiciously by the authors of the Bible, especially the Canaanites, who are associated with idolatry and various sexual offenses, but the ancestors of the Israelites are not exactly models of upright behavior themselves: Jacob resorts to trickery in order to secure his father's blessing. Jealous of Joseph, his brothers sell him into slavery. The Israelites who flee Egypt prove rebellious and unfaithful. Whatever their shortcomings, God recognizes something about the Israelites that moves him to single them out for special treatment. To Abraham, he promises many descendants and the land of Canaan; he intervenes to rescue the Israelites from slavery in Egypt; he uses his power to protect them in the wilderness from famine, plagues, enemies, and other threats; he leads them safely to Mount Sinai, where he reveals himself through the medium of the prophet Moses and instructs them in how to build a portable sanctuary where he can reside among them; and then, after 40 years of wandering in the wilderness, God permits the Israelites to enter the land of Canaan, described as a land of milk and honey, and take the land from its inhabitants.

   The central problem that preoccupies the Hebrew Bible, one might say, is how to sustain the special relationship with God established at Mount Sinai, a relationship that the Five Books of Moses describe as a covenant, a voluntary pact binding God and the people of Israel in a relationship of mutual obligation. The history of this relationship goes back to Noah and Abraham, who each establishes a covenant with God, but most of the Torah focuses on the covenant that God establishes with the Israelites at Mount Sinai through the mediation of Moses. The laws in Exodus, Leviticus, Numbers, and Deuteronomy are the stipulations of the covenant, the terms that Israel must abide by in its relationship with God.

   The importance of the Sinai covenant for understanding Jewish religious life and thought cannot be understated. The obligations it imposed on Israel established the ground rules for its society once it was established in Canaan, regulating how Israelites were to interact with their non-Israelites neighbors, slaves, enemies, criminals, and those foreigners who lived in their midst, but no less importantly, the commandments also established the framework for God's ongoing relationship with the Israelites—how the Israelites were to interact with God, the sacrifices they were to offer him, and all the other things they needed to do to sustain God's support.

   We cannot review all these commandments here—they cover the gamut from instructions for how to build the sanctuary where God was thought to have a presence (known as the Tabernacle) to rules governing how to observe the Sabbath and other holy days, to dietary and sexual prohibitions of various sorts, to laws governing the administration of justice and the treatment of the poor. What we can do is stress their importance: Following the commandments revealed at Mount Sinai was considered essential for maintaining the relationship that bound God and the Israelites together; it entitled the Israelites to the land of Canaan and ensured they would have or could regain divine protection in times of trouble. To this day, the revelation at Sinai and the establishment of a covenant with God there are the defining moments in the Jews' relationship to God, comparable in their significance for Jews to the role of the crucifixion for Christians.

2. *Israel's relationship with God depends on intermediaries, though these often turn out to be flawed.* One basic challenge of maintaining a close relationship with God is that it is impossible to see him. References here and there in the Hebrew Bible suggest that God may have some kind of physical body, but with the exception of Moses and a few other exceptional mortals, it is lethal for human beings to see him. Indeed, even hearing God's voice was considered an overwhelming experience: Deuteronomy tells us that the Israelites cannot bear to hear his voice at Sinai, which is why, according to this text, they turn to Moses to interact with God on their behalf.

Unable to see, draw near to, or communicate directly with God, the Israelites resorted to two ways of indirectly interacting with Him. First, they relied on certain objects to symbolize or convey the divine presence. The most famous of these is the Ark of the Covenant, a wooden chest that contained the tablets of the covenant inscribed at Sinai and which served as a throne or footstool for God, a resting place where some part of God's invisible self was present, flanked by the statues of two cherubs, winged creatures that served as his guardians or entourage. God did not appear directly to the Israelites, but his presence was radiated through the Ark, which, as a result, was so dangerous to look at or approach that it had to be kept hidden from the Israelites in a tent, the Tabernacle or Tent of Meeting. (Later, King David would move the Ark to Jerusalem, and it was soon thereafter deposited in the Temple built by Solomon. For more on the fate of the Ark, *see the box* "Five Questions About the Jewish Bible.") The Temple itself would become another symbol of God's presence: God was thought to reside there, present in the innermost sanctum, known as the Holy of Holies, and when the Israelites visited the Temple, as they would during the festivals of Sukkot, Passover, and Shavuot, they felt they were drawing near to God in a physical sense.

The second way in which the Israelites interacted with God was through the mediation of certain special people, individuals empowered to serve as go-between, to speak or act on God's behalf. The intermediaries they relied on—the prophet, the king, the priest—have all left their imprint on the Hebrew Bible. Many texts are ascribed to prophets; others are associated with the founding figures of Israel's monarchy, David and Solomon; and the priests have left behind ritual legislation and other material recorded in the Five Books of Moses. In every case, their authority derived from their status as a representative or servant of God.

The prophet was a kind of spokesperson for God with the ability to hear his voice and communicate with him in turn. Some prophets in ancient Israel would have visions of God, perhaps in the form of a dream; others heard his voice; while still others were able to decipher signs that he would send. We associate prophets with prediction, the supernatural ability to foretell the future, and a good portion of biblical prophecy does indeed involve predictions of the future, sometimes dire predictions of divine punishment and suffering, sometimes more optimistic visions of the future in which Israel overcomes its enemies, finds peace, and reconciles with God. The prophets in this sense were theological weather forecasters, predicting the good or bad things in store for the Israelites, but at least in some cases it was possible for the Israelites to influence the future, to change it by turning away from sinful behaviors toward doing what was right.

The prophets could serve other roles as well—they functioned as social critics, speaking on God's behalf to denounce the rich and the powerful for the sins and the injustices they committed, and they also acted as consolers, providing reassurance in times of danger or devastation. Sometimes, prophets also spoke back to God, pleading with him to spare

MODERN ENCOUNTERS WITH MOUNT SINAI

God's revelation at Mount Sinai has been the foundation of Jewish religious life since antiquity, but modern Jewish thinkers—those who feel committed to the Sinai covenant but also accept modern scholarship—face a daunting challenge: how to make sense of an experience at odds with a modern scientific understanding of reality. At the core of the Sinai experience, of course, is a supernatural being, and a secular-minded skeptic could question it on those grounds, but even the more historically plausible aspects of the story—the existence of a mountain named Sinai or of a prophet named Moses—cannot be verified historically. Some biblical scholars argue that the entire account of the Sinai revelation is a fiction, added secondarily to the Torah.

Beyond the historical problems with the biblical account, there are also the ways its representation of reality have been challenged or contradicted by modern experiences, like the Holocaust, which called into question the conception of divine justice associated with the Bible, and modern values like egalitarianism, at odds with the male-centered ethos of biblical books like Genesis. The Holocaust, in which millions of Jews perished, both secular and religious, called into question the commitment God had made to Israel at Sinai. Feminist Jews struggle with the Torah on other grounds: Its narratives marginalized women; its laws and rituals exclude them and can even be cited as a rationale for abusing them.

Modern Jewish thinkers have developed various ways to bridge between Mount Sinai and modernity. One way around the challenge of modern biblical scholarship was to minimize the Sinai revelation as a historical event and to emphasize instead its impact on the mind—how Sinai is experienced, felt, and remembered. For someone like the German Jewish theologian Franz Rosenzweig (1886–1929), for example, the Bible registers something genuine, but it did not particularly matter, for example, whether the Israelites actually crossed the Red Sea in the way the narrative claims—the original event might have been owing to some rare but naturally occurring weather phenomenon. What was crucial was the psychological-spiritual insights registered by the Torah's stories, like feeling one's birth as a gift that comes from beyond oneself (the emotional insight at the core of the Creation story), or feeling commanded—obligated to do something we probably would not choose to do on our own, an experience at the root of the Sinai narrative. Rosenzweig did not reduce religious experience to a mere projection of the mind—he saw in the

the Israelites from destruction, or seeking to understand why he acted as he did.

Moses is the model of the prophetic intermediary. His main role is to convey God's words to the people, to demonstrate God's power through the feats and wonders that he performs, and to intercede when God is angry with the people. Later prophets play a similar role, though according to one biblical text, they had less direct access to God than Moses, seeing God in visions and dreams rather than speaking to him "face-to-face" as Moses did (Numbers 12:6–8). The Bible tells us of several prophets active in the earliest centuries of the monarchy—Samuel and Nathan in the time of David, Elijah, and Elisha in the Northern Kingdom of Israel—but none of these figures appears to have written anything down (though Jewish tradition ascribes 1 and 2 Samuel to Samuel). Beginning in the age of Assyrian conquest, some prophets or their followers began to write down the words of prophecy, which is how we have the prophetic texts that comprise the Major and Minor Prophets (Isaiah, Jeremiah, etc.).

The two other kinds of intermediaries who help sustain Israel's relationship with God are the priest and the king, both defined by their

Bible a genuine revelation of God—but for him, the experience of revelation had no verbal content; all the words of the Torah were produced by human beings. This shows the influence of modern biblical scholarship on how he saw the Torah, but on the other hand, it did not matter to him that it challenged the veracity of the biblical account in a historical sense, because regardless of whatever really happened in history, he saw the act of reading the Torah as its own religious experience, drawing its interpreters into an encounter with God through the power of its narratives.

Others repurpose traditional Jewish interpretive techniques in order to rehabilitate the Sinai experience from a modern perspective. In Chapter 5, we will be introducing a mode of rabbinic interpretation known as midrash; we will leave most of our explanation for this approach for later, but one trait is worth noting now: Midrash often finds meaning in the silences of the biblical text, uncovering in the gaps of the Torah whole episodes nowhere directly recorded there, along with lessons and laws that go beyond anything that it explicitly promulgates. Adopting this technique, modern interpreters have reinterpreted the Sinai revelation in ways meant to address the challenges of modernity. The post-Holocaust philosopher Emil Fackenheim (1916–2003), a refugee from the Nazis, provocatively supplemented the Sinai experience by treating the Holocaust as a second revelation that threatened to decimate the Jews' faith in God but, at the same time, also issued a new kind of imperative for Jews to remain faithful to the Sinai covenant—to deny Hitler any posthumous victory against the Jews by not giving up on God and resolving to survive as a Jew. The feminist theologian Judith Plaskow, evoking midrash as a precedent, reimagines the Sinai experience in a way that casts aside the Bible's male-centric description of God and involves women as full partners in revelation.

For many Jews, these kinds of efforts are beside the point. Some religious Jews do not acknowledge the challenges of modern scholarship, dismiss its arguments and conclusions, or simply haven't learned about them. Secular Jews might not see the point of trying to salvage a story they take to be a myth. But a good number of Jews today find themselves somewhere in between a commitment to Jewish religious tradition and a secularized orientation, and the interpretations described earlier come from the struggle to integrate those clashing perspectives, efforts to reinterpret the experience of Sinai in light of modern values and doubts.

membership in a particular family. Priestly status was a matter of genealogy, of descent from Aaron, the brother of Moses. The larger tribe of Levi from which Aaron came was commissioned to play a supportive role in the sanctuary, a kind of lower class of Temple official who helped guard the sanctuary and maintain its cult (these are known in English as the Levites). The priest presented Israel's offerings before the Lord, protected the holiness of the sanctuary, and delivered messages from God through the Urim and Thummim, mysterious objects worn by the priests. They functioned as the servants of God, maintaining his Temple and overseeing the gifts made to him, and they also served as religious experts, with the know-how needed to construct and maintain the sanctuary, to protect against the impurity that was constantly threatening to contaminate the sanctuary and render it uninhabitable for God, and to oversee sacrifices and other rituals that Israel relied on to sustain its relationship with God.

The role of the king was assigned through genealogy as well: The only legitimate kings as far as the Bible is concerned are the descendants of David. The king led Israel into war on God's behalf, administered justice, and helped keep God accessible to Israel by building and sustaining the Temple. The king had a practical, political role as the leader of the army and government, but the Bible describes it as a religious role as well, describing David in particular as having a personal relationship with God. God even goes so far as to refer to David and his successors as his "sons," and in what amounts to a kind of covenant with David, he promises to establish his kingdom forever. Kingly status was conferred by a prophet who would effectively deputize the king as a representative of God through a ritual of anointment, the pouring of oil over the head or body. It was because of this ritual that the king was sometimes referred to as the "anointed one," the *mashiach* or messiah in English.

While Israel relies on these intermediaries to interact with God, however, the Bible often describes them as failing in their roles. The kings of Israel and Judah are consistently disappointing. Many abandon God for other gods, and even the greatest kings, David and Solomon, commit terrible sins that show their wavering commitment to God (David commits adultery with Bathsheba and murders her husband to cover up his wrongdoing; after a life of wise rule, Solomon turns to the foreign gods of his wives). The priests also often fall short, growing corrupt and self-serving; indeed, in the book of Ezekiel, God grows so incensed at what is happening in the Temple that he initiates its destruction himself. Even prophecy proves an unreliable connection to God, often failing to convince the Israelites to change their ways. Hence, another difficult question that the Hebrew Bible posed to its early Jewish readers, given the sinfulness of their ancestors and the failure of their leaders, is: How will their relationship with God survive?

3. *Although there are crises in Israel's relationship with God, they can be overcome.* The Bible establishes what it takes for Israel to sustain a relationship with God; it also dramatizes how easily that relationship can go awry. The Israel portrayed in the Bible, led astray by its leaders, frequently violates its obligations to God, straying after other gods and committing other sins against fellow Israelites. One main role of the prophets was to serve as a warning system, cautioning Israel against such behaviors, urging it to change its ways, but as we have noted, the prophets often fell short in this role, unable to persuade the Israelites to change their ways. Even Moses had a hard time getting the fickle Israelites to listen to him.

According to the Bible, in fact, the Israelites ultimately fail to live up to their side of the covenant, so alienating God that he allows their enemies to destroy the Kingdoms of Israel and Judah and to send them into exile. Much of the Bible is preoccupied with the misfortune that befalls the Israelites, with why God would allow his people to suffer so much if he is just and cared for his people. Different biblical texts handle this problem differently. The book of Job is famous for suggesting that mortals cannot understand why God acts as he does. Its central character, a righteous man named Job, is not an Israelite himself, but the misfortunes he suffers at the hands of God—the loss of his wealth, children, and health—make him a symbol of any God-believing person who must endure suffering without understanding why God would allow such a thing. Sometimes, the book of Job seems to suggest, God allows the righteous to suffer, and there is no explanation, or none that a mortal can understand. According to other biblical texts, however, the reason for Israel's suffering is clear: God is punishing it for its sins, or for the sins of its ancestors.

Even in the wake of disaster, however, biblical literature envisions a future in which Judah and, indeed, all Israel will be restored. Alongside their condemnations of the Israelites and their warnings of divine punishment, prophetic books often envision such a reconciliation sometime in the future, an age when God saves the Israelites from their enemies, restores what they had lost, and renews his covenant. These descriptions are the basis for what later Jews and Christians would understand as the eschatological age, an age at the end of time when God intervenes in reality in some dramatic way to punish his foes and restore his people.

But this future restoration is not necessarily foreordained: Prophetic literature repeatedly calls on its audience to change its ways, to turn away from wickedness to righteousness, from other gods back to God, as if its fate were in its own hands. In other words, it is not enough for the Israelites to wait for God's plans to unfold; they must make a change in their behavior to create a future for themselves beyond the misfortunes of the present. Later Jews came to believe that what keeps open the possibility of such self-correction is the Torah itself, from which the Israelites could learn what God expects of them and how to repent for their sins.

These observations scarcely qualify as a summary of the Bible's contents, but they may be enough to suggest why it proved such a valuable resource for Jews in the wake of Babylonian and Persian conquest. By reading scripture, Jews in this period could see all that had been lost because of their ancestors' sins, but they could also find hope for the future and guidance for the future.

The problem that Jews encountered as they tried to derive such guidance from the Bible was that it was not always so easy to make sense of its texts, which were written in an archaic language, were incomplete and did not always make sense, and were written for an age different from the one in which Jews now lived. The challenges of understanding and following biblical law are well illustrated in a recent book called *A Year of Living Biblically* by A. J. Jacobs, who tries to follow every law in the Bible literally. He soon finds that it is extremely difficult to actually implement most of these laws, partly because many of them are impractical, and partly because some of them conflict with modern American values, and thus, he has to behave in ridiculous ways to implement them or do some creative interpretation in order to do so without getting arrested, as when he tries to toss some small pebbles on the shoes of some Sabbath-breakers without them noticing to implement the penalty for Sabbath violation (see Numbers 15:32–36)—and even then he is not really following the law, which clearly mandates that the offender be stoned *to death*.

It is not just modern readers who encounter such problems; ancient readers of the Bible did as well. Consider the Bible's command to keep the Sabbath, part of the Ten Commandments. There is much at stake in keeping this particular command: Not only will God punish those who disobey them, he declares in the Ten Commandments, but also their descendants will be punished, while he will show kindness to those who obey them "to the thousandth generation" (Exodus 20:5–6). But to observe the Sabbath, one has to know things that the biblical text simply does not make clear. You shall not work on the seventh day, it orders, but what does it mean to work? Does preparing a meal count as work? Going to the bathroom? Caring for a child or a sick person? If the person died as a result of your decision to keep the Sabbath, would that not violate another command in the Ten Commandments, the command against killing? The Torah stresses the duty to follow God's commands clearly enough, but it often does not provide enough instructions for how to actually do so.

Yet another problem faced by early interpreters was the difficulty of applying by then ancient texts to the contemporary reality in which they happened to live. In 2 Samuel 7, God promises David that his descendants will rule forever. What did such a promise mean in a world in which there was no Davidic dynasty and Jews lived under the rule of foreign powers? The prophecies of Isaiah refer to the Assyrians. What did such prophecies mean when Jews faced not Assyria but the Greeks and the Romans? Early biblical interpretation is based on the assumption that the Bible is a perpetually relevant text, that it is God's way of addressing Jews as they live in the present, that it will speak to their needs or give them a sense of the future, but that assumption of relevance stood in tension with the fact that a good portion of the Bible was out of date by the time it was read by ancient interpreters, born of and referring to a bygone age.

Early Jewish readers of the Bible solved these problems in a way that can violate our sense of the Bible's intended or literal meaning. They saw meaning in tiny details that seem trivial by our way of reading. From a spare law, such as the command to keep the Sabbath, they derived numerous restrictions and rituals that do not seem to have any basis in the biblical text. They read prophecies addressed to the bygone era of biblical times as predictions of *their* future, or even as references to events happening in their own day. They did not read the Bible literally, sticking only to what it said explicitly, but filled in its gaps with fanciful stories and newly created laws. But while their interpretations do not always strike modern readers as very plausible, they did serve the needs of Jews themselves in this period, and there is a logic to them. Generally, even the most fanciful interpretations are responding to something in the text, some odd detail or troubling inconsistency that could not be understood without going beyond the information supplied in the Bible. Early Jews assumed that God had some reason for implanting these problems in the text, and biblical interpretation treated the Bible's inconsistencies and gaps as signals that a message, law, or lesson was there to be discovered between the lines of the text.

Let us return to the Sabbath command as an illustration. The Bible actually contains two versions of the Ten Commandments: one in Exodus 20, and a second version in Deuteronomy 5. The two versions are nearly identical, but there are several small differences, including how the Sabbath command is worded; thus, Exodus 20 commands Israel to *remember* the Sabbath day, whereas Deuteronomy 5 bids Israel to *keep* or *guard* the Sabbath. Why would God issue two different versions of the same command? Modern scholars have certainly noticed this inconsistency, and for them, the two versions of the Ten Commandments represent yet another doublet in the Torah, more evidence that it conflates material drawn from different sources. That is a plausible explanation, but it was inconceivable for early Jewish interpreters, who instead saw the inconsistency as evidence for something else, not a contradiction but a sign that God was trying to send two distinct messages:

> "Remember" and "Keep"—these two words were said by God as one word. . . . [A]s it is said [in Psalm 62:12]: "One [thing] God has spoken, two have I heard."
>
> (*Mekhilta de Rabbi Ishmael*)

In a communicative feat impossible for mortals, God gave both commandments at the same time, or rather, he said one thing but humans heard two. How is this possible? As suggested by Psalm 62 (as this interpreter reads that psalm), God can communicate in a way that humans cannot, surpassing the limits of human speech by making two statements at once. Jewish biblical interpreters believed that God's words more generally—the entire Torah—exceeded the limits of ordinary human communication and had to be read very deeply and creatively for the reader to be able to apprehend God's intentions or understand the full meaning of a word or verse.

The particular interpretation cited earlier is taken from a collection of rabbinic interpretations of the book of Exodus known as *Mekhilta de Rabbi Ishmael*. We will introduce the rabbis in Chapter 5, and we will see there that they practiced a form of biblical interpretation known as *midrash* that was distinctive in many ways, not least because of its repeated assertion that the biblical text could support more than one interpretation. But the rabbis were not alone in their assumption that the difference between "remember" and "keep/guard" was significant. Some early Jews, including the members of the Dead Sea Scrolls community, concluded that the command in Deuteronomy 5 to "keep" the Sabbath represented a distinctive commandment, not an inconsistent version of the command in Exodus 20, but another command revealed at the same time. According to their interpretation, Deuteronomy 5, the second iteration of the Ten Commandments, indicated that Jews had an obligation not simply to observe the Sabbath day itself but to safeguard its observance by stopping work *before* the Sabbath so as to avoid doing something that might cause one to miss its start time. Though in biblical times the starting point of the Sabbath was fixed as Friday at sunset, by the first century CE, many Jews were ending work even earlier on Friday, in the afternoon around three o'clock. What prompted this practice of preemptively stopping work a few hours before evening, it seems, was their interpretation of the Torah's command not just to keep but "to guard" the Sabbath.

While this reading might conflict with a modern secular reader's sense of what the biblical authors intended to communicate, early Jewish interpreters had their reasons for reading it in this way. Nowhere does the Torah indicate when the Sabbath actually begins, an ambiguity that places one in danger of violating it. This reading helps to address that problem by fixing a start point early enough to avoid any possibility of not resting on the Sabbath. To our eyes, such interpretation stretches a small discrepancy between two biblical passages well beyond any intended meaning, but early Jews did not operate according to our standards of plausibility. Early biblical interpretation becomes more comprehensible when one remembers that what may seem to us to be trivial details and inconsequential inconsistencies in the biblical text had serious religious and existential consequences for early Jews, who believed it was crucial to understand its content, even when puzzling, in order to sustain their covenant with God (*see the box* "Five Questions About the Jewish Bible").

The Bible and the Birth of Jewish Culture

One of the few constants in Jewish culture, persisting from the days of the Temple until the modern age, is an engagement with the Bible, the effort to understand its content and to relate it to the present. This is not to say that every Jew has engaged the Bible in the same way, but the engagement itself runs through all of Jewish history. Even today, long after modern scholarship has called the divine authorship of the Bible into question and many Jews have become secularized, the Bible remains central to Jewish life. The history it tells shapes how Jews remember their origins, its laws govern the lives of the religiously observant, and its prophecies and psalms continue to guide and inspire.

A case can be made that Jewish culture predates the creation of the Bible. In the Elephantine Papyri, after all, we have evidence of a Persian-period Judahite community with many of the attributes of later Jewish communities, but no sign of the Bible itself—evidence that suggests that Jewish culture was taking shape before the rise of the biblical canon. Alternatively, one can make the case that the Bible predates the Jews, first taking shape in ancient Judah before many of the events that would turn that culture into Jewish culture—for example, the Babylonian Exile, the Persian conquest, and the missions of Ezra and Nehemiah. Rather than try to solve the chicken-and-egg question of which came first, we end this chapter by simply emphasizing that the development of the Jews and the development of the Jewish Bible have been inextricably intertwined since the beginning, with Jewish culture generated through an engagement with the Bible even as it was giving shape to the Bible.

FIVE QUESTIONS ABOUT THE JEWISH BIBLE

1. You have been avoiding the term *Old Testament* to describe the Bible. Isn't the Old Testament the same thing as the Jewish Bible? If Jews don't use the term *Old Testament*, why not?

   Old Testament is a specifically Christian term. It originates from a prophecy in the book of Jeremiah that envisions that God would one day establish a "new covenant," and Christians believed this new covenant had been realized through Jesus. When there emerged a distinctively Christian biblical canon in the third and fourth century CE, the section having to do with Jesus—the Gospels, and so forth—was referred to as the *New Testament* because it was thought to set forth this new covenant (*New Testament* is from a Latin translation of the Greek for "new covenant"), and with that meaning, the term distinguished that part of the canon from what they referred to as the *Old Testament*, the covenant established at Mount Sinai as set out in what we have been calling the Jewish Bible. Christians believed that the Sinai covenant, limited to Israel, had been replaced by the covenant established through Jesus and extended to all peoples. In the view of early Christians, Jews were being blindly stubborn by adhering to its laws, whereas Jews understood themselves to be maintaining the obligations their ancestors had undertaken at Sinai. The Old Testament differs from the Jewish Bible in other ways as well. It orders the books differently than the Jewish Bible, and most Christians knew it from a Greek, Latin, or other translation rather than in the Hebrew original. The main reason that Jews do not use the word *Old Testament*, however, is that the term defines the content of the Hebrew Bible in light of the New Testament, which Jews do not accept as part of their Bible.

2. Why, then, don't Jews accept the New Testament as part of their Bible?

   Jews do not accept the New Testament as part of their Bible because they do not accept Jesus as the Messiah or the Son of God. There were Jews in the time of Jesus who looked forward to a messiah, a savior from the line of David, but for many, Jesus did not fit with their expectations of what this figure would be like or what he would accomplish, dying without delivering the Jews from their oppressors or making the other changes expected of the Messiah. Interestingly, it is possible that, by this point, some Jews might have expected not one but two messianic figures, the first suffering or dying before the second messianic figure would appear; Jesus's suffering and death could have fit into such an expectation, but early Christian belief posed another challenge to Jewish belief as well, developing the view that in light of Jesus, Jews no longer had to follow the laws of Moses as a condition of their relationship with God. This contradicted what Jews considered a fundamental obligation of their covenant with God (the obligation to abide by the laws of Moses was so intense that there were Jews in Jesus's day willing to die rather than to violate them). Since Jews did not believe that Jesus was who Christians claimed him to be, they did not accept the consequences of that belief, which included the redefinition of their canon to include a New Testament at odds with Jewish commitment to the laws of Moses.

3. How did Jews come to be known as the "People of the Book"?

   This label originated as a Muslim description of the Jews, but it was not applied only to them; it also described Christians and another group called the Sabians, some other kind of religious group defined by its commitment to a scripture. When applied to the Jews, the "Book" refers to the Torah, which describes people and events that Muslims regard as part of their sacred history, too, but in a written form that they believed to have been corrupted by the Jews who transmitted it. The Jews and others described in this way are considered non-Muslims subject to conversion, and if they refuse to convert, they are subject to a subordinate status that includes the payment of a special tax known as the *jizyah*. However, if they accept those terms, they were to be protected, and thus, being "People of the Book" was a better status than being a pagan, relatively speaking. In modern times, Jews have come to refer to themselves by this label, forgetting its negative connotation in Islamic tradition and applying it specifically to themselves (as opposed to Christians) in a positive sense. Today, the term is

FIVE QUESTIONS ABOUT THE JEWISH BIBLE (CONTINUED)

sometimes used to signal Jewish commitment to books in general rather to the Torah in particular.

4. You have mentioned that, according to the Bible, the penalty for what we might consider a minor religious violation, like gathering sticks on the Sabbath, was death. Do Jews impose such a penalty today, and if not, why not, if such a penalty is commanded in the Bible? At a more general level, why does Jewish religious practice today seem to assume all kinds of obligations and prohibitions nowhere mentioned in the Five Books of Moses?

The meaning of biblical law in Jewish culture has been shaped by ideas and interpretations developed by a group of scholars known collectively as the rabbis, who emerge in the centuries following the destruction of the Second Temple. Since we will not introduce the rabbis until Chapter 5, we cannot fully answer this question at this point, but to make a long story short, the rabbis saw Jews of their day as heir to the covenant established at Mount Sinai and thus believed that biblical law was still binding on them, including the cases where it applied the death penalty. However, they understood the Sinai revelation to have included something that they referred to as the Oral Torah, an aspect of divine revelation that was not recorded in the Five Books of Moses and was instead delivered orally, passed down in this way from Moses to Joshua and the prophets and from them to the rabbis themselves. The Oral Torah elaborates biblical law, working out details not addressed in the Bible, introducing qualifications and making exceptions. As far as the penalty on Sabbath violation is concerned, for example, the reason that rabbinic Jews today do not impose the death penalty is that they believe that no present-day religious court has the authority to impose such a penalty. Even if such a court existed, moreover, it seems doubtful that the rabbis would have enforced a death penalty for an offense like gathering sticks on the Sabbath, understanding that death was an excessively harsh penalty for a relatively minor violation of the Sabbath. Thus, they interpreted the Bible in ways that effectively ruled out the imposition of such a penalty, either by establishing a very high threshold to establish guilt (e.g., that a person could receive the death penalty only when a court is able to ascertain that the accused offender had been specifically warned not to commit the act) or by suggesting in this case that the penalty applied only to the days of Israel's wandering in the wilderness.

5. I do not know very much about the Bible, but I did once see *Indiana Jones and the Raiders of the Lost Ark*. What is the Ark, and how did it get lost?

The *Ark* refers to the Ark of the Covenant, described in the Five Books of Moses as a kind of chest in which the tablets of the covenant were kept. The Ark was dangerous to look into or to handle, and the Bible tells stories of God striking down those who mistreat it or get too close, but despite the danger, King David is able to relocate it to Jerusalem, and Solomon to place it in the Temple as the source of its holiness. What happens to it after that is unclear. When Solomon's Temple is destroyed by the Babylonians, there is no mention of it among the cultic items carried off to Babylon, nor does the Bible report it being removed or destroyed before then. So what happened to the Ark? No one knows. Some sources suggest it was concealed beneath the site where the Temple stood, or in a cave. Other sources report that it was carried off by the Romans after the destruction of the Second Temple. Ethiopian tradition claims that it was smuggled off to Ethiopia and is there to this day. All these are later traditions, however, and its actual whereabouts are unknown. In Jewish culture, the Ark persists in metaphorical form. Within the synagogue, the scrolls of the Torah are kept in a closet or niche known as "the holy Ark," the *aron ha-kodesh*, named in commemoration of the original Ark kept in the Holy of Holies. This "Ark" recalls the Temple, but its main function is to protect the holiness of the Torah scroll itself as the primary manifestation of God's presence among his people. The Ark's fate in Jewish tradition thus mirrors Judaism's evolution from a Temple-centered religion to one that looks to the Torah for access to God.

For Further Reading

For an authoritative scholarly history of the Persian Empire, see Pierre Briant, *From Cyrus to Alexander: A History of the Persian Empire* (Winona Lake, IN: Eisenbrauns, 1998). And for a briefer account, Matt Waters, *Ancient Persia: A Concise History of the Achaemenid Empire, 550–330* BCE (Cambridge: Cambridge University Press, 2014). For more on Jewish history in the Persian period, see William David Davies and Louis Finkelstein, *The Cambridge History of Judaism, Vol. 1: The Persian Period* (Cambridge: Cambridge University Press, 1984). *Oxford Bibliographies* offers a helpful annotated bibliography of relevant reference works and studies: Jenny Rose, "The 'Persian' Period" (last updated in 2020):

https://www.oxfordbibliographies.com/display/document/obo-9780195393361/obo-9780195393361-0194.xml.

There are many textbooks and surveys that review the content of the Hebrew Bible/Old Testament in more detail than we were able to do. See, for example, Michael Coogan, *The Old Testament: A Historical and Literary Introduction to the Hebrew Scriptures* (New York: Oxford University Press, 2006). For a translation of the Bible with supplementary information that explains its significance for Jews, see Adele Berlin et al., *The Jewish Study Bible* (Oxford, England, and New York: Oxford University Press, 2004), which contains helpful notes and essays. For an accessible introduction to how modern scholarship was able to figure out the authorship of the Torah, see Richard Elliot Friedman, *Who Wrote the Bible?* (San Francisco, CA: HarperSanFrancisco, 1997). For an introduction to the Bible as read by early Jews, see James Kugel, *The Bible as It Was* (Cambridge, MA: Harvard University Press, 1997), and for a contrast between ancient and modern ways of reading the Bible, Kugel's *How to Read the Bible, a Guide to Scripture, Then and Now* (New York: Simon and Schuster, 2007). For those interested in learning more about what the Bible has meant for Jews at different points in their history, we can recommend Benjamin Sommer, *Jewish Concepts of Scripture: A Comparative Introduction* (New York: New York University Press, 2012). For a translation of the Apocrypha, with some commentary from the perspective of Jewish studies, note Lawrence Wills and Jonathan Klawans, *The Jewish Annotated Apocrypha* (forthcoming from Oxford University Press). For a translation of biblical-style pseudepigrapha, see James Charlesworth, *The Old Testament Pseudepigrapha*, Vols. 1 and 2 (Garden City, NY: Doubleday, 1983–1985).

CHAPTER 3

Jews and Greeks

Sometime between the third and first centuries BCE, a Jew named Ezekiel composed a work that shows how important the Bible was for early Jews and yet also captures how different Jewish culture in this period was from that of ancient Israel. The subject of Ezekiel's composition was the Exodus, and his interest in this event shows his commitment to the biblical past. What reveals that we are in a different epoch is *how* Ezekiel recounted this story: In his version, the Exodus is a Greek tragedy.

The biblical account of the Exodus may not seem particularly "tragic" according to common understanding of that term, but the classical genre of tragedy was defined not by an unhappy ending but by formal traits that Ezekiel's play, written in Greek and known as the *Exagoge*, exhibits in the scant 269 lines that happen to survive. This is clear even from its opening lines, a monologue delivered by Moses that provides the audience with the background it needs to follow the story:

And when from Canaan Jacob did depart,
with threescore souls and ten he did go down
to Egypt's land, and there he did beget
a host of people: suffering, oppressed,
ill-treated even to this very day
by the ruling powers and by wicked men.
For Pharaoh, seeing how our race increased
in swarms, devised against us this grand scheme:
he forced the men to manufacture bricks
for use in building lofty walls and towers;
Thus with their toil he made his cities strong.
he ordered next the Hebrew race to cast
their infant boys into the river deep.
At which point, she who bore me from her womb
did hide me for three months.

The content is taken from Genesis and Exodus, but Ezekiel's version of the story is written in Greek, in a poetic meter typical of Greek tragedy. The very idea of beginning a play in this way, with a monologue that provides the audience with a historical overview, is one that Ezekiel probably borrowed from the great tragedian Euripides. Ezekiel borrowed other elements from Greek tragedy too. To dramatize the parting of the Red Sea, for example, he resorted to a cleverly cost-effective device, using a survivor of Pharaoh's army to describe what happened in retrospect—a theatrical trick for dealing with hard-to-stage spectacles developed by the Greek playwright Aeschylus.

The *Exagoge* illustrates the changes that Jewish culture went through in the wake of Alexander the Great. Alexander was born in Macedonia in 356 BCE, and before he was 30, he had managed to conquer the Persian Empire, defeating Darius III in 331 BCE. Alexander was not the first Greek to travel in the Near East, and he did not rule this empire for long (he died in 323), but the impact of his conquests transformed the cultures of the ancient Near East for centuries, initiating a

DOI: 10.4324/9781003611592-4

period known as the Hellenistic age (from *Hellas*, the Greek word for "Greece") that lasted until and beyond the Roman conquest of the Near East and Mediterranean in the first century BCE. Under the rule of Alexander's successors, Greek, or rather a dialect of Greek known as koine, became widely used, and Greek-style cities, distinguished by a distinctively Greek notion of citizenship, were established throughout the Near East. The most famous was the city of Alexandria in Egypt, founded by Alexander himself and renowned in antiquity for its architectural wonders and library, and many other cities were founded or reorganized in similar ways, including Jerusalem. Greek forms of education and the literature that formed the curriculum for this education—the writings of Homer, Plato, and so forth—spread with the Greek city-state, along with Greek artistic tastes, architectural conventions, and styles of dress. This is how our author learned the language and literary techniques that he needed to compose a "Tragedy of Moses"—Ezekiel probably lived in Alexandria or another Hellenized city, receiving an education that included the Bible but also Greek literature.

Not all early Jews were so receptive to Greek influence. In this same period, another Jewish author wrote the book of Jubilees, a pseudepigraphical text to which we referred in Chapter 2. Like the *Exagoge*, *Jubilees* is a retelling of the Pentateuch, but it lacks any obvious signs of Greek influence. Whereas the *Exagoge* was written in Greek, for example, *Jubilees*, though now preserved in full only in Ethiopic and Latin translation, was originally written in Hebrew (as known from Hebrew fragments found among the Dead Sea Scrolls). And it is not just Greek that its author avoids: He seems opposed to any kind of foreign influence on Jewish religious life as well, warning future generations of Israel, for instance, against "walking in the feasts of the gentiles after their errors and after their ignorance" (Jubilees 6:35)—apparently a reference to Jewish embrace of non-Jewish religious practice. Jubilees was written in the second century BCE, the same period as Ezekiel's retelling of the Exodus story as a Greek tragedy, but it illustrates a very different response to that culture, rejecting the imitation of foreigners as a betrayal of Israel's covenant with God.

Why did some Jews emulate Greek culture while others shunned it? A Jew living in Judea (the name used by the Greeks to refer to the territory of Judah/Yehud) was in a relative backwater compared to other places and may therefore have been more insulated from Greek influence than was a Jew living in a cosmopolitan center, such as Alexandria. However, scholars now realize that Judea in the second century BCE was also now subject to Hellenistic influence. In the same century when Jubilees was written, other Judeans were using Greek, studying in Greek educational institutions, and according to one source, even wearing Greek-style hats. Whether a Jew emulated the Greeks was not just a matter of geography but also depended on other factors, including one's economic circumstances (probably only the privileged could gain access to the kinds of schools where one could learn Greek) and whether one happened to live in the vicinity of a city where such schools and other Greek institutions could be found.

Part of what was attractive about Greek culture, at least for those with ambition to rise in society, is that it offered a new range of opportunities not available under earlier rulers. Greek identity as defined in the Hellenistic age was not restricted to people with a particular parentage or birthplace; in theory at least, it was accessible to any non-Greek willing to adopt the Greek language and follow Greek customs. By speaking, dressing, and acting in a Hellenized fashion, a Jew might gain stature, influence, or even more specific advantages, like employment from the government. The very accessibility of Greek culture also made it threatening, however, for Jews found that their adoption of Greek practices and ideas was sometimes at odds with the traditions linking them to their ancestors and to God. As the culture of those who ruled the Jews, moreover, a Hellenized way of life was linked in the minds of many Jews with the loss of independence, illicit taxation, and other forms of social humiliation and economic exploitation. Some Jews were in a position to be influenced by Greek culture and yet actively resisted it for political or religious reasons, seeking to revive the ancient traditions of Israel as a kind of alternative to the Hellenized world around them.

In reality, however, many Jews found options between the poles of complete resistance to Greek culture and complete assimilation, adjusting to life under Hellenistic rule even as they cultivated a Jewish identity. Our playwright Ezekiel is an example. Though his play is written in Greek in imitation of Greek literary models, his choice of subject matter is revealing. Retelling the Exodus story suggests an author who saw himself as faithful to the tradition established by Moses; indeed, perhaps he opted to recount the experiences of Moses—the story of an Israelite raised by a foreign princess but nonetheless remaining true to his Hebrew identity—precisely to demonstrate that it was possible to sustain a strong Jewish identity in a foreign setting.

Our focus in this chapter is this balancing act between adapting to Hellenized culture and sustaining a commitment to the biblical past and Jewish identity. The Jewish culture that emerges over the course of the Hellenistic period is the product of interaction with Greek culture, certainly not always embracing Greek influence in the obvious way that Ezekiel does, sometimes resisting it, but in one way or another transformed by the process of Hellenization. We aim to tell the story of this encounter, how Jews first encountered the Greeks, the people and events that were important in shaping their interaction, the varied ways in which Jews responded to the political and social changes introduced by Greek rule, and the impact of Hellenization on the formation of Jewish identity and culture.

Alexander and the Early Hellenistic Period

According to some accounts, it did not take long for the Jews and the Greeks to strike a rapport—it was happening already in the fourth century BCE. Clearchus, a Greek disciple of the great philosopher Aristotle who lived between 384 and 322 BCE, wrote of how his master once met a Jew during one of his visits and found the man to be wondrously strange and yet also like-minded. The Jew had a surprising and exotic background—his people were the descendants of Indian philosophers, Aristotle claimed, and their city had a strange-sounding name: *Hierusalem*—but he spoke Greek, and indeed, he impressed Aristotle as having the very soul of a Greek. If Clearchus's account of this encounter is to be believed, from their very earliest encounter, Jews and Greeks were able to overcome the linguistic and cultural differences dividing them very quickly and discovered an intellectual kinship.

But this story is probably *not* to be believed—Aristotle himself never mentions such an encounter in his own writings, and the true story of what happened when Jews and Greeks first encountered one another is unknown. Trade contacts between the Greek world and the Levant (a modern designation for the region that includes the former territories of the kingdoms of Israel and Judah) went back to the Persian period and even earlier, and a Greek military presence can be detected on the coast of Canaan as early as the seventh century BCE. When Alexander the Great conquered Judea, putting an end to Persian rule, certain cultural changes ensued—the Macedonians probably replaced Aramaic with Greek as the language of governance, for example. Still, it may not have

Figure 3.1 A depiction of a fateful battle, the battle of Issus, fought between Alexander the Great and the Persian king Darius III in 333 BCE, from a first-century BCE mosaic found in the Roman city of Pompeii. The partially effaced image of Alexander appears at the left side of the scene, seated on his famous horse, Bucephalus; Darius appears in the middle of the scene, with his arm outstretched, as if having just thrown a spear at him. Although Darius survived the battle of Issus, his defeat there marked the beginning of the end of Achaemenid power.

been clear to Jews at that time that they were living in a whole new epoch. Judea had been under foreign rule for centuries by that time, and Alexander probably continued Persian administrative practice, allowing the Jews of Judea to live according to their native laws and institutions as long as they avoided making trouble for him.

While we do not know very much about this period, there is reason to think not everyone was content to simply submit to Greek rule. To the north of Judea, in the territory of the former Kingdom of Israel, lived another people who believed in Yahweh; they were not Jews, however, but the ancestors of the people later known as the Samaritans (who we will introduce more fully later). Some reports state that they rebelled against the Greeks, seizing the official appointed by Alexander to oversee Syria—and burning him alive. Gruesome evidence also points to how the Greeks responded: the discovery in a cave at a site called Wadi Deliyeh of some 200 skeletons, perhaps the remains of refugees hunted down by Alexander's forces to suppress the revolt (Aramaic papyri found in the cave and dating between 365 and 335 BCE place these unfortunate inhabitants in the period of Alexander's conquest). We learn from the first-century historian Josephus that Jews, too, may have been reluctant to accept Greek rule, sustaining an allegiance to Persia, but there is no evidence of a rebellion in Judea at this time, and Josephus may well be right when he reports that the people soon decided of their own will to submit to Alexander.

Whatever Alexander's intentions for Judea (if he gave the area any thought at all), he did not live long enough to implement them himself. When he died in 323 BCE, his generals, known as the *Diadochi* or successors, fell to fighting over who would control the territory he had conquered, not just in the Levant, but also in Greece, Asia Minor, and Egypt. Judea, situated between Egypt and Mesopotamia, found itself in the middle of this conflict. After decades of warfare, Alexander's successors eventually divided his empire into separate kingdoms, two of which are relevant for Jewish history. His general Ptolemy secured control over Egypt, establishing a dynasty that lasted until Egypt was conquered by the Romans in 30 BCE. The Ptolemaic kingdom ruled Judea until 200 BCE, the year Judea was conquered by Antiochus III, ruler of the kingdom established by Alexander's general Seleucus I. Based in Syria, the Seleucid kingdom ruled Judea until the first few decades of the first century BCE, when the region came under Roman control (see Map 3.1).

The rulers in charge of these kingdoms were Greek, but they were different from those Greeks immortalized by classical literature: Pericles, Socrates, Euripides, and the like. Classical Greek culture was centered in Athens. Alexander and his successors were from Macedonia, to the north, a people regarded by the supercilious Athenians as barbarians in their own right. As we have noted, the Ptolemaic and Seleucid kingdoms promoted the establishment of Greek-style cities (the *polis*) whose citizens ran their own affairs, but unlike Athens of the classical age, these were not completely independent city-states. Situated within large kingdoms, these cities were granted their status by rulers who expected loyalty, taxes, and military support in return.

It is also important to keep in mind that the rulers of the Ptolemaic and Seleucid kingdoms were themselves transformed by their encounters with Near Eastern peoples, adapting to local culture, intermarrying with the local population, and aligning themselves with local tradition. The process began with Alexander himself, who, in Egypt, offered a sacrifice to the Egyptian god Apis and, when in Persia, wore the clothes of Persian

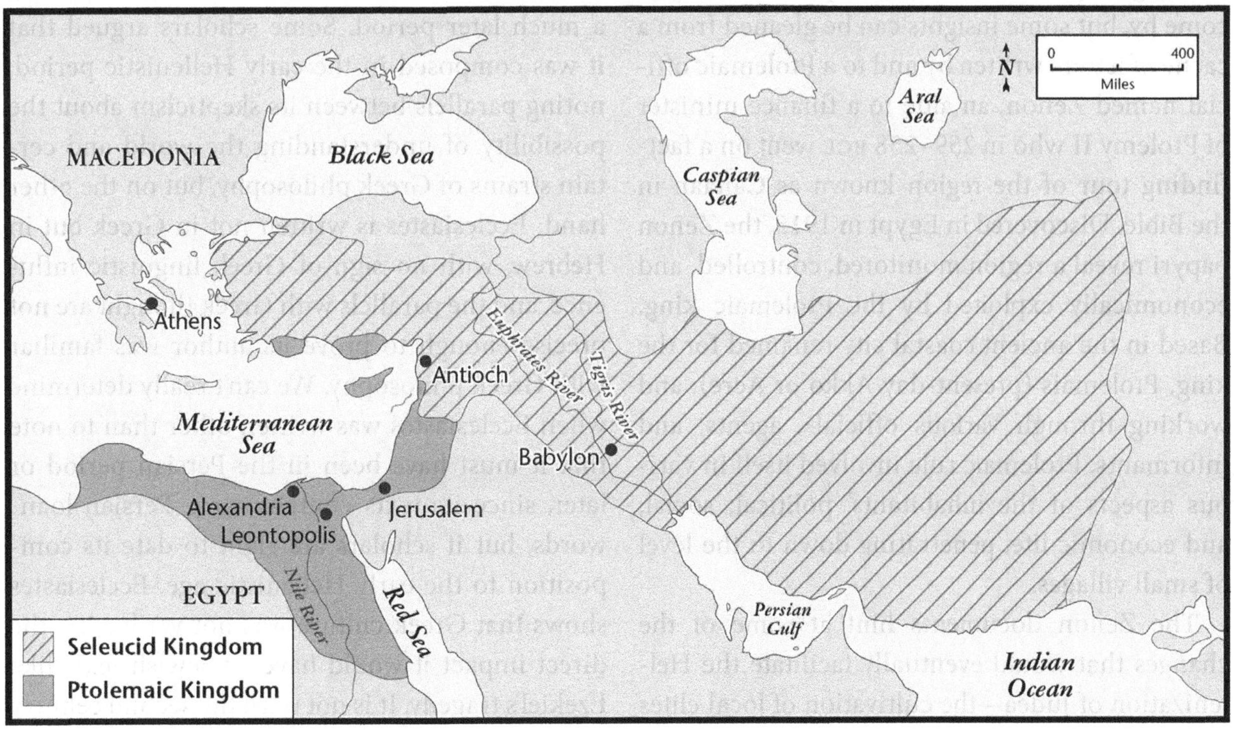

Map 3.1 The Seleucid and Ptolemaic kingdoms prior to the former's conquest of Judea around 200 BCE.

royalty. Best known for her doomed love affair with the Roman Marc Antony, Queen Cleopatra VII (69–30 BCE), the last Ptolemaic ruler of Egypt, provides another memorable example. Cleopatra's ancestry was Macedonian; even her name was Greek (it means "her father's glory"). Why, then, do we think of her as an Egyptian queen? Partly because that was how she presented herself: She learned Egyptian and identified with the goddess Isis, and even her suicide by cobra bite was an Egyptianizing touch (the cobra being a symbol on the Egyptian royal crown). *Hellenistic* has come to connote the kind of fusion of Greek with Near Eastern culture that Cleopatra exemplifies: not a one-way process in which the Near East adapted Greek culture, but a process of two-way influence in which Greeks and the peoples of the Near East adapted to one another.

Like the Persians before him, Ptolemy I, founder of the Ptolemaic line, probably allowed Jews in Judea to rule many of their own affairs according to their ancestral laws. At the same time, he and his successors introduced organizational changes that tied Judea more closely to the rest of the kingdom. Evidence from this period is hard to come by, but some insights can be gleaned from a cache of letters written by and to a Ptolemaic official named Zenon, an aide to a finance minister of Ptolemy II who in 259–258 BCE went on a fact-finding tour of the region known as Canaan in the Bible. Discovered in Egypt in 1915, the Zenon papyri reveal a region monitored, controlled, and economically exploited by the Ptolemaic king. Based in the ancient coastal city renamed for the king, Ptolemais (present-day Akko or Acre), and working through various officials, agents, and informants, Ptolemaic rule involved itself in various aspects of the inhabitants' political, social, and economic life, penetrating down to the level of small villages.

The Zenon documents hint at some of the changes that would eventually facilitate the Hellenization of Judea—the cultivation of local elites as intermediaries and the use of cities to channel their influence. They suggest that the Ptolemies relied on local aristocrats to help administer their rule, individuals like a figure named Tobias, whose family would become infamous over the course of the Hellenistic period for its members' role in tax collection in the area. They also suggest increased urbanization, and perhaps even the learning of Greek by some locals. Additional evidence for the influence of Hellenistic culture are the coins minted by Jerusalem authorities in the period between 300 and 250 BCE that bear the likeness of Ptolemy I and his wife, Berenice—evidence that Jerusalem itself was closely tied to Ptolemaic rule.

There is not a lot of other evidence for how Jews responded to Ptolemaic rule or for the process of Hellenization in this early period, and the fourth and third centuries BCE remain something of a dark age in our understanding of Judean history. An example of how difficult it is to pinpoint Greek influence at this time is the debate among scholars about how to date the biblical book of Ecclesiastes, a work traditionally attributed to King Solomon from biblical times but actually from a much later period. Some scholars argued that it was composed in the early Hellenistic period, noting parallels between its skepticism about the possibility of understanding the world and certain strains of Greek philosophy, but on the other hand, Ecclesiastes is written not in Greek but in Hebrew, with no sign of Greek linguistic influence, and the parallels with Greek thought are not precise enough to prove its author was familiar with Greek philosophy. We can't really determine when Ecclesiastes was written other than to note that it must have been in the Persian period or later, since its texts contain some Persian loanwords, but if scholars are right to date its composition to the early Hellenistic age, Ecclesiastes shows that Greek culture was not yet having the direct impact it would have on Jewish texts like Ezekiel's tragedy. It is not until the second century

BCE that Judean society begins to show clear signs of being significantly impacted by its exposure to Hellenistic culture.

A New Center of Jewish Life and Culture: Ptolemaic Egypt

As of this point in our history, we can no longer focus exclusively on what was happening in Judea. By this time, Jewish communities had long existed outside the land of Judah in Mesopotamia and Egypt. Some, like the Jewish community in Babylonia, arose as a result of exile, but we know that others, like the Elephantine community, formed in other ways, and Hellenistic rule intensified their size and dispersion throughout the Near East and Mediterranean. The reason for this growth seems to be both economic and political. Under Hellenistic rule, Jews found expanded economic opportunities beyond Judea's borders, and the support of Hellenized rulers like the Ptolemies helped create a place for them in societies like Egypt.

One such opportunity was the possibility of a military career under Ptolemaic rule, a role that we know relocated many Jewish males and their families to Egypt and other places. Like the Persians before them, the Greeks employed or conscripted Jews as soldiers, settling them and their families in places that they needed to fortify, something they may have done because, as non-native Egyptians themselves, the Ptolemies found it useful to rely on other non-Egyptians to help ensure their security. One example of how this brought Jews into Egypt comes from a Jewish text known as the *Letter of Aristeas* (discussed in more detail ahead), which reports that Ptolemy I brought to Egypt 100,000 captives from Judea and settled 30,000 of them in forts throughout the land. Though probably exaggerated, the numbers suggest one of the processes that contributed to the growth of a Jewish community in Egypt, eventually one of the largest Jewish communities in the Hellenistic period.

Jews were also drawn to places such as Egypt by other economic opportunities opened up under Hellenistic rule. Josephus notes that in addition to the Jews taken to Egypt by Ptolemy I as war captives, "not a few of the other Jews came to Egypt of their own accord, for they were attracted by the excellence of the country and Ptolemy's liberality" (Josephus, *Antiquities* 12.9). Josephus might be projecting the situation of his own day back onto an earlier period, but written evidence from Ptolemaic Egypt confirms that Jews there found a wide range of economic opportunities at this time, owning land, farming it as tenants, or working for the government as police and tax collectors. We know this in part thanks to Jewish inscriptions and papyri from Hellenistic Egypt, including documents discovered in a garbage dump near an Egyptian site called Oxyrhynchus, which hint of social and political tensions that faced the Jews of Alexandria and Egypt during the Roman period but also suggest that Jews were well integrated into the economy of Hellenistic Egypt before then, doing business, paying taxes, and achieving positions of status and influence. For the Jews mentioned by such evidence, Egypt was not a place of exile or servitude but simply a place where one could make a living, and its appeal in that regard might explain why Jews were drawn there from Judea, a place that offered a much narrower range of economic and social opportunities as well as greater instability and danger as a site of conflict between the Ptolemies and Seleucids. Similar opportunities elsewhere in the Hellenistic world may have been a factor in Jewish migration to places such as Syria, Asia Minor, and Greece.

As we mentioned briefly earlier, scholars once believed that Jews living in diasporic settings like Egypt were more susceptible to Hellenistic influence than the more religiously conservative Jews of Judea (for the meaning of the term *diaspora* as a description of Jewish communities outside Judea, *see the box* "Exile or Diaspora?"). Many scholars now reject the contrast as too simplistic—even within a single locale like Jerusalem, or even within a single family, Jews could respond in a variety of ways to Greek culture and Greek rule. Still, a case can be made that Jews in Alexandria faced the pressures and challenges of Hellenization a bit earlier than did their counterparts in Judah if only because, living at the seat of Ptolemaic rule, they would have encountered it earlier and would have been more integrated into the Hellenistic world than Palestine was in the third century BCE, with more opportunities for social and cultural interaction with Greek speakers.

By the time of Ptolemy II, the famous Library of Alexandria was in operation, and its treasure house of 200,000 books drew the best scholars of the day to Alexandria. Jews felt the city's attractions as well, judging from the large Jewish community that emerged in Alexandria by the end of the Hellenistic age. In the Near East in the same period, by contrast, Judea was a relative backwater, governed by a Hellenized elite of some sort based in Jerusalem but with a population that was still largely rural and with limited exposure to foreigners or Ptolemaic rule.

The Jews of Alexandria lived at the heart of Hellenistic culture, and especially their literary efforts give us our best opportunity to explore how Jews, or at least a wealthy and educated subset of the Jewish community, adapted to Greek culture in the third century BCE.

Only a thin slice of these literary efforts survives from this period, but enough has been preserved in the citations of later Christian authors to indicate that Jews were active participants in Alexandria's rich intellectual life. Ezekiel was not the only author to recast biblical history in light of Greek literature; we have examples of Jewish Greek histories, epics, and philosophy, and most of these works were probably written by Alexandrian Jews. The earliest known Jewish author to write in Greek is a historian named Demetrius, probably living at the end of the third century BCE, who tried to solve various chronological problems in his biblical sources in a way that recalls the historiographical methods of the Greeks. Another Jew, Philo (not to be confused with the more famous Philo of Alexandria, who lived in the first century CE), wrote an epic poem about Jerusalem. The earliest known Jewish philosopher, Aristobulus, lived in Alexandria in the second century BCE. His effort to explain the Bible in light of Greek philosophy includes the earliest examples of allegorical biblical interpretation, a reading technique borrowed from Greek scholars who had been using it to find insights into the universe and the human soul in the myths told by the poets Homer and Hesiod.

Allegorical biblical interpretation, first developed in Alexandria, is based on the assumption that the Bible, like the epics of Homer, as these works were understood by philosophers in the Hellenistic age, had two levels of meaning: (1) the surface meaning that tells a story of divine and human beings and (2) an implicit, allegorical meaning that the interpreter aims to bring out by reading the people and events of the text as coded symbols for abstract concepts. On the surface, a text like the Torah appears to be a book of stories and laws, but interpreters in the tradition of Aristobulus used allegory to show that its details also had a higher significance as a philosophical teaching about the nature of God. What, for example, does the Torah mean when it refers to God's hand? Someone reading the Bible literally might infer from this that God looked like a human being, but to Aristobulus who had likely studied the philosophy of Plato, such a claim would seem embarrassingly ignorant: How can an eternal being like God have a physical body which declines over time and eventually dies? By reading the expression "the hand of the Lord" not as a literal reference to a body part but as a metaphor for God's power, Aristobulus was able to reconcile the Torah with the Greek philosophical idea that the divine exists beyond the finite material realm of physical bodies.

What little we can tell from surviving evidence suggests that Jews, or at least the small percentage of the population that had access to education and writing, were very adaptive to the Hellenized environs of Ptolemaic Egypt, not seeming to draw very much from the indigenous cultural and religious traditions of Egypt that went back to the pre-Hellenistic age of Pharaohs but actively engaging Greek culture; adopting Greek literary genres, ideas, and ways of reading; cultivating a relationship with the Ptolemaic elite; and participating in and contributing to its administration of the land. It is also important to stress, though, that while the emulation of Greek culture helped Jews participate in the society of Ptolemaic Egypt, such adaption did not necessarily mean abandoning a Jewish identity or a commitment to the laws of Moses. To the contrary, it allowed for new ways to express this identity and fostered new forms of engagement with the Torah. While authors such as Demetrius, Philo, and Aristobulus (notice that all three names are Greek) tried to accentuate the similarity between Greek and Jewish culture, translating biblical history into a form familiar to Greeks, or finding similarities between the Torah and Greek philosophical thought, they seem to have remained strongly connected to Jewish tradition, focusing on the Bible, God, and Jewish history. To return to Aristobulus as an example again, he recognized the wisdom of philosophers, such as Plato, but he also believed that Moses was the better and more original philosopher—one that Plato was actually borrowing from.

EXILE OR DIASPORA?

Different terms are used to describe the Jewish communities that formed outside the Land of Israel, and each implies a different understanding of this experience. The Hebrew term *galut* translates as "exile" and is a description that implies that Jews living outside the land are not at home, and that their residence abroad is a kind of punishment imposed on them against their will. Many early Jews were indeed settled abroad against their will, exiled there by the Babylonians or taken as war captives during the Hellenistic period, and Jewish sources believed to have been written in the Hellenistic period—the apocryphal book of Tobit, for example—describe life outside the land as a divine punishment and a place of danger, a realm where Jews are subject to various kinds of peril and look forward to their return to their ancestral homeland. Other Jews resettled abroad of their own accord, however, moving for economic reasons or to take refuge from political conflicts in Judea, and life outside the land was not necessarily a negative experience from that point of view. Describing the Elephantine community as a community in exile is almost certainly misleading, since there is no evidence that its members ever suffered from exile, and the same is true of many Jews in the Hellenistic age. Relevant in this regard is the testimony of the first-century Jewish author Philo of Alexandria, who describes Jewish communities outside Palestine not as exiles but as colonists, a description that mirrors the settlement of Greeks throughout the Hellenistic world and suggests voluntary resettlement. And while these Jews revered Jerusalem as their motherland, he continues, they also regarded their new places of residence as a "fatherland," a cherished inheritance in its own right to which they felt a strong sense of kinship. This is why many scholars use another word to describe Jewish communities outside Judea that does not imply forced expulsion or divine punishment in the way that "exile" does: *diaspora*, from the Greek for "dispersion." Many Jews over the centuries have seen themselves as living in exile, hoping to return to their homeland someday, but that does not describe the experience of all Jews, and "exile" may not be the right term to describe the experience of Jews in Ptolemaic Egypt or other places where they felt at home in their environs.

The single most enduring attempt to bridge between Jewish and Greek cultures in Ptolemaic Alexandria was the translation of the Torah into Greek, the translation that we have referred to earlier as the Septuagint (introduced in Chapter 2). Many Jews in Ptolemaic Egypt probably spoke Greek as their first language, and knowledge of Hebrew may have been rare. Despite his erudition, for example, the first-century Philo of Alexandria does not seem to have known much Hebrew, perhaps knowing only the meaning of biblical names and little else about its vocabulary or grammar. One of the basic roles of the Septuagint was to render the Bible accessible to those Greek-speaking Jews, but it may have had another, nonlinguistic purpose as well: to further integrate Jewish tradition with Greek culture. One can detect the influence of Greek philosophy, law, and even mythology in its translation, adaptations that helped in subtle ways to diminish the differences between Greek and Jewish cultures.

The story of how the Septuagint came to be translated is preserved in the previously mentioned *Letter of Aristeas*, composed in Alexandria in the second or first century BCE. According to this letter, the Septuagint was an initiative of Ptolemy II, who commissioned a translation of the laws of the Jews as part of his effort to expand the number of books in the Library of Alexandria. To accomplish the task, the king sent a delegation to Judea to ask the high priest in Jerusalem to send six translators from each of the 12 tribes to help in the task. It was these 72 translators who inspired the translation's title, the Septuagint, which derives from the word for "seventy" in Latin. The *Letter of Aristeas* describes the delegates' journey to Jerusalem from the perspective of one of the king's envoys, a Ptolemaic official named Aristeas.

According to this text, it was not the Jews themselves who initiated this translation but the Ptolemaic king, out of a desire to fill out his library, but it is far from clear that the letter accurately describes the Septuagint's origins, and it is possible that it emerged from within the Jewish community, though perhaps with support from the Ptolemaic king. What is important here is the role that the letter assigns the Septuagint as a bridge between the Jews and the Greeks. As depicted by the letter, the Greeks and Jews of the story share much in common even before the Septuagint brings them closer together. Ptolemy shows great respect for Jewish tradition, making a costly gift to the Jerusalem Temple and showering honor on the translators, while for their part, the Jews in the story exhibit the virtues of cultured Greeks, sharing their appreciation for beauty, order, and truth. The narrative goes so far as to claim that the Jews and the Greeks worship the same God, though the latter call him Zeus. Even though the laws of Moses impose laws and practices that distinguish the Jews from other peoples—for example, special dietary laws—the *Letter of Aristeas* claims that when the Torah is fully understood, it demonstrates that the Jews share the same underlying commitment to wisdom, goodness, and beauty that characterizes Greeks such as Ptolemy II. By rendering the contents of the Torah accessible to them, the Septuagint could help Greeks appreciate that the Jews were not barbarians but an enlightened people like themselves.

For all that it does to translate Jewish culture into the philosophical and aesthetic categories of Greek culture, the *Letter of Aristeas* does not erase the boundary between Jewish and Greek culture. Through the voice of a Jewish high priest in the story, the narrative makes it clear that the very purpose of the law that was being translated was "to prevent [the Jews] from being perverted by contact with others or by mixing with bad influences." (line 142). The author of this text does not want to erase the boundary between Jewish and Greek culture, only to emphasize an underlying commonality that transcends their differences. What we can glimpse in the Septuagint, the *Letter of Aristeas*, and other Jewish texts composed in Ptolemaic Egypt is not the abandonment of a Jewish way of life for a Greek

Figure 3.2 An image from a mosaic in late Roman Palestine depicting a gate from the city of Alexandria. To the right of the gate is a tower with a flame coming out of its top—perhaps a depiction of the famous lighthouse of Alexandria, one of the Seven Wonders of the Ancient World. It was at the site of the lighthouse, on an island off the coast of Alexandria, that the Jews of Alexandria celebrated an annual festival in honor of the Septuagint, the Greek translation of the Torah. Perhaps seeking to associate the Septuagint with the lighthouse, Philo of Alexandria described the island as the place from which the "light" of its version of the Bible shone out to the world.

way of life but the effort to preserve a distinct Jewish culture by loosely aligning it with the culture of Alexandria's Ptolemaic rulers.

How did Jews in Ptolemaic Egypt manage this balancing act between integration and preserving a distinct culture? Part of the answer is segregation, not legally imposed segregation of the sort that was meant to prevent integration between Blacks and Whites in the United States, but the social segregation created by living in different neighborhoods, sustaining distinct institutions, and following different religious and cultural practices. Many Jews lived in separate, semiautonomous communities bound together by distinctive civic and religious institutions permitted them by their Ptolemaic rulers. By the first century CE, two of Alexandria's five quarters were predominantly Jewish—and the city's Jewish community was allowed its own court system and semiautonomous leader known (at least by the Roman period) as the *ethnarch*. This does not mean that Jews lived only within these communities; one should not imagine these neighborhoods as ghettos to which Jews were confined, but they were places where Jews could concentrate as communities and where they could more easily nurture a culture different from that of the Greeks or native Egyptians, a culture defined by its own customs and laws.

Jews in Egypt also developed distinct ways of worshipping. Many Jews in the Second Temple period regarded the Jerusalem Temple as the only legitimate temple, but we know of two other Jewish temples, both in Egypt. The temple at Elephantine, mentioned in Chapter 2, had been destroyed at the end of the fifth century BCE, and the Jews/Judahites there were evidently unable to rebuild it; but we know of another Jewish temple in Egypt established sometime in the second century BCE by Onias, a Jewish high priest (either Onias III or Onias IV; our only informant, the historian Josephus, seems confused about which Onias it was who built this temple). It functioned for several hundred years until it was shut down by the Romans in 74 CE, shortly after their destruction of the Second Temple. Josephus tells us how the temple came to be built. Having fled Judea, Onias secured the permission of the Ptolemaic king (probably Ptolemy VI) and his queen to build the temple at a place called Leontopolis, the site of a ruined Egyptian temple, and according to Josephus, the temple he established there was modeled on the one in Jerusalem, resembling it, albeit on a smaller scale. It is unclear whether Onias intended this temple to rival the one in Jerusalem or saw it as a complement to it, but either way, he evidently believed that he was acting at God's behest, claiming the temple fulfilled a prophecy in Isaiah 19:19 that forecast the construction of an altar to the Lord in the land of Egypt.

It is also in Ptolemaic Egypt, in the third century BCE, that we have our first evidence of the institution later known as the synagogue. The synagogue would eventually become the central meeting place for Jewish communities throughout the Mediterranean and Near East, a place of communal worship and other community activities. By the first century CE, it was already central to Jewish life both in Judea and in Alexandria. Our earliest evidence of this institution comes from Ptolemaic Egypt, in fact, though that doesn't necessarily mean that it originated there. There is a theory that it arose under the influence of Egyptian temples, which included annexes that served as places of study and writing, but that is conjecture, and there are other perfectly plausible explanations for its emergence—that it arose during the Babylonian Exile as a kind of mini-sanctuary to replace the Temple in Jerusalem, or even that it developed within Judea itself as a functional replacement for the city gate in pre-exilic Judah, the place where town elders would assemble to make various communal decisions. However it originated, the synagogue, like Onias's temple, allowed the Jews of Egypt a way to sustain a religious life different from that of Egyptians and Greeks.

What exactly the synagogue's role is in this early period is hard to say, however, and it is not clear that it had yet developed the roles that it would play in later antiquity. Actually, the term *synagogue*, from the Greek, meaning an "assembly place," wasn't yet in use in this period. Inscriptions from Ptolemaic Egypt refer to the institution as a "prayerhouse"—*proseuche*, from the Greek, meaning "prayer," a term that would remain in use until around the second century CE, when it was eclipsed by *synagogue*. As this earlier name suggests, the institution seems to have emerged as a center for communal prayer. What that would have entailed in this early period is anyone's guess, but it may have involved recitation of the kinds of prayers we know about from the book of Psalms and post-biblical literary sources—prayers for help, vows, expressions of gratitude, and perhaps prayers for God to support the Ptolemaic rulers. These prayerhouses are sometimes also described as "holy places," as if a god resided there, but there is no reason to think that they were temples, the site of animal sacrifice, like the temples of Elephantine and Onias. (It is possible that Jews made donations to these synagogues in fulfillment of vows made to God, but the evidence for that practice is from synagogues from the Roman period.) The synagogues of later periods would derive their holiness from the Torah scrolls kept within them, which were regarded as holy objects in their own right, and it is reasonable to suppose that the synagogues of Ptolemaic Egypt were the site of Torah-reading as well, but there is no clear evidence for that in this early period. What is clear is that these institutions developed a central role in the lives of the Jews of Egypt and Alexandria who invested significant resources in their construction. One synagogue in Alexandria was so immense and impressive that it was remembered by Jews centuries after its destruction during a war with the Romans in 115–117 CE.

Even as Jews developed their own institutions, however, they were also careful to cultivate a close relationship with their Ptolemaic rulers as protectors and patrons of their distinctive way of life. That dependence is reflected everywhere in our evidence from this period: in synagogue inscriptions that honor the Ptolemaic king and queen for their support, and in literary texts like the *Letter of Aristeas* that praise the Ptolemaic king as a generous patron. As different as their cultures were from one another, what Jews and the Ptolemies shared in common was that they had both originated from outside of Egypt, which made them allies in their relationship to Egypt's native population. The relationship thus followed a pattern set by the Persians during their earlier rule over Egypt, in which the government expected the allegiance and support of Jews, including military service, in exchange for its support of their communal institutions.

But while Ptolemaic rule appears to have been supportive of Alexandria's Jews—welcoming enough that Jews immigrated there from Judea—their situation was not completely secure. The Greek settlers of Egypt were only part of Egypt's population, which also included native Egyptians descended from those who had been there before Alexander's arrival, and some portion of this population was not happy about the Jews' presence in their midst and did what they could to discredit and displace them. We do not have clear evidence of anti-Jewish riots in the Ptolemaic period of the sort that beset the Jews of Alexandria when it was under Roman rule, but evidence does exist of the anti-Jewish resentment that would eventually boil over into such violence. In fact, the earliest known specimens of anti-Jewish literature come from Ptolemaic Egypt. An example of this literature is a history of Egypt written by Manetho, a Hellenized Egyptian priest. Manetho's account includes a kind of anti-Exodus story that, while it never mentions the Jews directly, was clearly written to ridicule them. In this topsy-turvy version of events, Moses is a renegade Egyptian priest whose commands to his followers are the very antithesis of what a Hellenized sensibility would value:

> He made it a law that they should neither worship the gods nor refrain from any of the animals prescribed as especially sacred in Egypt, but should sacrifice and consume all alike, and that they should have intercourse with none save those of their own confederacy.

One can recognize a grain of truth in Manetho's description—the laws of Moses do prohibit the worship of other gods and certain foods as well—but Manetho has spun Mosaic law into a sacrilegious rejection of Egyptian religion. And who are Moses's followers? In one passage, Manetho identifies them with the Hyksos, cruel invaders resented by native Egyptians; elsewhere, he suggests they included lepers the king wanted to cleanse from the land. Manetho's accusations call to mind later antisemitism, but the thinking involved was different from that of Christian anti-Judaism or modern antisemitism (*see the box* "Did Antisemitism Originate in Hellenistic Egypt?"). As an Egyptian living under foreign rule, he associated the Jews with Egypt's humiliation by foreign invaders and seems to have seen their expulsion from Egypt, as he suggests through his version of the Exodus story, as a way to revive his own culture.

This kind of claim endangered the Jews of Egypt in two ways. It could incite Egyptians themselves to acts of violence—this happened in Alexandria in the first century CE, when the Greek and Egyptian population of the city rioted against its Jewish community—and no less threateningly, it could also poison the relations between the Jews and the Ptolemies. As a member of the Ptolemaic court, Manetho was in a position to influence the king, and his Exodus story is probably an attempt to do just that by stressing the Jews' rebelliousness against an earlier king of Egypt. The Ptolemies claimed to embody the Greek value of *philanthropia*, a love of all humanity; as Manetho describes them, the Jews are the mirror image of this virtue, misanthropes whose history and ritual exude a hatred of humanity. Such rhetoric seems to have had little effect in the days of Ptolemy I or Ptolemy II, when Ptolemaic rule seems more supportive of the Jews than of native Egyptians, but we know that native Egyptians were allowed to play more of a role in the Ptolemaic government by the end of the third century BCE, and as their influence with

SEARCHING FOR JEWISH WOMEN IN PTOLEMAIC EGYPT

As is true of all of ancient Jewish history, it is a challenge to recover the experiences of women, because while they are mentioned frequently in literary and inscriptional sources, much of this evidence was written by men and reflects their perspective on women rather than the firsthand perspective of women themselves. An example is the story of Susanna, which appears as an episode in the Greek translation of the biblical book of Daniel and may have originated in Egypt, though its events are set in Babylonia (the story of Susanna now appears among the deuterocanonical books of the Catholic Bible, or the Apocrypha, as these works are known to Protestants).

Susanna is a pious woman who is sexually harassed by two elders who spy on her as she is bathing and seek to have sex with her. When she refuses, they have her arrested, falsely accusing her of having promiscuous sex with a lover, but Daniel is able to expose their lie. Susanna is depicted as a positive and virtuous figure, but the story has clearly been written from a male perspective, making Susanna a passive beneficiary of male heroism.

Despite the skewed nature of the evidence, however, it is possible to catch a glimpse of women exercising some measure of control over their lives, as in the cause of a papyrus dated to 218 BCE which reports the complaint to the Ptolemaic king from a woman named Helladore. She may not have been Jewish herself, but she had married her husband, Jonathas, according to the laws of the Jews, and that law had also allowed him to divorce her unilaterally. This was why she was now petitioning the king, going outside the legal system of the Jewish community in the hope of seeking redress. Jewish women in the Hellenistic period, as in earlier periods, lived in a world controlled by men, a world that devalued and severely disadvantaged them in many ways, denying them educational access and subjecting them to sexual abuse, as the story of Susanna attests. There is reason to think that in the Roman period, Jewish women in Alexandria were kept sequestered in their houses to avoid exposing them to the sight of men. Despite these circumstances, women found ways to assert agency and protect themselves, as Susanna does by refusing to submit to the sexual advances of the elders and calling on God to help her.

the Ptolemies grew, the status of Egyptian Jews became more precarious.

Much of the Jewish literature that survives from this period can be understood as a response to this pressure, an effort to enhance or safeguard the status of the Jews by aligning them with the Ptolemies or fitting them into Egyptian society. Some works, such as the *Letter of Aristeas*, stress the cultural affinity between the Jews and the Hellenized Ptolemies in both an explicit and implicit way. Aristobulus's philosophical work was dedicated to the Ptolemaic king. Still other works implicitly rebut the accusations of some Egyptian authors by stressing the Jews' positive contributions to Egyptian society. A narrative written by a Jew named Artapanus is an example: In its account of the biblical past, Abraham is welcomed into the home of the Egyptian king, to whom he teaches astronomy; Joseph is beloved by the Egyptians for organizing the way they farm the land; and Moses is honored by the priests of Egypt as a god. The Jews were not misanthropic foreigners, Artapanus shows through his history; on the contrary, they had been welcomed guests, benign and pious benefactors of their non-Jewish neighbors, and deserve credit for some of Egypt's greatest accomplishments.

Whatever the inherent attractions of Greek culture, such evidence suggests, Egyptian Jews also embraced it for pragmatic reasons, to secure their place in Hellenized Egyptian society. Hellenization should not be understood as simply a process of assimilation, the process whereby a minority group abandons its distinctive identity as it adopts the behaviors and values of a prevailing culture. It certainly has elements of such a process, but it could also serve as a way of preserving Jewish culture, allowing Jews to sustain their identity, culture, and community in an environment where they were resented by the native population and highly dependent on their Greek rulers. During this period, Egyptian Jews translated the Torah into Greek; recast biblical history in the form of such Greek literary genres as tragedy, history, and epic; and used Greek interpretive techniques such as allegory to turn the Bible and its laws into a philosophical text. All these practices mimic Greek practice and make Jewish culture more Greek-like, but they also helped Jews preserve their own distinct identity and ancestral traditions within a Hellenized context.

Seleucid Rule and the Maccabean Revolt

Little is known in general about life in Judea in the third century BCE, and it is hard to discern the impact of Hellenistic rule or the influence of Greek culture. As we have noted, important changes were certainly occurring in this period; it is just that they do not surface in obvious ways in Judean literature composed prior to around 200 BCE.

One text, known as *The Wisdom of Ben Sira*, written by a sage named Jesus ben Sira around 200 BCE, offers a rare glimpse into the experience of a Jewish intellectual from this period. The "discovery" of this text is a fascinating story. It was never really lost, having been preserved in the Apocrypha in a Greek translation known as Ecclesiasticus (not to be confused with the similarly spelled Ecclesiastes, discussed earlier in this chapter).

DID ANTISEMITISM ORIGINATE IN HELLENISTIC EGYPT?

The answer depends on what one means by *antisemitism*. If one means prejudice against Jews that stereotypes and ridicules them, ascribes to them malevolent motivations, suggests something wrong and harmful about their practices and beliefs, and sometimes manifests itself in violence against Jews and their communal institutions, *antisemitic* fits as a description of the rhetoric of Manetho and other later Egyptian Hellenistic writers, like Lysimachus and Apion. But some recent scholars have resisted using that label, which was coined in the nineteenth century, for the anti-Jewish attitude of ancient authors like Manetho on the grounds that it is anachronistic, and they have proposed other terms like *Judeophobia* as a better description, a fear of the Jews. They argue that projecting the term *antisemitism* onto antiquity falsely suggests continuity between ancient hostility toward the Jews and more recent antisemitism, born of modern racial theories and political ideas, or, for that matter, Christian antisemitism, fueled by distinctive theological ideas unique to Christianity. Ancient Judeophobia seems to have been born of communal rivalry among groups competing with the Jewish community for political and social status under Hellenistic rule, and the use of ridicule and stereotyping should be understood as part of a more widespread practice of ethnic caricature wielded against various peoples, including the Egyptians and the Greeks, who were also the object of stereotyping by Jews. It would be wrong to disconnect pagan Judeophobia in the Hellenistic Roman period from later Christian anti-Judaism, which perpetuated some of its tropes, but it is also wrong not to notice the differences between ancient hatred of the Jews and medieval and modern antisemitisms—for example, that ancient Judeophobia was based not on alleged religious sins or racial traits but on a perception of the Jews as a people who rejected widespread Hellenistic values.

However, it was only at the end of the nineteenth century that substantial fragments of the original Hebrew were discovered in a synagogue in Cairo, in a forgotten storage room used in the Middle Ages for the deposit of sacred texts (the number of texts found in this storage room, known as the Cairo Genizah, and their implications for understanding Jewish history dwarf the more famous discovery of the Dead Sea Scrolls, but they pertain mostly to the Middle Ages, not antiquity). Yeshua son of Eleazar son of Sira was a scribe who lived in Jerusalem around 200 BCE, and the work transmitted in his name records poetically expressed teachings on proper social conduct, family relations, wealth and poverty, and advice regarding women and children, among other topics, and it concludes with extended praise of Israel's biblical ancestors. The work was translated into Greek by his grandson, who brought it to Egypt around 132 BCE.

If one compares *The Wisdom of Ben Sira* to a work like Ecclesiastes, composed a century or two earlier, there are clear differences (*Ben Sira* clearly presupposes a biblical canon, whereas Ecclesiastes does not), but it is hard to pinpoint what difference Hellenization has made. Is the book's association of the Torah with wisdom a sign of such influence, suggesting that the study of the Torah was being remodeled on philosophy? There is no consensus on how to answer this question, since *Ben Sira* never refers to philosophy or cites the writings of any particular philosopher. If *Ben Sira* is any indication of what sages in Judea were thinking about around 200 BCE, it tells us they were interested in finding wisdom like their Greek counterparts, an interesting coincidence, but not one that necessarily reflects the process of Hellenization.

At about the time that Jesus ben Sira was writing this work, however, something was happening that would soon bring the influence of Hellenistic culture out into the open. In 202–200 BCE, Judea was wrested from the Ptolemaic kingdom by the Seleucid kingdom under Antiochus III. Far from trying to change the cultural status quo, Antiochus III seems to have followed the practice of earlier foreign rulers and affirmed the Jews' right to live according to their ancestral customs, a policy that persisted under his successor, Seleucus IV. There soon emerged signs of conflict, however. Seleucus IV, who ruled from 187 BCE to 175 BCE, reportedly made an effort to rob the Jerusalem Temple, reflecting a desperation for funding that made him oblivious to Jewish religious sensibilities. His official Heliodorus was unsuccessful for some reason—according to the Jewish account, because angelic beings blocked his way into the Temple and knocked him off his horse—but after Seleucus's assassination (allegedly by Heliodorus), he was succeeded by his brother Antiochus IV, who was not so easily deterred. It was during his reign that the emerging conflict between Seleucid rule and the Jews of Judea erupted into a war known as the Maccabean Revolt.

The Maccabean Revolt is remembered today in connection to Hanukkah, a holiday celebrated through the lighting of a special nine-branched lamp or *menorah* over an eight-day period. Hanukkah commemorates the rededication of the Temple after it was defiled by the Greek king Antiochus IV, understood as a miracle, and those who celebrate it may have only a sketchy understanding of the historical events that lie behind the holiday, which in America has absorbed some of the qualities of Christmas (observed on the 25th day of the month of Kislev in the Jewish calendar, Hanukkah always falls around Christmastime) and in Israel has been given a Zionist spin. But some of those events are known to modern-day historians thanks in large part to two narratives preserved in the Apocrypha, known as 1 Maccabees and 2 Maccabees. Neither text can be relied on as unbiased or complete account of events—in fact, they contradict each other on some key points—but they form the basis of what we know about this period of Judean history, and they reveal enough about the period to allow us to situate the Maccabean Revolt in the larger history of Seleucid Judea, and to recognize it as a response not just to a cruel ruler but to broader changes introduced through the process of Hellenization.

The causes and course of the Maccabean Revolt are hard to pin down, but what 1 Maccabees and 2 Maccabees suggest is that the revolt was a response to what Jews in Judea perceived to be a threat to their ancestral way of life. Antiochus is blamed for introducing some of the most offensive and dangerous of these changes, but others were introduced earlier by Jews themselves, especially by the high priests in charge of the Jerusalem Temple.

At this time, the most powerful position in Judean society was the high priest, the person in charge of the Jerusalem Temple and its staff. It was a position that seems to have been confined in this period to a single family known as the Oniads, but there arose in this period a struggle over who would hold it, with a priest named Jason displacing Onias III and securing the position for himself by offering a bribe to Antiochus (it was this Onias or his son Onias IV who would go on to establish the temple at Leontopolis in Egypt). A few years later, Jason was replaced by another ambitious priest seeking the high priesthood named Menelaus, who offered the king a bribe of his own, which he could afford only by plundering the Temple treasure. The violation of the Temple's sanctity left the population of Jerusalem deeply upset. These were the figures who introduced offensive Greek practices into Jerusalem according to 1 Maccabees, laying the groundwork for the more intrusive changes that Antiochus sought to impose. In Ben Sira, the high priest at that time, a figure named Simon is extolled as "the pride of his people," renowned for fortifying Jerusalem and improving its water supply. The fact that the high priests in 1 Maccabees are such corrupt and treacherous figures shows that from the perspective of this author at least, the Jerusalem priesthood had lost its moral and religious legitimacy, and that seems to have helped ignite the ensuing revolt, a rebellion not just against foreign rule but also against the priestly elite in Jerusalem for betraying its sacred duties out of ambition.

Among the most offensive of the changes introduced by these priests was Jason's establishment of a gymnasium in Jerusalem, a Greek institution for the physical and intellectual training of young men. What was so offensive about an educational institution like the gymnasium? We do not know exactly, but we can guess. The word comes from the Greek for "to train naked," referring to the fact that the young men there exercised in the nude. Our sources do not actually describe the young men training in Jason's gymnasium as nude, but historians have made such an inference. The text known as 2 Maccabees mentions that these young men began to wear Greek-style hats, and since it doesn't mention them wearing any other clothing, scholars have surmised that they were otherwise naked, wearing a hat to protect them from the sun, but nothing else, as was the practice of Greek athletes. Since we know from later sources that religiously observant Jews were offended by nudity, especially in the presence of God, it is plausible to suppose that what was offensive about this gymnasium was its exposure of male bodies. Beyond that, their nudity exposed the fact that Jewish males were circumcised—for some, an embarrassing point of difference from non-Jews, which they sought to cover over through a procedure known as epispasm, a technique to cover over or reverse the act of circumcision (this according to 1 Maccabees).

The adoption of Greek customs offended Jewish religious sensibilities in other ways as well. The introduction of Greek-style athletics created problems, for example. The priests, who were supposed to be the guardians of the ancestral traditions of Judea, are said to have abandoned their duties to join in athletic contests in pursuit of Greek-style prizes, while Jason's desire to participate in athletics led to an even more serious offense when he sent delegates to an Olympics-style contest with money intended to support a sacrifice to Hercules, venerated as a god. Had the delegates followed his instructions (which they did not), Jason would have been supporting the worship of a foreign deity, the greatest of offenses according to the Bible.

Jason's embrace of Greek athletic culture was part of a still larger change that he was trying to introduce—the transformation of Jerusalem into a Greek-style city, a *polis*, with all the trappings of a city as the Greeks understood that institution. To be recognized as a polis by the Seleucid authorities was to win certain privileges—certain rights for its male inhabitants, the ability to mint coins, and other benefits—and it may well be that Jason sought this status for Jerusalem as a way of strengthening its status within the Seleucid kingdom and of integrating it into the larger Hellenistic world. For many Jews, however, these changes threatened the Jews' traditional way of life, replacing it with new customs contrary to the laws of Moses, to paraphrase the view of the author of 2 Maccabees. Menelaus went even further: He stole golden vessels from the Temple to bribe a Greek official and to sell to other cities and went so far as to arrange for the murder of Onias, a former high priest who had been critical of his actions.

Nothing symbolized the threat to Jewish tradition more than the effort by Jews in this period to cover over the marks of their circumcision. Circumcision was the sign of the people's covenant with God, and it also served as a marker of a distinct religious and ethnic identity, distinguishing Jews from the Greeks. But the latter had a hard time understanding the practice, thought it barbaric, and made fun of it, so it became a barrier for Jews trying to align themselves with the Greeks and their cultural value. Judging from 1 Maccabees, some Jews in Jerusalem in this period tried to address this problem by removing or hiding the marks of their circumcision in order to conform with what Greeks thought a male body should look like.

We can thus see how the period of Antiochus's rule became a period of crisis for Jews in Jerusalem, associated with the disruption of religious tradition and the violation of the Temple's sanctity, but what pushed things over the edge into full-scale war was the direct intervention of Antiochus himself. Especially after Menelaus took over, the political situation began to deteriorate. He and Jason fell into fighting, creating a disturbance that Antiochus took to be a revolt and which he sought to suppress, and it was this intervention that sparked the Maccabean Revolt. Antiochus not only sacked the Temple, another violation of its sanctity, but also is said to have erected some kind of sacrilegious object within it, an idol or an altar, in an effort to rededicate it to the god Zeus. So many religious taboos were being violated that some believed an orgy was happening within the Temple itself, or so suggests 2 Maccabees, which reports that during this period non-Jews were having sex with prostitutes in its precincts.

To establish order, Antiochus also established a citadel in Jerusalem manned by non-Jewish soldiers, taking direct control over the city. The aspiration of every major city within the Seleucid kingdom was to secure from its rulers a formal recognition of its autonomy along with a related status that sources at this time refer to as "inviolability," the right not to be intruded into by outside powers. None of this amounted to full-fledged independence—it was a kind of favor that cities were seeking from Seleucid rule in exchange for their deepened support—but such recognition meant that a city could govern its internal affairs and command the respect of other cities. Though the Seleucids may never have officially acknowledged this status for Jerusalem, they had respected its sanctity in practice, and this was what Antiochus was threatening—the city's ability to control its own affairs and guard the inviolability of its temple. Especially, his incursion into the Temple must have left many Jews feeling powerless, humiliated, and outraged at the insult to their god and their ancestral way of life.

And even his violation of the Temple's sanctity isn't by itself what makes Antiochus so infamous in Jewish memory, for he took an even more drastic step. Alongside his other offenses, the king issued an edict that banned Jewish religious practice in general, outlawing circumcision, the Sabbath, and the Torah. Antiochus's forces destroyed whatever copies of the Torah they found and executed those found adhering to its laws, including women, who were punished for circumcising their sons by being forced to parade around the city with their babies hanging from their necks and then hurled down headfirst from its wall. Antiochus also apparently tried to compel Jews to break the laws of Moses by threatening and torturing them to death. We have reports of Jews in this period being forced to walk in a procession in honor of the Greek god Dionysius and of being forced to eat swine's flesh, which was taboo according to the laws of Moses. Some refused, choosing to die rather than betray the law, and the memory of their defiance seared itself into Jewish memories, producing the earliest accounts of Jewish martyrdom, of Jews choosing to die out of a sense of religious commitment (*see the box* "Is Martyrdom a Jewish Invention?"). Assaulting the Temple was bad enough, but Antiochus went even further, seeking to suppress Jewish religious tradition in a way that might have ended Jewish culture itself had it succeeded, especially given that according to one account, an order was sent to other cities that they should also execute Jews who did not change over to a Greek way of life.

Antiochus's motive for these measures remains a historical puzzle. Why did he believe that he had to intervene so drastically into the affair of Jerusalem? Why attack Jewish religious practice if he thought he was dealing with a political uprising? How did such an idea occur to him, given that there was no clear precedent for religious persecution in earlier history, and especially given that earlier rulers were usually respectful of local religious tradition? We do not know the answers to these questions, but scholars haven't stopped trying to answer them. Some have theorized that Antiochus suffered from mental illness, and as support, they point to his reputation for bizarre behavior (a reputation reflected in a joke at that time that made fun of Antiochus by changing his title *Epiphanes* to *Epimanes*, or "madman"). Perhaps, as suggested by the same title *Epiphanes* (Greek for "the revealed god"), he truly thought himself a divine being and resented the Jews for not worshipping him as did other peoples. A later Roman emperor named Caligula would punish the Jews for refusing to recognize him as a god, attempting to have a statue of himself installed in the Jerusalem Temple, and maybe such divine ambitions drove Antiochus as well.

Alternatively, perhaps Antiochus was influenced by the anti-Jewish prejudice of his day. According to a first-century Greek writer named Apion (whose criticisms of the Jews prompted Josephus to write a refutation called *Against Apion*), Antiochus was motivated by outrage at the barbarity of Jewish religious practice, believing that the Jews kidnapped Greek youths, fattened them up, and then sacrificed them. He sought to abolish Judaism, this story suggests, as a kind of humanitarian intervention, to stop kidnapping and cannibalism. In all likelihood, though, this report probably tells us more about Apion's own anti-Jewish prejudices than it does Antiochus's actual motives—in fact, it is an eerie anticipation of the blood libel of the much later medieval period that accused Jews of murdering children in order to consume their blood during Passover.

Other scholars have tried to discern a more pragmatic motive for the king's behavior, arguing that he was driven by financial, political, or military considerations, using an attack against Jews to reassert himself after a humiliating withdrawal from Egypt under pressure from the Romans, or driven by a desperate need for the funding that the Temple could provide. One approach to the question depicted the rebellion as a civil war: Antiochus was drawn into an internal religious conflict

IS MARTYRDOM A JEWISH INVENTION?

A *martyr* is a person who willingly submits to death, allowing others to kill him or her, or even taking his or her own life, out of a sense of commitment to God or religious principle. In recent times, martyrdom is often associated with Islam, but the term itself, from the Greek *martyrein*, "to witness," arose in Christianity, where martyrdom was seen as an exemplary way to express one's commitment to God and a way to emulate Jesus's death. In fact, the practice of dying for one's religion is rooted in still earlier Jewish culture. The earliest known accounts of people choosing to die for their religion appear in a 2 Maccabees account of Antiochus's persecution, leading scholars to conclude that what would come to be known as martyrdom originated in this period. The Bible does not contain accounts of people willing to sacrifice their lives out of devotion to God or the laws of Moses—a few suicides, yes, but not religiously motivated self-sacrifice out of religious commitment. The behavior appears to be new to the Hellenistic period, first recorded in sources written in Greek, like 2 Maccabees. Why does such behavior emerge in this period? Part of the explanation is political. As depicted in 2 Maccabees, martyrdom is an act of resistance, a refusal to betray God's laws under any circumstance, an attempt to preserve a measure of Jewish self-determination in a context where Jews found their lives controlled by others. Jews might not control their political destiny under a foreign ruler like Antiochus, but martyrdom gave them a way to control something—their dignity and the manner of their death.

But we don't have any accounts of martyrdom during the period of Assyrian, Babylonian, and Persian rule, when Israelites or Jews also found themselves under foreign domination. Was there something specific about the Hellenistic period that fostered this behavior? Perhaps it was Greek culture itself that served as a catalyst, for the Greeks had their own martyrs of a sort, people who chose to die rather than betray their principles. The most famous case, probably known to some Jews by the second century BCE, was Socrates, who chose to commit suicide rather than abandon his calling as a philosopher, and it is quite possible that this example exerted an influence on Jewish thinking, introducing a new ideal of what it meant to live a truly committed life.

So did Jews invent martyrdom? In a sense, yes, but the Greeks had an important role in its development too, a conclusion that further complicates our understanding of the relationship between Jews and Greeks in this period: Even in the act of resisting their Greek rulers, Jews could be emulating their culture.

among two Jewish factions, between cosmopolitan "reformers," like the priests Jason and Menelaus, who were seeking to align Judaism with Hellenistic values by eliminating its exclusiveness and self-isolation, and a more religiously conservative faction. The idea to outlaw religious practices like circumcision and Sabbath observance did not come from Antiochus himself, according to this reconstruction, but from the Jewish reformers with whom the king had aligned himself. This theory is different from other attempts to explain the events of the period because it casts the Maccabean Revolt as an internal conflict among different ideological factions within Judean society rather than as a rebellion against a foreign power.

Many of these theories have some evidence to support them, but none is completely persuasive, because they depend on sources that we have reason to be suspicious of and involve a lot of speculation. There are many reasons for such suspicion. Sources like 1 and 2 Maccabees were written long after the events they report, and it is not clear how their authors knew what they claim to know. They describe miraculous events that can seem fictionalized—stories of angelic beings intervening to save the Jews or of Antiochus IV converting to Judaism on his deathbed—and they sometimes contradict the other narrative's account. It is thus possible that they exaggerate Antiochus's impieties to make him look bad. We know that such exaggeration was used against earlier kings, described by hostile sources as arrogant and disrespectful of religious tradition so as to justify replacing them with another ruler. The Cyrus Cylinder, mentioned in the last chapter, is an example of such an account: Written by a supporter of the Persian king Cyrus, it seeks to discredit the Babylonian king that he was replacing, a ruler named Nabonidus, and it does so by describing as sacrilegious what the Babylonian king himself might have intended as acts of piety. It is possible that the same strategy shapes our sources' description of Antiochus IV, similarly accentuating his impieties to discredit him as a ruler. This is not to deny that Antiochus did injurious things to the Jews and their culture; it is to call attention to the fact that everything we know about him comes from sources that aren't completely reliable and may have their own reasons for describing things as they do.

Easier to understand than Antiochus's behavior is why a Jewish leader like Jason and Menelaus might collaborate in an effort to introduce Greek customs and institutions into Jerusalem. As we have noted, Hellenistic culture offered new opportunities to the ambitious, who could improve their lot in life by learning Greek and adopting Greek behavior. It also offered new opportunities to communities, who could improve their status by aligning themselves with their Hellenistic rulers. The more Jerusalem could approximate a Greek polis, for example, the more likely it was to secure the king's respect, which could mean greater autonomy, royal investment in the city's institutions, and financial benefits, like tax breaks and the right to mint coinage. The behavior of a Jason or a Menelaus in Jerusalem may not have been all that different from that of Aristobulus or Ezekiel in Alexandria: Their adoption of Greek institutions and customs was not necessarily an abandonment of Jewish tradition, as 1 and 2 Maccabees claim, but a pragmatic effort to improve Jerusalem's status within a Hellenized world and to deepen the connection between Jews and Seleucid rule.

Figure 3.3 A coin depicting Antiochus Epiphanes (Antiochus IV) being crowned king by the goddess Athena.

Clearly, however, many Jews did not see things in this way. While some embraced the changes taking place, others strongly opposed them, and the reason is that they were seen as a threat to what is referred to for the first time in this period as *Judaism*, originally a Greek word for a Jewish way of life, defined by commitment to the laws of Moses and distinctive religious practices like circumcision, Sabbath observance, and worship in the Jerusalem Temple. There is no evidence that Jews resisted Seleucid rule as long as they could practice this way of life. Even when Seleucus IV threatened to invade the Temple, they did not openly rebel but tried to talk him out of it. Antiochus's intervention forced the issue, however, by forcing Jews to choose between their commitment to the law and the adoption of a Greek way of life, and that was when there emerged a sharp conflict between the two cultures. Some Jews tried to avoid confrontation by running away, seeking refuge in Judea's wilderness, but they were hunted down, according to

A BRIEF HISTORY OF HANUKKAH, FROM ANTIOCHUS IV TO ADAM SANDLER

How did Hanukkah (or *Chanukah*, as it is often spelled in English) evolve from a Maccabean holiday into the gift-giving holiday that Jews celebrate today as a kind of answer to Christmas? The festival began during the Maccabean period as a celebration of the rededication of the Jerusalem Temple from the Seleucids, and it came to be associated with the lighting of the Temple lamp very early on but has undergone many changes since. In the Bible's instructions for how to build a sanctuary for God, the objects it describes include a seven-branch candelabrum, or "menorah" in Hebrew. The menorah in the First Temple was destroyed or looted, but the Second Temple had its own menorah, and this was what the Maccabees rekindled as part of their effort to rededicate the Temple to God and restart the sacrificial cult. The eight-day festival of Hanukkah was a celebration of this moment.

The rabbis of the Mishnah and the Talmud, introduced in a later chapter, played down the connection to the Maccabees and introduced the famous miracle story that explains why a lamp (menorah) is lit during Hanukkah for eight days. According to the story, the supply of oil needed to light the Temple lamp, enough for just one day, lasted for eight days, long enough for the oil to be replenished. By the days of the Talmud (by which the Jerusalem Temple had been gone for centuries), it had become a custom for Jews to light such lamps within their homes to commemorate the holiday, placing it outside their door or in the window closest to the street. Other customs associated with the holiday developed in the much later Middle Ages or modern times. The custom of eating of *latkes*, potato pancakes, originated among the Jews in Italy in the fourteenth century, though the word itself is Yiddish. The origin of the *dreidel*, the spinning top used in a Hanukkah children's game, is unclear, but it may have been modelled on a game called totum played in Europe during Christmas season.

As Jews in America began to successfully integrate into the broader non-Jewish culture of the country, Hanukkah continued to develop under the influence of Christmas. Gift-giving became important; companies began to commercialize the holiday, selling holiday cards and decorations; and some families even began to display within their homes a "Hanukkah bush," a Jewish version of the Christmas tree. The holiday as celebrated today is evidence of how much American Jews have adapted to their environs, but it also remains a celebration of Jewish tradition and distinctiveness. The "Chanukah Song," first performed by comedian Adam Sandler in a 1994 episode of *Saturday Night Live*, captures the holiday's significance in America as an alternative to Christmas, humorously seeking to make Jews feel better about being left out during Christmas by listing Jews who have become successful celebrities.

1 Maccabees. Others resisted, but passively, choosing to die rather than agreeing to violate the law. But a good number of Jews turned to yet another option—rebellion, seeking not necessarily to end Seleucid rule completely in this way but to secure a measure of autonomy, to win back the right to live in accordance with their own laws and traditions.

First Maccabees tells the story of how this rebellion began. According to its narrative, Antiochus's officials came to the town of Modi'in, not far from Jerusalem, to compel the Jews there to offer a sacrifice in accordance with the king's decrees. The officers turned first to a Jew named Mattathias, a priest and an important leader in the town, and demanded that he be the first to offer the sacrifice, but Mattathias openly defied them, not only refusing to offer the sacrifice but also brazenly striking down a Jew who had stepped forward to offer the sacrifice, along with a Seleucid officer. He and his five sons then took to the hills and began a kind of guerilla war against the Seleucids. They were not the only ones involved in the ensuing uprising—we have indications of another group that seems to have been active in the revolt at an even earlier period, known as the Hasidim, or "The Pious," but its leaders were at some point eclipsed by Mattathias and his family. After Mattathias's death, his son Judah took command, and it is from Judah's nickname, "The Maccabee" or "The Hammer," that the Maccabees and the Maccabean Revolt get their name.

The Maccabees may have been initially targeting Jewish collaborators rather than the Seleucids themselves. As they gained more of a following, however, they began to challenge the Seleucid kingdom more directly, with Judah winning several victories that allowed him to retake Jerusalem and restore the Temple cult—the event commemorated by Hanukkah (*see box*). It may seem remarkable that Judah was able to defeat the much larger armies of the Seleucids, but he seems to have been a skillful guerilla commander and motivator, with the leadership skills to grow a small band of followers into a large, highly enthused army. It did not hurt that Antiochus was distracted by what was happening in the eastern part of his kingdom, or that Judah recruited the support of the Romans, whose might was all too apparent to the Seleucids since it was their intervention that had forced Antiochus to withdraw from Egypt.

From Rebels to Vassals: The Rise and Fall of the Hasmonean Dynasty

Judah was soon killed in battle, but the fight with the Seleucids continued under his brothers Jonathan and then, after his death, Simon. It is not clear when to date the end of the Maccabean Revolt: In 161 BCE, Judah defeated Nicanor, a Seleucid general who had threatened to destroy the Temple, and this is where 2 Maccabees ends its story. But that didn't mean that Judea was now independent of Seleucid rule (Judea was the Greek name for the region known as the kingdom of Judah in the Bible and as the province *Yehud* in the Persian period). In truth, the Maccabean Revolt was not an independence war. The Maccabees sought greater political and religious autonomy, and they and their successors became the rulers of Judea, but they did not achieve a state that was fully independent of the Seleucid kingdom that controlled the region.

That said, by around 140 BCE, following the account in 1 Maccabees, the Maccabees had consolidated their control over Judea, restored the temple, and driven the non-Jews from the land. Simon was honored for this feat by being declared the high priest and ruler of the Jews "forever," which meant that this position would pass down to his descendants and that the Maccabees would now represent a political dynasty, not a line of kings—according to Jewish tradition, the role of king was limited to the dynasty descended from King David—a powerful elite in charge of the Temple as priests and considered the political leaders of Judea. Known as the Hasmoneans (a name perhaps inspired by the place where the Maccabean family was from), this new dynasty was comprised of successors of the Maccabean family that had left the revolt, and it controlled Judea until it came under Roman control in 63 BCE. First and Second Maccabees, likely emanated from Hasmonean circles or from people sympathetic to them, tell the story of the revolt in a way that makes a case for why the Maccabees and their Hasmonean successors were entitled to displace the high priests in charge at that time and become the guardians of the Temple and Judean tradition.

As historians once described this period, the Maccabees protected Judea from the encroachments of Hellenization, undoing the changes introduced by Antiochus and his Jewish collaborators and restoring the traditions of the Jews. In fact, even after the death of Antiochus IV, even after the Seleucids restored the Jews' right to practice their laws, the Hasmonean campaign to re-Judaize Judea continued. Simon continued his military conquests, capturing sites like Gezer, expelling its non-Jewish inhabitants, and resettling it with Jews. Simon was succeeded by his son John Hyrcanus, who ruled from 134 to 104 BCE, and he went on to subdue peoples living on the borders of the Hasmonean state, including the Idumeans, descendants of the Edomites. Rather than expelling them, however, he gave them a choice: They could remain in the land if they became Jews, an act of forced conversion that imitated Antiochus's effort to force the Jews to change their way of life. His son Aristobulus I would offer the same choice to the Itureans, a people settled in what is now Lebanon. Hasmonean power reached its height under Aristobulus's brother Alexander Janneus, who ruled from 103 to 76 BCE, a cruel ruler resented by many of his subjects, but an effective conqueror. He continued this policy of Judaization as well, conquering adjacent regions and forcibly converting their inhabitants.

Both literary and nonliterary evidence confirms an effort in this period to restore what was seen as the traditional Jewish way of life. First Maccabees closely imitates the style of biblical narratives like Joshua and Samuel. The holiday later known as Hanukkah, an eight-day festival now observed with the lighting of a lamp known as a menorah, was newly introduced by the Maccabees (*see box* "A Brief History of Hanukkah"), but it, too, seems to have been based on a biblical model, patterned on the biblical festival of Sukkot and on Solomon's dedication of the First Temple as described in 1 Kings. Hasmonean coins are inscribed in the ancient Hebrew script from the time of the First Temple, and an avoidance of foreign wine and other imports is reflected in the pottery found in Judea at the time of the Maccabees, as if a boycott of foreign goods was in effect. The effort to Hellenize Jewish culture seems to have provoked a backlash against foreigners and foreign influence: Non-Jews were driven out or forced to convert, and there were efforts to revive the ancestral culture of Judea as it was known from the Bible.

None of this means that the Hasmoneans were able to reverse the broader process of Hellenization, however. The sources are focused on the adoption of Greek customs and the abandonment of Jewish practices, as if these were mutually exclusive lifestyles, but the process of Hellenization is much more complex than that, reshaping Jewish culture in ways that Jews themselves did not always recognize. For one thing, the Jews, including the Maccabees, did not sever their contacts with the world around them. The Maccabees had a conflict with Antiochus IV, but they sustained relationships with other peoples, other Greeks, like the Spartans, the Romans, and eventually, the Seleucid kingdom itself, reconciling with it during the reign of John Hyrcanus—all of which required a knowledge of Greek and Hellenistic diplomatic etiquette.

The Hasmoneans also took Greek names, such as Alexander or, in the case of the one female Hasmonean ruler, Alexandra; built palaces and tombs modeled in their design and decoration on Hellenistic prototypes; and minted coins with Greek legends and symbols that emulated Seleucid coinage. One Hasmonean ruler even merited the nickname *Philhellene*, "Lover of the Greeks." For all their effort to retrieve the ancient traditions of biblical Israel, the Hasmoneans themselves participated and even facilitated the process of Hellenization in Judea.

This might seem like a contradiction at first. Why did the Maccabees/Hasmoneans resist Hellenized culture so strenuously during the Maccabean Revolt, only to behave like typical Hellenized rulers themselves? Were they two-faced politicians who abandoned their ideals as soon as they gained power and wealth? It is tempting to draw such a conclusion, especially given that many of the Hasmoneans do seem rather two-faced in their political behavior, continually switching political and religious allegiances, but in the Hasmoneans' defense, it should also be pointed out that they might not have seen the inconsistency that we do. It became a cliché in modern European thought to describe the cultures of

FORGOTTEN HEROINES OF HANUKKAH: WERE THE TRUE HEROES OF THE MACCABEAN REVOLT WOMEN?

The best-known heroes of the Maccabean Revolt are males—Mattathias, Judah the Maccabee, Simon—but there is also evidence that women played an important role in the revolt as well. Women were among those who voluntarily surrendered their lives rather than follow Antiochus's decrees. Second Maccabees tells the story of one such woman, an unnamed mother who urges her seven sons to die resisting Antiochus before accepting death herself (in later Jewish tradition, she is given the name of Miriam or Hannah), and other women were martyred as well, including the two women paraded around Jerusalem with their circumcised babies hanging from their necks. Such women stand up to Antiochus before Mattathias and Judah appear.

Later Jewish legend preserved the memory of women playing other roles in the revolt. A medieval text tells of a daughter of Mattathias who shamed her brothers into fighting Antiochus through a very brazen action. According to this story, the Greeks had required all new brides to be deflowered by the Greek governor. Mattathias's sons were going to go along with this, proceeding with a marriage ceremony for their sister, until she stood up at the ceremony, exposed her breasts, and challenged them to do something to stop her defilement—the incitement that started the revolt. This is a much later legend, but it may have its origins in a story composed during the Hasmonean period, the story of Judith, a widow who steps forward to defend Israel against an attacking enemy army while all its men stand by helplessly. Judith's story is set in biblical times (the enemy she fights are Assyrians), but a number of parallels with Judah the Maccabee—their similar names and their parallel beheadings of an enemy general—suggest the story reflects the events of the Maccabean Revolt. In later Jewish tradition, Judith was sometimes made a sister of the Maccabees, and her story read during Hanukkah, suggesting that Jews themselves saw the connection, and she may actually have been inspired by the heroism of Hasmonean women, like the mother of John Hyrcanus, who died a defiant death.

Given that Judean society in this period, like earlier Israelite society, was male-dominated, how do we account for the emergence of stories like the book of Judith which describe women acting more bravely than men and getting the better of male enemies? The Hasmonean line included one prominent female ruler, Salome Alexandra, or *Shelamzion* in Hebrew. The Hasmoneans seem to have believed that widows were eligible to assume the throne, and though brothers and sons usually seized this role, infighting within the Hasmonean family allowed Alexandra to rise to power, becoming the leader of Judean society (not its high priest, but the one who appointed this position) between 76 and 67 BCE. It is possible that these stories reflect her impact, but they may also tell us something about gender more broadly in this period. The women in these stories step forward because the men are unable to defend against the enemy, passively accepting its commands or too afraid to challenge it, and the contrasting bravery of mothers, sisters, and widows only underscores that powerlessness. In other words, while these stories focus on female heroes, they were still viewing things from a male perspective: The role they ascribe to female heroines like Judith may have been a way to underscore the ill effects of foreign rule, the passivity of the men an indication that something was very wrong in Judean society.

Judaism and Hellenism as incompatible opposites, as symbols of faith versus reason, tradition versus modernity, or East versus West, but such ways of imagining this period anachronistically polarize Jewish and Greek culture. The Hasmoneans themselves probably did not see the rivalry that much later Europeans did 2,000 years later; their objective was winning the right to practice their ancestral customs, and they seem to have had no compunction about allying themselves with Greeks or adopting Greek practices, provided that they could do so without violating Jewish laws or customs. Whether they succeeded is a different story. The Hasmoneans eventually grew unpopular with many of their Jewish subjects, but this needn't have been because of their adoption of Greek ways: There was plenty else for their subjects to be upset about, namely, the Hasmoneans' questionable claim to the high priesthood, the taxation and conscription probably necessary to support their wars, their cruelty (Josephus claims that Alexander Jannaeus alone slew 50,000 Jews, an improbably large number, but that one suggests how brutal they were remembered to be), and their misuse of communal funds, as when John Hyrcanus took money from David's tomb to pay for mercenaries to control the population.

The Hasmoneans' fusion of Jewish traditionalism and the embrace of Greek culture may not have been unique, for there is evidence that other Jews also saw no inherent contradiction between Greek and Jewish culture. A good example is one of the sources we have been relying on for our knowledge of the Maccabean Revolt—2 Maccabees—which is actually an abridged account of a longer, five-volume work written by a certain Jason of Cyrene that no longer survives. The first known work to use the terms *Judaism* and *Hellenism* is 2 Maccabees, which uses those Greek terms to refer to two distinct ways of life. By *Judaism*, 2 Maccabees means adherence to Jewish law: circumcision, the Sabbath, and the other customs and practices that Antiochus tried

Figure 3.4 Judith holding the head of General Holofernes, as illustrated in the "Doré Bible" from 1866. The episode calls to mind the beheading of General Nicanor by Judah the Maccabee as described in 2 Maccabees—one of several parallels that suggest the story of Judith was inspired by the Maccabean Revolt.

to abolish. *Hellenism* refers to participation in the gymnasium and other foreign customs associated with the Greeks. Pitting these ways of life against one another, 2 Maccabees would seem to support the view of Judaism and Hellenism as incompatible lifestyles, but the work itself complicates this distinction because it itself is written in Greek and emulates the conventions of Greek historiography. Antiochus had forced Jews to choose between Jewish tradition and foreign practices, a situation that left those committed to Jewish tradition no choice but to rebel or accept death rather than betray the law. In the absence of such compulsion, it was not necessary to choose between cultures. Some Greek practices—eating unclean food—were clearly forbidden by the laws of Moses, but others were not expressly prohibited, and so Jews might engage in those without feeling they had violated their covenant with God.

It is also worth remembering that Hellenization could be extremely subtle, affecting Jewish culture in ways that Jews themselves did not realize. In fact, the very conception of Jewish identity itself, of what it was that Jews were trying to preserve, changed in this period under the influence of Hellenization. The term *Jew* as it was used in this period still bears geographical and genealogical significance, tying Jews to the land of Judea or identifying them as descendants of the ancestor and tribe of Judah, one of Jacob's sons, but it also now implies something else—a commitment to a way of life defined by adherence to certain laws and customs. This shift in Jewishness from an identity ascribed to people at birth or by virtue of their birthplace to one that they generated through their own actions and convictions is so significant that some scholars see this period as the transitional moment when Judean culture evolved into something we can think of as a religion, Judaism, a voluntarily undertaken form of identity constituted not by descent or geography but by religious belief and ritual practice.

The strongest evidence for this argument is the fact that this period gives us our earliest stories of conversion, of non-Jews *choosing* to become Jewish by adopting a Jewish way of life. There is the conversion of the Idumeans and other non-Jews at the behest of the Hasmoneans—a choice made under the threat of expulsion but nonetheless cast as a choice—as well as fictional stories of converts, like one in the apocryphal book of Judith about an Ammonite named Achior who converts after he witnesses Judith's defeat of her enemies. Second Maccabees features such stories as well, including an episode in which Antiochus himself decides to become Jewish shortly before his death. Such stories reflect the same shift from a location-based or tribal conception of identity to a conception of Jewishness as an identity available to anyone of any ancestry or geographical background willing to commit to God and follow the laws of Moses.

Some Jewish sources in this period describe this way of life by the Greek term *politeia*, "citizenship," and that might reveal something about the origins of the shift in question. The Hellenistic definition of citizenship, spread through the Near East as the institution of the polis itself spread, was often tied to birthplace and descent, but it also allowed for the possibility of someone not born into a community to become a member of it by adopting its laws. This notion of citizenship colored how Jews defined what it meant to be a Jew, as reflected in Josephus's description of the Jewish community as a *politeia* to which Moses invited "all who desire to come and live under the same laws with us, (the prophet) *holding that it is not family ties alone which constitute membership but agreement in the principles of conduct*" (*Against Apion*, 2.210). The laws that defined this community, the laws of Moses, were not an invention of the Hellenistic age, but their significance as the basis of Jewish identity—adherence to these laws making one a Jew regardless of whether one was born in Judea—may have developed in light of the Hellenistic conception of what it meant to be a citizen, a free member of a community.

(Slaves were a different story. Slavery continued as an everyday, taken-for-granted reality among Jews in antiquity, as it did among Greeks and Romans. The Bible imposed limits and protections in terms of how the Israelites treated fellow Israelites who had fallen into slavery, but it did not question the institution itself, and Jews in the Hellenistic period accepted slavery as a divine punishment for sin that enslaved peoples had brought on themselves. It is not at all clear that slaves had a choice to practice a religion different from that of the household they served.)

In our review of the Ptolemaic period, we noted that Jewish embrace of Greek culture did not necessarily entail an abandonment of their identity as Jews. The history of the Maccabees helps to illustrate a related point: Even those Jews who were highly resistant to foreign culture and were willing to risk death to protect their ancient tradition against such innovations were transformed by the encounter with Hellenistic culture. Those Jews, too, were in the orbit of Greek language and social convention, drawing on it when it was in their interest to do so, and ironically, their effort to battle the Greeks in the Maccabean Revolt only intensified their exposure to Greek culture, bringing them into direct contact with Greek rulers and their ways. Jews could choose the degree to which they emulated the Greeks, deciding not to speak, eat, or worship like them, but the very idea that one had such a choice, that one became a Jew by acting Jewish or a Greek by acting Greek, is yet another effect of Hellenistic influence.

Emerging Religious Differences

We have seen that an important value in Jewish culture of this period was tradition, which in this context we can define as a commitment to preserve what the Jews had inherited from their ancestors, including the laws of Moses, the Temple, and other connections to their biblical forebearers. The changes we have been charting—the imposition of foreign rule and Hellenization—threatened these connections, but the rupture was neither complete nor irreversible in the minds of Jews, and they invested tremendous effort—and sometimes risked their lives—to preserve them.

A deep attachment to tradition was widespread among Jews in this period. We have already noted the revival of archaic Hebrew script, both in coins and in biblical texts from this period, and a similar engagement with the past is reflected in Jewish literature from this time, virtually all of it engaged in the Bible, often emulating its genres and style. The Dead Sea Scrolls give us some of our earliest evidence of the prayers that Jews recited, and these, too, routinely evoke precedents from the biblical past, employ biblical phraseology, and yearn for God to act in the present as he did in biblical times. The most influential social class in this period, the priesthood, was one that derived its authority from its connection to biblical figures like Aaron, and the Jerusalem Temple, though newly constructed in the Second Temple period, also linked Jews to the biblical past through its cultic vessels, vestiges of Solomon's Temple that survived its destruction. With Jews spread now over several continents, divided by the languages they spoke and the different political contexts in which they lived, what seems to have united their culture is this allegiance to tradition, to the laws of Moses, to the customs of the ancestors, and to the Temple.

But the importance of such tradition also introduced new divisions, differences over what it consisted of and how to sustain it. The most important inheritance from the past were the laws of Moses, the Torah, but Jews differed over how to interpret and apply their commandments. For many Jews, moreover, tradition was more than just the Bible; it might include other sacred texts that purported to record divine revelation, or unwritten traditions transmitted from generation to generation by word of mouth or by example. Also at the center of Jewish tradition was the Temple. At the same time, however, Jews were divided by struggles over who was entitled to be high priest, how to enact sacrificial and purity law, and even what calendar to follow when scheduling the festivals.

One of the schisms that seems to have emerged at this time was that between Jews and the descendants of the northern tribes of Israel, the people later known as the Samaritans. The Samaritans also saw themselves as the descendants of Israel bound by the law of Moses, but they believed that the cult it established was now located not in Jerusalem, as the Jews believed, but in the north, on Mount Gerezim, a mountain near the modern-day Palestinian city of Nablus. The Bible, of course, places this cult in Jerusalem, claiming that it was located there by David and Solomon, but that was a belief based in Jewish interpretation of the laws of Moses.

Figure 3.5 Members of the contemporary Samaritan community of Nablus in the act of offering a Passover sacrifice.

Source: Photo courtesy of Stefan Schorch.

The Samaritans developed a different conception of Mosaic law, which never specifies Jerusalem as the intended location of the Temple cult. In the Samaritan understanding of biblical history, they were the ones to continue the covenant established by Moses, and the Jews were Israelites who had gone astray. What we know about Samaritan belief comes from a later period (the Samaritan community survives to this day, albeit with a population of a few hundred; see Figure 3.5), but the origins of their conflict with the Jews seem to go back to the Persian period, as corroborated by the excavation of a temple first established on Mount Gerezim in this period.

By the second century BCE, the Hasmonean age, there had also emerged sharp differences within the Judean community itself, among different religious groups. The catalyst for some of this conflict appears to have been the political and social turmoil caused by the conflict between Antiochus and the Maccabees. For centuries, the high priest in Jerusalem had come from the line of a revered biblical priest, Zadok, a high priest from the time of David and Solomon. The Zadokite line lost this position in the time of Antiochus's persecution, and when the high priesthood was eventually claimed by the Maccabees—making them and their Hasmonean successors the ultimate guardians of the Temple cult—this seemed wrong to many Jews. Doubts about the Temple and the legitimacy of its priesthood seem to have fueled the rise of dissident religious groups, some founded by displaced priests like Onias, who went on to establish a Jewish temple in Egypt, others perhaps constructing alternatives to Temple worship, as we will see may have been the case of the Dead Sea Scrolls sect.

Apart from the disruption caused by Antiochus's actions and the Maccabean Revolt, other factors contributed to the rise of these divisions as well, such as the rising influence of a new kind of religious leader. The priestly class had the authority to define proper religious behavior, but only within the precincts of the Temple, and even there its authority became increasingly suspect in the wake of Antiochus's persecution and the Maccabean Revolt. To understand their obligations as Jews, many turned to other kinds of religious authorities, charismatic teachers, and prophets with different ideas about God, the Torah, and how to live one's life. In many cases, such leaders derived their authority from their ability to interpret the biblical text, but their authority might also derive from their knowledge of oral traditions. The main point to grasp is that they functioned as authoritative guardians of tradition: Through their interpretive efforts, they determined the particulars of biblical law and the meaning of biblical stories, they guided their followers in their understanding of the past and the future, and they functioned as intermediaries between Jews and their ancestors, and between Jews and their God. The priests by no means lost their influence in Hellenistic Judea, but they had to compete for that influence with figures whose influence came from their expertise, their communication skills, in some cases their supernatural or prophetic ability, and the devoted efforts of their followers.

Under the influence of these leaders, most of whom are unknown to us as named individuals but whose influence we can piece together from our textual evidence, there emerged in this period several competing groups of Jews bonded together not by kinship, as were the priests and the Maccabees, but by a shared understanding of tradition. We know of three of these groups by name: the Pharisees, the Sadducees, and the Essenes, groups best known to us from the writings of Josephus from the first century CE but arising much earlier in the second century BCE. Scholars often refer to these groups as sects, but whether that label is appropriate depends on what one means by *sect*. The definition we accept here is a small, well-organized group that breaks away from a larger community in the belief that it alone embodies the ideals of that community. By this definition, the Essenes probably qualify as a sect. Josephus reports that they had special rules of admission, and they often lived together in tightly organized communities bound together by the shared ownership of property and ritualized communal meals.

The label does not apply quite as well to the groups known as the Sadducees and the Pharisees. The Sadducees may have been more a social class than a sect. Their name connects them to Zadok, the legendary priest, and they may have consisted mostly of wealthy priests. The Pharisees bear a name that seems to have originally meant "separatist," as if they had withdrawn from the larger society, but they, too, don't quite adhere to our definition of a *sect*. They were a larger group than the Essenes, and they seem less marginal, drawing a lot of support from the larger community, not separating themselves from politics but exerting significant influence over it. Even the Hasmoneans, though sometimes at odds with the Pharisees, ultimately felt compelled to align themselves with their perspective because of their popularity. Were the Pharisees organized or distinct enough as a group to classify as a sect as we have defined that term here? The question has to remain an open one: It may be more accurate to describe them as a network of teachers who shared common traditions and beliefs.

Perhaps a better label than *sect* is "schools of thought" or "philosophies," the original meaning of the Greek term *haireseis* that Josephus uses to describe these movements. Many of the differences he notes do indeed seem philosophical, reflecting different ideas about the nature of human existence, and the term becomes even more appropriate when one notes that Greek philosophical schools in this period—Cynicism, Epicureanism, and Stoicism—were not just intellectual perspectives but specific groups of teachers and their disciples who socialized and sometimes lived together. Like such schools, groups like the Pharisees and Essenes were marked by distinctive beliefs and ideas. The Pharisees held that everything is determined by fate but also allowed room for humans to make their own decisions. They also believed that the soul survives the death of the body: The virtuous received a new life, while the sinful suffered eternal punishment. The Sadducees denied the immortality of the soul and the governance of fate, believing that humans have free choice between good and evil. Like the Pharisees, the Essenes believed in the immortality of the soul and in divine providence, but they did not make the same allowance for humans to determine their own fate. Described in this way, these groups sound like philosophies, and in fact, seeming to clinch the connection, Josephus likens the Pharisees to the Stoics.

To define such groups only by their beliefs is also misleading, however, because what also distinguishes these groups is what they define as the proper way of life. The Pharisees' conduct was governed by the laws of Moses, but also by what

Figure 3.6 Aerial view of an ancient settlement at Qumran near the Dead Sea where, according to many scholars, the sect that produced the Dead Sea Scrolls once lived.

Josephus calls the "tradition of the fathers," laws not written in Scripture that may have been transmitted orally from elders to disciples. This may refer to the oral tradition that would come to be known as the Oral Torah in rabbinic Judaism (see Chapter 5), in which case it conceivably governed many aspects of life not explicitly addressed in biblical law, ranging from Sabbath observance to conversion to the laws of purification to the distinctions between various kinds of oaths (all subjects of debates between Jesus and the Pharisees according to the New Testament). Josephus also tells us that the Pharisees were recognizable by a kind of shared ethos: They simplified their lifestyle and avoided luxury, were supportive of each other and the community, laid great emphasis on the observance of the commandments—a quality that the New Testament's references to the Pharisees stress as well—and were very deferential to their elders. The Essenes, too, were distinguished by their lifestyle: common ownership of property; the exclusion of wives from the community; no ownership of slaves; devotion to menial labor; a regimented daily life of prayer in the morning, work, and communal meals conducted in an environment of respectful silence; and an extremely strict understanding of the law that entailed executing anyone blaspheming the name of Moses and prohibited going to the bathroom on the Sabbath.

One of the reasons the Dead Sea Scrolls are so important—apart from what they reveal about the history and evolution of the biblical text—is that they include documents produced by one of these communities. Which community, though, is a matter of recent scholarly controversy. A Roman writer named Pliny placed an Essene settlement between Jericho and the En-Gedi oasis, near where the scrolls were found, and the discovery of a settlement in that area at a site called Qumran may be the remains of that settlement. The community described by the scrolls also resembles the Essenes in many ways: It, too, had strict initiation procedures, communal ownership of property, overlapping theological beliefs, like its conviction that everything had been determined by God in advance, and even similar toilet habits. Though most scholars identify the Dead Sea Scrolls sect as Essene, the Essene hypothesis is not without its weakness, and some scholars have argued for identifying the sect as a branch of the Sadducees. Whoever this community was, the textual remnants it left behind offer us a chance to view one of these groups from the inside out, not as this group appeared to outsiders, but from the perspective of those who belonged to it.

Although we do not know how this community came to be, scholars have drawn out some insights about its origins and history from the scrolls themselves. Sometime in the first half of the second century, probably after Antiochus's persecution, the sect coalesced around a leader known as the Teacher of Righteousness. His identity is unknown, but he seems to have been a priest or a religious expert who fell into conflict with the Jerusalem authorities, especially a figure known as the "Wicked Priest," who may have been the high priest at that time (the "Wicked Priest" has been identified with one of the Maccabees, Jonathan or Simon, but his identity is a mystery, and the title "Wicked Priest" might have been applied to multiple priests). For reasons that are unclear, in 150 BCE or so, the Teacher and his followers withdrew into the Judean wilderness, where, scholars believe, they established the settlement near the Dead Sea uncovered at Qumran, located very close to where the scrolls were found (Figure 3.6).

Many of the Dead Sea Scrolls were not written by this community. Works found there, like 1 Enoch and Tobit, were known from translations into other languages that survived into the present and were available to scholars well before the discovery of the scrolls. Their discovery in the caves of Qumran revealed the Hebrew or Aramaic original of these texts, but they weren't composed by the Dead Sea Scrolls community itself. Other texts found in the caves do seem to come from this community, however, reflecting its specific beliefs and practices, and among other insights, these reveal it to have been a sect as we have defined that term. The community of the scrolls was highly organized, disciplined, communitarian, and hierarchical; its members ate, prayed, and studied together, and their behavior was strictly regulated under the supervision of specially appointed officials and teachers. Texts like the *Community Rule* and the *Damascus Document*, found in multiple copies, lay out the rules and rituals that this community was to follow, including rituals to allow initiation into the group and its secrets, expel transgressors, and stage the periodic renewal of one's commitment to the community.

Contrary to what scholars used to believe, members of the community may not have practiced celibacy—some of the scrolls assume the permissibility of marriage and children—but the community was dominated by men closely bonded to one another by their shared religious life and studies. Evidence for the community's social organization is a cemetery excavated at Qumran where men are not buried with their families but together in the main part of the cemetery, while women (and one child) were found buried in extensions from the main section.

In another common manifestation of a sectarian orientation, the members of this community seem to have been very alienated from the outside world. One of the last scrolls to have been published, a composition known as the *Halakhic Letter*, suggests there was a period in the community's history when it tried to reach out to the authorities in Jerusalem to resolve its disagreements with them. The letter dissents from their views on religious matters, like the status of non-Jewish offerings in the Temple, sexual practice, and purification rules, but it does so diplomatically. The letter might reflect a stage in the community's history before it was completely alienated from Jerusalem. Other documents express more hostility to outsiders, however.

Biblical commentaries among the scrolls, using a distinctive interpretive technique to detect hidden prophetic meanings in the biblical text that scholars have come to refer to as pesher, complain of conflict with the Wicked Priest and another unnamed foe known as the "Liar" or the "Scoffer," a rival of the Teacher of Righteousness. Other sectarian texts also allude to persecution or tensions with outsiders. Even apart from its grievances against specific individuals, there is much that upset the community about the religious conduct of other Israelites, including their use of what the community believed to be the wrong calendar, a 354-day lunar calendar that followed the cycles of the moon instead of a 364-day solar calendar. Jubilees—not written within the community but very important to it, judging from the number of copies found among the scrolls—describes the use of the lunar calendar as an imitation of foreigners and their festivals. This perception of the lunar calendar as a religious mistake had serious consequences: From the perspective of the author of this text, it meant that the sacrifices and festivals observed in the Jerusalem Temple were being practiced on the wrong days and were therefore not in accord with God's commands in the Torah. This might well have represented one of the grievances that alienated the Dead Sea Scrolls community from the priests in Jerusalem, preventing them from participating in the sacrifices offered in the Temple.

One interesting insight that has emerged from the study of the scrolls is the role of language as a kind of social barrier used to insulate the community from the outside world. The scrolls composed within the community itself are written in a purified dialect of Hebrew modeled on that of the Torah and purged of loanwords from other languages. It can also use code words like "Wicked Priest" that only a member of the community could understand. One scholar has described its Hebrew as an "anti-language," a deliberate attempt to use language to distinguish itself from other Jews believed corrupted by their exposure to foreign culture.

The Dead Sea Scrolls community grew so antagonistic toward the outside world, in fact, that it seems to have imagined itself at war with it. The reader might recall that the Bible contains prophecies of a future time when God will intervene in the world to save his people and punish the wicked. Such ideas developed in the Second Temple period into what is known as eschatology, speculation about the final events of history. Many Jews were keen to know what would happen then, reading "apocalyptic" texts like Daniel and 1 Enoch to learn what lay in store for them (the term apocalypse, from the Greek for "the lifting of a veil," was used as a title for one such text, the New Testament book of Revelation, and from that it came to be used to describe the end of days or texts that forecast the end of days). People's visions of the end included a final catastrophic war between God and his enemies, a final judgment of those enemies and of all that had been lost over the course of Israel's history—the rebuilding of the Temple, a return of the exiles to the Promised Land, the restoration of the Davidic king.

The Dead Sea Scrolls sect went a step further, however, not merely trying to visualize the eschatological future, but also actively preparing for it. Indeed, its members believed that they themselves were living at the beginning of the end of days, the final era of judgment and deliverance, and imagined this age coming about through a battle, what we would now call an apocalyptic war, in which it would join with God's forces to help defeat the enemy. A description of this war appears in a text called the *War Scroll*, which describes it as a

ANSWERING SOME QUESTIONS ABOUT THE DEAD SEA SCROLLS

Where and How Were the Scrolls Discovered?

The scrolls were hidden in a series of caves in the Judean wilderness near the northwest shore of the Dead Sea. Most of the scrolls were discovered in the period between 1947 and 1956, with one notable exception that had been discovered much earlier and in an unexpected location. In 1896, Solomon Schechter (a scholar of Judaism in Cambridge who eventually went on to play an influential role in shaping the Jewish Conservative movement in America) found two manuscripts of what would later be recognized as the *Damascus Document* in a storehouse of sacred texts in a Cairo synagogue known as the Cairo Genizah. It was not until the latter discovery of this same composition among the Dead Sea Scrolls that scholars realized what it was. How it got from Judea to a Cairo synagogue is unclear, but we do know that people have been finding hidden scrolls in the Judean wilderness since antiquity. Apart from the Damascus Document, the Dead Sea Scrolls began to come to light after a chance discovery in 1947, when a Bedouin shepherd in search of lost sheep found seven scrolls concealed in large jars in what would later be labeled Cave 1. They were passed on to antiquities dealers, who sold them to scholars, and the latter began to excavate that cave and others nearby. The nearby site of Qumran was also excavated in the 1950s, and finds there seemed to associate the ancient settlement there with the scrolls, including what scholars thought were tables used by scribes and two inkwells, but the link between the Qumran settlement and the scrolls is debated to this day.

Are the Dead Sea Scrolls the Greatest Manuscript Discovery of All Time?

The scrolls are significant for many reasons. They give us our earliest evidence of the biblical text and help us understand its development. They give us an insider's view into an early Jewish sect. Although not mentioning Jesus and not Christian texts themselves, they illumine the Jewish background from which Christianity emerged, including concepts like "the new covenant." Prayer texts from Qumran shed light on the early history of Jewish liturgy, and the legal and interpretive texts among the Dead Sea Scrolls generate interesting connections with later rabbinic Judaism. It has now been 70 years since their discovery, and scholars are still learning from the scrolls.

But are they the *greatest* manuscript discovery of all time? That is debatable. For all the insights they offer, they have not fundamentally changed our understanding of Jewish history in this period. Scholars still pretty much rely on sources like 1 and 2 Maccabees and Josephus for our basic understanding of this period, including our understanding of early Jewish sectarianism. Meanwhile, other manuscript discoveries have revealed many more manuscripts than the 900 or so texts discovered among the Dead Sea Scrolls (of which about 115 compositions have been attributed to the Dead Sea Scrolls sect). The aforementioned Cairo Genizah has yielded more than 200,000 fragmentary texts that cover a period of 1,000 years, shedding new light on everything from ancient texts like *Ben Sira* and the *Damascus Document* to medieval social, economic, and religious life. The Cairo Genizah dwarfs the Dead Sea Scrolls in what it tells us about Jewish history. There is no doubt that the scrolls are a priceless intellectual treasure, but a sensationalist media has slighted the significance of other discoveries, and the public's fascination with them may be damaging the scrolls themselves since there are now reports that the almost-nonstop traveling exhibition of the scrolls, while stoking the curiosity of hundreds of thousands of people, is threatening their preservation.

Was There an Attempt to Cover Up the Dead Sea Scrolls?

It is true that by the late 1980s, many of the Dead Sea Scrolls had not yet been published, including important documents, such as the *Halakhic Letter*, their appearance delayed by the small size of the publication team, lack of funding, and other haphazard factors. The delay was frustrating, but the work of piecing together and deciphering the thousands of fragments involved was painstaking, and many scholars were content to wait for the official team of scholars charged with publishing the scrolls to complete their work. After decades, however, some lost patience and accused the team of being too controlling—or, worse, of deliberately suppressing the scrolls for fear that their content would undermine Christianity. Pressure from such groups, and especially the publication of unofficial reconstructions and photographs, helped speed up official publication in the 1980s and 1990s. While the original team was not faultless, there is no reason to think there was a calculated plot to suppress the scrolls for fear of what they might reveal.

What Is the Most Interesting Newly Discovered Text Among the Scrolls (Apart From Biblical Manuscripts and Other Texts Previously Known From Other Sources)?

That depends on what you find interesting. Many people are intrigued by the *Copper Scroll*, a text inscribed on copper sheets rolled up in the form of a scroll, because it represents a kind of treasure map, instructions for how to find an assortment of treasure hidden in Jerusalem and its vicinity. This treasure might represent the wealth of the Temple hidden in the time of its destruction by the Romans, but some believe that the treasure never existed since none of it has been found (and many people have looked). Texts that seem to anticipate Christian beliefs—texts like the so-called *Aramaic Apocalypse* that contains the phrase "son of God" or a text that purportedly referred to a "pierced messiah"—generated excitement initially but have proven disappointing, not actually saying what people thought they said. The scrolls include astrological texts, exorcistic texts, and texts written in secret code, but these are too fragmentary to tell us very much. Some of the most informative texts are probably the least interesting to read, at least to those looking for some kind of adventure story or profound spiritual insight. If one is interested in the history of Jewish law and legal interpretation, works like the *Halakhic Letter* can draw you in. If one is interested in the history of Jewish worship, one might study texts like the *Word of the Luminaries*, a collection of supplicatory prayers that anticipate later rabbinic prayer in some respects, or *The Songs of the Sabbath Sacrifice*, a collection of angelic hymns recited on successive Sabbaths that reflects the sect's belief that it was capable of interacting with the angels and joining them in heavenly praise. The best sources for understanding the community itself are works like the *Damascus Document* and the *Community Rule*, which give us insight into its organization and activities. Virtually all of the Dead Sea Scrolls are fascinating for one reason or another; what makes them interesting are the kinds of questions we bring to them.

Are There More Scrolls Yet to Be Discovered?

Many of the caves in the Judean wilderness have been searched, but there may be others that have yet to be found, and who knows what can yet turn up in the antiquities market? A controversial Israeli expedition called "Operation Scroll," happening in the 1990s, just as Israel was poised to withdraw from the territory of Jericho, found documents in caves in that region (though nothing as dramatic as the Dead Sea Scrolls). More recently, an intriguing text dubbed *The Vision of Gabriel* showed up in a private collection, a Hebrew text inscribed onto a 3-foot-tall stone tablet and possibly connected to the Dead Sea Scrolls (its origins are unknown, however, and it is hard to make sense of its partially preserved content), and archaeologists have uncovered a twelfth cave that probably once held Dead Sea Scrolls that were looted. Most recent of all (at the time that we write this) is the discovery of fragments preserving a Greek text of the biblical books of Zechariah and Nahum, though the cave where these fragments were found was not connected to the Qumran community but to a somewhat later group.

There is no doubt people will continue to search for additional scrolls, but the desire to satisfy one's curiosity does come at a cost, encouraging the unscrupulous to loot sites and to fabricate forgeries, like a recently publicized collection of 70 metal books supposedly found in a cave in Jordan that are very likely to be fakes. Perhaps the most promising way to find new textual material is suggested by the recent use of advanced imaging photography developed by NASA to detect previously unnoticed writing on already-recovered Dead Sea Scrolls fragments. This approach seems to have uncovered traces of a previously unknown manuscript and may yet yield other discoveries and insights.Another recent and intriguing development is the use of Artificial Intelligence (AI) to distinguish different scribe handwriting styles in the scrolls, showing that there are new insights to be drawn from scrolls that have already been discovered.

40-year battle between the "sons of light," God and his army of angels and righteous Israelites, and the "sons of darkness," an army of foreigners and their demonic allies. The *War Scroll* was possibly consulted by the sect as it prepared for a battle that it believed already underway.

Given its effort to withdraw from the outside world and its antagonism to foreigners, did the Dead Sea Scrolls community somehow escape the process of Hellenization that we have been describing in this chapter? Certain aspects of Greek culture it did keep at bay, but even the Dead Sea Scrolls community was not immune to the effects of Hellenization. We have seen that over the course of the Hellenistic age, Jewish identity developed from its origins as a form of kinship and ethnicity into a commitment to a particular way of life motivated by belief and expressed through ritual practice and scriptural interpretation. A practice like conversion, new to this period, is rooted in the belief that people can redefine their identity through their choices and actions, that they can overcome the identity imposed on them by birth and align themselves with a new community. The Dead Sea Scrolls community is born of this same sense of identity, constituted by initiates who freely and publicly affirm their commitment to the community in a covenant ceremony and can be kicked out of the community if they don't adhere to its rules. The sect may have included families, but it was itself an alternative to the family, a group held together not by kinship but by beliefs and rituals. It was what scholars now label a voluntary association, similar to the non-Jewish philosophical schools, clubs, and mystery cults so prevalent in the Hellenistic world, and their resemblance is probably not a coincidence, for what made all these kinds of social organizations possible was the same Hellenistic ethos that reshaped Jewish culture itself at this time, a sense of the community as a *mini-polis* constituted of freely associating individuals, and of membership in that community as a status open to all (or at least open to all adult males) willing to abide by its laws.

The Afterlife of Jewish Hellenistic Culture

The historical period we have been concerned with in this chapter stretched from the fourth century BCE to the first century BCE, but the Hellenization of Jewish culture continued well beyond those years. To illustrate the persistent influence of Greek culture, we conclude this chapter with an example from a later period of history, a Jewish tradition that is both traditional and Hellenized at the same time: the ritualized retelling of the Exodus during Passover.

Even as the Israelites were departing from Egypt, the Bible reports, Moses was commanding them to remember the experience, establishing the rites of the Passover festival as a commemoration of the Exodus. Passover as practiced today, reflecting changes that can be traced back to the third century CE, is very different from the biblical festival, however, when the festival was celebrated with a sacrifice of a lamb. Now, the central act of the Passover festival is a banquet structured by a service known in Hebrew as the *seder* that consists of blessings, prayers, stories, questions, and comments as laid out in a kind of scripted recitation of the Exodus story known as the Haggadah (from the Hebrew for "telling"). One reason for the change in the Passover ritual is the destruction of the Temple, which made it impractical for Jews to offer the Passover sacrifice, but the difference also reflects the impact of Hellenization.

In fact, the Passover meal, as structured by the Haggadah, shares many traits with the customs of the Greek symposium, a ritualized banquet devoted to philosophical discussion. Participants in a symposium would recline for the meal while being served by servants. As they drank wine (the word *symposium* comes from Greek, meaning "to drink together"), they might sing a song in honor of a god or give a speech enumerating the god's special gifts to humankind. When the food was served, its arrival might occasion a question, or one might pick up a piece of food to discuss its origins. All these customs are paralleled in the Haggadah's script for the Passover meal: Jews are to recline at the table and drink four cups of wine. Participants sing songs and recite speeches in praise of God for what he did during the Exodus, and they ask questions about the foods eaten during the meal. The Haggadah even incorporates Greek words, such as *afikomen*, a special piece of matzoh eaten at the end of the seder, which comes from a Greek word for the entertainment after the meal.

None of this means that the Haggadah was consciously modeled on the Greek symposium. To the contrary, its authors deliberately avoided the imitation of Greek practices at odds with their own tradition—the invocation of foreign gods or the kind of excessive revelry and drinking at the end of a meal that might lead to an orgy, as happened in some symposia. Participants in the seder saw themselves as fulfilling an age-old biblical injunction to commemorate the Exodus, and the stories, songs, symbols, and rituals of the Haggadah are mostly modeled on or drawn from the Bible. From the perspective of its participants, in other words, the Passover seder was a traditional Jewish act. But as we have seen, even when Jews resisted Hellenistic influence or sought to insulate themselves from foreign contact, they were still participants in Hellenistic culture. Its influence can be detected in every aspect of Jewish life, even in how Jewish tradition itself was enacted, as the Haggadah illustrates when it draws on the conventions of the Greek symposium to commemorate the Exodus.

The impact of Greek culture on the formation of Jewish culture has been obscured by the passage of time. At its height, the Jewish community in Alexandria—the most influential Jewish community outside of Judea in the Hellenistic period—probably numbered in the hundreds of thousands, yielding such great intellectuals as Philo of Alexandria, a prolific Jewish philosopher active in the first century CE. That community went into decline in late antiquity, however—overshadowed in its influence on Jewish culture by the rabbi-led Jewish communities that developed in Palestine and Babylonia at this time, communities also influenced by Hellenistic culture but not using Greek in the same way. We know of the Septuagint, the writings of Philo, and other accomplishments of the Alexandrian Jewish community only to the extent that its literature was preserved by later Christians.

But the influence of Hellenistic culture transcends the fate of any particular author or community, and its impact on Jewish life was both intensified and broadened by the Romans, who were themselves Hellenized by the time they established an empire that encompassed most of the world's Jewish population. A Jew might oppose Hellenistic influence or be unconscious of that influence, but for Jews living in the Roman Empire, it was not possible to operate completely outside the cultural and social framework that Hellenism had established. Greek language, ideas, laws, and customs would have a major impact on early Christians, such as Paul (yet another Jew who wrote in Greek), and, less obviously but no less importantly, on the sages who would shape rabbinic Judaism—even those who opposed studying Greek and taking Greek names. There was no escaping the influence of Hellenistic culture, because Judaism itself was an outgrowth of that culture, inheriting a distinct identity from the Hebrew Bible but reshaping that identity under the influence of—and in response to—the Greeks.

For Further Reading

For important, if dated, studies of the Jewish encounter with Greek/Hellenistic culture, see Elias Bickerman, *The Jews in the Greek Age* (Cambridge, MA: Harvard University Press, 1962), Martin Hengel, *Judaism and Hellenism: Studies in Their Encounter in Palestine During the Early Hellenistic Period* (London and Philadelphia: SCM Press and Fortress Press, 1974), and William David Davies and Louis Finkelstein, *The Cambridge History of Judaism, Vol. 2: The Hellenistic Age* (Cambridge: Cambridge University Press, 1989). On the impact of Hellenization, see John Collins, *Between Athens and Jerusalem: Jewish Identity in the Hellenistic Diaspora* (Grand Rapids, MI: William B. Eerdmans Publishing, 2000), and Erich Gruen, *Heritage and Hellenism: The Reinvention of Jewish Tradition* (Berkeley: University of California Press, 1998). *Oxford Bibliographies* contains several bibliographies relevant for the study of Hellenistic Jewish history, literature, and religion, but those require a paid subscription. Freely accessible bibliographies do exist, however, such as is provided by Yale University Library. See https://guides.library.yale.edu/hellenisticjudaism/bibliographies.

This chapter's depiction of sectarianism is indebted to Shaye Cohen, *From the Maccabees to the Mishnah* (Philadelphia: Westminster John Knox Press, 1987). On diasporic Jewish life, see John Barclay, *Jews in the Mediterranean Diaspora: From Alexander to Trajan (323* BCE*–117* CE*)* (Edinburgh: T & T Clark, 1996). On the Samaritans, see Reinhold Pummer, *The Samaritans: A Profile* (Grand Rapids, MI: William B. Eerdmans Publishing, 2016).

For surveys of Jewish literature in this period, see George Nickelsburg, *Jewish Literature Between the Bible and the Mishnah* (Philadelphia: Fortress Press, 1981), and Michael Stone, ed., *Jewish Writings of the Second Temple Period* (Philadelphia: Van Gorcum and Fortress, 1984). For a reliable introduction to the Dead Sea Scrolls, see James VanderKam, *The Dead Sea Scrolls Today* (Grand Rapids, MI: William B. Eerdmans Publishing, 1994), and Lawrence Schiffman, *Reclaiming the Dead Sea Scrolls: The History of Judaism, the Background of Christianity, and the Lost Library of Qumran* (New York: Doubleday, 1994). For an accessible translation of Greek Jewish texts, which is also the source of the translation of Ezekiel's tragedy described at the beginning of this chapter, see James Charlesworth, *Old Testament Pseudepigrapha*, Vol. 2 (Garden City, NY: Doubleday, 1985), especially 7–34 (*Letter of Aristeas*); 35–142 (Jubilees); and 775–919 (Ezekiel's tragedy and other Jewish texts in Greek). One can now add to these books online resources, like the website of the Orion Center for the Study of the Dead Sea Scrolls and Related Literature at the Hebrew University, which offers a bibliography and other kinds of information for those interested in the Dead Sea Scrolls: http://orion.mscc.huji.ac.il.

CHAPTER 4

BETWEEN CAESAR AND GOD

In this chapter we move into the era that produced two distinct religions that remain alive to this day: rabbinic Judaism and Christianity. *Rabbinic Judaism* refers to the version of Judaism that, in the centuries following the destruction of the Second Temple in 70 CE, spread from rabbi-led academies in Palestine and Babylonia to the rest of the Jewish world and now shapes the religious beliefs and practices of Jews today. Christianity emerged from its origins as a movement within Jewish society to become a distinct religion, with some 2.5 billion adherents presently, about a third of the world's population. Both movements began in the same period and have many similarities, but they developed in different directions, and by around 100 CE, Christianity was drawing more non-Jewish followers than Jewish followers. Covering a period that moves from the age of the Second Temple into the period that scholars refer to as "Late Antiquity," this chapter introduces the political, religious, and social changes that produced the early Christian movement and set the stage for the emergence of rabbinic Judaism.

Roman Conquest and Its Impact on Jewish Life

The Maccabees claimed to have the support of God in their battles with the Greeks, but there was another, more earthly power that they turned to as well: the Romans. The Romans were already so powerful by this time that the mere possibility they might intervene was intimidating, and the Maccabees' efforts to cultivate a "friendship" with them (a euphemism used at that time to describe political alliances) may help explain why the Seleucids, who had been defeated by the Romans in the past, were willing to end their conflict with the Jews. In the end, however, it was not the Jews' Greek foes but their Roman "friends" who proved more dangerous. In the next century, the help that Rome offered the Jews became a pretext for taking over Judea, and Roman rule would prove to have devastating consequences for their traditional way of life that went beyond anything that happened in the Seleucid period.

The event that opened the door for the Romans was a feud that broke out between two Hasmoneans, Aristobulus II and Hyrcanus II, over who would succeed their mother, Salome Alexandra, who died in 67 BCE. By then, the Roman general Pompey was in the area, having taken over the territory that had belonged to the former Seleucid kingdom, and he used the conflict between Aristobulus and Hyrcanus to insert himself into Judean politics as a kind of impartial arbiter. After hearing the claims of each side, he initially deferred making a decision, but when Aristobulus proved uncontrollable, Pompey moved against him. In 63 BCE, he arrested Aristobulus

DOI: 10.4324/9781003611592-5

and marched on Jerusalem to root out what was left of his support.

Pompey scandalized the Jews by entering the Temple, a space forbidden to all but the priests, but according to Josephus, he was otherwise highly respectful of Jewish tradition, refraining from looting the Temple's contents and ordering the resumption of its sacrifices. While definitely intent on eliminating any resistance, he seemed to want to respect Jewish religious sensibilities. He also seemed to want to restore self-rule to the Jews, establishing Hyrcanus as ruler of Judea. Even as he did so, however, Pompey made it clear that he was really in charge now, taking much of the territory the Hasmoneans had ruled and putting it under a Roman governor and reducing Judea to the status of a tribute-paying dependent. Judea was not fully incorporated into the Roman Empire for some time, but it was from this moment, as Josephus would later note, that the Jews became subject to Rome.

The ensuing centuries of Roman rule saw many momentous changes in Jewish culture. It was during the Roman period, in the wake of major Jewish revolts in the first and second centuries CE, that Judea lost much of its Jewish population, and there was a shift in the center of Jewish communal life from Jerusalem to a region north of Judea and to diasporic locations, like Babylon and Rome. During this period, Jewish religious life became more diffuse as well. After the destruction of the Temple in 70 CE, Jews developed new ways of worshipping and interacting with God that were not dependent on the offering of sacrifice or the physical building of the Temple: new forms of prayer, for example, that could be practiced in the synagogue. Many of the Jewish groups we encountered in Chapter 3—the Hasmoneans, Pharisees, Sadducees, and Essenes/Dead Sea Scrolls sect—disappeared by the second century CE, while new non-Temple-centered movements began to flourish, including those which generated what we now call Christianity and rabbinic Judaism.

Too much happened during the Roman period to fit into a single chapter, and so we have opted to divide our coverage of this period into two. The present chapter covers the early Roman period, from 63 BCE to 135 CE, from Pompey's conquest to the Jewish revolts of the first and second centuries CE. Chapter 5 follows Jewish culture into the seventh century CE, by which time its center of gravity had shifted from a Roman-controlled Palestine to a Persian-controlled Babylonia. Along the way, we will touch on significant political and religious developments: the rise and decline of the Herodian dynasty, Jewish revolts against Rome and their impact, the birth of Christianity and its split from Judaism, and the eventual "rabbinization" of Judaism.

In some ways, the Romans were not that different from the Jews. Like Jewish society in antiquity, Roman society was agrarian-based, patriarchal, and highly traditional. The Romans revered their gods and cherished the traditions bequeathed to them by their ancestors. Like Jewish culture, Roman culture, too, had been transformed by its encounter with the Greeks, still using Latin in Rome itself but embracing Greek in the eastern part of its empire and, especially among its elite, adapting its own cultural traditions in light of Greek culture. By the second century BCE, however, Jewish culture and Roman culture were on sharply divergent paths because, by then, the Romans were operating in the Hellenistic world from a position of much greater power than the Jews. By dint of its military power and manipulation of alliances, Rome reshaped the Hellenistic world, establishing itself as the supreme power by the first century BCE.

How the Romans achieved this position of supremacy is a subject for another book, but a few important turning points bear mentioning. By the fourth century BCE, the Romans had largely consolidated their control over the other peoples of Italy, expanding their reach into the larger Mediterranean. In the Western Mediterranean,

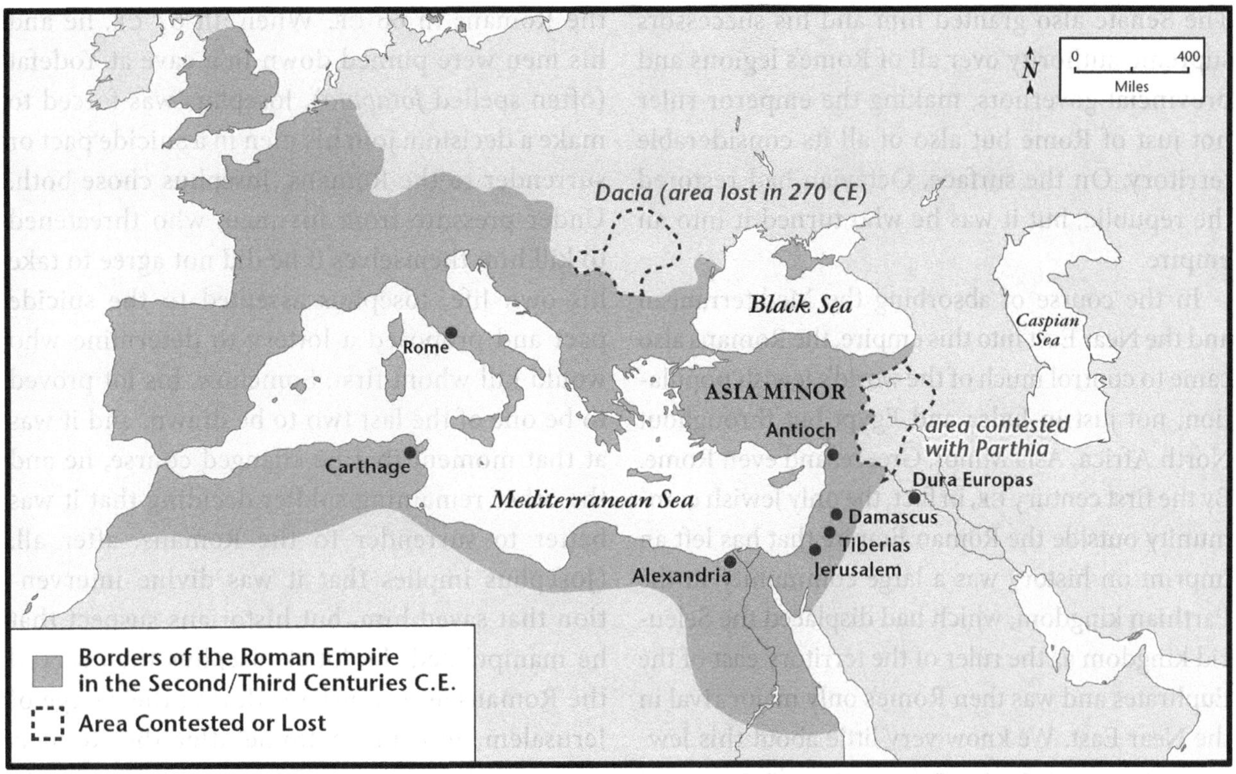

Map 4.1 The Roman Empire in the second/third centuries.

they faced a serious rival, the Phoenician colony of Carthage in North Africa, but by the second century BCE, after three harrowing wars known as the Punic Wars, Rome was able to subdue Carthage once and for all, gaining unchallenged control over Spain and North Africa. In the Eastern Mediterranean and the Near East, it faced the Seleucids and the Ptolemies, among other kingdoms, but it soon overcame their resistance as well. Together with her Roman lover, Marc Antony, Cleopatra VII, the last of the Ptolemies, had hoped to re-energize her kingdom, but Cleopatra and Antony's ambition collided with that of Julius Caesar's posthumously adopted son, Octavian, who, after defeating them in 31 BCE, added the title of Pharaoh of Egypt to his expanding powers. Under Octavian, Rome would control a territory that stretched from Spain in the west to the Euphrates in the east (see Map 4.1).

It was also under Octavian that Rome completed its transformation from a republic to an empire. *Republic* in this context was a kind of oligarchy presided over by the Roman Senate, a council of elders (the word *senate* is related to the Latin *senex*, meaning "old man"). The Roman Senate did not pass legislation, as the US Senate does, but made recommendations and appointed various offices. Pompey's conquest of Judea occurred only a few decades before the Roman republic came to an end in the time of Julius Caesar and Octavian. The latter ostensibly acted to restore the republic, but he purged senators he did not like and packed the Senate with those he did, and the result was a compliant body that voted him more and more offices, powers, and titles, including "Imperitor," from which the word *emperor* derives, and "Augustus Caesar," the reason Octavian is also known as Augustus.

The Senate also granted him and his successors supreme authority over all of Rome's legions and provincial governors, making the emperor ruler not just of Rome but also of all its considerable territory. On the surface, Octavian had restored the republic, but it was he who turned it into an empire.

In the course of absorbing the Mediterranean and the Near East into this empire, the Romans also came to control much of the world's Jewish population, not just in Judea and Egypt but throughout North Africa, Asia Minor, Greece, and even Rome. By the first century CE, in fact, the only Jewish community outside the Roman Empire that has left an imprint on history was a large community in the Parthian kingdom, which had displaced the Seleucid kingdom as the ruler of the territory east of the Euphrates and was then Rome's only major rival in the Near East. We know very little about this Jewish community, however, for our main source of information is the Babylonian Talmud, a source that took shape in the sixth and seventh centuries CE, centuries after the period we are focused on in this chapter (for more on the Talmud, see Chapter 5). Since historians are limited in what they can say about the past by the sources that happen to be available to them, Jewish history between 63 BCE and the age of the Babylonian Talmud is almost completely limited to what happened within the Roman Empire.

Among the sources we do have, the most important for understanding Jewish history in the early Roman period is one we have already mentioned on several occasions: the historian Flavius Josephus. Born in 37 CE to a family of priestly and Hasmonean descent, Josephus was in an excellent position to report on Jewish–Roman relations in the first century CE, fighting against the Romans for the first part of his career, then aligning himself with them in the second half of his life. We know from his own account of his life that he had been a general in the Jewish army during the Jewish Revolt against the Romans in 66 CE. When, in 67 CE, he and his men were pinned down in a cave at Yodefat (often spelled *Jotapata*), Josephus was forced to make a decision: join his men in a suicide pact or surrender to the Romans. Josephus chose both. Under pressure from his men, who threatened to kill him themselves if he did not agree to take his own life, Josephus assented to the suicide pact and proposed a lottery to determine who would kill whom first. Somehow, his lot proved to be one of the last two to be drawn, and it was at that moment that he changed course, he and the other remaining soldier deciding that it was better to surrender to the Romans, after all. (Josephus implies that it was divine intervention that saved him, but historians suspect that he manipulated the lots.) Josephus then served the Romans as a translator during their siege of Jerusalem, moving to Rome after the Romans destroyed Jerusalem in 70 CE and beginning to publish, first, an account of the revolt, then an even lengthier "prequel," the *Jewish Antiquities*, which recounts Jewish history from the biblical age to the time just before the Jewish Revolt, along with a smaller work titled *Against Apion* (a defense of the *Antiquities* against critics) and an autobiography. Since the latest of these sources seem to come from the 90s CE, we assume that Josephus died around 100 CE.

Josephus's writings are the main sources from which our knowledge of this period is derived, but he is by no means our only source of information; we have several other textual sources: the copious writings of the Jewish philosopher Philo of Alexandria, the Dead Sea Scrolls, pseudepigraphical texts written in this period, references to the Jews in Greek and Roman sources, and the New Testament, an invaluable source for early Christian history, of course, but also an important source for understanding Jews and Judaism in the first century CE. Anyone who has traveled to Israel and seen the excavated portion of the Temple complex in Jerusalem, or wandered among the

THE OLDEST JEWISH COMMUNITY IN EUROPE: JEWS IN THE CITY OF ROME

After the destruction of the Second Temple in 70 CE, Josephus moved to Rome, where he produced his writings, and he would have found there a Jewish community that had been in existence for two to three centuries by that point. The earliest Jews in Rome may have been drawn there by trade contacts with Alexandria and by political contacts with Judea, but we do not know for certain when a community there first arose, and the earliest testimony for a Jewish community living in Rome indicates that, at that point, they were not welcome in the city: In 139 BCE, a Roman official expelled the Jews for attempting to spread their sacred rites to the Romans. One can infer that Jews were allowed to return, however, because a robust Jewish community was in existence in Rome by the first century BCE. While there were other periods of hostility, including other periods when Jews were expelled, a Jewish community took root in Rome and became part of the life of the city, along with Christians after they emerge in first century CE.

Julius Caesar grew up in a part of Rome with a substantial Jewish population, and it is possible that that background helps explain how he developed a favorable relationship with Jewish leaders and communities both in Judea and in cities elsewhere in the Roman Empire, issuing decrees that granted them various privileges, including the ability to practice their traditions. After his assassination in 44 BCE, one source reports, Jews mourned his death more than they did any other people. Augustus, the first emperor, developed a similarly positive approach to the Jews.

The oldest known synagogue in Europe was established in the first century in Ostia, the seaport of Rome, which remained in use until the fifth century CE, and scholars have gained some insight into the Jews who lived in the city from its excavation and from ancient catacombs from the period between the second and the fourth century CE—underground cemeteries where Jews buried their dead. According to one estimate, some 100,000 Jews were buried in the catacombs of Rome (only two are extant, but they have not been properly excavated, are not easy to visit, and have been so neglected that, very disturbingly, some of the skeletal remains of the dead still remain there). Inscriptions and graffiti found in these catacombs preserved the names of the people buried there, revealing a bit of information about who they were, their social and economic status, and even a bit about their religious life. There is not a lot of evidence for Jewish life in Rome in the first centuries of its empire, but what little we know suggests a community able to weather or bounce back after various crises in Jewish–Roman relations, continuing into the Middle Ages.

ruins of Caesarea on the coast north of Tel Aviv, or climbed up to the fortress of Masada overlooking the Dead Sea, will know that the Roman period also left behind substantial archaeological evidence. And a fair number of inscriptions and coins offer additional insights into Jewish social, political, and economic life. But without the narratives of Josephus, it would be much harder to fit all this evidence into a larger picture, for he provides us with our only extended narrative of Jewish history in the first 150 years or so of Roman rule.

As dependent as modern historians are on Josephus, however, they have also learned to be cautious in their use of his writings. Some of Josephus's historical claims have been partially corroborated by other sources or by archaeology: His description of the Essenes corresponds in many ways to the Dead Sea Scrolls sect, the excavation of the southwest corner of the Temple

Mount corroborates some of what he says about its architecture, and the discovery of Masada has done much to confirm his account of the battle that happened there after the fall of Jerusalem. But Josephus was an ancient historian, not a modern one: his understanding of how to reconstruct the past was in line with the standards of Greco-Roman historiography of the day, but not with our own standards. He often simply paraphrased the testimony of earlier sources without questioning them or seeking to corroborate their claims, accepted explanations that many historians today would find implausible or simplistic, and even invented speeches and other details to spice up his narrative or make a point.

Also undercutting Josephus's credibility is the evidence suggesting his goal was public relations, both for himself, to defend against accusations of treason, and for his Roman patrons, who saw in their victory against the Jews an opportunity for self-promotion. Josephus's ability to publish his works—indeed, his very survival in Rome, where he had many rivals and critics unhappy with him—depended on his ability to curry favor with the emperor Vespasian and his sons Titus and Domitian, a new imperial dynasty that owed much of its stature to its victory against the Jews during the Jewish Revolt of 66–70 CE. The fact that Josephus took the first name "Flavius," inspired by the family name of his imperial sponsors (the Flavians), reflects his desire to be closely associated with them. Josephus tells us that Titus personally endorsed his account of the Jewish Revolt, designating it the official account. We cannot be certain that he actually had Titus's personal endorsement (this might be another of Josephus's dubious boasts), but it is not hard to see why the emperor might have approved: His historical accounts are clearly works of pro-Roman (and, more precisely, pro-Flavian) propaganda, glorifying Rome's heroism in defeating the Jews, extolling the leadership of Vespasian and Titus, and clearing them of blame for the Temple's destruction (Josephus's account assigns responsibility to the recklessness and sinfulness of the Jewish rebels).

Figure 4.1 Statue of Augustus, the first Roman emperor.

But while his pro-Roman bias undermines Josephus's credibility as a historian, Josephus's pro-Roman sympathies illustrate one way in which Jews responded to Roman conquest; many other like-minded Jews in both Palestine (the Roman name for the region between the Mediterranean Sea and the Jordan River) and diasporic communities like Alexandria adopted a similar attitude toward Roman rule, not just opting to accept it but actively participating in it. The family of Philo of Alexandria, the first-century Jewish philosopher, is an example; one of his nephews, Tiberius Julius Alexander, even became an important governor-general under the Romans, serving as Titus's second-in-command during his siege of Jerusalem in 70 CE. Philo himself may have tried to remain aloof from politics, but he, too, reflects this attitude toward Rome, describing emperors like Augustus as ideal rulers who mirrored the qualities of God in their just and peaceful administration of the world.

The praise of the Romans one can find in the writings of Josephus and Philo may seem fawning and insincere to us, but it reflects a survival strategy that goes back to the Persian period and is reflected in biblical sources, like Deutero-Isaiah, which describes the Persian Cyrus as an agent of God. The Roman Empire brought many advantages—improved infrastructure, relative peace, and a well-developed legal system, along with support and protection for Jewish religious practice and civic rights—and it was also extremely dangerous to try to resist it, as Jews could learn by observing what had happened to other peoples who had attempted to fight the Romans. In their heart of hearts, Jews like Philo and Josephus may have privately detested Roman rule, but whatever secret resentment they nursed, they concluded that outwardly submitting to Rome was the safest course for the Jews, and they may have sincerely believed that the Romans' great power derived from God himself, who was using them to serve his own ends, just as, according to the Bible, he had used the Persians to help the Jews return from exile and rebuild the Temple.

For its part, Rome had reasons of its own to try to win the goodwill of its Jewish subjects. Like the empires that had preceded it, Rome preferred to build its empire on the existing political structure of the societies it ruled, relying on the local aristocracy to rule on its behalf. At first, it did this in Judea as well, but when the Hasmoneans proved too much trouble, Rome pushed them aside in favor of a more pliant ruler, Herod, a descendant of Idumeans who had converted to Judaism under duress during the Hasmonean period and who would go on to rule Judea from 37 BCE until his death in 4 BCE. Herod worked hard to cultivate a good relationship with the Romans, building Caesarea and other cities in honor of Augustus and visiting with him and other high-ranking Romans on several occasions. They, in turn, depended on Herod to keep the peace in Judea, which he was able to do with an army that included Romans, Gauls, and Germans. He kept tight control over the priesthood, appointing a friend to the high priesthood, and also over the Sanhedrin of Jerusalem (from the Greek for "meeting" or "assembly"), a kind of supreme court or ruling council that seems to have played an important role in religious and civic affairs in the city (this organization is infamous for its role in the trial of Jesus, but its history and workings are very murky). In exchange for Herod's loyalty, the Romans granted him additional territory and high status within the empire.

Herod is best known for two reasons: his rebuilding of the Temple and the role he plays in the story of Jesus. Both tell us something about the nature of his rule. He was an extremely active builder, initiating the construction of cities like Caesarea, fortresses such as Masada, palaces, theaters, and other kinds of buildings, not just in Palestine, but also as far away as Greece. His expansion of the Temple, a project he undertook in 20 BCE, was his most ambitious project (see Figure 4.2). Employing 10,000 workers and taking years to complete (according to John 46), the project involved the demolition of the existing temple building and the erection of a new complex atop a platform big enough to accommodate courts, gates, porticos, a fortress known as the Antonia, and other large buildings. The newly constructed Temple complex, its massive dimensions now confirmed by excavations of the Temple Mount's support walls, was one of the most awe-inspiring spectacles of the day—so magnificent that, according to Josephus, Titus hesitated to destroy the Temple, because he judged it an "ornament" for the empire.

Herod's interest in the Temple creates the impression of a ruler deeply committed to Jewish tradition, and he might have undertaken the

Figure 4.2 A modern reconstruction of Herod's Temple complex. For a more updated, "virtual" tour of Herod's Temple, see https://www.youtube.com/watch?v=HHLD6RXVLaM.

project to encourage just that perception. Despite the support of Rome, Herod could not take his legitimacy as a Jewish ruler for granted. From the perspective of Jewish tradition, he had no claim to the kingship or the high priesthood since he was not a descendant of David or Aaron; his very Jewishness was in question since his grandfather was an Idumean convert, and not everyone may have accepted the legitimacy of such conversion, especially one that had been undertaken under compulsion (the Idumeans had been forced to convert by the Hasmoneans as part of their effort to Judaize the land of Judea and its bordering regions). To lend stature to his rule, Herod did try to associate himself with the Hasmoneans, taking as his second wife a princess from that family named Mariamne, but their relationship soured, and Herod had her executed. Herod offended his Jewish subjects in other ways as well, introducing various Hellenistic or Roman innovations into Jerusalem, such as athletic games and Greek-style entertainment arenas. His subjects were so suspicious of such undertakings, in fact, that they assumed the theater he built in Jerusalem contained the sort of decoration that violated the biblical command against making images in the likeness of God—and he had to take his critics on a tour of the theater to assure them this was not the case. Herod's rebuilding of the Temple seems another effort to shore up his reputation with his Jewish subjects, casting him as a champion of Jewish piety while also creating a significant public works project that kept a lot of artisans and laborers employed for several decades.

The other reason that Herod is so famous (or rather infamous) is that he appears in the

Gospel accounts in Matthew and Luke of Jesus's birth, and his image there reflects another side of the king. According to Matthew 2:1–18, Herod learned that the king of the Jews had been born in Bethlehem (which, if true, would have undermined his own status as king of the Jews), and, unable to find the child, he ordered the death of all the children of Bethlehem. The story, absent from the other Gospel accounts, does not necessarily record an actual historical event (it may have been composed to suggest a parallel with the Exodus story, recalling Pharaoh's effort to slay Israel's male babies), but it does capture something genuine about Herod's ruthless suppression of rivals. Deeply suspicious of those around him, when Herod sensed that someone was a threat, he did not shirk from killing him or her. Herod's victims included his wife, three of his children, his mother-in-law, John the Baptist, and countless others—a record of ruthlessness that stood out even by Roman standards. A story told centuries later claimed that when Augustus heard that Herod had slain a number of baby boys, including his own child, he quipped that he would sooner be Herod's pig than his son.

In fairness to Herod, though, we might note that his paranoia was not that delusional. He had many rivals, including what was left of the Hasmoneans, and several attempts were made to assassinate him. As a master of the art of survival, however, he was often able to anticipate his enemies and knew how to protect himself, building fortresses at Masada and elsewhere and developing an extensive spy network. Herod managed to rule for more than three decades through a combination of skillful public relations, good intelligence, and sheer brutality.

Herod's successors continued to stay close to Rome, and the family stayed in power through much of the first century CE, but its rule was fractured, and the Herodians were ultimately unable to keep a lid on the tensions within Jewish society. After Herod's death, his sons essentially divided his kingdom. Archelaus (who ruled from 4 BCE to 6 CE) took control of Judea, Samaria, and Idumea; Herod Antipas presided over the Galilee and Perea, areas north of Judea, from 4 BCE to 39 CE; and Herod Philip took responsibility for the Golan in the northernmost part of the country, ruling from 4 BCE to 33/34 CE. Archelaus was a particularly ineffective ruler, so outraging his subjects that Augustus banished him to Gaul, in what is now France, but his brothers fared better in their parts of the Herodian kingdom. A few decades later, in 37 CE, a grandson of Herod, Herod Agrippa I, known as Agrippa I, came to power and briefly revived the fortunes of the Herodian line, winning popular support in Judea through his pious commitment to Jewish tradition, but his reign was relatively brief, as he died in 44 CE. His successor, Agrippa II, and his sister Berenice were unable to sustain control over their subjects in Jerusalem, which broke out in revolt in 66 CE. Herodian rule did not really survive the Jewish Revolt of 66–70 CE, essentially disappearing with the destruction of Herod's Temple in 70 CE.

The Herodians were able to rule for as long as they did, over a century, largely because they had the support of the Romans, but that association may have been part of what cost them their legitimacy with many of their subjects. When a Herodian failed as a ruler, moreover, the Romans had to step in more directly, and that only increased the tensions. After the ill-fated reign of Archelaus, Rome sent officials of its own to administer Judea more directly on its behalf, minor-league governors known first as a prefect and later as a procurator, but these only exacerbated tensions through their cruelty, venality, and disdain for Jewish tradition. The most infamous of these officials was Pontius Pilate, prefect of Judea between 26 and 37 CE (or perhaps 19–37 CE, according to some recent scholars). Pilate is remembered today for his role in Jesus's trial but was notorious among Jews at that time, in Philo's words, because of "the briberies, the insults, the robberies, the outrages and wanton injuries, the executions without trial constantly repeated, the ceaseless and supremely grievous cruelty" (*Embassy to Gaius*, 302). Not every Roman administrator was this bad—Philo has a lot of respect for a governor named Petronius, who helped avoid a major conflict during the reign of Caligula—but Pilate seems to have been typical of many of the procurators who administered Judea in the decades before the great revolt: capable of brutality in the pursuit of maintaining order, understaffed, perhaps venal, and at a loss to understand the Jews and their customs (*see the box* "The Jews in Roman Eyes").

The fact that the Romans had such a hard time ruling the Jews means that Josephus's pro-Roman attitude is not a reliable index of how Jews in general responded to Roman rule. Rome did successfully cultivate close relationships with the elite of Jewish society—the Herodian dynasty, the high priests in Jerusalem, aristocrats like Philo, and others who the Romans hoped would serve as intermediaries with the broader Jewish community. Yet beyond that upper echelon, and even within it, there were many Jews who were deeply resentful of Roman rule, detested the Romans as cruel oppressors, resented their indifference to

THE JEWS IN ROMAN EYES

As we noted earlier, Romans like Julius Caesar developed a positive relationship with Jews, but the Romans could also be very hostile to the Jews, expelling them from Rome itself on several occasions (though allowing them to return) and coming into conflict with Jews in Judea and other communities. The following is a sampling of how the Romans saw the Jews, as voiced by some of Rome's leading thinkers and writers. Note the variety of attitudes reflected in these texts, ranging from Varro's admiration to the hostility of the historian Tacitus and encompassing responses that combine a little of both admiration and hatred.

Varro (Roman scholar living between 116 and 27 BCE): "Yet Varro . . . thought the God of the Jews to be the same as Jupiter, thinking that it makes no difference by which name he is called, so long as the same thing is understood."

Cicero (Roman orator and statesman who lived between 106 and 43 BCE): "Even while Jerusalem was standing and the Jews were at peace with us, the practice of their sacred rites was at variance with the glory of our empire, the dignity of our name, the customs of our ancestors."

Seneca (Roman philosopher who killed himself in 65 CE): "The customs of this accursed race have gained such influence that they are now received throughout all the world. The vanquished have given laws to their victors."

Tacitus (Roman historian living between 56 and 117 CE): "The Jews are extremely loyal to one another, and always ready to show compassion, but toward every other people they feel only hate and enmity. They sit apart at meals and they sleep apart, and although as a race, they are prone to lust, they abstain from intercourse with foreign women; yet among themselves, nothing is unlawful. They adopted circumcision to distinguish themselves from other peoples by this difference. Those who are converted to their way follow the same practice, and the earliest lesson they receive is to despise the gods, to disown their country, and to regard their parents, children, and brothers as of little account."

Source: From Menahem Stern, *Greek and Latin Authors on Jews and Judaism, Jerusalem*: The Israel Academy of Sciences and Humanities, vol I (1974), pp. 210, 197–198, 431; vol II (1980), p. 26. © The Israel Academy of Sciences and Humanities. Reproduced by permission.

Jewish religious tradition, and chafed under the taxes they imposed. We cannot conduct a poll of political attitudes in this period, but it is clear from the uprisings that broke out after Herod's death that something was not working in how Rome was managing the Jews under its control. At least this was the case for Judea. Jews living in other regions might have had a different relationship with Roman rule—Jews in the Galilee seem a bit more willing to come to terms with Roman rule than the Jews of Judea, for example—but what happened between Jews and Rome in Judea had repercussions for Jews throughout the Roman Empire and brought to the surface tensions that were by no means restricted to a particular geographical region.

RESISTING ROME—AND THE AFTERMATH

We have seen that some Jews in this period, including our two most important sources, were ready to argue that Roman rule was good for the Jews. Indeed, Philo describes Emperor Augustus as an ideal ruler—a peacemaker who unified the world, brought civilization to the barbarians, and ended piracy and other social problems. Not every successor lived up to his example, but many did prior to the Christianization of the Roman Empire in the fourth century BCE, professing benevolence toward the Jews. Thanks to archaeology, one can see the constructive impact of Roman rule that might have led Jews like Philo to a positive assessment: the improvement of the water supply in cities like Jerusalem and Caesarea through the building of aqueducts, for example, or the development of better roads, streets, and ports.

Why is it, then, that Roman rule was so unpopular among many Jews? Like other peoples, the Jews wanted to be free, to control their own lives, but that wasn't the only issue. By this point, Jews had lived under foreign rule for many centuries—under the Babylonians, the Persians, and the Greeks—and if anything, Rome was even more adept at controlling large populations, knowing better than to rely on force to control its subjects but using patronage, the bestowal of benefits, to win their gratitude and loyalty. It used this method with the Jews as well, granting Jewish communities special privileges, making donations to the Temple, and developing close relationships with Jewish leaders, like Herod. What is it, then, that led so many Jews not just to hate Roman rule but also to risk and often sacrifice their lives to defy it?

One motive for such resistance was the commitment the Jews felt to traditional practices that the Romans sometimes infringed upon, accidentally or willingly. Some Jews felt that belief in God itself prevented them from submitting to Roman rule. One such group emerged during an uprising that broke out in 6 CE, led by a teacher named Judas, who was opposed to Roman rule as a matter of principle. Only God was king, he proclaimed, and no Jew should submit to a human ruler. Judas seems to have died early on in this conflict, and his supporters scattered, but his message resonated for many Jews, leading to the rise of a movement described by Josephus as the Fourth Philosophy, a kind of revolutionary religious ideology that would survive into the period of the Jewish Revolt, motivating rebel groups like the Sicarii and the Zealots.

This view seems to have been in the minority, and most Jews probably saw no inherent religious conflict with Roman rule despite the Romans' polytheism and use of cult statues. Over time, however, their experience of Roman rule gave many Jews other reasons to see it as a threat to their traditions. During his initial conquest of Judea, the general Pompey had sacked and looted the Temple, resulting in the death of priests, and there were other moments of religious crisis to follow. The most dire was triggered by Emperor Caligula, who, because he was suspicious of the Jews' loyalty to him, sought to install a statue of himself as Jupiter in the Temple, an act that would have probably provoked a rebellion had not the Roman governor Petronius stalled the order long enough for the problem to go away when the emperor was assassinated. That kind of direct threat by an emperor was rare, but more local offenses were more common, committed either through insensitivity or deliberate provocation, and it did not take much to trigger a crisis. Indeed, even a single action of a single soldier could trigger a major confrontation, as when, according to Josephus, a Roman soldier once sparked a riot when he turned his back to a crowd of Jews and, to put things nicely, emitted a loud noise in their faces.

But religion was not the only source of conflict: Jewish restiveness was also fueled by economic hardship. While some Jews prospered under the Romans, which facilitated trade and the accumulation of wealth in the trans-Mediterranean economy that developed under their rule, many Jews fell into poverty. First-century Judea was afflicted with periodic famines and widespread unemployment. Herod's reconstruction of the Temple can be seen as a kind of employment program, giving thousands of laborers work for several decades, but judging from sources like the Gospels, poverty and class divisions were major social problems in first-century Palestine. Roman rule made economic survival much more difficult by confiscating land and imposing various kinds of taxes and tolls (according to one estimate, about 30 percent of a typical farmer's income went to paying taxes). There is not a lot of evidence from which to reconstruct the causes of poverty in this period, but it seems that a number of other causes also contributed to it: famine in the 40s, heightened unemployment after the completion of Herod's Temple, and the consolidation of wealth as Herod and other wealthy people took ownership of much of the land in Palestine.

As a result, many Jews found themselves landless or in debt. Some sold themselves or their children into slavery out of desperation, while others turned to banditry, a rampant problem in Judea during this period. It would be wrong to suggest that conflicts like the Jewish Revolt were peasant uprisings—the rebels included upper-class people, like Josephus himself—but economic grievance was a factor, with the conflict offering an opportunity to end onerous taxation, to loot the palaces of the wealthy, and to get access to the resources of the Temple.

What made Roman rule even harder to bear is that many Jews could imagine a much better reality. Drawing on the traditions of apocalypticism that had taken shape in the Hellenistic period, some Jews in this period also looked forward to a future when God would intervene against the Romans. A number of apocalyptic texts come from the Roman period, including the aforementioned *War Scroll*, which imagines a final battle between the sons of light, perhaps the Dead Sea Scrolls sect itself, and the sons of darkness, which might include the Romans. Many scholars read apocalyptic literature from this time period as a kind of passive resistance, a fantasy that encourages waiting for God to intervene to save his people from their enemies, but it can also be read as an incitement, encouraging Jews to believe that God was about to step in and that they should be prepared for change. We cannot tell for certain, but some Jewish uprisings, perhaps even the Jewish Revolt itself, might have been fueled by the belief that the end-time had arrived or was soon to do so, that God and his angels were about to enter the fray against the enemy and re-establish divine rule over the earth. Texts like the *War Rule* might even have been used as a kind of training manual for such a conflict.

All this helps us understand why Jews resented Roman rule and wanted to bring it to an end, but it does not fully explain why they were so ready to act on this impulse. As Josephus would observe, Roman rule was virtually invincible, and resisting it was suicide. Other peoples had tried to rebel against it and failed, and Rome could be brutal to those who resisted its rule. Among its enforcement practices, the most notorious was the act of crucifixion—the "most wretched of deaths," in the words of Josephus. It was applied specifically to slaves, mutinous troops, and non-Romans who were deemed enemies of the state, and it was meant to be terrifying, staged at the busiest of roads so that many people would see and be deterred from any subversive thought. It was one thing to grumble about the Romans in private or to fantasize in secret about Rome's future destruction at the hands of God; it was another thing to defy the Romans openly, and Josephus was not the only Jew to conclude that it was better to submit to Rome than to heroically resist and perish.

And yet, by 66 CE, many Jews—not all, by any means, but many—were convinced that it was both necessary and feasible to rebel against Rome and were confident enough that they declared their rebellion in the most public of ways: halting the sacrifices offered in the Temple on behalf of the emperor and the Roman people. Thus began what is known by modern historians as the First Jewish Revolt against Rome in Judea, which soon spread to the rest of Palestine. This is the war that Josephus participated in and would go on to describe at such length, and it is arguably the best-documented rebellion of any that occurred under Roman rule.

The event that triggered the revolt was a conflict that broke out between the Jewish and Greek inhabitants of Caesarea, and the subsequent overreaction of the procurator Florus. But what really fueled it were deeper religious, economic, and social grievances that had been taking root in Judean society since Pompey's invasion in 63 BCE. The widespread sense of grievances helps explain why so many Jews supported the revolt. Although Jews in the Diaspora do not seem to have become very involved in the revolt, it drew support from every corner of Jewish society within Palestine itself, from Judea in the south to the Galilee and the Golan in the north, from the poor as well as from members of the wealthy elite, from priests and non-priests. For a time, the rebels were able to shake off Roman rule, forming a kind of government that was able to mount a defensive army and even mint coins, until the Romans sent a force large enough to violently suppress the rebellion.

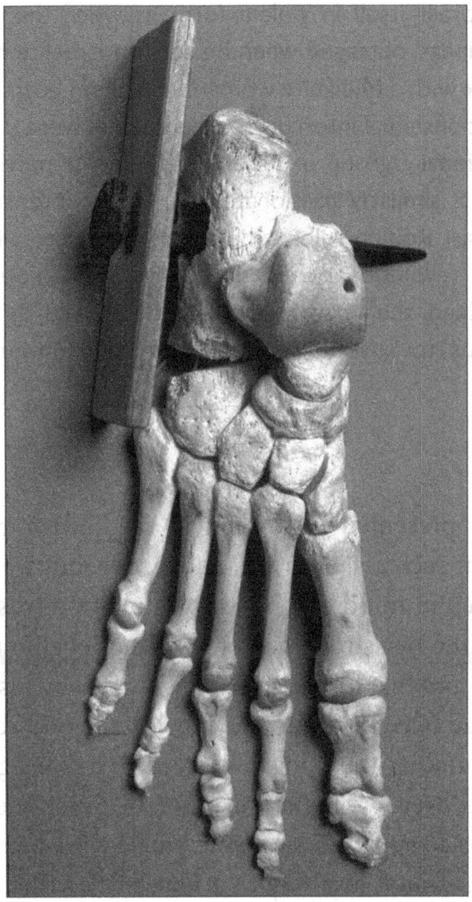

Figure 4.3 A reconstruction based on a foot found with a nail piercing its heel bone discovered in a Jerusalem suburb in 1968. The skeletal remains of the man in question were found in a tomb with a Hebrew inscription reading, "Jehohanan the son of HGQWL." He was in his 20s when he was crucified. We have many accounts of crucifixion, but they lack many details. This find is a very rare piece of archaeological evidence of crucifixion, and the dearth of evidence for the practice makes it difficult to figure out how it was actually carried out or how death occurred. One possible reason that more evidence for crucifixion has not been identified is that the nails used in such executions seem to have been considered a powerful medical amulet and were removed from bodies for that reason.

WHO WERE THE ZEALOTS?

The word *zealot* as used today refers to someone fanatically committed to a cause, and it derives from the name of one of the militant groups active during the Jewish Revolt. *Zeal* in a biblical context refers to a kind of jealous commitment to protect one's God and people, and it could sometimes express itself in violent form, as when the priest Phineas, outraged when he sees an Israelite having sex with a Midianite woman, slays them both in the act of sexual intercourse. The Zealots were a revolutionary group in the first century CE motivated by a similarly passionate and violent intensity to resist Roman rule. Some scholars refer to all Jewish revolutionaries in this period as Zealots, and indeed, the term *zealous* can be applied by Josephus to anyone showing passionate enthusiasm for a cause, but the revolutionary group that he refers to as the Zealots was a specific faction that emerged in the final stages of the revolt, the best remembered of several revolutionary factions that included groups like the Sicarii, named for their use of a certain kind of dagger, and the followers of leaders like Simon, son of Giora. At the end of the revolt, at a point when the Zealots were lodged within the Temple, they came into conflict with some of these rival groups and also turned against the city's provisional government for deciding to surrender to the Romans, killing the high priest and executing others they suspected of treason. Some Zealots were eventually dislodged from the Temple by a rival faction; others remained and died fighting the Romans.

As presented by Josephus, the Jewish rebels appear reckless, even self-destructive, but we have to keep in mind that he was writing in retrospect, after the disastrous outcome of the rebellion was clear, and that his description is shaped by his pro-Roman bias. In reality, the rebels had good reason for thinking they might succeed in a war against Rome. Nero sent the governor of Syria, Cestius Gallus, to suppress the revolt, but he was unexpectedly defeated in a way that boosted Jewish confidence. The Romans were further distracted by the political instability that followed Nero's death in 68 CE, an event that triggered a power struggle in which, in a single year, power quickly passed through three emperors until, finally, Vespasian, the military commander in charge of operations in Judea, established himself in the role. While Rome was distracted in such ways, the Jews in Judea made the most of their advantages: They were far more numerous than the few thousand Roman troops stationed in Palestine on the eve of the revolt, and they could also rely on their knowledge of the terrain and on the formidable defenses of Jerusalem, a city protected by three walls, as well as other Herodian fortresses, such as Masada. The first battle with the Romans would have boosted their confidence even more when, unexpectedly, the rebels were able to rout the enemy. While Rome could have been expected to send a larger force, it had a powerful enemy in the region—the Parthian kingdom, based in present-day Iran, which had once briefly conquered Jerusalem in 40 BCE—and the rebels hoped to draw the Parthians into the war through the mediation of the large Jewish community living in Mesopotamia beyond the Roman Empire.

Aside from the Parthians, the rebels also counted on another powerful ally, one that had helped their ancestors in many previous battles: God. In the decades prior to the revolt, the Romans had had to put down a number of mini-insurrections led by prophet-like figures who had convinced their followers that God was on their side by promising to perform various miracles or to show them divine visions. One such figure, a prophet named Theudas, claimed he could part the Jordan River as if he were Moses or Joshua; another unnamed Egypt prophet led thousands of followers in a failed attempt to take Jerusalem. These movements were inevitably quashed, and their leaders killed, but their failure did not discredit the belief that God himself might one day intervene against the Romans. In fact, just before the revolt, rumors that such intervention was imminent spread like wildfire. Sages discovered in the Torah a prophecy that someone from Judea would rule the world, and people witnessed all kinds of uncanny events that seemed to signal victory: a sword-shaped star appearing over Jerusalem, a bright light appearing around the sanctuary during Passover, and armed battalions hurtling through the clouds. The rebels still believed that God would defend them even at the very end of the war, when the Romans had them pinned down in the Temple Mount.

We know from reading Josephus's retrospective account that their confidence was tragically mislaid. Vespasian's return to Rome to assume the role of emperor temporarily halted Rome's effort to suppress the revolt in Judea, but it was soon resumed under his son Titus. Leading an immense force to subdue Jerusalem, Titus achieved victory within the year, and what helped him in this effort was internal dissension among the rebels themselves. By the time the Romans placed a siege on Jerusalem, the remaining rebels in the city—the Zealots and other groups—had turned on one another, launching attacks against one another as they vied for control over the Temple Mount (*see the box* "Who Were the Zealots?"). It did not help that the city was full of refugees and pilgrims who happened to be there for the festival of Passover, putting greater pressure on the limited resources of a city under siege.

After about six months of this, Titus's army was able to break through Jerusalem's walls and take control of the city and the Temple Mount. In August of 70 CE, the Romans destroyed the Temple. According to Josephus, it had been destroyed against the will of Titus, consumed in a fire started by a soldier acting on his own, but some scholars suspect that Josephus, who sought to curry favor with the imperial family after he switched sides to the Romans, was trying to make excuses for Titus, and they argue that the general did, in fact, order the burning of the Temple. Whatever led to its destruction, the loss of the Temple was a disaster that left such a deep imprint on Jewish memory that it is mourned by Jews to this day, commemorated on the ninth day of the Jewish month of Ab (a fast day known as Tisha B-Av), and its loss wasn't the only reason the Roman destruction of Jerusalem was so devastating. Josephus claims that a million Jews died during the siege of Jerusalem, a number which is probably unrealistically high but which nonetheless suggests the revolt's devastating impact on Judea.

It did take a few more years for Rome to quash all the remaining rebels, but quash them it did. At the fortress atop Masada, some 960 rebels (not the Zealots, but the Sicarii) withstood a Roman siege until 73 CE, but when they saw that the Romans were about to capture the fortress, they decided to kill themselves rather than become slaves (*see the box* "The Mass Suicide at Masada"). After this and a few other mop-up operations, the Romans went to violent extremes to make sure the Jews never rebelled again. Rebel leaders were paraded through the streets of Rome before being executed; the Romans looted the Temple of its vessels, which were carried off to Rome, and did not allow the Temple to be rebuilt; and the Jews were further humiliated by a special tax that redirected funds once intended for the Second Temple to a temple of Jupiter in Rome. In case all this was not enough to get the Jews to think twice about another revolt, Rome stationed an entire legion in Jerusalem to control things there and closed down the temple at Leontopolis in Egypt, lest it, too, become the center of a rebellion.

Yet even these efforts were not enough to convince many Jews to accept Roman rule. Jerusalem had been defeated, but there were Jewish communities now throughout the Roman Empire, some with their own grievances against their non-Jewish neighbors or the Roman authorities and who were not deterred by what happened in Judea. North Africa was one such place. Jews in these places lived alongside large Greek-speaking and native populations, and their tense relationship often became violent. The situation we know best is Alexandria, but it could well have been typical of multiethnic cities in North Africa more broadly. The Greeks and Egyptians of the city had long resented their Jewish neighbors, and Roman rule seemed only to feed their resentment, choosing sides or playing one side off against another. For their part, the Jews—their status in the city precarious—feared and resented their non-Jewish neighbors and occasionally struck out at them as well.

The result was decades of ethnic conflict that sometimes became violent: In 38 CE, Alexandria erupted in anti-Jewish rioting, in which many Jews were killed and synagogues destroyed; in 41 CE, with the death of Caligula, the Jews struck back in a riot of their own; and in 66 CE, the Jews and Greeks fought again in a conflict that ended with a Roman massacre of the Jews. A few years later, some of those involved in the Jewish Revolt evidently recognized that such tensions might allow them to transfer their rebellion to such places, for Josephus tells us that after the Roman victory in Judea, surviving rebels went to Egypt and Cyrene (what is now Libya) and tried to stir things up there. They failed, betrayed to the Romans by fellow Jews eager to avoid trouble, but they weren't completely off base in their feeling that these communities were ripe for their own rebellion against their non-Jewish neighbors and rulers—just a few decades too early.

Indeed, far from marking the end of Jewish resistance to the Romans, the Jewish Revolt is really the first in a series of major uprisings that encompassed both diasporic Jewish communities and Judea itself. We know less about these revolts than we do about the First Jewish Revolt because we lack a Josephus to tell us what happened—that is, a source that records the sequence of events—but they may have posed an even greater threat to Roman control over the Jews and provoked a greater backlash.

One of these rebellions, known by modern historians as the Diaspora Revolt, was actually a series of (eventually) interconnected Jewish uprisings that occurred in 115– 117 CE during the reign of Emperor Trajan. The foment seems to have started in Libya, beginning like earlier riots in Alexandria between Jews and Greeks, but this time, the Romans were not able to contain the violence, and it quickly spread to other parts of the Jewish world—to Egypt, Cyprus, and perhaps as far as Mesopotamia. The Roman historian Cassius Dio claims that the Jews perpetrated all kinds of atrocities during this war, even eating the flesh of their victims. The cannibalism charge is probably concocted—decades before the war, Greco-Egyptian writers such as Apion had been accusing the Jews of kidnapping Greeks to sacrifice and eat them—but what it does tell us nonetheless is that the revolt was serious enough to cause a level of hysteria within the non-Jewish population. Another measure of how threatening this revolt became was the backlash it provoked. To quell the uprising in Mesopotamia, the Romans put thousands to death. In Cyprus, Jews were banned from the island. In Egypt, the great Jewish community of Alexandria was devastated. Jews continued to live there, but for all intents and purposes, the Alexandrian Jewish community—the community that produced the Septuagint, Philo, and much else—came to an end at that time.

But even that devastating outcome did not suppress Jewish hopes of throwing off Roman rule.

Some 15 years later, in 132 CE, yet another major Jewish uprising exploded in Judea itself, the Bar Kochba Revolt. As is true for the Diaspora Revolt, we have just enough evidence to sense how important this revolt was, but not enough to reconstruct a clear picture; in fact, the causes of the revolt are a matter of ongoing and probably irresolvable debate. The sources—really just a few references in later Roman, Christian, and rabbinic texts—point to at least two possibilities:

1. The revolt might have been triggered by an imperial decree against circumcision or perhaps a ban against castration, conflated with circumcision. One problem with this theory, apart from the fact that there is not much evidence of such a ban, is that it is not clear why the Roman Empire would try to ban circumcision, given the number of Jews in the empire that it would have affected, not to mention non-Jews who practiced circumcision. Hence, many scholars are inclined to accept another explanation also suggested by the sources.
2. The revolt was a reaction against an attempt by Emperor Hadrian to turn Jerusalem into a pagan city with the name Aelia Capitolina. The name Aelia Capitolina—*Aelia* in honor of Emperor Hadrian's family, and *Capitolina* in honor of the Roman god Jupiter Capitolinus—associated the city with a pagan god, and it is even possible that a temple might have been dedicated to Jupiter on the site of the Temple. The construction of such a city and temple would have deeply offended Jews, both obstructing the hope of rebuilding a Jewish temple in Jerusalem and erasing the traditional Jewish identity of Jerusalem. One can imagine such a move stirring a revolt—Jews had nearly risen up when Caligula tried to install a statue of Jupiter in the Temple a century earlier—but it, too, suffers from its share of historiographical problems, including indications that the city was refounded as a pagan city *after* the Bar Kochba Revolt rather than before it.

We have far less literary evidence for the Bar Kochba Revolt than we do for the Maccabean Revolt or the First Jewish Revolt against Rome, so the truth is that we just do not know what caused it. We also do not know very much about its leadership. According to rabbinic literature, the leader of the revolt, Simon bar Kosiba—or Bar Kochba, as he was known to his followers—was recognized by the great rabbi Akiba as a messianic figure, a divinely sent redeemer predicted by Scripture; indeed, the nickname Bar Kochba, or "Son of a Star," refers to a messianic prophecy in Numbers 24:17: "[A] star shall come out of Jacob." Perhaps then the rebels' goal was not just to assert their independence from Rome but also to initiate the messianic age. The evidence we have from the rebels themselves never makes such claims, however—there Bar Kochba appears as a pious military leader but nowhere makes claim to the kind of messianic or supernatural status ascribed to him in certain rabbinic legends (*see the box* "Letters From a Rebel"). We do know that Bar Kochba ran a kind of provisional administration able to mint coins—or rather recycle Roman coins, by erasing their imperial images and reinscribing them with Bar Kochba's name. From these coins, moreover, we know that Bar Kochba held an official position known as the *nasi*, variously translated as "prince," "patriarch," or "president," further suggesting that he and his followers set up some kind of provisional government.

Some coins also feature the name of a priest, Eleazar, and that, together with the coins' depiction of the Temple's façade, suggests that the rebels' goals may have been religious as well as political, possibly even the restoration of the Temple, though that, too, is just an educated guess. In many ways, the Bar Kochba Revolt was more consequential than even the First Jewish Revolt, but without a Josephus to tell us its story, we know very little about those involved in the conflict, either the Jews or even those in charge of the Roman forces.

THE MASS SUICIDE AT MASADA

One of the most memorable moments in Josephus's description of the Jewish Revolt (though he may have poached it from a source) is his account of the Roman siege of Masada. The episode includes one of the most eloquent speeches in Josephus's narrative, that of Eleazar ben Yair, the Sicarii leader at Masada, an impassioned (but reasoned) argument for suicide as the only way for the rebels to preserve their freedom and honor. Then follows one of his narrative's most horrifying moments—a description of how the rebels carried out the act:

> While they caressed and embraced their wives and took their children in their arms, clinging in tears to those parting kisses, at that same instant, as though served by hands other than their own, they accomplished their purpose, having the thought of the ills they would endure under the enemy's hand to console them for their constraint in killing them. . . . Wretched victims of necessity, to whom to slay with their own hands their own wives and children seemed the lightest of evils! Unable, indeed, any longer to endure their anguish at what they had done, and feeling that they had wronged the slain by surviving them if it were but for a moment, they quickly piled together all the stores and set them on fire; then, having chosen by lot ten of their number to dispatch the rest, they laid themselves down each beside his prostrate wife and children, and flinging their arms around them, offered their throats in readiness for the executants of the melancholy office . . . then, the nine bared their throats, and the last solitary survivor, after surveying the prostrate multitude, to see whether haply amid the shambles there were yet one left who needed his hand, and finding that all were slain, set the palace ablaze, and then collecting his strength drove his sword clean through his body and fell beside his family.
>
> (*Jewish War* 7:391–397)

Modern historians have asked whether such a dramatic incident really happened. We have reason to think that it did. Evidence uncovered during the excavation of Masada corroborates aspects of Josephus's account. Skeletal remains of men, women, and children may be the remains of the site's defenders and the families they killed before they killed themselves. Eleven pottery pieces, each inscribed with a name or the nickname of a man, may have been the lots used by the rebels to determine who would slay whom (though Josephus claims that only ten lots were drawn). In recent years, however, some scholars have expressed doubts about Josephus's account, pointing to details that Josephus or his source may have made up to make his story more appealing for his audience, which included Greeks and Romans. Eleazer's speech, for example, echoes elements of what Socrates says before he takes his own life.

Regardless of whether the mass suicide at Masada unfolded in the way Josephus describes, what is clear is that the story addresses an issue that preoccupies the historian throughout his account of the Jewish Revolt—what we might call the ethics of voluntary death. Josephus's narrative includes many episodes of Jews choosing to die for the sake of God or to escape defeat and subjugation, and his interest in this act reflects a broader admiration for voluntary death that he shared with both his fellow Jews and the Romans. Jews in this period esteemed those willing to die rather than betray God or the laws of Moses—recall our discussion of martyrdom in Chapter 3. For their part,

From the little evidence that survives, we can only piece together a very incomplete picture of how the Bar Kochba Revolt unfolded. It appears to have begun in the summer of 132 CE, spreading to much of Judea—whether it extended farther afield into places like the Galilee is disputed,

Romans also admired those willing to die to preserve their honor and freedom, who used suicide to exert a final measure of control over their lives and to avoid the humiliation of defeat. Josephus's description of what happened at Masada is admirable from both perspectives.

What adds an interesting twist is that Josephus mixes this admiration for voluntary death together with grave reservations about the choice to die. Another famous episode in his account of the revolt is his description of his own brush with suicide when trapped in a cave by the Romans. His fellow soldiers wanted to kill themselves rather than surrender, just as the rebels would later do at Masada, but Josephus resisted, offering an argument against suicide that represents a kind of counterpoint to Eleazar's later argument in favor of suicide. Josephus's arguments did not persuade his fellow soldiers, who then forced him to participate in a suicide pact, but he managed to survive nonetheless (he persuaded his men to use a lottery system to decide who would slay whom and somehow found a way to be among the last two to be chosen in the lottery, at which point he persuaded the other soldier to surrender with him to the Romans), and he claims that he was able to survive because God did not want him to die. In light of this account, it becomes difficult to tell whether Josephus thought that the suicide at Masada was the right thing to do. He may have admired the rebels' courage, but it is striking that when it came time to consider such a fate for himself, it was the argument against suicide that prevailed.

Figure 4.4 The fortress of Masada.

as is whether the rebellion ever captured Jerusalem. Some of the coins feature the legend "for the freedom of Jerusalem," and it is unknown whether this means that Jerusalem's liberation was something that the rebellion achieved at some point or merely aspired to. It is also unknown how the

LETTERS FROM A REBEL

The rebel leader Bar Kochba was long shrouded behind a veil of myth. Greek and Roman sources give us some information, but few details. Christian literature and rabbinic literature give a more colorful portrait of Bar Kochba, portraying him as a bandit and a failed messiah, but their testimony dates from long after the revolt, reflecting an awareness of the revolt's tragic outcome, and the stories they tell incorporate recognizably legendary motifs and exaggerations. So little information can be gleaned from these sources, or even from the thousands of coins left behind by the rebels, that until fairly recently, even Bar Kochba's name remained unclear. Was it *Bar Kochba*, "Son of a Star," as in Christian sources, or *Bar Kozeba*, "Son of a Liar," as registered in rabbinic sources?

Beginning in the 1950s, documents from the time of the Bar Kochba Revolt began to come to light, and then, in 1961–1962, came the most remarkable discovery of all: the discovery of 15 letters that recorded correspondence between Bar Kochba himself and his followers, found in a cave in the Judean desert where some of those followers had apparently taken refuge (the cave, uncovered by the archaeologists Yigael Yadin, was dubbed the "Cave of Letters"). These letters do not reveal as much as we would like, but they do tell us some things. The leader's real name, they show, was Shimon Bar Kosiba (Bar Kochba and Bar Kozeba were nicknames, the latter sarcastic), and they reveal something of what he was like as a leader. Also discovered in the cave were the remains of human skeletons, including that of a child; some of the oldest textiles known from the Roman period, dated to the time of the Bar Kochba Revolt and telling us something about what Jews wore in this period; and a cache of legal documents belonging to a woman named Babatha (discussed later).

The following two letters show Bar Kochba struggling to sustain the discipline and motivation of his followers:

> From Shimeon bar Kosiba to the men of En-Gedi. To Masabala and to Yehonathan bar Ba'ayan, peace. In comfort you sit, eat, and drink from the property of the House of Israel, and care nothing for your brothers.
>
> From Shimeon ben Kosiba to Yeshua ben Galgoula and to the men of the fort, peace. I take heaven to witness against me that unless you mobilize [destroy?] the Galileans who are with you every man, I will put fetters on your feet as I did to ben Aphlul.

Some scholars believe that such letters reflect a war taking a turn for the worse, coming from Bar

rebellion came to an end, though it does seem that the last major battle occurred at Bethar, southwest of Jerusalem. Inscriptions suggest that up to 11 or 12 Roman legions were involved in the subjugation of Judea—by one estimate, more than 50,000 soldiers. The remains of a 10-meter triumphal arch built by the Romans near the city of Beth Shean, inscribed with letters some 15 inches in height, hint at what a great victory they believed they had achieved.

Like the Diaspora Revolt, the Bar Kochba Revolt provoked a terrible backlash from a Roman government intent on re-establishing its control. Rabbinic sources depict this period as an age of terrible persecution: The Romans forbade circumcision, the teaching of the Torah, and other Jewish religious practices, and they executed in horrifying ways those who defied them by publicly keeping the commandments. The executions of Rabbi Akiba and nine other sages became legendary in later Jewish tradition, their deaths remembered as acts of heroic martyrdom, a "glorifying of God's reputation" (kiddush ha-shem, more precisely the sanctification of God's name), as such practice came to be

Figure 4.5 A coin minted by the Bar Kochba rebels. The side pictured on the left depicts what seems to be the façade of the Temple, including what may be the lost Ark of the Covenant in the interior. The side pictured on the right features a lulav and etrog, symbols of Sukkot, a festival associated with the inauguration of the Temple. Such imagery raises the possibility that one of the goals of the Bar Kochba Revolt was to restore the Temple.

Kochba at a time when he was having to rebuke his troops for declining discipline and commitment. Since the letters are undated, however, it is impossible to put them into any kind of sequence in relation to each other or the overall course of the war. The second passage's reference to "Galileans" is another intriguing but ultimately elusive aspect of these documents. Some believe it might refer to Christians, who were occasionally known as Galileans because of Jesus's association with that area, but we do not know who they really were or how they related to the rebels.

For these translations, and for more about Bar Kochba, see Yigael Yadin, *Bar-Kochba: The Rediscovery of the Legendary Hero of the Last Jewish Revolt Against Imperial Rome* (London: Weidenfeld and Nicolson, 1971), which also describes the discovery of the Babatha letters, which come from the period between 93 and 132 CE.

known in rabbinic sources, since the executed were thought to have bravely submitted to torture and death rather than betray their allegiance to God.

Scholars have questioned whether such a persecution ever took place, but this was certainly a very difficult time for Judea, which lost much of its Jewish population during the war. If one believes the Roman historian Cassius Dio, 985 villages were razed to the ground, 580,000 people were slain, and so many people were taken slaves that the price of slaves fell throughout the empire. Jews were forbidden on pain of death from entering Jerusalem except for one day a year, the ninth of Ab, when they were allowed into the city to mourn the Temple. Jewish culture survived in other areas—in the Galilee and in Diaspora settings, such as Babylonia and Rome—but in Judea, it was largely devastated.

Beyond Submission and Revolt

Josephus had concluded that it was folly to rebel against the Roman Empire. The Bar Kochba Revolt seems to have led later Jewish intellectuals also to rethink rebellion as a tactic of communal survival. Rabbinic literature, our principal literary source for Jewish culture in the period between 200 and 650 CE, records a range of views about Roman rule. Some sages extolled the benefits of Roman rule, and some collaborated with the Roman government—leading sages, such as Judah the Patriarch, are even said to have enjoyed a close relationship with the emperor—but others criticized its oppressiveness and moral failings. To the extent it is possible to generalize, however, rabbinic literature seems to back away from a posture of open resistance, distancing itself from such rebels as Bar Kochba and greatly narrowing the scenarios in which *kiddush ha-shem*, martyrdom, was justified. In fact, in a story that is probably not historical but nonetheless speaks volumes about the rabbinic attitude to Roman rule, rabbinic literature traces the pedigree of rabbinic culture back to Yohanan ben Zakkai, a sage who chose not to join in the Jewish Revolt but rather to escape from Jerusalem by concealing himself in a coffin taken out of the city and to place his personal fate and that of his tradition in the hands of the Romans rather than to die with the rebels. There were other Jewish uprisings against Roman rule in the following centuries, but those are even less well documented than the Bar Kochba Revolt, and it was not until the rise of Islam many hundreds of years later, in the seventh and eighth centuries CE, that Jews living within the Roman Empire would see a viable alternative to its rule.

We should also note, however, that submission and rebellion weren't the only two options available to Jews. Recognizing the danger of rebellion did not necessarily mean that one had to willingly embrace Roman rule, and other, less-confrontational ways were available to resist it. Some Jews may have adopted a kind of deliberately ambiguous posture toward Roman rule, not challenging it directly but not exactly yielding to it either. A possible example is Jesus's response when asked whether Jews should pay taxes to the Roman Empire (Matthew 22:15–22; Mark 12, 14–17; Luke 20:20–26). The question put Jesus in a very perilous situation. Saying yes would seem to endorse Roman rule, potentially making Jesus look like a collaborator at a time when many Jews were extremely resentful of Roman taxation, but saying no would amount to a rejection of imperial rule, which could get Jesus in serious trouble with the Roman authorities. Jesus avoided the pitfalls of either response by finding an answer in between them: "Give to Caesar the things that are the Caesar's, and to God the things that are God's." On the surface, Jesus seems to be saying that Jews should pay their taxes to Rome, but on closer examination, the statement is actually quite equivocal and could be understood to be saying the opposite: Yes, pay Caesar his due, but since God is the only true king (or so many Jews in Jesus's day believed), nothing is really due Caesar, while Jews' true loyalty remains with God, to whom they owe everything. A Roman could thus hear one thing, while an anti-Roman Jew might hear something more subversive. We will not get into the vexed question of whether this incident really happened, but the kind of equivocal response it describes may well illustrate one of the techniques that Jews used in their interaction with the Romans, seeming to acquiesce to them, but in an ambiguous way that reflects a refusal to completely yield to the Romans.

Another form of what we might think of as nonconfrontational resistance was the continued production of apocalyptic literature, which looked forward to a time beyond the end of foreign domination. We know of apocalyptic texts composed in the immediate aftermath of the First Jewish Revolt, pseudepigraphical texts now known as 2 Baruch and 4 Ezra that were attributed to biblical figures living in the aftermath of the First Temple's destruction but were really composed in the wake of the Second Temple's demise, probably at the end of the first century CE or early second century CE. Such texts ponder the question of why

God would have allowed the destruction, accepting it as divine punishment for Israel's sins, but they also include visions of the future that foresee the defeat of God's enemies and the restoration of his people. According to such texts, while the Temple was destroyed, its essential core persists untouched by the enemy, in the form of the Ark of the Covenant hidden underground from the enemy or as a heavenly shrine accessible only to those select few to whom God reveals it. These are reflections of the author's imagination, but they may reflect a real development in this period: the emergence of an underground Jewish culture kept a secret from outsiders, a culture nursing hopes for revenge and restoration but concealing itself behind the veneer of telling stories about the biblical past.

Yet another way to resist Roman rule without directly challenging it was simply to leave the empire, and many Jews did this as well. The devastation of the Bar Kochba Revolt and its aftermath, along with other economic troubles in third-century Palestine, seems to have prompted even some rabbinic sages to leave for Syria, Asia Minor, and Babylonia (which was especially enticing because it was outside the Roman Empire)—a "brain drain" that the sages of Palestine were not able to reverse despite their efforts to restrict migration and extol life in the Holy Land. Compared to Rome, Babylonia was a veritable refuge for Jews—so appealing that one sage explained the Babylonian Exile not as divine punishment but as God's effort to save the Jews from the decrees of the Romans (Babylonian Talmud, *Gittin* 16b–17a).

While all this suggests that Jewish resistance to Roman rule probably continued well beyond the revolts of the first century CE, it is also clear that many Jews now avoided direct confrontation with Rome. Indeed, it is probably not irrelevant for understanding their long-term survival that the two most successful movements to emerge out of Jewish culture in the aftermath of the Bar Kochba Revolt—Christianity and rabbinic Judaism—both developed a nonconfrontational approach to Roman rule. Jews never forgot the destruction of the Second Temple, and we know that many looked forward to a messianic age, when God would intervene to punish the Romans and deliver the Jews from them, but the communities that endured the longest under their rule seem to have been those willing to acquiesce to its power or else relocate beyond its reach.

Jewish Life Before and After the Temple's Destruction

We again pick up the thread of Jewish political history after the second century CE in Chapter 5. Before then, we turn our attention to Jewish social and religious life in the period just before and after the Second Temple's destruction. The destruction of the Temple is recognized today as a major turning point in Jewish history, not just for political reasons, but also because of its impact on how Jews lived their lives, how they worshipped, and how they connected to one another. Jews knew from the Bible that the Temple had been destroyed before by the Babylonians, but it had been rebuilt within a century and the sacrificial cult restored, and something similar was true following the desecration of the Second Temple by Antiochus IV. The Romans' destruction of the Second Temple proved permanent, imposing a major disruption of Jewish religious and social life and laying the groundwork for the emergence of new ways of interacting with God. In what remains of this chapter, we will try to convey this change by offering snapshots of Jewish life before and after the Second Temple's destruction.

Jewish Life Before the Temple's Destruction

What was it like to be a Jew in the decades before the Second Temple's destruction? The answer depends on what kind of Jew we are talking about—a Pharisee or an Essene, a priest or a non-priest, a man or a woman, a denizen of Jerusalem or a resident of a

Galilean village? There had developed many variations of being Jewish in this period.

Unfortunately, much of this diversity of experience is lost. Just a slice of it is preserved in the surviving written evidence, which consists of either literary texts composed by members of the intellectual elite or inscriptions, papyri, and coins that record mostly a narrow range of public, economic, and legal activities. Consider some of the many people whose perspectives are not registered in this evidence. We know from sources like the Gospels that there were many poor people in Palestine in the first century—people who were hungry and sick, who were sometimes driven to begging, prostitution, and thievery—and we know as well that at least some in society were greatly concerned about such poverty: Both Jesus and the later rabbis would express great concern for the poor and encourage charity and other ways to help them (though there was also suspicion of those who gave charity too publicly, as a way of making themselves look good). But although we know that poverty was a major social problem, we do not have any sources from the poor themselves. Wealthy Jews in this period, like other wealthy people in the Roman Empire, often put their wealth on display, in well-decorated houses and tombs. The poor were not in a position to leave monuments to the lives they endured.

The same is true of other figures at the bottom of the early Jewish social ladder. With the exception of a few unconventional groups like the Essenes, who refused to own slaves, most Jews in this period were like the non-Jews of the Roman Empire in their attitude toward slavery, accepting it as an established part of life, enlisting slaves, interacting with them, or serving as slaves themselves, but slaves, too, didn't leave behind any accounts from which we can learn of their experience. We know as well that many Jews served as menial laborers, free in status perhaps but forced by economic dependency to toil on the farms of wealthy estates, or to quarry stone for Jerusalem's stone industry, mine salt near the Dead Sea, or make a living as fishermen if they lived near Palestine's other great body of water, the Sea of Galilee (as did some of Jesus's disciples). We do not have first-person testimony for any of these experiences either.

An immense gap in the record is the perspective of women. Some women do emerge in the sources, but in general, women are relegated to the margins, and we almost never hear them speaking in their own voices. In some communities, women may have been discouraged from having any kind of public presence. Speaking of the situation in Alexandria, for example, Philo of Alexandria remarked that women are best suited to the indoor life and should never stray from the house. It is not clear that women elsewhere abided by such a restriction—Jesus encounters many women during his travels who seem to freely approach him—but they seem to have been expected to cover their heads with a mantle as a sign of their unavailability. Archaeology has uncovered some unexpected glimpses of the lives of women, though what it tells us is limited. Perhaps the most remarkable discovery occurred in 1961 when, in the same cave where he discovered the Bar Kochba letters, the Israeli archaeologist Yigael Yadin uncovered a cache of legal and business documents now known as the Babatha archive, named for the young Jewish widow from the second century CE to whom these documents belonged. The documents are a fascinating glimpse of Babatha's life, telling us about her marriages, her fight for child support, and her business transactions. But the rarity of this evidence, found tucked away in a crevice in a remote cave, is a reminder of how little testimony we have from ancient Jewish women.

As limited as our evidence is, however, we can draw from it a number of insights into Jewish social, religious, and cultural life in the decades before the Second Temple's destruction. What is of special interest here are those aspects of Jewish culture that distinguished the Jews from non-Jews, that marked their culture as different from that of Greeks, Romans, and others. Philo and Josephus are both very proud of these differences, claiming that Jews would sooner die than betray their ancestral customs, and securing the right to practice them was always an important issue in the Jews' interaction with their Roman rulers. It is true, as we noted in the last chapter, that Jews did not agree on the content of their religious tradition, and sectarian disputes continued in the Roman period, but despite such differences, many Jews were united by their commitment to the laws of Moses and the traditions of the ancestors.

At the center of this tradition was the Jerusalem Temple itself, which drew Jews together annually on the three great festivals of Passover, Shavuot, and Sukkot. In the period of the Second Temple, these three festivals were all pilgrimage holidays that required Jews to travel to Jerusalem to worship in the Temple. We do not know if Jews felt an obligation to attend these festivals every year, but we know that in the Roman period, tens of thousands of pilgrims visited Jerusalem for the festivals, forcing an expansion of the Temple complex and its walkways to accommodate the large crowds. Although synagogues existed by this point, it seems to have been impossible for Jews to imagine worshipping God without the Temple. Even the Dead Sea Scrolls community, though it may have rejected how the Jerusalem Temple cult was managed, looked to the Temple as a model for its own religious practices and envisioned its restoration in the eschatological future.

Reflecting the importance of the Temple in this period was the stature of those associated with it, the priests. In the absence of the Davidic dynasty, the priesthood, or at least the priestly families at the upper echelons of the priestly class, emerged as Judea's preeminent social elite—not just as a religious caste, but also as a ruling class. For this reason, Herod and the Romans took great care to control the office of the high priesthood, intervening in appointments and assuming control over the priestly vestments that the high priest needed to perform his duties. Despite this cooptation of the high priesthood, however, the priesthood in general retained its authority and status. Josephus cites his priestly pedigree as proof of his noble origins, and the titles *priest* and *priestess* (the latter a title bestowed on the wives and daughters of priests) would continue to function as signs of high status centuries after the Temple's destruction.

Apart from the Temple, many Jews also shared in common a distinctive lifestyle that distinguished them from non-Jews. Sabbath observance was important, as was the synagogue, and the right to maintain these and other traditions was important to Jews whether they lived in Palestine itself or in a diasporic setting. For reasons that remain unclear, sustaining a state of purity seems to have become important for many Jews, at least for those living in Jerusalem or Palestine. Impurity was conceived of as a kind of infection that one could contract by exposure to bodily fluids, the dead, and non-Jews rendered impure by their worship of idols. It was not an illness, but one had to get rid of it in order to interact with holiness, God's presence, as manifest in the Temple and other holy people and things. For reasons we do not fully understand, cleansing oneself of impurity seems to have become a preoccupation for many Jews in Palestine in this period, not just for priests, but also for others, who tried to avoid impurity by using stone vessels (unlike a metal vessel or an open clay vessel, stone was thought resistant to impurity) and by immersing themselves in a ritual bath known as the mikveh (plural: *mikva'ot*) (Figure 4.6). The different groups that we have noted developed different approaches to handling impurity: The Pharisees stressed the importance of handwashing before meals, while the Essenes avoided oil, which other Jews used for bathing but which they saw as a source of impurity. The Essenes also developed distinctive toilet habits, defecating in private and burying their excrement, whereas other

Figure 4.6 The earliest dated *mikveh*, or ritual bath, found in a Hasmonean palace at Jericho, believed to have been in use in the period between 150 and 100 BCE. It has been surmised that priests were the ones to introduce the *mikveh* to ensure the state of purity they needed to be in to enter the Temple, but they eventually came to be used by Jews in general. After the Temple's destruction, ritual bathing retained its importance for other reasons, including the purification of women after menstruation and as part of the conversion process for non-Jews, the latter use suggesting that Jewish ritual bathing may have been the origin of Christian baptism.

Jews, evidently not seeing excrement as a source of impurity, were less concerned about it and didn't mind doing it in public.

Another distinguishing trait of early Jewish culture was the rejection of cult images, statues, and other divine images venerated by non-Jews in this period. It was once assumed that early Jews rejected images altogether. The Ten Commandments in Exodus 20 and Deuteronomy 5 prohibit the Israelites from making idols "in the image of anything in the heavens above, or on the earth below or in the sea under the earth" (Exodus 20:3; Deuteronomy 5:7), and that command was sometimes taken in Jewish tradition as a blanket ban on depicting God in any form, along with humans. The prohibition need not be interpreted in such a broad way, however, and we know from later in the Roman period that synagogue art did sometimes feature images of people. For the earlier Second Temple period that we are focused on in this section, however, Jewish art avoids anthropomorphic representation: What survives of Jewish art from this time—wall paintings, mosaic floors, decorated vessels, coins—exhibits geometric patterns; images of plants, birds, and fish; and religious symbols, like the menorah (a seven-branch lamp used in the Temple), but such art consistently avoids the presentation of people, foreign gods, or God himself, appearing to interpret the biblical prohibition against images as one that applied to images of God and to human beings, who, according to Genesis 1, were created in the image of God. Part of what we learn from examples like the mikveh and the restrictions on artistic representation is that Jewish religious life in this period was not defined solely by Jewish allegiance to the Temple and its sacrifices. It was also manifest in other behaviors in day-to-day life—an ongoing ritualized regime of purification, and other religiously motivated practices to which Jews could adhere whether they lived in Judea itself or in a community in another locale.

The Temple itself remained a central, unifying force in Jewish culture, as suggested by Philo, for example, who describes the three pilgrimage festivals as times when Jews transcended the geographical differences that divided them, coming together from all four corners of the earth:

> Countless multitudes from countless cities come, some over land, others over sea, from east and west and north and south at every feast. . . . Friendships are formed between

Figure 4.7 A 2,000-year-old religious symbol. Detail from the Arch of Titus in Rome, built to honor Titus's defeat of the Jews during the First Jewish Revolt. Depicted here is a procession carrying the Temple menorah and other artifacts looted from Jerusalem following the Temple's destruction. Although these objects were deposited in a Roman temple and then eventually looted or destroyed, the menorah and other objects associated with the Temple would continue as important religious symbols for Jews well after the Temple's destruction, especially the menorah, which was used as a symbol in synagogues ancient and modern and appears on the emblem for the State of Israel and on the seal of Mossad, Israel's national intelligence agency, among other places, where it has come to serve as a symbol of the Jewish nation, the Jewish tradition, or the vision of Judaism as a source of universal enlightenment.

> those who hitherto knew not each other, and the sacrifices and libations are the occasion of reciprocity of feeling and constitute the surest pledge that all are of one mind.
>
> (Philo, *Special Laws* 1:69–70)

As this description suggests, the Temple was an important source of Jewish unity, bringing Jews together from all over the world into a shared experience of goodwill and common purpose (in theory at least; in reality, the festivals were sometimes unruly events, characterized by overcrowding and periodically disrupted by rioting and other kinds of violence). Jews unable to visit the Temple themselves could still express their support for it by sending their payment of an annual half-shekel Temple tax, used to support the daily sacrifice. By this point, Jews were dispersed throughout the Roman Empire and beyond, divided by geographical, political, and economic differences, and it is not an exaggeration to say that what held them together despite these differences, sustaining the sense of common identity, was their shared allegiance to the Temple, their commitment to it as the ideal model of worship even if they had problems with the priests running the Jerusalem Temple or dissented from how it was being administered.

Jewish Life After the Temple's Destruction

The Temple's centrality in the religious life of Jews explains why its destruction was such a significant turning point in Jewish history. We do not have many sources from the century or so following the Temple's destruction, but the few that we do give us some glimpses of the grief and devastation that this event generated. Thus, for example, in 2 Baruch, an apocalypse from this period that we mentioned earlier, life continuing without the Temple can scarcely be imagined:

> Blessed is he who was not born, or he who was born and died. But we, the living, woe to us, because we have seen those afflictions of Zion and that which has befallen Jerusalem. . . . You farmers, sow not again. And you, o earth, why do you give the fruit of your harvest? Keep within you the sweetness of your sustenance. And you, vine, why do you still give your wine? For an offering will not be given again from you in Zion, and the first fruits will not again be offered. And you, bridegrooms, do not enter and do not let the brides adorn themselves. And you, wives, do not pray to bear children, for the barren will rejoice more. And those who have no children will be glad, and those who have children will be sad. For why do they bear in pains only to bury in grief?
>
> (2 Baruch 10:6–15)

The loss of the Temple meant that Jews could no longer practice the sacrificial rites mandated by the Torah, and that meant that Jews could not interact with God in the way that the Bible instructed, no longer able to offer the requisite sacrifices needed to atone for their sins or to thank God for his generosity. How would Jews be able to continue their relationship with God without the access that the Temple provided? The social structure of Jewish life was greatly affected by the Temple's loss as well. The priesthood, the religious elite of first-century Jewish society, was deprived of its reason for being, and Jews no longer had the opportunity to connect to Jews from other places, as they had done during the festivals of Passover, Shavuot, and Sukkot, threatening the communal unity that tied Jews to one another across the divide between the Diaspora and the homeland. For some, like the author of the foregoing passage, the loss of the Temple must have seemed like the end of the world.

And yet Jews found ways to sustain their religious life in the absence of the Temple. Many Jews probably did not give up on the hope of restoring the Temple, but there also developed, in the wake of its destruction, new forms of religiosity, new ways of sustaining Israel's covenant with God and interacting with him, that did not depend on sacrifice. Some of these were long familiar to Jews—circumcision, the observance of the Sabbath, the avoidance of forbidden foods. They were not dependent on the Temple cult, and Jews simply continued to practice them in the absence of the Temple. By this point, the synagogue was also a well-established institution in many communities in both Palestine and the Diaspora, and it would prove to offer an important venue for communal religious practice in the post-Temple age—the public reading of the Torah, prayer, donations in honor of God, and other religious activities. The two centuries following the Temple's destruction are not well documented, but it seems to be during this period that Jews began to develop lasting alternatives to the Temple cult that would allow them to interact with God without sacrifices and from wherever they happened to live.

How was Jewish culture able to adapt so successfully? We do not know, but it seems likely that part of the answer has to do with changes already beginning to take place before the Temple's destruction. Well before 70 CE, some Jews had grown disenchanted with the Temple and its priesthood and began developing alternatives to its cult. This is one reason that the religious life of the Dead Sea Scrolls community is so intriguing—alienated from the Jerusalem Temple, its members turned to prayer as a substitute for sacrifice. Those who developed these practices may not have seen themselves as replacing Temple ritual, but the institution of the synagogue and non-Temple-centered religious practices offered alternative modes of worship to which larger numbers of Jews could turn in the wake of the Temple's destruction.

Also important is what had begun to happen to the priesthood in the Second Temple period. The priesthood did not come to an end with the Temple's destruction, but its situation changed significantly. From at least the time of Antiochus's persecution and the Maccabean Revolt, events that disrupted the priestly succession and raised doubts about how the Temple was being managed, there were Jews who questioned the legitimacy of the priests in charge of the Temple—whether this or that high priest had a right to the office, or whether this or that rite was being properly performed. During the Roman period, when Herod and the Romans often interfered in the appointment of the high priesthood, its credibility suffered even more.

While all this was happening to the priesthood, other kinds of leaders were emerging who offered alternative ideas about religious life: wonder-workers, prophets, and sages who derived their authority not from a priestly lineage or their role in the Temple rite but from their supernatural and interpretive abilities and who introduced conceptions of the Torah or God that did not necessarily depend on the Temple. The Teacher of Righteousness, the founder of the Dead Sea Scrolls community, was one such figure from the Hellenistic period, and Jesus was another from the Roman period, a teacher of humble origins who was nonetheless able to exert an influence on fellow Jews by performing marvelous feats, teaching, and predicting the eschatological age, and they were not the only such figures to emerge in the decades before the Temple's destruction. That event was devastating to the priesthood, which lost the institution from which it derived its authority, but by that point, there existed other forms of religious leadership that filled the vacuum, not tied to the Temple and thus able to operate in its absence.

While Jewish religious life was already beginning to change in profound ways before the Temple's destruction, however, that event is still a major turning point in Jewish religious life, dislodging the priesthood from its position of authority and creating a pressing need for alternatives to the sacrificial cult. Or rather, we might say that it was the combination of the Temple's destruction and the Bar Kochba Revolt that marked a major change, for it was probably the latter event, which saw the transformation of Jerusalem into a pagan city, that ended the possibility of restoring the Temple in the way that it had been restored after the destruction of the First Temple. We are more or less guessing here because of how little evidence survives from this period, but it seems likely that in the wake of these events, it became clear to many Jews that the Temple's restoration was not going to happen anytime soon, and that they would need alternative ways of worshipping God. For Jews living in places outside Jerusalem, that simply meant sustaining the local religious practices and institutions they had had before the Temple's destruction, but there also now emerged new conceptions of religious life that, while never abandoning the memory of the Temple, ultimately replaced it as a way of relating to God.

As it happens, the changes in Jewish culture of this period proved to be a harbinger of changes that would set in throughout the Roman world, for over the next centuries, there seems to be a much broader trend away from temple-centered religion. By the second and third centuries CE, pagan intellectuals like Lucian of Samosota and Porphyry were voicing criticisms of sacrifice as an ignorant form of worship and offering contemplation and a disciplined lifestyle as the best way to interact with the divine. By the end of the fourth century CE, public sacrifices were abolished by a

Christianized Roman Empire. As sacrifice went into decline, so too did other manifestations of a temple-centered culture. Temples themselves suffered neglect or destruction or were turned into churches and (after the rise of Islam) mosques, where the central act of worship was not sacrifice but prayer. Priests found their authority eclipsed by other kinds of intermediaries—the philosopher, the monk, and the spiritual master, whose authority derived from insight and an exemplary lifestyle rather than from ritual expertise. In this new terrain, it became more important to have access to one's spiritual master, by following him as a disciple, by reading his writings, or by venerating his remains, than it was to have access to any particular place. There also developed religious practices that made temples far less necessary than they had been in the earlier Roman Empire: Especially noteworthy is the increasing importance of the reading of sacred texts as a way to interact with God.

The reasons for this move away from the Temple to the sacred text as the focus of religious attention are not fully understood. The most obvious catalyst was the rise of Christianity, which we will describe ahead, but its success and influence were intertwined with other factors. One was a change in the technology of writing: the development of the codex (the precursor of the modern book) and a corresponding decline in the use of the scroll. A codex was less expensive to produce than a scroll, easier to transport and to circulate, and its embrace may help explain the emerging importance of sacred texts in the religions that developed under Roman rule, not just Christianity, but also other communities, like the Manicheans, followers of a prophet named Mani, for whom sacred texts were also important. No less important was a shift in the nature of religion itself in this period: a greater emphasis in Christianity and other religions on personal internal transformation, the care for others, and a sense of community based on shared beliefs rather than shared ancestry or a shared birth in a particular city or region.

The Temple's destruction forced many of these changes onto Jews earlier than was the case for other peoples. The change was not welcome—Jews would grieve the Temple's destruction on the ninth day of the month of Av (*Tisha b'Av*), fasting, performing other mourning rites, and even visiting the site where the Temple stood, and many would pray for its restoration. In retrospect, however, we can see that having to live without the Temple forced Jews to make changes that helped their culture survive in the non-temple-centered environment that emerged in the Roman world, necessitating the turn away from sacrifice to the study of sacred texts as the primary religious act, and the eclipse of the priest by other religious leaders who based their authority not on their association with the Temple but on their access to divine knowledge.

One of the consequences of this transformation was the emergence in Jewish culture of a new kind of religious authority known as the rabbi, not a priest or a prophet, but a teacher who derived his authority from his knowledge of the Torah and his pious religious observance. Possibly emerging out of the Pharisees or other Second Temple period groups, such sages eventually formed a kind of scholarly network of teachers and disciples defined by a distinctive attitude toward Jewish tradition and religious practice. These sages were very interested in the Temple and its rituals, studying them in great detail, but part of what distinguishes them from earlier Jewish scholars of the Second Temple period is that they saw the act of study itself, rather than the Temple cult, as the most important form of interaction with God, a kind of substitute for the Temple cult. Through their interpretation of the Torah, these early rabbis helped reconceptualize Jewish religious tradition in ways that ensured its continued vitality in an age without temples and sacrifices.

The rabbis who emerge in the Roman period merit much more sustained attention than we can squeeze into this chapter, and thus, we will make them our focus in the next chapter. But rabbinic Judaism was not the only non-Temple-centered religious community to emerge in the wake of the Temple's destruction: We have started to refer to Christianity, which originated as a form of Jewish culture that took shape in the years just before and after the Temple's destruction. Christianity and Judaism are now two separate religions, but the boundary between them was not clear in the beginning: Christianity's founding figures—Jesus, his 12 disciples, Paul—were all Jews and saw themselves as continuing the tradition started by Abraham and Moses. Christianity's origins are thus part of the story of Jewish culture in this period, not only because Christians would go on to shape the world in which many Jews lived but also because Christianity itself is an outgrowth of Jewish culture in the Roman period, reflecting the very changes we have been describing in this section. We cannot describe the life of Jesus or the early history of the movement he inspired with the detail such important subjects deserve, but a brief look at how Christianity evolved out of Judaism will serve us as a way to transition from Jewish culture as it existed in the days of the Second Temple period to what developed in the wake of its destruction.

Christianity's Emergence From Jewish Culture

Christianity traces its origins back to an itinerant Jewish teacher and wonder-worker put to death in Jerusalem during the administration of Pontius Pilate. In Hebrew, his name seems to have been Yehoshua or Yeshua, but he is better known by the Greek form of this name, Jesus. (*Christ*, the other name by which he is known, did not originate as a personal name but rather as a title, *christos*, a Greek rendering of the Hebrew word "anointed one," applied to Jesus by his followers to signal his status as a royal figure in the line of David.) Today, Jesus is regarded by Christians as a divine being, but he spent his life as a Jew amid other Jews in the Galilee and Judea and drew on earlier Jewish tradition in what he taught and how he behaved. Much can be learned about the origins of early Christianity by placing it in a Jewish context.

Although he is the first century's most famous Jew, Jesus is largely a mystery from a historical point of view. We have no writings from Jesus himself, nor is he mentioned by any contemporary author, and so we must rely on later sources—the letters of Paul and the Gospels of Matthew, Mark, Luke, and John—written 30–60 years after his death. There are certainly Christians who accept the Gospels as unerringly accurate, but modern scholarship is more skeptical because these sources are hard to corroborate, make inconsistent claims, and tell their stories in ways that seem to have been colored by the beliefs, literary goals, and circumstances of their authors. But the nature of the Gospels as historical sources deserves far more attention than we can devote to it here.

We can say a few things about Jesus with relative certainty. Although the traditional Christian calendar places his birth in 1 CE, it is possible he was born at any point between 4 BCE and 6 CE (the Gospel of Matthew argues for an earlier date, reporting that Jesus was born while Herod the Great was still alive, and Herod died in 4 BCE). He hailed from Bethlehem, the city of King David's birth, but he was known as Jesus of Nazareth, a town in the Galilee, because that is where his parents were from. The Gospels report that Jesus had an early association with John the Baptist, a popular teacher and prophet, who facilitated the baptism of Jesus, an immersion in water that allowed for the forgiveness of sin. We cannot confirm that association from sources outside the New Testament, but we have independent testimony from Josephus that John really existed—he was reportedly executed by Herod—and that he really championed baptism, which seems to have developed out of earlier Jewish use of immersion in water as a form of purification. We also can corroborate the existence of other important figures mentioned in the Gospels: Herod, Pontius Pilate, and even Caiaphas, the high priest at the time of Jesus's death. Scholars have no reason to doubt that Jesus was crucified; this was a sadistic form of execution that the Romans used against outlaws and slaves as a warning to those who would consider challenging the order of things. The Gospels depict his execution differently, however, even disagreeing about when it happened (*see the box* "The Quest for the Historical Jesus").

While Jesus himself is largely beyond the historian's reach, what we know about Jewish culture in the first century can help explain the rise of the movement he inspired. In Chapter 3, we noted the rise among Jews in Judea of various "philosophies" or sects—the Pharisees, the Sadducees, and the Essenes/Dead Sea Scrolls sect—movements that continued into the first century. The Pharisees appear to have exerted the most influence on the broader population, but no single movement represents the definitive form of Judaism. Christianity arose as one of these movements, initiated by a Jew and drawing its earliest followers from the Jewish community. In some respects, the early Christians bear a particularly close resemblance to the Pharisees—they were both popular movements organized around teachers and held similar beliefs, such as their shared expectation of a resurrection of the dead—but in other respects, the Christians resembled the Essenes. Joining a community like the Pharisees or the Essenes was a way to live an ideal lifestyle—to avoid the distractions of ordinary life in order to draw closer to God or study his laws. The group formed by Jesus and his followers was of a similar character.

Many Jews in the late Second Temple period believed the troubles of the present would soon give way to a different, better age. Israel was supposed to enjoy God's protection, and yet the lives of Jews were full of suffering and injustice: disease, drought, famine, and oppression at the hand of foreign rulers. Why did God allow the righteous to suffer in this way? Why did God not intervene to save them? As noted in Chapter 1, the prophets of the Hebrew Bible answered these questions by interpreting Israel's troubles as punishment for Israel's sin, a disciplining or chastising that would end one day. Some prophetic passages even refer to a specific time when everything would be set right—a "day of the Lord," or "the end of days," when God would deliver his people. Jews in the Greco-Roman period took even more of an interest in what would happen in that final period of divine judgment, battle, and deliverance—the "eschatological age," as scholars now refer to it. Some Jews, believing that time to be close at hand, actively prepared for it.

While it was probably widely assumed by Jews that God would come to their rescue in the end, they differed over how exactly the eschatological age would play out. In some Jewish apocalyptic texts from the first or second century CE, God intervenes directly, or through his angels or other supernatural beings. In others, God works through special humans—either the Davidic messiah, a kingly figure from the line of David, or a priestly messiah, an alternative savior figure from the line of Aaron. The Dead Sea Scrolls community seems to have anticipated these two messiahs, and there were probably other conceptions of the Messiah and the apocalyptic age circulating in first-century Judea as well. Underlying these ideas was the belief that the present was a transition between the biblical past and a messianic future, and that the progress from one to the other had been determined in advance, following a scripted sequence of events that had been determined by God in advance. God had hinted at this future in scriptural texts that revealed their eschatological secrets to certain divinely elected, knowledgeable humans, like the Teacher of Righteousness mentioned in the Dead Sea Scrolls.

Like the Teacher of Righteousness, the Jesus of the Gospels knows the plan for the eschatological future, revealing glimpses of it to his followers, but more than that, he had a special role in that plan, not just as a herald, but as a divine deliverer, the Messiah long expected by Jews. The descriptions of Jesus preserved in the New Testament actually combine several Jewish messianic traditions from this period. Jesus is identified as the Davidic messiah—hence the importance of associating him with Bethlehem, the city of David's birth—but he is also ascribed some of the characteristics of other eschatological figures, such as the priestly messiah (see the *Letter to the Hebrews*, which describes Jesus as a priestly figure). One of the distinctive elements of early Christian messianism is its claim that Jesus would act out his messianic role in two stages, fulfilling some of it in an initial appearance ended by his death and then returning in the eschatological age to complete the work. The belief in a messiah that comes in two stages can be seen as similar in a way to the earlier Jewish belief that God will send two messiahs.

We also know from the book of Revelation, an early Christian apocalypse believed to have been written in the first century CE, during or shortly after the First Jewish Revolt against Rome, that early Christians envisioned the eschatological age as one of violent conflict between God and his forces against the Devil and his forces (*see the box* "The Origin of Satan"). This conception is very similar to the one recorded in the *War Scroll* and other Jewish apocalyptic texts that anticipate a final eschatological battle, as are many other elements of early Christian eschatology—the expectation of a final judgment of the righteous and the wicked, for instance, and the anticipated resurrection of the dead.

To be sure, not every element of early Christian messianic belief has a demonstrably Jewish origin. One distinctive idea with no clear Jewish antecedent was the belief in Jesus as a divine being, the son of God, which seems to be born of the Greek idea of the "divine man," rulers and heroes who combine divine and mortal attributes. Earlier Second Temple sources feature many supernatural beings, but none refers to a human being regarded as a god, and that way of conceiving Jesus might reflect the influence of a non-Jewish conception of apotheosis—the transformation of certain special human beings into gods. The best-known example from this period is the Roman emperor, who was believed to become a god after his death. The Romans practiced a ritual where they would release an eagle into the sky to signify the ascent of the divinized person into the heavens, and they depicted that ascent in art and coinage. The idea of Jesus as the Son of God may reflect some fusion of this idea of the divinized human ruler with the biblical conception of the king as an adopted son of God, a status conferred on King David when God selects him and his descendants to rule Israel (see 2 Samuel 7:14).

Yet another possible connection between Jesus and early Judaism is his most famous meal, the "last supper" that he had with his disciples on the night before his crucifixion. Since this meal happened on or near Passover, some scholars argue that what Jesus and his disciples were in fact doing on this occasion was celebrating the Passover meal (indeed, two of the Gospels identify it as a Passover meal), and they have tried to explain what transpired during the Last Supper in light of the rituals of the Passover meal as known from rabbinic sources and the Dead Sea Scrolls. Thus, for example, Jesus's efforts to explain the wine and bread at the meal can be understood in light of a later rabbinic custom of explaining the unleavened bread, wine, and other food items consumed during the Passover meal, while the singing of a hymn at the end of the Last Supper parallels the singing of certain psalms at the end of the Passover meal. During the meal, Jesus makes certain references to the eschatological age, and such references call to mind a description in a Dead Sea Scrolls composition known as the *Rule of the Congregation* of an

THE QUEST FOR THE HISTORICAL JESUS

The quest for the historical Jesus, to understand what he really did and said as a person, has been frustrated by the small amount of firsthand evidence. Certainly, more direct evidence exists for Jesus's world than for the ages of Abraham, Moses, or David, and yet a close examination of this evidence renders Jesus himself nearly as inaccessible. The following are the sources that scholars work with in reconstructing the historical Jesus:

1. Writing in the 50s, Paul is the earliest extant source to speak of Jesus. Encountering Jesus only after the latter's death, however, he is not an eyewitness to his life or crucifixion and has little to say about Jesus before his death.
2. The Gospels provide us with four accounts of Jesus's life, and they are the indispensable basis for any biography of Jesus. Their testimony is even later than Paul's, however, and does not always match up with what one can infer from his letters; they report nothing about Jesus that can be directly corroborated by extrabiblical evidence in the way one can confirm the actions of figures such as Herod; and they are sometimes inconsistent among themselves in what they report. (An example of an inconsistency is the timing of Jesus's death. According to the Gospel of Mark, he is crucified at 9:00 a.m., the morning after the Passover meal is eaten, while according to the Gospel of John, he was crucified after noon, the day before the Passover meal was eaten.) By comparing the Gospels to one another and noting their differences, scholars have come to recognize that each shapes the information it has inherited from earlier sources, sometimes even inventing reported details in the way that Josephus invents details in his historical accounts. As an example of how a gospel depiction of Jesus can be shaped to reflect the beliefs of its author, consider the description of Jesus by the author of John as "a lamb of God who takes away the sins of the world" (John 1:29). The author's perception of Jesus as a lamb offered up as a sacrifice may explain why he preferred a different chronology for Jesus's crucifixion than that found in Mark. In John's chronology, Jesus dies on the same day, at the same time that the Passover lamb was sacrificed, thus deepening the sense of Jesus as a "lamb of God."
3. Josephus refers to Jesus in a brief passage in *Antiquities* 18:63–64:

> About this time [Pilate's day], there lived Jesus, a wise man, if indeed one ought to call him a man. For he was one who wrought surprising feats and was a teacher of such people as accept truth gladly. He won over many Jews and many Greeks. He was the Messiah. When Pilate, upon hearing him accused by men of the highest standing among us, had condemned him to be crucified, those who had in the first place come to love him did not give up their affection for him. On the third day he appeared to them restored to life, for the prophets of God had prophesied these and countless other marvelous things about him. And the tribe of the Christians, so called after him, has till this day not disappeared.

Here we would seem to have clear-cut corroboration for the existence of Jesus, and it has been cited as such by Christian historians since the fourth century CE. But since the sixteenth century, scholars have suspected that the passage was forged by a later Christian, or at least tampered with, for its implication that Josephus was Christian ("He was the Messiah") seems unlikely, given what Josephus says elsewhere about his religious beliefs (not to mention that Josephus's description of Jesus as the Messiah is missing from an Old Arabic version of the *Antiquities*). Even if Josephus wrote this passage, he did so in the 80s or 90s, decades after Jesus's death, so like the Gospels, it does not represent firsthand or contemporary information either.

4. Supposed archaeological evidence for Jesus's existence has proven very dubious as well. In 2002, for example, an artifact was made public that seemed at first to be powerful corroboration: a burial box inscribed in Aramaic with the words "James, son of Joseph, brother of Jesus." For about a year, scholars tried to determine whether the Jesus referred to here was the

famous Jesus, but their efforts bore no fruit in the end, because, while the burial box is probably authentic, the inscription written on it has been shown to be a forgery.

5. Various noncanonical gospels, including a recently published gospel attributed to Judas Iscariot, have come to light, offering another potential source of information about Jesus. These have proven to be later and less credible than the canonical gospels, however. The Gospel of Thomas might be an exception: Depending on who you believe in the debate over when it was written, it might predate some of the canonical gospels. But even if it is early, it does not offer as much help as one might expect, for it is a collection of Jesus's sayings, not a narrative, and while it may reveal something of Jesus's original teachings and beliefs, it does not supply biographical information.

While there is plenty of reason to be skeptical of the sources, one can say this in favor of the Gospel accounts: Their authors know too much about Judea in the period between Herod and Pontius Pilate to be discounted in the way some biblical scholars discount Genesis and Exodus. They have proven a better gauge of what early Christians believed about Jesus than a source for what Jesus was really like, but for now, their depictions of Jesus are as close as we can come to the historical Jesus.

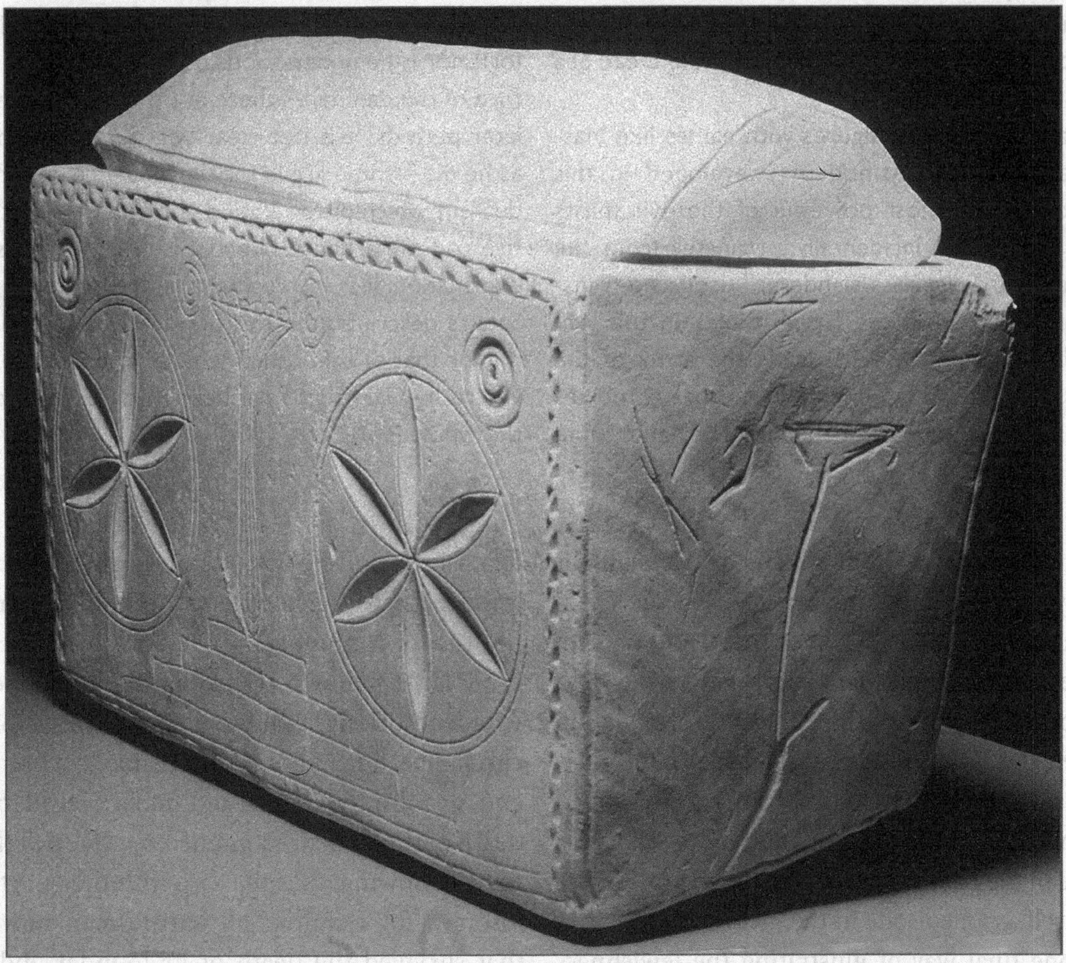

Figure 4.8 An ossuary (a box where the bones of the dead were gathered) inscribed with the name Caiaphas. An individual named Caiaphas was a high priest in Jerusalem at the time of Jesus's trial.

THE ORIGIN OF SATAN

By the Roman period, many Jews believed the world to be populated by various supernatural beings in addition to God. Belief in angels was widespread—the belief that God had at his command various supernatural servants and messengers that he dispatched on various missions, that intervened on behalf of pious humans, or that would fight on their behalf against God's enemies during the eschatological war. Angels appear in the Hebrew Bible, but by the Roman period, they had come to acquire individual personae, names, and specific roles. Something similar was true of evil spirits, the demons Jews blamed for various medical and mental problems. The Gospels' depiction of Jesus suggests that exorcism—the eviction of demons from people's bodies—was a much-in-demand skill in Palestine in the first century CE, and we have evidence of exorcistic techniques from the Dead Sea Scrolls and Josephus.

Satan—or similar figures with names like Mastema, Belial, and Asmodeus—developed in this period as the most powerful of the evil spirits (the word *devil*, incidentally, originates from the Greek word *diabolos*, "slanderer," used as a translation for Satan in the Greek Bible). In the *War Scroll*, for example, Belial leads the army of the sons of darkness, an enemy force that combines human and supernatural enemies. The name Satan in particular, from the Hebrew word for *adversary*, appears here and there in the Hebrew Bible, sometimes functioning as a celestial being hostile to God, but he doesn't seem particularly important; the name does not function as a personal name for the most part, and he doesn't play the kinds of roles ascribed to him in later Judaism and Christianity.

By the first century, however, Satan is a much more developed figure, playing some of the roles we now associate with him—a being fallen from heaven, an enemy who seeks to harm or control people, a force that has to be vanquished by God in the final battle at the end of days. However, even then, he still does not have many of the qualities associated with Satan today; he wasn't described as red or depicted with horns or holding a pitchfork, nor is he understood to preside over the torture of the damned—these are traits developed in later periods. It is not clear why Satan developed as he did—some argue for the influence of Persian dualism, which pitted a good god against a destructive god of darkness, but that is only one possible explanation. It is interesting to note, however, that Satan's description in this period does sometimes mirror that of the Roman emperor, as in Luke 4:6, where he claims to have been given control over the whole world.

eschatological banquet, at which the Messiah (or actually, the two messiahs expected by the Dead Sea Scrolls community) will eat bread and wine in the presence of the leaders and sages of the Israelite community. The debate over the connection between the Last Supper and Passover continues, but a link to the eschatological banquet envisioned by some Jews would explain a lot about what was at stake in the Last Supper, including the role of the meal itself as an episode in the messianic age.

As one final way of illustrating the Jewishness of the early Jesus movement, let us consider Jesus's death itself and how it was understood by his followers. As we have noted, the first century saw the rise of a number of charismatic figures who drew large followings through their prophetic or wonder-working ability or with promises of radical change. Such figures often came to a premature end, as John the Baptist did under Herod, but the death of the leader did not necessarily spell the end of his following, as is the case with the Fourth Philosophy, for example, an anti-Roman movement that survived the death of its founder, Judas the Galilean, who disappears after a failed insurrection against the Romans in 6 CE but was still influential decades later during the Jewish Revolt and is even mentioned in the New Testament (Acts 5:37), written around 80 or 90 CE.

The Jesus movement followed this same pattern, persisting beyond Jesus's death, but this was not just because its members were particularly loyal. They understood Jesus's execution in light of earlier Jewish understandings of death. Before God's final deliverance, many apocalyptic texts disclose, the righteous would have to endure a period of tribulation, a time of suffering, and even death. What made this suffering bearable was the knowledge that it was only temporary: The suffering would end, the dead would be restored, and evil would be vanquished. In fact, the death of the righteous could be instrumental to this happy ending: In a first-century text known as the *Testament of Moses*, the prophet foresees an age of persecution when Jews will be crucified because of their commitment to the law. During this period, the testament continues, a Levite named Taxo will withdraw into a cave, resolving to die so as to trigger God's intervention in history. Early Christians drew on such ideas to make sense of Jesus's death, interpreting it as a sacrifice undertaken to save others, and the trigger for the eschatological age. Jesus's death wasn't the end of the early Christian movement, in part because, by that point, death itself was not seen as an end but rather as a transition to a new phase of existence, and as a catalyst for ultimate salvation.

For the purposes of this sketch, we have chosen to accentuate the parallels between the Jesus movement and the Dead Sea Scrolls and other eschatologically oriented literature, but we could have easily drawn parallels also with other kinds of Jewish cultures. Some scholars are prone to stress Jesus's connections not to Jewish apocalyptic tradition but to Jewish wisdom tradition, stressing Jesus's role as a teacher and his formulation of parables and other wise sayings. Others have discerned connections between Jesus and Jewish revolutionary groups from this period, noting traces of anti-Roman sentiment in some of his behavior and sayings that suggest the Romans were not completely wrong to suspect him of being opposed to their rule. One of Jesus's disciples, Judas Iscariot (infamous for betraying Jesus), has a name that resembles "Sicarii," the rebel group that ended up on Masada, fueling speculation that Jesus had direct contacts with this anti-Roman group.

But while the discovery of connections like these has helped to better situate early Christianity within the Jewish cultural and religious context out of which it emerged, they also sharpen a longstanding question that is not of minor significance for understanding the course of Jewish history: Given Christianity's Jewish origins, why aren't Christians today Jews? In other words, how did Christianity grow into its own religion as opposed to continuing as a kind of Judaism?

The Parting of the Ways

Scholars stress that the "parting of the ways" between Judaism and Christianity—that is, their development into two discrete, often antagonistic religious communities—was not a simple or immediate development, taking many centuries to unfold, but the reasons for this split go back to the very beginning of Christianity, if not to Jesus himself, then certainly to Paul, his earliest and most influential interpreter.

Paul was a Jew who identified with the Pharisees before his conversion to Christianity, but the experience he had of Jesus took him, and Christianity, in a very different direction from that being followed by other Jewish followers of Jesus. In a series of letters written between 50 and 60 CE (only some of the Pauline letters in the New Testament are believed by scholars to have been written by Paul himself), Paul helped organize the Christian communities taking shape in Asia Minor, Greece, and Rome.

Through those letters, Paul introduced his understanding of what it meant to be a Christian. In his view, Jesus's death and resurrection had introduced a radical change in the relationship between God and humanity. Before Christ, the Jews enjoyed a special relationship with God by virtue of their participation in the covenant established at Mount Sinai, which, through the laws and rituals it imposed, established a way for Jews to achieve salvation not available to non-Jews, but the Sinai covenant was a temporary measure, Paul reveals; God had never given up on the rest of humanity, however sinful it may have been, and had sent Jesus to extend the possibility of salvation beyond the Jews to the rest of the peoples. Now that Christ had been resurrected, Paul claimed, the law, like a teacher whose job was done, was no longer necessary, for one could overcome sin and achieve salvation by trusting what God had done through Jesus. Along with this change came another one, no less radical: After Jesus's resurrection, it was possible for non-Jews to join in this new relationship with God, a "new covenant." Salvation was no longer a matter of being Jewish or adhering to Mosaic law but of faith in Christ.

Christianity's acceptance of non-Jews did not, of itself, mark the rupture between Judaism and Christianity. Though some Jews at this time may have looked askance even at converts, not to mention non-Jews, many Jewish communities in this period had room not just for proselytes but also even for "God-fearers"—non-Jews who venerated God and adhered to Jewish law but did not convert to Judaism. Early non-Jewish followers of Jesus may well have fallen into this latter category, but Paul's theology did much more than

FROM THE SABBATH TO SUNDAY

One example of how early Christianity came to distinguish itself from Judaism is reflected in the calendar, in the Christian shift from Saturday to Sunday as the most important day of worship during the week. Like other Jews, Jesus and his followers observed Saturday, the seventh day of the week in the Jewish calendar, as the day of rest commanded in the Torah. Jesus does allow for certain activities that other Jews might have prohibited—for example, he allows his disciples to pluck grain on a Sabbath when they are hungry (Matthew 12:1–8)—but Jews in general debated what activities were allowed on the Sabbath, so Jesus was not unique in having a controversial view, and nowhere in the Gospels does he suggest that Sunday should be made a day of worship instead of Saturday. That change only took place later, sometime after Paul, as Christians sought to differentiate themselves from the Jews. Some Christians continued to follow Jewish law, but most, coming from non-Jewish backgrounds and following Paul's understanding of the "Old Covenant" as no longer binding, did not feel obligated to follow the Torah's command to keep the Sabbath, turning to Sunday, which had taken on newfound significance as the day of Jesus's resurrection. We cannot fully reconstruct the process by which Sunday came to replace the Sabbath for Christians, but a turning point came in the fourth century CE, when Sunday was officially adopted as a day of rest. Shifting the most sacred day of the week from the seventh day to the following day, the first day of the new week, not only signaled that Christians were distinct from the Jews but also conveyed the message that their religion marked a new beginning, a new era in God's relationship with humanity that superseded the covenant established at Mount Sinai.

However, by transferring elements of the Sabbath to Sunday, including sometimes referring to Sunday as the Sabbath, Christians also acknowledged a continued sense of connection to Judaism.

welcome non-Jews into the Jewish relationship with God in this way; it allowed them to bypass Judaism and its laws altogether in their pursuit of a relationship with God. To the extent that Jewish religious life in this period was defined by the laws of Moses, what Paul was advocating was not a Judaism to which non-Jews were welcome but a new relationship with God in which, as Paul put it, "[t]here is no longer Jew or Greek" (Letter to the Galatians 3:28).

Paul's theology left open the possibility of a Christianized Judaism—Jews who identify as Jews and adhere to Jewish law but believe in Christ as well—and indeed, Paul never seems to have abandoned his own Jewish identity, depicting his embrace of Christ as a transformation *within* a religious tradition rather than as a conversion from one religion to another. But although there continued to be Jewish Christians for some time (a vague category that encompasses born Jews who converted to Christianity and also Christians who felt they should follow Jewish law), Paul's theology provided a compelling rationale for accepting non-Jews into the movement without requiring them to become Jews. By the time the canonical Gospels were written (between 70 and 100 CE), many Christians regarded themselves as something other than Jewish. By the second century, Christians like the soon-to-be-martyred Ignatius were condemning Judaizing Christians for blurring the line between two communities they considered utterly distinct (for an example of Christianity's emerging distinction from Judaism, *see the box* "From the Sabbath to Sunday").

Though Christianity soon detached itself from Jewish culture, it was still rooted in Jewish tradition. It laid claim to the Bible, understanding Christians rather than the Jews as the true successors to the tradition established by Abraham and Moses. In this way, early Christians can be compared to a group briefly introduced in previous chapters, the Samaritans. The Samaritans were not Jews—they did not live in Judea, worship in the Jerusalem Temple, or accept the Jewish biblical canon—but they professed an overlapping identity, venerating the Five Books of Moses (but not other biblical books), tracing their descent to the Israelite tribes of Ephraim and Manasseh, and viewing their temple on Mount Gerizim as the cult ordained by Moses. What fueled the antagonism between the Jews and the Samaritans was not just their differences but also their similar self-image as descendants of biblical Israel. The Jews faced a similar rival in the Christians, a people with its own way of worshipping God, its own understanding of the Bible, and its own claim to the status of God's people.

It is in the context of this rivalry that one must understand the emergence of a virulent anti-Judaism in early Christian culture, a hostility already evident within the Gospels and coming into sharp relief by the second century. Christians inherited some of the suspicions and prejudices of earlier pagan Judeophobia, which focused on Jewish religious practices as evidence of Jewish malice and barbarism, but Christian antisemitism was not a simple continuation of earlier pagan ideas. Christians did not belittle Jews for rejecting cult statues or worshipping an alien God—Christians behaved similarly, after all. What emerged in place of these motifs was a theological and moral critique of the Jews for their alleged role in the death of Jesus and their rejection of his status as the Messiah and Son of God. Christian anti-Judaism is perhaps best conveyed in the words of those who promulgated it—say, the fourth-century theologian Gregory of Nyssa (while perhaps falsely assigned to Gregory, the passage ahead nonetheless sums up Christian grievances against the Jews):

> Murderers of the Lord, murderers of the prophets, rebels, and full of hatred against God, they commit outrage against the law, resist God's grace, repudiate the faith of their fathers. They are confederates of the devil, offspring of vipers, scandal-mongers, slanderers, darkened

DID THE JEWS KILL JESUS?

One of the accusations that early Christians lodged against Jews is that they were guilty of deicide, of killing the Son of God. Responsibility for his death was placed not just on individual Jews living at that time but on the Jewish people as a whole, past and present, as if today's Jews somehow participated in Jesus's trial and execution too. The earliest known accusation of this nature is found in the writing of the bishop Melito of Sardis, who died around 190 CE, and it is a charge sometimes leveled against Jews to this day. As recently as 2011, Pope Benedict XVI found it necessary to publish a work that laid out the reasons that the Jews were not to be held responsible for Jesus's death.

So were (are) the Jews responsible for the death of Jesus? Let us address this question historically. Although the Romans were the ones to actually execute Jesus, some of the Gospels do what they can to transfer guilt to the Jews—not just individual Jews, but the whole people, reporting that it voluntarily accepted responsibility (see, for example, Matthew 27:25). As we have noted, however, it is not clear that we can rely on the Gospels for an understanding of what really happened. As scholars have pointed out, their authors (writing between 70 and 100 CE) may have been seeking to distance themselves from the Jews, at that period involved in rebellion against the Romans, or else being punished for that rebellion, and thus dangerous for Christians to be identified with. Since they were seeking non-Jewish converts, the authors of the Gospels may also have wanted to exonerate the non-Jews involved in the Crucifixion, lest they antagonize their non-Jewish (and especially Roman) audience. This is how secular scholars explain the Gospels' efforts to assign collective responsibility to the Jews: Religious readers might not be so quick to question the New Testament's reliability, but in recent decades, authorities like the Catholic Church have re-examined the New Testament and found no reason in it to hold the Jews collectively responsible for the death of Jesus, now or at that time.

It is certainly credible from a historical perspective that individual Jews might have informed on Jesus or supported his execution. We know of Jews in this period, including Josephus himself, who threw their support to the Romans and informed on or worked against fellow Jews: Such Jews did this to protect themselves or to get the better of their rivals or because they sincerely supported the Romans, and their behavior is similar to that of modern defectors and informers who ally themselves with a foreign power, sometimes for self-serving reasons, but sometimes out of a sincere sense that cooperating with that power is a better course for their people than defiance. We have no way to confirm the testimony of the Gospels, but on the basis of an example like Josephus, there is nothing historically improbable about their claim that Jesus was betrayed to the Romans by Judas Iscariot or other fellow Jews.

It is a far step from such individual cases, however, to holding the Jews collectively responsible for Jesus's death as a people. The vast majority of Jews, living throughout the Roman Empire, would not have even heard of Jesus, much less consented to his death at the hands of an enemy conqueror, and there were probably many Jews who would have balked at handing over a fellow Jew to the Romans. The absurdity of the accusation becomes clear when one considers whether it would be fair to hold all Italians today responsible for the death of Jesus simply because there were Romans involved in his execution. The issue is not simply a matter of setting the historical record straight: The accusation of deicide has long served as a rationale for prejudice in the Christian world, fostering the impression of Jews as persecutors even at times when they were the ones being persecuted.

in mind, leaven of the Pharisees, Sanhedrin of demons, utterly vile, quick to abuse, enemies of all that is good.

(*In Christi Resurr.* Orat. 5, PG 46, 685)

Concentrated in the preceding passage are some of the main themes of Christian anti-Judaism: (1) The Jews had refused to accept Jesus as the Messiah and Son of God, (2) the Jews had murdered God by conspiring to kill Jesus (a view that plays down the fact that Jesus had actually been executed by the Romans; *see the box* "Did the Jews Kill Jesus?"), and (3) the Jews were "confederates of the devil," perpetrating various sins under the cloak of piety.

In the first two or three centuries of the Common Era, Christian hostility toward the Jews may have posed no more of a threat to them than Samaritan hostility did. Despite the legal and economic sanctions that followed the revolts of the first and second centuries, Judaism's legal status remained basically the same: It was recognized by imperial rule as a legitimate religion entitled to protection. Christianity did not enjoy such protection and, in fact, suffered through several periods of intense persecution by the Roman government.

However, unlike the Samaritans (who still endure but number only a few hundred today), the Christian community was a rapidly growing and increasingly influential one, and the more influence it gained, the more its anti-Jewish tendencies posed a threat to Jews. Already by the first century, the Christians were making inroads in Syria, Asia Minor, Greece, and even Rome (where Christian missionizing efforts evidently created such a disturbance that the Jews of the city were expelled yet again in the 40s); they had even begun to win African converts. By the second century, Christians were living throughout the empire and beyond—the Christian historian Eusebius places a Christian community as far away as India at this time. It is not clear when Christians first became the majority in the empire—they were still facing bouts of persecution in the early fourth century—but by this period, their influence was such that even the emperor became an adherent. In 312, as he prepared for battle, Emperor Constantine I had a vision that inspired him to order his troops to affix a sign of Christ on their equipment. Under his rule and that of almost all his successors, the Church had a defender in the Roman Empire.

Even after its Christianization, the Roman Empire never declared Judaism illegal, continuing legal protections for the communities within its domain. But Jewish culture was now vulnerable in its conflict with Christianity in a way that it had not been before. Christian mobs, sometimes riled up by local leaders, attacked synagogues as they did pagan temples, turning some of them into churches. They could also drive Jews from the communities in which they lived, as happened in Alexandria in 414. Although such violence was not necessarily endorsed by the Roman authorities—indeed, they sometimes intervened to protect the Jews—even the emperor could not always save the Jews. After the burning of a synagogue in the Mesopotamian town of Callinicum in 388 CE, Emperor Theodosius initially tried to intervene to have it rebuilt but then gave up the attempt under pressure from St. Ambrose. The Church did not seek to exterminate the Jews—they were to be preserved as the Old Testament was preserved—but those Jews living under Christianized Roman rule were now a marginalized minority in a society premised on their purported theological failings.

By this time, Christians and Jews clearly saw the other as Others, a distinct community regarded as evil. But that is a distinction that crystallized only after the first century. For the first few decades of Christian history—in the days of Jesus and his immediate disciples, perhaps still in the time of Paul—the early Christian community was still hard to distinguish from the Jews, one of several competing understandings of God, the Torah, Jewish tradition, and the eschatological future. The Jewish origin of Christianity means that what we have described in this chapter is as much a part of Christian history as it is Jewish history—indeed, much of what we know about this time period comes from scholars not of Jewish studies but of early Christianity seeking to understand the religious and social background of the New Testament.

What we want to emphasize here, however, is that the earliest Christian community is, at the same time, a part of the history of the Jews. It is only because of what we know in retrospect—Christianity's development into a separate religion and its subsequent antagonistic relationship with Judaism—that we may balk at the idea of treating the earliest Christians as Jews, but they were, and the written evidence they have left behind tells us many things about early Jewish culture that we would have had a hard time seeing without such evidence. There is still a lot of debate among scholars about what is and isn't "Jewish" about early Christianity—what it inherited from Jewish tradition and what it absorbed from Greek and Roman culture—but one could have the same debate about other forms of Jewish culture known from this period, the Judaism of Philo or Josephus. What distinguished Christianity from other kinds of Judaism was not its commingling of Jewish and non-Jewish culture per se but the fact that it was so successful at integrating non-Jews and worked so hard to distinguish itself from earlier Jewish tradition that it eventually came to see itself as distinct from Judaism.

The Transition to Late Antiquity

In the period between Pompey's invasion of Judea and the Bar Kochba Revolt, Jewish culture was forced into a series of changes by its conflicts with Roman rule. The destruction of the Temple during the First Jewish Revolt compelled Jews to develop alternatives to the act of sacrifice and the institution of the priesthood. The backlash triggered by the Diaspora Revolt precipitated the decline of large Jewish communities, like that of Alexandria, which had exerted so much influence during the Second Temple period. The de-Judaization of Jerusalem and Judea in the wake of the Bar Kochba Revolt ended the hope of restoring the Temple and shifted the center of Jewish life in Palestine to the Galilee. The Jewish culture that emerged from all this change was very different from that of 100 BCE, shaken and reorganized by two centuries of Roman domination and Jewish resistance.

It would be a mistake, however, to attribute all the change of this period to the violent conflict that developed between Jews and Romans in the first two centuries of the Common Era. The Roman world itself was not a static thing—it, too, underwent continuous change and development, splitting into western and eastern halves in the third century CE and acquiring in its eastern half a new capital at Constantinople in present-day Turkey. It absorbed various migrations and invasions, struggled under periods of economic decline, and underwent a process of gradual Christianization that eventually penetrated into every aspect of religious and social life. The differences are so marked, in fact, that it has become common among historians to label the period between the third century CE and the Islamic conquests of the seventh and eighth centuries as "late antiquity," considered a kind of transitional age between the pagan Roman Empire and the cultures that developed in Europe, North Africa, and the Near East in the Middle Ages. Late antique culture was continuous with the Hellenistic and Roman culture that we have been concerned with in the last two chapters, but it saw major new developments as well, including the emerging dominance of monotheistic faith and its role as a driving force of empire. The impact of this period on subsequent history is reflected in the fact that the two religions that emerge as most dominant at this time, Christianity and Islam, shape the culture of much of the world's population to this day.

To give some sense of Jewish history in late antiquity, we thus need to move beyond the revolts of the first and second centuries CE to the following centuries. Our focus in the next chapter will be the development of what is now known as rabbinic Judaism, which is often described as a response to the destruction of the Second Temple but really developed only many centuries after the Temple's loss, probably long after many Jews had adapted to living without it. To understand its emergence, we need to place rabbinic Judaism in the context of the Mediterranean and Near Eastern culture that developed in late antiquity, a culture distinguished from earlier antiquity by a number of developments, including the decline of temples and sacrifice; the rise of a new conception of community defined by shared religious belief rather than by ethnicity or citizenship; and a heightened reverence for holy men revered for their knowledge and disciplined lifestyle. Our goal in the next chapter is to introduce rabbinic Judaism within the context of these broader cultural changes and to explore how it became the most influential form of Judaism to emerge from late antiquity.

For Further Reading

The Roman period, and especially the first century, has been the focus of extensive scholarship, in part because of its role as background for early Christianity and in part because of sensational archaeological discoveries, such as those at the Temple Mount and Masada. For more about Jewish history and culture in this period, see classic studies by Emil Schürer, *The History of the Jewish People in the Age of Jesus Christ*, as updated by Geza Vermes and Fergus Millar (Edinburgh: T & T Clark, 1973), Shmuel Safrai and Menachem Stern, *The Jewish People in the First Century*, 2 vols. (Assen: Van Gorcum & Co., 1974, 1976), and William Horbury, William David Davies, and John Sturdy, *The Cambridge History of Judaism, Vol. 3: The Early Roman Period* (Cambridge, England: Cambridge University Press, 1999), but the research has continued since then and has broadened its focus. See, for example, Erich Gruen, *Diaspora: Jews amidst Greeks and Romans* (Cambridge, MA: Harvard University Press, 2002); Martin Goodman, *Rome and Jerusalem: The Clash of Civilization* (New York: Vintage Book, 2007), and the studies included in Catherine Hezser, ed., *The Oxford Handbook of Jewish Daily Life in Palestine* (Oxford: Oxford University Press, 2020).

For further discussion and a bibliography of more specific topics, see John Collins and Daniel Harlow, *The Eerdman's Dictionary of Early Judaism* (Grand Rapids, MI: William B. Eerdmans Publishing, 2010), which covers the period through the second century CE. A number of online entries from *Oxford Bibliographies* are relevant, although these are behind a firewall. Examples include the entries "Flavius Josephus" by Steve Mason and Eelco Glas, and "Late Antique (Roman and Byzantine) History" by Haym Lapin.

Translations used here of both Philo and Josephus can be found in the Loeb Classical Library of Harvard University Press. Translations of Dead Sea Scrolls material are taken from Elisha Qimron and James Charlesworth, *The Dead Sea Scrolls: Hebrew, Aramaic and Greek Texts with English Translations, Vol. 1: Rule of the Community and Related Documents* (Tübingen: J. C. B. Mohr [Paul Siebeck] and Louisville, KY: Westminster John Knox Press, 1994).

Much research has been devoted to understanding Jesus, Paul, and early Christianity against an early Jewish backdrop. See, for example, Paula Fredriksen, *Jesus of Nazareth, King of the Jews: A Jewish Life and the Emergence of Christianity* (New York: Knopf, 1999), and Parish Sanders, ed., *Paul and Palestinian Judaism: A Comparison of Patterns of Religion* (Philadelphia: Fortress Press, 1977). Also helpful for understanding the connections between the New Testament and early Judaism is Amy-Jill Levine and Marc Brettler, eds., *The Jewish Annotated New Testament* (Oxford, England: Oxford University Press, 2011).

There now also exists a wealth of online resources for those who want to learn more about Jewish history in the Roman period. There are websites devoted to Josephus, like Flavius Josephus Online, and still other resources bearing on other sources from this period, like *4 Enoch: The Online Encyclopedia of Second Temple Judaism, and Christian and Islamic Origins*: www.4enoch.org, not to mention innumerable sites related to the Roman Empire and Christianity. A good way to keep up with current trends in the field is the website Ancient Jew Review, which contains articles and reviews on topics relevant to the study of Judaism in this period.

CHAPTER 5

TALMUDIC TRANSFORMATIONS

IN THE CENTURIES that followed the destruction of the Second Temple, there emerged a community of scholars now known by the title *rabbi* who have had a transformative effect on Judaism into the present. These scholars introduced a new conception of the Torah and how to study it very different from anything that had existed previously. They developed ways of interacting with God that did not depend on the Temple, and their scholarly activity produced a wealth of new compositions—the Mishnah, Midrashic literature, and the Talmud—that would become as important to guiding Jewish life as the Hebrew Bible. It is hard to determine how influential these sages were in their own day, but their efforts had such an impact on the later development of Jewish culture that Judaism today is really "rabbinic Judaism," Judaism as reshaped by ideas and practices originating in the late antique context, which we will be exploring in this chapter.

Who were "the rabbis," and how did they come to exert such an influence on Jewish life? It might have been easier to answer these questions if the rabbis themselves had left us a historical account like the ones that biblical authors produced for ancient Israel or that Josephus wrote for the Second Temple period, but they did not. In lieu of such a narrative, however, one text can serve as a starting point for rabbinic history—it will not help us pin down the actual origins or development of rabbinic Judaism, but it does tell us something of how the rabbis placed themselves in history.

The work in question, *Pirkei Avot*, or the "Chapters of the Fathers," is included in a larger document known as the Mishnah that we will examine later in this chapter. *Pirkei Avot* is not a history but a kind of anthology that gathers together the pithy observations and teachings of early rabbinic sages. The name *Avot*, or "Fathers," might refer to the "fathers" or early authorities in the rabbinic movement or, else, to the teachings themselves, as the fundamentals of wisdom. Its opening chapter is what is of interest here, as it presents an intellectual genealogy that establishes the credentials of the rabbinic sages by tracing their authority back to the biblical age. *Pirkei Avot* traces the transmission of the Torah from Moses to Joshua, from Joshua to the prophets and elders of the biblical period, and from the prophets and elders to the sage Yohanan ben Zakkai and his students, founding figures in the rabbinic movement who lived in the transitional period between the Second Temple period and the age that followed the Temple's destruction. According to the rabbis' own understanding of their history, in other words, they were the successors to Moses, continuing a tradition that reached all the way back to Sinai.

Pirkei Avot makes it appear as if rabbinic Judaism flowed directly out of the wisdom of sages in the Second Temple period, but in fact, it differed from what it grew out of in many ways. In the Jewish

DOI: 10.4324/9781003611592-6

culture of the Second Temple period, the central religious authority was the priest, whose primary role was not to interpret the Bible or preach to the people, though he might do such things, but to perform the rituals that allowed Israel to interact with God in the Temple. In rabbinic Judaism, formed in the wake of the Temple's destruction, the priest was eclipsed by the rabbi, the scholar and teacher, whose place in Jewish society was based on intellectual merit rather than on coming from a particular family line and whose authority was based not on his role in the rituals of the Temple but on his study and interpretation of the Torah. This shift in the nature of religious authority had momentous consequences for the development of Judaism as a religion and culture, allowing for very different understandings of the Jewish past and of how to continue its traditions into the present.

The focus of this chapter is the rabbinic movement and its transformative impact on Jewish culture in late antiquity. The term rabbi ("my teacher") was used as a general term of respect in Jewish antiquity, applied to various sages, judges, and teachers (including Jesus) by their disciples and followers. In the context of this chapter, what we mean by *rabbi* is not just a respected Jewish teacher in a general sense but a sage within a particular social network that emerged after the Second Temple's destruction: the community of sages reflected in the Mishnah, the Talmud, and other texts that came out of this movement. Jewish culture in general is not extensively "rabbinized" until long after the death of these sages, but they were the ones to initiate this transformation, and that is why we make them our focus in this chapter.

The Late Antique Context of Rabbinic Judaism

Before we introduce the rabbis, however, it is important to put their movement into a larger context, and here we run into a familiar problem that has obstructed us repeatedly in our attempt to reconstruct ancient Jewish culture. Most of what we know about these figures comes from texts that are very hard to contextualize or to connect to evidence from other sources. If we try to move beyond rabbinic literature, we find that we do not know very much about Jews or Jewish culture in a broader sense. To be sure, we have references in Christian sources along with the archaeological remnants of synagogues, tombs, and inscriptions that generate a lot of insight, but all this evidence is not enough to give us a very complete picture of Jewish life beyond what is represented in rabbinic sources, or of how the rabbis fit into Jewish society. Still, the evidence we do have does allow us to sketch in at least some of the larger context in which rabbinic culture developed—or, rather, *contexts*, since that culture developed in two settings: in Palestine, controlled by the Roman Empire, and in Babylonia, ruled by a dynasty known as the Sasanians.

Jewish Life in a Christianized Roman Context

What we know of Jewish life in the Roman Empire after the Bar Kochba Revolt suggests that many Jews in subsequent centuries probably saw themselves as continuing the traditions of their ancestors—the laws of Moses and other ancient traditions inherited from the biblical past. It is true that Jewish religious life in this period differed in one glaringly obvious respect from that of earlier periods—there was no longer a Temple—but even so, the Temple remained important for Jews, if only as a memory or symbol of what Jews had lost and what they might yet regain. In fact, we know that Jews still had reason to think the Temple's restoration was within the realm of possibility centuries after its destruction. In 362 CE, a Roman emperor named Julian—known in Christian sources as "the Apostate" because of his hostility to Christianity—undertook to rebuild the Temple as part of his effort to reverse the Christianization of the Roman Empire and also perhaps to recruit Jewish support for his war against Persia. It is hard to know what Jews made of Julian's attempt, but some evidence of Jewish support has been identified. An inscription discovered on the "Wailing" Wall in Jerusalem (a remnant of the wall that surrounded Herod's Temple complex) uses a verse from Isaiah 66 to express the rejuvenation some Jews may have felt at that time: "When you see it [i.e., the Temple], your heart will rejoice and your bones will sprout like green grass." This seems to be someone's hopeful reaction to Julian's attempted restoration of the Temple.

As it happens, Julian died before he finished the project, assassinated by a Christian or slain in battle, depending on which sources one believes, but the hope of rebuilding the Temple persisted long after antiquity. Jews developed rituals and customs that kept alive the memory of its loss—the observance of the fast day of Tisha B'Av falling during summertime and the shattering of glass during Jewish weddings were two ways that they commemorated its destruction. In their prayers and blessings, Jews continued to express the hope that the Temple would be restored one day, though they looked not to foreign rulers but to the long-anticipated Messiah to rebuild it. What is also important to note, however, is that the hope of a restored Temple did not prevent Jews from adapting to a world without it. Many laws and rituals could be observed without it or were newly developed in its absence, and those sustained a vital Jewish religious life no longer dependent on the Temple. Indeed, the most telling aspect of Julian's attempt to rebuild the Temple from the perspective of Jewish history may well be that its failure did not make much of a difference to Jews—rabbinic sources never mention it, as if the rabbis had never heard of the attempt. By this point, Judaism had evolved to the extent that the actual presence or absence of the Temple in Jerusalem made little difference to how many Jews lived their lives or expressed themselves religiously.

It is also clear that even as Jews continued to find ways to maintain their distinct identity, they also participated in the non-Jewish world around them. Much of Jewish life in this period mirrors non-Jewish culture and can sometimes be indistinguishable from it. The economy of Jewish life—Jewish involvement in agriculture and other ways of making a living; what Jews produced, used, and purchased—often cannot be neatly differentiated from that of non-Jewish neighbors; their basic wardrobe seems similar to that of Romans (tunics and mantles), and they engaged in similar leisure activities. For example, going to the public bathhouse—not just to get clean but also to socialize, receive medical treatment, and seek various forms of pleasure—became a part of social life for Jewish males as it was for non-Jewish males in this period.

But at the same time, Jews also found ways to engage in the broader culture of late antiquity in a way that also reflected a distinctly Jewish orientation. To return to the subject of clothes, for example, what a Jewish man or woman in this period wore might be basically the same as that of non-Jews, but Jews did introduce differences that marked their distinct identity. Their clothing could be produced in distinctive ways—in adherence to biblical law, for example, Jews might avoid mixing linen and wool—and some Jewish men visibly distinguished themselves by adding fringes (*tzitzit* in Hebrew) to their mantles in fulfillment of another biblical command (this kind of fringed mantle, known in Hebrew as a *tallit*, has become a regular part of the dress of religiously observant Jews today, worn under the clothes throughout the day and over the clothes during prayer).

Both of the trends we have been describing here—the abiding commitment of Jews to their ancestral culture and their adaption to the late antique Roman world around them—are well illustrated by the synagogue. As was noted earlier, the synagogue was an institution that originated as early as the third century BCE and further developed after the destruction of the Second Temple. By the first century, synagogues (or structures given other names but serving analogous functions) were established throughout the Eastern Mediterranean—not only in Palestine, but also in Egypt, Asia Minor, Greece, and Italy. The large number of synagogues in late antiquity (we have indications of at least 11 in the city of Rome alone), their wide distribution around the Mediterranean and Near East, and the resources invested in their construction and decoration all indicate they were central to Jewish communal life.

As noted in the chapter on the Hellenistic period, the synagogue served as a kind of community center, and its importance in Jewish society only increased in the Roman period as measured by the resources invested in their construction. The synagogue was the setting for many public activities, like the administration of justice, business transactions, and the manumission of slaves, but its most basic role was to connect Jews to the Torah. Scrolls of the Torah were kept there, the synagogue was where Jews publicly read from the Torah during Sabbaths and other religious occasions, and some synagogues may have featured a "seat of Moses," a special chair where the synagogue leader or a respected elder may have been seated as a sign of honor. The synagogue was not invented to take the place of the Temple—it emerged before the Second Temple's destruction—but it came to be seen as a kind of virtual Temple, replicating in its design some of the elements of the Temple. Thus, the niche where the Torah scrolls were kept came to be known as the *holy ark*, or *aron hakodesh*, a sacred chest in Solomon's Temple where the tablets of the covenant were kept. The synagogue is thus an excellent illustration of a widespread Jewish commitment to tradition, to the Bible, and even to the now-absent Temple.

But the example of the synagogue also illustrates the ways in which Jewish culture had adapted to its cultural surroundings in the Hellenized Roman world of late antiquity. The architecture and decorations of late antique synagogues often imitate the elements of non-Jewish public buildings. Some synagogues feature mosaic floors decorated with images from the zodiac, a Greco-Roman way of imagining the heavens that included the personification of the seasons and the sun god himself, Helios. Evidently, those who frequented such synagogues did not perceive such images to be a violation of the biblical prohibition against divine images; they were simply emulating widespread non-Jewish imagery. Other architectural or decorative elements were borrowed from churches after the spread of Christianity. An example is the use of a screen or partition to separate off and hide the Torah scroll. This element seems to emulate Solomon's Temple, where the Ark of the Covenant was concealed within the Holy of Holies, but it is at the same time an imitation of the contemporary Christian practice of using screens to separate the priests and their activities around the altar from the lay congregation. It is known that some synagogue and church screens were actually made in the same workshops.

From such evidence, we can see how it was that Jewish culture continued in late antiquity and even flourished in some settings. Jews were able to find ways to maintain a distinct cultural and religious identity—to engage the Bible, to build and sustain communal institutions, to practice their laws and traditions—and they did so in ways that were also adapted to their cultural environs in a late antique world. Some Jewish communities within the Roman world were devastated by the uprisings of the first two centuries of the Common Era, but others thrived, and new communities could emerge even in remote regions, like Germania and Gallia, far from where Jews had lived in the past.

And yet in many ways, the late antique Roman world was not a hospitable one to Jews and Jewish culture. Jewish communities thrived in some places, but there is also evidence of an overall

Figure 5.1 A mosaic floor from a sixth-century synagogue at Beth Alpha, near Beth Shean, in modern-day Israel, depicting a Greco-Roman zodiac. The central figure is the sun god Helios, while the symbols in the surrounding wheel, labeled with Hebrew names, are the classic 12 zodiac signs of Greco-Roman astrology, corresponding to the 12 months of the year. Such zodiacs may have been used to help measure the passage of the year as in non-Jewish communities, but the zodiac eventually developed into a conventional Jewish decoration of its own and is still used in such a way by some Jewish communities.

political and cultural decline, especially after the fourth century CE. Some historians have argued for a dramatic Jewish demographic downturn over the course of late antiquity, a claim that is hard to prove, but there are certainly indications of declining political fortunes. After the end of the Herodian dynasty, there emerged in the second or third century CE a kind of national leadership based in Palestine known as the patriarch or the *nasi* in Hebrew, which had some kind of legal authority and official recognition by the Roman government, though nothing like the power of Herod or his influence with the Romans. The patriarchs claimed Davidic lineage, which elevated their status to that of a quasi-royal figure; they seem to have been wealthy and respected; and they had influence over Jews in Palestine and even the Diaspora, but the nature of their authority and their status in the eyes of the Roman government are debated by scholars, and their powers seem to have been quite limited, restricted to internal communal matters—judicial and religious matters like overseeing the Jewish calendar (which had to be carefully regulated by judges who determined when each lunar month began). And whatever influence this institution might have exerted at its height in the third and fourth centuries CE, it did not survive for very long: The patriarchate was abolished by 429 CE, perhaps replaced by local Jewish councils or some other form of leadership, but nothing as stable or as visible as the earlier Herodian dynasty or the high priesthood.

Another possible reflection of decline are the various indications we have of Jews in this period seeking to escape their circumstances. For some Jews, escape took the form of apocalyptic or messianic fantasy, looking beyond the present for savior figures who could deliver them from the travails of the world around them. Many Jews may have converted to Christianity in this period, but Jesus was not the only messianic figure that Jews looked to for a way out. Around 450 CE, for example, there emerged a Jewish messianic movement led by a figure known as Moses of Crete, who reportedly claimed he was the original Moses, returned to once again deliver the Israelites from their enemies. His followers suffered a tragic end when the sea failed to part for them as it had for the biblical Israelites, but such experiences did not discredit the hope for a future savior. Texts like the *Book of Zerubbabel*, a seventh-century composition, show that Jewish messianism continued to the very end of antiquity, in part as a way to imagine a life beyond the end of Roman rule. As this composition depicts things, the biblical figure Zerubbabel meets the Messiah in Rome itself, though he is unrecognized by anyone else because he is disguised as a poor beggar. The Messiah's woes are temporary, however: Zerubbabel learns he will eventually reveal himself as a new emperor who will displace Rome and re-establish the Kingdom of Israel.

Of course, as mentioned in the last chapter, there was also a way to escape that did not involve supernatural intervention—moving beyond the control of the Roman Empire. This became all the more feasible in the third century CE thanks to the rise of the Sasanian kingdom in Iran and Mesopotamia, a successor to the Parthian kingdom. During the reign of Shapur I between roughly 240 and 270 CE, the Sasanian kingdom had been able to defeat the Romans in a decisive battle, even capturing the emperor himself, and conquered territory from the Romans on its eastern frontier, territory inhabited by many Jews. Shapur himself, along with subsequent rulers, seemed hospitable to Jews; rabbinic literature depicts Shapur as a close friend of the rabbinic sage Samuel. We will have more to say about the situation for Jews in the Sasanian kingdom later in the chapter; suffice it to say for now that, compared to what Jews faced in the Roman Empire, the Sasanian kingdom could seem a kind of refuge.

Although many Jews may have been seeking a way out of the Roman Empire, however, we know of no revolts comparable to the Jewish rebellions of the first and second centuries (though there were occasional uprisings, such as a Jewish revolt in 351/352 during the reign of Gallus). Perhaps this was because the consequences of those earlier rebellions were so terrible that few Jews wanted to risk rebellion, but there is also reason to think that things may have improved for Jews a bit within a few decades of the Bar Kochba Revolt.

In 193 CE, a soldier named Septimus Severus became Roman emperor, initiating a dynasty that lasted until 235 CE. Certain measures by Septimus suggest hostility to the Jews, including possible legislation that forbade conversion to Judaism and Christianity, and there might even have been a local Jewish uprising in Palestine during his reign, but the evidence for all that is rather thin, and in other respects, he seems to have treated the Jews quite favorably, evidently allowing native-born Jews to assume high-ranking public positions without having to take on duties at odds with their religious faith and throwing his support behind the institution of the patriarch, who served as an intermediary between the Jews and the Romans. Severus is remembered as sympathetic to the Jews, and something similar is true of the last in the Severan line as well, Alexander Severus, emperor between 222 and 235 CE, who seems to have had a sufficiently positive relationship with Jews that a synagogue in Rome was named in his honor. In other words, relations between Jews and Romans may have improved under the Severans.

Following the end of the Severan dynasty in 235, however, came a period of political and economic chaos that made life difficult not just for Jews but also for many people—half a century of crises and catastrophes that included inflation and the collapse of currency, invasions in various parts of the Roman Empire, assassinations, civil wars, and plagues. Recent historians have challenged the idea of an empire-wide crisis in the third century CE, but it was certainly a period of significant and disruptive changes for many. In fact, the empire itself became sufficiently destabilized over the course of the century that Emperor Diocletian, in 285 CE, thought it necessary to appoint a co-emperor to help rule it, a splitting of the empire into two parts—a Western Roman Empire and an Eastern Roman Empire—that became permanent after the death of Emperor Theodosius I in 395 CE. To be sure, the eastern part of the empire, where the majority of Jews lived, did not suffer the sharp decline the western part did. The city of Rome, the capital of the Western Empire, was sacked in 410 CE, and the Western Empire itself had fallen by the end of the century, whereas the Eastern Roman Empire, later known as the Byzantine Empire, continued all the way into the fifteenth century. It, too, faced its share of political, economic, and military problems, however, shrinking in size until basically it was confined to a region in present-day Turkey, the

Figure 5.2 A relief found in Iran depicting Shapur I's victory over the Roman emperor Valerian.

Balkans, and southern Italy. The decline of Jewish life in the Roman Empire can be understood to some degree to reflect the broader decline of the Roman Empire itself.

Beyond these political and social changes, there was another development that made life extremely difficult for Jews under Roman rule: the Christianization of the Roman Empire. Although it originated out of Judaism, Christianity developed a competing understanding of the Bible and God's relationship with humanity that could demonize Jews. Christians had not been a major threat to the Jews through the first three centuries of the Common Era. Indeed, Christians themselves were a persecuted minority through the end of the third century, especially during the reign of Diocletian, when churches were dismantled and Christians executed. Christianity's influence nonetheless grew throughout this period, winning more and more adherents and exerting more and more influence on the broader society, and this eventually changed the relationship between Christians and Jews.

A major turning point came during the rule of Constantine the Great (324–337 CE), famous for establishing a new capital of the empire, known as Constantinople (present-day Istanbul). On the eve of a battle, Constantine had a divine vision that convinced him to become a defender of Christianity, and he and virtually all of his successors deployed imperial power to do so, using legislation and other instruments of the state to support Christianity and undercut the influence and status of the Jews. With the exception of the aforementioned emperor Julian "the Apostate," who, during a brief reign lasting from 361 to 363 CE, tried in vain to revive the Temple, Christianity would have imperial backing in its struggle with Judaism from the fourth century onward (*see the box* "Converting the Land of Israel into the Christian Holy Land").

The Christianized Roman Empire never sought to abolish Judaism, continuing to recognize it as a legally sanctioned religion even as it sought to disempower it. Some Christians were sympathetic to the Jews or drawn to Jewish religious traditions, attending synagogues and Jewish festivals, and in some places, synagogues were built in close proximity to churches, more evidence of close social relations. Christian theology was hostile to Jews, for reasons we have noted in the last chapter, but it, too, developed a kind of tolerance for Jews, thanks in large part to the influence of Augustine of Hippo, the great Christian theologian who lived between 354 and 430. Augustine had sharp religious differences with Judaism, believed the Jews had misunderstood the Bible, and interpreted their suffering and dispersion as divine punishment for their rejection of Christ, but he did not advocate the violent opposition to the Jews characteristic of other Christian thinkers of the day, arguing that they should be permitted to exist, albeit in a miserable state, as living testimony to the truth of Christian belief. The influence of Augustine's view of the Jews is probably a major reason that Jews were able to survive under Christian rule through the end of antiquity and the Middle Ages. There were Christian leaders who wished to convert Jews to Christianity—in some cases, Jews were forced to convert under threat of expulsion or death—but by and large, the Augustinian approach prevailed, allowing for the continuation of Jewish communities, albeit in a weakened state.

Despite this tolerance, proponents of the Church and Christianized Roman rule did act on their hostility to the Jews. Constantine himself did not introduce major changes in the legal status of the Jews—in fact, he lifted the prohibition that barred Jews from visiting Jerusalem or mourning the Temple's loss—but his legislation adopted a very nasty tone against the Jews, describing their religion as a "nefarious sect." Subsequent emperors and church counsels, independent of the emperor but often working in consultation with him, introduced legislation that was designed to discourage or prevent the kind of close social interaction that had developed between Jews and Christians in many places: Christians were forbidden from attending synagogues, and Jews were not allowed to marry Christians, own Christian slaves (to avoid the slave's conversion to Judaism), or hold certain high offices.

A measure of the growing separation between the two communities was the detachment of the Christian holiday of Easter from Passover. Because the Gospels associate Jesus's death and resurrection with Passover, the two holidays were often celebrated in conjunction, which meant that Christians had to follow the Jewish calendar to know when to celebrate Easter. By the fourth century, Christians came to object to the idea that a Christian holiday could be dependent on the timing of a Jewish holiday and turned to a new system for determining the date of Easter that made its timing independent of Passover. Christianity after the fourth century was no longer a minority religion—it was in charge—and the effect of its laws was not just to contain the Jews as competitors but to turn them into pariahs, socially segregated from the Christian population, without some of the legal protections they had enjoyed under a pagan Roman Empire and now dependent on a government hostile to their religious beliefs.

Their weakened legal position also made Jews more vulnerable to the attacks of local Christian communities now under the leadership of bishops, local church leaders who became increasingly powerful in the fourth century CE and thereafter. Such attacks, often targeted at the synagogue, could be highly destructive. Although Roman law officially protected the synagogue from destruction or seizure, the fact that the government had to intervene to protect synagogues is one measure of the extent to which Jews were subject to violence from the local Christian community. In 388 CE, to cite one of the most infamous examples, a synagogue at Callinicum in present-day Syria was destroyed by a mob at the instigation of the local bishop. The incident suggests the level of hostility that some Jewish communities faced in this period; it also registers the bishop's growing influence over the fate of local Jewish communities, for while the emperor at that time, Theodosius the Great, had intended to rebuild the synagogue of Callinicum, he was talked out of it by Ambrose, the highly influential bishop of Milan.

It is very difficult to generalize about Christian Roman treatment of the Jews in this period—sometimes the Roman government would intervene against the Jews, and sometimes it would act to protect them—and the situation became only more complex as the Roman Empire began to fragment from the fifth century onward. In the Western Roman Empire, as centralized imperial power came to an end, bishops exerted even more influence, sometimes acting on anti-Jewish or proselytizing impulses in a way that could devastate the local Jewish community. An example is what happened in the sixth-century town of Clermont (in present-day France), where, with instigation from the local bishop, Avitus, who hoped to convert the town's Jews, a conflict broke out between Jews and Christians that resulted in the destruction of the synagogue and the forced conversion of the Jewish community under the threat of expulsion. Other Christian leaders, however, were more tolerant, such as Gregory the Great, who became pope in 590 CE (the *pope* is the bishop of Rome, always a powerful position because of Rome's importance and eventually becoming the most important authority in the Roman Catholic Church). Though wanting Jews to convert to Christianity, Gregory is known to have ordered bishops to compensate Jews for the seizure of synagogues and condemned forced conversions.

Alongside the history of persecution we have been describing, we also have to factor in the ways in which the development of Jewish culture was stimulated by its exposure to Christianity. Christians and Jews continued to live in close proximity in many communities, allowing for interaction and mutual influence. We have already noted that synagogues could emulate the design of churches, and that was only one of many ways in which Jewish culture was reshaped through its interaction with Christianity. In addition to the bishop, another group of religious authorities who emerged in this period were the monks, individuals who withdrew from society to live alone or in small communities, embracing a kind of deliberate poverty that shunned normal social life and worldly pleasure. No exact equivalent to the monk developed in Jewish culture, which never embraced a complete renunciation of sexuality or withdrawal from social life, but it is probably not a coincidence that the rabbi of late antiquity mirrors many of the qualities of the monk. Both the rabbis and many monks participated in communities defined by a close bond between teachers and disciples, and both functioned in similar ways as mediators—mediators between humans and God and also mediators among humans, as arbitrators of communal disputes. They did not share the practice of celibacy, but the rabbis of late antiquity did practice a kind of bodily self-denial, not disavowing sex and marriage but seeing their life of study as an alternative to sexuality, or highlighting the tension between study and married life.

While Jews certainly adapted their culture to a Christian context, however, the fact is that Christianized Roman rule posed many new threats. Christian theologians and writers fostered negative stereotypes, Jews were subject to pressure to convert, and they were vulnerable to harassment and physical attack—and all this in a political context, where the government was less willing or able to protect them, where Jewish communities were hemmed in by anti-Jewish legislation and sometimes caught in between the conflicts that divided Christians or that broke out between the Roman Empire and the Sasanians or, later, the Muslims. Jews fared better than the pagans did in a Christianized Roman Empire—the latter more or less disappeared—but their situation certainly seemed to deteriorate, at least when compared with the condition of Jews living beyond the Roman Empire, and especially in Babylonia.

The Babylonian Jewish community seems to have been a large one well before the end of the Second Temple period, but we can scarcely follow its history after the end of the biblical period—what we know of its intervening history in the Second Temple period comes from some brief references in Josephus's writings, a bit of archaeological evidence, and much later rabbinic sources. Over the course of late antiquity, however—after the third century CE—Babylonian Jewry found a voice of its own, developing into a major center of Jewish life that eventually overshadowed the Jewish culture of the Christian world. Because of its success in this Babylonian context, Jewish culture there developed in a different direction from that of the Jewish communities in the Christianized contexts of Palestine, Alexandria, Rome, and Constantinople. We turn now to a sketch of the Babylonian/Persian Jewish community as the second important context for understanding rabbinic Judaism, a context in

CONVERTING THE LAND OF ISRAEL INTO THE CHRISTIAN HOLY LAND

Among the consequences of the Christianization of the Roman Empire was a major change in the cultural profile of Palestine, now not just the ancestral homeland of the Jews but also a sacred place for Christians (the name Palestine, originally referring to the coastal part of Canaan associated with the Philistines, was first used of the region that included Judea by Greeks, and was later adopted as an administrative name by Roman/Byzantine Empire who passed it on in turn to the later Muslim empires who wrested control of the area in the seventh century).

Christians inherited from Judaism a reverence for Palestine as the Holy Land, but it had different meanings for the two communities. For Jews, Palestine, or that part of it that corresponded to the biblical Canaan, was a gift bestowed on their ancestors by God as part of his covenant with the Israelites. Jerusalem was especially significant as the capital of the Davidic kingdom and the location of the Temple, where God was thought to have a physical presence on earth. Early Christians understood the Temple, Jerusalem, and the Holy Land in a metaphorical way, or else, they were interested in the heavenly Jerusalem and did not see their relationship with God as tied specifically to geography in any literal sense. Eventually, however, the geographical Holy Land became important to Christians as well. By the third century, Caesarea, on the coast of Palestine, had become a center of Christian activity, and Christianity soon made inroads into the rest of Palestine too. Jerusalem had been the site of the most important events in the Christian conception of history—the crucifixion and resurrection of Jesus—and even before the fourth century, it had become important to many Christians to make pilgrimage there as a way of remembering the sacred events of Jesus's life and of feeling close to God.

The fourth century was a turning point, however, especially during the reign of Constantine, who, in addition to building a new Christian capital for Rome at Constantinople, aimed to restore the hidden tomb of Christ. After a journey by his mother, Helena, to Jerusalem, during which she uncovered the relics of what was believed to be the cross on which Jesus was crucified, Constantine initiated the construction of a church at the site of the discovery, which came to be known as the Church of the Holy Sepulchre. By the fifth century, churches were built in other places in Jerusalem as well, and

which it developed from the subculture of a small network of scholars into a nearly worldwide Jewish culture, stretching in its influence from Babylonia to North Africa and, eventually, into Europe.

Jewish Life in Sasanian Babylonia

In some respects, the Jews of Babylonia were in the same basic situation as Jews living under Roman rule—they, too, faced the challenge of sustaining their culture under foreign domination—but the political and cultural environment in Babylonia was different in important ways. For many centuries, the Jews of Babylonia lived under the same rulers that governed Judea—the Babylonians, the Persians, the Seleucids—but that changed in the first century BCE, when they came under the rule of the Parthian confederacy, based in Iran. When the Parthians fell in the third century CE, the aforementioned Sasanian kingdom, another multiethnic empire based in Persia, took control.

Research on Jewish life in the Sasanian kingdom is less developed than the corresponding study of the Christian Roman world, and scholars' understanding of the Sasanian kingdom has changed in recent years. What was once thought to be a relatively decentralized political system where ethnic at other places associated with Jesus, in the Galilee and elsewhere, which drew even more Christian pilgrims and immigrants.

Despite the Christianization of the Holy Land, Jews continued to live there and perhaps even thrived. They were prosperous enough as a presence to build and restore impressive synagogues at over 100 sites (the influx of Christian pilgrims and immigrants might have actually benefited local Jewish communities economically even as it swamped them demographically). While it would be misleading to describe this period as one of clear decline for Jews in Palestine, however, Christianity clearly came to dominate: Christian churches appeared everywhere, even remote regions like the Judean wilderness became the site of Christian monasteries, and Jews became a demographic minority. Christians would continue to dominate the Holy Land until the Sasanian and Muslim conquests of the seventh century CE, and their sense of connection to the Holy Land would continue long after that, ultimately motivating the wars known as the Crusades, a centuries-long effort that began in the eleventh century CE as an effort to regain Christian access to Jerusalem.

Figure 5.3 The "Madaba map" was part of a mosaic floor discovered in the nineteenth century in a Byzantine church at Madaba, Jordan. Dating to the sixth century CE, it depicts a Christianized Holy Land with Jerusalem at its center, pictured here, and one can see a number of the Christian shrines that had been built there by this time, including the Church of the Holy Sepulchre (a large structure in the center of the city perpendicular to the Cardo, the columnated roadway stretching across the city). Other parts of the map not visible here depict sites associated with stories from the Hebrew Bible and New Testament venerated by Christian pilgrims.

and religious communities like the Jews enjoyed a lot of autonomy may, in truth, have been more centralized and integrated, with Jews less insulated from their environs than once assumed. Still, Jews in the Sasanian world existed in a different political, cultural, and religious environment than did their counterparts in the Roman world, and that led Babylonian Jewish culture to take its own path even as it remained in contact with Jews in the Roman Empire.

The Sasanians closely identified themselves with a religion known as Zoroastrianism, which traced its history back to an ancient Iranian prophet named Zarathustra (or Zoroaster, as the Greeks referred to him), who taught about a supreme god named Ahura Mazda and his epochal battle with an evil spirit named Angra Mainyu. Zoroastrian priests could be very zealous in defense of their religion, and their royal allies are mentioned in sources as sometimes prohibiting certain Jewish religious observances and persecuting the Jews (along with Christians, Buddhists, and others). Fire was a very sacred symbol in Zoroastrian faith associated with Ahura Mazda and considered a source of goodness and purity, and Jews had to take care to avoid offending their religious sensibilities by keeping their use of Hanukkah candles out of sight. All in all, however, the relationship between Jews and their Zoroastrian Sasanian rulers seems not to have been as antagonistic as that between Jews and Christians—what Sasanians found most threatening about Christians was their missionizing activity, and that was less of an issue for Jews, who did not actively seek converts in the same way. Although religious conflicts and bouts of persecution still occurred, Zoroastrians never accused the Jews of betraying or killing their gods, did not proselytize or forcibly convert them, and did not engage in as consistent and prolonged polemic and persecution that Jews suffered through in a Christianized Roman Empire. For their part, Jewish (or at least rabbinic) sources seem more positively inclined toward Sasanian rule than they do toward Roman rule.

Key to this relationship with Sasanian rule was a kind of Jewish leadership that traced its history back to the Babylonian Exile but that really emerged in the third century CE: the exilarch. In some ways, the exilarch resembles the institution of the patriarchate—both were semi-royal representatives of the Jewish people who claimed Davidic descent, both exercised some level of control over the Jewish court system, and both served as intermediaries with the foreign government that ruled the Jews. Of the two, however, the institution of the exilarch proved far more durable than the patriarchate, surviving into the Muslim period and continuing in one form or another into the fifteenth century CE.

The exilarch not only played a diplomatic and judicial role but also exerted economic power, overseeing a kind of court, hosting lavish banquets as a way to display his wealth and assert social influence, and playing a semi-governmental role as when he appointed the official who oversaw the marketplace. An exilarch known as Mar Zutra II, in power between 512 and 520 CE, felt sufficiently powerful that he rebelled against the Sasanians, setting up an independent state that survived for seven years—a reminder that Jewish/Sasanian relations were not always so cordial, or the exilarch so loyal. For the most part, though, the exilarch functioned as an intermediary between the Jewish community and the Sasanian state, helping to maintain good relations. The relationship could be so close that, according to a Persian source, the fifth-century Sasanian ruler Yazhgird I, son of Shapur III, was married to a daughter of the exilarch.

Jews had a stake in maintaining a good relationship with the Sasanian authorities, and for their part, the Sasanians had a stake in sustaining good relations with the Jews, though that did not mean that they lavished a lot of attention and resources on them. Many Jews in this period lived in Mesopotamia, what is now Syria and Iraq, and the region was a kind of frontier zone between the Sasanian kingdom and the Roman Empire, a site of frequent conflict (for the impact this could have on Jews living in the region, *see the box* "A Synagogue in a War Zone"). The fact that the Christians living under the Sasanians in this region had reason to sympathize with their coreligionists in the Christianized Roman Empire made them more politically suspect than the Jews. By contrast, Sasanian rule found in the Jews a population with a history of good relations with earlier Persian rulers and a history of bad relations with Rome, and that made them easier to let be than was the case for Christians, who posed more of a political and religious threat.

Although it was once thought that Jews in the Sasanian kingdom were siloed from their surroundings, there is more and more evidence that they were in fact enmeshed in their cultural environs while still able to preserve a distinct identity. In places like Mahoza, a city on the bank of a canal connecting the Euphrates and Tigris Rivers, Jews interacted with non-Jews on a daily basis.

More evidence of integration is the language that Jews in Babylonia used, not a Hebrew unfamiliar to non-Jews or the Persian of the Sasanian elite but the Aramaic used by the general population. Not that Jews completely assimilated into their surroundings—it has been noted that there are fewer Persian loanwords in Babylonian rabbinic literature than Greek loanwords in Palestinian rabbinic literature—but there were many opportunities for interaction with non-Jews, and the result is a Jewish culture adapted in many ways to a Babylonian environment.

Two examples can illustrate this process of adaptation. The first emerges from the different sex lives of Jews in Palestine and Babylonia. For Jews in general, being fruitful and multiplying were a biblical commandment, and getting married and having children were considered a duty. Rabbinic sources composed in a Roman context, however, sometimes register an ambivalence about getting married. Marriage was thought to be in tension with higher obligations, especially Torah study, and some sages seem inclined to put off marriage so that they could pursue those other obligations. Babylonian sources reflect a different attitude, preferring that the sage get married as early as possible. Thus, it is said of one Babylonian sage who married at the age of 16, Rav Hisda, that his one regret was that he did not get married at the age of 14.

The difference between Palestinian and Babylonian rabbinic culture may well reflect the difference between a Hellenized Christian Roman Empire and a Sasanian one, for the Palestinian view mirrors the attitude of Greco-Roman philosophy and monasticism, which valued sexual self-restraint and celibacy, whereas the Babylonian view mirrors the attitude of Persian/Zoroastrian culture, which valued childbearing as a form of immortality. Another contrast between Roman and Sasanian sexual culture might explain a difference between Palestinian and Babylonian Jewish attitudes toward monogamy: Palestinian rabbinic sources incline toward monogamy, whereas Babylonian rabbinic sources are more open to polygamy and even to having "a wife for a day" (i.e., of marrying a woman for a temporary period to sanction brief sexual relations with her while being married to someone else). The former view mirrors the monogamous tendencies of Roman society, and the latter, Sasanian sexual ethics.

A second example of Jewish culture adapted to Babylonian Sasanian culture involves magical practice. Despite a biblical prohibition of magic, Jews employed what we would think of as magical practices to protect themselves in a dangerous and unruly world, consulting the stars, seeking to protect themselves from demons, and using incantations and amulets to summon divine or angelic help. We have evidence of late antique magical practice from both Palestine and Babylonia, and it, too, speaks to some of the cultural differences that developed between Jews in these regions. A compilation of Jewish magical recipes known as *Sefer Ha-Razim* (the book of secrets), composed in Palestine in the fourth or fifth century, reflects its Greco-Roman environment: It is written in Hebrew but contains an invocation of the Greek sun god Helios in a Greek-transcribed-into-Hebrew script. Jews in Babylonia practiced magic too, but much of what we know of their practice, coming from hundreds of Jewish magic bowls discovered in Mesopotamia and Iran, reflects the influence of Babylonian/Persian culture.

The purpose of the bowls was to imprison evil spirits, probably by trapping them within the bowl (such bowls were often found upside down, as if to catch something underneath). What is significant here is that the names of some of the demons are of Mesopotamian or Persian origin, as in the case of Lilith, a figure known from rabbinic sources as a temptress demon responsible for nocturnal emissions and miscarriages (in later rabbinic legend, she is identified as Adam's first wife, before

A SYNAGOGUE IN A WAR ZONE

Jews living in the borderland between the Sasanian and Roman Empires sometimes found themselves caught in the center of conflict, and the precariousness of their situation is reflected in the history of a remarkably preserved synagogue found in 1932 at a site known as Dura-Europos. Located on the Euphrates River in present-day Syria, the city of Dura-Europos was established during the Seleucid period, and its inhabitants found themselves passing from the control of one empire to the next, first back and forth between the Parthians and the Romans, and then between the Romans and the Sasanians. The synagogue was located just inside the city wall, and during a final defense of the city around 256 CE, its inhabitants tore off the roof and filled the building with sand in order to strengthen the wall. They thereby buried what was inside the building, including magnificent murals that depict various biblical scenes, and thus preserved them. For historians of Jewish art, these murals are important evidence that Jews in this period did not necessarily interpret the biblical commandment against divine images as a prohibition against representational art—the murals depict many humans, including a nude daughter of Pharaoh bathing in the Nile. Among the other reasons that these illustrations are fascinating is the way they reflect the site's borderline status between the Romans and the Sasanians; some of the biblical figures are dressed in Roman garb, and others in Persian garb.

But the Dura-Europos synagogue also attests to something else: the peril of life in a war zone between empires. The murals themselves have been subject to violence, with the eyes of some of the biblical figures gouged out. It is possible that the perpetrators were pious Jews offended by the presence of human images in the synagogue and mutilating them once they took control over the synagogue, but that is speculation, and other explanations are possible. Noting that several of these mutilated figures are dressed in Persian garb, in fact, one scholar has suggested that the perpetrators were not Jews but Roman soldiers symbolically striking out at images they took to be Persian enemies. Whatever one makes of all that, the synagogue itself came to a violent end during a battle between the Romans and the Sasanians, a terrible fight that, as archaeologists have recently discovered, may have involved the use of poisonous gas against the Roman defenders of the city.

God created Eve, fleeing Adam after a fight and menacing newborns ever since). Lilith seems to be an outgrowth of a class of demon known from Babylonian sources.

Such differences between the Jewish cultures of the Roman and the Sasanian Empires should not obscure the many personal, cultural, and religious connections that cut across the political boundary. There were trade routes that connected the Roman world to the Sasanian kingdom, and many kinds of people traveling from one realm to the other: soldiers, diplomats, traders, and even intellectuals, like the Athenian philosophers who sought refuge from Christianity in the Sasanian court after the closure of their academy in 529 CE. The Jews themselves were an important intermediary, and their ability to move from Palestine to Babylonia in late antiquity was crucial in the relocation of rabbinic culture from one context to the other. Despite such overlap, however, there were also physical, political, and social barriers that divided the two cultures—a political boundary between Rome and the Sassanians, but also geographic distance, a different relationship to the majority religion, and other cultural and religious differences that would leave an imprint on the rabbinic culture that developed in Babylonia and distinguish it from the rabbinic culture that developed in Roman-controlled Palestine.

The fate of the Dura-Europos synagogue captures the vulnerability of Jews in this region compared to the Jews of southern Mesopotamia, the region of Babylonia. Living closer to the center of Sasanian power, the Jews of Babylonia were able to establish a more stable and secure community than was possible for the Jews of Dura-Europos, a community devastated by the conflict between the Romans and the Sasanians. Unfortunately, the region today has proven no less volatile and dangerous: although the wall paintings of the Dura Europa synagogue were removed by archaeologists for museum display, the remnant of the synagogue itself appears to have been destroyed in 2014 by the militant group ISIS in the context of the Syrian civil war.

Figure 5.4 A scene from the wall painting of the Dura-Europos synagogue depicting Mordechai and Haman from the book of Esther dressed in Persian garb.

The world we have been describing was changed in significant ways in the seventh century CE in the wake of Islamic conquest. The Byzantine Empire persisted but lost much of its territory to Islamic rule, and the Sasanian kingdom came to a complete end in the mid-seventh century CE, when it was conquered by Arabs. Islamic rule marks a new period in Jewish history; it is certainly the end of the story we are telling in this chapter, but it did not end the Jewish culture that had developed in Sasanian Babylonia. Not only did that culture continue into the Islamic period, but its influence also grew as Islamic rule expanded into a fractured Roman Christian world.

Putting the Rabbis Into the Picture

How do the rabbis fit into the two historical contexts that we have briefly sketched?

Not very clearly. Rabbinic literature does reflect many of the cultural developments we have described, but what is less clear is the impact that rabbis had on the larger community. Nonrabbinic sources do occasionally mention figures identified as rabbis—for example, the magic bowls mentioned earlier sometimes refer to Yehoshua bar Perahya, a rabbi known from rabbinic sources—but for the most part, there is little trace of the celebrated rabbis of the Mishnah and

Figure 5.5 A bowl with an Aramaic magical inscription used to protect individuals from evil spirits.

Talmud, the most important rabbinic texts, in any of the archaeological and inscriptional evidence we have from Palestine or elsewhere. At a large cemetery found next to the town of Beth Shearim in the Galilee, a site where some 30 catacombs were discovered dating from the second to the fourth centuries, the tombs of several rabbis were found, including three successors of the great sage Judah the Patriarch, who we will encounter in a few pages as the reputed editor of the Mishnah. Another fourth-century inscription from northern Israel marked the building on which it was posted as the study house of Rabbi Eliezer ha-Qappar, another figure known from rabbinic sources. Such inscriptional testimony establishes the rabbis as a presence in late antique Palestine, but they do not tell us very much about them and their activity or clarify their influence on the surrounding Jewish community.

This near invisibility of the rabbis beyond the bounds of rabbinic literature generates one of the mysteries of rabbinic history that preoccupies scholars today. We know in retrospect that the rabbis eventually redefined what it meant to be Jewish in much of the Jewish world. How did it happen that a small group of sages who, in their own day, had little discernible impact beyond their own study circles came to transform Jewish culture? The historian's answer to this question spills over into the medieval period, the subject of later chapters, but it begins in late antiquity, and it is that part of the story that we aim to reconstruct in the rest of this chapter.

Rabbinic literature is vast in its size and scope—the Talmud is described as a "sea" for good reason—and it yields all kinds of information about Jewish life in late antiquity, but it is a very tricky historical source. Rabbinic texts like the Babylonian Talmud, weaving back and forth between Hebrew and Aramaic, are highly technical in the terms they use, and their argumentation follows a logic only the initiated understand. The stories preserved in this literature contain all kinds of information about family life, economics, the relationship with non-Jews, people's sense of humor, how the rabbis regarded the animal world, and the study culture of the rabbis themselves, among numerous other topics, but it is hard for historians to access this information if they are not trained in how to read rabbinic literature.

A much-discussed illustration of the problems involved in reconstructing rabbinic history from these kinds of sources is a famous story told of one of the founding figures of rabbinic Judaism, the sage Yohanan ben Zakkai. Yohanan lived in Jerusalem in the time of the Jewish Revolt, but he was also known for his activities at a place called Yavneh (or Jamnia, as it is known in Greek sources from the Roman period), a coastal town, and this story explains how he got from one place to another. Yohanan had been trapped in Jerusalem by the rebels, who were watching to make sure no Jews defected to the Romans, but he managed to escape by hiding in a coffin that his disciples carried outside the city. Making his way to the Roman general Vespasian, Yohanan predicted that the general would become ruler, a prophecy that was immediately confirmed by a messenger coming from Rome to announce that Vespasian would now be emperor. A grateful Vespasian allowed Yohanan to make one request, and in one version of the story, Yohanan asks permission to move to Yavneh with his disciples, thus establishing this place as the first center of rabbinic learning and judicial authority after the Second Temple's destruction.

Is this how rabbinic Judaism emerged in the wake of the Temple's destruction? While we cannot rule out such a possibility, the story as we have it dates from long after the time of Yohanan, and it has been preserved in rabbinic sources in multiple forms that differ from one another in many ways. Might the story preserve the memory of real events transmitted orally from Yohanan's disciples to their successors until the time it was written down? Possibly, but many of the story's details seem more legendary than historical. Yohanan's prophecy of Vespasian's kingship, for example, bears a suspicious similarity to a story that Josephus tells about himself in his account of the Jewish Revolt. If one visits Yavneh today, there is a tomb there believed by religious Jews to be that of Gamliel II, Yohanan's successor, but it has its origins in the much later Islamic period, and there is no archaeological evidence of any kind of rabbinic activity at Yavneh or elsewhere at such an early period. It seems more likely that the Yohanan story grew out of some version of Josephus's story as it was circulated in Palestine after 70.

The story of Yohanan's escape from Jerusalem illustrates the challenge of reconstructing rabbinic history: It is hard to know when the sources are describing what really happened and when they reflect later legend. Though scholars have not always been able to overcome this challenge, however, they have not stopped trying, extracting from rabbinic texts many clues about who the rabbis were and how they came to exert an influence over the larger Jewish community. The following survey, informed by recent scholarship, focuses on three key moments in the development of rabbinic Judaism: (1) the emergence of the rabbinic movement after the Second Temple's destruction, (2) the establishment of rabbinic authority in the larger

Jewish community sometime in the following centuries, and (3) the relocation of rabbinic culture to Babylon and its development into a worldwide Jewish culture. It is misleading to describe rabbinic history in such a straightforward manner. Scholars vary widely on how they reconstruct the origins and development of early rabbinic culture, and the sources do not even permit one to reconstruct a clear chronology of events. Important rabbinic figures like Yohanan, Akiba, and Judah the Patriarch are largely beyond our reach as real-life people, and we can reconstruct only a partial picture of the institutional and cultural contexts in which they operated. What we aim to do here is merely to introduce some significant moments in the development of rabbinic culture in a way that will help you situate the rabbis and the literature associated with them in a history that begins with the Temple's destruction in 70 CE and ends in the Islamic age.

The Emergence of Rabbinic Culture

The emergence of the rabbis, occurring between the end of the Second Temple period and 200 CE, is really a matter of speculation, since we have no rabbinic literature from this early period in their history, only traditions found in rabbinic sources from later centuries that are questionable as to their historical accuracy. Nevertheless, by putting this testimony with what we know from Josephus and other Second Temple period sources, it is possible to make educated guesses about where the rabbinic movement came from and how its development was tied to the Jewish Revolt and other events in the first and second centuries CE.

According to *Pirkei Avot*, the rabbis' pedigree goes back to sages living in the period of the Second Temple, such as Hillel and Shammai, who probably lived in the first century BCE. Hillel, supposedly born in Babylonia and a contemporary of Herod's, is an especially important sage in rabbinic memory. The earliest list of rabbinic rules for interpreting the Torah is associated with him, as are many wise sayings, including the famous "If I am not for myself, who will be for me, but if I am for myself alone, what am I?" Both Hillel and his contemporary Shammai are remembered as the founders of schools—probably like the circle of disciples who gathered around Jesus rather than an institutionalized school in the sense that we use the term today—and it was these disciples who seem to have transmitted the teachings of their masters to later generations. The debates between Hillel and Shammai and their respective schools, covering legal issues ranging from how to recite certain blessings to what it took for a non-Jew to convert to Judaism, loom large in how rabbinic literature recalls the Second Temple period. Hillel, for example, is remembered as the ancestor of the line of sages who held the office of the patriarch.

Attempts have been made to link Hillel's teachers, Avtalion and Shema'ayah, with two important sages known from Josephus, a Pharisee named Pollion (perhaps originally Ptollion) and his disciple Samais, but that identification is far from certain, and there is no pre-rabbinic evidence for Hillel himself. Even assuming there was a real Hillel and Shammai, images of the two in later rabbinic texts are fictionalized portraits that may not reflect what they were actually like.

While we cannot say much about the pre-rabbinic Judaism of the first and second centuries CE, there do appear lines of continuity between rabbinic Judaism and what preceded it in the Second Temple period. To begin with, there is the title *rabbi* itself, which literally means "my master." The rabbis used the term to refer to one another, but the term itself seems to go back to the Second Temple period as a way for disciples to address respected teachers (it is used in the New Testament by people addressing Jesus). The rabbis put their own spin on the title, deciding who merited it and reserving it for sages who lived after the Temple's destruction (e.g., they don't call Hillel a rabbi), but they were building on a title, and a tradition of how teachers and students should interact, that took shape in the pre-rabbinic period.

Some of the Second Temple figures whom the rabbis cite as revered predecessors are described in other sources as Pharisees. An example is Gamliel I (or Gamliel the Elder), a grandson of Hillel. He is an important figure in rabbinic literature, responsible for rulings like one that allowed women to remarry on the evidence of only one witness to the death of her husband (as opposed to the two witnesses often required by the rabbis to establish the truth of something). What is relevant about him is that he is also known to us from the New Testament, from the book of Acts, Chapter 5, where he is depicted as a Pharisee, and from Acts 22 as the teacher of Paul himself. (Gamliel is so important for Christianity that he was sainted by the Catholic Church, which deemed him a convert, and his body supposedly interred in a cathedral near the Leaning Tower of Pisa.) Beyond corroborating the existence of Gamliel I, these references establish a direct identification of a Pharisaic sage with a sage known from rabbinic sources.

Beyond links between certain pre-Temple sages in rabbinic lore and historical individuals known from other sources, the rabbis also resemble the Pharisees in several of their religious views. One of the Pharisees' distinguishing traits is their respect for an extrascriptural tradition of legal and religious practice transmitted from teacher to disciple, a tradition that seems to anticipate the central role of oral tradition in later rabbinic culture. Rabbinic records of Pharisaic conflicts with the Sadducees usually side with the Pharisees, and the beliefs and legal positions attached to the Pharisees often have parallels in rabbinic sources. According to Josephus, for example, the Pharisees held a view moderating between predestination and free will, believing that human destiny is determined by fate while also allowing that humans can nonetheless control what is in their power. This is consistent with a teaching attributed to Rabbi Akiba in *Pirkei Avot* 3:19: "Everything is foreseen, yet freedom of choice is granted." Such parallels are cited as evidence that rabbinic Judaism developed as a post-Temple offshoot of Pharisaic Judaism.

While a Pharisaic origin for rabbinic Judaism seems very likely, however, scholarship has complicated things. The rabbis never actually identified themselves as Pharisees (in contrast to Paul and Josephus, who acknowledged their affiliations with this group), nor did they identify themselves with any other specific sect from the Second Temple period. In fact, it has been argued that the rabbis were opposed to sectarianism in general, reconceiving Jewish tradition in ways designed to overcome the factionalism that divided Judean society in the Second Temple period. It is possible that the early rabbinic movement absorbed various kinds of religious affiliates, Pharisees but also priests, Zealots, the religious authorities referred to in the New Testament as scribes, and perhaps even some early followers of Jesus (such an identity has been suspected for Rabbi Eliezer ben Hyrcanus, who is said to have told Rabbi Akiba of a teaching he learned from a Yeshua son of Pantera, a figure tentatively identified as Jesus).

Whatever ties they had to Second Temple period Jewish culture, early rabbinic sages adapted their understanding of Jewish legal and ritual tradition in light of the Temple's destruction, reinterpreting it in a way that allowed for religious practice without a temple or the act of sacrifice. Rabbinic literature attributes this transformation to none other than Rabbi Yohanan ben Zakkai, the sage who escaped Jerusalem just before its destruction:

> As Rabban Yohanan ben Zakkai was coming from Jerusalem, Rabbi Joshua (Yohanan's leading student) followed him and beheld the Temple in ruins. "Woe unto us," Rabbi Joshua cried, "that this, the place where Israel atoned for its sins is laid waste." "My son," Yohanan said to him, "Be not grieved; we have another

> atonement as effective as this. And what is it? It is acts of loving kindness, as it is said [in Scripture], 'For I desire mercy and not sacrifice.'"
> (Hosea 6:6, *Avot de Rabbi Nathan* 4:18)

According to this story, Yohanan recognized a way for Israel to sustain its relationship with God without the Temple, substituting acts of loving-kindness—*gemilut hasidim*—for the act of sacrifice. Like other rabbinic stories told of Yohanan, this one is probably better classified as legend than history, but the real Yohanan may indeed have worked to revise Jewish worship in light of the Temple's destruction, although in very specific ways tied to how to implement certain religious duties dependent on the Temple cult. Before 70 CE, for example, when the shofar (a ram's horn used as an instrument) was blown on Rosh Hashanah (the Jewish New Year), it was permitted to do so only in the Temple. Yohanan decreed that after the Temple's destruction, it could be blown anywhere. There are only a few such measures attributed to Yohanan, but they represent a first step toward adapting to the loss of the Temple, allowing Jews to continue religious practices that had been dependent on it until that that point.

The Bar Kochba Revolt and its aftermath also had a major impact on the development of rabbinic Judaism. While some rabbis supported the revolt, others did not, and their desire to avoid another such disaster seems to have had an influence on early rabbinic views on subjects like messianism, the belief that God would soon send someone to deliver them from their enemies. Bar Kochba was reportedly recognized as a messiah by none other than Rabbi Akiba. His nickname, Bar Kochba, "son of a star," cast him as a fulfillment of a messianic prophecy in the book of Numbers: "[A] star shall come out of Jacob" (Numbers 24:17); and that perception of him as a divinely appointed savior with supernatural powers might have given some Jews the confidence they needed to join him in a fight against a far more powerful enemy like the Romans. But the disastrous outcome of the Bar Kochba Revolt called such messianic expectation into question—the rebels were defeated, and Akiba and other sages were executed.

Formulated in the aftermath of the revolt, rabbinic literature registers the reassessment all this caused, expressing disillusionment with Bar Kochba. One rabbi is remembered as claiming that the prophecy in Numbers predicted not a savior but a liar (*kozav*, a pun on Bar Koseba's actual name)—that is, that Bar Kochba was a messianic impostor rather than the real thing. Many scholars believe that in the wake of the Bar Kochba Revolt, rabbis tried to curb messianic expectation, discouraging speculation about when he was going to arrive, postponing the messianic age indefinitely, or playing down the difference that the Messiah would make.

Rabbis in this period also backed away from martyrdom, the willing decision to accept death at the hands of the enemy or to take one's own life rather than betray one's commitment to God. Jews had been emboldened during the Maccabean Revolt and the anti-Roman wars that followed by the belief that being willing to die for God and his laws would redeem their death, that they would be resurrected, and that their sacrifice would atone for the sins of their people and redirect God's wrath against the enemy. Martyrs were venerated figures in late antiquity, most conspicuously among Christians, for whom martyrs who accepted suffering and death in imitation of the sufferings of Christ were considered heroes and an inspiration for the faithful.

Admiration for the martyr is evident in rabbinic literature as well, but one also detects there an effort to curtail the practice. According to a rabbinic view, for example, a Jew was required to die for the law, but only if being compelled to commit the most serious offenses—murder, idolatry, and incest; otherwise, he was permitted to break the law to save his life (this makes for an interesting contrast with Philo's and Josephus's claim that Jews would sooner die than violate even the smallest detail of their laws). The founding figure of the rabbinic movement, Yohanan ben Zakkai, exemplified through his escape from Jerusalem to Yavneh a Judaism that rejected rebellion and defiant death in favor of submission to Rome and a life of study.

Unfortunately, beyond the questionable anecdotes preserved in much later rabbinic sources, we possess no evidence for Yohanan and other rabbinic figures who lived in the first two centuries of the Common Era, making it impossible to know for certain what happened in this important phase in the development of rabbinic culture. It is not even certain that we can speak of a rabbinic movement in this early period, for the rabbis may not yet have had a clear sense of themselves as a group, operating individually or in small circles, but without a sense of being part of a particular community. What we are referring to as "the rabbinic movement," a coherent, semi-organized network of scholars distinguished by a common lifestyle, belief system, ways of interpreting scripture, and institutions of learning, may actually describe a situation that does not crystallize until after Yohanan and Akiba.

Connecting the rabbis to the Pharisees answers the question of where the rabbis came from originally, but it also raises another question: What is it that allowed this movement to flourish in the centuries after the Second Temple's destruction while other Jewish groups did not? This was a time when the central institutions of Jewish life in Jerusalem—the Temple and the Herodian dynasty—were destroyed or drained of influence. The priesthood probably continued in this period, but its role in society was eclipsed by that of the rabbi (*see the box* "What Became of the Priests after the Temple's Destruction?"). Why were the descendants of the Pharisees—if that is who the early rabbis were—so successful in the post-Temple period?

We do not know the answer to this question, but we can make an educated guess. The power of the Herodian line was tied to the Roman support it enjoyed. When the Herodians failed as mediators between the Jews and the Romans, they lost that support. The priests' authority was tied to the Temple, and its destruction deprived them of a clear role in society, not to mention an important source of income, the priesthood deriving its funding from the offerings contributed to the Temple. The authority of the Pharisees and then the rabbis was tied to their role as legal and scriptural experts. Their influence did not come from a central institution but was tied to the expertise, reputation, and charisma of individual sages respected for whom they learned from, their knowledge of the law, perhaps in some cases their supernatural and healing power (the second-century disciple of Akiba Rabbi Meir was one such sage known for his wonder-working power). Like Jesus, an individual sage might be executed, but the movement was able to continue because his disciples would carry on the teachings of their master.

Also significant in the wake of the Bar Kochba Revolt was the relocation of the center of rabbinic activity to the Galilee, in the north. According to rabbinic lore, Yohanan ben Zakkai moved from Jerusalem to Yavneh, a city on the coast south of where Tel Aviv is today, but after the Bar Kochba Revolt, the center of rabbinic activity shifted to Usha and then to other sites in the Galilee, a calmer and more prosperous region than a war-torn Judea.

It was probably also crucial to the success of rabbinic Judaism that the early rabbis came to accept life under Roman rule. Some, including probably the famous rabbi Akiba, were supporters of the Bar Kochba Revolt, but in the wake of its disastrous outcome, the rabbinic movement in general seems to have come to terms with Roman rule—if not actively aligning with it, at least avoiding open rebellion. Rabbinic literature can be extremely critical of Roman rule, but in stories like that of Yohanan ben Zakkai, it distances itself from rebellion, recommending submission, or at least

WHAT BECAME OF THE PRIESTS AFTER THE TEMPLE'S DESTRUCTION?

The Second Temple period was a time when the priesthood flourished. The high priest was, in effect, the ruler of Judean society until the rise of the Herodian dynasty, and even then, the upper echelons of the priesthood continued to be at the center of Judea's elite class, enjoying considerable wealth, status, and cultural influence. With the destruction of the Second Temple, the priesthood lost the chief rationale for its existence: the role it played in offering sacrifices and guarding the Temple's sanctity. Still, the priesthood did not disappear or lose its prestige, and it may have made a partial comeback in late antique Palestine as a cultural elite.

One of the most intriguing sources of evidence for a priestly resurgence in late antiquity is the composition in this period of complex and allusive synagogue poems known in Hebrew as *piyyutim* (singular: *piyyut*). Usually written in Hebrew, early *piyyutim* were composed to accompany the public reading of the Torah, in connection with Sabbath, holiday worship, and other public occasions in the life of the synagogue. What connects them to the priesthood is that some were composed by Galilean priests, including figures with such names as Yohanan the Priest, and others by persons with close social connections to the priestly families who settled in the Galilee after the Temple's destruction. They often incorporate Temple-centered themes, yearning for its reconstruction or alluding to the 24 "priestly orders," the names of the priestly watches that served in rotation in the Temple when it stood. The offering of the Yom Kippur sacrifice, used to atone for the community's sins and sustain God's presence in the Temple, inspired *piyyutim* that glorify the Temple cult and the priest (these poems form the basis of a Yom Kippur service followed to this day in many communities).

Priests may also have been the ones to produce *Hekhalot* literature, a late antique offshoot of apocalyptic literature whose descriptions of the heavens and the angelic worship there are modeled on the Temple cult (the term *Hekhalot* refers to the chambers of this heavenly Temple). While priests sustained their interest in the Temple, they were never able to restore its cult or recover their status within Jewish culture. To this day, in religiously observant communities, priests are granted certain privileges during worship (e.g., the right to be called up, first, in reading the Torah and to recite the priestly benediction), but it is rabbinic law that has determined these privileges, signifying the priesthood's subordination to rabbinic authority.

stopping short of public defiance of Rome. This political posture spared the rabbinic movement the fate suffered by Jewish movements, such as the Zealots and the Bar Kochba rebels, which did not survive the rebellions they waged.

Such historical background helps illumine where the rabbinic movement came from, but it does not explain rabbinic influence on the broader Jewish culture. We can understand how someone like Paul was able to exert an influence: He and other early Christian missionizers engaged in active outreach, traveling throughout the Roman world to its largest cities and writing in the Greek that many people, including the many Greek-speaking Jews of the Diaspora, could understand. The early rabbis did not operate in this way; they used a scholarly Hebrew and Aramaic that many Jews beyond Palestine probably did not understand, and even within Palestine itself, they seem to have mostly operated in this early period in the more rural parts of Palestine, villages and towns rather than urban centers. It is hard to know what kind of influence such figures had or how they would have exerted influence beyond their circles.

Thus, we find that the beginnings of rabbinic history do not answer the question we have posed for ourselves. We can make educated guesses about where the rabbis came from, but at this early point, there is no clear evidence that they were able to influence Jewish culture in general, no imprint of rabbinic influence on any inscriptions or archaeological evidence from this time. We cannot even tell how much impact the rabbis had on one another in this period, since the details of how they interacted with each other, what their study life was like, and how they were organized remain murky in a period that we know about only from much later rabbinic texts. To understand how the rabbinic community had such an impact on Jewish culture, we have to look to developments that took shape after the end of the second century CE, and to a key turning point that occurred at this time: the composition of a work known as the Mishnah.

The Creation of Rabbinic Literature

The Mishnah is the foundational document of rabbinic Judaism. It is so important, in fact, that it enjoys a kind of scriptural status in Jewish religious life to this day, second in importance only to the Bible. As a composition, it is very different from the Bible. It is not a book of prophecy, nor does it contain any kind of history like the one recorded in the Five Books of Moses. It is a compilation of originally oral traditions attributed to various sages from the end of the Second Temple period through to the beginning of the third century, the time of the Mishnah's composition. Like the Bible, however, its content was endowed with great significance, becoming a subject of study, interpretation, and debate, and like the Bible as well, its content would go on to shape how Jews live their lives and interact with God.

The name "Mishnah" comes from a Hebrew word meaning "to repeat" or "to study" and perhaps refers to how the Mishnah was learned or transmitted through repetition. Much of it is a record of legal opinions, some presented anonymously, some attributed to named rabbis, though it also includes anecdotes, biblical interpretation, wise sayings, and other miscellaneous material. It is organized into six divisions known in English as orders, each of which focuses on a different category of religious law. The order *Zeraim* (Seeds) addresses the handling of agricultural products from the Land of Israel, considered divine property. *Moed* (Sacred Time) pertains to the Sabbath, the major festivals, and other holy days. *Nashim* (Wives) encompasses laws having to do with marriage and divorce. *Neziqin* (Damages) addresses courts, criminal, and civil law. The subject of *Qodashim* (Holy Things) is the Temple cult, and *Toharot* (Purities), how to maintain the state of purity and avoid impurity. Each of these orders is divided into tractates that cover more specific topics, making for 63 tractates in all.

It is tempting to compare the Mishnah to codifications of Roman law from the same period, but some of its characteristics make it hard to imagine how it could have functioned as a law code in any practical sense. Some of its material—the order having to do with the Temple, for example—had no practical application in a world without a Temple. Also noteworthy is that the Mishnah frequently records dissenting opinions, as in the opening lines of the first tractate, *Berachot*, a tractate concerned with various blessings and prayers:

> From when does one recite the *Shema* in the evening? From the hour when the priests enter to eat their *terumah* [a kind of Temple offering] until the end of the first watch [about a third of the way into nightfall] so the words of Rabbi Eliezer. The sages say, "Until Midnight" Rabbi Gamliel says, "Until the sun rises in the morning."

The *Shema* is a scriptural passage from Deuteronomy 6:4–9 that Jews recite every day, morning and evening, as an affirmation of their faith in

God. To fulfill this law, one has to know when the evening begins and ends, a practical issue that the foregoing passage seeks to address, but note that it doesn't quite resolve it, instead reporting three different views about when the evening ends. The recording of different opinions, and of the majority view along with the minority view, would become one of the hallmarks of rabbinic literature from this period and suggests that its purpose was to preserve and convey the differing views of multiple sages.

A tenth-century scholar named Sherira Gaon, the venerated head of an important rabbinic academy in Babylonia who lived sometime between 900 and 1000 CE, developed the first known explanation for the Mishnah's origins—he attributed its organization to the third-century patriarch Rabbi Judah (active around 200 CE), though Sherira also concludes that Rabbi Judah himself did not compose the words of the Mishnah but was working with the teachings of earlier rabbis and building on earlier attempts to organize them. For much of the period prior to Judah, Sherira explains, the sages had been able to personally transmit these teaching directly from one generation to another, but the Temple's destruction and other crises, along with the continued growth of the oral tradition, required an intervention. While earlier generations agreed on the content of the tradition, they understood and formulated these traditions in different ways, and as these teachings were passed from one generation to the next, they grew even more varied, causing Judah to be concerned that parts of the tradition would be lost—hence his effort to conserve and organize the tradition in the form of the Mishnah.

Sherira was writing some seven centuries after the Mishnah's composition and probably projects onto its history the role of the Mishnah in his own academic culture. The Mishnah does seem to draw on earlier oral sources, but it does not tell us who compiled it, why, or in what circumstances. Rabbi Judah does figure prominently in it, but he is not identified in the Mishnah itself as its editor. Complicating things still further is the existence of another rabbinic work from this time known as the Tosefta, which overlaps with the Mishnah in its organization and content but differs from it in many ways and is not attributed to Judah (it was associated with the sages Hiyya and his student Oshaya). Is the Tosefta some kind of supplement to the Mishnah, as its name suggests (*Tosefta* means "addition"), or an alternative version of the Mishnah? Scholars debate what motivated its composition, and how it relates to the Mishnah, and the bottom line is that we do not understand much about the composition of either work.

The remembered connection with Judah does suggest that the Mishnah's composition is tied to the institution of the patriarchate. The Hebrew equivalent to "patriarch" is *nasi*, the very title that Judah bears, and it may well be the backing of the patriarchate that gave this document its original authority. There is a lot of debate among historians of this period about the nature of the patriarch's/nasi's authority and when he emerged as an important figure in the Jewish community, but it seems clear that the position had become important by the third century CE, precisely the period when the Mishnah was being composed

Judah might well have been the most influential of these figures. There is reason to think that he was the first patriarch to operate beyond rabbinic circles, sending rabbis to serve as judges and scribes in local communities. By moving the patriarchate to Sepphoris, an important Galilean city, he played an important role in the transition of the rabbinic movement to a more urbanized setting, where it could exert more influence on the larger population, and he may also have made the rabbinic vocation itself more accessible to people by creating salaried positions for certain sages and by establishing a tithe to support poor disciples. Enhancing these efforts to reach outside rabbinic circles, Judah also seems to have cultivated a political relationship with the Roman Empire that gave his office authority not just in Palestine but also in other Jewish communities in the Roman world. Judah is remembered in rabbinic literature as a personal friend of the Roman ruler Antoninus—perhaps the Severan emperor Caracalla. Whether there is any truth to that memory, we do not know, but it may well be the case that he had some kind of close relationship with at least the local Roman government.

The compilation of the Mishnah, whether Judah was its editor himself or it was produced by loyal disciples, can be seen as another extension of the patriarch's emerging influence. It does not impose Judah's particular legal views in any direct way, allowing for dissenting opinions from other sages, but it asserts a subtler kind of authority simply by organizing the collective teachings of the rabbis up until that point and deciding what was worth transmitting. We know from the Tosefta of rabbinic teachings left out of the Mishnah that the Mishnah preserves only a part of a much larger body of rabbinic teaching. That might tell us something about the purpose of the Mishnah, that it was an effort not simply to preserve but also to determine what made it into the tradition in the first place, whose perspective counted as worth studying.

The Mishnah's emergence represents an important step in the consolidation of rabbinic Judaism. For the rabbis who operated in the Mishnah's wake, its composition marked a major division in their history. Those sages who were recorded in the Mishnah came to be known as the Tannaim, from the Aramaic word *tanna* ("repeater"), referring to one who studied the tradition. Rabbinic sages living after Judah to 500 CE or so came to be known as the Amoraim, from the Aramaic word *amora* ("speaker"), referring to one who repeated the words of a sage aloud as a kind of spokesperson or translator. An *amora* was someone who stood by the teacher when he taught, receiving the master's words and then trying to make them clear to a larger audience. That was the role of the Amoraim, to receive the teaching of their Tannaitic teachers—the Mishnah—and then explain it to others.

We know of the Mishnah's stature in the following centuries because we have some of the interpretation that it inspired or actually quite a bit of that interpretation. The Palestinian and Babylonian rabbinic communities each developed their own interpretive response to the Mishnah. The Palestinian response is preserved in what is known as the Palestinian Talmud, the Talmud of the Land of Israel, or the Jerusalem Talmud, completed by the fourth or early fifth century CE (not in Jerusalem, as the latter name implies, but probably in Tiberias in the Galilee, to which the seat of Palestinian rabbinic activity eventually moved). The Babylonian response is recorded in the Babylonian Talmud, completed in the sixth or seventh century CE. Talmudic commentary has become so interwoven into how the Mishnah is understood that the Mishnah, once it was incorporated into the Talmud, was not published as a separate text until the sixteenth century, when Christian authorities in Europe decided that the Babylonian Talmud needed to be burned but were still willing to permit the Mishnah to exist.

We will return to the Babylonian Talmud later; what is important here is the Palestinian Talmud.

The Palestinian Talmud is not *the* Talmud you may have heard of before—that shorter term refers to the later Babylonian Talmud, which has eclipsed the Palestinian Talmud in its impact on subsequent Jewish culture—but it is the earlier of the two Talmuds, and it is our best evidence for the Palestinian rabbinic culture that developed in the afterglow of the Mishnah. It is written in Hebrew and a Galilean dialect of Aramaic, with many Greek and Latin loanwords that reflect a rabbinic culture influenced by the cultural environment of a Hellenized Roman Palestine. Its basic organization is tied to the Mishnah, with the

Palestinian Talmud as it exists now covering a little more than half of its tractates.

The Palestinian Talmud suffers from a comparison with the later Babylonian Talmud, which was much more carefully organized and more fully elaborated, better integrating its source material into a well-orchestrated whole, but such comparison is anachronistic, judging the Palestinian Talmud by a literary standard that did not exist yet in the time of its composition. For us, what is important about this text is what it tells us about the status of the Mishnah by this period: It had become the focus of rabbinic activity, as if the Mishnah were a kind of quasi-scripture in its own right, drawing efforts from rabbinic readers to explain its text, resolve apparent contradictions between it and other Tannaitic sources, and derive legal conclusions.

We should hasten to note that the Mishnah was not the only focus of rabbinic scholarly activity. The rabbis sustained an interest in the Bible itself, of course, developing distinctive ways of reading it, known as midrash, which we will explore a bit later. Sometime during the Tannaitic period in Palestine, several rabbinic works of scriptural interpretation were composed especially focused on the legal sections of the Torah, including the *Mekhilta of Rabbi Ishmael* (focused on Exodus), *Sifra* (on Leviticus), *Sifre Be-Midbar* (on Numbers), and *Sifre Devarim* (on Deuteronomy). Such works show that the rabbis thought very carefully about how to make sense of the biblical text, developing a very sophisticated range of techniques for understanding it. But part of what distinguishes rabbinic biblical interpretation from earlier forms of Jewish biblical interpretation is the existence alongside the Torah of another authoritative source, the rabbinic tradition articulated by the Mishnah and elaborated upon in the Palestinian Talmud.

Such laws, as the Mishnah itself suggests, were like mountains hanging by the hair—that is, there were many laws, but they seemed very thinly connected to the Torah, with little or no support in its text. How exactly did this extrabiblical legal teaching in the Mishnah relate to the Torah? Did it somehow derive from the laws of the Torah, arising through some kind of biblical interpretation that the Mishnah does not make explicit? This seems to be the view of some early sages who endeavored to identify the scriptural origins of extrabiblical rabbinic traditions through midrashic interpretation, but other rabbis developed an alternative view—that this tradition originated independently of the Torah, that it represented a distinct inheritance. A preoccupation with this problem, of how to relate rabbinic teaching to the Torah, is one of the animating goals of rabbinic interpretation as it emerges in the wake of the Mishnah.

It is very difficult to trace the development of rabbinic authority in Palestine over late antiquity, but what evidence we have suggests a movement that continued to develop and grow in influence. We have noted that Palestine in this period seems to have become less hospitable for Jewish culture as it became more and more Christianized, but there is also evidence that Palestinian Jewish culture, including rabbinic, seems to have flourished, at least in some places. Not only did Jews in Roman and Christian Palestine produce the Palestinian Talmud, and many works of Tannaitic and Amoraic biblical interpretation, but they also created Aramaic translations of the Bible that could add a lot of material in the renderings of the Bible (such translations were known by the term targum, from the Aramaic word for "translation"), the liturgical poems known as *piyyut* (from the Greek word for "poetry"), magical texts, and the earliest examples of Jewish mystical literature, known as Hekhalot literature.

Late antique Palestine also saw the emergence, beginning in the seventh century, of the Masoretes, a group of scribes initially based in Tiberias who endeavored to preserve the Hebrew biblical text in what they regarded as its correct form and to ensure its proper pronunciation and liturgical chanting in the synagogue. To do this, they

THE OTHER ANCIENT JEWISH LANGUAGE

For Jews, Hebrew was not just an ancestral language; it was a sacred language, the language of the Torah, and its special status explains why they continued to use it for literary and religious purposes well beyond the end of late antiquity, even when it was no longer used in everyday life. By the onset of late antiquity, however, most Jews in the Near East used another Semitic language, Aramaic, which is closely related to Hebrew. Aramaic was not considered as holy as Hebrew, but it, too, plays a very important role in Jewish religious, social, and cultural history from the biblical period into modern times.

Already in the period of Persian rule, the age of Cyrus and Darius, Aramaic was widely used in Babylonia and elsewhere. Biblical books from this age, like Ezra-Nehemiah and Daniel, contain sections in Aramaic, and the Elephantine Papyri are written in Aramaic as well. Such was its impact that it changed Hebrew itself: At some point in the Persian period, for example, the Canaanite script used to write Hebrew was replaced by the square script of Aramaic.

Aramaic continued to be widely used by Jews into late antiquity, in both Palestine and Mesopotamia, and many Jewish texts from this period were composed in the language.

Aramaic was so widely used, in fact, that it became necessary for Jews to produce Aramaic translations of the Bible, known as *targumim* (singular: *targum*). The earliest known Aramaic translations are found among the Dead Sea Scrolls, and Aramaic translations continued to be produced in late antiquity, including works probably composed in Palestine, like *Targum Pseudo-Jonathan* and *Targum Neofiti* (the most important targum, *Targum Onkelos*, is from Babylonia). One noteworthy characteristic of late antique *targumim* is that they often expanded greatly on the Hebrew biblical text. As a tiny example, compare the wording of Genesis 1:1 with how it is rendered in *Targum Neofiti* (the italicized words indicate the differences):

> In the beginning God created the heavens and the earth, the earth was a formless void and darkness covered the face of the deep, while a wind/spirit from God hovered over the surface of the earth.
>
> (Genesis 1:1–2)

> In the beginning *and in great wisdom*, God created *and finished* the heavens and the earth. And the Earth was void and formless, *desolate from humans and animals alike. It was emptied of all planted vegetation and trees.* Darkness was spread on the surface of the depths, and a *merciful* spirit from before the Lord blew across the waters.
>
> (this translation is taken from Sefaria.com) (*Targum Neofiti*)

The Aramaic translations add various details to the biblical text inspired by midrash—for example, the idea that God had the assistance of wisdom when creating the heavens and earth.

There aren't many Jewish speakers of Aramaic today (though there are some, like Kurdish Jews in northern Iraq), but it still exerts an influence on Jewish life. Important works in Jewish mystical tradition, like the *Zohar*, are written in Aramaic. The traditional form of the wedding contract that lays out the responsibilities of the groom to the bride—the *ketuba*—is cast in Aramaic. When a Jew remembers the dead during the prayer service, the traditional hymn recited for such a purpose, known as the Kaddish, is mostly in Aramaic.

developed a complex system of vowel and punctuation signs added above and below the consonants of the biblical text involving scores of signs and requiring extensive grammatical and interpretive analysis. The result of the effort that they initiated, a development over many centuries and spanning the divide between late antiquity and the Middle Ages, is an astonishing act of scholarship on a par with the production of the two Talmuds. It has been observed that the Masoretes felt it necessary to add 14 signs to just the first word of the Bible, *bereshit* ("In the beginning"), and they exerted a comparable level of intellectual effort for every single word in the Hebrew Bible—a half million words! (For the oldest biblical manuscript bearing the imprint of Masoretic activity, from around 930, see the image of the Aleppo Codex in Chapter 2.) The creation of the Palestinian Talmud is another manifestation of this Jewish cultural flourishing.

By the end of this same period, there is also reason to think that the rabbis' understanding of Jewish religious tradition was exerting an increasing influence over the broader Jewish community. One piece of evidence for this influence is an inscription from a synagogue at a site called Rehov in the Beth Shean Valley and dated to the sixth or seventh century CE. The inscription cites religious laws bearing on tithing and agricultural practice, and these directly parallel material in the Tosefta and the Palestinian Talmud, evidence that, by this time, rabbinic literature was indeed influencing synagogue life in at least some Palestinian Jewish communities. The inscription even alludes to "Rabbi," which could well be a reference to the patriarch Judah, since the title "Rabbi" without a name is how rabbinic sources refer to him.

But this is not very much evidence to go on, and it is relatively late, from the sixth or seventh century CE. When did the rabbis and their scholarly efforts begin to exert influence on the larger Jewish community beyond rabbinic circles, and how did they manage to acquire that influence? Did the rabbis control whatever court system existed in this period, as rabbinic sources might lead one to think?

Figure 5.6 An inscription from a synagogue in Rehov, Israel, from the sixth or seventh century CE. The inscription cites agricultural laws also known from rabbinic texts—evidence for rabbinic literature's growing influence on Jewish culture in late antiquity.

When did they begin to shape what was happening in synagogues, or the way non-rabbis prayed, or how the Torah was understood beyond the study house? Despite much scholarship on these questions, their answers remain elusive. A find like the Rehov inscription testifies to rabbinic influence by the end of late antiquity, but it amounts to only one piece of evidence, and it hardly fills in the picture for earlier centuries. To better understand the rabbinization of Judaism, therefore, we have to shift our attention to Babylon.

Turning the Page With the Babylonian Talmud

The origins of the Jewish community in Babylonia go back to the time of the Babylonian Exile in 586 BCE, and its history runs throughout the period covered by the four previous chapters, though little is known about that history. After the third century CE, Babylonia began to emerge as a major center of rabbinic activity. This shift is reflected in the career of a single sage named Rav Abba, known simply as Rav in rabbinic literature. From what rabbinic sources suggest, Rav was born in Babylonia, but like other sages from there, he went to Palestine to study, reportedly receiving his ordination from Judah ha-Nasi. But then around 219 CE, Rav returned to Babylonia and established a *bet midrash*, or study house, at Sura, which became one of the most important rabbinic academies in Babylonia. For later Babylonian rabbis, Rav's return to Babylonia was a turning point in their relationship with Palestine as the center of rabbinic authority: "From the time Rav arrived in Babylonia," declared one sage, "we in Babylonia have put ourselves on the same footing as Israel" (Babylonian Talmud, *Bava Kama* 80a).

Like with Yohanan ben Zakkai and Judah ha-Nasi, Rav's portrayal in rabbinic literature may not be an accurate depiction, but it does tell us something about how the sages of Babylonia saw themselves: While they never broke from their roots in Palestinian rabbinic Judaism and held Palestinian figures such as Yohanan ben Zakkai and the patriarch Judah in esteem, they saw themselves as having a comparable authority and were willing to act independently in developing their own distinctive brand of rabbinic culture.

As the rabbinic movement began to coalesce in Babylonia, it began to assert itself vis-à-vis its Palestinian counterpart, emboldened perhaps by the fact that Babylonia happened to fall beyond the jurisdiction of Roman law and hence beyond the patriarch's legal authority and enforcement powers, whatever those were. Babylonian independence is detectable already in the second century, when a sage named Hananiah, having immigrated to Babylonia after the Bar Kochba Revolt, made an attempt to regulate the calendar from there—a direct challenge to Palestinian legal supremacy. A threat of excommunication was enough to stifle Hananiah's challenge, but the episode was an early sign of the self-confidence that led later Babylonian sages to claim a legal authority equivalent to the sages of Palestine.

The sages of Babylonia could not ignore the centrality of Palestine in Jewish history, but they asserted an almost-equivalent status for themselves. They boasted of the fact that their roots in the biblical past predated those of their Palestinian colleagues—after all, as the site of the Garden of Eden and the original home of Abraham, Babylonia was arguably where Jewish history had begun. Yes, Babylonia was also a place of exile, but since their arrival in Babylonia, Babylonian sages claimed, the Jews there had jealously preserved their pedigree by avoiding intermarriage, keeping their line purer than did the Jews of Palestine. In other words, Babylonian sages saw themselves as in no way inferior to their counterparts in Palestine, and some may have seen themselves as preserving Jewish tradition in a less-corrupted form.

The intellectual vibrancy of the Babylonian rabbinic community has been extensively preserved in the Babylonian Talmud, a composition that is extremely difficult to describe because of its scope, breadth, and intricate argumentation.

WADING INTO THE SEA OF TALMUD

The Babylonian Talmud is as important for understanding the religious development of Judaism as the Bible, but it is much harder to interpret. From the moment one begins to read it, one is already swimming in the deep end.

In a nutshell, the Talmud (or Gemara, an Aramaic term that describes the Talmud's analysis of the Mishnah) is a kind of commentary or response to the Mishnah, an effort to understand the reasons for what it says, to raise questions about things that are unclear, and to resolve apparent discrepancies between the Mishnah and other rabbinic traditions. Its basic unit of organization is not the book or the chapter but something that is not clearly marked in the text: the *sugya*, an analysis launched by some issue in the Mishnah that follows a back-and-forth between different claims and counterclaims, with lots of digressions or apparent digressions. It can be hard to pinpoint where exactly a *sugya* ends, but it has a structure, initiated by a particular topic, question, or issue posed by the Mishnaic text that it seeks to relate to Scripture or other rabbinic traditions through a kind of back-and-forth argument, *shakla ve-tarya*, as it is known in Aramaic. The discussion can seem meandering, but part of the fun of reading the Talmud is learning to recognize how the component parts fit together into a logical flow.

To give you a taste of how the Talmud works, let us consider a famous—and disturbing—passage from the tractate known as *Qiddushin* (39b—that is, page 39; the *b* signifies the back side of the page). The passage begins with an interpretive observation about the Torah attributed to a rabbi named Jacob, a sage from the late second century CE who was thought to have been a teacher of Judah the Patriarch:

> It was taught: Rabbi Jacob says, "There is not one commandment in the Torah where the reward for keeping the commandment is laid out right next to the command which does not presuppose the doctrine of the resurrection of the dead" (or in other words, whenever the Torah explicitly specifies the reward for following a command right next to the command, it is implying that the reward is actually bestowed in the World to Come, the afterlife). Thus, when it talks about honoring parents (in the Ten Commandments), it is written: "that your days may be long, and that it may go well with you" (Deuteronomy 5:15). Again in connection with the law of letting the mother bird go from the nest, it is written: "That it may go well with you and you may live long."
>
> (Deuteronomy 22:7)

What Rabbi Jacob is seeking to demonstrate in this passage is that the Torah endorses the doctrine of resurrection, the idea that God rewards those who follow his commandments by granting them life after death. The Torah itself never suggests such an idea explicitly—we know from our much later vantage point that it is something that Rabbi Jacob is projecting onto the biblical text—but he claims that it is being referred to in two biblical verses, which he cites here: Deuteronomy 5:15 and Deuteronomy 22:7.

> Honor your father and your mother, as the Lord God commanded you, *so that your days may be long and that it may go well with you.*
>
> Deuteronomy 5:16

> If you come to a bird's nest, in any tree or on the ground, with fledglings or eggs, with the mother sitting on the fledglings or the eggs, you shall not then take the mother with the young. Let the mother go, taking only the young for yourself, in order *that it will go well with you and you will live long.*
>
> (Deuteronomy 22:7)

The two commandments may not seem all that similar to each other. The first is the commandment to honor one's parents; the second requires the Israelites to let the mother bird go when taking eggs or baby birds from its nest so as not to eat the mother and its offspring at the same time. What the two commandments share in common is that they both explicitly state the reward right after presenting the commandment, and it is the same reward—the person will do well and live a long life. This is why Rabbi Jacob has zeroed in on these particular commandments, but why does he think they are referring to life after death? Neither mentions the afterlife explicitly. Why not read them more straightforwardly as promises of a long life in this world? In the ensuing passage, the Talmud will offer an argument for why Jacob's less-obvious afterlife interpretation must be right.

Having put Rabbi Jacob's position on the table, this passage then proceeds to a disturbing story that seems at first to call into question whether there is any reward at all for following these commandments:

> Now, there was an incident when a man's father said to him, "Ascend to the top of the building and bring me down some young birds," and (the son) went up to the top of the building, shooed the mother bird away and took the young ones, and on his return he fell and he died. Where is this man's "it will go well with you," and where is his "you will live long"?

What is relevant about this story is that the man it depicts is fulfilling *both* of the commands mentioned by Rabbi Jacob—he honors his father by obeying his instruction to find him some young birds, and he follows the other command by letting the mother bird go before taking them. By all rights, then, if the Torah's promise of a reward is true, the man should have gone on to a long life, and yet not only does he suffer an untimely death but he also dies after just completing the very commandments that ought to have guaranteed him a long life—*if the Torah's reference to a long life applied to life in this world.*

We learn from later in this Talmudic passage that some rabbis believed that Jacob's own grandfather, Elisha ben Abuyah, witnessed a similar episode, and that it shook his faith in the Torah so profoundly that he became a heretic (because of this heresy, Elisha is shunned by the rabbis: They won't even mention him by name, referring to him only as *Aher*, "The Other"). The man's death raises disturbing questions about the value of obeying the Torah's commandments and believing its promises: The world does not seem to be a place where people are rewarded for following the Torah.

But the Talmud is not citing this story here to cast doubt on the Torah. As it interprets this episode, it actually supports Rabbi Jacob's position that the reward for fulfilling these two commandments is life after death. How so? The death of the young man proves that the Torah's references to living a long life cannot possibly be a reference to long life in this world—otherwise, the man would not have died—and the only other possibility, if one assumes, as the rabbis did, that the Torah is always truthful, is that the reward must come in the afterlife. The Talmud continues: "'*[T]hat it will go well with you' means in the world where all is well and 'you will live long' means the world where life is completely long.*" The Torah keeps its promises; it's just that the reward is not the temporary reward of extended life in this world but a truly long life in the next world.

The Talmud is not done yet, continuing (the comments in brackets are meant to help explain the passage):

> But perhaps such a thing never happened? Rabbi Jacob actually saw this occurrence. Then perhaps that man was having sinful thoughts [while he was performing the commandments, thus bringing punishment down on himself]? But the Holy One, blessed be

WADING INTO THE SEA OF TALMUD (CONTINUED)

He, does not link thoughts to actions [and hence thinking a sinful thought would not have been enough to trigger divine punishment]. Perhaps then what he was thinking about was idolatry [the worst possible sin], as it is written: "That I may catch the house of Israel in their own heart" (Ezekiel 14:5), which means that one is punished for idolatrous thoughts.

What is going on here? The Talmud is posing challenges to Rabbi Jacob's position. First, someone suggests that the incident didn't really happen, in which case the argument it supports doesn't stand, but that objection is brushed away; Jacob saw it with his own eyes. Then another possibility is floated that would neutralize Jacob's analysis from another direction: Yes, the man was performing the commandments that entitled him to a reward, but perhaps he was secretly sinning at the same time by thinking evil thoughts, which would have neutralized his righteous actions. If this is what happened, the son's death was of no relevance for determining whether the reward is given in this world or the next, because the son wasn't entitled to the reward at all; he had forfeited it by thinking sinful thoughts. The Talmud then mentions a possible objection to this objection. It is accepted among the sages that God doesn't punish people for merely thinking evil thoughts, but there is an answer to that in turn: Perhaps the man was thinking *idolatrous* thoughts, idolatry constituting such a terrible sin that God is willing to punish Israel for merely thinking about committing it.

The discussion has gotten very convoluted, but that is characteristic of the back-and-forth dialectic of the Talmud which goes on through several more challenges and responses that we will not try to reproduce here. The Babylonian

For Babylonian sages after the Tannaitic period, as for Palestinian sages in the same period, the Mishnah had become a canonical document, but Babylonian sages developed their own interpretive response to it, building on earlier Palestinian tradition but adapting it, elaborating it, and injecting their own voice through the inclusion of Babylonian Amoraim, who are cited by name in its text alongside Palestinian Amoraim. The successors to the Amoraim in Babylonia are the unnamed sages known as the Saboraim ("explainers") or, in a term coined by modern scholarship, the *Stamaim* ("anonymous ones")—who finalized the Talmud in the period between 500 and 700 CE. Their accomplishment, reflecting the work of generations, is stunning for its very distinctive and carefully structured argumentation, a record of complex and clever interpretation, back-and-forth dialectic, storytelling, and more that runs for some 2.5 million words (for the challenge of reading even a snippet of this massive work, *see the box* "Wading into the Sea of Talmud").

The Babylonian Talmud intermixes Palestinian and Babylonian traditions in a way that makes it appear as if the sages of the two places were all engaged in one conversation. But by comparing the two versions of the Talmud, scholars have been able to distinguish differences between the two variants of rabbinic Judaism. By the time of the final editing of the Babylonian Talmud in the sixth and seventh centuries CE, the sages of Babylonia had developed their own distinctive intellectual culture. They studied in large academies that were more institutionalized than the study circles or study houses of Palestinian sages. The more centralized nature of study meant that students had to travel greater distances and spend more time away from home than did their predecessors, leading to prolonged absences that had implications for their

Talmud is all about this back-and-forth: the intellectual jousting among sages and the "aha!" moments that come when someone successfully parries an objection or is able to overcome all his opponent's defenses.

This back-and-forth—once one learns how to follow it—is what makes the Talmud so fun to read, but as this example also shows, there are often larger issues at stake in the dialectic. Here the rabbis are confronting problems that threaten their very commitment to the Torah: Why is it that bad things happen to those who keep God's commandments? Why does God make promises in the Torah that he doesn't seem to keep? What is the purpose of obeying his commands if doing so doesn't protect one from harm? Why not conclude, as Elisha ben Abuyah did, that there is no point to following the Torah? What can seem like academic argumentation for its own sake frequently reveals scholars willing to intellectually wrestle not just with their colleagues but also with how to make sense of life itself, including the question of why keep the Torah's commandments in a world where there is no clear reward for doing so.

For those who want to study the Talmud, it has never been more accessible. The entire text of the Talmud, and other classic rabbinic texts, along with English translations, can now be found online, for free, at a site called Sefaria, a witty fusion of the word *safari* with the Hebrew word for book, *sefer* (www.sefaria.org). There are now English commentaries as well. But it is difficult to understand the Talmud's argumentation by reading it on one's own, so the best way forward is to follow the advice of the rabbis themselves and find oneself a teacher.

families back at home. Even if its details are exaggerated, some historical truth probably lies behind the Babylonian legend that Akiba had a wife willing to wait 24 years while he finished his studies—the experience of Babylonian sages who had to leave their spouses for long periods to pursue their studies.

Rabbinic study, as it is reflected in the Babylonian Talmud, was governed by a highly developed ethos of argumentation tempered by scholarly etiquette. Sages debated one another not necessarily to resolve the issue at hand but, rather, for the love of debate and for the respect that one could attain through intellectual acuity. It is not unusual for a debate in the Babylonian Talmud to lead to no clear conclusion: The point was to develop arguments, objections, and responses to objections, not necessarily to reach a clear judgment about the law. A story told in the Talmud of a famous rabbinic duo captures this aspect of Babylonian rabbinic culture. After the death of his study partner, Resh Lakish, the sages provided Rabbi Yohanan with a new study partner. Unlike Resh Lakish, this colleague was willing to acknowledge when Yohanan was correct. Rather than being consoled, however, Yohanan missed his old partner:

> "When I made a statement, he [Resh Lakish] would pose twenty-four difficulties, and with twenty-four solutions I would solve them and thus our discussion expanded. But you [Yohanan's new partner] say, we learned a teaching that supports you. [In other words, the new partner would simply agree with Yohanan, ending any debate]. Of course I [Yohanan] know that I am right."
>
> [Yohanan] would go out and tear his clothes, crying "Where are you the Son of Lakish, where are you the Son of Lakish?"
>
> (Babylonian Talmud, *Bava Metsia*, 84a)

What Yohanan yearns for in this story is not to win the dispute but to debate a sharp colleague willing to counter his every argument so that the dispute will never end. This ethos helps explain the form of the Babylonian Talmud, which can go on at great length, moving from argument to counterargument to counter-counterargument, because its editors were interested not in conclusions but in keeping the argument going for as long as possible.

It was this particular form of rabbinic culture, the one reflected in the Babylonian Talmud, that had the greatest impact on later Jewish culture. As noted earlier, when we refer to the Talmud today, we are referring to the Babylonian Talmud, and it is the Babylonian Talmud's conception of rabbinic culture—the way it reframes and understands the Mishnah and rabbinic scriptural interpretation—that became authoritative for later Jewish culture. To understand how it achieved that status, however, it is not enough to learn about the Babylonian Talmud itself: We also have to understand how Babylonian rabbinic culture developed in its wake.

Historically, what follows the composition of the Talmud is the emergence in Babylonia of scholarly leaders known as the Geonim (singular: Gaon), who were Babylonian rabbinic sages at the head of the two most important rabbinic academies in Babylonia, Sura and Pumbedita. These academies and the scholars who led them intensified their influence after the Sasanians were defeated by Muslims in the seventh century, and it was through their religious authority that rabbinic culture—and, more specifically, the Babylonian rabbinic culture articulated by the Talmud—began to exert influence on Jewish communities throughout the rapidly expanding Islamic world. All this is to jump ahead a few centuries, and we will be looking at the Geonim in more depth in the next chapter. All that we would note here are some of the factors that helped the rabbis of Babylonia exert such an influence on the Jewish world.

To begin with, as noted elsewhere, the rabbis benefited from a more favorable social and political environment that gave them an edge over their counterparts in Palestine. Whereas the rabbis of Palestine found themselves hemmed in by Roman legislation and Christian anti-Judaism, the rabbis of Sasanian Babylonia were able to find a relatively secure environment to develop their culture. And whereas the rabbis of Palestine lost an important source of institutional backing when the patriarchate disappeared, the rabbis of Babylonia benefited from an association with a more enduring community leader, the exilarchate, which, as it turns out, lasted longer than the Sasanian kingdom itself.

Second, the rabbis of Babylonia benefited from an event that happened after the completion of the Talmud: the Muslim defeat of the Sasanian kingdom in the mid-seventh century CE. We will introduce Islam and its relationship to the Jews under its rule in the next chapter; suffice it to say for now that Islamic conquest had the effect of unifying most of the territory where Jews lived, politically reconnecting the Jews of Babylon with the Jews in Palestine, and also Egypt, North Africa, and even faraway Spain. They also found in Islam an example to follow: the efforts of Muslim scholars who were also trying to establish a religious-legal system for a population settled over the same expanse of territory.

Third, the rabbis of Babylonia benefited from a technological advance that set in during the Islamic period: the introduction of paper manufacturing to the Middle East in the eighth century. In 762, a Muslim dynasty known as the Abbasid caliphate established a capital in Iraq at the newly constructed city of Baghdad, which also became the center of Babylonian rabbinic activity when the academies of Sura and Pumbedita both relocated there. The establishment of a paper mill in Baghdad in 794 greatly boosted the production and circulation of books in the environment in which the Geonim were operating, and while the

Geonim continued to value the oral transmission of tradition, they also took advantage of this new technology to communicate their views, developing a genre known in English as the responsum, a written answer to a question posed by a correspondent, to stay in touch with far-flung communities.

Because these far-flung communities could not engage in the interpersonal instruction that happened within Babylonia's rabbinic academies, they needed to find another way of gaining access to the learning there if they were to understand rabbinic tradition, and that seems to have been what prompted Gaonic-era sages to authorize the writing down of the Talmud in the eighth century CE, even though as part of the Oral Torah, it was originally transmitted orally. To some degree, putting the Talmud in writing weakened the authority of the Geonim, as Jews elsewhere began to think themselves able to draw their own legal conclusions from the Talmud without needing to follow the remote guidance of Gaonic scholars, but the circulation of a written Talmud also helped disseminate Babylonian rabbinic Judaism throughout Islamic lands.

For such reasons, the rabbis of Babylonia gained enough legal and religious influence that, by the ninth century, their leaders were ready to cast themselves as the supreme legal authority within the Jewish world (by "Jewish world" we mean in this context the Jewish population living under Islamic rule, an estimated 90 percent of the worldwide Jewish population during the Middle Ages). It was then that a Geonic scholar named Pirkoi ben Baboi, in a letter addressed to the Jews of North Africa, claimed that it was the Babylonian sages, not the Palestinian rabbis, who preserved Jewish tradition in its purest form. The Palestinian Jewish community had allowed the Torah to be corrupted, he argued, whereas the rabbinic academies of the Babylonian community had preserved it intact and, for this reason, should have ultimate legal authority. Sometime in the same period, the 920s, this authority was put to the test when Palestinian and Babylonian rabbis had another dispute over who would set the calendar, long the jealously guarded prerogative of the Palestinian community. Some communities followed the Palestinian reckoning for a time, but in the end, it was the Babylonians' calculation—and, by extension, Babylonian legal authority—that prevailed.

There were Jews in this period who resisted the authority assigned to the rabbis and rabbinic sources—most notably, the community known as the Karaites, to whom we will return in the next chapter—but that resistance is itself evidence of the impact that rabbinic culture was having by the end of antiquity. The Geonic effort to establish rabbinic authority was achieving such success that by the time late antiquity was giving way to the Middle Ages Jewish culture was now settling into two basic camps: rabbinic Judaism and an anti-rabbinic Judaism that developed in reaction to the Judaism of the Babylonian sages.

The Impact of the Rabbis on Jewish Culture

We have tried to explain the origin of the rabbis, who they were, and how they came to exert an influence over the broader Jewish world, but there is another question we have yet to address: How is a *rabbinized* Jewish culture different from the Jewish culture that preceded it? The following attempt to answer this question is largely based on the Babylonian Talmud as mediated through later Geonic understanding (unless otherwise noted, the Talmudic references in what follows are to tractates from the Babylonian Talmud).

The most fundamental change introduced by rabbinic culture, arguably the root of all the others, was the establishment of the rabbi as the authoritative interpreter of Jewish tradition. Biblical tradition establishes three kinds of

ARGUING WITH GOD

The rabbinic love of debate and dialectic is reflected in how the rabbis understood God: The Talmud contains many stories of biblical figures, or even the rabbis themselves, arguing with God, and this is not considered an act of impiety. The idea was not exactly new. The Bible itself records cases of prophets or other biblical figures, like Abraham and Job, complaining to God, negotiating with him, and even challenging him in a way. Only in rabbinic literature, however, are there stories of humans engaging God in intellectual, scholarly debate, challenging him on interpretive or legal grounds in the way the rabbis might challenge their teachers or peers, and such acts are not considered heretical or impious.

A famous example involves a legal dispute between Rabbi Eliezer and the other sages in which Eliezer commands wondrous acts to support his position.

> "If the law agrees with me," he tells his colleagues, "let this carob tree prove it," and the carob tree is lifted up and transported a hundred cubits from its place. The other sages do not question the miracle, but it has no effect on their position. And so Eliezer summons another supernatural witness: "If the law agrees with me, let this channel of water prove it." The water in the channel begins to flow backward, but the sages reject this proof too. Finally, an exasperated Eliezer declares, "If the law agrees with me, let it be proved from heaven," at which point a heavenly voice rings out, "Why do you dispute Eliezer, with whom the law always agrees?" One might think this settled the matter in Eliezer's favor, but the other sages

A WHO'S WHO OF THE ANCIENT RABBIS

To help sort out all the rabbinic names we have been mentioning, here is a list of some of the most prominent sages featured in rabbinic literature, important for their role within rabbinic literature itself and/or for their place in later Jewish culture.

- **Tannaim**
  - **Rabbi Yohanan ben Zakkai.** A first-century sage, Yohanan ben Zakkai is remembered in rabbinic literature for going over to the Roman side during the Jewish Revolt and convincing the new emperor to allow him to relocate to Yavneh, the first seat of rabbinic learning.
  - **Rabbi Eliezer ben Hyrcanus.** A disciple of Yohanan and peer of Gamliel II, remembered, among other things, for a legal dispute against his fellow sages, when the latter even voted against the heavenly voice that supported Eliezer's position. Eliezer was also remembered for being accused of heresy and punished with excommunication.
  - **Rabbi Akiba ben Joseph.** A second-century sage of humble origins, honored for his modesty and for his martyrdom during the Bar Kochba Revolt. Akiba is remembered for his role in systematizing rabbinic legal tradition and developing new hermeneutical principles that stressed the significance of every detail in the biblical text. Akiba's peers and disciples included many other prominent sages, like Ishmael ben Elisha, Shimon Ben Azzai, Shimon bar Yohai (later known as the supposed author of the *Zohar*, a mystical commentary on the Torah), and Meir (also a disciple of Elisha ben Abuyah, who became a heretic after the failure of the Bar Kochba Revolt).
  - **Rabbi Judah Ha-Nasi.** Traditionally, the patriarch credited with the composition of the Mishnah and so revered that, after his death, Jews across the Roman Empire wanted to be buried near him in the necropolis of Beth Shearim.
- **Amoraim**
  - **Rabbi Yohanan bar Nappaha.** An orphan who became a master of the Torah and, eventually, the head of the academy in Tiberias in third-century Palestine, remembered for his

counter, "We do not heed the divine voice because long ago, at Sinai, you wrote in the Torah, 'After the majority you must incline.'"

(Exodus 23:2)

The sages in the story establish by means of scriptural interpretation that the resolution to disputes such as the one with Eliezer should follow the majority view even when the minority can plausibly claim divine support for its views. How does God respond when challenged by the sages in this way? Laughing, he concedes, "My sons have defeated me, my sons have defeated me" (Babylonian Talmud, tractate *Bava Metsia* 59b).

This story registers the way the love of back-and-forth dialectic in Babylonian rabbinic culture colored the rabbis' understanding of God. Remember that who wins the debate does not matter all that much in this culture; what does matter is how one debates, and here the sages do so brilliantly, outwitting God by citing his own words against him, a divine decree in the Torah that trumps any present-day miracle. This is why, rather than taking offense at their challenge, God is delighted to have been defeated in the argument, for like the rabbis themselves, he values opponents willing and able to challenge him with a smart objection.

According to the rabbis' interpretation of the Torah, it was God's will that the sages resolve disputes according to their own interpretive ability and communal consensus, and that meant that it was theologically acceptable for them to come into intellectual conflict with God himself, as they do in this story, provided that they did so in a respectful tone, with the right motives, and with strong arguments to support their position. For the rabbis, God was a fellow scholar, which meant that they could challenge him in the way they challenged one another.

intellectual exchanges/debates with Resh Lakish, another Palestinian sage remembered for having been a bandit and gladiator before he became a sage.

- **Rav.** A title that the Talmud uses for Abba bar Aybo, the founder of the Babylonian academy at Sura, a trading town on the Euphrates. His migration to Babylonia around the year 220 CE marks the beginning of that rabbinic community's ascendancy.
- **Samuel.** Head of the academy in Nehardea in third-century Babylonia and friend of King Shapur I of Persia; his disputes with Rav play a central role in the Babylonian Talmud. Samuel established an important political principle for later Jewish tradition: "[T]he law of the land is the law"—that is, the law of the societies where Jews lived is binding on Jews, even in some cases taking precedence over Jewish law.
- **Rav Ashi.** As the head of the academy at Sura in the early fifth century, he cultivated good relations with the Persian government. The Talmud states that from Judah Ha-Nasi to Ashi, no one combined learning and high office in such perfect harmony. Following the views of later Geonim, he is also credited with much of the scholarly and organizational work that led to the Babylonian Talmud, along with Ravina, though this work was completed by subsequent generations.

This list leaves out scores of rabbis mentioned in the Mishnah and the Talmuds, and we can't cover them all, but it is important to note one group almost completely excluded from rabbinic circles altogether: women. While rabbinic literature acknowledges the learning of a few exceptional women, such as Beruriah, wife of Meir, the rabbis did not generally allow women into their circles as teachers or disciples. The question of whether women could be rabbis was not articulated until the nineteenth century, and the first female rabbis in the Reform, Reconstructionist, and Conservative movements were not ordained until the twentieth century. Today, however, there are many women, including Orthodox women, seeking to enter the culture of Talmud study, and there are even now several volumes of a feminist Talmud commentary on its way to being completed in the next few years. See www.geschkult.fu-berlin.de/e/judaistik/Forschung/talmudbavli.

intermediaries between God and Israel: the Temple and its priesthood, the king, and the prophet. Rabbinic literature justifies the role of the rabbi in Jewish society by aligning it with all three figures even as it also casts the rabbi as their replacement. While they did not challenge the prerogatives of the priestly class, the rabbis usurped its role by developing Torah study into a substitute for sacrifice. They did not claim to be kings, but the patriarch claimed Davidic descent, and the rabbis in general further identified themselves with kingly tradition by reimagining David as a sage preoccupied with the study of the Torah, just as they were. As *Pirkei Avot* suggests, rabbinic tradition also cast itself as heir to the prophets, not claiming prophetic powers, but casting rabbis as the heirs to the Torah revealed to Moses and the other biblical prophets. Sometimes, the Talmud intimates that the rabbis eclipse even Moses himself. In one well-known story, God permits Moses a glimpse of Akiba teaching the Torah to his disciples. After listening to and not comprehending Akiba, the prophet can only express astonishment that God chose to reveal the Torah through him rather than so learned a sage (*Menahot* 29b). Taking over the roles played by other leaders in earlier Jewish society, the rabbi was cast as the primary intermediary between God and Israel.

The central activity of the rabbi was Torah study, depicted in rabbinic sources as a lifelong commitment to God. Some sages held that the very reason God created humanity was for it to labor in study (cf. *Sanhedrin* 99b), and the sages debated whether such study took precedence over other important commandments and responsibilities, such as the duty to preserve one's own life. Fulfilling this duty to study was not quite like becoming a monk—rabbis got married and worked for a living—but as noted, it did require a deferral of worldly pursuits, or existed in tension with them, and rabbinic literature struggles to reconcile the demands of study with other obligations, such as a man's duty to satisfy his wife's sexual needs.

The rabbis were not the only Jews committed to the Torah, but their understanding of the Torah was distinctive in many ways. The rabbis developed their own way of interpreting the Hebrew Bible, known as midrash. Deriving from a Hebrew root meaning "to seek" or "to investigate," *midrash* is not an easy term to define. It can refer to collections of rabbinic interpretations of the Bible, but it also describes the mode of interpretation reflected in these collections (these midrashic collections, incidentally, come from Palestine, not Babylonia; in Babylonian rabbinic Judaism, midrash is incorporated into the Talmud). Like other early Jews, the rabbis assumed that every detail in the Torah was significant, but midrashic interpretation is even more preoccupied with those details, its commentary triggered by small gaps and redundancies in the text. For the rabbinic interpreter, even small deviations in how a word is spelled hint at a story or message that the rabbi aims to draw out through interpretation.

Scholars today distinguish two types of midrash: halakhic midrash and aggadic midrash, reflecting a distinction between two modes of rabbinic expression, known as Halakhah and Aggadah. Halakhah, from the root meaning "to walk," involves the study of law and custom, while Aggadah, from the root "to tell," is a much looser category that encompasses stories, wisdom, and other nonlegal teachings (in truth, the category of Aggadah only fully developed after the Talmud and was projected onto it retroactively, but it remains a useful way to refer to the non-legal material in the Talmud). Accordingly, halakhic midrash focuses on the legal sections of the Torah or on sections from which one can derive legal conclusions, while aggadic midrash addresses nonlegal sections, like the stories of Genesis, and seeks to draw nonlegal conclusions from its interpretation. While the two kinds of midrash approach the biblical text with different kinds of interest, they use a similar creativity, and similar interpretive techniques, to draw out the implications they discover there, finding in biblical literature all manner of legal guidance and moral, social, and cosmological insight nowhere made explicit in the text.

How midrashic interpretation responds to the Bible can strike the modern reader as wildly fanciful. It transforms biblical figures—Adam, Jacob, and David, for example—into rabbinic-like sages, draws connections between far-flung biblical verses that seem to have nothing to do with another, and even sometimes reverses what you or I might regard as the "plain sense" meaning of a biblical text. Even so, midrashic interpretation has rules: Specific assumptions and reasoning techniques allowed the rabbis interpretive freedom but also constrained how they drew meaning from the biblical text (*see the box* "Cracking the Bible's Code Rabbinically").

One of the most conspicuous characteristics of midrash is that there is no such thing as *the* midrashic reading of the biblical text; rabbinic literature can assign different, even contradictory, meanings to a biblical verse, sometimes presenting different interpretations of the same verse side by side without any indication that one is considered correct and the other wrong. The rabbis believed that God is able to communicate different things to different perspectives simultaneously, and thus, it is possible to draw different but equally valid conclusions about the meaning of the Torah:

> "It is taught in the school of Rabbi Ishmael: 'Behold, my word is like fire, declares the Lord, and like a hammer that shatters rock'" (Jeremiah 23:29). As this hammer produces many sparks, so a single verse has many meanings (*Sanhedrin* 34a).

God's "word"—understood in this midrash not as prophecy but as Scripture—is like a fire that can spark different meanings when the text is subject to interpretation.

In this regard, midrash mirrors the nature of rabbinic culture, which allowed for and even celebrated disagreement and fierce argumentation among the rabbis, debate that could be sharp enough to be described in the Babylonian Talmud as "the war of Torah." In fact, it is the process of argumentation, not the particular legal conclusions that it might lead to, that most interests the editors of the Babylonian Talmud; as we have already noted, much of its back-and-forth does not lead to a clear decision about the legal issue at stake. Even when rabbinic literature comes down clearly on one side of a legal dispute, it does not discredit the dissenting view. To the contrary, it grants that the losing view has value too, as suggested by the following episode:

> For three years there was a dispute between the school of Shammai and the school of Hillel. One side said, "The law is according to our views" and the other side said, "the law is according to our views." A divine voice declared, "Both sides are the words of the living God, but the law is according to the school of Hillel."
>
> (*Erubin* 13b)

As a practical matter, the law was to be determined according to the views of the school of Hillel, but the views of both schools were thought to reflect the divine will—the reason that even the losing side of a rabbinic dispute is worthy of respectful transmission.

This is not to say that the rabbis liked losing debates. Failure to argue properly, to parry an objection or answer a question, was a source of shame for the rabbis, and it was important to avoid shaming an opponent precisely for that reason. Why is it that God preferred the school of Hillel to the school of Shammai? the story asks. "Because they were gracious and modest, and would teach their words and the words of the House of Shammai." As in other stories we have seen, what rabbinic culture valued was not winning the argument so much as knowing how to make it in the right way, and that includes showing respect to opponents.

What most distinguishes the rabbinic approach to the Torah is not just its interpretive approach but also its very understanding of what the Torah consists of. By the time of the Babylonian Talmud, rabbinic sages had come to believe that the Torah revealed to Moses had two forms, the Written Torah, preserved in the Bible, and an Oral Torah, transmitted by the sages. The latter is now preserved in written form—the Mishnah and the Talmudic commentary it inspired—but its transcription into writing was relatively late, and it was originally transmitted orally from rabbis to their disciples through face-to-face teaching. We noted earlier that the Pharisees venerated an unwritten tradition, and the Oral Torah may represent a later offshoot of that tradition, but for the rabbis of the Talmud, this tradition was more than just an ancestral inheritance: It was the Torah itself—part of what God revealed to Moses at Mount Sinai:

> Rabbi Levi son of Chama said in the name of Rabbi Shimon the son of Lakish, "What is the meaning of the verse, 'I will give thee the tablets of stone and the Torah and the commandment which I have written to teach them'?" [Exodus 24:12]. "'Tablets' refers to the Ten Commandments. 'Torah' refers to the Five Books of Moses. 'And the commandment' refers to the Mishnah. 'Which I have written' refers to the Prophets and the Writings. 'To teach them' refers to the Gemara [another word for the Talmud but here not the Babylonian Talmud, which does not exist yet, but rather the rabbinic study of the Mishnah]." [The verse] teaches all of them were given to Moses at Sinai.
>
> (*Berakhot* 5a)

In a manner that is typical of midrash, Rabbi Shimon ben Lakish responds to the apparent wordiness of the text cited from Exodus 24:12, which piles on a long, seemingly redundant series of phrases in reference to God's revelation at Mount Sinai. According to the midrash, this verse actually contains no redundancy, since each phrase refers to a different aspect of God's revelation to Moses, some referring to the component parts of the Written Torah, and others referring to the components of the Oral Torah—the Mishnah and its study by the rabbis. According to this and other rabbinic texts, to read the Hebrew Bible is to encounter only a part of what God had revealed to Moses. To *fully* understand God's revelation at Sinai, one needs to study the Oral Torah as manifest in the teachings of the rabbis themselves.

The concept of the Oral Torah, like much else in rabbinic culture, is paradoxical. It consists of orally transmitted teachings of the sages themselves: their legal debates and rulings, biblical interpretations, wise sayings of the sort collected in *Pirkei Avot*, and stories of the rabbis' own exploits. This tradition was not fixed like the written biblical canon; it grew over time, becoming larger and more complex through the rabbis' rulings, argumentation, and interpretive activity. It also incorporated within it alternative, even contradictory, views of the meaning of the Torah. The rabbis knew that Moses would scarcely have comprehended what the Torah had come to encompass in their own day, and yet they also believed, paradoxically, that all this interpretive creativity on their part was already revealed at Sinai: What rabbis taught their students, the questions students asked their teachers, the debates among colleagues—all were part of what was revealed to Moses, though Moses himself hadn't realized it.

Why wasn't the Written Torah sufficient? Why did God need to reveal himself through the Oral Torah? Jewish scholars would ponder these questions long after the rabbinic age, answering them in different ways, but what their answers share in common is that the two Torahs were interdependent, that Jews needed one to fully understand and enact the other. This point is illustrated in *Shabbat* 31a by means of a story about the great sage Hillel. A non-Jew seeking to convert insists that Hillel teach him only the Written Torah, not the Oral Torah, and Hillel agrees to teach him in a manner that cunningly demonstrates the indispensability of the Oral Torah. In the first lesson, Hillel recites to him the Hebrew alphabet in its conventional order, beginning with *aleph*. On the next day, he reverses the order, beginning with the last letter of the alphabet, *tav*. When the convert objects that this was not how things were presented the day before, Hillel makes his point explicit: just as a student is dependent on a teacher and interpersonal instruction for how he understands the alphabet, so too must he rely on the guidance of the Oral Torah, the teachings of the rabbis, to understand the Written Torah.

The Oral Torah was necessary in the rabbis' view because, from their perspective, the Written Torah hinted at but did not reveal all that God wanted to teach Israel, including gaps and interpretive difficulties that required supplementation. As noted in Chapter 2, the wording of a biblical command—for example, the injunction to keep the Sabbath—is too vague by itself to put into practice without elaborating on it in some way and filling in its gaps. The Oral Torah provided that supplementation, helping to make sense of what could not be understood by reading the biblical text alone. Indeed, more than merely helping to explain biblical law, the concept of the Oral Torah allowed the rabbis

CRACKING THE BIBLE'S CODE RABBINICALLY

For modern readers of the Bible, midrash appears to be a very strange way of making sense of the text. Often, it seems to invent the interpretive problem that it is purportedly solving, and the "solutions" it comes up with can go far beyond anything that the text could have been intended to mean. An example can help illustrate how midrash differs from how you or I might read the biblical text. A modern reader would probably not be puzzled by the fact that the first letter of the Torah happens to be the Hebrew letter *bet* (in the word *bereshit*, "in the beginning"), but this did puzzle rabbinic interpreters, who wondered why God began his Torah with the *second* letter of the alphabet rather than the first (*aleph*):

Yonah in the name of Rabbi Levi [said]: "Why was the world created with a *bet?* [in other words, what was God teaching by beginning Genesis 1 with the second letter of the alphabet, not the first?]: Just as a *bet* is closed on its side and open from its front, so also you are not permitted to inquire about what is above [in the heavens] and what is below [on the earth]." Rabbi Judah son of Pazzi explained the Creation according to the words of Bar Qappara: "Why [was the world created] with a *bet?* To make known to you that there are two worlds" [by which is meant this world and the afterlife, implied by the numerical value of bet, the second letter of the alphabet and used as a symbol for the number two]. Another interpretation: "Why [was the world created] with a *bet?* Because [*bet*] is an expression of blessing [the Hebrew word for "blessing" begins with *bet*]. And why not *aleph* [the first letter of the alphabet]? Because it is an expression of curse" [the word for "curse" begins with *aleph*].*

Not only does the problem that provokes these responses seem contrived, but also the sages' solution seems to stray wildly from the Bible's intended meaning as we might reconstruct it, positing that God purposely used the letter *bet* to communicate some message not expressly stated by the text if read literally—to warn against metaphysical speculation, to hint at the existence of an afterlife, or to imply the blessedness of creation. For many modern readers, the first sentence of Genesis, but not the first letter, certainly bears significance. For the rabbinic reader, even the shape of that letter was significant.

* Genesis Rabba on Genesis 1:1; adapted from the work of Gary Porton, "Rabbinic Midrash," in *A History of Biblical Interpretation*, vol. 1, eds. Alan Hauser and Duane Watson (Grand Rapids, MI: William B. Eerdmans, 2003), 215–216.

CRACKING THE BIBLE'S CODE RABBINICALLY (CONTINUED)

But this way of reading the text does not mean that the rabbis were simply making up their interpretations of the Bible without concern for logic or reason. Certain rules govern their interpretation, though the rabbis themselves seem to have disagreed over those rules. One difference had to do with whether the language of the Torah could be understood in the same way that human language is. The view that "[t]he Torah speaks in human language" was associated with Rabbi Ishmael, a second-century sage who rejected his contemporary Akiba's efforts to find divine meaning in the tiniest elements of the biblical text, including redundant words and even the appearance of individual letters. Such differences notwithstanding, the rabbis shared the belief that scriptural language required special techniques of interpretation.

Rabbinic literature sometimes gave specific labels to these techniques, which it referred to as methods or rules (*middot*). An example of such a rule is *gematria*, the calculation of the numerical value of letters (*aleph* = 1, *bet* = 2, etc.) to understand a word's meaning (an interest in the mathematical value of letters is evident in the preceding passage, which draws on the fact that *bet* has the value of 2 to argue that God begins with this letter to teach that *two* worlds exist, this one and the next one). A list of 7 such rules was attributed to Hillel, and another of 13 rules was ascribed to Rabbi Ishmael. In actuality, midrashic interpretation is not limited to these 7 or 13 interpretive techniques, but the formulation of such lists suggests that rabbinic culture was highly self-conscious about how it read Scripture.

to develop a new kind of revelation alongside the Written Torah, an unfolding, ever-expanding multigenerational revelation that they themselves helped create through their intellectual effort. Rabbinic culture was a conservative one, revering what it had inherited from the Bible, but it was also highly creative, valuing legal, interpretive, and argumentative innovation. The concept of the Oral Torah helped resolve the tension between these conservative and creative impulses by allowing the rabbis to understand their own creativity as part of the tradition they were preserving.

But what difference did all this make to the actual lives of Jews? In a very real sense, the understanding of the Torah we have been describing here was limited in late antiquity to a small and highly insulated group of intellectuals, and there is very little evidence of their interpretations having much of an effect on the broader Jewish community in the age of the Mishnah and Talmud themselves. That began to change by the end of late antiquity, however, and certainly by the Islamic period, and through the influence of the Geonim, rabbinic concepts like the Oral Torah would come to shape what would become medieval Jewish culture. This chapter concludes with one example of that influence, a brief description of how the rabbinization of Jewish culture transformed the way Jews worshipped God.

It is very difficult to reconstruct the history of how Jewish worship became rabbinicized. The Dead Sea Scrolls include prayers and blessing that illumine the prehistory of rabbinic religious practice, but there is a big chronological gap between this evidence and the earliest rabbinic evidence from 200 CE and later, and it is not possible to explain the origins of many of the innovations that the latter introduces—for example, the obligation to recite the *Shema* assumed by the Mishnah. There is a bit of evidence to suggest that the rabbis themselves did not invent this practice, but we simply do not know when Jews began to understand the instructions in Deuteronomy 6:4–8 as a commandment to recite those verses twice a day. The emergence of the *Shema* as a ritualized liturgical performance predates the Mishnah, as did many other Jewish ritual practices, but we cannot reconstruct this history. What we want to focus on here is how the rabbis transformed the ritual inheritance they received from earlier Jews.

As we noted, the rabbis emerged in the wake of the Temple's destruction, facing circumstances that ruled out any immediate prospect of rebuilding the Temple: first, the defeat of the Bar Kochba Revolt in the second century CE, and then Emperor Julian's failure to rebuild the Temple in the fourth century CE. This does not mean that the Temple cult was not important to the rabbis. Rabbinic literature shows that they developed a keen interest in the intricacies of the Temple's rituals and mourned its destruction, and that the Temple remained a model of worship for them. The rabbis tied the timing of their three daily prayers to the timing of the daily sacrifices in the Temple, adopted liturgical practices taken from the Temple (e.g., the use of "Amen" as a response), showed deference to priests and Levites, and required those engaged in prayer to face in the direction of the Temple—all signs of their continuing reverence for the Temple. What there is no evidence of the rabbis doing, however, is trying to rebuild the Temple itself: The religious life they developed was premised on its absence.

In lieu of the Temple, the rabbis accepted the synagogue as the main setting for communal worship, seeking to regulate the kind of worship that took place there. Some elements of the prayer service they developed were drawn from or inspired by the Temple cult, but much of it involved practices that originated independently of the Temple cult or after its demise (*see the box* "A Brief Introduction to Jewish Prayer"). But the synagogue was not the only setting for the new forms of worship that rabbinic literature introduced; the home was also an important setting, as in the case of the rabbinic reformulation of the Passover ritual. In the Second Temple period, Passover was a pilgrimage festival that revolved around a visit to the Temple and a special kind of sacrifice. Under rabbinic influence, its celebration came to focus on a meal conducted in the home, adopting the Greco-Roman customs of the symposium into a retelling of the Exodus that turned it into a kind of study session.

The reason the rabbis were able to adapt Jewish worship in these ways has to do with their conception of the Torah. Midrash allowed the rabbis to tease out details of religious practice not made explicit in the biblical text, and the Oral Torah allowed for much additional supplementation. The rabbinic understanding of the Sabbath is a classic example, including all kinds of prohibitions not found in the Bible. The rabbis identified 39 categories of labor within the Bible's prohibition against work, including activities such as writing two letters or even erasing in order to write two letters. They regulated with great precision what objects could be handled or carried during the Sabbath, how food was to be prepared, even what kinds of shoes one could wear (e.g., sandals with nails protruding from the soles were forbidden). Some of these rules could be derived from or connected to specific biblical verses, but many could not and were developed instead through rabbinic teachings transmitted as part of the Oral Torah.

When the Mishnah and Talmud were canonized during the Geonic period, so too were the religious practices that were developed through these compositions. Citing earlier rabbinic tradition as their authority, the Geonic sages developed and disseminated the first Jewish prayer book that standardized the wording and sequence of the synagogue prayer service (the first siddur, or Jewish prayer book, actually originated from the order of prayers as spelled out by the ninth-century Gaon Amram ben Sheshna, better known as Amram Gaon, in a responsum probably meant for Jews in Spain). It was also in this period that the Haggadah was canonized as well, the text that lays out the order (or seder) of the rabbinic Passover service:

A BRIEF INTRODUCTION TO JEWISH PRAYER

The prayers of biblical figures are often depicted as spontaneous acts, calls for help in times of need or to express gratitude. Prayer was not always spontaneous, however. The book of Psalms preserves prayers that were artfully crafted and, in some instances, were meant for use as part of Temple worship. By late antiquity, after the Temple's destruction, prayer took the form of a structured, communal activity. The form of the prayers recited in this communal context was developed by the sages of the Mishnah and the Talmuds, and it was the Geonim who standardized them as a prayer book followed during religious services to this day.

Since at least the time of the Mishnah, it has been the practice for communal prayer to happen three times a day, though in the Mishnah, there was a debate over whether the third evening prayer was obligatory. Every act of communal prayer follows the same basic script, built around two building blocks:

1. The *Shema* and its blessings. The *Shema* ("Hear"), a title taken from the opening word of Deuteronomy 6:4–9 ("Hear O Israel, the Lord is our God, the Lord is one"), involves the recitation of that and two other scriptural passages to emphasize God's relationship to Israel. The blessing celebrates God's role in the creation of the world, the Exodus, and the giving of the Torah.
2. The *Amidah*, also known as the *Tefilah* or "Prayer." Consists of a series of blessings that combine praise and thanksgiving with petition for forgiveness, healing, the restoration of Jerusalem, and other benefactions from God.

Several times a week, including Shabbat, the prayer service also incorporates a ritualized reading from the scroll of the Torah following a fixed schedule of readings. The rabbis required a quorum of ten adult males, a *minyan*, for the performance of communal prayer, and it was only in the twentieth century that some Jewish communities began to count women as a part of the quorum. None of this prevents Jews from praying privately and spontaneously, but it makes prayer a different kind of experience than it is for many contemporary Christians—an everyday, communal activity.

the blessings, prayers, rabbinic comments, and psalms recited during the Passover meal. Although it draws on material from the Mishnah, the Haggadah is a Geonic creation: It was Amram Gaon who codified its contents in his siddur, and the earliest known versions come from this period.

Through Geonic influence, in other words, the rabbinic understanding of how to worship God became the way many Jews actually worshipped God, establishing the wording of the prayers to be recited three times a day, the blessings recited before and after meals in gratitude to God, traditions for how to read the Torah in the synagogue, and so on. The Geonim were building on material that they inherited from earlier sages through the Mishnah and Talmud, but they are the ones who deserve the credit for spreading rabbinic teachings within the broader Jewish community, using their legal authority, cultural influence, and international contacts to disseminate it among Jewish communities throughout the Islamic world.

This is only to describe the initial formation of rabbinic worship, which is still evolving as you read this, and we must be careful not to project rabbinic religious practice as it developed in later periods onto the period of late antiquity that we are recounting in this chapter. Many religious practices now part of rabbinic tradition—the requirement to cover one's head with a *kippah* (a small cap) as a sign of humility before God, the bar mitzvah, and the practice of reciting the Kaddish prayer for the dead—were developed only in the medieval or early modern periods. But the development of these later practices occurred in a culture thoroughly shaped by the interpretive and textual legacy of earlier rabbinic culture, and it is fair to say that even today, Jewish worship remains thoroughly rabbinicized, as illustrated by the Passover Haggadah, now considered so essential to Passover observance that even Jews who know little of rabbinic tradition otherwise rely on it to celebrate the holiday. As the most widely circulated Jewish text outside the Bible, the Haggadah is living proof of the lasting legacy of rabbinic culture.

So too is the role of Talmud study in contemporary Jewish culture. The study of the Talmud is actively pursued today in the yeshiva, a traditional Jewish educational institution that has its origins in medieval Europe but sees itself as continuing the tradition of study initiated by the rabbis of late antiquity. For centuries, the yeshiva has been a place where Jewish men study the Talmud, a practice that remains alive and well in Orthodox communities, but in recent decades, the study of the Talmud has expanded. Hundreds of thousands of Jews worldwide engage in a practice called *Daf Yomi*, reading one page a day until the entire Talmud is completed after seven and a half years. There are now yeshivas where women can study the Talmud, and in 2003, a rabbi named Benay Lappe founded a yeshiva named SVARA that aims to empower queer and trans people to engage in Talmud study. These developments reflect shifting norms in modern society, but they also speak to the continued vitality of the study-centered Jewish culture initiated two millennia ago by Hillel, Shammai, and their disciples.

For Further Reading

Because rabbinic literature is so vast, and its usefulness as a historical source so vexed, it is harder to find readable surveys of rabbinic history than for biblical history. Still, good introductions are available. See Shaye Cohen, *From the Maccabees to the Mishnah* (Philadelphia: Westminster John Knox Press, 1987); Hershel Shanks, ed., *Christianity and Rabbinic Judaism: A Parallel History of Their Origins and Development* (Washington, DC: Biblical Archaeology Society, 1992); and Steven Katz, *Cambridge History of Judaism, Vol. 4: The Late Roman-Rabbinic Period* (Cambridge, England: Cambridge University Press, 2006). Our understanding of the rabbinic/late antique period is constantly changing in light of new approaches and information. For more on rabbinic Judaism within a broader late antique landscape, see the studies in Gwynn Kessler and Naomi Koltun-Fromm, *A Companion to Late Ancient Jews and Judaism* (Hoboken, NJ: Wiley and Sons, 2020). For recent perspectives on rabbinic literature, see Charlotte Fonrobert and Martin Jaffee, *The Cambridge Companion to the Talmud and Rabbinic Literature* (Cambridge: Cambridge University Press, 2007), and Eyal Ben Eliyahu et al., *Handbook of Jewish Literature From Late Antiquity* (Oxford, England: Oxford University Press, 2012).

For a sense of the wider religious context, see Peter Brown's classic, *The World of Late Antiquity* AD *150–750* (New York: Harcourt Brace Jovanovich, 1971), or more recently, Glen Bowersock et al., *Late Antiquity: A Guide to the Post-Classical World* (Cambridge, MA: Belknap Press of Harvard University Press, 1999), or for a shorter introduction, Guy Stroumsa, *The End of Sacrifice: Religious Transformations in Late Antiquity* (Chicago and London: University of Chicago Press, 2009). For recent research on the Iranian context of the Babylonian Talmud, see Simcha Gross, *Babylonian Jews and Sasanian Imperialism in Late Antiquity* (Cambridge: Cambridge University, 2024). For more on the scholarly culture reflected in the Babylonian Talmud, see Jeffrey Rubenstein, *The Culture of the Babylonian Talmud* (Baltimore, MD: Johns Hopkins University Press, 2005).

On religious life in antique Judaism, see Lee Levine, *The Ancient Synagogue: The First Thousand Years* (New Haven, CT: Yale University Press, 2000). For the history of Jewish prayer, see Stephen Reif, *Judaism and Hebrew Prayer: New Perspectives on*

Jewish Liturgical History (Cambridge, England: Cambridge University Press, 1993). Though dated in its approach, Ephraim Urbach's *The Sages: Their Concepts and Beliefs*, 2 vols. (Jerusalem: Magnes Press, 1965) provides an overview of rabbinic religious belief.

Translations of representative rabbinic narratives from midrashic works and both Talmuds can be found in a volume from the Talmudist Jeffrey Rubenstein, *Rabbinic Stories* (Mahwah, NJ: Paulist Press, 2002). For an introduction to how to read rabbinic texts, see Barry Holtz, ed., *Back to the Sources: Reading the Classic Jewish Texts* (New York: Simon and Schuster, 1984), 129–211; Holtz has also recently published an engaging volume that can serve as an introduction to the challenge of reconstructing the lives of individual rabbis: Barry Holtz, *Rabbi Akiva: Sage of the Talmud* (New Haven, CT: Yale University Press, 2017).

CHAPTER 6

Under the Crescent

Was there a "medieval" period in Jewish history? The term *Middle Ages* was first used by Christian writers in the fifteenth century, and it was intended as pejoratively as it sounds: nothing more than an intermediate stage separating the period of classical antiquity from the period of the Renaissance, the "revival" of classical civilization in modern Europe. In European historiography, the Middle Ages, extending roughly from the fifth to the fifteenth century, were therefore long treated as a dark age, a long twilight, and it is this negative view that informed writings on the Jewish Middle Ages as well. Historians have come to acknowledge, however, that the notion of a "medieval" period is problematic: First, it is Eurocentric and makes little sense when applied to other parts of the world, and second, it seems to dismiss an entire millennium as little more than an interlude. Nonetheless, the concept of the "Middle Ages" is by now so deeply rooted in the historical imagination that one can hardly avoid using it, but when we employ it in the following two chapters, it will be with the understanding that there was nothing particularly second-class or dark about this period in Jewish history.

When do the Jewish Middle Ages begin? The common point of departure in European history is the fragmentation and reconfiguration of the Roman Empire in late antiquity. In 286 CE, Emperor Diocletian divided the empire into a western and an eastern part, a division that eventually became permanent. Reeling under pressure from the "barbarian" invasion of Germanic tribes, Slavs, and other non-Greco-Roman peoples, the Western Roman Empire persisted until the fifth century CE, when the last emperor of Rome, Romulus Augustus, was deposed and exiled in 476 CE. From the perspective of Jewish history, however, the collapse of the Western Roman Empire was of secondary importance, as most Jews at that time lived elsewhere: in the Eastern Roman Empire (the Byzantine Empire), with its capital, Constantinople, which outlived its western counterpart by centuries (it survived, though in its last couple of centuries only a shadow of its former self, until the conquest of Constantinople by the Ottoman Turks at the end of the medieval period, in 1453), and in the Persian Empire. In this part of the world, another development took place that undoubtedly inaugurated an entirely new era, also in Jewish history: the rise of Islam in the seventh century.

Within a few decades after the death of Muhammad, the founder of Islam, in 632, his successors had established an empire that stretched far beyond the Arabian Peninsula, where the new religion had been born. In 636, Muslim Arab forces routed the Romans at the battle of Yarmuk and established control over Syria and Palestine by 641; from there, they went on to conquer Iraq and Persia, defeating the Persian army in 637 at the battle of Qadisiyya. The conquests of Egypt

DOI: 10.4324/9781003611592-7

and North Africa followed, and by the early 700s, the Muslims had extended their empire all the way from Spain in the West to Afghanistan in the East. Having dismantled the ancient Persian Empire and taking possession of the Byzantine territories in the Near East, this vast empire now included the overwhelming majority of world Jewry under the shared roof of Islamic rule. For centuries, the major centers of Jewish life—Palestine and Babylonia—had been divided by the political frontier that separated the Roman and the Persian Empires. After the rise of Islam, the Jews of both areas were now, for the first time since the days of Alexander the Great in the fourth century BCE, united under one empire. Unlike Alexander's empire, however, the Islamic caliphate lasted for centuries, and most areas conquered in the early decades of Islamic history, with the notable exception of Spain, remain part of the Muslim world to this day.

It is estimated that about 90 percent of all Jews lived under Islamic rule in the early Middle Ages, until at least around the year 1200; however, this balance began to shift, ever so slowly, partly because of immigration to Christian Europe, but mostly due to the successful push of Christian forces on the Iberian Peninsula who reclaimed the territories conquered by the Muslims in the eighth century, thus bringing more and more Iberian Jews into the realm of Christendom. Uniting most Jews under the umbrella of Islamic rule alone seems to warrant the widely accepted convention to recognize the onset of a new period in Jewish history in the seventh century. This period also corresponds, not coincidentally, with other major social and cultural changes transforming the Jewish world. As we saw in the previous chapter, one of the most striking differences from late antique Jewish culture was the pervasive impact of rabbinic writings on Jewish life in the Middle Ages, which had now become central to the Jewish scriptural canon. As interpreted and expanded upon in this period, rabbinic texts and their influence came to reshape Jewish culture, with Jews looking to the Mishnah and Talmud as a source of juridical, religious, and legal authority. For much of the early medieval period, Jewish leaders in Palestine and in Iraq competed for influence and authority among the far-flung Jewish Diaspora. At the end of this process, which was of course by no means as inevitable and straightforward as it might appear in hindsight, the Babylonian Talmud had been established as the primary work of reference for the rabbinic culture that was to define the Jewish experience of the medieval period and beyond.

As we will see in the introduction to Chapter 8, the end of the fifteenth century—in particular, the expulsion of the Jews from Spain in 1492—can be seen as a transitional moment into a new historical period, the early modern era. The Jewish Middle Ages, then, are a conspicuously long period, unfolding over more than eight centuries on a very broad stage in multiple geographic settings and cultural contexts. It therefore goes without saying that the present overview will be able to explore only some of the basic conditions that shaped Jewish life in the Middle Ages and offer some glimpses into the rich cultural creativity of medieval Jewry, a legacy that continued to shape Judaism in subsequent centuries. Whereas Jews everywhere in the medieval world were tied by a shared textual tradition—the Bible, the Mishnah, and the Talmud—and maintained a sense of shared destiny, their experiences were also influenced by the Muslim and Christian environments in which they lived. The current chapter will focus on the Jews of the Islamic world, the vast majority of the Jewish population in the early part of the Middle Ages, and Chapter 7 will then turn to the Jews of Christendom, in particular in western and northern Europe.

At the beginning of the Middle Ages, Jewish communities, mostly living in the lands of the Mediterranean basin and in the Middle East, oriented themselves toward one of the spiritual centers in

Palestine or Babylonia. Many cities—for example, Cairo in Egypt or Ramla in Palestine—even hosted a number of different communities: a Palestinian and a Babylonian synagogue, alongside the synagogue of the Karaites, a group that challenged the authority of rabbinic "oral tradition" (represented most importantly in the Talmud). Each of these communities was tied to its spiritual and political leadership in Palestine or Babylonia, with whom they maintained intensive contact by seeking guidance regarding questions of religious law, sending financial contributions for the maintenance of the scholarly academies operating in Tiberias (later Jerusalem) and Baghdad, and receiving honorary titles bestowed by the Palestinian and Babylonian leaders on their supporters in the lands of the Diaspora.

As the Islamic world fragmented into smaller political units, from the tenth century on, and as a growing number of Jews moved westward and established thriving communities in North Africa and in Spain, as well as beyond the realm of Islam in Christian Europe, the Jewish world witnessed the emergence of new communal identities. By the late tenth and early eleventh centuries, we see the rise of independent Jewish centers—for example, in Egypt, Tunisia, and Spain—that emancipated themselves from the hegemony of the older spiritual centers in the East. As a result, the later medieval period was marked by the emergence of various territorially defined Jewish subcultures, which continued to be in contact with one another, but which also each developed their own cultural identity. The Jewish Middle Ages, then, began with the unification of most of the Jewish world under the roof of Islamic rule, organized around the two spiritual centers of Babylonia and Palestine. By the tenth century, a new pattern began to emerge, the rise of territorial, culturally distinct Jewish communities around the Mediterranean and in Europe, each of which developed its own unique flavor and set the stage for an increasingly diverse Jewish world in the modern period.

THE JEWS AND EARLY ISLAM

Muhammad and the Jews

Muhammad was born in 570 CE and is said to have received his first revelation at the age of 40, in the year 610. He continued to receive revelations throughout his life, which were collected after his death in 632 and together make up the holy book of Islam, the Qur'an. Muhammad's prophetic message represented a radical kind of monotheism that did not sit well with his contemporaries in his hometown, Mecca, which at that time served as a major pagan pilgrimage site and trading hub. Facing growing hostility, Muhammad eventually abandoned Mecca together with his followers and relocated to the oasis of Yathrib, later known as Medina, some 250 miles north of Mecca. This migration, known in Arabic as *hijra*, marks the beginning of the Islamic calendar. In Medina, Muhammad founded the first community of believers (*umma*) and established himself as both a prophet and a political leader. It was there that he encountered a large number of Jews.

The Qur'an is full of characters and stories that are familiar from the Hebrew Bible and the New Testament. Abraham appears as the spiritual ancestor, the first monotheist; he was, in the words of the Qur'an,

> not a Jew, not yet a Christian; but he was an upright man who had surrendered [in Arabic, '*muslim*,' to God]. Those of mankind who have the best claim to Abraham are those who followed him, and this Prophet [Muhammad] and those who believe [with him].

Islam recognized figures like Moses, David, Solomon, and Jesus as true prophets; Muhammad, however, was to be the "seal of prophecy," the last prophet whose task it was to re-establish the true, pure divine revelation that, according to Islamic theology, had been corrupted by Jews and Christians. The striking appearance of so many elements of Jewish and Christian tradition in Islam was due to the influence of members of both religions living on the Arabian Peninsula with whom Muhammad would have had contact, first during his life in Mecca, which saw the coming and going of traders from throughout the peninsula, and later in Medina, where, as noted, he encountered a large number of Jews. The influence of Jewish beliefs and rituals on the teachings of Muhammad can be discerned not only in the pages of the Qur'an but also in early Muslim religious practice. The Islamic reverence for Jerusalem, from where Muhammad was believed to have ascended on a miraculous journey to heaven, is a case in point, and in the early days of Islam, Muslims prayed facing Jerusalem, until another revelation changed the direction of prayer (*qibla*) toward Mecca.

Whatever the expectations of Muhammad and his followers, the Jews of Medina did not embrace the leader of the Muslims as a prophet and did not join the new religion. At first, coexistence between the "believers"—that is, the Muslims—and the Jews was ensured by Muhammad's ordinance for Medina, which stipulated that "the Jews have their religion and the Muslims have theirs," though it also included an ominous warning against "those who act wrongfully and sin, for they bring destruction upon themselves and their households." The ensuing confrontation between Muhammad and the Jews of Medina has sometimes been described as the earliest anti-Jewish persecution in Islamic history; in reality, though, the conflict is probably best understood in terms of clashing political and economic interests. As Muhammad sought to consolidate his authority in Medina and extend his power beyond, waging a battle against the pagan Arab tribes of the Peninsula and eventually conquering his hometown, Mecca, in 630, he also confronted his Jewish detractors, who failed to accept his prophetic mission and were accused, justly or not, of not being loyal to Muhammad and threatening his rule. As a result of this largely political confrontation, two of the major Jewish clans were forced to leave Medina in 624 and 625, and their lands were distributed to Muhammad's allies. In 627, the members of a third Jewish clan, the Banu Qurayza, were accused of conspiring with forces from Mecca that had laid siege to Medina, and Muhammad resolved to make an example of them; several hundreds are said to have been killed.

The following year, Muhammad took on the oasis of Khaybar, where some of the expelled Jews of Medina had relocated. The battle of Khaybar ended with the capitulation of the Jews, who accepted the terms of surrender dictated by the victorious Muslims, who "made peace with them in return for fifty percent of their produce." This set an important precedent for the treatment of Jews and Christians in places conquered by Muhammad and, later on, by his successors, validated by a Qur'anic revelation. The Jewish and Christian "People of the Book" were granted peace and protection in exchange for paying a tribute, called *jizya*, to the Muslims: "Fight against those to whom Scriptures were given," the Qur'an says in reference to Jews and Christians, who were recognized as having received previous divine revelations, "until they pay the tribute out of hand, and are humbled" (Qur'an, 9:29).

On the one hand, then, the Muslim community was expected to wage battle against those who did not accept Islam—to engage in *jihad*, or holy war. But on the other hand, it was also clear that whereas pagans had no choice, at least in theory, but to accept Islam or face death, Jews or Christians would be left alone as long as they acknowledged the supremacy of the Muslims, paid their tribute (which later became a regular form of poll tax), and accepted an inferior, humbled status within the order of Islamic society. The earliest encounter between Muhammad and the Jews was, then, one of conflict and, indeed, warfare. The outcome of this conflict also laid the foundations, however, for a remarkably stable modus vivendi that allowed Jews and Christians to live (and often thrive) under Muslim rule throughout the Middle Ages. Pronouncements on Jews and Christians in the Qur'an and the prophetic traditions attributed to Muhammad (*hadith*) reflect the ambivalent attitude that arose out of the early political confrontations yet also highlight the potential for toleration that medieval Islam would display toward these older religious traditions (*see the box* "The Qur'an and the Jews").

The Umayyad Caliphate and the "Pact of Umar"

As we saw in the introduction to this chapter, the Muslim commonwealth expanded rapidly in the decades after Muhammad's death in 632. The first four caliphs (as the leaders of the Muslim community were known, from the Arabic *khalifa*, or "successor") ruled from Medina until the fifth caliph, Mu'awiya, established the first caliphal dynasty, the Umayyad caliphate, and moved the capital to the Syrian city of Damascus. The Umayyad caliphate endured until 750; by that year, the Muslims had created a formidable empire that extended from the Atlantic coast in the west to the Indus delta in the east. The expansion into Christian Europe was checked only when the Muslim forces were defeated at the Battle of Tours in 732 and their siege of the Byzantine capital, Constantinople, failed in 717–718. Within their vast empire, however, Muslims long remained a relative minority of the population as Islamization lagged behind the swift establishment of military-political control. This was certainly true for the first two centuries of Islamic rule, and it is estimated that as late as the tenth century, the majority of the population in Egypt were Coptic Christians, and in northern Syria, Christians represented a majority until the twelfth century. Even after more substantial numbers of Christians embraced Islam in Egypt and Syria in the fourteenth century, large Christian minorities remained.

This meant that the Muslim rulers had to be pragmatic in dealing with their non-Muslim subject population. The Qur'an declared that "there is to be no compulsion in religion" (Qur'an 2:256), and it would have been impossible to impose the new religion by force in as broad a territory as the one that was conquered by the early Islamic Empire. Building on the precedence of Muhammad's treatment of the Jews of Khaybar, Islamic law (*shari'a*), therefore, recognized the continued existence of Jewish and Christian communities under Muslim rule. Treated as dhimmis—literally, "protected people"—Jews and Christians were granted protection of life and religious freedom in exchange for the payment of a special poll tax (the *jizya*). Conditions defining the parameters of coexistence between dhimmis and Muslims were spelled out in a document referred to as the Pact of Umar, traditionally attributed to the second caliph, Umar ibn al-Khattab (r. 634–644), though the oldest version of this text that we know of comes from the tenth century. Under these circumstances, the transition to Islamic rule was likely not particularly traumatic, and perhaps was even a welcome change, from the point of view of many non-Muslim populations in the territories conquered by the Muslims. The Jews, of course, had long been used to living as a religious minority, and their legal status under Islamic rule turned out to be rather similar to what it had been in Roman and Byzantine law. For the Christian populations in the Middle East, too, Islamic rule may not have represented as big a change as one might have imagined, as most Christians in the Middle East were Monophysite Christians, who were separated theologically from the Orthodox Christianity of the Byzantine emperors, whose rule they often resented.

What is most striking about the Pact of Umar, even more so than its various stipulations, is its form. It was phrased as a treaty, as a pact, which obligated both sides of the agreement: the Jews and Christians, who were expected to submit to the restrictions spelled out in the Pact, and the Muslim state, which recognized a specific slot for the Jewish and Christian communities within Islamic society. In other words, the legal protection of the Jews (and the Christians) did not depend on the whims of the individual ruler but was inscribed as a basic principle in Islamic law. Several of the stipulations found in the Pact of Umar reflected the conditions of the early years of the Muslim conquest: Dhimmis were not allowed to "shelter any spy" or "wear swords or bear weapons," conditions that arguably served the security interests of the young Islamic Empire rather than any theological considerations. Other stipulations were more explicitly discriminatory: for example, the rule not to build new houses of worship or restore those that had fallen into disrepair. This law was likely derived from a similar restriction against the building or restoration of synagogues that had existed already in Byzantine law. But it is clear that, over time, exceptions were made and ways around the wholesale prohibition of new non-Muslim houses of worship were found: The synagogues and churches in cities established by Muslims, such as (new) Cairo, Kufa, and Baghdad, are testimony to that.

Still, other conditions in the Pact of Umar were designed to symbolically enforce a social hierarchy in which the dhimmis occupied a clearly defined and legally secured but inferior position. Jews and Christians, for example, had to promise thus:

> [To] show deference to the Muslims and to rise from our seats when they wish to sit down. . . . We shall not ride on saddles. . . . We shall not take any slaves that have been allotted to the Muslims. . . . We shall not build our homes higher than theirs.

The public display of dhimmi religions was also restricted, initially perhaps to avoid their influence on the young Muslim community, and later as a way to mark the social hierarchy. The sale of wine to Muslims was not allowed (as consumption of alcohol is prohibited to them); neither the public display of non-Muslim religious symbols and books nor the "raising [of their] voices" during prayers or funeral processions was to be permitted. At the same time, a certain anxiety seems to have persisted about the mingling of Muslims and non-Muslims, and several stipulations of the Pact of Umar were intended to ensure the maintenance of social boundaries separating Muslims and dhimmis. "We shall not attempt to resemble the Muslims in any way with regard to their dress," the Christians and Jews pledged, and "shall always adorn ourselves in our traditional fashion. We shall bind the *zunnar* [a kind of belt] around our waists."

Not all these conditions were always implemented. In fact, despite an enjoinder "not to speak as [the Muslims] do," Arabic quickly became the vernacular language shared by members of all religions, including the Jews, throughout the Islamic world west of Iran. Also in their dress, the dhimmis seem to have assimilated to Muslim customs, so that, in 850, Caliph al-Mutawakkil, ruling in Baghdad, felt the need to prescribe a special kind of dress to be worn by Jews and Christians so they could readily be distinguished from Muslims. More generally speaking, it appears that the basic conditions of the Pact of Umar—maintaining social boundaries and the social hierarchy, no new synagogues and churches, and so on—were, more often than not, observed in the breach. Numerous Muslim rulers employed dhimmis in public office and put them in a position of authority over Muslims, which clearly ran counter to the principles of the Pact of Umar, and complaints about Jews or Christians violating the conditions of their status as dhimmis were frequent.

Around the beginning of the twelfth century, for example, an Islamic legal scholar in the Moroccan city of Tangiers was approached with a complaint

THE QUR'AN AND THE JEWS

Muhammad, the prophet of Islam, experienced his first revelation when he was around 40 years old. The holy scripture of Islam, the Qur'an, was not revealed in one single instance but, rather, in portions throughout the prophet's lifetime, from around 610 until his death in 632. A chapter in the Qur'an is called a sura; when the text of the Qur'an was standardized, the individual chapters were arranged according to their length, with the second sura being the longest one and the shortest chapter appearing at the end (the first chapter, a brief statement of the main Muslim credo in the unity of God, is an exception). Being revealed over two decades, the individual portions of the Qur'anic text often respond directly to specific historical events, and thus, the pronouncements dealing with Jews (and Christians) that one finds in the Qur'an need to be understood as a response to Muhammad's own encounter with the Jews of Arabia.

In 628, the Muslims of Medina defeated the Jews living in the nearby oasis of Khaybar, and the battle ended with the surrender of the Jews, who were granted protection of life and property in exchange for paying an annual tribute to the Muslims. This became an important precedent for the Muslim treatment of Christians and Jews in territories that were conquered by the expanding Islamic Empire, and it was duly confirmed in the following Qur'anic passage revealed after the battle of Khaybar:

> Fight against those to whom the Scriptures were given, who believe not in God nor in the Last Day, who forbid not what God and his messenger have forbidden, and follow not the true faith, until they pay the tribute out of hand, and are humbled.
>
> (Sura 9:29)

This is the classical proof text in Islamic law establishing the basis for the interaction between Muslims and the so-called People of the Book—namely, Jews and Christians—who possessed their own divine revelation (the Torah and the New Testament, respectively) and were thus in a different category than were the pagans. Jews and Christians had to pay a special tax (the poll tax, or *jizya*) and recognize the superiority of the new Islamic order in exchange for being granted toleration and protection. In fact, the Qur'an mandated the political expansion of the Muslim state, but it prohibited the use of force to spread the new religion: "There is no compulsion in religion" (Sura 2:256).

Some passages in the Qur'an display a rather positive attitude toward the Jews and Christians and seem to express an early expectation that the Jews of Medina, Muhammad's residence after leaving his native Mecca in 622, may be drawn to the new religion. Consider the following:

> Children of Israel, remember the favor I have bestowed upon you. Keep your covenant, and I will be true to Mine. Dread My power. Have faith in My revelations, which confirm your Scriptures, and do not be the first to deny them.
>
> (Sura 2:40–41)

In fact, Jews, Christians, and a somewhat-mysterious group referred to as "Sabeans" were reassured in the Qur'an:

> Believers, Jews, Christians, and Sabeans—whoever believes in God and the Last Day and does what is right—shall be rewarded by their Lord; they have nothing to fear or to regret.
>
> (Sura 2:62)

But it soon became clear that the Jews rejected Muhammad's claims as a prophet, and relations between Muslims and the Jews in Medina deteriorated quickly. Other passages in the Qur'an reflect the tensions that emerged at that time:

THE QUR'AN AND THE JEWS (CONTINUED)

> O you who believe! Take not the Jews and Christians as friends. They are friends to one another. Whoever of you befriends them is one of them. God does not guide the people who do evil.
>
> (Sura 5:51)

Another passage singles out the Jews, no doubt because of the political rivalry between the early Muslims and the Jews of Medina and Khaybar, who were accused of conspiring against Muhammad with the pagan inhabitants of Mecca:

> You will find that the most implacable of men in their enmity to the faithful are the Jews and the pagans, and that the nearest in affection to them [the Muslims] are those who say: "We are Christians." That is because there are priests and monks among them; and because they are free from pride.
>
> (Sura 5:82)

The most serious accusation against Jews and Christians in the Qur'an is the suggestion that they had been unfaithful to their own divine revelations, while some of the Qur'an's exhortations are not unlike the criticism familiar from the admonishments of the biblical prophets:

> Do you [Muslims] then hope that they [the Jews and Christians] will believe in you, when some of them have already heard the word of God and knowingly perverted it, although they understood its meaning? . . . There are illiterate men among them who, ignorant of the Scriptures, know of nothing but lies and vague fancies. Woe to those that wire the scriptures with their own hands and then declare: "This is from God," in order to gain some paltry end. . . . When We [i. e., God] made a covenant with the Israelites We said: "Serve none but God. Show kindness to your parents, to your kinsfolk, to the orphans, and to the destitute. Exhort men to righteousness. Attend to your prayers and render the alms levy." But you all broke the covenant except a few, and gave no heed.
>
> (Sura 2:75–83)

The attitudes toward Jews and Christians in the Qur'an are thus ambiguous: On the one hand, those traditions were recognized as legitimate religions based on earlier divine revelations; at the same time, the Qur'an accused Jews and Christians of having tampered with God's Word, and political tensions between the groups led to some clearly hostile statements, particularly against the Jews. Overall, however, it was the Qur'anic mandate for tolerating the "People of the Book" in exchange for payment of the *jizya* and acceptance of an inferior social status that shaped Muslim–Jewish relations throughout the Middle Ages.

---

against a Jewish doctor living in Fez, also in Morocco, who

> wears a turban and a ring, rides on a saddle on a beautiful riding animal and sits in his shop without a distinguishing mark and without a belt (*zunnar*), and he also walks around in the market streets without a distinguishing mark which would allow him to be recognized [as a dhimmi]. Rather he [wears] the most exquisite dress, like the Muslim notables or even better.

The Jewish doctor was thus in clear violation of the fundamental principles of *dhimma* law, marking religious difference and inferior status. The Muslim legal scholar responded by restating the conditions of the Pact of Umar, chastising the Jew for transgressing its rules and urging the Muslim authorities in Fez to implement them. He also prefaced his remarks to the Muslims who had addressed this question to him and who were clearly upset with the Jewish doctor's behavior, by reminding them of a saying of the prophet Muhammad regarding the dhimmis: "Humiliate them, but do not oppress them." What was at stake, then, was the implementation of the law, not some kind of arbitrary repression against the Jews. For most of the medieval period, moreover, it was only when additional interests were at stake—political rivalry, for example, or economic tensions—that the Muslim authorities were pushed to rigidly enforce the more restrictive rules of the Pact of Umar. The most striking difference between the legal situation of the Jews under Islam and Christendom in the Middle Ages, then, was not so much a greater or lesser degree of discrimination or tolerance but, rather, the stability and continuity of the legal status accorded the Jews under Islamic law.

The Pact of Umar was as notable for the restrictions it imposed as it was for those it did not: It curtailed neither economic freedom nor the freedom of residence and travel. This represents an important contrast with the situation of the Jews in many parts of Christian Europe, where Jews were often excluded from certain (or even most) professions and where they could not simply establish residence wherever they wanted. In the Islamic world, by contrast, all a Jew (or Christian) needed was a receipt that he had paid his yearly poll tax in his regular place of residence, and this allowed him to freely move about everywhere in the vast territory that was under Muslim rule. We find the Jews of medieval Islam engaged in a wide range of economic activities, from trade to metalworking, weaving, tanning, sugar manufacture, and silkwork, to owning agricultural land, vineyards, and orchards. The elite of the community were often doctors, the most prominent of whom might be employed in the services of various Muslim rulers, trading families engaged in large-scale international trade, and religious leaders.

THE ABBASID CALIPHATE AND THE BABYLONIAN GEONIM

In the year 750, the Umayyads were defeated by the Abbasids, a rival dynasty who, in their bid for power, almost exterminated the Umayyad ruling clan. The new Abbasid rulers moved the caliphate from Damascus to Baghdad (founded in 762), and with that move they realigned the political geography of the Middle East (see Map 6.1). From the perspective of Jewish history, this change was important, as the Babylonian Jewish leadership, the Geonim—the heads of the Babylonian rabbinic academies in Sura and Pumpedita (introduced in Chapter 5)—now found themselves right in the political center of the Islamic Empire. By the ninth century, the two yeshivot of Sura and Pumpedita had relocated to Baghdad, where their respective leaders competed for power and influence with the nominal head of the Babylonian Jewish community, the so-called exilarch (*rosh ha-golah*), who claimed to be a descendant of the biblical Davidic dynasty and represented the community to the caliphal authorities.

Baghdad under Abbasid rule became the largest city in the Islamic world and, indeed, is estimated to have been, at that time, the largest city of the world outside China. Baghdad was not only the seat of the caliphate but also a hub of commerce and trade, attracting immigrants from all over the Islamic Empire and beyond. The Abbasid dynasty did away with the policy of their Umayyad predecessors, who had favored the old Arab elites; in fact, the numerous non-Arab Muslims of the Islamic East had been a driving force behind the Abbasid rebellion against Umayyad rule. The remarkable confluence of ethnic groups and religious cultures made Abbasid Baghdad into a cosmopolitan center, a hub of international commerce, and also a center of cultural creativity. Caliph al-Mansur (ruled 754–775) sponsored the translation of a wide range of texts into Arabic, making pre-Islamic Persian literature and ancient

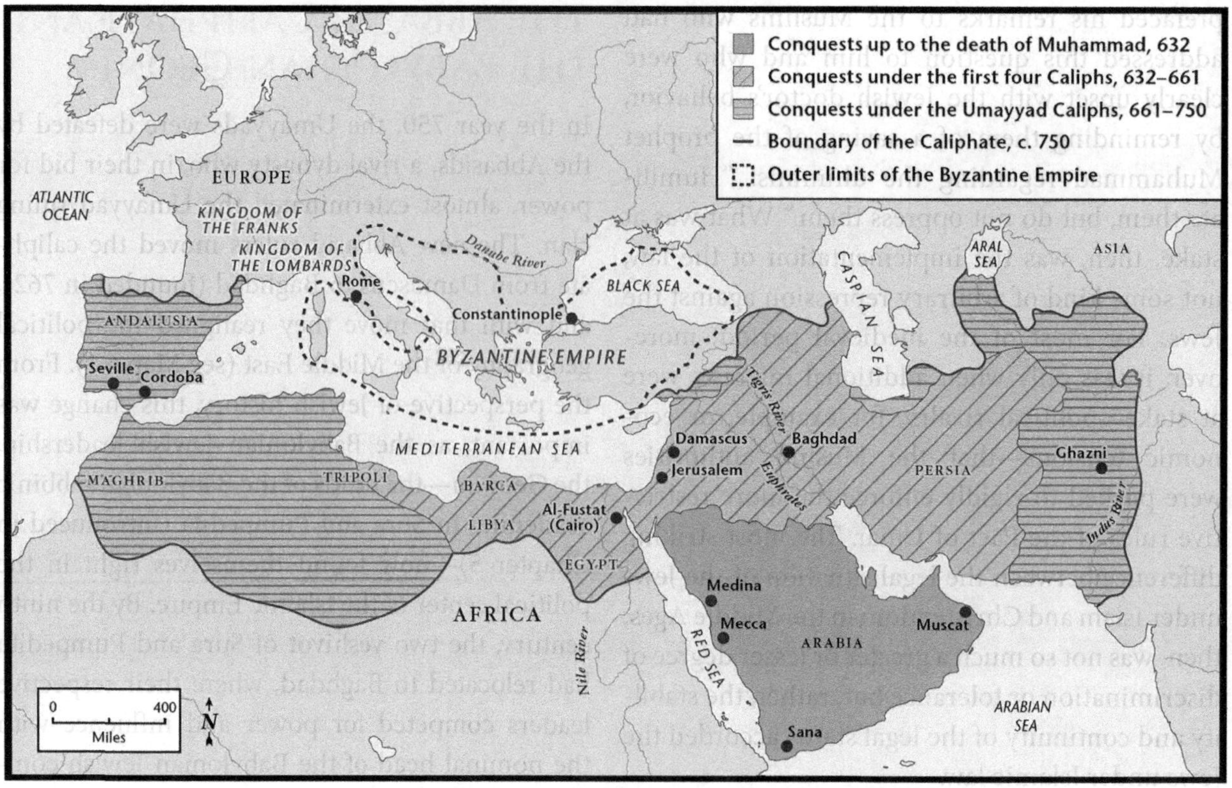

Map 6.1 The expansion of Islam, from Muhammad to the beginning of the Abbasid caliphate (750).

Greek philosophy and science part of the Muslim cultural canon. The Jews, with their two yeshivot and the exilarch, also were an important element of the cultural and ethnic mix of Abbasid Baghdad, and they joined the theological-philosophical discussions that arose out of the encounter between ancient Greek philosophy and monotheistic religion. It is striking how Muslims, Jews, Christians, and Zoroastrians all participated in Arabic *kalam*, as the rational theology developing in the Abbasid period was known. One Spanish Muslim scholar visiting Baghdad at that time was taken aback when he attended a discussion of *kalam* that included Muslims of various sects as well as members of other religions, Jews among them.

> Each group had its own leader, whose task it was to defend its views, and every time one of the leaders entered the room, his followers rose to their feet and remained standing until he took his seat. In the meanwhile, the hall had become overcrowded with people. One of the unbelievers rose and said to the assembly: we are meeting here for a discussion. Its conditions are known to all. You, Muslims, are not allowed to argue from your books and prophetic traditions since we deny both. Everybody, therefore, has to limit himself to rational arguments. The whole assembly applauded these words.

The Muslim visitor from Spain did not like what he saw: "You can imagine," he concluded, "that after these words I decided to withdraw."

The most prominent representative of the flourishing Jewish culture of Abbasid Baghdad was Saadya ben Yosef (882 or 892–942), who presided as Gaon over the academy of Sura from 928 until his death (hence, he is often referred to as Saadya Gaon). Saadya was born in Egypt and was the first outsider to be appointed head of one of the two Babylonian yeshivot. He translated most of the Bible into Arabic and made major contributions to the study of Hebrew philology (composing the first known Hebrew dictionary), Jewish liturgy, and rabbinic law. He authored an influential theological treatise, called the *Book of Beliefs and Opinions*, which he wrote in Arabic and which was stimulated by *kalam* and the intellectual climate of the early Abbasid caliphate. Saadya began this book with a discussion of epistemology (how people know what they know and the mistakes to which they are vulnerable) and then continued, among other topics, to provide proof that the world was created (rather than of infinite existence), to define the nature of God and his attributes, to explain the reasons for divine law, and to reconcile free will with divine providence, all as a way of establishing the Written and Oral Torah on rational grounds.

If reason can attain the truth in this way, however, why does one need revelation? According to Saadya, revelation imparts the truth to those incapable of rational investigation and provides guidance for those engaged in philosophical speculation. Ultimately, however, reason and revelation always led to the same truth, and for Saadya, there could be no contradiction between reason and faith, between philosophical thinking and the revealed truth of the Torah. Talking about miracles and prophecy, for example, he noted that:

> [T]he reason for our belief in Moses lies not in wonders or miracles only. . . . Only *after* we heard the prophet's message and it was right, Saadya explained, did we ask him to produce miracles in support of it. . . . If we hear [the prophet's] call and at the onset found it to be wrong [i.e., being against reason], we do not ask for miracles, for no miracle can prove the [rationally] impossible.

Saadya was not only a thinker comfortable with the principles of rational theology as it was developed at that time by Muslim scholars but also a champion of Babylonian over Palestinian rabbinic leadership. A key moment in the competition between the two centers was the calendar controversy of 921–922, during which Saadya ben Yosef played an important role (though he was appointed as head of the Sura academy only a few years later). Historian Marina Rustow explains:

> The basic problem facing the ancient Israelite calendar—and the later Jewish one based on it—was how to reconcile the lunar months the Torah presumes with the agricultural or solar cycle it commands. Twelve lunar months add up to a span roughly eleven days shorter than the solar year.

Without making any adjustments, therefore, the festival of Passover, for example, would move through the solar year, but the Bible prescribes it as a spring festival. Therefore, the rabbis followed a system of intercalating an extra month (during 7 years out of every 19-year cycle).

Declaring the beginning of a new lunar month and of the occurrence of a leap year had long been the prerogative of the Jewish leadership in the Land of Israel. Upon the sighting of the new moon, the rabbinic court in Palestine would declare the beginning of a new month and used a system of beacons to announce the beginning of the month to Jewish communities elsewhere. The calendar could also be determined, of course, on the basis of fixed astronomical calculations, but until the controversy in the 920s, it was understood that if there was any discrepancy between the lunar tables used by Jewish communities elsewhere and the actual observation of the new month in Palestine, one would follow the latter. In 921, however, when Meir Gaon of Tiberias announced the calendar and leap years for the following three years, it differed from the mathematical calculation of the calendar of the Babylonians. Rather than deferring to the authority of the Land of Israel, Saadya understood this as an opportunity to assert the independence and, indeed, primacy of the Babylonian academies over their counterparts in Palestine. A controversy ensued when Jewish communities celebrated the Jewish New Year in the fall of 922 on different days, depending on whether they followed the Palestinian or Babylonian rabbinic authorities. In the end, it seems, the Babylonian reckoning emerged victorious (the Jewish calendar today still follows it), though even in later years, the conflict flared up on a few occasions and some communities continued to resist the dominance of the Babylonian rabbis.

At the heart of Babylonian rabbinic culture stood the two academies of Sura and Pumpedita. These institutions functioned as something more than academies of rabbinic learning, including as a supreme court. They competed, as in the calendar controversy, over the loyalty of Jewish communities the world over with their counterpart in Palestine, the rabbinic yeshivah in Tiberias (which moved to Jerusalem in the tenth century). Twice a year, in late winter and late summer, the Babylonian academies hosted *kallot* ("gatherings"; singular: *kallah*), in which scholars arrived from far and wide, bringing donations from their home communities and, in exchange, hoping to receive honorific titles bestowed upon them by the Babylonian Geonim.

The Gaonic practice of writing responsa (singular: *responsum*) was perhaps the most important way in which a Gaon exerted his authority across a great geographic expanse. The responsum was a method of justice-by-correspondence, in which a given Gaon wrote out a judicial opinion in response to a specific legal inquiry and thereby established a legal precedent to which subsequent legal scholars might refer. The responsum has served as an important component of Jewish law ever since, dealing with matters such as the correct order of prayers, dietary laws, marriage and divorce, personal injury, and business liability. Maintaining such channels of correspondence over often vast geographical distances owed much to the establishment of the Islamic Empire, which united the overwhelming majority of medieval Jewry under the roof of a common legal system and a shared Arabic-speaking culture (*see the box* "The Gaonic Standardization of Jewish Prayer").

The influence exerted by the Babylonian Geonim over a far-flung Jewish Diaspora was formidable. This is not to say that they entirely vanquished the authority of the rabbinic leaders of Palestine, but it was a clear indication of their growing success when Isaac ben Jacob Alfasi (1013–1103), a rabbinic scholar in North Africa, ruled that if there was a disagreement between the Palestinian and the Babylonian Talmud (discussed in Chapter 5), the latter would take precedence. While the Palestinian Talmud continued to be considered an authoritative source as well by later scholars, even today, when people talk about "the Talmud," they invariably mean the Babylonian Talmud that came to define, more than any other work, rabbinic culture. Why was it that the Babylonian tradition emerged dominant when the rabbis of Palestine could lay claim to representing the authority of the Holy Land? Historians have generally linked this to the political dynamics of that time: After all, the Babylonian Geonim found themselves at the very center of the Islamic Empire once the Abbasids had established their capital there. While there is no evidence that their physical proximity to the caliphs itself enhanced their political power, it is clear that their location in the political, cultural, and commercial hub of the empire could only enhance their reach throughout the Jewish world, whereas Palestine was more of a provincial backwater within the Islamic Empire.

In part, however, the spread and dominance of the Babylonian school were linked, ironically, to the declining power of the Abbasid caliphate and, indeed, to the decline of the Babylonian academies themselves. The late ninth and the tenth centuries witnessed a sizeable migration of Jews from the eastern Islamic lands (Persia and Iraq) to the west, including Egypt, North Africa, and Muslim Spain, which paralleled the shift of political power away from the seat of the Abbasid caliphs and toward emerging centers in the west, such as Cairo in Egypt, Kairouan in Tunisia, or Córdoba in Spain. The Muslim geographer al-Maqdisi (d. around 990) noted, for example, how Fustat (old Cairo) had "superseded [Baghdad] until the day of Judgment" and had "become the greatest glory of the Muslims." As Babylonian Jews, and among them rabbinic scholars, established themselves elsewhere, they brought with them their traditions and practices and facilitated the spreading of Babylonian rabbinic Judaism. Thus, by the time the Babylonian academies themselves folded, around 1040, the Babylonian rabbinic tradition had come to dominate medieval Jewish culture as far away as North Africa or Spain.

However, the Palestinian tradition did remain dominant in another area—that is, in establishing the authoritative text of the Bible. The Masoretes, who were active in Tiberias in the eighth and ninth centuries (see Chapter 2), established the correct

Figure 6.1 The Dome of the Rock in Jerusalem, built under the Umayyad caliph Abd al Malik ibn Marwan (r. 685–705) on the site of the Temple. Jerusalem achieved a status of religious significance in Islam and became a major pilgrimage destination for Muslims as much as it was for Jews and Christians.

THE GAONIC STANDARDIZATION OF JEWISH PRAYER

The Bible establishes prayer—praise, petition, confession, and thanksgiving—as an important form of communication with God, but the idea of prayer as a continuous religious obligation, one to be performed by Jews several times a day and following a fixed sequence of prescripted blessings and prayers, seems to have developed over the course of the Second Temple and the rabbinic period. The rabbis of late antiquity developed the central communal prayers recited to this day and even ordered them in a fixed sequence, but that was not the end of the process. It was not until the Gaonic period that the first prayer book, the siddur (from the Hebrew word for "ordering"), was developed. The earliest systematic ordering of the prayers, compiled by the ninth-century Gaonic leader Amram, from material in the Talmud and earlier Gaonic sources, established that prayers were to be recited throughout the year on weekdays, Sabbaths, the new moon, and special fast days and festivals. Saadya developed another siddur about a century later.

The prayer book established by the Geonim has been substantially supplemented throughout the centuries with *piyyutim* (liturgical poems) and other materials. In addition, the Hebrew poetry of medieval Spain left its impact on Jewish liturgy, as did the Jewish mysticism of the Kabbalah. Regional differences developed over time, with the Ashkenazi, Sephardi, Italian, Yemenite, and other traditions each acquiring their own particular liturgical flavor. In the modern era, the prayer book underwent revisions in the liberal strands of modern Judaism. However, the influence of Gaonic efforts is still evident in the basic structure of the prayer service and, indeed, in the very existence of the prayer book.

And what is the structure of Jewish communal worship? Jewish men (the obligation of communal prayer was imposed only on males until the rise of the Reform and Conservative movements) are required to pray at certain hours three times a day in correspondence to the time of communal sacrifice in the Temple. One need not worship in a synagogue, but communal prayer requires a quorum or minyan of at least ten adult Jewish males. Prayer follows a precisely scripted sequence of recitations organized around two major components: the Shema, a declaration of faith in God derived from the biblical books of Deuteronomy and Numbers, and the Amida (from the Hebrew for "standing"), a sequence of 19 petitionary prayers uttered while standing. The Kaddish, a well-known part of the service, is a largely Aramaic recitation said at the close of individual sections of the service and at its conclusion; the one at the end, the Mourner's Kaddish, is recited by close relatives of the deceased and seems to have become part of the Jewish mourning process in the Middle Ages. The service also includes a public Torah reading on Mondays, Thursdays, and the Sabbath.

reading of the biblical text and added vowels and symbols for the chanting of the text. The oldest manuscript text of the Hebrew Bible that has come down to us from the medieval period is the so-called Aleppo Codex, produced by the Tiberian Masoretic scholar Aharon ben Asher and completed around the year 900.

Egypt, Palestine, and the Karaite Challenge

In 909, the Fatimid rulers of Ifriqiya, modern-day Tunisia, established a counter-caliphate in defiance of the Abbasid caliph residing in Baghdad. Sixty years later, they conquered Egypt and, soon after, took control over Palestine as well. Thus, by the tenth century, the Islamic Empire, once united under the caliphs of Damascus and, later, Baghdad, began to fragment into smaller political units. Though the Abbasid caliphate nominally existed until 1258, when the Mongolian invaders sacked Baghdad, power shifted to competing dynasties, especially in the Western part of the Islamic world, and even in Iraq, the Abbasid caliphs lost much of their political and military clout.

Belonging to the Shi'ite branch of Islam, the Fatimid caliphs of Egypt were themselves something of a religious minority in the predominantly Sunni areas where they ruled; that and the large percentage of non-Muslims living in Egypt at that time may account for what is often described as a rather tolerant attitude toward the dhimmi population under the Fatimids. In fact, non-Muslim courtiers, or those who had only recently converted to Islam, were so prominent in their administration that the Fatimids were criticized for relying on the services of dhimmi officials in apparent violation of the inferior status of non-Muslims. One Muslim author in the eleventh century denounced the situation and wrote sarcastically:

The Jews of this time have reached
The pinnacle of their desires, for they rule.
They have power and wealth,
And have produced councilor and king.
O people of Egypt! I advise you:
Become Jews, for heaven itself has become Jewish.

We know, indeed, of quite a few Jews and Christians who occupied important positions within the Fatimid administration. One Babylonian Jew, Ya'qub Ibn Killis, had converted to Islam before he ascended to become the chief minister of the Fatimid state, but other Jews and Christians served in less-prominent positions without ever embracing Islam.

Many of the Jews employed at the Fatimid court were Karaites. The Karaites (from the Hebrew root *qara'*, meaning "to read") differed from the mainstream of medieval Jewry in their rejection of the authority of the Mishnah and the Talmud. The Karaites insisted that law was to be derived through the critical interpretation of the biblical text, unmediated by an "oral tradition," as in rabbinic Judaism. For example, rabbinic tradition understands the biblical injunction not to "burn any fire throughout [one's] settlements on the Sabbath day" (Exodus 35:3) as a prohibition against kindling a new fire on the Sabbath day, but one could still sit by the light of a fire that had been lit *before* the onset of the Sabbath. The Karaites, by contrast, maintained that the biblical prohibition referred not only to lighting a fire but also even to allowing an already-lit fire to burn. Or consider another example: Rabbinic tradition maintains that it is prohibited to eat meat and milk products together, on the basis of the rather ambiguous biblical verse "You shall not boil a kid in its mother's milk" (Exodus 23:19). The Karaites did not accept this nonliteral interpretation and were often denounced by their rabbinic counterparts in the Middle Ages as "eaters of meat with milk." Another bone of contention was the calendar: The Karaites criticized the practice of rabbinic Jews who observed a second festival day on the biblical holidays of Sukkot, Passover, and Shavuot in communities outside the Land of Israel, and derisively called it a "festival of their own invention." The rise of Karaism is usually dated to the eighth century, and by the tenth century, Karaites began to trace the origins of their group to the eighth-century scholar Anan ben David, though historians today think that the followers of Anan ben David and the Karaites were originally different groups with different ideas and were merged, in the Karaite imagination, only at a later point.

By the tenth century, Karaite communities were well established throughout the Middle East and maintained their own synagogues, being especially prominent in Egypt and Palestine. They emphasized the obligation to dwell in the Holy Land and thus made up a significant portion of the Jewish population in Jerusalem. Cities like Cairo in Egypt or Ramla in Palestine counted not only two rabbinic synagogues—Palestinian and Babylonian—but also a Karaite one. In the wake of the Crusades, many Karaites relocated from Palestine to the Byzantine Empire, and some even went further north to medieval Poland and Lithuania. The Karaite leader of this movement toward the Byzantine Empire was Tobias ben Moses, credited with translating or organizing the translation of classic Karaite texts from Arabic to Hebrew. Despite the success of this relocation, the Karaites drew comparatively few members; according to the twelfth-century account of the wide-ranging traveler Benjamin of Tudela, only 500 Karaites lived in Constantinople. In the end, the rabbinic tradition of the large majority of medieval Jews withstood the challenge presented by Karaism, but in the tenth century, Karaite scholars made important contributions to the study of Hebrew philology, philosophy, and biblical exegesis.

The heated polemics between rabbinic Jews and Karaites in the Middle Ages notwithstanding, we should not imagine the two groups to have lived in clearly delineated, separate communities. Thanks to the vast evidence found in the Cairo Genizah (*see the box* "The Cairo Genizah"), we know, for example, that marriages between rabbinic and Karaite Jews were quite common in Egypt. Marriage contracts determined how to negotiate the different religious observances of the couple. The leaders of both communities recognized these marriages, and rabbinic officials even drew up legal documents according to Karaite rules. No less remarkable is the fact that political alliances could cut across the seemingly clear divide separating rabbinic and Karaite Jews: When the Gaon of the Jerusalem yeshivah needed to secure an official appointment from the Fatimid caliph in Cairo, supporting his claim to legal authority within the community, it was often members of the Karaite elite who employed their contacts at the caliphal court to help out. It is even more striking to see how the heads of the Babylonian rabbinic academies of Sura and Pumpedita employed the services of Karaite merchants, such as the Tustari family, as part of their network to dispatch responsa to communities in Egypt or North Africa. Ironically, then, Karaites were among those who assisted the Geonim of the Palestinian and Babylonian academies to establish their authority elsewhere in the Jewish world.

Given their proximity to the Holy Land, the Jews of Egypt were closely tied to the Gaonic leaders in Palestine. The yeshivah of Tiberias had moved to Jerusalem in the tenth century, and as a result of the Crusades (Jerusalem fell to the Crusaders in 1099), it moved first to Tyre (in modern-day Lebanon), and then Damascus, and eventually relocated to Fustat (old Cairo) in Egypt. In the last third of the eleventh century, competition arose to the Gaon of the Palestinian yeshivah as a leader of Egyptian Jewry with the establishment of the office of *ra'is al-yahud* ("head of the Jews" in Arabic, known as *nagid* in Hebrew). The *ra'is al-yahud* was appointed by the caliphal government, in the view of one historian, holding a function similar to the patriarch of the Coptic church, and represented the Jewish community to the Muslim authorities. Often, the position was held by Jews who also served the caliphs as court physicians, as in the case of the famous medieval scholar Moses Maimonides, who was the head of Egyptian Jewry in the 1170s and again from about 1195 until his death in 1204. From the twelfth through the fifteenth centuries, the position of *ra'is al-yahud* in Egypt was held by descendants of Maimonides.

The rise of the *ra'is al-yahud* as the head of a unified Egyptian Jewish community was an example of what some historians have described as the transition from the "ecumenical" to the "territorial" organization of medieval Jewish life. Whereas in the early Abbasid and Fatimid period, Jews the world over organized themselves around competing spiritual centers in Palestine and Babylonia, by the eleventh century, a new pattern of territorial community had emerged. Jews in Egypt were now united under a shared territorial leadership that transcended the loyalty to a declining Gaonic authority. In a similar fashion, other communities—in Tunisia, for example, or in Muslim Spain—emerged, and this led to the rise of local and regional Jewish identities. Jews continued to be in contact with one another across such political and cultural boundaries that separated them, but the later medieval period was marked increasingly by the rise of distinct Jewish subcultures in many different settings.

Writing in the ninth century, the Karaite author Daniel ben Moshe al-Qumisi admonished his Jewish readers to remember Jerusalem, the holy city of Judaism, and to consider the example of the Christians and Muslims who were flocking to the city as pilgrims.

> Do not the nations other than Israel come from the four corners of the earth to Jerusalem, every month and every year in the awe of God? What, then, is the matter with you, our brethren in Israel, that you are not doing even as much as is the custom of the Gentiles . . .? Hearken to the Lord, arise and come to Jerusalem, so that we may return to the Lord.

During the Fatimid period, Jews from Egypt, throughout the Mediterranean, and even from northern Europe went, indeed, to great trouble to travel to Jerusalem and participate in the annual pilgrimage on the occasion of the Sukkot festival. When the Crusaders conquered Jerusalem in 1099 (on the impact of the Crusades on European Jewry, see Chapter 7), however, they banned Jews from living in the city, and Jewish life in Jerusalem resumed only when the Muslim forces under Saladin retook the city 88 years later. One rabbi from the nearby Syrian city of Aleppo testified to the ravages wrought by the Crusaders in Palestine: "A haughty arm has struck, it has made way with the brooms of destruction, and has chased away all who unify the Name [i.e., Jews] from every border of the Holy Land." In general, however, the Crusaders had little choice but to come to terms with the local population of the territories they had conquered (they lost their last outpost, Acre, to the Muslims in 1291), and Palestine continued to attract Jewish pilgrims and immigrants even during this period. Judah ha-Levi, the Spanish poet and philosopher, set out for Palestine in 1140; in the thirteenth century, rabbis from northern Europe (England, France, and Germany) migrated to the Holy Land, and the prominent Spanish rabbi Nahmanides (Moshe ben Nahman) settled in the Land of Israel a few years before his death in 1270. Still, with the removal of the Jerusalem yeshivah to Syria and then to Egypt and the turmoil of the Crusades, the Land of Israel ceased to function as a cultural, much less political, center for the Jewish world in the later medieval period.

The "Golden Age" of Muslim Spain

The period of Islamic rule in Spain (known as *Sefarad* in Hebrew and *al-Andalus* in Arabic) is popularly remembered as a "golden age" in Jewish history. Like Egypt under Fatimid rule, Muslim Spain in the tenth/eleventh centuries emerged as a major center of Jewish culture in its own right. When the Umayyad caliphate was destroyed by the Abbasids, the surviving scion of the defeated dynasty escaped to Spain, where his descendant,

Abd ar-Rahman III (r. 912–961), eventually established a counter-caliphate, the Umayyad caliphate of Córdoba (in 929). Córdoba at that time was a vast and sophisticated city of 100,000 or more inhabitants and home to great libraries—the caliph's collection was said to hold 400,000 volumes—a magnificent mosque, and a huge royal palace constructed on the outskirts of the city at Madinat az-Zahra. Just as al-Andalus appeared like a land of unequaled riches and beauty in the medieval Muslim imagination, Jewish observers, too, praised the land for its natural bounty, and also as a center of trade and culture, attracting people and goods from throughout the Islamic world. Hasdai ibn Shaprut (919–970), who served as court physician and advisor to Abd ar-Rahman III and his successor, al-Hakam (r. 961–976), echoed those sentiments:

> The land is rich, abounding in rivers, springs, and aqueducts; a land of corn, oil and wine, of fruits and all manners of delicacies; it has pleasure-gardens and orchards, fruitful trees of every kind, including the leaves of the trees upon which the silkworm feeds. . . . There are also found among us mountains . . . with veins of silver, gold, copper, iron, tin, lead sulphur,

THE CAIRO GENIZAH

When Scripture and other sacred writings age to the point of disuse, Jews do not treat them as they would normal trash; rather, such texts are buried in consecrated ground. Since it is inefficient to prepare a hole in the ground for every old document and book, writings were deposited in a repository, called *genizah*, where they would remain until they would be buried all at once. For reasons unknown to us, the *genizah* of the Palestinian synagogue in Old Cairo was never emptied, and writings accumulated over the centuries. The Cairo Genizah, as it is commonly referred to, held thousands of books and documents of various length. Over the centuries, people had deposited a wide range of documents, from sacred texts to business letters, in the *genizah*, presumably because they were written using the Hebrew script. The documents from the Cairo Genizah have proved a veritable treasure trove for historians.

In the mid-nineteenth century, a scholar named Abraham Firkovitch began to mine the Cairo Genizah for books and documents, which he took back with him to his native Russia. There, in St. Petersburg, remains the largest collection from this remarkable cache. Firkovitch did not publicize the provenance of his finds, however, and he left much behind. Only later in the same century did Solomon Schechter, a Talmud scholar in Cambridge, England (and later president of the Jewish Theological Seminary of America in New York), recognize the monumental importance of the Cairo Genizah. Two Scottish women had traveled to Egypt and brought back with them the Hebrew text of the apocryphal book Ecclesiasticus (known in Hebrew as Ben Sira), which had been known until then only in Greek. Following the scent of this extraordinary discovery, Schechter found the treasures of the Cairo Genizah and systematically removed them. He brought thousands of pages back to Cambridge, and there he assembled an enormous collection of Judeo-Arabic and Hebrew documents—all written in Hebrew letters.

These documents, including letters, contracts, bills of sale, wills, and literature dating from the tenth to the twelfth centuries, have revolutionized not only medieval Jewish history but also the history of the region in general, by virtue of their astounding wealth of information about daily life, commerce, marriage, and Muslim–Jewish relations, to name only a few topics. Today, historians from many areas of specialization rely on the Cairo Genizah for a window into the Mediterranean world of 1,000 years ago.

> porphyry, marble and crystal. Merchants congregate in it and traders from the ends of the earth . . . bringing spices, precious stones, splendid wares for kings and princes and all the desirable things of Egypt.

The rise of the Umayyad caliphate in Córdoba coincided with the rise of an increasingly self-confident Andalusian Jewry thriving in Muslim Spain. The eleventh-century Muslim scholar Sa'id al-Andalusi (d. 1070) described how Hasdai ibn Shaprut led the Jews of Sefarad into a new age of cultural independence from the established centers of Jewish life in the East, in particular the Gaonic academies of Babylonia. The Muslim author could not help but notice, of course, how this development paralleled the changes in the larger Islamic world, with Umayyad Spain proclaiming its independence from the Abbasid caliphate in Baghdad.

> [Hasdai] was the first to open for Andalusian Jewry the gates of their science and jurisprudence, chronology, and other subjects. Previously, they had recourse to the Jews of Baghdad in order to learn the law of their faith and in order to adjust the calendar and determine the dates of their holidays. . . . When Hasdai became attached to [caliph] al-Hakam II, gaining his highest regard for his professional ability, his great talent, and his culture, he was able to procure through him the works of the Jews in the East which he desired. Then he taught the Jews of Spain that of which they had previously been ignorant. They were able as a result of this to dispense with the inconvenience which had burdened them.

What this Muslim observer described here as the singlehanded accomplishment of Hasdai ibn Shaprut, assisted by the caliph in Córdoba, was, of course, part of a larger development that we have already seen in the case of Fatimid Egypt: the decline of the Babylonian center of Jewish culture and the rise of new centers elsewhere.

Hasdai ibn Shaprut rose to his position of influence at the court in Córdoba, thanks to his reputation as a physician—in particular, his discovery of various antidotes to poison—and when he gained the confidence of the caliph, he came to serve as a diplomatic intermediary on a number of occasions. When the Umayyad caliph of Córdoba entered negotiations with the Byzantine emperor (their religious difference notwithstanding, both were enemies of the Abbasid caliphs of Baghdad), Hasdai played a role, as he did in establishing relations with various Christian rulers in Europe. He also corresponded with Joseph, king of the Khazars, a Turkic people on the northern shore of the Black Sea, whose leading families had embraced Judaism (which arguably seemed like a neutral position for a state wedged between the Muslim and Byzantine zones of influence). Like modern scholars of the Khazars, Hasdai was intrigued by the notion of a sovereign Jewish state in Khazaria, and he made sure to inquire whether the king of the Khazars had any information regarding the coming of the Messiah (as it turns out, he did not). Hasdai's skills as a mediator were not only beneficial in diplomacy; when the Byzantine emperor sent a rare Greek manuscript on pharmacology to the Umayyad caliph in Córdoba, he also dispatched a monk who would translate the work from Greek into Latin (its title in Latin was *De Materia Medica*), and it fell to Hasdai to then translate the Latin into Arabic.

Like the caliph himself, who sponsored Islamic and secular scholarship, Hasdai also became a patron of the arts and sciences. Among his protégés were two of the leading scholar-poets of the Hebrew language, Menahem ben Saruq and Dunash ben Labrat, who helped to lay the foundations of the "golden age" of Hebrew poetry in medieval Spain and whose work was emblematic of the cross-cultural encounter between Jewish/Hebrew and Islamic/Arabic culture. Menahem ben Saruq (c. 920–970) moved from Tortosa, in northeastern Spain, to Córdoba, sometime toward the middle of the tenth century, to become Hasdai's personal secretary. In that position, he was responsible for penning Hasdai's letter to the king of the Khazars, but later, he fell out of favor and wrote a lengthy poem lamenting the abuse he had suffered. Menahem ben Saruq was an accomplished poet, but one of his greatest achievements was the creation of a Hebrew dictionary, the *Mahberet*, or "notebook," which was notable because of the pioneering way in which it defined biblical words in Hebrew, as opposed to translating them into another language, such as Arabic. Written in Hebrew, it had a widespread impact because it served as the chief source of Hebrew philological instruction for Jews who did not know Arabic. It was thus especially important in Christian Europe, where the great sage Rashi and his grandson Jacob Tam, among others, were reliant on the *Mahberet*. From a philological point of view, the book's lasting claim to fame was to establish that Hebrew is a language with cogent, identifiable rules. Another one of Hasdai's protégés was Dunash ben Labrat (920–990), who had been a student of Saadya Gaon in Iraq and is credited with introducing Arabic meter into Hebrew poetry. Like Menahem ben Saruq, Dunash also was a notable Hebrew grammarian. One of his contributions was to distinguish between transitive and intransitive verbs in the Hebrew language and to identify Hebrew verbs as being composed of three-letter roots. He was deeply critical of Menahem's dictionary, claiming its misunderstandings would lead to impiety.

The rise of Hebrew poetry in al-Andalus is a prime example of how the Jews of medieval Islam embraced the cultural values of their surrounding society and made them their own. The celebration of Hebrew, whether in pioneering grammatical studies or the creation of new Hebrew poetry, was, in a way, the Jewish version of the Islamic celebration of Arabic as the language of the Qur'an. Jews used Arabic as well, to be sure, both as their vernacular language and for philosophical and scientific writing. But at the same time, the grammarians and poets of medieval al-Andalus adapted the ideal of *arabiyya*, the idea of Arabic as the perfect, divine language, to Hebrew, the language of the Bible. As a result, Hebrew came to be seen as a "holy tongue," holding a place analogous to that of Arabic in Islamic culture.

Menahem ben Saruq and Dunash ben Labrat disagreed on the proper adaptation of Arabic grammar and literary rules to Hebrew poetry. Menahem argued that one could not superimpose standards of Arabic poetry onto Hebrew poetry, rooted in his observation that the Hebrew poetry of the Bible has no discernible meter, in contrast to Arabic poetry (how biblical poetry works, and whether it has any kind of meter, continues to puzzle scholars), and it was his belief that biblical, not Arabic, poetry should be the model for Hebrew poetry in the present. Dunash ben Labrat, in contrast, concluded from the close linguistic relationship between Hebrew and Arabic, which share grammatical structures and vocabulary, that Arabic poetry could and should function as a model for Hebrew poetry, and he worked to close the literary gap between them by developing a technique for imitating the quantitative metrics of Arabic poetry in Hebrew. In the end, Dunash's approach to adapt the meter of Arabic poetry to Hebrew came to dominate the production of secular (and some liturgical) Hebrew poems in medieval Spain.

The content of Hebrew poetry, too, was shaped by the conventions of its Arabic counterpart. What may appear its most striking feature, given the conventional image of the medieval period as a deeply religious age, was the blatantly secular character of much of the poetic creations of that time. It is true that the poets of medieval Spain wrote splendid religious poems as well, many of which are still a part of the Jewish prayer book, but much of their writing also celebrated the courtly life of al-Andalus, the joys of wine and love. Modern readers are often surprised by the homoerotic imagery of many of these poems: Clearly, homosexuality was not seen as a taboo, biblical prohibitions notwithstanding, a reflection of the surrounding Islamic Arabic culture that did not see a problem either with poetry celebrating homoerotic encounters or with the drinking of wine, both theoretically not allowed under Islamic religious law.

One of the great figures of Spanish Hebrew poetry at its heyday in the eleventh century was Samuel ha-Nagid (ibn Naghrela). Although he was a rabbinic authority in his own right, was a major benefactor of rabbinic scholarship, and made a point of donating olive oil for the illumination of synagogues in the holy city of Jerusalem, many of his poems reflect the secular, courtly culture of al-Andalus, in which he felt entirely at home:

Your debt to God is righteously to live,
And His to you, your recompense to give.
Do not wear out your days in serving God;
Some time devote to Him, some to yourself.
To Him give half your day, to work the rest;
But give the jug no rest throughout the night.
Put out your lamps! Use crystal cups for light.
Away with singers! Bottles are better than lutes,
No song, nor wine, nor friend beneath the sward—
These three, O fools, are all of life's reward.

The poem is a good illustration of the balance that the Hebrew poets of al-Andalus, and indeed, the Jews of the medieval Islamic world, struck between their devotion to religious, rabbinic culture on the one hand and a secular culture shared with their non-Jewish neighbors on the other. "Some time devote to [God], some to yourself," Samuel says: a curious invocation of secular time in an ostensibly religious age.

The Spanish caliphate lasted until the beginning of the eleventh century, when, once again, various local rulers shook off the central power of Córdoba. Spain descended into civil war, and the once-formidable Umayyad Spanish caliphate was succeeded by a plethora of small fiefdoms and emirates, known as the *taifas*. Their disunity and ongoing mutual warfare emboldened the Catholic rulers of the northern Spanish kingdoms, who overcame their own divisions and pushed back against the Muslim rulers of al-Andalus. By the late eleventh century, roughly the northern half of the Iberian Peninsula had been taken by the Christian Reconquista, or reconquest, with the city of Toledo falling into Christian hands in 1085 (see Map 6.2). Despite the changing political circumstances, however, the "golden age" of Jewish culture continued. Like Hasdai ibn Shaprut in the days of the caliphate, other Jewish scholar-leaders emerged, serving the courts of the *taifa* kings, with Samuel ha-Nagid being the most prominent example.

Not only a scholar and poet, Samuel also served as a close advisor and chief minister of the Muslim ruler of Granada. In several of his poems, Samuel ha-Nagid even intimates that he served as military commander in Granada's campaigns against various of its neighbors, and his achievements arguably represented the pinnacle of what a dhimmi could achieve in medieval Islam. The downfall of his son Joseph, who succeeded him in his political role, however, illustrates the limitations inherent in the social-religious order of that time, as well as the fact that medieval coexistence could always turn into violence. The medieval Jewish chronicler Abraham ibn Daud explained in his *Sefer ha-Kabbalah* (*The Book of Tradition*) the following about Joseph ibn Naghrela: "[O]f all the fine qualities which his father possessed he lacked but one. Having been reared in wealth and never having to bear the burden in his youth, he lacked his father's humility. Indeed, he grew haughty, to his destruction." Muslim sources corroborate the image of Joseph ha-Nagid as overly confident in his power, so that he got entangled in palace intrigues and ethnic tensions in Granada, and in 1066, a violent mob rose up against him and killed him along with many of the Jewish community in Granada. This pogrom-like event (which, curiously, is hardly known to us from Jewish sources but described in contemporary Muslim Arabic sources) shows that even in the "golden age" of medieval al-Andalus, an entire Jewish community could pay the consequences for the (real or alleged) wrongdoings of one of its leaders.

In the buildup to the violent attack of 1066, a venomous poetical attack against Joseph ibn Naghrela and the Jews of Granada written by a Muslim author, Abu Ishaq of Elvira, seems to have played a role. The text shows, incidentally, the social and political role of poetry at that time, and it illustrates the unease of many Muslims with the rise to prominence and power by Jews (and Christians) under Islamic rule.

He [Badis, the king of Granada] has chosen an infidel as his secretary
When he could, had he wished, have chosen a Believer [i.e., a Muslim].
Through him, the Jews have become great and proud
And arrogant—they, who were among the most abject
And have gained their desires and attained the utmost . . .
Put them back where they belong
And reduce them to the lowest of the low . . .
They dress in the finest clothes
While you wear the meanest.
They are the trustees of your secrets
—yet how can traitors be trusted . . .
Their chief ape [referring to Joseph ha-Nagid] has marbled his house
And led the finest spring water to it.
Our affairs are now in his hands
And we stand at his door . . .
Hasten to slaughter him as an offering,
sacrifice him, for he is a fat ram
And do not spare his people
For they have amassed every precious thing . . .
Do not consider it a breach of faith to kill them
—the breach of faith would be to let them carry on.
They have violated our covenant with them
So how can you be held guilty against violators?

What is no less remarkable than Abu Ishaq's violent language is the fact that even in this vitriolic, polemic attack against the Jews of Granada, the author felt obliged to invoke a quasi-legal argument: The Jews, he claimed, had violated "our covenant with them"—that is, the conditions set out in the Pact of Umar—and therefore, it was acceptable to take revenge against them. By appointing a Jew as chief minister, the Muslim ruler of Granada had inverted the social hierarchy, thus undermining his own legitimacy as well as the protection granted to the Jews.

Although unusual, one of the most severe episodes of persecution under medieval Islamic rule occurred as Muslim al-Andalus began to fall apart under the relentless pressure of the Christian conquest of the twelfth and thirteenth centuries. Two Berber dynasties from North Africa intervened and succeeded to temporarily counter the Christian Reconquista. First came the Almoravids, who entered al-Andalus in 1086, following the Christian capture of Toledo. During their rule, they established a harsh religious regime, destroying and dispersing the Jewish community of Granada (which had just recovered from the violence of 1066) when they took control of the city in 1090. In the 1140s, the Almoravids were replaced by the Almohads, also Berbers from North Africa, and driven by a religious zeal that exceeded that of their predecessors. Under Almohad rule, one of the few forced conversions to Islam of the medieval period decimated the Christian population of North Africa, while thousands of Jews in North

MEDIEVAL MESSIAHS

As at the end of the Second Temple period, many Jews in the Middle Ages continued to harbor messianic expectations, often heightened by tumultuous events, such as the Crusades, the Mongolian invasion, or the expulsion from Spain. Jewish culture had never developed a single coherent picture of the messianic age, and medieval Jews differed in how they envisioned it. Maimonides counted messianism among the essential doctrines of Judaism, stating that God "will send our messiah at the End of Days, to redeem those who await his salvation at the End, and God, in his loving kindness, will revive the dead," but others, like Joseph Albo (c. 1380–1445), in his work titled *Sefer ha-Ikarim* (Book of Core Beliefs), neglected to include messianism as a central Jewish tenet. Some believed that the messianic age would bring political deliverance for the Jews; others saw it as a more cosmic change. Some discouraged speculation about the timing of the messianic age; others tried to precisely calculate its arrival. While Jews could differ on these points, messianic belief in a general sense seems to have been widespread.

At particular times in the Middle Ages, various groups of Jews came to expect the Messiah's arrival in their lifetime—sometimes within a few brief years, or even months. We do not know very much about these messianic movements, but in general, they seem to focus on a charismatic individual, usually thought to have been of Davidic descent, who claimed (or who was acclaimed by others) to be the Messiah. Jewish historians generally call these figures "false messiahs," by virtue of the fact that—judged in retrospect—they did not bring about the messianic redemption. Their following certainly did not believe them to be false, however, and some won many such followers.

One of the earliest false messiahs in the Middle Ages, Serenus (or Severus), illustrates the threat such movements sometimes posed to the Jewish community, advocating not only subversive ideas but also the suspension of Jewish law. It is reported in one source "that many went astray after him and committed heresy—refusing to recite the core prayers, and disregarding the unsuitability of foods." Serenus, who also permitted working on the second day of festivals and abolished the *ketubbah* and certain incest laws, was eventually arrested and brought before the caliph, who handed him over to the Jewish community for execution. Another such figure was David Alroy, a messianic leader from twelfth-century Kurdistan whose followers sent a letter "to all Jews dwelling nearby and far off . . . [that] the time has come in which the Almighty will gather together his people Israel from every country to Jerusalem the holy city." Upsetting the social and political order, militant messianic movements like those led by Serenus and David Alroy could be very dangerous for their adherents. Maimonides tells of one messianic figure in Yemen who said, when asked for proof of his claims, "Cut off my head and I will come back to life immediately." His captor complied, and the anticipated resurrection did not follow, though according to Maimonides, many foolish people were still expecting the fellow to rise from the dead.

Medieval Jewish messianism can be seen as the mirror image of medieval Jewish everyday life. The Messiah, after all, embodied the hope that Jews would one day be redeemed from the conditions in which they lived in a diasporic present and returned to the Land of Israel. Even someone as prosperous as Hasdai ibn Shaprut, living a life of influence and prosperity in Córdoba, was nonetheless discontent enough to want to learn the date of God's promised redemption. The popularity of messianic belief is a reminder that, for medieval Jews, life encompassed more than merely earning a living or keeping a home.

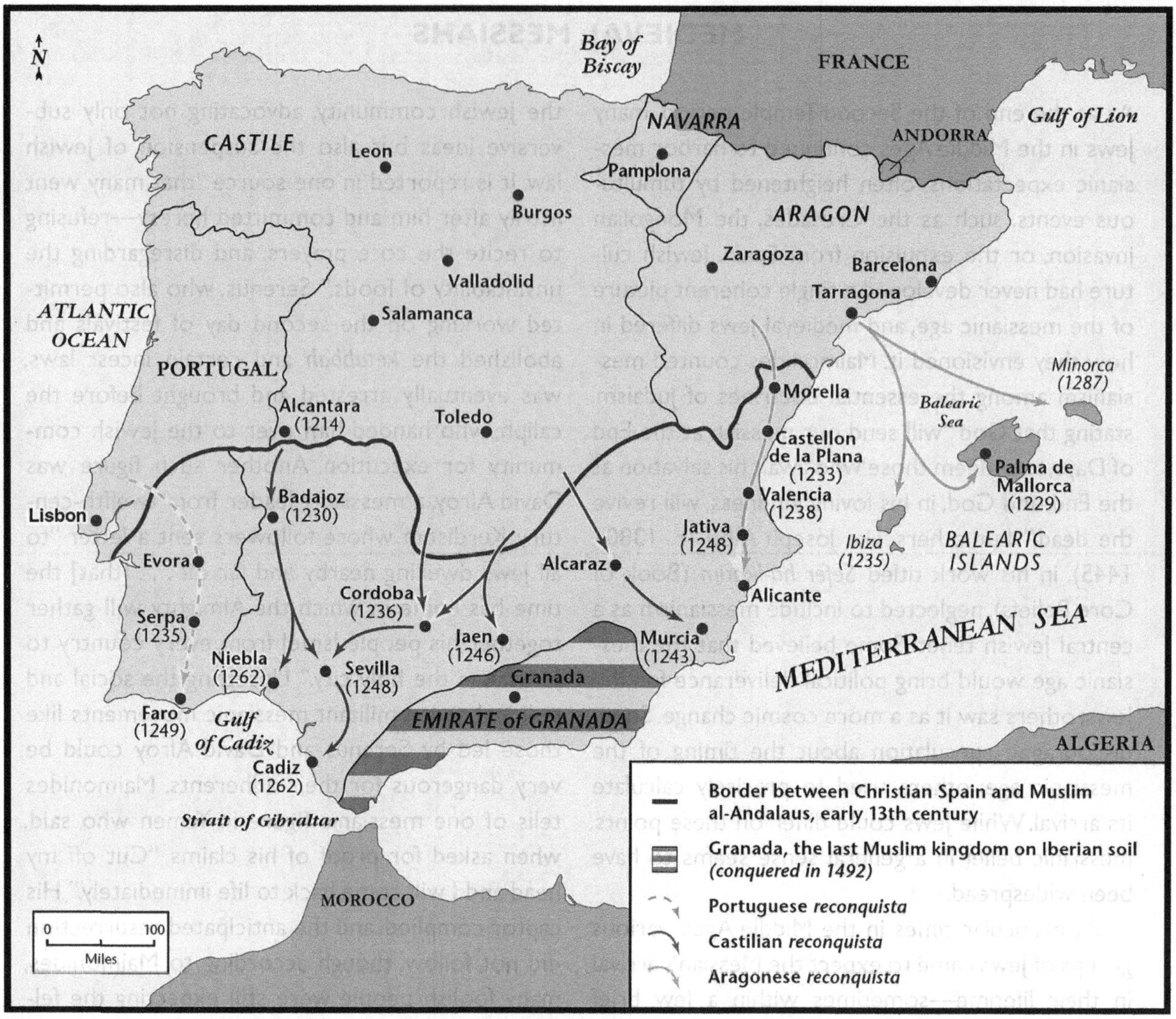

Map 6.2 The Christian reconquest (Reconquista) of Muslim Spain.

Africa and Muslim Spain likewise were obligated to embrace Islam or flee Almohad territory, either north into lands held by the Christians or east, to Egypt. The details of the Almohad persecution are not very well-known. In a letter written by a Jew of Moroccan origin living in Egypt, we read, "As to the congregations of the West [i.e., Morocco], because of [our] sins, they all perished. . . . [T]hey either apostatized or were killed." It was on account of this that the great scholar Maimonides, born in Córdoba in 1135, was forced to flee Spain, together with his family. What is puzzling is that they first moved to Fez, in Morocco, the heartland of the Almohads; he later moved on to Egypt. As to the Almohad forced Islamization, Maimonides ruled that temporary conversion was permissible to save one's life (since Islam, as a monotheistic religion, is not considered idolatry, from the point of view of Jewish law), with the caveat that one had to leave the land of persecution as soon as possible in order to return to Judaism elsewhere.

The Almohad persecution did not spell the end of Jewish life in Muslim al-Andalus, but it certainly meant the end of the "golden age" that the Jews had experienced under Islamic rule. The focus of Jewish life and culture on the Iberian Peninsula now shifted to Christian territory; we will return to Spain, therefore, in the following chapter when exploring the Jewish experience under Christendom.

Jewish Thought in the Islamic Middle Ages

As we saw earlier, Islamic culture in the Middle Ages facilitated the encounter with classical Greek philosophy, and like their Muslim or Christian counterparts, Jewish thinkers also wrestled with the implications of rational, philosophical, and scientific thinking for their religious tradition. Once again, Muslim al-Andalus proved a particularly fertile ground for a Jewish engagement with the main cultural trends of that time. One of the striking features of the period was the facility with which ideas about the nature of God, creation, or prophecy were exchanged between authors of different religious backgrounds. Thus, Bahya ibn Paquda, in the late eleventh century, adopted a portion of one chapter in his book *Hovot ha-Levavot* (*Duties of the Heart*) from a theological text written in Arabic by a Christian author (he copied the passage almost verbatim), and the same text appeared again in the writings of the Islamic thinker al-Ghazzali. To cite another example, Solomon ibn Gabirol (c. 1020–1057) penned a philosophical work whose translation into Latin under the title *Fons Vitae* (*The Fountain of Life*) proved to be more influential on later Christian theology than the original (which has been lost) ever was in Jewish circles.

At the risk of making things appear too schematic, there were two philosophical traditions that shaped medieval Jewish (as well as Muslim and Christian) philosophy: Neoplatonism and Aristotelianism. Neoplatonism, a reading of Plato's philosophy that developed in late antiquity, exerted great influence on Christian and Muslim mystics in the medieval period and, at least indirectly, on Jewish Kabbalah (we will discuss the emergence of kabbalistic literature in Christian Spain in Chapter 7). In the Neoplatonic view, all existence can be understood as the result of a process of "emanation" or "radiation" that has its origins in a pure, unqualified, spiritual "first principle." The further removed from its origin, the less spiritual and the more material does existence become, down to the material world that we inhabit. The human body, in its materiality, inhabits the lower rung in this hierarchical order of emanation, but the human soul, whose origin lies in the pure, spiritual first principle, has the potential to liberate itself from the body and to return to pure spirituality. Some of Solomon ibn Gabirol's poetry can be understood as an expression of Neoplatonic ideas, as in the following passage from a poem titled "Keter malkhut" (Royal Crown), in which he imagines human beings as extensions of the presence of God in the finite world:

> You bestowed upon it the spirit of wisdom
> and called it "soul" . . .
> And you placed it in the body to serve it and keep it . . .
> because from fire [the body] was created,
> evolving from nothing into something
> when God came to it in fire.

More influential was Aristotelianism, which dominated medieval Jewish philosophy from the twelfth century onward and well into the early modern period. Abraham ibn Daud of Spain first criticized the Neoplatonic view of Solomon ibn Gabirol in his book *Emunah Rabah* and developed a Jewish engagement with Aristotelian philosophy instead. For the great medieval scholar Maimonides, the ancient Greek philosopher Aristotle (fourth century BCE) had "reached the highest degree of intellectual perfection open to man, barring only the still higher degree of prophetic inspiration." Jewish thinkers of the medieval

Islamic world were exposed to the philosophy of Aristotle through Arabic translations of his work, as well as Arabic translations of Greek commentaries on Aristotle and the work of Islamic philosophers of the Aristotelian school, such as al-Farabi (d. 950), Avicenna (Ibn Sina) (d. 1037), and especially, Averroes (Ibn Rushd) (who was born in Córdoba; d. 1198).

The Jewish Aristotelians differed from the earlier practitioners of rational theology, or *kalam*, and from Neoplatonic thinkers, in that they posited a clear boundary between philosophical and prophetic knowledge. If earlier philosophers like Saadya Gaon had argued that reason and faith could always be reconciled, the Aristotelian philosophers maintained that these were two entirely different sets of knowledge and that philosophy had to operate without any regard to the revealed truths of the Bible and the prophets. Only what could be demonstrated following Aristotle's rules of logic could be accepted as philosophical truth, and only after the fact could one juxtapose—and perhaps harmonize—philosophy and religion. The question of creation, for example, was one that preoccupied the Jewish Aristotelians, much like it did their Muslim or Christian counterparts: Aristotle had maintained that the world was eternal and that one could not possibly assume a beginning point for prime matter; the Bible, of course, taught that the world had been created by God and therefore must have had a beginning. Some medieval Jewish philosophers were willing to accept Aristotle's idea of an eternal universe, whereas others tried to defend the biblical notion of creation from within philosophical discourse. Maimonides, though he rejected the arguments of the *kalam* in favor of creation as philosophically flawed, advanced his own theory refuting Aristotle's idea of an eternal universe with no beginning or end. Others, like Isaac Albalag (living in Christian Europe in the thirteenth century), were willing to accept the idea of an eternal universe, against the religious notion of creation in time, as a more reasonable proposition.

Judah ha-Levi (c. 1075–1141), who had been born in Christian Spain but lived most of his life in Muslim al-Andalus until he left the Iberian Peninsula to move to Palestine in 1140, was troubled by the implications of rational philosophy for rabbinic Judaism. He therefore wrote, in Arabic, a treatise titled *The Book of Argument and Proof in Defense of the Despised Faith*, which was subsequently translated into Hebrew and came to be known as the *Sefer ha-Kuzari*, or *Book of Kuzari*. Ha-Levi framed his defense of Judaism against Christianity, Islam, and the Karaites, but above all against rational philosophy, as a dialogue between the king of the Khazars and a rabbi. In the story (which was, of course, fictional, though the conversion of the Khazar ruling class to Judaism appears to be historical fact), the Khazar king has a dream in which he is told by an angel that his intentions are praiseworthy but his actions are not, and thus, he sets out to discover truth. The king summons, one after another, a philosopher, a Christian, and a Muslim but is unconvinced by all of them, until he finally invites a rabbi, who lays out the principles of Judaism. The Khazar king is persuaded, and the bulk of the *Kuzari* consists of the ongoing dialogue between the rabbi and his new pupil. Ha-Levi's imaginary philosopher, summarizing his view of the world, illustrates well the challenge presented by philosophy to traditional Judaism:

> God is, in the opinion of the philosophers, above the knowledge of individuals, because they change with the times and there is no change in God's knowledge. He does not know you, much less your intentions and actions, nor does He listen to your prayers or see your movements. Even if philosophers say that He created you, they only speak in metaphor, because He is the cause of causes in the creation of all creatures, but not because this was

> His intention from the beginning. He never created man, for the world is without beginning, and no man arose other than through one who came into existence before him. . . . Everything is reduced to the Prime Cause—not to a Will proceeding from it, but to an Emanation, from which emanated a second, a third, and a fourth cause.

Judah ha-Levi, through the voice of the rabbi (called the *haver* in the Hebrew version of his book), sets Judaism against philosophy. Unlike Saadya Gaon, who had maintained that, ultimately, there could be no contradiction between rational philosophy and revealed religion, the *Kuzari* clearly posits an insurmountable difference between philosophical and prophetic knowledge. Ha-Levi argues that the Jewish people alone possess the spirit of prophecy, and that God had revealed himself to them specifically. When Moses spoke to Pharaoh, ha-Levi's rabbi explains:

> [H]e did not say: "The God of heaven and earth" . . . sent me. In the same way God commenced His speech to the assembled people of Israel: "I am the God you worship, who has led you out of the land of Egypt." He did not say "I am the Creator of the world."

Much of the *Kuzari* enlists the superior qualities of the Jewish people and its land, the Land of Israel, as well as its language, Hebrew. Ha-Levi even goes so far as to declare that "any gentile who joins [them] sincerely shares [their] good fortune, but he is not equal to [them]," for he would not possess the spirit of prophecy that, in ha-Levi's understanding, was transmitted from Abraham to Isaac to Jacob and on to the Jewish people as a community tied by common descent, not merely a shared belief.

Judah ha-Levi responded not only to the onslaught of rational Aristotelian philosophy but also to a deteriorating political situation in which the Jews found themselves increasingly caught between their warring Christian and Muslim neighbors. Ha-Levi, living in Spain, longed for Israel. In one famous poem, he lamented:

> My heart is in the East, though I am at the westernmost end
> How can I savor and enjoy my food?
> How can I fulfill my vows and obligations, while Zion lies bound by Edom and I by the chains of Arabia.

Zion—Jerusalem—lying bound by Edom, a common name for Christianity in medieval Jewish literature, referred to the Crusaders who had conquered the holy city and banished its Jews, whereas the "chains of Arabia" invoked the turbulent times under Almoravid rule that Judah ha-Levi experienced in Spain. His pessimistic tone regarding life in Spain—"[H]ow can I savor and enjoy my food"—notwithstanding, Judah ha-Levi himself was still a representative of the literary "golden age" of Spanish Jewry. No fewer than about 800 poems written by him have come down to us, including secular poetry on wine, love, and the beauty of boys and women.

The towering figure of medieval Jewry in the Islamic world was Moses Maimonides (Moshe ben Maimon, also called the Rambam, 1135–1204; Figure 6.2). Born in Córdoba, Maimonides, as we saw, had to abandon Spain and eventually settled in Cairo, where he became a physician in the service of the Fatimid court and rose to power within the Egyptian Jewish community. Maimonides shaped Jewish culture in several important ways: First, he was one of its most accomplished philosophers (within the dominant trend of Jewish Aristotelianism), laying out his philosophical worldview in a book he wrote in Arabic, *The Guide to the Perplexed*. Second, in addition to many other writings and commentaries on rabbinic tradition, he authored a work, in Hebrew, that became a classic in the study of Jewish law, a comprehensive law code titled *Mishneh Torah*. And third, Maimonides was an important political leader within his community,

Figure 6.2 Statue of Maimonides (1135–1204), the eminent medieval scholar of rabbinic law and philosopher, in Córdoba, Spain, where he was born.

establishing what became, essentially, a dynasty of leadership for the Egyptian Jewish community that lasted several generations.

Maimonides's *The Guide to the Perplexed* (written in the late 1180s) dealt with all the common themes that preoccupied medieval philosophers: the relation between reason and prophecy, the question of creation, the rationale of the religious commandments, man's free will versus God's foreknowledge of all human action, the existence of evil, and of course, the nature of God. Maimonides acknowledged the limits of reason in understanding God: We can know only what God is *not*, but it would be philosophically wrong to attribute any positive traits to the divine. Thus, we know that God is *not* imperfect, he is *not* more than one, he is *not* material, and so on. The common anthropomorphic language of the Bible, which described God in positive terms—God speaks, wills, gets angry, and even is imagined in terms of the human body, as when he leads the Israelites out of Egypt "with an outstretched arm" (Exodus 6.6)—thus needed to be understood metaphorically. Projecting human attributes onto God, therefore, is philosophically erroneous (and idolatry is a philosophical error). The problem with this rationalistic approach was, of course, that a God as understood by the Aristotelian philosophers remained elusive, unknowable, and impersonal.

Saadya Gaon distinguished between those biblical commandments that could be understood rationally as promoting an ideal society or advancing one's spiritual perfection and those that could be accepted only on the authority of divine revelation but were beyond human reasoning. The ceremonial laws, for example, those prescribing the sacrifices in the Temple, were an example of such laws that seemed to elude rational comprehension. Not so, Maimonides argued: All divine commandments can ultimately be derived through reason. "It is fitting for man to meditate upon the laws of the holy Torah and to comprehend their full meaning to the extent of his ability," he taught in his *Mishneh Torah.* But he also made sure to warn that "[n]evertheless, a law for which he finds no reason and understands no cause should not be trivial in his eyes" and still needed to be fulfilled in its entirety. Maimonides's own rational explanation of ceremonial law that he offered in his philosophical work *The Guide to the Perplexed* was quite audacious: The animal sacrifices in the Temple that were prescribed in great detail in the Bible were essentially a concession to the times.

> As at the time the way of life generally accepted and customary in the whole world . . . consisted in offering various species of living beings in the temples, [God's infinite wisdom] did not require that He give us a Law prescribing the rejection, abandonment, and abolition of all these kinds of worship. For one could not then conceive the acceptance [of such a Law], considering the nature of man, which always likes that to which it is accustomed.

Such an essentially historical, rational explanation of the commandments seemed to suggest, of course, that the *real* purpose of religious law was something more profound, and that would raise the question as to why one should still practice the commandments once one had understood their actual, deeper, philosophical meaning.

Maimonides himself understood well the potential danger inherent in philosophical study. "It is not the purpose of this treatise," he clarified in the introduction to his *The Guide to the Perplexed*, to teach "the vulgar or the beginners in speculation, nor to teach those who have not engaged in any study other than the science of the Law"—that is, biblical and rabbinic tradition. Philosophy was the highest form of understanding and the loftiest goal one could achieve, but it was also dangerous for those uninitiated in philosophical thinking, as they could be led astray, away from Jewish law and tradition, by engaging in philosophical speculation. Maimonides put it thus:

> One of the parables generally known in our community is that comparing knowledge to water. . . . He who knows how to swim brings up pearls from the bottom of the sea, whereas he who does not know, drowns. For this reason no one should expose himself to the risks of swimming [i.e., philosophical speculation] unless he had been trained in learning to swim.

In the context of medieval Islamic culture, Maimonides's philosophical work was widely respected. Once his *The Guide to the Perplexed* was translated from Arabic into Hebrew, however, by Samuel ibn Tibbon in 1204, it also became known to Jewish readers in Christian Europe. Some embraced rational philosophy, and Jewish Aristotelian thought flourished among Jewish scholars of northern Spain and in southern France, with Levi ben Gershon (Gersonides) of fourteenth-century Provence the most notable example. Others, however, saw Maimonides's philosophy as a dangerous threat to Jewish tradition. A major controversy erupted among Jewish intellectuals of Spain and France in the 1230s, with excommunications and counter-excommunications traded between adherents of the pro- and anti-Maimonidean camps, and the polemic flared up again in the early 1300s, when the foes of Maimonidean thought issued a ban, forbidding the study of philosophy and science to anyone under the age of 25. (As can be imagined, the ban could hardly be enforced, not least because the decree itself provided a loophole and exempted students of medicine from the prohibition.)

Maimonides's contribution to rabbinic literature and, in particular, to Jewish law was no less important and daring than his accomplishments as a philosopher. In fact, for much of the medieval and early modern period—until the Jewish Enlightenment rediscovered his philosophical work in the eighteenth century—he was associated primarily with his *Mishneh Torah* (literally, "repetition of the law"). Maimonides was not the first medieval rabbi to compose a comprehensive digest of Jewish law—Isaac Alfasi, head of the rabbinic academy of Lucena, near Córdoba, had done so a century earlier—but his *Mishneh Torah* still was a major innovation in a number of ways: First, he chose to write in a clear Hebrew, modeled on the language of the Mishnah rather than biblical Hebrew or the Aramaic of the Talmud, in order to address as wide an audience as possible. Second, he rearranged a vast amount of material that he culled from classical rabbinic literature into chapters organized according to subjects, making his code more accessible and user-friendly than earlier texts. Finally, he decided to forego the ambiguity and back-and-forth of the argument that is so typical of Talmudic writing; instead, he presented his material in concise form and presented clear legal rulings rather than open-ended discussions. While this was neither the first nor the last attempt to create an all-encompassing digest of rabbinic law produced by a rabbinic authority, and though Jewish law today sometimes differs from the rulings established by Maimonides, the *Mishneh Torah* continues to be one of the great works of medieval rabbinic literature.

If philosophy and rabbinic law were among the preoccupations of medieval Jewish thinkers, the study of the Bible also saw a great deal of innovation in the medieval period, and once again, Muslim al-Andalus emerged as a major center. The medieval period saw the rise of a running commentary on the biblical text. Many of the commentaries written in the period still appear in the traditional Jewish printed edition of the Bible known as the *Mikraot Gedolot* (literally "big Scriptures") and continue to serve as an important tool for understanding the difficulties of the biblical text in the original Hebrew. Medieval Jewish commentators understood the biblical text in different ways, but two interpretive modes are especially important. *Derash*, related to the word *midrash*, is an attempt to go beyond the explicit meaning of the text and tease out latent meanings or knowledge hinted at in the grammar, word choice, or spelling of the Hebrew text. *Peshat*, often translated as "literal interpretation," "contextual interpretation," or the "plain sense" of the text, sought to understand the biblical text in its literary and linguistic context.

Medieval commentators made great advances in the understanding of the *peshat* of the biblical text with the tools of grammatical and philological study that they learned from Muslim scholars who developed these fields through the study of the Qur'an. Relying on *peshat* was also useful in combating rival interpretations of the biblical text—for example, by Christian theologians—as its principles were universally shared across religious boundaries, unlike the more figurative or metaphorical interpretations of the Jewish midrash or competing Christological readings of passages that appear in the Hebrew Bible (or Old Testament).

One of the most famous medieval commentators was Abraham ibn Ezra (1089–1164), a close associate of Judah ha-Levi, who drew on Arabic grammatical science to rationally derive the contextual meaning of the Bible. Although he was also a prolific poet, philosopher, mathematician, and astronomer, ibn Ezra is best remembered today for his biblical commentary—the first to appear in the Islamic world written in Hebrew rather than in Arabic. There he tried to strike a compromise between interpreters who relied on midrash for understanding the Bible and those who tried to understand the Bible independently of rabbinic tradition based on their own reasoning alone. He used grammar and his observations of the world to explain the "plain sense" meaning of the text while following rabbinic tradition in understanding biblical law. Some of what he suggests, or mysteriously hints at, about the authorship of the Bible—the idea that the second half of the prophet of Isaiah was written after the exile, for example—anticipates the findings of modern biblical scholarship.

The need for commentary demonstrates the peculiar mix of conservatism and innovation that marked the Jewish Middle Ages, innovation fostered by the encounter with Islamic intellectual culture. Both the Bible and the Talmud presented challenges to comprehension—sometimes even on a basic level. Most of the Bible was already over 1,000 years old by the onset of the Jewish Middle Ages; even a learned person might not be able to fully understand the text in its entirety. The Talmud was even harder to comprehend, requiring readers to work through highly technical and convoluted argumentation. Through the power of reason, medieval commentators were able to unravel the puzzles posed by these texts. Just as philosophy, science, and mysticism in this period were penetrating the secrets of the universe, biblical commentary of the sort that ibn Ezra exemplifies was revealing the secrets of the biblical text, whereas Maimonides sought to cut through the complex structure of Talmudic arguments to establish a clear and, in his view, rational summary of what the rabbis referred to as the Oral Torah. Like medieval Jewish philosophy and poetry, biblical commentary of the day manifests both the religious traditionalism of Jews in this period and their openness to new ideas from the outside world.

Jewish Lives Under Islamic Rule

While historians often dwell extensively on the accomplishments of small literate elites, most medieval Jews, of course, were neither poets nor philosophers, and the life of the average person in the Middle Ages was hardly shaped by the debates between Jewish Aristotelians like Maimonides and their detractors. Fortunately, however, a vast number of medieval documents survived the ages in a storage room in a synagogue in Old Cairo (*see the box* "The Cairo Genizah") and allow us a glimpse into the everyday lives of Jews living in the Islamic world between the tenth and the twelfth centuries. Beyond the highbrow culture reflected in the writings of rabbis, philosophers, and poets, we get a better sense of everyday life in a medieval Jewish community.

By the tenth century, the time when we begin to have an abundance of records from the Cairo Genizah, two important demographic developments had reshaped the Jewish world: the migration from east to west, which we have referred to earlier and which precipitated the relative decline of Babylonia and the rise of new centers of Jewish civilization in Egypt, North Africa, and Spain, and the urbanization of much of the Jewish world under Islamic rule. In pre-Islamic Babylonia, for example, many Jews had still lived an agrarian way of life in the countryside. The Islamic conquest, however, set in motion a gradual shift to the cities, partly because special taxes burdened non-Muslim owners of land and partly because of the new opportunities offered by the cosmopolitan urban centers that emerged throughout the Islamic Empire. Although we still read of Jews who owned orchards, fields, or livestock in the tenth or eleventh centuries, in such cases, they usually employed local agents to look after their land. By and large, though, theirs had become an urban community and, as far as we can tell from the evidence in the Cairo Genizah, a highly mobile one. The hundreds of letters preserved from the period show how Jewish merchants from Sijilmasa in Morocco or Seville in Spain maintained ongoing and close contact with their Jewish counterparts in Cairo and as far away as Samarkand in Central Asia, the Byzantine capital Constantinople, or the port cities of India.

Though far from typical in the scope of their operations, one great merchant family deserves to be pointed out: the Radhanites, who traded in silk fabrics, slaves, furs, and swords and had dealings that extended to Europe and China (see Map 6.3 and *the box* "Jewish Slave Trading"). This is how one Muslim chronicler described the Radhanite merchants, illustrating the fact that the medieval Islamic world stood at the very center of global

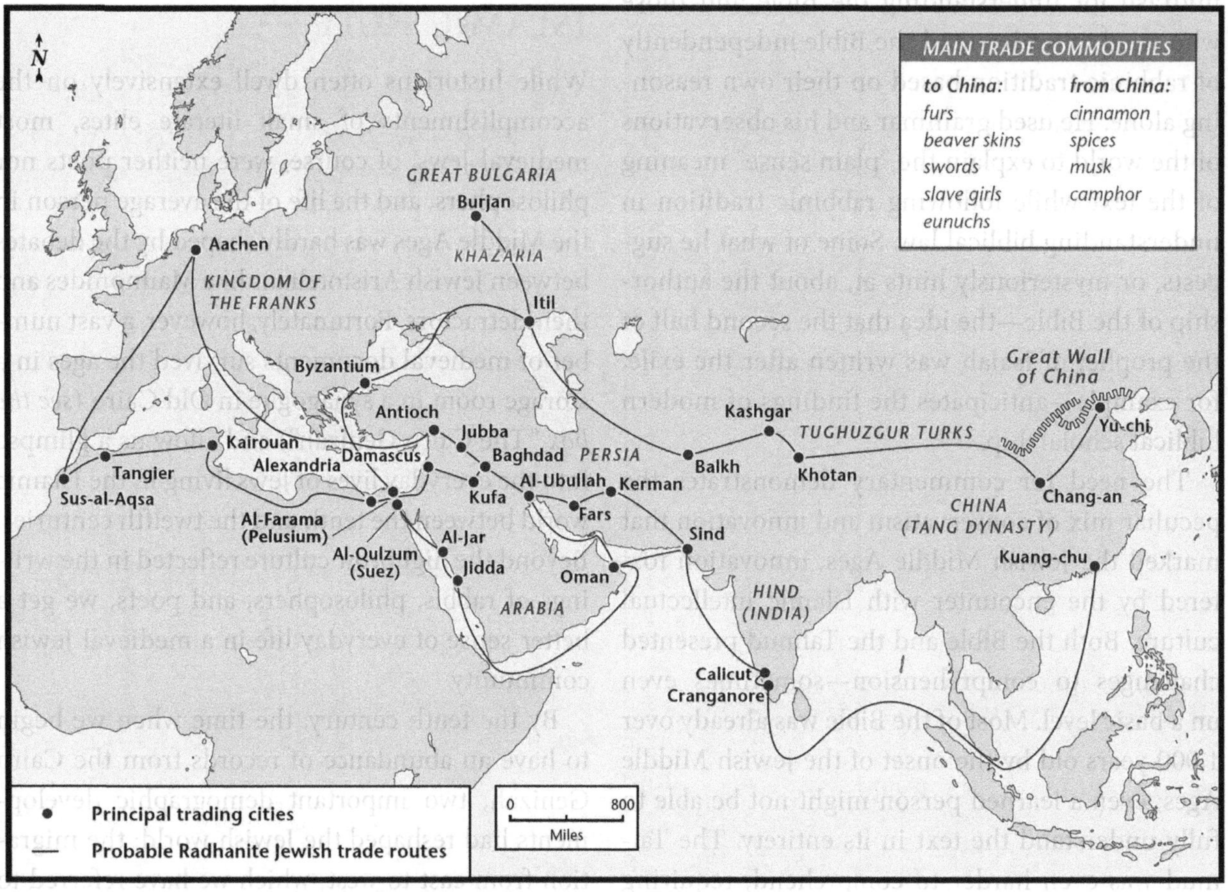

Map 6.3 The trading circuit of the Jewish traders known as the Radhanites.

commerce, as well as the important role played by Jewish merchants:

> They speak Arabic, Persian, Greek, Frankish, Andalusian, and Slavonic. They travel from East to West and from West to East by both land and sea. From the West, they bring adult slaves, girls, and boys, brocade, beaver pelts, assorted furs, sables, and swords. They sail from the Land of the Franks in the Western Sea [i.e., the Mediterranean] and set out for al-Farama [in the Nile Delta, in Egypt]. There they transport their merchandise by pack animal to al-Qulzum [a port on the Red Sea]. . . . At al-Qulzum they set sail for al-Jar and Jidda [on the Arabian Peninsula], after which they proceed to Sind, India, and China. From China they bring musk, aloeswood, camphor, cinnamon, and other products obtained from those regions. . . . Some go straight to Constantinople to sell their merchandise to the Byzantines, while others go to the capital of the king of the Franks [referring to the kings of western Europe] and sell their goods there.

Islamic rule did much to facilitate this kind of wide-ranging trade by introducing new, safer forms of vessels and building additional lighthouses while uniting a territory stretching from the Atlantic Seaboard all the way to India under the umbrella of an Islamic, Arabophone culture. Even after the demise of the Abbasid caliphate, the political borders did not permanently disrupt what could be described, in somewhat-anachronistic language, as a vast area of free trade.

Most Jewish merchants conducted their business on a more modest scale than the Radhanites, to be sure, but the Cairo Genizah preserves a large number of documents from numerous Jewish families maintaining close trading relations with Jews in other lands. Often, their trading partners were family members, while marriage politics were another way of forging alliances between merchant families in different locations. We should not imagine this as an exclusively Jewish operation, however, and merchant letters from the period are full of references to cooperation with Muslim traders, especially when it came to the organization of overland travel, which was usually conducted by caravan. On the other hand, the high-profile commerce in luxury goods also exposed Jewish traders to extortion, as they could be accused of subverting the conditions of dhimma inferiority. Consider one example from the early eleventh century, a letter from the Taherti brothers in Qayrawan, Tunisia, to the Tustari brothers in Cairo. (This, incidentally, also illustrates the often-close and cordial relationship between rabbinic Jews, like the Tahertis, and Karaites, like the Tustaris.)

> The cloaks sent by you have arrived, and I wish to thank you for your kindness and exertion in this matter. . . . All you have sent, my lord, is fine, but I wish to ask you to buy everything all over again, for the three robes striped with curved lines, as well as the white robe which I wanted to have for me as a mantle, were taken from me by a man who imposed on me. Present circumstances make such things necessary; I cannot go into detail about this. . . . I would like the robe to be deep red, as red as possible, and the white and yellow also to be of excellent color. I did not like the color of the yellow which arrived. Also, the white robe which is to serve as a mantle should be of the same quality.

Historian Shlomo Dov Goitein explained that Taherti had probably been forced to sell the merchandise to Muslims, perhaps a competitor, who may have threatened to invoke the principles of the Pact of Umar and denounce the Jewish trader for wearing luxury garments. This did not deter Taherti, however, from relying on the services of Muslim merchants otherwise:

> I have another wish, my lord. Should a caravan set out in which trustworthy Muslims,

> who have given you sureties, will travel, let the merchandise of my brothers be sent with them as if it were yours. They would profit from this in many respects. The balance for the garments ordered will be sent to you with the pilgrims' caravan in a purse of gold dinars.

Relations between Jews and Muslims were frequent at all levels of society. It has often been said that the Jewish communities enjoyed legal autonomy under Islamic rule. While the medieval state was certainly less involved in people's everyday lives than modern governments today, Jews still frequently had to deal with the Muslim state authorities. The documents preserved in the Cairo Genizah suggest that each individual dhimmi was himself responsible for paying his poll tax to the state, and while the government consulted the Christian and Jewish community leaders in assessing the overall tax burden, it was not the community that collected the poll tax (the practice may have been different elsewhere and in other periods). In legal matters, too, it was by no means infrequent that the Islamic courts got involved with internal Jewish affairs. For example, the Muslim government would seize part of an inheritance if a Jew had left only female heirs, for according to Islamic law, a daughter could never inherit more than half her father's estate, even though according to Jewish law the female heirs would have been entitled to the entire inheritance. But Jews appealed to Muslim courts on their own initiative as well. Again, differences in Islamic and Jewish laws of inheritance might prompt Jewish heirs to involve the Muslim courts when they would stand to benefit from the application of Islamic law.

In other instances, individuals directly challenged the authority of the rabbis by taking their case to a Muslim court. During Maimonides's time, for example, a Jewish man who was a *kohen* (i.e., of priestly descent) found himself unable to marry a divorced woman because such a union was prohibited in Jewish law, so he decided to contract marriage before a Muslim judge. When some community leaders wanted to introduce changes in the order of prayers in the synagogue by abolishing or reducing the number of poetic insertions into the regular liturgy, their opponents did not hesitate to involve the Muslim authorities. On another occasion, Moses Maimonides's son, Abraham Maimonides, also wanted to introduce certain reforms in the Cairo synagogue, including a new seating arrangement, banning cushions and reclining pillows, and reforming the text of the liturgy, but his adversaries denounced the plan to the sultan. More frequent, however, was the practice of Jews who turned to the Islamic courts to register contracts—for example, for the sale of a house—rather than to fight their legal battles.

As we saw in the merchant letter cited earlier, cooperation among traders and even stable business partnerships between members of different religious communities were common. Without any restrictions on places of residence, Jews and Muslims were often neighbors and, speaking the same language—Arabic—would have had extensive dealings with one another in their everyday life. In the twelfth century, a Jewish traveler from Christian Europe, Benjamin from the Spanish city of Tudela, visited numerous cities throughout the Middle East and wrote an extensive travelogue about his experiences. Benjamin noted with some amazement how Jews and Muslims even seemed to share religious practices, such as the veneration of the tombs of saints or other religious figures. On the pilgrimage to the burial site of the biblical prophet Ezekiel, in Babylonia, he noted, for example:

> People come from a distance to pray there from the time of the New Year until the Day of Atonement. The Jews have great rejoicings on these occasions. Thither also come the Head of the Diaspora [the *rosh ha-golah*] and the Heads of the academies [the

JEWISH SLAVE TRADING

One aspect of Jewish trading deserves special notice because of the role it continues to play in antisemitic charges against Jews: slave trading. The charge that Jews ran the slave trade in historical times is a willful distortion of history, but it is true that Jews in the Islamic world did participate in the slave trade, as did Muslims and Christians in the same era, all trading in and owning slaves. If anything was distinctive about Jewish slave owning, it is probably the legal issues generated by the possibility of conversion to Judaism. Biblical law made a distinction between Israelite and non-Israelite slaves, and the former were entitled to certain protections that the latter were not (and incidentally, it is not clear that medieval Jews ever owned fellow Jews as slaves). That gave non-Jewish slaves an incentive to convert to Judaism. It was forbidden for a master to compel the conversion of a slave, but a slave could convert voluntarily, and that, apparently, was a route to manumission for some. The conversion to Judaism of many slaves explains why Christians sought to prohibit Jewish ownership of Christian slaves.

> Babylonian yeshivot] from Baghdad. Their camp occupies a space of about two miles, and Arab merchants come there as well. . . . Distinguished Muslims also come there to pray, so great is their love for Ezekiel the Prophet.

This everyday interaction does not mean that a community like that of medieval Cairo did not know any tensions between Jews and Muslims. In fact, the Judeo-Arabic letters from the Cairo Genizah coined a term, *sinut* (a word of Hebrew origin that did not appear in biblical or Talmudic literature), to specifically denote anti-Jewish hatred. Maimonides, too, though he was a respected physician at the Fatimid court and head of the Jewish community in Egypt, noted rather darkly in a letter that he dispatched to the Jews of Yemen, "God has cast us into the midst of this people, the nation of Ishmael [i.e., the Muslims], who persecute us severely, and who devise ways to harm us and to debase us." The Jews in the period of the Cairo Genizah, then, knew good times and bad in the relations with the medieval Muslim state.

The prominent role of successful merchants should not divert our attention from the fact that much of the Jewish community, in medieval Cairo as elsewhere, was very poor. In the Middle Ages, providing welfare was not something that the government concerned itself with, though prominent members of the court privately made pious endowments for the benefit of the poor. The Jewish community also tried to mitigate the circumstances of poverty. In his *Mishneh Torah*, Maimonides ruled that people were

> commanded to give the poor man according to what he lacks. If he has no clothing, he should be clothed. If he has no house furnishings, they should be bought for him. If he has no wife, he should be helped to marry. If it is a woman, she should be given in marriage.

The highest form of charity, however, according to Maimonides, was to provide one's fellow Jew with an opportunity so he could earn his own living.

A frequent challenge was the need to provide support to poor foreigners—for example, refugees who had found their way to the thriving city of Cairo in hope of a better life. One letter of solicitation found in the Cairo Genizah suggests that such hopes were sometimes disappointed:

> I have no cover, and no couch, and no work to which I can resort. I am from a faraway place, namely Rahba [in Iraq]. I have been here three months and none of our coreligionists has paid any attention to me or fed me with a piece of bread. So I have turned to God the exalted and to my master to do for me what is appropriate for every wayfarer and give me as charity a little money to raise [my] spirits, for I am miserable and dying from hunger.

Another challenge was to provide support for Jewish communities elsewhere, most importantly in the Holy Land, and the need to provide ransom for Jews who had fallen captives to pirates. A letter sent from Alexandria to Old Cairo in the middle of the eleventh century noted, for example, that:

> Three captives arrived in the company of harsh masters from among the king's merchants. They announced, "We found these three people taken off a ship wherein Byzantine soldiers had plundered them and stripped them of all their merchandise." . . . We took upon ourselves the yoke of providing their food for about a month. We labored hard seeking the cost of one of them, but found only ten dinars in pledges. We request that of the fifty dinars needed, forty remain the obligation of the communities of Fustat.

Piracy was only one of the many dangers involved in medieval travel, and many a long-distance merchant lost his life while away on business. "Years have waned, but I still mourn and have not found solace," Moses Maimonides lamented long after he had received the news of his brother David, a merchant, drowning in the Indian Ocean. A frequent problem was the fate of the wives left behind by their traveling husbands. If the husband failed to return home but there was no conclusive evidence that he was, in fact, dead, the woman found herself tied to her missing husband, without any possibility of remarrying or of collecting the money guaranteed her in her marriage contract; she would become what is known in Hebrew an *agunah*. It was a widespread practice among both Muslims and Jews that the husband would grant his wife a conditional divorce before setting out on a long-distance trip, freeing his wife from any obligation if he did not return within a specified period of time.

We learn, in fact, quite a bit about family life, marriage, and the lives of women—matters that were rarely addressed in literary sources and that we otherwise know very little about—from the documents preserved in the Cairo Genizah. Marriage was typically a deal negotiated between two families, serving the economic interests of both, and endogamy, especially marriage between first cousins, was frequent and had the advantage of preserving capital (the dowry and the dower) within the wider family. In such circumstances, the choice of a marriage partner was largely preordained or, at any rate, likely to be the choice of the bride's father rather than her own. We do hear of cases, however, when the bride-to-be defied the plans that others made for her, and indeed, legally speaking, a woman could not be married against her will. In one example, about which we learn from a letter in the Cairo Genizah, a group of Karaites from Cairo went to Jerusalem and remained there for several months. Among the travelers was the young Rebecca, as well as two men, Abraham and Simon, both of whom wanting to marry her. The elders within the group preferred that she be joined to Abraham, but Rebecca herself wanted Simon. Abraham then swore to kill one of the two if she would not marry him, and the girl had to be careful not to leave her home unaccompanied. When the elders consulted with her father, back in Cairo, he insisted that Rebecca should marry whomever she preferred. Getting impatient with the situation, Simon bribed an official of the rabbinic (not the Karaite) community in Jerusalem to draw up a fake marriage contract betrothing Rebecca to Simon, with counterfeit signatures of the Karaite elders and all. The scheme failed, however, and after the ensuing scandal, the official was removed from his position. Rebecca, for her part, decided—quite sensibly, it seems—not to marry either of her suitors.

A Jewish marriage in the Middle Ages was usually formalized in a number of stages. First, parents chose future mates for their children and agreed on the formal terms, to be fulfilled later. Upon the couple's reaching marriageable age, they and their families would begin the two official stages of marriage (which were eventually combined into one): betrothal and wedding. At the betrothal, the families legally committed to the specific terms of the marriage contract, meaning, that the bride and groom had to divorce to break the betrothal (even though the marriage had not truly begun). The wedding ceremony marked the official beginning of the marriage and took place under the huppah, or wedding canopy, after which the couple would begin their life together. Marriage thus constituted a promise between two parties, which took the form of the marriage contract called the *ketubbah* (plural: *ketubbot*) and obliged the husband and wife to bear responsibility for one another's well-being. While many of the medieval *ketubbot* are formulaic and essentially the same as those used in a traditional Jewish wedding ceremony today, others, especially the ones drawn up by Karaites (or, in cases of Karaite–rabbinic mixed marriages), were often much more personalized and detailed. One such Karaite document declared:

> I, Hezekiah, the bridegroom, will provide her with clothing, cover, and food, supply all her needs and wishes according to my ability and to the extent I can afford. I will conduct my life toward her with truthfulness and sincerity, with love and affection. I will not grieve nor repress her and will let her have food, clothing, and marital relations to the extent habitual among Jewish men.

In the Islamic realm, polygamy was still permitted, while monogamy had become the norm for Jews in Christian Europe. Since it is common in the Bible and allowed in rabbinic law, as well as in Islamic law, the Jewish communities of medieval Islam took it for granted that a husband could have more than one wife, as long as he provided for all of them and met the conditions set out in the marriage contract. In reality, however, it seems that this was not a very common practice and most families consisted of a husband, wife, and an average—according to one rough estimate based on data from the Cairo Genizah—of four children. What was frequent, however, was for divorced or widowed women to remarry. Almost half (45 percent) of all women who appear in the Genizah documents were married more than once. While a few independent women—a wealthy widow, for example—could afford to live on their own and participate in the city's economic life, this was still a patriarchal society, in which most women depended for their livelihood on men—their fathers and husbands.

That is not to say, however, that women did not play an important role in economic life: Some owned real estate that they leased, lent money, or entered into business partnerships. Women who left their houses were expected to cover their hair and dress modestly, but unlike Muslim women, they were not required to veil their faces. They were, indeed, by no means confined to the privacy of the home, and the synagogues of medieval Cairo, for example, featured women's galleries, and women's attendance of synagogue seems to have been common. Like elsewhere in the traditional Jewish world, of course, women were excluded from active participation in the synagogue service. They would usually know the basic Hebrew prayers, though few received any kind of formal education and the study of Bible and rabbinic learning was considered a privilege of the men. Still, there were examples of particularly learned women among the Jews of medieval Islam, though few references have survived in our sources. One poem discovered in the Cairo Genizah has been identified as having been written by the wife of the famous Spanish Hebrew poet Dunash ben Labrat (her name, unfortunately, is not known to us). A space where women would socialize with one another was the public bath, an important feature of any city in the medieval Islamic world, and women were also known to travel, often unaccompanied by their husbands—for example, to visit relatives or to make the pilgrimage to a holy shrine or to the holy city of Jerusalem.

As in late antiquity, the synagogue remained the central communal institution of the Jewish community. It was not just a place for public prayer or the reading from the Torah but also the focal point of all communal affairs. This was where the rabbinic court met, classes for schoolchildren were held, travelers were hosted, and public charity was dispensed: In Cairo, bread was distributed to the poor twice a week in the synagogue, and wheat, clothing, or cash on an occasional basis. The different subcommunities each maintained their own synagogues—as we saw, Cairo featured Babylonian, Palestinian, and Karaite synagogues—though the division was not as clear-cut as we might imagine, and people sometimes shifted adherence from one congregation to another. As the main public space of the community, the synagogue was where social hierarchies were put on display (e.g., through the seating arrangement), and public bans against transgressors of rabbinic authority were declared. They were also the space, however, where individuals—including women—had the right to voice their grievances if they felt wronged by the legal system, and at least in exceptional cases, they were entitled to interrupt the public prayer service and voice their complaints in front of the entire community.

The merchant letters preserved in the Cairo Genizah made a clear distinction between the lands of Islam and the Christian countries in Europe, both the Byzantine Empire and western Europe. That should not suggest an impermeable boundary separating the worlds of medieval Islam and Christendom, however, and Jewish traders from northern Europe and the Byzantine Empire appear frequently enough in the documents of the Cairo Genizah. Travel also occurred in the opposite direction: A Spanish-Jewish traveler in the tenth century, Ibrahim b. Ya'qub, marveled at the fact that when he visited the German city of Mainz, he had no trouble finding spices from India and the Far East, which were imported via the trade routes traversing the Muslim world. More surprisingly, he also encountered a man in Mainz who was able to translate a manuscript on the proper cantillation of the Bible from Arabic into Hebrew.

We should not, therefore, exaggerate the division between Jews living "under the Crescent" and those living "under the Cross." It is to the latter, the increasingly important Jewish communities of Christian Europe, that we turn in the next chapter.

For Further Reading

For Jewish life under Islamic rule, of particular importance is the classic six-volume work of Shlomo Dov Goitein, *A Mediterranean Society: The Jewish Communities of the Arab World as Portrayed in the Documents of the Cairo Genizah* (Berkeley: University of California Press, 1967–1993), and Shlomo Dov Goitein, *A Mediterranean Society: An Abridgment in One Volume*, ed., Jacob Lassner (Berkeley: University of California Press, 2003). For a one-volume history, see Bernard Lewis, *The Jews of Islam* (Princeton, NJ: Princeton University Press, 1985). For a comparative view of the Christian and Muslim Middle Ages, see Mark R. Cohen, *Under Crescent and Cross: The Jews in the Middle Ages* (Princeton, NJ: Princeton University Press, 2008). For a survey and translation of primary sources, see Norman Stillman, *Jews of Arab Lands* (Philadelphia: Jewish Publication

Society of America, 1979). On the Cairo Genizah, see Adina Hoffman and Peter Cole, *Sacred Trash: The Lost and Found World of the Cairo Geniza* (New York: Schocken Books, 2011) and Marina Rustow, *The Lost Archive: Traces of a Caliphate in a Cairo Synagogue* (Princeton, NJ: Princeton University Press, 2020).

For the poorly documented Gaonic period, see Robert Brody, *The Geonim of Babylonia and the Shaping of Medieval Jewish Culture* (New Haven, CT: Yale University Press, 1998). For the more richly illumined Jewish history of Islamic Spain, see the classical treatment by Eliyahu Ashtor, *History of the Jews in Muslim Spain* (Philadelphia: Jewish Publication Society of America, 1973–1984). See also Ross Brann, *Iberian Moorings: Al-Andalus, Sefarad, and the Tropes of Exceptionalism* (Philadelphia: Penn University Press, 2021).

For the Fatimid period and Karaism, see Marina Rustow, *Heresy and Politics of Community: The Jews of the Fatimid Caliphate* (Ithaca, NY: Cornell University Press, 2008). On women, see the pertinent material in Judith Baskin, *Jewish Women in Historical Perspective* (Detroit, MI: Wayne State University Press, 1998). For medieval travelogues, see Elkan Nathan Adler, ed., *Jewish Travellers* (New York: Hermon Press, 1966). For Karaite authors, see Leon Nemoy, *Karaite Anthology* (New Haven, CT: Yale University Press, 1952). For more on Jewish communal life and self-rule, see Marc R. Cohen, *Jewish Self-Government in Medieval Egypt: The Origins of the Office of Head of the Jews, ca. 1065–1126* (Princeton, NJ: Princeton University Press, 1981). On Jewish merchants and the economy of the Genizah period, see Jessica Goldberg, *Trade and Institutions in the Medieval Mediterranean: The Geniza Merchants and Their Business World* (Cambridge: Cambridge University Press, 2012). On poverty and charity in medieval Cairo, Marc R. Cohen, *Poverty and Charity in the Jewish Community of Medieval Egypt* (Princeton, NJ: Princeton University Press, 2005). For studies of Jewish literature and thought, consult Raymond Scheindlin, *Wine, Women and Death: Medieval Hebrew Poems on the Good Life* (Philadelphia: Jewish Publication Society of America, 1986), and Dan Pagis, *Hebrew Poetry of the Middle Ages and the Renaissance* (Berkeley: University of California Press, 1991). For studies of medieval Jewish thought, see Colette Sirat, *A History of Jewish Philosophy in the Middle Ages* (Cambridge, England: Cambridge University Press, 1985), and Daniel Frank and Oliver Leaman, *The Cambridge Companion to Medieval Jewish Philosophy* (Cambridge, England: Cambridge University Press, 2003). On Maimonides, see Isadore Twersky, *A Maimonides Reader* (New York: Behrman House, 1972), and Sarah Stroumsa, *Maimonides and His World: Portrait of a Mediterranean Thinker* (Princeton, NJ: Princeton University Press, 2009). On the emergence of regional Jewish "subcultures" in the Middle Ages, see Javier Castaño, Talya Fishman, and Ephraim Kanarfogel, eds., *Regional Identities and Cultures of Medieval Jews* (Liverpool, UK: Littman Library, 2018).

CHAPTER 7

UNDER THE CROSS

Dividing the medieval Jewish world between the lands of Islam and the lands of Christendom, as we have done here, is not without its problems. There was much that Jewish communities in both areas had in common. Their legal status, for example, was partly derived in both cases from the precedent of Roman law. Cultural contact between the Jews of the Islamic world and Christian Europe was also frequent, and as a result, they influenced each other. The interplay between the different cultural centers in the medieval Jewish world can be seen in the case of the rise of the Babylonian Talmud as the prime (though never exclusive) authoritative source of rabbinic culture. Produced by the academies in Babylonia and disseminated throughout the Jewish Diaspora in the days of the Islamic Empire, the Talmud was made by the scholars of medieval northern Europe Rashi (1040–1105) and his successors into the ultimate work of reference for rabbinic culture and the Jews, in the words of historian Talya Fishman, into the "people of the Talmud." The unique situation of Spain serving as the frontier and battleground between Islam and Western Christendom for the better part of the Middle Ages is another case where a clear distinction between the Jews of the Muslim world and those of the Christian world hardly captures the experience of people living at that time. What is more, while the juxtaposition between Jews "under the Crescent" and "under the Cross" may be too stark, internal differences within each of these political-cultural areas were significant and make broad characterizations problematic. What did the isolated Jewish merchants of the Carolingian Empire in northern Europe have in common with centuries-old urban communities, like those of Constantinople or Rome? Can we really assume that the well-documented Jewish community that left behind the Cairo Genizah had a similar experience as the Jews of so many other places in the Islamic world, about whom we know precious little? Local circumstances and contingencies often determined the day-to-day experience of medieval Jews, and any broad picture that we can draw here will have to simplify a complex and ever-evolving reality.

Nevertheless, if we are mindful of the potential problems with organizing medieval Jewish history in this way, we can still make the case that the Jews, in their everyday experience, their interaction with their non-Jewish neighbors, and their cultural creativity, were deeply influenced by the Islamic and Christian civilizations among which they lived. The relation between Christianity and Judaism, for example, was unique and produced an encounter between medieval Christians and Jews that was both particularly intimate and particularly prone to tension, and even violence. The fact that Christians did not only recognize the Jewish Bible as part of their own holy scriptures (the "Old Testament") but also saw themselves

DOI: 10.4324/9781003611592-8

as nothing less than the "new Israel," as having replaced the Jews as God's chosen people, shaped their relation to the older religion. Jews and Christians were equally concerned with establishing social and theological boundaries around and between their religious communities. Yet they also influenced each other, and the fact that this dialogue was often couched in the language of polemics or overshadowed by outbreaks of violence should not obscure the fact that medieval Christian culture constructed itself in important ways as a direct response to Judaism, and that Judaism, too, was shaped and reshaped by its interaction with Christianity.

If the "Middle Ages" have a negative connotation in Jewish history, this is largely due to the dark view of the experience of medieval Jewry under Christian rule. Many years ago, the American Jewish historian Salo Baron spoke of the "lachrymose" tendency of much of Jewish historiography. Baron took issue with a view that understood medieval Jewish history as a string of one persecution after another, from the Crusades to the Black Death, and medieval Jewry as a culture that was doomed from the outset and went under with a series of expulsions that marked the end of the European Jewish Middle Ages. Such a pessimistic view does not do justice to the centuries of Jewish life and cultural flourishing in medieval Europe. Violence and expulsions punctuated Jewish life in medieval Europe, and as the historian David Nirenberg has argued, "anti-Judaism"—defining oneself against the notion of "Judaism," real or imaged—became a central feature of Western thought. But neither Jewish life nor Jewish–Christian relations can be reduced to moments of cataclysmic violence, nor should the focus on the negative aspects of the Jewish–Christian encounter in medieval Europe obscure the fact that, as a percentage of the world's Jewish population, the Jewish communities of Christian Europe would eventually outnumber their coreligionists in the Islamic world.

Any population figures for the medieval period can provide only a rough estimate. Although numbers appear in the writings of Jewish travelers such as Benjamin of Tudela in the twelfth century, as well as other Jewish and non-Jewish sources, they are not usually reliable. A modern "guesstimate" (by historian Salo Baron) suggests the following picture for medieval Christian Europe: In the year 1300, France and the "Holy Roman Empire" (mostly German-speaking lands in Central Europe) each had about 100,000 Jews. By the end of the medieval period, around 1490, this number was much smaller in the case of France (20,000), due to the expulsion of the Jews from much of France in the fourteenth century, and also somewhat smaller in the case of the Roman Empire (80,000). By contrast, the Jewish communities of southern Europe had grown significantly between 1300 and 1490 (i.e., before the large-scale expulsion of the Jews from Spain in 1492, which marked the end of the medieval period): The numbers rose from 50,000 to 120,000 in Italy, from 150,000 to 250,000 in Spain, and from 40,000 to 80,000 in Portugal. An area that saw a spectacular growth in its Jewish population, largely due to emigration from France and the German-speaking lands, was eastern Europe: Poland-Lithuania had about 5,000 Jews in 1300, and that number increased to 30,000 by 1490; in the case of Hungary, it rose from 5,000 to 20,000. (This, by the way, compares to an estimate of anywhere between 20,000 and 40,000 Jews in twelfth-century Egypt.) As we said, these numbers have a very large margin of error, but they demonstrate a general trend of Jewish demographic expansion in Europe (with the obvious exception of those countries that expelled their Jews during this period). At the same time, it is important to point out that the Jews never represented more than 1 percent of the total population in any medieval kingdom, except Spain. (This is less significant than it seems, though, for the Jews were often a far larger percentage of the urban population, even if not in the kingdom at large.)

Given the varied and rich experience of the Jews under medieval Christendom, the following pages cannot provide anything close to a comprehensive overview. Because of the important ways in which they have shaped Jewish cultures in later centuries, the focus here will be on the communities of Ashkenaz—northern France and the German Empire—as well as Sefarad—that is, the Christian kingdoms of medieval Spain. We will also hear about the Jews of medieval Italy and other areas (e.g., *see the box* "In the Byzantine Empire"), but the main narrative will concentrate on these two cultural areas that bequeathed a particularly rich legacy to the Jews of the modern world.

From Roman Law to Royal Serfdom

The Christian attitude toward Judaism and the Jews had always been ambiguous. Consider the following passages written by the apostle Paul in the first century, in his letters to the Romans and to the Galatians, respectively:

> So I ask, have they [the Jews] stumbled so as to fall? By no means! But through their stumbling salvation has come to the Gentiles, so as to make Israel jealous. Now if their stumbling means riches for the world, and if their defeat means riches for Gentiles, how much more will their full inclusion mean! . . . [I]f some of the branches were broken off, and you, a wild olive shoot, were grafted in their place to share the rich root of the olive tree, do not boast over the branches.
>
> (Romans 11:11, 17)

> Abraham had two sons, one by a slave woman and the other by a free woman. One, the child of the slave, was born according to the flesh; the other . . . was born through the promise. Now this is the allegory: these women are two covenants. One woman, in fact, is Hagar, from Mount Sinai, bearing children for slavery. Now Hagar is Mount Sinai in Arabia and corresponds to the present Jerusalem, for she is in slavery with her children. But the other woman corresponds to the Jerusalem above; she is free, and she is our mother. . . . You . . . are . . . like Isaac [the son of a free woman]. But just as at that time the child who was born according to the flesh persecuted the child who was born according to the Spirit, so it is now also. But what does the scripture say? "Drive out the slave and her child; for the child of the slave will not share the inheritance with the child of the free woman" [Genesis 21:10].
>
> (Galatians 4:22–30)

If we unpack these texts, we see how closely Christian self-understanding was intertwined with the Christian view of the Jews. Though the Jews had temporarily "stumbled" and thus given the gentiles the opportunity to find salvation, God had by no means rejected them altogether. "Do not boast [over the Jews]," Paul admonished his readers in the letter to the Romans, for the Jews, at the end of days, would once again occupy their place as God's chosen people. The letter to the Galatians, however, spoke a different language: God's bond with the Christians had, in fact, superseded the old covenant with the Jews. Paul did not hesitate to equate the Christians with the descendants of Abraham's chosen son, Isaac, relegating the Jews to the place held by Isaac's brother Ishmael in the biblical story, who, being deemed a negative influence on Isaac, had been driven out, along with his mother, Hagar, into the desert. In the same way, Paul seemed to suggest, the vestiges of Judaism had to be removed so that the new faith, Christianity, could be fulfilled. He associated Judaism with blind obedience to the law, with the "flesh," and construed Christianity as its direct opposite, faith in Christ taking the place of the law, the "spiritual" taking the place of the alleged Jewish attachment to the material. This binary was to echo through centuries of Western thought, well into the modern era.

Medieval Christendom oscillated between the two poles defined in the writings of Paul: On the one hand, the Jews were seen as living in error but ultimately indispensable, and thus having a place in Christian society; on the other hand, they were seen as a potential threat to the purity of Christian faith and society. Applied to political and legal practice, theological arguments could be marshaled in favor of extending tolerance to the Jews or to support their exclusion from medieval society. For much of the medieval period, the more pragmatic, tolerant attitude prevailed, but the alternative view of Paul in the letter to the Galatians, which held the Jews to be a threat and unhealthy influence, was always there to be acted upon.

Saint Augustine, who can be seen as the founding father of Western Christianity (354–430), codified what became the dominant attitude toward the Jews. Citing the verse from Psalms 59:12, "Kill them not, lest my people forget," Augustine argued that the Jews had an important role to play within Christian society and needed to be tolerated. According to Augustine, the Jews served as "witnesses" to the truth of Christianity. On the one hand, they testified to the antiquity of biblical prophecy, which was important, because Christians interpreted passages from prophetic writings like Jeremiah as foretelling the coming of Jesus. On the other hand, the Jews served as a foil for Christianity. Their life as a discriminated minority living in exile proved, in Augustine's view, that they had been punished for their rejection of Jesus and demonstrated a life in the absence of grace. Drawing a stark contrast between "carnal" Judaism, indentured to the law, and "spiritual" Christianity, liberated through grace, the fate of the Jews provided living proof of the truth of Christendom.

This theological construct was embraced by later leaders of the Christian Church and was translated into a basic toleration—though not "tolerance"—of the Jews in medieval law. Pope Gregory I ("The Great," pope between 590 and 604) declared, for example, that "the Jews are not to be [unjustly] restrained; nor shall injustice be done to them." A balance needed to be established between imposing restrictions and an inferior position on the Jews and not treating them arbitrarily and unjustly. In the words of Gregory I: "Just as license ought not be granted to the Jews to presume to do in their synagogues more than the law permits them, just so ought they not suffer curtailment of those things which have been conceded to them." The canon (a law promulgated by the pope) known as *Sicut Iudaeis non*, first issued in the twelfth century and repeated by nearly every pope thereafter, spelled out the idea of the Augustinian equilibrium again, prescribing an inferior position for the Jews but also providing basic guarantees and legal protections to them. This treatment of the Jews differed radically from the attitude of the medieval Church toward other religions, most importantly Islam, which was seen as an enemy of Christendom. In a letter from 1063, Pope Alexander II expressed this contrast clearly: "The matter of the Jews is entirely different from that of the Saracens [Muslims]: the latter actively engage in war against Christians; the former are everywhere ready to be subservient."

The peculiar place of the Jews in medieval Christian society was not only present in theological writings or Church legislation but also communicated through images and art, bringing the message of not only Jewish subservience but also the necessity of the Jews as witnesses of the triumph of Christianity into public places. Numerous sculptures on church facades, as well as images on stained-glass windows or illuminated manuscripts from the medieval period, depicted two women representing *Ecclesia* (i.e., Christendom) and *Synagoga* (i.e., the Jews). The figure symbolizing the "synagogue" looks

Figure 7.1 The statue on the left is a medieval representation of the Church (i.e., Christianity), depicted as a proud and victorious woman. On the right, the synagogue (i.e., Judaism) is depicted as a blindfolded woman bearing a broken scepter. These particular statues are from a thirteenth-century cathedral in Bamberg, Germany, but similar images appear in many other places in Christian Europe—for example, Notre Dame in Paris.

downcast, holds a broken staff, and wears a blindfold, showing the Jews being chastised by God for their failure to accept the truth of Christianity. The opposite figure, representing *Ecclesia*, looks proud, is wearing a crown, holds onto a scepter that is intact, and clearly stands for the triumph of Christianity. But whereas the two figures draw a clear contrast between the old and the new covenant, just as in Augustine's doctrine, one requires the presence of the other. It is only in the contrast between the victorious church and the downtrodden synagogue that the message of the images emerges; only the juxtaposition of the two images conveys the idea that the triumph of Christendom lies precisely in its having "superseded" Judaism (see Figure 7.1).

In the case of the Islamic Empire, religious and political leadership had been closely intertwined since the days of Muhammad. Christianity, on the other hand, began as the religion of a small minority within the Roman Empire, and only in 313 did Emperor Constantine become a Christian, and Christianity eventually became the empire's official religion. (The process was by no means a straightforward and linear one; the last pagan emperor, Julian, who ruled briefly in the early 360s, unsuccessfully tried to turn back the Christianization of the Roman Empire.) Roman imperial law had long recognized the status of Judaism, and Jews had been citizens of the empire. Even after the Christianization of the empire, the interests of the state and of the church were never perfectly aligned, and throughout the medieval period, state and church were often pitted against each other when it came to exercising authority over the Jews. In 388, conflict arose when a bishop in Mesopotamia allowed the burning of a synagogue, but he was reproached by Emperor Theodosius I, who ordered the synagogue to be rebuilt. The emperor's intervention provoked the anger of the bishop of Milan, Ambrose, who excommunicated Theodosius; the emperor relented at first, only to declare a few years later that all attacks against synagogues were considered a major crime.

In the 430s, Theodosius II (ruled 408–450) redefined the legal status of the Jews in a way that reflected the new reality of the Roman Empire as a Christian state. While his code of law, the Theodosian Code, reaffirmed Jewish citizenship and granted protection against any arbitrary cancelation of their legal rights, it also lumped together "Jews, Samaritans, Heretics, and Pagans" in one section and imposed new restrictions. Jews were not to be permitted to hold public office or any kind of position of authority over Christians. They were also not allowed to build new synagogues, nor could they, under the threat of death and loss of property, convert any Christian to Judaism. Later imperial law codes, such as the one promulgated by Justinian (ruled 527–565) in the Eastern Roman (or Byzantine) Empire, included further restrictions. Because Justinian saw himself as the head of both church and state, his law code further undermined the status of the Jews, who, for example, were no longer to enjoy any kind of legal autonomy and whose testimony against Christians was not to be accepted in court.

Medieval Charters and Royal Authority

In 286 CE, Emperor Diocletian divided the Roman Empire into a western and an eastern part. This split eventually became permanent, with the western part of the empire falling to the successive waves of invasions from the north. The last emperor in the west, Romulus Augustus, was deposed and exiled in 476 CE, and new dynastic kingdoms emerged in Spain, England, France, and other parts of formerly Roman Europe. In the year 800, the Carolingian king Charles the Great (Charlemagne, ruled 768–814) was crowned as the "Holy Roman Emperor" by the pope, but after the death of his son and successor, Louis the Pious, in 840, the empire was split into three parts (which subsequently fragmented even further). The eastern part came to be known as the "Holy Roman Empire" (after 1512, the "Holy Roman Empire of the German Nation") and encompassed much of central Europe, reaching from the Netherlands in the northwest to northern Italy in the south, and from Belgium in the west to the Czech lands in the east, including all of what is today Germany at its center.

In the Carolingian Empire, Jews continued to enjoy the collective rights that they had under Roman law. The Carolingian emperors, especially Louis the Pious, however, went further and issued privileges to individual Jewish merchants by granting them special rights and protection in order to promote trade and commerce.

A typical example of such a charter of privileges from the Carolingian period stipulated:

> [W]e have taken under our protection the following Hebrews, R. Domatus and his nephew Samuel. . . . Do not presume to exact from the above Hebrews taxes, horse fees, residence fees, and road tolls. In addition, we permit them to trade and freely to sell their possessions to whomever they will. They have the right to living by their own laws. And they may hire Christian [men] to work for them, except on Christian feast days and

> Sundays. They are also free to acquire foreign slaves and to sell them within our borders. If a Christian has a dispute or litigation with them, he must bring in his behalf three acceptable Christian witnesses, in addition to three Hebrew ones. . . . If Jews have a dispute or litigation with a Christian, they must produce Christian witnesses in their behalf. These Hebrews complained to us about certain Christians, who . . . have induced slaves of the Hebrews to despise their masters and to have them baptized. . . . They urge these slaves to be baptized in order to free themselves from their masters. The sacred canons in no way ordain such manumission. . . . Further, you are to make it known that anyone who plots against their lives [of these Jews] or actually murders one of them will have to pay our palace ten pounds of gold, for we have taken these Hebrews into our protection so long as they remain faithful to us.

Such ample rights, and especially the fact that the emperor sided with the Jews when it came to the question of releasing or not pagan slaves who had turned to Christianity, drew an angry response from church leaders, like Agobard, the bishop of Lyon, who joined a rebellion against Louis the Pious in 833. Louis the Pious had issued a decree that, in the spirit of the foregoing charter, prohibited anyone from baptizing a slave owned by a Jew without the consent of the slave's owner, and Agobard denounced it, saying, "[A] decision has gone out from the court of the most Christian and most pious emperor which is so contrary to the law of the Church." The bishop of Lyon juxtaposed the attitude of the emperor with what he perceived as the imperative of church law, which insisted on the inferiority of the Jews and "forbade all fraternization with Jews . . . [and] prohibited . . . anyone who has become impure through fraternizing and dining with the Jews from breaking bread with any of [their] priests."

Until about the tenth century, the Jews of the Carolingian Empire collectively had a defined legal status that was informed by the legacy of Roman law. Over time, however, their position began to erode. Although Louis the Pious had issued charters with special privileges to individual Jewish merchants, such charters increasingly became the *only* foundation of Jewish existence in the empire. "From the late eleventh century onward," historian Kenneth Stow observed, "Jews no longer resided in a given territory by inherent right. Instead, their residence came to hinge on a charter that the ruler offered the entire Jewish community." The conditions set out in such charters were at times quite beneficial, to be sure. The problem, however, was that now the entire Jewish community, not only certain individuals, depended for their protection and legal status entirely on such privileges. The Jews, in other words, who had collectively enjoyed an inherent legal status in Roman law, now came to depend on individual benefactors. Moreover, as political power in the medieval Holy Roman Empire fragmented, by the late eleventh century, it was local rulers rather than the central imperial authorities who issued privileges to the Jews—thus being responsible for providing protection—and who were now also in a position to revoke such privileges whenever it seemed opportune to them. A good example of an eleventh-century charter offering protection to an entire Jewish community was that issued by the bishop of Speyer, a town in the German Rhineland, in 1084:

> When I wished to make a city out of the village of Speyer, I Rudiger, surnamed Huozmann, bishop of Speyer, thought that the glory of our town would be augmented a thousandfold if I were to bring Jews. Those Jews whom I have gathered I placed outside the neighborhood and residential area of the other burghers. In order that they not be easily disrupted by the insolence of the mob, I have encircled them with a wall. . . . I have accorded them the free right of exchanging

> gold and silver and of buying and selling everything they use. . . . I have, moreover, given them out of the land of the Church burial ground to be held in perpetuity. . . . Just as the mayor of the city serves among the burghers, so too shall the Jewish leader adjudicate any quarrel which might arise among them or against them. If he be unable to determine the issue, then the case shall come before the bishop of the city. . . . They [the Jews] may legally have nurses and servants from among our people. . . . In short, in order to achieve the height of kindness, I have granted them a legal status more generous than any which the Jewish population have in any city of the German kingdom.

As we will see ahead in the discussion of the First Crusade that ravaged the Jewish communities of the Rhineland, the protection promised in local charters was tenuous, as it depended on the enduring goodwill of the authorities who had granted them, as well as on their power to enforce the promises made to the Jews. The legal status of the Jews remained ambiguous, and it set them apart from everyone else: On the one hand, they were not treated the same as the townspeople, yet on the other, they were not foreigners either. Over time, as European monarchs tried to assert their power and centralize control, the Jews increasingly came to depend on the central royal authorities for their security and their rights (or "privileges," as they were called in the Middle Ages). Frederick I (Barbarossa), emperor of the Holy Roman Empire, made this legal dependence of the Jews explicit when he declared, in 1157, that the Crown had taken the Jews under its protection "because they pertain to [Roman] chamber." In the following century, in 1236, Emperor Frederick II pronounced the Jews of the empire to be *servi*, or "serfs," of the royal treasury. In other European kingdoms, too, the royal authorities—for example, King Richard I of England in 1189, Duke Frederick II of Austria in 1244, and King Bolesław of Poland in 1264—asserted that the Jews were to be considered "property" of the Crown. A legal compilation from thirteenth-century Castile (one of the Christian kingdoms of medieval Spain), the *Libro de los fueros de Castilla*, explained thus:

> The Jews belong to the king; although they might be under the power of nobles or with their knights or with other men or under the power of monasteries, all should belong to the king under his protection and for his service.

Royal protection no doubt could prove beneficial for the Jews, but it also meant that they were subject to a unique legal status that set them apart from the remainder of medieval society. Since the Jews were so closely identified with royal power in the eyes of the regular townspeople, attacking them became one way of expressing dissatisfaction with the Crown. In the Catalan city of Girona in 1320, for example, it was reported that "some people, *in contempt of royal authority* . . . threw rocks and harmed Jews." At the same time, exclusive dependence on royal protection also meant that Jews were subject to unchecked exploitation. The Jews could be taxed at the discretion of the king: In England, for instance, a series of tallages were imposed in the course of the thirteenth century, leading to the ruin of much of English Jewry and, in the process, reducing its economic usefulness to the Crown. In 1290, when King Edward I needed additional tax revenues from the landed nobility, he seized the debts owed to the Jews and allowed the knights to repay them to the royal treasury minus the interest; in exchange he received the immediate tax payment from the nobility that he sought, and agreed to give in to religiously and economically motivated pressures to permanently expel the Jews from the kingdom. Bleeding the Jewish moneylenders and financiers as much as possible and eventually expelling the

Jews from England in 1290 altogether illustrate the peril of the legal status of the Jews as it had developed in medieval Europe.

The Thirteenth Century

The thirteenth century witnessed not only the expulsion of the Jews from England but also a hardening in the attitude of the Catholic Church. When Pope Innocent III (1198–1216) reaffirmed the canon *Sicut Iudaeis* of his predecessors, he introduced it in terms that left no doubt about his feelings about the Jews:

> Although the Jewish perfidy is in every way worthy of condemnation, nevertheless—because through them the truth of our own faith is proven—they are not to be severely oppressed by the faithful. Thus, the prophet says, "Do not slay them, lest they forget your law."

In 1215, Innocent III convened the Fourth Lateran Council, which, among many other issues, addressed the proper place of the Jews in Christian society. Next to the censure of Jewish "immoderate usury"—the lending of money at excessive interest—and the renewed assertion of the longstanding prohibition of Jews holding positions of authority, the Fourth Lateran Council emphasized the importance of social segregation. It noted:

> In some provinces, a difference in dress distinguishes the Jews or Saracens [Muslims] from the Christians, but in certain others such a confusion has grown up that they cannot be distinguished by any difference. Thus it happens at times that through error Christians have relations with the women of Jews or Saracens, and Jews or Saracens with Christian women. Therefore, that they may not, under pretext of error of this sort, excuse themselves in the future for the excesses of such prohibited intercourse, we decree that such Jews and Saracens of both sexes in every Christian province and at all times shall be marked off in the eyes of the public from other peoples through the character of their dress.

The council's decree suggests, of course, that socializing across religious boundaries must have been frequent and that, in many parts of Christian Europe, it was impossible to tell the difference between Jews and Christians. Especially the possibility of sexual relations between a Jewish man and a Christian woman—even if she was a prostitute—was seen as endangering the purity of Christian society. A law code compiled in thirteenth-century Castile expressed the same concern when it stipulated that:

> Jews who live with Christian women are guilty of great insolence . . . [and] shall be put to death. For if Christians who commit adultery with married women deserve death on that account, much more so do Jews who have sexual intercourse with Christian women, who are spiritually the wives of Our Lord Jesus Christ.

The theological thinking underlying the anxiety about sexual encounters between members of the two religions was thus spelled out clearly: Contact with Jews presented a danger to the purity of the body of Christian society, not only to the integrity of Christian faith. In fact, the concern regarding Jewish–Christian interaction was not limited to the realm of improper sexual encounters. The same thirteenth-century legal code from Castile, Alfonso X's *Siete partidas*, also stipulated, "We forbid any Christian man or woman to invite a Jew or a Jewess, or to accept an invitation from them, to eat or drink together, or to drink any wine made by their hands." Any social contact, in other words, was liable to violate the ideal order of Christian society (though, it needs to be pointed out, Jewish leaders were no less worried by unrestrained socializing, not to mention sexual encounters, between Jews and Christians). The solution ordained in the Fourth Lateran Council, familiar from Islamic stipulations regulating the proper place of religious minorities, was that Jews had to be distinguished by their dress. Secular Christian rulers implemented this rather vague injunction by ordering Jews to attach a special badge to their clothes so they would easily be distinguished and marked as Jews—and thus as social outcasts. The degree to which such rules were enforced is difficult to ascertain, to be sure, and it varied from one place to another.

Though the Church of the thirteenth century grew more apprehensive about the place of the Jews in Christian society, it was still beholden to the traditional stance set out by Pope Gregory I. Thus, Pope Gregory IX, in the 1230s, saw it fit to defend the Jews against arbitrary treatment and undue exploitation at the hands of the secular authorities. "Certain of these lords," the pope warned in a letter to the archbishops and bishops of France, "rage against these Jews with such cruelty that, unless they pay them what they ask, they tear their fingernails, pull out their teeth, and inflict upon them other kinds of inhuman torments." The same Gregory IX, however, also oversaw a new chapter in the confrontation with Judaism when he responded to a charge brought forward against the Talmud, the foundational work of rabbinic Judaism, by one Nicholas Donin in 1236. Donin was a Jewish convert to Christianity, and he composed a text with 35 accusations against the Talmud, which he portrayed as blasphemous, insulting of Christianity, proving that the Jews had strayed from their own religion as contained in the books of the Old Testament. As a result of Donin's denunciation, the pope wrote to the kings throughout Catholic Europe with the request to confiscate all copies of the Talmud, but only in Paris did action ensue. In 1242, a trial against the Talmud was staged in Paris. Predictably, the Inquisition concluded that the accusations were justified, and 24 cartloads of Talmud manuscripts and other rabbinic writings were burned in public.

CONVERSION TO JUDAISM

Although less common than Jewish converts to Christianity, examples exist of conversion from Christianity to Judaism. The converts to Judaism who do occasionally appear in the sources often found their way to Judaism through their training in Scripture as Christian clerics. Bodo, the chaplain to the Holy Roman emperor Louis the Pious (r. 814–840), converted to Judaism in 838 and adopted the Hebrew name Eliezer before fleeing to Muslim Spain, where he remained for the rest of his life. Proselytes also came to Judaism from other corners of society. As was the case with medieval Christians and Muslims, Jewish households could include slaves and servants, and they would sometimes convert to the religion of their masters. In fact, Jewish law encouraged the circumcision and conversion of non-Jewish slaves, and in all probability, the bulk of converts to Judaism came from this population.

Once converted and eventually freed, these slaves held full standing as formal converts and enjoyed the protection that Jewish law afforded them. The conversion of slaves was deeply troubling to Christian authorities, who sought to impede it. The Fourth Council of Toledo in 633 issued a document titled "On the Keeping of Slaves," in which it was stated:

> Jews should not be allowed to have Christian slaves nor to buy Christian slaves, nor to obtain them by the kindness of any one; for it is not right that the members of Christ should serve the ministers of Antichrist. But if henceforward Jews presume to have Christian slaves or handmaidens they shall be taken from their domination and shall go free.

The boundary between Christianity and Judaism remained as clear as it did not just because Jews sought to defend it but also because Christian authorities patrolled the boundary.

Some Christian theologians, however, preferred that the Talmud (and other rabbinic writings) be censored, not destroyed: The new Christian interest in the Talmud had led them to believe that the texts of rabbinic tradition themselves could be used in the polemical assault on Judaism. Just like earlier Christian theologians had interpreted the Hebrew Bible in a Christological way, they now claimed that the Talmud and other ancient Jewish texts also contained veiled references to Jesus that proved the truth of Christianity. Spain in the thirteenth and fourteenth centuries saw a series of staged public debates in which a Christian—usually a Jewish convert to Christianity familiar with both traditions—sought to prove that a proper reading of the Talmud confirmed Jesus as the Messiah and that the Jews were wrong in their rejection of Christianity. The most famous of these disputations took place in the summer of 1263 in Barcelona, where the Jewish convert Pablo Cristiani faced one of the leading rabbis of that time, Moses ben Nahman (Nahmanides), in a debate convened by the king of Aragon, James I.

Two accounts—a Christian one, in Latin, and Nahmanides's response, in Hebrew—were written about the disputation. Nahmanides turned out to be a brilliant debater, and his own account certainly makes it appear that he "won" the debate. Nonetheless, his own written polemic was considered a blasphemous insult to Christianity when it came to the attention of the Dominican friars, and Nahmanides was forced to leave Spain, eventually moving to the Holy Land. Other such debates ensued elsewhere in Spain (it appears that Nahmanides had, indeed, intended his own written response as a guide for Jews finding themselves in the situation of having to refute Christian religious polemics), for example, in Majorca in 1286, in Avila in the 1370s, and in Pamplona in 1375. Meanwhile, King James I of Aragon, who saw no problem with employing Jews (and Muslims) in the administration of his kingdom, actively supported the missionary effort to convert the Jews. In 1242, he went so far as to issue a decree that compelled Jews and Muslims to attend missionary sermons delivered by Dominican and Franciscan friars, even promising that state officials would compel the attendance of any reluctant Jew or Muslim who failed to show up for these occasions.

ASHKENAZ

Jewish Communities in Northern Europe

Considering that today most Jews are Ashkenazi Jews and that Jewish culture as we know it now, especially in North America, is dominated by the flavor of Ashkenazi traditions, it is easy to forget that until at least the eleventh century, Ashkenaz was a remote backwater of Jewish life. Most Jews of antiquity and the early medieval period lived in the lands around the Mediterranean and in the Middle East, whereas a Jewish presence in northern Europe emerged only gradually. For medieval Jews, "Ashkenaz"—a place-name that appears three times in the Bible—was understood to refer to an area that included the Jewish communities of the German Empire and of northern France (the latter sometimes was also called "Tzarfat"). Under the Carolingian emperors (Charlemagne and his successor, Louis the Pious), a number of Jewish merchants made their way from Italy across the Alps and established themselves in towns in the German Empire, especially in the Rhineland. Until the eleventh century, the most important of these northern Jewish communities was the one in Mainz (in today's southwestern Germany), while other communities emerged in Speyer, Worms, Cologne, Regensburg, and Trier. Jewish settlement was small in the towns of medieval Ashkenaz, in contrast to the large urban communities one could find in the Islamic world, and the overall number of Jews in Ashkenaz paled in comparison to the sizeable Jewish population of medieval Spain. Eventually, however, the number of Jews began to grow, and by the fourteenth century, Jews lived spread out over hundreds of different towns in the empire.

A similar trend holds true for the Jewish presence in northern France: While the Jewish communities of southern France, in particular in Provence, had a long and venerable tradition and were closely tied to the Jews of Catalonia and Christian Spain, we know very little about Jewish life in northern France before the year 1000. Thereafter, however, northern France (especially the regions of Normandy and Champagne) emerged as an area of settlement that attracted Jewish merchants, later drawn into moneylending, and as a center of Jewish learning. The city of Troyes, for example, was the home of the famous rabbi Solomon Yitzhaki, commonly known by his acronym Rashi, one of the most important scholars of medieval Ashkenaz and, indeed, of medieval Judaism in general (more on Rashi ahead). By the twelfth century, the cultural identity of the Jews in the German Empire, Ashkenaz, and of those in northern France, Tzarfat, became more distinct, but the two areas continued to be in close contact. Yet another area in northern Europe that witnessed Jewish settlement around this time was England, where Jews of French origin began to establish themselves following the Norman conquest in 1066.

As we saw in the privilege extended to the Jews of Speyer by the bishop of that town in the late eleventh century, Jews generally had the right to adjudicate their own internal affairs. "Just as the mayor of the city serves among the burghers," the charter from Speyer read, "so too shall the Jewish leader adjudicate any quarrel which might arise among them or against them." The Jews, like everyone else, were ultimately subject to the royal authorities, of course, and they even found justification for this in the Talmudic legal principle of *dina de-malkhuta dina*, or "the law of the land is the law." As a tight-knit group legally and religiously set apart from the surrounding Christian society, however, the Jewish communities also had ample room to run their own affairs according to the dictates of Jewish law. In Ashkenaz, as elsewhere in the Jewish Diaspora, communities were guided by rabbinic and lay leaders, though the two were more closely intertwined than in other parts of the Jewish world. Generally, each community was independent, and local custom was particularly cherished in Ashkenaz, and nowhere did a supreme, supralocal religious authority or clear hierarchical structure of religious leadership emerge. In certain places, kings appointed individuals to oversee the affairs of the Jews, to be sure—for example, the *Presbyter* of the Jews in England or the *Rab de la Corte* in Castile—but even then the task of these officials was to serve as intermediaries between the central government and the Jews, not as superior authorities in matters of Jewish law. In Ashkenaz and elsewhere, rabbis of various locales sometimes gathered in irregular synods, or meetings, to determine legal matters of common interest. By and large, however, authority rested with the local community rabbi or with individual rabbinic leaders, whose prestige and power derived from their scholarly reputation, not from a specific office.

A number of such rabbinic scholars exerted great influence over the Jews of Ashkenaz in their own and subsequent generations, including Gershom ben Judah (Rabbenu Gershom, d. 1040), Solomon Yitzhaki (Rashi, d. 1105), Jacob ben Meir Tam (Rabbenu Tam, d. 1171), and Meir ben Barukh of Rothenburg (d. 1293). Rabbenu Gershom is credited with a number of decrees, or *takkanot*, that defined the legal contours of medieval Ashkenazi culture—for example, the prohibition of polygamy or the prohibition against divorcing one's wife against her will. Another rule attributed to Gershom ben Judah was the principle that once the majority of the community leadership had consented to an ordinance or decree, the entire community was bound by the majority's decision.

One of the legal innovations of the medieval Ashkenazi communities was the so-called *herem ha-yishuv*, which allowed the local Jewish community to regulate the settlement of Jews and keep out newcomers, in order either to defend itself against outside competition or to allow it to exclude individuals believed to undermine public morals. Jewish communities in the Islamic world, by contrast, did not, as a rule, claim any such prerogative, probably a reflection of the different legal status enjoyed by Jews under Christian and Muslim rule in general. Another common legal arrangement was the *maarufiya*, essentially a monopoly that allowed a Jew to enter into an exclusive business relation with a Christian and protected him against competition from other Jews doing business with the same person. This practice needs to be understood in a context where Jewish merchants or financiers often conducted major transactions for Christian patrons, primarily from among the nobility.

Rabbinic Culture in Medieval Ashkenaz

A long-established narrative claims that the two centers of Jewish culture in medieval Europe, Ashkenaz and Sefarad, had their roots in the two competing centers of antiquity, Palestine and Babylonia: Ashkenazi culture, it is said, had its origins in Palestine, whose traditions were transmitted through the Byzantine lands and Italy by merchant families who established themselves north of the Alps in the Carolingian period. The most prominent of these families was the Kalonymus family of Lucca in Italy, who originally hailed from the southern part of Italy that was part of the Byzantine Empire and, ultimately, from Palestine. Medieval Sephardi culture, on the other hand, is said to have its roots in that other center of late antique Jewish culture, Babylonia. Recently, however, historians have challenged this account as overly simplistic: The rabbis of both medieval Ashkenaz and medieval Sefarad received the teachings of the Talmud from the Geonim in Babylonia. However, if they applied these teachings differently, that was mostly due to the influence of the surrounding medieval cultures among which they lived, not because of the genealogy of their respective traditions. The same holds true for the Ashkenazi and Sephardi variants of Jewish liturgy. While some scholars have claimed that the Ashkenazim preserved the Palestinian traditions whereas the Sephardim followed Babylonian liturgy, this interpretation relies primarily on poetic insertions (*piyutim*) that were preserved meticulously in Ashkenaz, many of which can be traced back to Palestine. This view ignores the fact that the basic structure and wording of *all* prayer rites, including the Ashkenazi one, essentially follow the Babylonian model.

Considering the geographic distance from the centers of rabbinic learning in the Mediterranean and in the Middle East, it is astonishing not only how innovative the rabbis of medieval Ashkenaz were in their study of the Jewish textual traditions but also how influential their teachings turned out to be for the subsequent development of rabbinic scholarship. The towering figure in this regard was Rabbi Solomon Yitzhaki, active in the eleventh century (1040–1105). Widely known as Rashi, he was a native of Troyes, in northern France, and studied at the rabbinic academies in Mainz and Worms in Germany. When he was about 25 years old, he returned to Troyes, where he established a school of his own. His scholarship had a tremendous impact on the study of both the Bible and the Talmud throughout the Jewish world. Rashi penned a commentary on most of the books in the Bible as well as a comprehensive commentary on almost the entire Babylonian Talmud. His biblical commentary was the first Hebrew book ever to be printed, in 1475, and practically all subsequent Jewish editions of the Hebrew Bible included Rashi's commentary. His explanation of the Babylonian

Talmud likewise had an impact everywhere in the Jewish world: Within half a century after his death, his Talmudic glosses were known to rabbis throughout Europe, and within a century, they were read by scholars everywhere, including Christian Hebraists who sought to understand the text of the Talmud. When the complete Babylonian Talmud was printed in Italy in the 1520, Rashi's glosses were printed on the inside margin of the text, and all standard editions of the Talmud since have included the commentary by the medieval Ashkenazi sage.

In his commentary on the Bible, Rashi combined midrashic interpretation (on *Midrash*, see Chapter 5) with an exploration of the "plain meaning" (called *peshat*) of the biblical text and generally chose that midrashic reading that was most faithful to the plain sense of the text. He elucidated difficult passages, translated obscure words into contemporary French, and presented essentially a digest of the traditional rabbinic understanding of the biblical text. Consider Rashi's gloss on the following well-known passage: "You shall not take vengeance or bear a grudge against your countrymen. Love your fellow as yourself: I am the Lord" (Leviticus 19:18). In his commentary, Rashi explains what "taking vengeance" means, a concept whose implications are not spelled out in the biblical text, and he wonders why the biblical verse speaks of both "vengeance" and "grudge," which one could think mean the same thing:

> *You shall not take vengeance.* A person says: "Lend me your sickle," and the other fellow answers, "No." On the following day the other fellow asks: "Lend me your axe," and the person answers: "I won't lend you, just as you didn't lend me." This is vengeance. But how then would you define a grudge? A person says: "Lend me your axe." The other fellow answers, "No." But the very next day the other fellow says: "Lend me your sickle" and the man answers: "Surely, here it is. I am not like you who wouldn't lend me your axe." Now this is a grudge, because this man was treasuring up hatred in his heart, even though he didn't take vengeance.

Elsewhere in his commentary, Rashi's explanation straddles further from the close, contextual reading of the text, following instead the way it has traditionally been understood by the rabbis. Thus, for example, Rashi's explanation of the very first verse of the Bible: Why, the commentator wonders, does the Torah begin with an account of creation, rather than with the first commandment that God issued to the Israelites, namely, the sanctification of the new moon (in Exodus, Chapter 12), implying, of course, that the purpose of Scripture is, above all, to impart the mitzvot that the Jews are supposed to live by?

> *In the beginning.* Said Rabbi Isaac: was it not necessary to begin the Torah except from "This month is to you" [Ex 12:2], which is the first commandment that the Israelites were commanded. Now for what reason did He commence with "In the beginning"? Because [as it says, in Ps. 111:6): "The strength of His works He related to His people, to give them the inheritance of the nations." For if the nations of the world should say to Israel, "You are robbers, for you conquered by force the lands of the seven nations [of Canaan]," they will reply, "The entire earth belongs to the Holy One, blessed be He; He created it [which is the point of the beginning of the Torah] and gave it to whomever He deemed proper. When He wished, He gave it to them, and when He wished, He took it away from them and gave it to us."

While Rashi relied here on an old midrashic tradition, there surely was a contemporary context that made his gloss on the opening verse of the Torah all the more relevant. As Rashi was writing, the pope was preparing for the first Crusade (see ahead), and Christians and Muslims alike laid claim to Jerusalem and the "Holy Land" as their possession. Not so, suggests Rashi; it is to the Jews that God has given the land, and despite all odds, it will be theirs once again in the future.

Rashi's commentary on the Talmud was a similar tour de force. Rashi established the correct reading of the Talmudic text. (In an age before printing, a large number of different manuscripts were in circulation, presenting all kinds of small or major variants, so a first act of interpretation was to determine which version was the correct one.) As in his commentary on the Bible, he elucidated difficult words and passages and explained technical terms. Designed to be used alongside the written text of the Talmud, Rashi's commentary was thus an important step in the textualization of a rabbinic tradition that had been carried on orally in Ashkenaz far longer than in the Sephardi communities of Spain or North Africa. In the end, Rashi's glosses allowed students of rabbinic culture to read the Talmud as a coherent narrative and the Talmud to emerge as the centerpiece of traditional Ashkenazi education and jurisdiction. Rashi was followed by his sons-in-law, grandsons, and students, who continued the systematic study of the Talmudic text, taking Rashi's commentary as a point of departure. These additional glosses are called tosafot, and their authors, who were active in France and Germany in the twelfth and thirteenth centuries, are therefore referred to as the "tosafists." Like Rashi's commentary, the *tosafot* were subsequently included in practically all printed copies of the Talmud, and already in the thirteenth century, their method of Talmud study was introduced to the world of Sephardi Jewry by Nahmanides (Rabbi Moshe ben Nahman, d. 1270) of Girona, a center of Jewish learning north of Barcelona.

The tosafists, in the words of one recent historian, "regarded the entire Talmud as a unified and inherently coherent corpus." They "identified textual parallels and created a comprehensive system of cross-referencing," guided by two assumptions: "the notion that the Talmud's language was fixed and authoritative, and the notion that the Talmud was internally consistent." The tosafists developed a sophisticated method of dialectic study of the Talmudic text and relied on a wide range of scholarship, from Gaonic writings to studies of Hebrew grammarians in medieval Spain and the Talmudic dictionary of Natan ben Yehiel of Rome (known as *Arukh*, completed in 1101). Their method involved identifying the smallest inconsistencies and making the most subtle logical distinctions in the Talmudic text (or in Rashi's commentary on the Talmud), trying to reconcile contradictions and establish the best possible reading of the text. The tosafists were also aware of the tension between religious precepts as they appeared in the Talmud and the actual customary practice of Ashkenazi Jews; taking both the Talmudic text and Ashkenazi custom to be authoritative, their endeavor included the harmonization of apparently incompatible understandings of Jewish law. In one sense, Rashi and the tosafists contributed to the rise of a uniquely Ashkenazi culture that was distinct from its Sephardi counterpart. At the same time, however, their approach to the study of the Talmud, precisely because it came to occupy such a central place in their own intellectual endeavors, shaped the encounter of Jews with the Talmudic text elsewhere in the Jewish world and to this day.

Whereas the tosafist engagement with the Talmud involved the open-ended dialectical study of the smallest details of the text, they were also concerned with providing practical legal guidance. One of Rashi's students, Simha ben Samuel of Vitry, France (who died sometime before Rashi himself—that is, before 1105), composed an invaluable collection of liturgy and law called Mahzor Vitry. This work included the prayers for the whole year, along with laws pertaining to liturgy, the observance of the Sabbath and the holidays, marriage, and ritual slaughter, making it a unique book of reference for the legal traditions and customs of northern French Jewry in the late tenth and early eleventh centuries. Other members of the tosafist school engaged in the systematic collection of the religious customs (*minhag*) of the medieval Ashkenazi Jews, a society particularly sensitive to the authority of local and family custom even when it might contravene established halakhic practice: *minhag mevatel halakhah* ("custom nullifies law [or legislation]"), a phrase that appears in the Jerusalem Talmud, was frequently invoked by Ashkenazi authorities. One such collection of customs was that of Jacob Molin of Mainz (d. 1427).

As we saw in the previous chapter, the towering achievement in the realm of legal codes had been Maimonides's *Mishneh Torah*, an all-encompassing, encyclopedic guide to Jewish law. The intersection of tosafist culture with that of medieval Spain produced, in the fourteenth century, another law code that proved, in some ways, even more influential than Maimonides's work. In 1303, the tosafist scholar Asher ben Yehiel (known as the "Rosh") left his native Germany and moved to Toledo, the capital of the Christian Kingdom of Castile in Spain. There, his son, Jacob ben Asher (d. 1340), penned a new comprehensive code of Jewish law, called the *Arba'ah Turim*. The work was the result of the remarkable encounter of medieval Ashkenazi and Sephardi culture, following Maimonides and the author's father, the Rosh, in its legal decisions, introducing the scholarship of the Ashkenazi rabbis to medieval Spain, and adopting a novel, thematic organization of Jewish law that departed both from the structure found in the Talmud and from that proposed by Maimonides. The four-part division of Jacob ben Asher's *Arba'ah Turim* became the standard for all subsequent codes of Jewish law, the most influential (to this day) being the law code written by Joseph Caro (and annotated for Ashkenazi readers by Moses Isserles) in the sixteenth century.

The Ashkenazi Pietists

Around the same time that the tosafists transformed Talmud study into the cultural ideal of medieval Ashkenaz, a very different religious movement emerged in the towns of the Rhineland as well: the so-called Hasidei Ashkenaz, or "Ashkenazi pietists," a group that should not be confused with the latter-day Hasidism that began in eighteenth-century eastern Europe. The teachings of the Hasidei Ashkenaz are associated with three descendants of the prominent Kalonymus family, Samuel, Judah, and Eleazar. The pietists produced a great deal of esoteric writings, but their most important and most well-known work is a collection of some 2,000 *exempla*, or moralizing stories, and exegetical vignettes, known as the *Sefer Hasidim* (*The Book of the Pious*). The book's authorship is attributed to Samuel the Pious and his son Judah the Pious (d. 1217), and it not only presents the ideals and virtues of Ashkenazi Hasidism but also allows a glimpse into the lives of medieval Ashkenazi Jews more generally. According to Eleazar of Worms, the Hasidei Ashkenaz preserved an ancient, esoteric tradition that had been transmitted by a certain "Abu Aaron," who had received his learning in Babylonia. Abu Aaron had brought "the secret of ordering the prayers and the other secrets" to Italy, from whence they had been transmitted down to the Kalonymus family of Lucca, who had subsequently moved to Ashkenaz.

The pietistic ideal of the Hasidei Ashkenaz derived from the uncompromising desire to fulfill the "will of the Creator" (*retson ha-bore*), beyond the requirements of religious law itself. The Ashkenazi pietists invoked the Talmudic dictum "You shall forever be resourceful in fearing God" and developed an ideology of piety that involved an intense sense of self-sacrifice in the service of God's will. "Pay attention to how some people risk their very lives for the sake of personal honor," *Sefer Hasidim* explained.

> For example, knights go into the thick of battle and even sacrifice themselves to enhance their reputations and to avoid being humiliated. Moreover, consider how many stratagems respectable women adopt in order to avoid being discovered after they become pregnant as the result of an affair. Not to speak of thieves. If these people work so hard for only monetary benefits, how much the more should [a pietist] be resourceful for the sake of his Creator's honor.

The pietists invoked the ideal of martyrdom that had emerged out of the tragedy of the First Crusade (see ahead) and suggested that if one was willing to make the ultimate sacrifice and give up one's life for the "sanctification of God's name" (*kiddush ha-shem*), how much more so should the righteous Jew be willing to accept the burden of piety in his or her everyday life? Submission to the "will of the Creator" meant to go beyond the letter of Halakhah (though not against it), accepting prohibitions and embracing pious acts that were stricter than what religious law actually prescribed.

The greater the suffering, the Hasidei Ashkenaz taught, the greater the reward: This was the reason the Creator had endowed mankind with the "evil inclination," and only by overcoming one's desire to sin could one achieve the ideal of true piety. The flipside of this idea was a highly original understanding of repentance. The Ashkenazi pietists taught that there were different kinds of atonement, with ritualized penitential practices not only matching the severity of the transgression and its deserved punishment but also counteracting the pleasure that had been derived from committing the sin in the first place. One example was a person who had transgressed religious law by having sexual intercourse with an unmarried woman who was ritually impure (i.e., had not immersed herself in the ritual bath following her menstruating days). "He should not participate in social activities with women for a year or two," Eleazar of Worms taught, "nor look at a woman's face, breasts, or genitals, even those of his wife when impure, before she has ritually bathed." Another form of atonement involved matching the suffering from the acts of penance to the pleasure derived from the transgression:

> He should suffer remorsefully in proportion to the pleasure he experienced when he kissed, fondled, and had intercourse with her. He should fast at least forty days, eat no meat, drink no wine during the night preceding or following the days he fasts.

Yet another form of penance—which, according to Eleazar, was "not found in practice"—consisted of entering into a situation similar to the one that had led to the original transgression and resisting the temptation of sinning again: If he found himself again alone in the same woman's company and both desired to sleep with each other but he resisted the temptation of doing so, he would prove that he had truly repented and defeated his evil inclination. One can imagine why the pietists did not want to encourage seeking out opportunities to practice this latter kind of penance.

Judah the Pious, author of the greater part of *Sefer Hasidim*, wanted to mold the pietists into a socially distinct group, a sect of sorts that separated itself from the mainstream Jewish community. He did not hesitate to distinguish the "righteous," that is, those who followed his pietistic ideal, from the "wicked," that is, all other Jews; nor did he shy away from counting the most learned rabbinic scholars, if they were not part of the Hasidei Ashkenaz, among the "wicked." The pietist took it upon himself to engage in ever more demanding practices of devotion and penance that would atone for the sins of his generation.

Sefer Hasidim recounts, illustrating the extreme nature of the pietistic ideal:

> It once happened [that] a Pietist used to sit on the ground among insects in the summer, and in the winter, he would put his legs into a container filled with water until his legs became stuck in the ice. His friend asked him: "Why do you do that? . . ." [The Pietist] said to him, "I myself have not sinned that much, but it is impossible that I have not committed minor sins. For those, I would not have to undergo such acts of suffering. But the Messiah suffers because of our sins. . . . Also, the perfectly Righteous bear suffering. . . . When the Righteous endure suffering, many benefit."

Eventually, Judah's sectarian program failed; it is not clear how large of a movement, if it ever became one, the Hasidei Ashkenaz were. It fell to his cousin Eleazar of Worms to transform Judah's sectarian idea into a personal, individual form of pietism that appealed to Ashkenazi society as a whole and not only to a small elite.

Crusades

In 1095, Pope Urban II called on all Catholic Christians for a campaign to wrest control over Jerusalem and the Holy Land from the Muslims. The following year, the first wave of Crusaders set out from northern France, and by 1099, the Crusading armies had conquered Jerusalem from the Muslims and established the Kingdom of Jerusalem, which would last until the Muslim forces under Saladin took it back in 1187. In the spring of 1096, as the first Crusading knights marched through the Rhineland, they turned their wrath against the Jewish communities that they encountered on their way. One Hebrew chronicle describing the events identified the motivation of the Crusaders as a vendetta against all those they considered enemies of Christendom:

> When they passed the cities where Jews dwelled, they said: Behold, we are going far away, to take our vengeance on the Ishmaelites [the Muslims]. But the Jews live among us, whose fathers unwarrantedly slew and hanged him on the cross. First, we will take our vengeance on them, and blot them out. The memory of Israel will no longer exist.

Indeed, in the spring of 1096, marauding Crusading knights and bands of rabble who joined them attacked the Jewish communities of the Rhineland and elsewhere in Central Europe, leaving about 1,000 Jews dead and many forcibly baptized. Only in Speyer was the local bishop able to protect all but 11 of the Jews in his city. In Regensburg, the city's Jews were driven into the Danube River and baptized. Many other communities, such as those of Mainz and Worms, were destroyed.

Despite the widespread violence, forced conversions, and gruesome acts of martyrdom, the Ashkenazi communities of the Rhineland recovered more quickly from the onslaught than might have been expected. Though many historians have seen the First Crusade as a turning point in medieval Jewish history, it did not permanently derail the expansion of Jewish life in northern Europe, nor did the events inaugurate a period of sustained persecution. In fact, the German emperor Henry IV issued an edict in 1097 allowing those Jews forcibly converted the previous year to return to their old religion, and the violent attacks against the Jews were not repeated during the subsequent Second and Third Crusades, in the 1140s and the late 1180s. Bernard de Clairvaux, the spiritual leader of the Second Crusade, actively protected the Jews of the Rhineland, and Ephraim of Bonn, who wrote a chronicle of the Second Crusade, reported nothing like the widespread violence of the Crusade half a century earlier. Rabbi Eleazar of Worms, for his part, related in a brief memoir of events during the Third Crusade that the Jews had obtained a decree from Emperor Frederick Barbarossa that "anyone who kills a Jew will be killed" and that participating

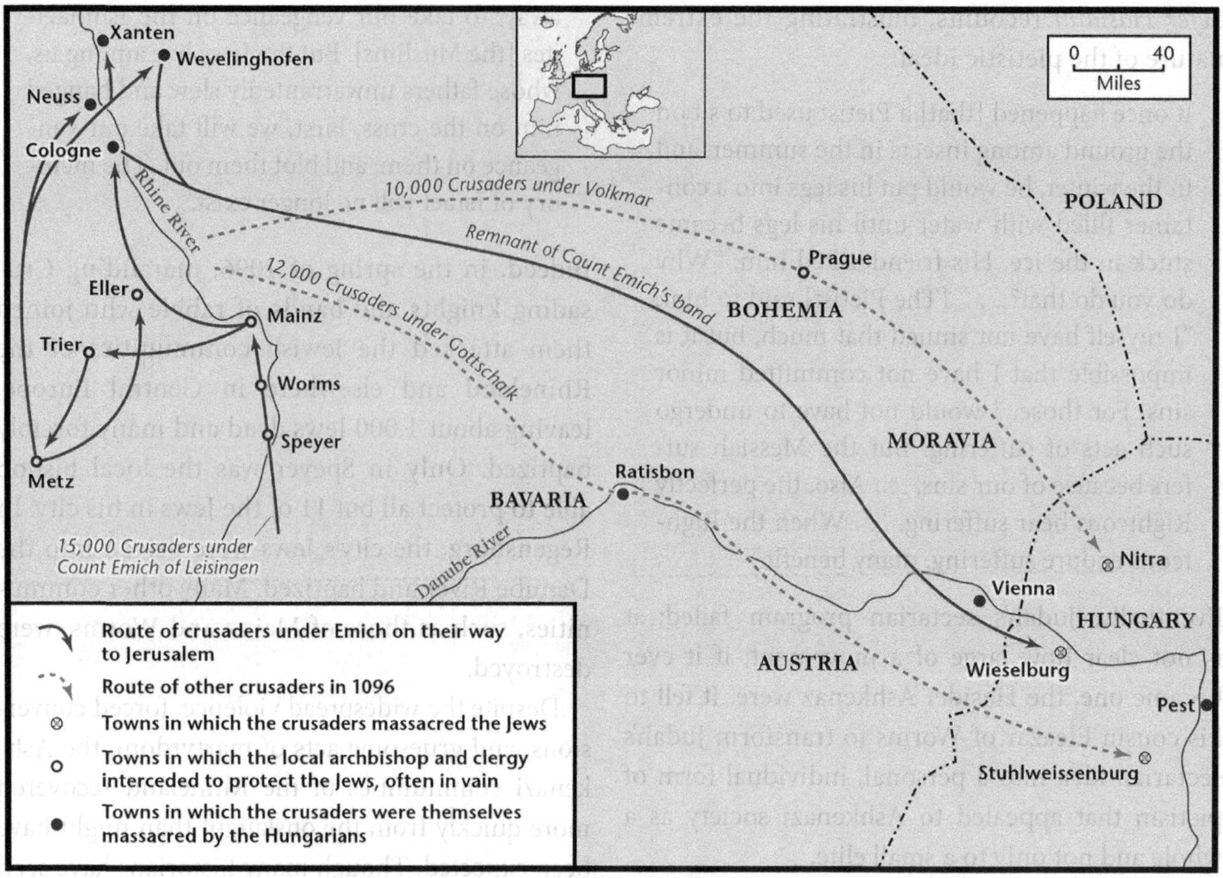

Map 7.1 The route of the First Crusade, 1096.

in the Crusade could not be invoked as a justification (see Map 7.1).

When considering the lasting impact of the First Crusade, what matters perhaps more than the events of 1096 was the way they were remembered in subsequent generations. The onslaught of the Crusade—or, rather, the Jewish response to the violence that enveloped them—shaped Ashkenazi culture in important ways. The central image that was expressed in liturgical poems, memorial lists of those who died, and a number of rather detailed chronicles describing the events was an ideal of martyrdom and self-sacrifice. The narrative accounts of the Crusade, the longest of which an anonymous account traditionally (but mistakenly) attributed to a Solomon ben Samson, as well as another, shorter chronicle called *Mainz Anonymous*, dwell at length on the presumably heroic conduct of the Ashkenazi Jews in places like Mainz and Worms, who had chosen martyrdom and, indeed, suicide rather than falling into the hands of the Crusaders or being baptized. Historians are still debating how reliable these chronicles or the accounts preserved in liturgical poems really are: There is no doubt that many Jews were killed and others killed themselves and their families, but how widespread was this behavior? It is clear that the texts celebrating the self-sacrifice of the Jewish martyrs of 1096 were written, sometimes decades after the events, not as objective historical accounts; instead, the authors may have wanted to find justification for the acts of murder and suicide that could not really be reconciled with Jewish law yet were painted in the glowing colors of sacrifice and martyrdom. They may also have wanted to address the growing threat of voluntary conversion to Christianity among Jews in the twelfth century, a reading suggested by historians Jeremy Cohen and Avraham Grossman. However reliable the details presented in the Hebrew Crusade narratives, they did engrave the image and ideal of martyrdom—*kiddush hashem*, or "sanctification of [God's] Name," as it was called in Hebrew—into the collective memory of Ashkenazi Jewry.

Not that the acts of self-sacrifice escaped the attention of contemporary Christian observers of the Crusades. Albert of Aix, for example, noted as follows:

> The Jews, seeing that their Christian enemies were attacking them and their children, and that they were sparing no age, likewise fell upon one another, brothers, children, wives, and sisters, and thus they perished at each other's hands. Horrible to say, mothers cut the throats of nursing children with knives and stabbed others, preferring them to perish thus by their own hands rather than to be killed by the weapons of the uncircumcised.

The accounts in the Hebrew narratives provide some rather gruesome and disturbing descriptions, which, of course, are impossible to verify and which may be implausibly detailed, given the fact that those who had gone through the events did not live to tell the tale. Nonetheless, the chronicles capture the image of a community caught up in extreme violence and an equally extreme ideology of religious martyrdom. Consider the story reported in *Mainz Anonymous* about one Jewish family in Worms:

> There was a certain young man, named Meshullam ben R. Isaac. He called out loudly to all those standing there and to Zipporah his helpmate: "Listen to me both great and small. This son God gave to me. My wife Zipporah bore him in her old age, and his name is Isaac. Now I shall offer him up, as did our ancestor Abraham with his son Isaac." Zipporah replied: "My lord, my lord. Wait a bit. Do not stretch forth your hand against the lad, whom I have raised and brought up and whom I bore in my old age. Slaughter me first, so that I not witness the death of the child." He then replied: "I shall not delay even a moment. He who gave him to us will take him as a portion. He will place him in the bosom of Abraham." He then bound Isaac his son and took in his hand the knife with which to slaughter his son and made the benediction for slaughtering. He then slaughtered the lad. He took his screaming wife from the chamber, and the crusaders killed them.

While in this case the woman, Zipporah, responded in a way that one may have expected from a mother, other examples highlight the particularly active and heroic role played by women, a prominent feature of the Hebrew accounts of the Crusade. The chronicle attributed to Solomon ben Samson tells of Rachel, a Jewish woman of Mainz who was determined to sacrifice her four children. First, her older son Isaac was killed, then:

> When the child Aaron saw that his brother Isaac was slain, he screamed again and again: "Mother, mother, do not butcher me," and ran and hid under a chest. [Rachel] had two daughters also who still lived at home, Bella and Matrona, beautiful young girls, the children of her husband Rabbi Judah. The girls took the knife and sharpened it themselves that it should not be nicked. Then the woman bared their necks and sacrificed them to the Lord God of Hosts who had commanded us not to change His pure religion. . . . When this righteous woman had made an end of sacrificing her three children to their Creator, she then raised her voice and called out to her son Aaron. . . . [S]he dragged him out by his foot from under the chest where he had hidden himself, and she sacrificed him before God, the high and exalted.

Eventually, Rachel herself was killed by the Crusaders when they entered the home, and when the father witnessed the scene, he threw himself upon his sword and killed himself too.

The last detail is significant: The father was carrying a sword, he was armed, and indeed, the chronicles tell us that the Jews had been by no means passively awaiting disaster only to sacrifice themselves. When Mainz was attacked by the Crusaders led by Count Emicho, the Jews,

> although they saw the great multitude, an army numerous as the sand on the shore of the sea, still clung to their Creator. Then young and old donned their armor and girded on their weapons, and at their head was Rabbi Kalonymus ben Meshuallam, the chief of the community. Yet because of the many troubles and the fasts which they had observed they had no strength to stand up against the enemy.

Besides the praise for the heroic conduct of the Jews of Mainz, who were willing to defend themselves but were willing to bear the burden of martyrdom too, can one detect here a subtle critique of the religious leadership that had exhausted the community by imposing upon it pious but, ultimately, counterproductive acts, such as continued fasting, in the vain hope of averting disaster?

When trying to make sense of the acts of martyrdom reported in the Hebrew chronicles, it is important to realize that many Jews did not really face a choice between baptism and death, but that in many instances, the Crusaders and the mob were set to kill, not to convert, them. What is more, the ideology of self-sacrifice that was attributed to the generation of the Crusade in the later chronicles is, of course, primarily an expression of the ideology that formed *after*, and in response to, the events, an ideology constructed and propagated in the chronicles themselves. We should not assume, in other words, that individuals like "Rachel" in Mainz or "Meshullam" in Worms were fanatics motivated by an uncompromising ideology of *kiddush ha-shem*; they may simply have been desperate. Be that as it may, the ideal of martyrdom that emerged out of the violence and destruction of the First Crusade would shape medieval Ashkenazi culture for many generations to come. The Hasidei Ashkenaz of the thirteenth century, for example, still promoted *kiddush ha-shem* (though of a spiritual kind) as an all-encompassing ideal that should guide the behavior of the pious.

Where did this ideology of martyrdom come from? Ironically, it seems to have been influenced by the cultural values of Christian society. A Crusading knight, for example, could not necessarily expect to ever return home alive: His participation in the struggle to conquer the Holy Land from the Muslims was a sacrifice, both in material terms and by putting his life in danger. It is no coincidence that one of the draws to participate in the Crusade was the indulgence promised by the pope, according to which engaging in the holy war against the enemies of Christendom would atone for the individual's sins and be rewarded in the afterlife. As one Muslim writer at that time observed about the European Crusaders, "[t]he Franks said: 'Here our heads will fall, we will pour forth our souls, spill our blood, give up our lives.'" In this heated atmosphere of religious sacrifice, it may not have been so strange to see Jews embrace a similar ideal of martyrdom, if only to prove that Judaism was by no means inferior to Christendom, for the glory of which the Crusading knights were willing to give their life.

Related to the celebration of the martyrs was a greater sensibility toward memorializing the dead. As historian Ivan Marcus explains:

> [T]he [Ashkenazi] custom of reciting annually the list of the local righteous dead—and, later on, the anniversary of one's parents' death—is mainly derived from the Christian monastic practice of compiling and reading necrologies, lists of the dead arranged by date of death.

Like their Christian neighbors, Ashkenazi Jews began to create memorial books (*Memorbücher*) recording the names of the departed, and they

A JEWISH POLEMIC AGAINST CHRISTIANITY

The anti-Jewish strain in medieval Christian culture had a marked impact on Jewish culture and demography. For one thing, it stirred in many Jews a deep hatred of Christianity, a sentiment often kept concealed from outsiders but sometimes surfacing in Jewish ritual and literature. Jews developed their own anti-Christian polemical literature or parodied Christianity in works such as *Toledot Yeshu*, a derogatory history of Jesus that inverts the Christian practice of using Jewish sources against the Jews by using the New Testament against Christians. In the following passage, for example—which depicts Jesus in a disrespectful debate with the rabbis about the Talmud—the narrative uncovers something unusual about Jesus's paternity, not that he was born of God, but that he was the fruit of an unlawful and illegitimate sexual union:

> One day Yeshu [Jesus] walked in front of the Sages with his head uncovered, showing shameful disrespect. At this, the discussion arose as to whether this behavior did not truly indicate that Yeshu was an illegitimate child and the son of a *niddah* [a menstruant not supposed to have sex]. Moreover, the story tells that while the rabbis were discussing the [Talmudic] Tractate *Nezikin* [Damages], he gave his own impudent interpretation of the law and in an ensuing debate he held that Moses could not be the greatest of the prophets if he had to receive counsel from Jethro. This led to further inquiry as to the antecedents of Yeshu, and it was discovered through Rabban Shimeon ben Shetah that he was the illegitimate son of Joseph Pandera. Miriam admitted it. After this became known, it was necessary for Yeshu to flee to Upper Galilee.

Christian sources complain of other blasphemous practices, of Jews relieving themselves on Christian symbols or hanging an effigy of Haman during Purim in mock emulation of the Crucifixion. At first, one is tempted to dismiss such reports as akin to the host desecration accusation—trumped-up charges concocted to justify anti-Jewish violence—but recent scholars think they may actually bear some truth. Purim, in particular, a raucous, carnivalesque holiday, may have been a time when Jews expressed pent-up resentment of Christianity in a mockingly subversive, if not directly confrontational, way.

embraced rituals of commemorating the dead, such as the liturgical memory service (*yizkor*) on the Day of Atonement and the three festivals of Sukkot, Passover, and Shavuot, as well as the recitation of the ancient *Kaddish* prayer (which, in and of itself, has nothing to do with death) as the mourner's prayer (*also see the box* "A Jewish Polemic Against Christianity").

A Disastrous Fourteenth Century

As traumatic as the events of the First Crusade must have been, the level of violence was still relatively localized and abated quickly, and incidents of attacks against Jews remained an exception until the late thirteenth century. Then, however, two major series of widespread violence erupted: first, the Rindfleisch massacres, thus called after the leader of a mob that went on a rampage for five months and ravaged over 40 communities throughout Bavaria in 1298, with the memorial books listing no fewer than 3,400 victims. This outbreak was followed a few decades later by the Armleder massacres of the 1330s, like the previous wave of violence sparked by an accusation that Jews had desecrated the host. The Armleder massacres reached an even larger geographic area, including more than 100 Jewish communities in Alsace (in France), and turned into violence against part of the Christian population as well (*see the box* "The Blood Libel and Other Lethal Accusations").

An even greater frenzy of anti-Jewish violence erupted in the late 1340s as Europe was reeling from the effects of the bubonic plague, the Black Death, which left, according to some estimates, as much as one-third of Europe's population dead. Unable to understand the causes of the plague, Christians turned once again against the Jews, who were accused of poisoning wells and whose presence among Christians was believed by many to have provoked the wrath of God. In Provence and Catalonia, it is said, the massacres caused more deaths than the plague itself, and the violence quickly spread throughout much of Western and Central Europe, affecting hundreds of Jewish communities from France and northern Spain and throughout the German Empire, all the way to northern Italy and Hungary. The events, which oddly did not spark the same kind of expansive literary response among Jews as the Crusades, were no doubt the single most disastrous anti-Jewish persecution that the medieval world had seen to that date. After the massacres had abated, many towns that had chosen to cxpel their Jewish population during the plague readmitted them to assist in reconstructing a normal life, but violence against Jews now remained a factor on a relatively high level, in terms of both frequency and geographic spread.

By the time of the Black Death in the mid-fourteenth century, Jewish life in most of France, as well as in England, had already come to an end: In 1290, as we saw earlier, King Edward expelled the Jews from England when he was pressed to do so by the landed nobility, who were the primary debtors of Jewish moneylenders. The situation in France was more complicated, as political control was more fragmented; when King Philip IV expelled the Jews in 1306, the decree applied only to the royal lands in central France (around the capital, Paris), and subsequent kings allowed the return of some Jews, only to expel them again a few years later. The expulsion from France thus became final only in 1394, under King Charles IV, and even then Jews continued to live in southeastern France until 1501 and were never permanently ejected from the territories of the pope around Avignon, in southern France.

The factors behind these expulsions varied, but there were a few common factors that impelled the monarchs of England and France to remove the Jews from their realms. There was, of course, the increased hostility from the Church, as well as public anti-Jewish feelings. These were made worse by the fact that in both England and France, Jews had come to play an important role in moneylending, and since the Jews were seen as "property" of the royal treasury, the nobility who defaulted on their debt essentially lost their lands to the central royal authorities. By extorting taxes and all kinds of irregular payments from the Jews, the kings indirectly imposed new taxes on the Christian customers of the Jewish moneylending business as well, and the more the Crown exploited the Jews, as it was wont to do, the more it undermined the very possibility for the Jews to continue to render useful services to the economy in general and to the Crown in particular. Popular anti-Jewish feelings arose as a consequence of the interplay of these factors—religious apprehension, economic pressure, political tensions—and found their expression in repeated, localized outbreaks of violence. A ritual murder accusation in the French city of Blois in 1171, for example, led to the trial and execution of more than 30 Jews in the town. In 1190, when the English king was away on a Crusade, Jews were attacked in numerous places throughout England; in York, they took refuge in the king's tower and eventually committed mass suicide—as many had done a century earlier in Germany during the First Crusade—and their attackers finally burned all the bonds of debts owed to Jews that had been deposited in the town's cathedral. As a result, the king ordered that all debt obligations to Jews had to be recorded in duplicate, with one copy remaining in the royal treasury. That, of course, also gave the king direct knowledge of all business dealings of his Jewish subjects, as well as the opportunity to exploit this information against the nobility indebted to Jewish creditors. Thus, when the English barons agreed to advance King Edward the sum of 115,000 pounds that he urgently needed in exchange for expelling the Jews and canceling all debts owed to them (and which would have been claimed by the Crown), he alone knew how beneficial the deal was for the monarchy, as only about 10,000 pounds of outstanding Jewish loans remained.

The fourteenth century was bookended by major disasters that befell the Jews of Europe: A decade before the turn of the century, all Jews were expelled from England. A century later, in 1391, the Jews of Spain fell victim to a wave of massacres and forced conversions that left behind a severely traumatized community. In the middle decades of the century, especially during the Black Death, most Jewish communities in Europe—in France and the German lands in particular—were affected by widespread persecution. This is not to say that Jewish life throughout the century and everywhere was a litany of suffering, but the fourteenth century certainly did see the unraveling of the earlier medieval order, and it would take time for Jewish life in western Europe to recover, a process that would unfold in the early modern period (Chapter 8).

Sefarad

Life on the Frontier

The Jews of medieval Spain lived on the frontier between Islam and Christendom. The Christians understood the centuries-long battle to gain control over those parts of the Iberian Peninsula that had fallen under Muslim rule after 711 as a Crusade, a holy war to return those lands to the realm of Christendom. Invoking this notion of restoring a political order that had been disturbed by the eighth-century expansion of Islam, they called the military campaign against the Muslims the *Reconquista*, or "reconquest." The Jews living in Muslim al-Andalus and in the Christian territories of the northern part of the Iberian Peninsula naturally were affected by the conflict, and though they had no stake in the confrontation between the warring parties, the changing political fortunes on the peninsula obviously impacted their lives as much as they affected the lives of their Christian and Muslim neighbors.

The famous Hebrew poet and philosopher Judah ha-Levi, for example, lamented in a poem, "Between the hosts of Seir [i.e., Christendom] and Kedar [i.e., Islam], my host is lost; Israel's host vanishes. They wage their wars and we fall when they fall—thus it was ever in Israel." Another poet and philosopher of medieval Spain, Moses ibn Ezra, likewise referred to the political vicissitudes of the time in his poetry. In one text, he decried his own displacement from his native city of Granada after it had fallen to the Almoravids, a Muslim dynasty that wrought a period of religious intolerance and persecution in Muslim al-Andalus in the late eleventh century. Moses ibn Ezra found refuge in the Christian territories of northern Spain. Reflecting on his fate, he compared the sophistication of Arabic-speaking al-Andalus to what he considered a culturally inferior and backward Jewish community in the lands of Christian Spain. For the Jews of the Christian north, he had little else but scorn:

> Fortune has hurled me to a land where the lights of my understanding dimmed
> And the stars of my reason were beclouded with the murk of faltering knowledge and stammering speech.

THE BLOOD LIBEL AND OTHER LETHAL ACCUSATIONS

In 1144, the Jews of Norwich, England, faced a strange accusation: When the body of a Christian boy named William was discovered in the woods, the Jews of the town were rumored to have abducted, tortured, and ritually murdered him, just like their ancestors were believed to have killed Jesus. The ritual murder accusation of 1144 was probably the first of its kind, but it was soon followed by a similar libel in the French city of Blois in 1171, and throughout the medieval period and even to modern times, Jews of different places were subjected to ritual murder charges. In Norwich, the local sheriff investigated the case but determined that it had been a false accusation.

In 1235, in the German town of Fulda, an additional accusation was made: that the Jews had not only murdered a Christian child but also, in fact, used his blood for ritual purposes. Thus, the blood libel against Jews was born, and Jews throughout Europe found themselves exposed to similarly outlandish accusations on dozens of occasions. Often, a blood libel would lead to popular violence against the Jewish community that stood accused. Sometimes the authorities intervened and defended the Jews; at other times, they seemed to give credence to the libel. Given the strict prohibition against consuming even the blood of kosher animals, it was patently clear to anyone who knew anything about Jewish laws and traditions that the blood libel could be only a fabrication. In fact, several kings, emperors, and popes intervened and declared that these accusations against the Jews were false, but to no avail: The blood libel remained, was still used by the Nazis in the twentieth century, and can be found even today in antisemitic and anti-Zionist propaganda in the Middle East.

In the Middle Ages, the association of Jews with blood was further complicated by the claim that Jews used Christian blood as a palliative. Medicine and magic were closely linked, and the Jewish application of Christian blood was said to effect miraculous cures. In the Middle Ages, it was said that if a blind Jew were to smear his eyes with the blood of monks, his eyesight would be restored. According to popular wisdom, Constantine was

I have come to the iniquitous domain of a people scorned by God and accursed by man
Amongst savages who love corruption and set an ambush for the blood of the righteous and innocent.
They have adopted their neighbors' ways, anxious to enter their midst,
And mingling with them they share their deeds and are now reckoned among their number.
Those nurtured, in their youth, in the gardens of truth, hew, in old age, the woods of forests of folly.

Ibn Ezra clearly had little regard for his new Christian environment and its Jews: the "lights of . . . understanding" are "dimmed," "stars of . . . reason . . . beclouded," and his coreligionists of Christian Spain are described as "savages who love corruption." But there is something else in his text, a cursory remark that deserves our attention: "They," the Jews of Christian Spain, he writes, "have adopted their neighbors' ways"; they "mingle" with Christian society and are "reckoned among their number." As unsophisticated as their culture appeared to the Andalusian poet-philosopher, in other words, the Jews of northern Spain seemed to be quite at home in Christian society. There were no shadows of looming persecution; quite to the contrary, the Jews in *Reconquista* Spain were deeply integrated into general society, and though ibn Ezra did not think this was a good thing, they said to have been stricken with leprosy for his persecution of Christians and was advised by his Jewish physician to bathe in the blood of Christian children. The leprotic Richard the Lionhearted was said to have been given similar advice to cure his disease. Other medievals firmly believed that Christian blood applied topically cured Jews of the wound of circumcision. In Hungary, it was claimed that once a year, Jews strangled a child or virgin with phylacteries, drew blood from the victim, and smeared it on the genitals of their children to ensure fertility. Finally, belief was widespread that Jewish males menstruated, a view articulated by the Italian astrologer Cecco d'Ascoli, who declared that "after the death of Christ all Jewish men, like women, suffer menstruation." This would be a charge repeated with some consistency for centuries to come. Christian blood was said to cure Jewish male menstruation, and thus, it was necessary for Jews to procure it.

A related anti-Jewish accusation known as host desecration follows a similar trajectory. The precipitant for this kind of accusation was the Fourth Lateran Council in 1215, which officially recognized the belief that the wafer used in the Catholic ceremony of the Eucharist, the *host*, actually became the body of Christ during the ceremony, a doctrine known as *transubstantiation*. Some Christians maintained that Jews, believing in this doctrine themselves, stabbed and mutilated the host in a kind of re-enactment of the Crucifixion of Christ, allegedly causing it to shed blood. Such accusations—the first known case occurred in 1243—often had two consequences: A cult would be established on the site of the desecration, and the community would seek retaliation against the local Jewish community; many Jews were tried and executed for this reason. In 1290, for example, a Jewish moneylender in Paris was accused of host desecration, an event commemorated in a chapel built on the site and probably also the trigger of an expulsion of Jews from France in 1306. Another accusation in 1370 led to the virtual end of the Jewish community in medieval Belgium. The last Jew killed for the "crime" of host desecration died in the seventeenth century.

were almost indistinguishable from their Christian neighbors. If we do not reduce medieval Jewish history to intellectuals, poets, philosophers, and rabbinic scholars, and if we consider Jewish society at large—Jewish merchants, owners of vineyards, butchers, and artisans, and not to forget Jewish women, who were, by and large, excluded from the pursuits of the much-celebrated literary high culture—then a different, more nuanced picture of medieval Jewish life emerges.

The first major victory of the Christian Reconquista was the capture of the city of Toledo in 1085. Long after the Christians had established their rule and made Toledo the capital of the Kingdom of Castile, the Jews of the city continued to display a highly Arabized culture, and their language skills allowed their elites to engage in the cross-cultural and diplomatic exchange between the Christian and Muslim states of the Iberian Peninsula. Still, in the thirteenth century, Jews played an important role in the translation work sponsored by the Castilian king Alfonso X, making works of Arabic scholarship on mathematics, philosophy, medicine, astronomy, and other topics available to a Christian readership in Europe. Jews would collaborate with Christians in this endeavor by translating texts from Arabic into the Romance vernacular (e.g., Castilian), and a Christian scholar would then translate the Romance texts into Latin.

The cross-cultural contact that endured for centuries, the wars of the Reconquista and sectarian violence notwithstanding, was expressed in other ways too: Consider the example of the synagogue built at the behest of Samuel ha-Levi Abulafia in 1357 in Toledo, a wealthy court Jew who served as the treasurer of the Castilian king Pedro I. The wall stucco decoration presented a blending of Islamic art, with geometric and floral motifs as well as Hebrew and Arabic script as decorative elements, and the symbolism of the Christian Kingdom of Castile, with the royal coat of arms of Castile and Leon and a Hebrew inscription celebrating the prominence of the building's patron, Samuel ha-Levi (see Figure 7.2). The model for this kind of decorative art can be found in the architecture and artwork in the Christian royal palace in Seville, the fourteenth-century *Alcázar*, which, in turn, was inspired by the magnificent palace, also dating from the fourteenth century, of the Muslim rulers of Granada: the famous *Alhambra*, built by the Nasrid sultans of the last remaining Muslim kingdom on Iberian soil.

The Reconquista gained momentum in the thirteenth century, and by mid-century, the kingdoms of Castile, Aragon, and Portugal had gained control over the vast majority of the Iberian Peninsula. Córdoba was conquered in 1236, Valencia in 1238, Seville in 1248, and Murcia in 1266. As a result of the accelerated pace of conquest in the thirteenth century, a growing number of settlers were needed to repopulate the areas that came under Christian rule. The newly conquered territories drew a large number of migrants, and among them were many Jews. In fact, Spain attracted Jewish immigrants from across the Pyrenees as well in this period, with Rabbi Asher ben Yehiel, a native of Cologne who moved from Germany to Toledo early in the century, arguably the most famous example. When he first arrived in Castile, Asher ben Yehiel was surprised to learn the extent of legal autonomy that the Jewish communities of the kingdom seemed to enjoy. He noted:

> [I]n all countries with which I am familiar, capital cases are not judged [by Jews] except here in Spain. I was greatly surprised when I came here, that it was possible to judge capital matters. . . . I accepted this custom for them, but I never agreed with them in the destruction of life.

The Jewish communities in Christian Spain, in other words, had the right to impose capital punishment—the death penalty—on members of their community, a right that no Jewish community of the medieval or early modern period ever held.

Figure 7.2 Interior of El Transito synagogue.

This should not lead us to overstate the power of the community over the lives of individual Jews, however, nor should we mistake the prerogatives granted to the Jewish community for genuine legal autonomy, which remained, after all, subject to the ultimate authority of the Crown. As elsewhere in Europe at that time, the monarchs of the Christian kingdoms in Spain claimed the Jews living under their rule as "property" of the royal treasury. This reality allowed individual Jews to circumvent the juridical institutions of the community and its rabbis, appealing to the Christian authorities instead. At least during the initial phase after the Christian conquest, many Jews established themselves in places where there was no organized community or established religious infrastructure at all.

Jews played a role in the colonization effort of the Reconquista from the outset. Two Jewish moneylenders, for example, appear in the famous medieval epic celebrating the adventures of the Christian nobleman and warrior known as "El Cid Campeador," who conquered Valencia from the Muslims in the 1090s (Valencia subsequently reverted to Muslim rule and was finally reconquered by King James I of Aragon in 1236). According to the epic "The Song of the Cid" (*El Cantar del mio Cid*), the warrior hero, who had fallen into disfavor with King Alfonso VI, sought out the help of two Jewish moneylenders, Raguel and Vidas. A supporter of the Cid, Martin Antolinez of Burgos (in Castile), explained his master's request to the two Jews:

> Is it you, my good friends, Raguel and Vidas? I should like a word with you two in private. . . . Both of you give me your hands and promise to keep this secret from everyone, Moors [Muslims] and Christians alike, and I shall make your fortune so that you will be rich for life. When the [Cid] Campeador went to collect the tribute, he received vast sums of money and kept the best part of it. For this reason accusations were brought against him. He has in his possession two chests full of pure gold. The King, as you know, has banished him and he has left his properties, holdings, and manors. He cannot carry the chests with him, for then their existence would be revealed. The [Cid] Campeador will entrust them to you and you must lend him a suitable amount of money. Take the chests and keep them in a safe place.

Jewish financiers could provide a crucial service: Not identified a priori with the political interests of the Christians or the Muslims, they were seen as politically neutral actors who could be trusted to be above the fray of political intrigues and military confrontation. Throughout the Christian kingdoms of the Iberian Peninsula, Jews were also employed as tax farmers, a role that essentially consisted of advancing capital to the government and then collecting the tax revenue from the local population, retaining a profit. A common arrangement in all premodern states, Jews were often employed in this capacity. As historian Javier Castaño argued, Jews were not as prominent in tax farming in Christian Spain as often believed, but they still played a role far greater than their share of the overall population. Jews were about 3 percent of Castile's population in the late fifteenth century, but of the 500 tax farmers that we know of in the years between 1439 and 1469, 15 percent were Jews. It is important to add, though, that most Jews were, of course, not engaged in moneylending or tax farming, and Jewish economic activities in *Reconquista* Spain were significantly more diverse than in many other parts of Europe. Jews worked in many professions of the urban economy, as tailors, butchers, goldsmiths, or merchants, but they also owned agricultural land and engaged in the making of wine or olive oil.

As the major Christian kingdoms—Castile, Aragon, and Portugal—extended their conquests over the thirteenth century, leaving only a rump state under Muslim rule until they completed the Reconquista with the capture of Granada in 1492, the royal authorities increasingly asserted their power in the newly conquered territories. Laws were codified, and legal practices unified, throughout the various kingdoms, with the crowning accomplishment arguably the compiling of the law code known as *Las Siete Partidas* ("the seven parts") under King Alfonso X of Castile in the thirteenth century (though they would be fully implemented only in the following century). As the Crown asserted its direct oversight over the Jewish communities, however, its interests inevitably clashed with those of other political players: the baronial authorities, the Christian municipalities, and the Catholic

Figure 7.3 An illuminated Hebrew manuscript of the Jewish prayer book from Spain (c. 1300). The image depicts knights on horseback, a reflection of a culture celebrating chivalric virtues during this period's Christian "reconquest" of Spain.

Church. Each had its own claims on exercising oversight over the Jewish minority, and each competed for its share of taxes collected from the Jews. The Church, for example, insisted that Jewish landowners also pay the tithe (*diezmo*) that had to be paid by all Christian landowners to the Church, but even where the Crown acceded to such claims from the Church, it enforced the rules unevenly. In the towns, where most Jews lived, local municipal authorities saw direct, exclusive royal sovereignty over the Jews as an intrusion on their own rights, and Jewish communities often found themselves at the center of power conflicts between the central royal government, city leaders, the Church, and the landed nobility. What is more, because they were seen as royal property, the Jews were particularly susceptible to bearing the brunt of any popular anger and discontent with the Crown, and anti-Jewish violence was often informed by traditional kinds of anti-Jewish prejudice as much as it was motivated by political circumstances.

A good example of this dynamic is the attacks suffered by Jews in the late 1340s, during the bubonic plague, which led to violence against Jews throughout Europe. Jews were attacked in the city of Barcelona, for instance, and the king of Aragon, Peter IV, tried to assert his authority and enforce the protection of the Jews against popular hostility, which apparently was whipped up by certain preachers in the local churches. In late May 1348, Peter IV wrote to the "faithful councilors and citizens of the city of Barcelona"—that is, the leaders of the city's government—noting that:

> [T]hrough information supplied to us by the Jews of the *aljama* [community] of the aforementioned city, we have learned that recently, when the populace of the aforesaid city had been aroused, certain men of that city . . . invaded the Jewish quarter and there killed several of the Jews.

He lauded the city leaders who had tried to protect the Jewish quarter, but he saw it fit to remind them nonetheless, "[W]e wish that the aforesaid Jews, who live under our special protection, be preserved unharmed as our royal subjects from improper oppression and disturbance." Ten days later, the king sent another missive to Barcelona, this time addressing the bishop and clerical leaders of the city. He expressed his concern about the incitement of the population against the Jews and admonished the church leaders that they make, "to the extent of [their] power . . ., provisions through which the Jews of the aforesaid quarter might be protected from undeserved persecution." In particular:

> [W]e require and entreat, since you care to provide in such a manner for the dignity of our honor, that the sermons offered by preachers and others in the churches of the aforesaid city, through which incitement against or danger to the aforesaid Jews might develop, be completely suppressed.

The royal warning, however, seems to have failed to ensure the protection of Barcelona's Jews, and the following year, in February 1349, Peter IV wrote to the municipal councilors of the city concerning "the rash intrusion carried out this year against the *aljama* of the Jews of the aforesaid city by several men of that city." He continued:

> We are impressed deeply with the gravity of the matter . . . since the justice by virtue of which we live and reign has not yet been done. Indeed, what is worse, those intruders despise the sting of our aforesaid discipline as a result of this lack of punishment for their crime and continue their evil design. They do not hesitate to spread covertly threats against those Jews, that during the coming Holy Week they will attack them and destroy them totally. . . . You must take care to make such provisions and ordinances concerning these matters as may seem necessary to you, so that the aforesaid *aljama* and all its members will be protected.

Religiously motivated anti-Jewish sentiment, therefore, could be mobilized and lead to violence against the Jewish minority, but this mobilization always happened in a particular local political context, in which the Crown, the Church, the city's government, and the Jewish community itself all played a role.

In many areas of *Reconquista* Spain, the social reality was even more complex, as a sizeable Muslim minority ended up living under Christian rule, alongside the Jews. While many Jews retained their Arabized culture long after the Christian conquests, this did not necessarily translate into good relationships with their Arabic-speaking Muslim neighbors. Relations between the two minorities were tense at times, as they clashed with one another over matters such as competing economic interests, religious conversion, or sexual encounters between members of the two religious groups. The conversion of Christians to Islam or Judaism was not something that the medieval Christian authorities would have tolerated, of course, but the competition over converts from Islam to Judaism or vice versa was another matter. Other problems arose when Jews were allowed, like their Christian counterparts, to own Muslim slaves, or when Jewish men frequented Muslim prostitutes. At times, inter-minority relations deteriorated into violence and mirrored the patterns of anti-minority confrontation found in Christian society. A striking example of this were Muslims who participated in Christian assaults on the Jews during the Holy Week of Easter. Thus, King James of Aragon noted that, in the early fourteenth century,

> some Muslims living in Deroca, despite a proclamation that no one, during the eight days of Easter, dare stone or throw stones at our castle of Deroca where the Jews live, scaled the walls of that castle and then attacked the Jews living in that castle with rocks and swords, seriously injuring some of them.

Sefarad and the Rise of Kabbalah

The literary culture produced by the Jews in Christian Spain represented both a continuation of the legacy of Muslim al-Andalus and the integration of influences that reached Spanish Jewry from Europe north of the Pyrenees. Consider the example of Hebrew poetry by individuals like Todros ben Judah Abulafia (d. 1306), which both represented a continuation of the Andalusi tradition of Hebrew poetry and experimented with new styles that were inspired by the troubadour poetry of Christian Europe.

Arguably, the most renowned scholar of medieval Christian Spain was Moses ben Nahman, known also as Nahmanides (1194–1270), who was born in Girona, Catalonia, and who departed for the Holy Land in 1267 and lived the last years of his life in Jerusalem and Acre. Nahmanides played a central role in the controversy over Moses Maimonides's philosophical writings in the 1230s (see Chapter 6), and the king of Aragon summoned him to a public disputation with Pablo Cristiani, a Jewish convert to Christianity, in Barcelona in 1263. Nahmanides was an extraordinarily prolific writer: About 50 of his works have been preserved. He left his imprint in several areas, in particular through his commentary on the Bible and his writings on the Talmud. He was responsible more than anyone for introducing the kind of Talmud study to the Sephardi world that had been developed by the tosafists of northern France, and he created a new synthesis of the Talmudic scholarship of Spain, northern France, and Provence (southern France). Like the tosafists, he was concerned with the close study of the Talmudic text for its own sake, and not primarily for the sake of determining legal practice, which had been the focus of the Sephardi approach to the Talmud. At the same time, Nahmanides insisted, as Isadore Twersky has described it, "that study of Talmud must be supplemented by study of kabbalah whose concepts and symbols infuse the normative system with spirituality and theological vision."

Kabbalah, a form of Jewish mysticism, then, was the second area in which Nahmanides had a major impact. He did so primarily through his seminal commentary on the Bible, which joined those of his predecessors, Abraham ibn Ezra of Spain and Rashi of northern France, as one of the classical commentaries that have shaped traditional Jewish biblical scholarship to this day. Nahmanides was the first to integrate the teaching of Kabbalah into his glosses on the Bible, and he made ample use of midrashic interpretations in his biblical commentary, which reflected his broader theological understanding of God, the role of the Jewish people, and the Torah. He often cited the interpretation of a verse "by way of the plain meaning of Scripture," followed by another interpretation that he introduced with the words "by the way of Truth"—that is, its interpretation in the spirit of Kabbalah.

Kabbalah literally means "tradition," something that has been "received," and refers to the mystical teachings that developed in Provence and Spain in the twelfth and thirteenth centuries. Forms of "mysticism" can be found in all religious traditions, and the term usually refers to a religious experience of communion (or unity) with the divine, transforming the individual's consciousness and leading to the disclosure of "secret," "hidden" knowledge. Mysticism was part of the Jewish tradition since antiquity, and various forms of Jewish mysticism developed over the centuries. In the mid-twelfth century, a new Jewish mystical literature emerged in Provence, in southern France. It was probably not a coincidence that this very area also was the scene of a controversy over the teaching of Jewish philosophy, in particular the writings of Maimonides, and in a sense, the lore of Kabbalah was a response to the challenge of philosophy.

For the Aristotelian philosophers like Maimonides, the divine commandments primarily served an educational purpose; they were designed for the benefit of humans, whereas a self-sufficient and all-powerful God clearly did not really "need" individuals to perform ritual or address God in prayer. But what was the rationale for the commandments once their philosophical message had been learned? What was the point of praying if God could not be moved by prayer? Kabbalah offered an altogether different understanding of prayer and the commandments: For the kabbalists, the words of prayer and the deed of performing the commandments not only were beneficial for the individual Jew but also had an actual impact on the life of the divine realm itself; they literally sustained the universe, and they were more than mere symbols.

One of the earliest works of Kabbalah was the strange and obscure *Sefer ha-Bahir* (which, ironically, translates roughly as the "book of clarity"), composed in twelfth-century Provence. The *Sefer ha-Bahir* was written, at least at first sight, in the form of an ancient midrash, expounding on each verse of the Bible. It raised more questions than it answered, however. "You think you know the meaning of this verse?" the *Bahir* asks its reader at one point, and continues: "Here is an interpretation that will throw you on your ear and show you that you understand nothing of it at all." For all its obscurity, the *Bahir* had a great impact on subsequent kabbalistic literature. It enumerated, for example, a series of ten "potencies" of God, according to the ten phrases "Let there be . . ." in the biblical story of creation. Later Kabbalah developed this idea of ten potencies (or spheres)—*sefirot*, as they were called—into a complex system of interrelated powers that together made up the divinity (Figure 7.4). Kabbalah presented a mythical universe in which "God," the divine realm, was the scene for the interplay of the ten *sefirot*, and all ten were contained within the one God.

Nahmanides, Jonah Gerondi (d. 1263), and others developed this kabbalistic lore further in thirteenth-century Catalonia, on the Spanish side of the Pyrenees. Another school of Kabbalah developed in Castile in the late thirteenth century. The single most influential work of Jewish mysticism—the *Zohar*, or "book of splendor"—emerged within this circle of Castilian kabbalists toward the end of the century, around 1290. Moses de Leon was the central figure in the composition and circulation of what became known as the *Zohar*, a mystical text written as a midrashic homily on the text of the Pentateuch in archaic Aramaic. In fact, the Castilian kabbalists claimed that the text preserved a tradition that dated back to the days of Rabbi Simeon bar Yohai and his disciples in the second century CE, and though certain critical spirits questioned the ancient pedigree of the work, it came to be widely accepted throughout the Jewish world as containing divinely inspired truths, no less authoritative than those conveyed in the Mishnah or the Talmud.

For the kabbalists, God's revelation in the Torah is not designed to convey historical knowledge about the origins of the world or of the Jewish people, nor is its only purpose the teaching of law or the communication of the divine commandments. Below the surface of the text, the kabbalists believe, there is a hidden, more profound message: the essence of God himself, not just the manifestation of his will in history or law, is encoded in the biblical text. Kabbalah provides the key to unlock the secrets of the divine; understood in a kabbalistic way, the Torah reveals the nature of God himself and discloses the secrets of the cosmos. In the words of the *Zohar*:

> Rabbi Simeon said: If a man looks upon the Torah as merely a book presenting narratives and everyday matters, alas for him! . . . the Torah, in all of its words, holds supernal truths and sublime secrets, . . . Thus the tales related in the Torah are simply her outer garments, and woe to the man who regards that outer garb as the Torah itself. . . . See now. The most visible part of a man are the clothes that he has on, and they who lack understanding, when they look at the man, are apt not to see more in him than these clothes. In reality, however, it is the body of the man that constitutes the pride of his clothes, and his soul constitutes the pride of his body. So it is with the Torah. Its narrations which relate to things of the world constitute the garments which clothe the body of the Torah; and that body is composed of the Torah's precepts [i.e., the commandments]. People without understanding see only the narrations, the garment; those somewhat more penetrating

Fig. 174. JEWISH CABBALIST HOLDING THE SEPHIROTIC TREE
Paulus Ricius, *Porta Lucis hæc est porta tetragrammaton, justi intrabunt per eam* (Augsburg, 1516).
Author's collection.

Figure 7.4 A diagram of the ten *sefirot*, or emanations of God in kabbalistic tradition, and their relationship to one another. Keter is the highest of the *sefirot*, the point beyond which the mind cannot go. The uniting of Hokhmah and Binah, masculine and feminine aspects of God, produced the lower seven *sefirot*. Jewish mystics believed humans mirrored this structure and their soul originating from within it and are thus in a position to influence God through their actions, promoting a harmonic and integrated relationship between the different parts of the *sefirotic* system through ethical and ritual practice.

> see also the body. But the truly wise, those who serve the most high King and stood on Mount Sinai, pierce all the way through to the soul, to the true Torah which is the root principle to all.

It is impossible to summarize the thinking of the *Zohar* and the Castilian kabbalists in the limited space available here. To get a taste of the poetic imagery used in the *Zohar*, consider this comment on the first verse of the Bible, Genesis 1:1, outlining the origins of all existence, the beginnings of creation:

> "In the beginning"—when the will of the King began to take effect, he engraved signs into

> the heavenly sphere. Within the most hidden recess a dark flame issued from the mystery of the Infinite (*ein-sof*), like a fog forming in the unformed—enclosed in the ring of that sphere, neither white nor black, neither red nor green, of no color whatever. Only after this flame began to assume size and dimension, did it produce radiant colors. From the innermost center of the flame sprang forth a well out of which colors issued and spread upon everything beneath, hidden in the mysterious hiddenness of *ein-sof*.

According to the kabbalists, the world came into being through a process of "emanation." The ultimate root of all being is the *ein-sof*, the "Infinite," and from this root spring forth the layers of emanation, described variably as beams of light, flows of water, and the like, in kabbalistic writings. The ten *sefirot* are the first products of this emanation. They are arranged, in the kabbalist's imagination, in a specific order of emanation and descending proximity to their point of origin, and the result is a complex structure of ten "potencies," or manifestations of the divine, that interact with one another—and which all are part of the divine realm itself.

There are several important ideas related to the structure of the ten *sefirot*: First, there are two sides, the left side and the right side. The two are often depicted as the "male" and "female" sides of the divinity, and kabbalistic literature employs the image of a sexual union to describe how the *sefirot* of "wisdom" (*hokhmah*, on the right, male side) and that of "understanding" (*binah*, on the left, female side) unite to produce the lower seven *sefirot* of the divine realm. Ideally, there is a perfect balance between the two sides. At the top of the lower seven *sefirot*, for example, there are the potencies of "love" (or "greatness") and of "power" (or "judgment"): The former, on the "male" or right side, represents God's mercy, whereas the other, on the "female" or left side, represents his power to pass judgment and inflict punishment. If both are in perfect harmony, everything is in order, but if the side of "judgment" becomes too strong, for example, it produces and gives strength to the forces of evil. The task of the kabbalist, ultimately, is to restore the perfect harmony and effect the union of the *sefirot*, and it is through prayer and performance of the commandments that this can be achieved.

At the lower end of the sefirotic structure is the potency of *yesod*, "foundation," which the *Zohar* describes in shockingly explicit language as the "phallus" of the divinity. It is through this *sefirah* that the divine energy, or "light," is channeled all the way down from the highest *sefirah*, *keter* ("crown"), and passed on to the lowest potency, known as *malkhut* ("kingdom") or *shekhinah* (a term that denotes God's presence in the world). This is where the divine world is connected with the lower worlds, all of which ultimately emanate from their shared point of origin: the worlds inhabited by angels and, at the very bottom, the material world inhabited by humans. Just as it is the task of the kabbalist to facilitate the union and balance of the female and male *sefirot*, it is necessary to ensure the flow of energy from the world of the *sefirot* down, through the union of *yesod* and *malkhut*.

The strength of this complex theosophical structure was that it allowed the kabbalists to relate to the personal God of revelation. Whereas philosophers like Maimonides had tried to argue away the anthropomorphic language that the Bible employs to describe God (having a face, getting angry, etc.), the kabbalists embraced precisely this language as providing a clue into what "God," understood as the divine realm encompassing all ten *sefirot*, "looked" like. This allowed them to experience the divine through mystical practice and to believe that their prayers and performance of commandments had a direct impact on the structure of the *sefirot* in the divine world above, and thus on the proper functioning of the cosmos.

The rise of Kabbalah in thirteenth-century Christian Spain should not obscure the fact that other facets of Jewish literary creativity remained as well. In the realm of philosophy, for example, Hasdai Crescas of Barcelona (c. 1340–c. 1411) continued what had long been a distinguished tradition of Spanish Jewry. Crescas wrote a philosophical treatise called *Or Adonai* ("the light of the Lord"), which he completed in 1410 and which presented a systematic exposition of the central dogmas of Judaism. He criticized medieval Jewish Aristotelianism, for example, as it was developed in the philosophy of Maimonides, and some scholars have noted the striking modernity of Crescas's philosophy and how his thinking "foreshadows the scientific revolution about to transform European thought in the sixteenth and seventeenth centuries" (Robert Seltzer). Crescas argued, for example, against the Aristotelian notion of space. Whereas the Jewish Aristotelians had maintained that the universe was finite, Crescas suggested that it was open and infinite. To cite another example, the Aristotelians had argued that matter was the potentiality for being, but for Crescas, matter was a primary entity that existed in actuality. Philosophical speculation continued among the Jews who were displaced by the expulsion from Spain in 1492, but in the end, it was Kabbalah that had the more significant and lasting impact on Jewish culture in subsequent centuries (*see the box* "Banning Jewish Philosophy").

Toward Expulsion

During the summer of 1391, Jewish communities throughout the Iberian Peninsula were attacked; tens of thousands, it seems, were killed or converted to Christianity to escape the violence. The riots began in Seville in June of that year, and while their rapid spread throughout Castile and beyond its borders into the Kingdom of Aragon is still not very well understood, there were certainly plenty of precedents elsewhere in medieval Europe. The violence of 1391 was followed by enduring conversionist pressure, in particular as the result of another staged disputation, this time in the city of Tortosa, which lasted for several months, from February 1413 to November 1414. As a result of this persistent onslaught, an even larger number of Jews embraced Catholicism and depleted the ranks of Spanish Jewry. We will take a closer look at the consequences of this wave of conversions, which created a whole new social class of converted Jews, known as *conversos* (or, in a derogative term, as *marranos*), in the beginning of the following chapter. Here, we will briefly consider the last century of what remained of Spanish Jewry in the wake of the violence of 1391 and the widespread conversions that ensued.

Historians in the past have pointed out the difference between the apparent readiness of Ashkenazi Jews in the Rhineland to die as martyrs rather than undergo baptism during the First Crusade and the mass conversions of Spanish Jews in 1391 and later. The comparison is problematic to begin with, of course, as we are talking about two entirely different historical contexts, in different parts of Europe, and involving events separated by three centuries. The juxtaposition of Ashkenazi martyrdom and the conversions in Spain is wrong on another account as well: There was, after all, widespread "martyrdom" in Spain and thousands died, whether at the hands of their attackers or by sacrificing their own lives. Rabbi and philosopher Hasdai Crescas described the events that rocked Spanish Jewry in 1391 in a moving letter that he sent to southern France:

> On the day of trouble and distress . . . God's anger was kindled against the holy city . . ., the community of Toledo. . . . There, its rabbis who were the pure and choice seed of Rabbi Asher, fathers, children, and disciples, sanctified the Name in public. There were many who were converted as they could not bear

BANNING JEWISH PHILOSOPHY

Among those with reservations about the study of philosophy was the great Spanish rabbinic scholar Solomon ben Adret (1235–1310). However, ben Adret, who was conversant with the work of Maimonides and other philosophers, was not completely opposed to philosophical speculation. The following ban represents something of a compromise, prohibiting the study of philosophy up until the age of 25, but not going as far as others who would have banned it altogether:

> Woe to mankind because of the insult to the Torah! For they have strayed far from it.
> Its diadem have they taken away.
> Its crown they have removed
> Every man with his censer in his hand offers incense Before the Greeks and Arabs.
> Like Zimri [a biblical Israelite who had sex with a Midianite woman; Numbers 25], they publicly consort with the Midianitess
> And revel in their own filth!
>
> They do not prefer the older Jewish teachings
> But surrender to the newer Greek learning
> the prerogatives due their Jewish birthright.
> Therefore have we decreed and accepted for ourselves and our children, and for all those joining us, that for the next fifty years under the threat of the ban, no man in our community, unless he be twenty-five years old, shall study, either in the original language or in translation, the books which the Greeks have written on religious philosophy and science . . . We, however, excluded from this our general prohibition the science of medicine, even though it is one of the natural sciences, because the Torah permits the physician to heal.

Source: Jacob Marcus, trans., *The Jew in the Medieval World: A Sourcebook 315–1791*, rev. ed. (Cincinnati, OH: Hebrew Union College Press, 1999), 215–216.

the pressure. The following Sabbath, the Lord poured out his anger like fire, shook his sanctuary and desecrated the crown of his Torah, that is the community of Barcelona which was overtaken on that day. The number of the dead reached two hundred fifty. The rest of the community escaped to the fortress where they took refuge while the enemies looted the Jewish streets and put some on fire. The governor of the city had no hand in the attack. On the contrary he did his best to save them. . . . Then the masses and the mobs rebelled against the city leaders, they attacked the Jews who were in the fortress with bows and catapults. Many died as martyrs. . . . All the rest were baptized. Only a few escaped to baronial cities. . . . They were the elite. Because of our sins there is today no one known as a Jew in Barcelona.

While Crescas speaks of hundreds of victims, other sources mention thousands; one historian, Haim Beinart, even estimated that as much as one-third of Spanish Jewry was killed, and another third baptized, in 1391. In any event, given the traumatic experience of the summer of 1391 and the fact that merely 100 years later, in 1492, the Jews were finally expelled from Spain, it is easy to see the last century of Spanish Jewry as a period of inevitable decline.

We will discuss the matter of the expulsion further in the next chapter. What is surprising, however, is the fact that the surviving Jewish communities of Spain actually seemed to regain their footing once they had recovered from the initial trauma of 1391. The Jewish map of Christian Spain, to be sure, looked very different now: Some cities, like Barcelona, or the island of

Mallorca, ceased to have a Jewish community at all, and others were only a shadow of their former selves. But by 1480, one recent estimate still puts the number of Jews in the Kingdom of Castile alone at about 100,000 (about 3 percent of the population), with most Jews now living in smaller towns rather than the large urban centers of the Iberian Peninsula. Cultural creativity continued, and even peaceful Jewish–Christian cooperation did not come to an end. In the 1420s and 1430s, for example, Rabbi Moses Arragel of Guadalajara produced a Romance Bible and commentary at the request of the grand master of the Order of Calatrava (a military order established in the twelfth century). A Hebrew printing press was established, in the city of Guadalajara, in 1476, and Hebrew book printing was well underway in Spain by the time of the expulsion. In terms of a reviving economy, too, the Jewish communities of fifteenth-century Spain were rebuilding: One historian even speaks in a recent study of the Jews in fifteenth-century Morvedre, north of Valencia, of a "Jewish renaissance."

In Castile, Abraham Benveniste was appointed in 1421 as *Rab de la Corte*, a sort of "chief rabbi" representing the Jews of the kingdom, and convened a conference of the Castilian communities in Valladolid in 1432. A range of ordinances were passed, and Jewish community life was reorganized. The continued effort of centralization, which continued under the subsequent leader Abraham Seneor, a prominent banker of the royal court, led to what historian Javier Castaño has described as a "development of proto-national consciousness of the Jews in Castile in a process similar to processes undergone by other churches in the West." Ironically, as Jewish history in medieval Spain was approaching its end, the Jews of Castile and Aragon may have identified more than ever with the respective kingdoms in which they lived (and not only with their local or regional environment). It is therefore, perhaps, not altogether surprising to see how tenaciously the exiled Spanish Jews held on to their Iberian legacy even after they were expelled in 1492 (see Map 7.2).

A People Apart?

The image that we have of Jewish society in medieval Christian Europe is often one of a community living in isolation from its non-Jewish environment, frequently subject to persecution, and guided by religious tradition. On all three accounts, Jewish life in the Middle Ages was more complicated than that. It is true that the basic religious difference between Christians and Jews was taken for granted by everyone and shaped the encounter between members of the two religious communities. It is also true, as we have seen throughout this chapter, that Jews were often the victims of violence. The Jewish religious tradition, finally, did indeed provide the foundation for the way Jews lived and thought about themselves, the world around them, and their place in history, and nobody would have ever thought of Jewish identity in the medieval period as anything but tied to the teachings of the Jewish religion.

The eminent American Jewish historian Salo Baron argued in an article he published in 1928 that the situation of the Jews in medieval society is often misunderstood. The Jews, Baron reminds us, were, for the most part, an urban population and thus belonged to a small minority whose legal status (and privileges) set them apart from the overwhelming majority of people, the peasants. Peasants were, most everywhere in medieval Europe, treated as serfs, tied to the land they tilled, and if a landowner sold his possessions, he also sold the peasants living on his estate along with the land itself. Jews never enjoyed "equal rights," of course, in medieval societies, whether Christian or Muslim—but nobody really enjoyed "equal rights," a concept that would have made

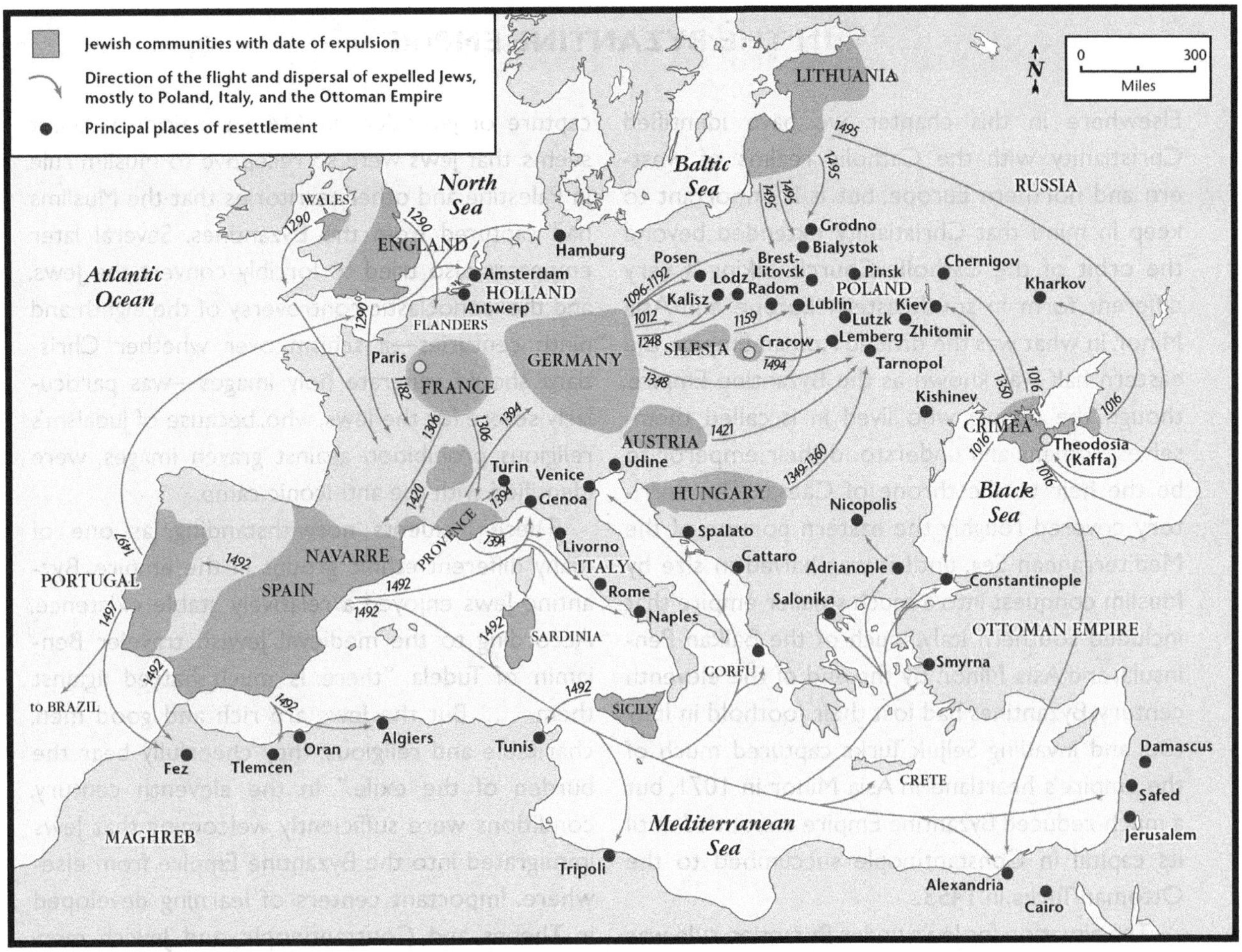

Map 7.2 The expulsion and migration of Jews from western Europe, 1000–1500.

no sense to anyone at that time. Instead, Jews constituted a clearly defined group that enjoyed certain privileges and that offered them opportunities unavailable to the bulk of the population, the peasants. At the same time, of course, Jews as a group were always subject to certain restrictions, but that, too, was the case for pretty much everyone else in medieval society, at least outside the nobility.

Both Christian and Jewish authorities were equally interested in maintaining clear dividing lines between their communities. Anyone who violated the boundaries separating Jews from Christians was seen as a threat to the existing social and religious order by both Jewish and Christian leaders. The Church and the state, of course, were in a much stronger position than the Jewish community to set rules and enforce them. But when the Church insisted, as it did on numerous occasions throughout the medieval period, that Christians should not partake of Jewish food or drink wine made by Jews, they demanded nothing that the rabbis would not have endorsed too. Dietary restrictions in Jewish law, after all, also served the purpose of maintaining clear social boundaries between Jews and gentiles.

Everyday reality, however, was another matter; consider, for example, the problem of sharing wine. Talmudic rules regarding the production

IN THE BYZANTINE EMPIRE

Elsewhere in this chapter, we have identified Christianity with the Catholic realms of western and northern Europe, but it is important to keep in mind that Christianity extended beyond the orbit of the Catholic Church, taking a very different form in southeastern Europe and Asia Minor. In what was the divided Roman Empire, the eastern half was known as the Byzantine Empire, though the people who lived in it called themselves Romans and understood their emperor to be the heir to the throne of Caesar. This territory covered roughly the eastern portion of the Mediterranean Sea, until it was halved in size by Muslim conquest into a much smaller empire that included southern Italy, much of the Balkan Peninsula, and Asia Minor. By the end of the eleventh century, Byzantines had lost their foothold in Italy too, and invading Seljuk Turks captured much of the empire's heartland in Asia Minor in 1071, but a much-reduced Byzantine Empire continued until its capital in Constantinople succumbed to the Ottoman Turks in 1453.

The situation for Jews under Byzantine rule was different from that of Jews in Catholic Europe. In a kingdom that understood itself as a continuation of the Roman Empire, Byzantine Jews, like their non-Jewish neighbors, understood themselves to be Romans and did not hesitate to assert the ancient legal status of Judaism as an officially recognized religion as a source of protection. On the other hand, they also faced legal discrimination and persecution under Byzantine rule. On the eve of the Muslim capture of Palestine in 634, Jews found themselves reeling from the persecution imposed on them by Emperor Heraclius (610–641) because they (allegedly) had aided the Persians in their capture of Jerusalem in 614—a major reason, it seems, that Jews were so receptive to Muslim rule in Palestine and other territories that the Muslims had captured from the Byzantines. Several later emperors also tried to forcibly convert the Jews, and the iconoclastic controversy of the eighth and ninth centuries—a schism over whether Christians should venerate holy images—was particularly severe for the Jews, who, because of Judaism's religious prohibition against graven images, were identified with the anti-iconic camp.

These incidents notwithstanding, as one of many different ethnic groups in the empire, Byzantine Jews enjoyed a relatively stable existence. According to the medieval Jewish traveler Benjamin of Tudela, "there is much hatred against them. . . . But the Jews are rich and good men, charitable and religious; they cheerfully bear the burden of the exile." In the eleventh century, conditions were sufficiently welcoming that Jews immigrated into the Byzantine Empire from elsewhere. Important centers of learning developed in Thebes and Constantinople, and Jewish merchants excelled in the textile trade despite efforts to exclude them from the silk business. Byzantine Rabbanite Judaism did not produce many great scholars of the legal tradition, though many poets and midrashists hailed from the empire. Byzantine Karaite legalists, on the other hand, set the agenda for their entire movement for four centuries (on the Karaites, see Chapter 6). The Rabbanite Tobias ben Eliezer penned a well-known midrashic compilation, *Midrash Leqah Tov*. He also participated in a messianic movement that took the Jews of Greece by storm as the Crusaders made their way eastward from Europe.

and handling of wine are quite strict. It is therefore not surprising to see that many Jews, from northern France to southern Spain, were engaged in wine making, thus supplying the Jewish community with a beverage that was used for religious ritual (e.g., Sabbath observance includes the blessing over wine on Friday evening and Saturday morning), and that served as a staple in everyday life as well. (According to the calculations of one historian, a Jewish family in late fifteenth-century Umbria, in central Italy, drank, on average, between 1.5 and 3 liters of wine a day.) Despite all theoretical restrictions imposed by religious law, however, it was also widely known that some Jews in Italy were not too strict when it came to tasting non-Jewish wines: "I have known that from time immemorial our forefathers in Italy habitually drank ordinary [i.e., non-Jewish] wine," the Venetian rabbi Leone da Modena explained in the seventeenth century. On the other hand, Christians were wont to ignore the admonishments of the Catholic Church when it came to enjoying a nice glass of Jewish wine. In the fourteenth century, for example, Father Taddeo, abbot of a monastery in Umbria, praised the Trebbiano red wines of a Jewish winemaker as the best in the area, and the monks of the confraternity of S. Stefano were among the regular patrons of a tavern operated by a Jew in the 1380s in Assisi and often purchased their wine there.

Jewish–Christian interaction was manifest in all walks of life, from the elite of "court Jews" all the way down to the lower classes of society. Within highbrow culture, there are many examples of cross-cultural influence, from the fields of philosophy and theology to literature. The Hebrew poet Immanuel of Rome (d. 1328), for example, was influenced by the Hebrew poetic tradition that had developed in medieval Spain, but he was also clearly aware of Italian poetry of his time. His *Mahberet ha-tofet ve-ha-eden* (a poem on "hell and paradise") reflected the influence of Dante's great epic, the classic of Italian literature. Cross-cultural cooperation can be found at the opposite end of the social order, too, among individuals who were outcasts from both Jewish and Christian societies. A surprising example is the case of Abramo di Ventura da Roma, a Jew who made a living as a professional criminal in the 1430s in Perugia, Italy, as the head of a band of criminals that included both Jews and Christians and that specialized in kidnapping the children of wealthy Jewish merchants and bankers to extort ransom payments.

While historians have long acknowledged that relations between Jews and Christians in Spain or Italy may not have always followed the letter and spirit of religious laws trying to keep them apart, Ashkenazi Jewry has at times been seen as more traditional and subservient to rabbinic authority. Also in medieval Ashkenaz, however, social reality was more complicated. Thus, Rabbi Isaac of Corbeil in thirteenth-century France was asked about the case of a Jewish woman who had been baptized and had taken a Christian lover. Subsequently, she had second thoughts, returned to Judaism, and her Christian partner converted to Judaism. Were they allowed to marry? Rabbi Corbeil ruled that they were not. This was hardly a typical case, to be sure, but it does suggest, as other examples from rabbinic legal discussions of the period, that also in Ashkenaz, Jewish–Christian relations could not always be as closely monitored as both the Jewish and the Christian authorities would have wanted, and that individuals did at times defy the authority of their religious leaders.

Interaction with Christianity even informed the development of religious ritual in medieval Ashkenaz. As they incorporated cultural practices and values from surrounding Christian society, Ashkenazi Jews transformed those practices and values and made them their own, providing a good example of the nature of interreligious exchange in the Middle Ages that always involved elements of both accommodation and resistance. Thus, the Jewish rite of circumcision, the ritual by which baby boys are initiated as members of the Jewish community, underwent changes in the medieval period that, in some cases, seem modeled on the Christian rite of baptism. During the age of Charlemagne, the institution of godparents—adults not related to the infant who participated in the baptism ceremony along with the biological father—was introduced from the Byzantine East into the Catholic West. It is probably not a coincidence that a similar honorific role developed in the medieval Ashkenazic circumcision rite: the *ba'al ha-brit* or *sandek* is an adult male (women could play a similar role as well) who passes the child to the father and holds the baby during the circumcision.

Another ritual of childhood, one used to introduce young boys to Torah study, may have been influenced by Christianity as well. As part of the ceremony, the young boy would be given cakes baked with honey and inscribed with verses from the Bible, thus symbolically enacting a passage found in Ezekiel 3:3: "I ate it, and it tasted as sweet as honey to me." Historian Ivan Marcus has suggested that this practice of eating the sweet cakes with verses from Scripture on them may have been "a Jewish transformation of the central liturgical mystery of the church, the Eucharist," when Christians partake of the host as a symbol of Christ. Thus, Jews were influenced by the rituals and religious ideas of their Christian neighbors. Their adapting them to Judaism, however, was not a process of imitation or cultural assimilation but involved a process that transformed the meaning of the rituals and symbols they adopted and made them their own.

For Further Reading

For recent overviews of Jewish history under medieval Christendom, see Kenneth Stow, *Alienated Minority: The Jews of Medieval Latin Europe* (Cambridge, MA: Harvard University Press, 1991); Robert Chazan, *The Jews of Medieval Western Christendom* (Cambridge, England: Cambridge University Press, 2006); and Robert Chazan, *Reassessing Jewish Life in Medieval Europe* (New York: Cambridge University Press, 2010).

For the history of Jews in particular regions, see Yitzhak Baer, *A History of the Jews of Christian Spain*, 2 vols., trans. L. Scheffman (Philadelphia: Jewish Publication Society of America, 1961–1966); Jane Gerber, *The Jews of Spain* (New York: Free Press, 1992); Jonathan Ray, *The Sephardic Frontier: The Reconquista and the Jewish Community in Medieval Iberia* (Ithaca, NY: Cornell University Press, 2006); Jonathan Ray, *Jewish Life in Medieval Spain* (Philadelphia: Penn University Press, 2023); Cecil Roth, *The History of the Jews of Italy* (Philadelphia, PA: Jewish Publication Society of America, 1946); Ariel Toaff, *Love, Work, and Death: Jewish Life in Medieval Umbria* (London: Littman Library of Jewish Civilization, 1998); David Malkiel, *Reconstructing Ashkenaz: The Human Face of Franco-German Jewry, 1000–1250* (Stanford, CA: Stanford University Press, 2009); and Joshua Holo, *Byzantine Jewry in the Mediterranean Economy* (Cambridge: Cambridge University Press, 2009). On the Crusades and martyrdom, see Robert Chazan, *European Jewry and the First Crusade* (Berkeley: University of California Press, 1989).

On Jewish–Christian relations, see Joshua Trachtenberg, *The Devil and the Jews: The Medieval Conception of the Jew and Its Relation to Modern Anti-Semitism* (Philadelphia: Jewish Publication Society of America, 1943); Solomon Grayzel, *The Church and the Jews in the XIIIth Century* (New York: Hermon Press, 1966); David Berger, *The Jewish-Christian Debate in the High Middle Ages* (Philadelphia: Jewish Publication Society of America, 1979); Jeremy Cohen, *The Friars and the Jews* (Ithaca, NY: Cornell University Press, 1982); Robert Chazan, *Daggers of Faith: Thirteenth-Century Christian Missionizing and Jewish Response* (Berkeley: University of California Press, 1989); Israel Yuval, *Two Nations in Your Womb: Perceptions of Jews and Christians in Late Antiquity and the Middle Ages* (Berkeley: University of California Press, 2006); Jonathan Elukin, *Living Together, Living Apart: Rethinking Jewish-Christian Relations in the Middle Ages* (Princeton, NJ: Princeton University Press, 2013); David Nirenberg, *Communities of Violence: Persecution of Minorities in the Middle Ages* (Princeton, NJ: Princeton University Press, 1996); and David Nirenberg, *Neighboring Faiths* (Chicago: University of Chicago Press, 2014).

On Jewish communal life, see Louis Finkelstein, ed., *Jewish Self-Government in the Middle Ages*, reprint (Westport, CT: Greenwood Press, 1972). For Jews and the economy, see Joseph Shatzmiller, *Shylock Reconsidered: Jews, Money-Lending and Medieval Society* (Berkeley: University of California Press, 1990). On medieval Jewish families, see Elisheva Baumgarten, *Mothers and Children: Jewish Family Life in Medieval Europe* (Princeton, NJ: Princeton University Press, 2004); Elisheva Baumgarten, *Practicing Piety in Medieval Ashkenaz* (Philadelphia: Penn University Press, 2014). On medieval Jewish ritual and Christianity's influence on it, see Ivan Marcus, *Rituals of Childhood: Jewish Acculturation in Medieval Europe* (New Haven, CT: Yale University Press, 1996). On medieval rabbinic culture, see Talya Fishman, *Becoming the People of the Talmud* (Philadelphia: University of Pennsylvania Press, 2011). On medieval Jewish literature, see Susan Einbinder, *Beautiful Death: Jewish Poetry and Martyrdom in Medieval France* (Princeton, NJ: Princeton University Press, 2002). On the Hasidei Ashkenaz, see Ivan Marcus, *Piety and Society: The Jewish Pietists of Medieval Germany* (Leiden, The Netherlands: E. J. Brill, 1981). For major studies of Jewish mysticism by Gershom Scholem, see his *Major Trends in Jewish Mysticism* (New York: Schocken Books, 1941), *On the Kabbalah and Its Symbolism* (New York: Schocken Books, 1965), and *Origins of the Kabbalah*, trans. A. Arkush (Philadelphia, PA: Jewish Publication Society of America, 1987); Moshe Idel, *Kabbalah: New Perspectives* (New Haven, CT: Yale University Press, 1988).

For an online collection of medieval Jewish sources in translation, see www.fordham.edu/jewish/jewishsbook.asp.

CHAPTER 8

A JEWISH RENAISSANCE

THE EXPULSION OF the Jews from Spain in 1492 marked in many ways the end of one period in Jewish history and the beginning of another. As we have noted, the expulsion from Spain was the culmination of a long process of a Jewish exodus from western Europe and the decline of Jewish communities that had once defined medieval Jewish culture. England had expelled its Jews as early as 1290; a series of expulsion orders, especially in 1306 and 1394, evicted the Jews from most parts of France. The German lands of central Europe lacked a strong central authority, which is perhaps one reason that a wholesale expulsion of the Jews from medieval Germany never occurred, yet numerous German regions and cities likewise expelled their Jews in the course of the fifteenth century, and a final wave of expulsions in the wake of the Protestant Reformation and the Catholic Counter-Reformation ended Jewish life in many of the remaining areas of western and central Europe. By 1570, the only free imperial city in Germany where Jews still lived was Frankfurt, and the remnants of a Jewish presence in western Europe were restricted to a few ecclesiastical states (administered by the Church) in German-speaking lands and some principalities in northern Italy.

But these expulsions also marked a new stage in Jewish history characterized by the emergence of two major Jewish communities in the east: in the Ottoman Empire, where many of the Spanish Jews sought refuge, and in Poland-Lithuania, which emerged as the new center of Ashkenazi Jewry. The Polish-Lithuanian and the Ottoman Jews left their imprint on the Jewish culture of the early modern period. These demographic and cultural centers of early modern Jewish life showed a remarkable resilience in the reconstruction of Jewish culture in the generations after the forced mass migrations from the west, but it was also a culture profoundly transformed by its relocation in new eastern European and Middle Eastern settings. We see in the rise of these new cultural centers the beginning of modern Jewish history, and so before we turn to their specific histories, we begin this chapter with a broad consideration of the changes that helped transform medieval Jewish culture into early modern Jewish culture.

What was the *early modern* period in Jewish history? Does this term, typically used by historians of Europe to describe the era from the fifteenth to the eighteenth centuries, make any sense when applied to the Jewish historical experience? The *modern* age in Jewish history was a time of revolutionary changes, by the end of which Jewish life, religion, and society looked completely different from what they had been before the onslaught of modernity. By contrast, the *early modern* age was one of transition or gradual change. Profound changes occurred throughout the Jewish world in the two centuries between the Spanish expulsion and the eighteenth century, but Jewish identity and culture remained

DOI: 10.4324/9781003611592-9

largely intact. The first fissures appeared in the culture's foundations, but the overall structure of Jewish tradition remained strong.

The main factors in the transformation of Jewish culture in the early modern period were several and came from both outside and inside the Jewish world:

1. The forced migrations themselves played an important role, as they led not simply to the relocation of individuals and entire communities but also to encounters between different Jewish traditions. The Spanish Jews "exported" their own cultural heritage to those places where they settled after the expulsion, whether in North Africa or the Ottoman lands in Turkey and the Balkans. After a few generations, they had imposed their cultural hegemony over the local Jewish communities, the Sephardi tradition deeply transforming and, in many cases, replacing the traditions of, for example, the Greek-speaking Romaniot Jews of the formerly Byzantine lands.
   Both the Spanish Jews and the Ashkenazi Jews of France and Germany also took their languages with them, so that Yiddish became the predominant language of the Jews in eastern Europe, and Ladino (Judeo-Spanish) the dominant language of the Jews in the Ottoman Balkans and Turkey. What was striking in both cases was that now, perhaps for the first time ever, Jews spoke a language that was completely different from the language of their non-Jewish environment. Unlike the situation in medieval Spain and Ashkenaz, the Arabic-speaking lands, or Persia, Jews did not speak their own variety of the local language but rather a separate, "Jewish" language. (This is the significance of Yiddish, which means "Jewish.")
2. Different was the fate of those who remained on the Iberian Peninsula: In Spain, many Jews converted to Catholicism in the wake of the violence of 1391 and through the year of expulsion in 1492. That year, many more embraced Christianity, whereas others made their way across the border to Portugal. There, they faced another forced mass conversion a mere five years later, in 1497. This mass conversion of Jews created an entire class of people who were nominally Catholics but many of whom retained a sense of Jewishness. Thus, between 1391 and 1497, a significant portion of Iberian Jewry came to live under the guise of Christianity. Many, perhaps most, of these so-called *conversos* (sometimes also referred to as *marranos*, a derogatory term literally meaning "swine") ultimately assimilated into Christian society, but others continued to see themselves as Jews (in an ethnic, if not a religious, sense), maintained some Jewish practices, and created an entire subculture of their own. They generated a constant trickle of emigrants who left the Iberian Peninsula in subsequent centuries, settling in various parts of Europe and the Mediterranean, and many returned openly to Judaism when they had an opportunity to do so. For the conversos, assimilation into the surrounding Christian society was a lived reality. They were the first collective of Jews (or former Jews), for whom "Jewishness" held an ethnic rather than a religious meaning, and for whom the affirmation of their Jewishness in a religious sense became a matter of choice rather than an accident of birth. This presented an entirely new challenge and anticipated the modern Jewish predicament when Jewish identity could no longer simply be taken for granted.
3. Another factor that transformed Jewish culture profoundly, just as it did with European culture in general, was the invention of printing. Print, one of the most important technological innovations of human history, arguably marked the end of the Middle Ages and the beginning of a new era as much as anything else. The new possibilities for communicating knowledge to a growing number of people had a transformative impact on the development of Jewish culture in the early modern age. Different Jewish traditions that had maintained only sporadic contact now began an exchange of knowledge on an unprecedented scale. Ashkenazi Jewry, for example, was exposed more

systematically than ever before to the traditions of the Sephardi "golden age" in medieval Spain, as well as the new cultural trends to be found among the Spanish Jews living in Ottoman lands after 1492. Printed books not only enabled the spreading of ideas and information across cultural divides but also made information far more accessible to a much broader audience (*see the box* "The Hebrew Printing Revolution").

4. The early modern age saw the spread of new ideas generated within Jewish culture, most importantly the unprecedented dissemination of the esoteric teachings of medieval and early modern Jewish mysticism (Kabbalah), knowledge of which had previously been restricted to a small elite in the Middle Ages. Early modern European Jews, like their Christian neighbors, also began to grapple with the impact of the scientific revolution. Medieval Judaism, to be sure, had not necessarily been hostile to "secular" knowledge. Some, like Maimonides, the great philosopher and scholar of medieval Sephardi Jewry, had tried to reconcile Jewish and "secular" learning. Others had been indifferent to what they perceived as "foreign" wisdom, deeming it to be of little consequence for Jews. In the early modern age, many Jews encountered a whole universe of scientific knowledge that challenged traditional notions, for example, the discovery that Earth was not the center of the cosmos but rotated around the sun and not the other way around, as had been the traditional understanding according to the Bible, classical Greek philosophy, Talmudic Judaism, and medieval Christianity. The fight between the traditional and the Copernican worldviews was the early modern equivalent of the contemporary fight over evolution. Early modern Jews, like non-Jews, had to come to terms with a new scientific understanding of the world that was no longer easily reconcilable with their religious traditions.

   An important role in the dissemination of scientific knowledge and its transformative impact on early modern Jewish culture was played by doctors. Beginning in the sixteenth century, Jews from Poland, Tunisia, Germany, and Turkey came to Italy to study medicine at the universities at Pavia and Padua, an entire cadre of Jews to be exposed to science in a secular setting, and returning to their communities after their medical studies with a very different outlook and understanding of Jewish tradition and its relation to secular, scientific knowledge.

5. Political changes in Christian Europe further transformed Jewish life and reversed the trend of expulsion from the west by the end of this period. Partly as a result of the stalemate in the religious war ravaging Europe in the wake of the Protestant Reformation and the Catholic Counter-Reformation, Christian rulers began to give precedence to the political and economic interests of the state over religious considerations. The new economic politics of mercantilism, each ruler trying to attract as much capital and trade as possible to his own territory, reshaped attitudes toward Jews: The Christian state began to consider the potential economic use of Jews as outweighing their religious status. The expanding financial needs of European states during and after the Thirty Years' War led many Christian sovereigns to regard Jews not as a religious threat but, rather, as an economic asset. Whether focused on merchants attracted to the port cities of the Atlantic Seaboard and Italy or "court Jews" serving as financiers to Christian monarchs, the perception that Jews would be useful to the economic interests of the state transformed the political conditions of Jewish life significantly.

In this chapter, as well as Chapter 9, we explore these issues in greater detail. We ask how the exodus of the Jews from the west and the establishment of new centers of Jewish life in the east changed the contours of Jewish culture in the early modern age. And we explore how early modern Jewish culture changed in this age of discovery, when some—like the conversos or the medical students at Italian universities—found themselves immersed in a non-Jewish environment, when scientific developments undermined traditional certainties, and when the printing revolution reshaped the patterns of communication and the transmission of knowledge in the Jewish Diaspora.

Until around 1700, Sephardi and Middle Eastern Jews still represented the majority of the world Jewish population. Throughout the period, however, the demographic growth of the Ashkenazi Jews in eastern Europe was impressive, and even the widespread massacres afflicting eastern European Jewry in the mid-seventeenth century turned out to be a temporary setback. Estimates for Polish-Lithuanian Jewry suggest a population growing from around 30,000 in 1500 to 100,000 (perhaps even more) in 1575. Around the beginning of the eighteenth century, Ashkenazi Jews represented, for the first time in Jewish history, a majority of the Jewish population, and Polish-Lithuanian Jewry became the largest Jewish community in the world (*see the box* "Sephardim and Ashkenazim").

The largest urban Jewish communities in the early modern period were in the cities of the Ottoman Empire, with Salonika (in modern-day Greece) and the imperial capital, Istanbul (Constantinople), both having about 20,000 Jews in the mid-sixteenth century. Most Jewish communities in Europe, including those in eastern Europe, were much smaller, with only a few communities—Prague, Vienna, Frankfurt, Cracow, Lviv, Lublin, Mantua, Rome, Venice, and Amsterdam—exceeding 2,000 souls before 1650. Throughout the German lands, where most cities had expelled their Jews by the sixteenth century, the remaining Jews lived dispersed, often in very small rural communities. In the decades after 1650, communities living in important port cities in western Europe and in Italy expanded significantly: The Jewish population of Amsterdam grew from just over 3,000 in 1650 to over 6,000 by 1700, while in the Italian port city of Livorno, it rose from about 1,250 in 1645 to 2,500 in the late seventeenth century. The largest communities in central Europe were Frankfurt, Prague, and toward the end of the period, the sister communities of Hamburg-Altona-Wandsbek in northern Germany. In eastern Europe, the vast expansion of the Jewish population occurred primarily in a large number of small and midsize communities, especially in the eastern part of the Polish-Lithuanian lands.

Iberian Jewry Between Inquisition and Expulsion

The summer of 1391 was a fateful moment for Spanish Jewry. From early June through August, one Jewish community (known as aljama) after another was attacked by local Christians. By the end of the widespread violence, many synagogues throughout Spain had been made into churches (e.g., the two synagogues that can still be seen in the city of Toledo), thousands of Jews had either undergone conversion to escape popular wrath or fled, and many had been killed. The events of 1391 and the continuing pressure in subsequent years led to a mass conversion of Jews to Christianity, creating an entirely new substratum in medieval Spanish society. Next to the established Christian and Jewish communities (the latter showed a remarkable resilience and regeneration in the remaining century before the expulsion), there was now a third group: the conversos, also often referred to at that time as "new Christians." In some places—for example, in the cities of Barcelona and Valencia—no Jewish community remained after 1391, and all the former Jews now lived as conversos.

The attacks on the Jews of Spain had not been the result of an orchestrated push toward mass conversion. In many places, the Crown and its representatives tried, as they had before, to protect the Jews against violence, but incited by lower-ranking clergy and popular preachers, such as Ferrant Martínez in Seville, the mob invaded Jewish quarters and made a point of attacking the Jews precisely because they were seen as protégés of the

Crown. The new situation would have seemed like a dream fulfilled for Christians: At last, after years of missionary fervor, a large portion of the Jews had undergone baptism, albeit under pressure.

Yet in reality, the mass conversion soon created a whole set of new problems. On the one hand, the new Christians (recent Jewish converts) could not all necessarily be expected to fully embrace their new faith. It is true that some were sincere in their embrace of Catholicism. A former rabbi of Burgos, Solomon ha-Levi (1351–1435), converted to Christianity in 1391, went to Paris to study theology, and years later, returned to Burgos as the bishop of the city. Under his Christian name, Pablo de Santa María, he penned a historical work, *The Seven Ages of the World*, for the education of the Castilian king John II. On the other hand, many of the Jewish converts never fully integrated into

THE HEBREW PRINTING REVOLUTION

The invention of printing in Europe around the middle of the fifteenth century was perhaps the single most important technological innovation of the early modern period. The cultural consequences of print were numerous and revolutionized the ways in which information was exchanged. The innovation in Europe (printing in China preceded the invention of printing in the West by several centuries) is generally associated with the printing workshop of Johannes Gutenberg of Mainz in southwestern Germany. Gutenberg began to print in the 1440s and produced his famous two-volume printed Bible in 1455. As early as 1444, we already hear of a business contract between a Christian goldsmith and a Jew in Avignon, in southern France, who wanted to engage in the "art of artificial writing" (i.e., print). Nothing came of this first endeavor (only 48 movable Hebrew letters had been made), but it is clear that Jews experimented with this new technology from the very beginning and were eager to use it for Hebrew printing.

The first printed Hebrew works that we know of were produced several decades later in Italy: The medieval code of Jewish law known as *Araba'a Turim* was printed in 1475 near Padua, whereas the eleventh-century biblical commentary by Rashi came off the press in Reggio di Calabria in southern Italy. Spanish Jews developed Hebrew printing in the 1480s and then introduced the new technology to the Ottoman Empire after the expulsion from Spain (a Hebrew printing press was opened by Sephardi exiles as early as 1493 in Constantinople). For centuries, Italy—particularly the city of Venice—was the center of Hebrew printing, whereas printing presses proliferated in other parts of the Jewish world—the Ottoman Empire, Cracow and Lublin in Poland, and Prague—in the sixteenth century. In the seventeenth century, successful Hebrew printing houses operated in various German and Polish cities as well, whereas Amsterdam, Holland, became a new center of Hebrew print in the seventeenth century, and Livorno, Italy, in the eighteenth century.

Among the most well-known Jewish printers was the Soncino family, which began its business in 1484 in the Italian city of Soncino (from which the family name is derived). They later expanded and opened printing houses in Salonika and Constantinople in the Ottoman Empire (in the 1520s and 1530s, respectively). It was, however, a Christian printer, Daniel Bomberg, who was responsible for some of the most influential Hebrew printing ventures of the period: Working in Venice, in 1517–1518 he produced a "rabbinic Bible" (i.e., the Hebrew text of the Bible, together with its classical Aramaic translation, and the most influential commentaries printed on the margins of the page). In the early 1520s, he printed a complete edition of the Talmud. The pagination of every Talmud printed even today still follows the pagination of Bomberg's edition, making it possible to navigate this vast compendium and give precise citations.

Bomberg's editions of the Bible and the Talmud are only one example of the profound impact of their new community, never truly embraced the new faith, and continued to think of themselves as Jews. In fact, the conversions of 1391 and the following years created an odd situation that was unprecedented in the medieval period: Religious differences now divided families, one spouse having converted to Christianity, the other having remained a Jew. Siblings and cousins were divided by religion as well. Further complicating matters, most conversos continued to live in close proximity to their former coreligionists. They continued to inhabit the same houses, to do business with each other, and to socialize with Jewish friends and family members. Those conversos who wished to continue to live secretly as Jews could do so, because their Jewish neighbors provided them with books, kosher food, and information about holidays and religious practice.

printing on the development of Jewish culture in the early modern period. First of all, printing greatly expanded the readership of books. The printed book was still an expensive commodity in the sixteenth and seventeenth centuries, to be sure, but it was infinitely more accessible than the hand-copied manuscripts of the Middle Ages. More people had access to more books, and it was precisely this "democratizing" effect that made printing perhaps the most important technological innovation of the period. Literacy rose significantly as printed books became more widely accessible, and knowledge of Jewish texts—from the Bible to the Talmud to the prayer book—became much broader.

Books were not only more widely available but also studied differently. Before print, few people had direct access to written texts, so knowledge was primarily transmitted orally in a teacher–student relationship. Important texts were memorized, whereas the distinction between the "original" text and its interpretations or commentaries was blurred when they were studied orally, rather than from a written page. Printing changed all this as it established an authoritative and widely available text, and it standardized Jewish practices more than before. The unifying impact of print is particularly noticeable in the synagogue liturgy. Differences remained between various traditions, to be sure, but a trend evolved toward unifying practices in both the Sephardi and the Ashkenazi worlds.

Moreover, printing exposed more readers to more ideas by making the exchange of knowledge and information possible across large geographic distances and in less time. Exchange of information no longer had to rely on the personal contact made through travel or letters; rather, wide audiences could be reached in many different places. In eastern Europe, for example, printing exposed Ashkenazim to the cultural production of the Sephardi world, and it played a major role in the broad reception of new works, such as the *Shulhan Arukh* (see Chapter 9).

However, printing posed a new challenge to the authority of the rabbis. Before, the individual Jew would consult his or her rabbi with all questions relating to correct Jewish practice. Teaching and learning constituted a personal interaction between the rabbi and his students. Print made books more easily available, and individuals could begin to learn by themselves without the guidance of the rabbis. It is true that study in pairs or groups continued to be a typical feature of Jewish learning, but individual reading, for study or for pleasure, also became more feasible.

None of this should be exaggerated. The impact of print did not change Jewish life overnight. Books continued to be a relatively rare commodity, and traditional practices of reading and learning were not dismantled at once. But printing did initiate a process of democratizing Jewish culture, the consequences of which could still be felt centuries later.

SEPHARDIM AND ASHKENAZIM

Sephardi

The term *Sephardi* derives from *Sefarad*, a word that appears in the biblical book of Obadiah and has been used in reference to Spain since the Middle Ages. In the strict sense of the word, *Sephardim* are the Jews of the Iberian Peninsula (Spain and Portugal) and their descendants. After the expulsion of the Jews from Spain in 1492 and the forced conversions in Portugal in 1497, Sephardi Jews established communities in the Ottoman Empire (which they eventually came to dominate culturally and linguistically), in North Africa, in various cities of Italy and northwestern Europe, and in the Americas of the colonial period. The Sephardim of northern Morocco continued to use their Spanish Jewish dialect, known as *Haketia*; the Ottoman Jews spoke Judeo-Spanish, known as *Ladino*; and the Sephardi Jews of Europe and the Atlantic Seaboard continued to use Portuguese and Spanish throughout the early modern period.

Ashkenazi

The name *Ashkenaz* appears in three biblical books (Genesis, Chronicles, and Jeremiah). In the Middle Ages, the term was applied to the Rhineland, and by the early modern period, "Ashkenaz" included the Yiddish-speaking communities of western, central, and eastern Europe. If France and Germany were the center of the medieval Ashkenazi world, its demographic and cultural epicenter had moved to Poland and Lithuania by the sixteenth and seventeenth centuries.

The terms *Sephardi* and *Ashkenazi* are also applied to describe the different liturgic and religious-legal traditions that developed in Spain and the Middle East on the one hand and in northern and eastern Europe on the other. In this broader sense, *Sephardi* would include Jewish communities from the Middle East (e.g., Syria, Egypt, or Iraq) who were not of Spanish or Portuguese origin but shared liturgic and religious-legal traditions with the Iberian Jews. In terms of their liturgical practice, it has been suggested that the Sephardi tradition is a continuation of the practice of Babylonia, whereas the Ashkenazi tradition was transmitted from Palestine through Italy to northern Europe. In reality, however, the division is not as clear-cut as this model suggests. In today's usage, the term *Sephardi* is often misleadingly employed to refer to all non-Ashkenazi or all non-European Jews.

Several other groups within early modern Jewry have a historical experience and religious-cultural heritage that set them apart from both the Sephardi and Ashkenazi Jews. These include, in Europe, the Italian Jews, who continued to follow their own Italian Jewish traditions and who lived side by side with the Sephardi and Ashkenazi immigrants who made Italy their home. Outside Europe, these include, for example, the Jews of Yemen, India, Iran, and Muslim Central Asia, as well as the Jews of Ethiopia.

At the same time, the "old" Christians (people with no Jewish ancestry) now faced formidable competition in practically all areas of life from "new" Christians. Jews could be, and were, restricted to certain economic and social roles. As Christians, however, the conversos were able to rise high in Christian society and compete with Christians for positions in the state and, as in the case of Solomon ha-Levi, even in the Church. Together with the (probably not unjustified) suspicion of the sincerity of their religious convictions, this created new tensions, which erupted in 1449 in a violent attack that was directed not at the Jews but at the conversos of Toledo.

In response to these events, and given the fact that many conversos continued to occupy commercial and professional roles that were identical to those they played when they were Jews, the municipal council of the city—then the seat of the Castilian king—adopted new legal statutes that introduced a novel distinction between "old" and "new" Christians:

> We declare the so-called conversos, offspring of perverse Jewish ancestors, must be held by law to be infamous and ignominious, unfit, and unworthy to hold any public office or any benefice within the city of Toledo . . . or to have any authority over the true Christians of the Holy Catholic Church.

Known as the statutes of "purity of blood," or *limpieza de sangre*, this legislation introduced an entirely new concept that ran counter to established Church law and, more generally, against medieval sensibilities. Personal status had been defined by one's religion, and just a century earlier, the major law code of Castile, *Las Siete Partidas*, had explicitly prohibited reminding a Jew or Muslim converting to Christianity of his or her pre-conversion background. *Limpieza de sangre* racialized Jewish identity and disassociated it from religion and theology. Initial opposition by the Crown and the Church notwithstanding, and though the particular law of 1449 was later revoked, the standard of "purity of blood" was gradually adopted throughout Spain and Portugal over the course of the sixteenth century.

The violence of 1391 was followed by an unabated conversionist movement, led largely by Dominican and Franciscan friars. One aspect of the process was the staging of disputations between Christians and Jews. One such public "debate," the most important of its kind during the medieval period, took place in Tortosa from February 1413 to November 1414. The Christian side, led by a converso to add insult to injury, set out to repudiate Judaism by focusing on the question of whether the Messiah had come yet. By the disputation's end, the Christian side predictably declared victory over the Jewish representatives, with contemporary reports stating that hundreds of Jews ended up converting to Catholicism. Violence, forced conversions, and endless persuasion had devastating consequences for Spanish Jewry.

Group identity is often expressed by exclusion: We know who we are and what we have in common as a group primarily by defining who we are *not*, defining ourselves against the foil of the "other." It might be difficult at any given time to clearly pinpoint what it means to be Jewish, for example. The easiest way of defining Jewishness is to identify what it is not. If a basic distinction in medieval Spanish society between "us" and "them" was a religious one, setting Jews apart from Christians and Muslims, the mass conversions of the fifteenth century eroded this certainty. The conversos now represented a group that was somewhere in between, whose status was ambiguous: Christian in name yet still bearing the stigma of Jewishness.

In 1478, the Catholic monarchs of the recently united Spanish kingdoms of Castile and Aragon decided that it was time to tackle the problem of converso religious ambiguity. They requested authorization from the pope to establish a national Inquisition, which began its work in 1481. The Inquisition was not concerned with Jews, as is often believed, but with Christians—including, of course, the "new" Christians. Its task was to root out "heresy," beliefs and practices that were seen as contrary to Church doctrine, and the most important "heresy" of them all was the secret practice of Judaism—Judaizing, as it was known.

Inquisition tribunals were set up throughout the Iberian Peninsula, and inquisitors established traveling courts, visiting places that lacked a permanent court. When the Inquisition came to town, the process began with a "grace period" of 30 or 40 days, during which people could come forward, confess their "crime," and be reconciled with the Church. This was still a public and humiliating process, and confession did not necessarily spare one of punishment, except for eluding the death penalty. The inquisitors would also provide the public with a list of practices that were supposed to be indicators of secret Judaizing—for example, people refraining from eating certain foods, avoiding labor on Saturdays, doing extra shopping before Jewish holidays, slaughtering animals in a certain way, or observing rites of mourning that were seen as Jewish.

Once the Inquisition process began, the accused was presumed guilty, unless she or he could prove otherwise. The Inquisition tried to get a full, voluntary confession because, although it had recourse to torture, confessions given under torture were of little value and were notoriously unreliable. The records kept by the Inquisition meticulously documented the evidence provided by witnesses and the declarations by the defendants. Today, they represent a fascinating and rich source for historians trying to reconstruct the lives of conversos and other victims of the Inquisition, providing many surprising insights into daily life. One historian has even published a book of recipes based on Inquisition records, for culinary traditions were often identified as signs of Judaizing. Refraining from pork might be an obvious example, but a whole converso cuisine developed and was documented by the inquisitors themselves.

In a testimony before the Inquisition court of Ciudad Real, dated December 30, 1483, a certain María Días declared that she had observed the following:

> In the house of the said Pedro de Villarruia they were keeping the Sabbath and they dressed in clean and festive cloths of linen [in honor of the Sabbath]. And she knows and saw that they were praying on those Saturdays from a book. . . . And they prepared food on Friday for Saturday, and they prepared the entire house on that day, cleaned and washed, and lit new candles. . . . They kept the holidays of the Jews and were fasting on their fast days until the night. And one never saw them eating rabbit or hare or eagle [which are unkosher animals].

The defendants could prove their innocence only by proving that the witnesses were unreliable and motivated by personal revenge and enmity. The problem for the accused, however, was that the identity of the witnesses was not disclosed. If convicted of the "crime" of Judaizing heresy, the "guilty" party was handed over to the secular authorities, their property was confiscated, and they were burned at the stake (Figure 8.1). In fact, the public spectacle, at once restoring the injured honor of the Church and staging a powerful warning for all other Judaizers, was so important that even if someone was found guilty of heresy after he or she had died, the Inquisition would have their body exhumed and burned in public, and their property confiscated. With all that, it is important to remember that Judeo-Conversos were only *one* of the groups that were singled out by the Inquisition, which continued to operate for several centuries, on the Iberian Peninsula officially until the 1830s, and in the Spanish colonies in the Americas until the 1820s. The overall number of individuals killed was smaller than the grim popular image of the Inquisition might suggest: According to some modern historians, the Inquisition carried out some 44,000 trials between 1540 and 1700, but less than 2 percent of the individuals put on trial were burned at the stake. The fate of Judeo-Conversos seems to have been disproportionately dire, however. Another modern study suggests that, under the jurisdiction of the Inquisition of Aragon, 25,890 cases were tried. Of those, 942 involved crypto-Jews—and of that number, 520 (2 percent of the total, but 55 percent of those accused of "Judaizing") were executed.

When, in January 1492, Catholic Spain conquered the last Muslim stronghold in southern Spain, the emirate of Granada, a new political

Figure 8.1 Portuguese Inquisition at work: the burning of heretics after an auto-da-fé in Lisbon, as depicted in an eighteenth-century print by Bernard Picart.

situation had been created on the peninsula. Most of what is modern-day Spain was now under one unified rule, that of the "Catholic monarchs" Ferdinand and Isabella. In March of that year, the monarchs signed an edict that ended the history of a community that had lived in Spain since Roman times, and it was not until the late nineteenth century that individual Jews began to "return" to Spain, and not until 1954 that another synagogue would be built there. The edict declared, "[W]e have been informed that in our kingdoms there were some bad Christians who judaized and apostasized against our holy Catholic faith, mainly because of the connection between the Jews and the Christians." The edict then enumerated steps that had been undertaken to solve the "problem," from the segregation of Jews and Christians enforced in 1480 to the establishment of the Inquisition a year later and on to the partial expulsion of Jews from cities in southern Spain in 1483. All this, they concluded, "proved to be insufficient as a complete remedy," and "in order that there should be no further damage to [their] holy faith, . . . [they] have decided to remove the main cause for this through the expulsion of the Jews from [their] kingdoms."

A moving force behind the edict of expulsion was, no doubt, the Inquisition and its chief inquisitor, Tomás de Torquemada. Historians still debate the real purpose of this edict: Did the Catholic monarchs use the religious reasoning as a pretext, did they even mean what they said when ordering all Jews to leave, or did they secretly hope that this would be the last incentive for the remaining Jews to also convert to Christianity, thus removing Judaism as a religion without necessarily removing the Jews? It has been shown that little was gained economically by expelling the Jews, while little direct damage resulted to the Spanish economy from the expulsion. The real motivations thus seem to have been religious and political. Whatever the purpose, probably half the Spanish Jews decided to convert and stay; the other half left, most of them for neighboring Portugal; while smaller numbers went to North Africa, Italy, and Ottoman Turkey. Historians disagree about the actual numbers of Jews who left Spain at that time, but probably around 100,000 Jews went into exile.

Portugal provided a logical refuge, an exile that could be reached by land, since traveling overseas was impractical for many. However, it was only a few years later that the Jews of Portugal faced their own demise. The marriage contract between the Portuguese king Manuel and Isabella, daughter of the Spanish monarchs Ferdinand and Isabella, stipulated that Portugal would have to follow the Spanish example and likewise expel its Jews. On December 5, 1496, the Portuguese king gave all the Jews, many of them Spanish refugees from 1492, ten months to abandon his kingdom. In reality, however, the Portuguese Crown preferred conversion. In early 1497, Jewish children up to 14 years of age were seized by the state and baptized. Many were sent to the island of São Tomé, a Portuguese possession off the coast of Angola—a part of Portugal's colonial settlement policy that ended, according to contemporary Jewish chronicles, in the death of the children involved. Then, in March 1497, the order of expulsion was essentially transformed into a forced mass conversion of *all* Jews, and instead of being expelled, the new conversos were now prohibited from leaving Portugal at all. The Portuguese knew that the transformation of an entire community of former Jews into Christians would take time, and it was not until 1536 that the Inquisition began to operate in Portugal. Certainly, many conversos ultimately assimilated into Christian society and forgot about their Jewish origins. However, some—especially in Portugal, where the entire community had been forced into conversion—maintained a distinct crypto-Jewish converso culture that survived for many generations.

The Inquisition continued its obsessive attempt to root out all Judaizing, and its activities were soon expanded to the newly gained Spanish and Portuguese possessions overseas. In 1569, the Spanish Crown established the Inquisition in Lima (Peru) and Mexico City. These efforts notwithstanding, still several generations later, many conversos had not integrated into Christian society, were still rejecting the Christian faith, and continued to perceive themselves as Jews (as an ethnic group, if not religiously).

When the Portuguese first opened their borders to converso emigration in 1506, a constant trickle of conversos left the country. Many went to join communities established by the Spanish Jewish exiles of 1492—for example, in the Ottoman Empire—whereas others sought opportunities in northern Europe, establishing new communities in the early decades of the seventeenth century in places such as Amsterdam, Hamburg, and London (see Map 8.1).

The Sephardi Jews of the Ottoman Empire

The demise of Spanish Jewry coincided with the expansion of the greatest Islamic empire of the early modern period, the Ottoman Empire, in the

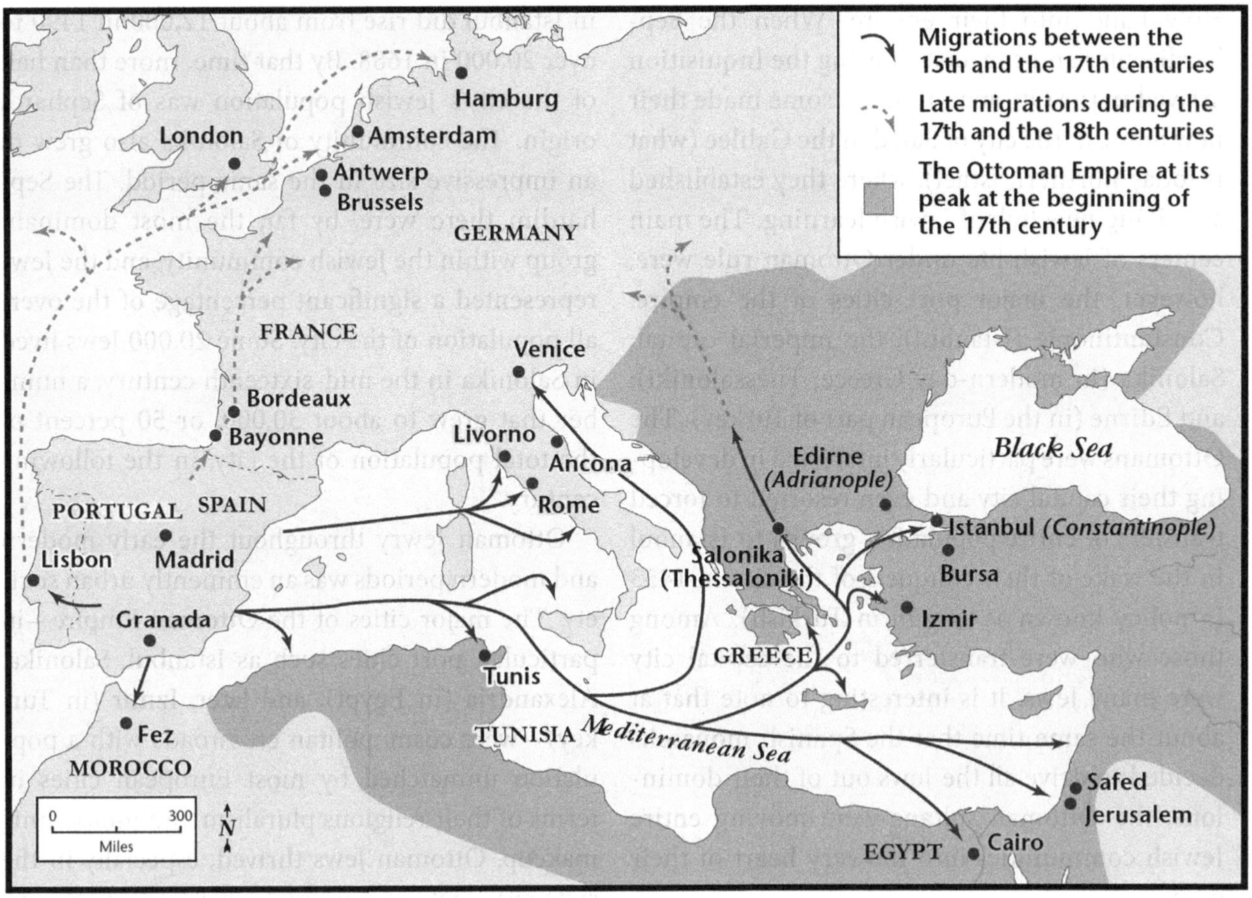

Map 8.1 Expulsion of the Jews from Spain, with major Sephardi communities in the Ottoman Empire.

Eastern Mediterranean. The origins of the Ottoman state go back to around 1300. Constantly expanding at the cost of other Muslim principalities in Anatolia and of the major Christian power of the east, the Byzantine Empire, the new Ottoman state finally conquered the city of Constantinople in 1453. Later known as Istanbul, Constantinople had once been the capital of Christianity. It then was converted into the capital of an Islamic empire that, at its peak, stretched from Algeria in the west to Iraq in the east, from Hungary in southeastern Europe to Yemen at the southern tip of the Arabian Peninsula. The Ottoman Empire survived until after World War I, though it began losing territory on its European front beginning in the late seventeenth to the early eighteenth century.

It was in this vast empire that many Spanish, or Sephardi, Jews found a new refuge. Some arrived in the major cities of the Ottoman Empire soon after the expulsion from Spain in 1492, whereas others immigrated in the following decades and were later joined by conversos escaping the Inquisition in Portugal and Spain. They established a new and thriving nucleus of Jewish life under the protection of the Ottoman sultans. Jewish chroniclers of that time went out of their way to praise the hospitality of their new home, and a popular (but historically inaccurate) myth developed that the Ottoman sultan Bayezid II had actually invited the Spanish Jews to settle in his empire.

By 1516–1517, the Ottomans had conquered Syria and Palestine and incorporated the Jewish

Holy Land into their empire. When the Sephardi exiles and conversos fleeing the Inquisition arrived in the Ottoman Empire, some made their new home in the city of Safed in the Galilee (what is today northern Israel), where they established a thriving new hub of Jewish learning. The main centers of Jewish life under Ottoman rule were, however, the major port cities of the empire: Constantinople (Istanbul), the imperial capital; Salonika (in modern-day Greece: Thessaloniki); and Edirne (in the European part of Turkey). The Ottomans were particularly interested in developing their capital city and even resorted to forced transfers of entire population groups to Istanbul in the wake of their conquest of the city in 1453 (a policy known as *sürgün* in Turkish). Among those who were transferred to the capital city were many Jews. It is interesting to note that at about the same time that the Spanish monarchs decided to drive all the Jews out of their dominions, the Ottoman sultans were moving entire Jewish communities into the very heart of their empire.

One of the most renowned rabbis of Ottoman Salonika was Moses Almosnino (d. c. 1580), a Sephardi Jew. In the 1560s, Almosnino was part of a Jewish mission from Salonika to the sultan in Istanbul to negotiate more favorable economic conditions for his community. During the lengthy visit to the imperial capital, Almosnino wrote a short history about the Ottoman sultans and a description of the city, all of it in the Judeo-Spanish language of the Sephardi Jews.

> The population in Constantinople [Istanbul] and its surrounding areas . . . grew ten times during the reign [of Sultan Suleyman the Magnificent, r. 1520–1566]. One can certainly call this city of Constantinople and its surrounding areas a kingdom and climate unto itself . . . for the immeasurable number of its people.

If the tenfold increase of the population was probably an exaggeration, the Jewish population in Istanbul did rise from about 12,000 in 1490 to over 20,000 in 1688. By that time, more than half of the city's Jewish population was of Sephardi origin. The community of Salonika also grew to an impressive size in the same period. The Sephardim there were, by far, the most dominant group within the Jewish community, and the Jews represented a significant percentage of the overall population of the city. Some 20,000 Jews lived in Salonika in the mid-sixteenth century, a number that grew to about 30,000, or 50 percent of the total population of the city, in the following century.

Ottoman Jewry throughout the early modern and modern periods was an eminently urban society. The major cities of the Ottoman Empire—in particular, port cities such as Istanbul, Salonika, Alexandria (in Egypt), and later, Izmir (in Turkey)—were cosmopolitan crossroads with a population unmatched by most European cities in terms of their religious pluralism and multiethnic makeup. Ottoman Jews thrived, especially in the sixteenth century. Jews and Christians were considered *dhimmis*, non-Muslims protected by the Islamic state who had to abide by certain restrictions and paid a special poll tax (*jizya*). In reality, some restrictions that Islamic law imposed on the non-Muslim population were ignored even in the capital city, Istanbul. For the most part, the Ottoman authorities were interested in securing the regular payment of taxes and in maintaining public order. The administration of daily life, economic activities, and the exercise of religious authority all were the prerogative of the Jewish and Christian communities, who could otherwise expect little interference in their affairs on the part of the state.

One can learn much about Jewish life under Ottoman rule from responsa written by the rabbis at that time. (*Responsa* are legal opinions written by rabbis to address questions submitted to them by individuals or by Jewish communities.) One such text, which says a lot about the economic situation of Ottoman Jewry, was sent by the Salonikan rabbi Samuel de Medina (1505–1589) to the Jews of Janina, a city in northern Greece. The question addressed to Rabbi de Medina was as follows:

> The Jews of Janina complain about visiting Jewish merchants who compete with the local shopkeepers. . . . Would it be permissible for the Jews of Janina to use their influence with the local government officials to forbid these non-resident merchants to sell their merchandise in the city?

Samuel de Medina's lengthy and carefully worded responsum started out by declaring:

> [T]he opinions expressed in the Talmud and by the legal scholars of former generations regarding such cases do not apply to our own time. . . . [Today,] we [Ottoman] Jews live under one sovereign who imposes no restrictions on travel or on commercial activities on any of his subjects. We see, for instance, that merchandise from Sofia [Bulgaria] is sold in Angora [Turkey]. . . . The same is the case regarding the sale of Turkish products in Egypt. . . . And considering the fact that Moslem and Christian merchants are permitted to sell their wares all over the Empire, why should Jews discriminate against Jewish merchants?

He therefore declared the exclusion of nonresident Jewish merchants from Janina illegal and added:

> This is all the more true in the case of the Ottoman Empire where no trade barriers whatsoever are put in the way of foreign merchants. Surely, the Jews of one city cannot legally keep out Jewish merchants of another city or of another kingdom.

Samuel de Medina's responsum is interesting from a variety of perspectives. To begin, it reflects the self-confidence of the Sephardi rabbinate just a few decades after the trauma of the expulsion from Spain. Boldly declaring that certain opinions expressed in the Talmud "do not apply in our own time," Samuel de Medina interprets Jewish law with an eye to the requirements and conditions of his age and feels at liberty to rule against opinions and precedents established by earlier generations of rabbis.

In addition, Rabbi de Medina identifies the Ottoman context as one of essentially unrestricted commercial freedom, as one large economic area under a single political administration without any kind of economic discrimination. If Jews were pushed into certain marginal sectors of the medieval and early modern European economies—for example, moneylending, banking, peddling, and petty trade—no such restrictions existed in the Ottoman Empire. Jews were excluded from many trades and crafts in Christian Europe because, as Jews, they could not become members of one of the guilds that controlled access to most professions. In the Ottoman lands, Jews could form their own guilds, and even more surprisingly, guilds with a mixed membership of Muslims, Jews, and Christians were not uncommon.

In the sixteenth century, Salonika and several other cities in the empire, including Safed in northern Palestine, became major hubs of Ottoman manufacture and commerce of textiles. Spanish Jews moving to the Ottoman Empire brought with them new techniques for producing stronger broadcloth at a lower cost. The textile sector emerged as the economic basis of the Sephardi communities in Salonika and Safed and came to be identified so much with the Jews of Salonika that by the mid-sixteenth century, the Ottoman government required them to pay their poll tax in cloth to provide for the Janissary corps, a key part of the Ottoman military. As the century progressed, however, the competition of cloth manufactured in England, both of superior quality and at better cost, led to a slow decline in the Ottoman Jewish textile industry. The sector collapsed in Safed, though it held out longer in Salonika. In Europe, the textile and garment trade was also crucial to the Jewish economy, and thus, Jewish involvement was, by the early modern period, an international phenomenon.

The trading network that Samuel de Medina alluded to in his responsum was concerned with internal trade within the confines of the empire. The Sephardi Jews, however, also emerged in the sixteenth century as intermediaries between Ottoman lands and Europe. Sephardi Jews living in the Ottoman Empire knew European languages (Spanish/Judeo-Spanish or Portuguese), and they maintained a network of family and business relations throughout the emerging Sephardi Diaspora. Spanish Jews and Portuguese conversos established themselves in port cities throughout the Mediterranean (outside the Ottoman Empire, primarily in Italy, in cities such as Venice, Ancona, and Ferrara, as well as in North Africa), and in new communities that emerged in the cities of the Atlantic Seaboard (Amsterdam, Hamburg, and London in northwestern Europe, and Bordeaux and Bayonne in southwestern France). These communities formed one of the most impressive trading diasporas in the early modern period, spanning various continents and straddling the cultural divide between the Islamic world and the various Christian powers of western Europe.

The Jews of the Ottoman Empire contributed to the economic development of the major Ottoman cities and perhaps the empire more generally, and their fate was tied to the fortunes of this vast Muslim state. Throughout the sixteenth century, the Ottomans moved from one military triumph to another and even twice laid siege (though unsuccessfully) to the Habsburg capital, Vienna, first in 1529, and again in 1683. This period of Ottoman imperial expansion also was the golden age of Ottoman Jewry, a period of economic well-being and remarkable religious freedom. It was under these circumstances that the Sephardim and former conversos, after settling in the Ottoman Empire, were able to overcome the trauma of expulsion or forced conversion and to generate an unexpected Sephardi renaissance under Ottoman rule.

Living in Spain, the Jews had interacted quite freely with their neighbors and were very much part of the dominant culture—interreligious violence and forced conversions after 1391 notwithstanding. But the Ottoman Empire was a multiethnic and multireligious empire, especially in its provinces in the Balkans and in the major port cities in which the Jews settled. Thus, the Sephardim maintained their own traditions and even their own language: Judeo-Spanish, or Ladino. In the European provinces of the empire and in Turkey, Ladino eventually became the predominant Jewish language. In places such as Salonika, even non-Jews would speak some Ladino, as it soon emerged as a dominant language in the marketplace. Elsewhere—for example, in Istanbul or Janina—Greek-speaking Jewish communities that had lived in the city since late antiquity continued to exist side by side with the more recent Sephardi arrivals. (In the Middle Eastern parts of the empire, on the other hand, the Spanish Jews generally assimilated into the local Jewish culture and adopted Arabic as their primary language.)

The fact that Spanish Jews continued to maintain their original language does not mean that Jews were isolated from their non-Jewish environment. Certainly many Jewish men living in places like Istanbul or Edirne had at least some knowledge of Turkish or another local language, and many Jewish traditions were clearly influenced by the Ottoman environment. Popular culture is a good example of the cultural mix that was generated by the mass immigration of Sephardi Jews into the Ottoman Empire: Bringing with them old traditions from Spain, they continued to sing ballads whose origins were in medieval Spanish culture. But the tunes they used were influenced by Ottoman musical traditions.

If some Jews spoke at least some Turkish or other languages outside their homes, within Sephardi families and communities, Ladino remained the principal idiom. Many women, in fact, probably did not speak any other language. What emerged in the Ottoman lands of the sixteenth century was a unique Hispano-Jewish culture transplanted, as it were, to the multiethnic empire of the Ottoman sultans. Ladino, like other Jewish languages written in Hebrew characters, borrowed extensively from Hebrew and languages spoken in Ottoman lands, such as Turkish and Greek, but it remained close enough to Spanish that even today a Spanish speaker would be able to understand most of it without major difficulties. It is curious, however, that Ladino remained largely the language of popular culture, whereas rabbinic elites continued to write almost exclusively in Hebrew—in fact, a flourishing Ladino literature did not emerge until the early eighteenth century, when, in 1730, the Istanbul rabbi Jacob Huli published the first volume of an encyclopedic commentary on the Bible written in Ladino, the *Me'am Lo'ez*. In the sixteenth century, only relatively few works were written and printed in Ladino, Moses Almosnino of Salonika being the most prominent author.

It was not only Spanish Jews exiled in 1492 who arrived in the Ottoman Empire. Throughout the sixteenth century and beyond, a constant trickle of conversos continued to leave Portugal and Spain, often escaping the Inquisition but, at times, simply in search of a better life. These former conversos established a far-flung Diaspora, providing an important link between the Islamic and the Christian worlds, especially in the commercial realm, where, in the early modern period, they undertook the lion's share of trade between these two regions. One outstanding example of the networks established by former conversos is Doña Gracia Mendes. Born into a converso family in Portugal in 1510, her husband had been the owner of one of the most important banking houses in Lisbon and was involved in overseas trade. When he died in 1535, Doña Gracia inherited his large estate. With the establishment of the Portuguese Inquisition a year later, Gracia Mendes decided to leave. She went first to Antwerp (in today's Belgium). The family fortune was so significant that the Holy Roman Emperor Charles V tried to have the estate confiscated, but bribing the emperor and providing him a generous loan, Gracia Mendes was able to save most of her assets and procure a passage of safe conduct from the Venetian government and moved to Venice.

The family later moved to Ferrara and, around 1553, began to live openly as Jews. Soon afterward, Doña Gracia left for Istanbul in the Ottoman Empire. It was there that she and her nephew Joseph rose to unprecedented prominence. Joseph was appointed duke of the island of Naxos, which the Ottomans had recently conquered from the Venetians, and controlled a large network of tax farms in the empire. Tax farming involved advancing the tax income for a given region to the government and leasing the right to collect those taxes from the local population. It was a common practice in premodern states and an economic sector in which the Spanish Jews had been active during the medieval period.

In 1555, Joseph and Gracia Mendes demonstrated their international connections when they tried to organize an Ottoman boycott of the Italian port of Ancona, which is part of the papal states. Previous popes had invited Jews and conversos to settle in Ancona to promote trade with the Ottoman Empire. In 1555, however, a new pope, the Counter-Reformation pope Paul IV, came to power and initiated a crackdown on conversos who were secretly practicing Judaism in his lands. When two dozen conversos were burned at the stake in Ancona, Gracia Mendes and her nephew Joseph convinced the Ottoman sultan to formally protest and tried to organize a boycott of the papal port city. The effort ultimately failed, but it illustrates the close connections of the Sephardi converso Diaspora, often based on family and kinship ties, linking the major port cities of the Mediterranean and—increasingly in the seventeenth century—the Atlantic world.

OTTOMAN SAFED IN THE SIXTEENTH CENTURY

Palestine, or Eretz Yisrael ("The Land of Israel"), as it was known to the Jews, came under the rule of the sultans of Constantinople when the Ottomans conquered it, along with Syria and Egypt, from the Mamluks in the early sixteenth century. Soon afterward, the city of Safed (*Tsfat*), in the region known as the Galilee in northern Israel, began to attract a growing number of Jewish immigrants. Former conversos fleeing the Inquisition in Spain and Portugal—along with Jews from other parts of the Ottoman Empire, from the neighboring Arabic-speaking lands, from North Africa and Italy and other parts of Europe—were drawn to Safed and established there what became the leading Jewish community in the Holy Land in the sixteenth century. One reason was the flourishing of Safed's economy in the first century after the Ottoman conquest. Its Jewish population peaked in the late 1560s, when it reached perhaps as many as 1,800 households, though it declined as the economic situation deteriorated in the following decades.

For many of the rabbis and scholars who moved to Safed at that time, however, it was more than its favorable economic environment that attracted them to the city. Consider this account by an anonymous Jewish traveler from the year 1495, before the Ottoman conquest and the great expansion of the city:

> Safed is built on the slopes of a mountain and is a great city. The houses are small and modest, and when the rain falls it is impossible to walk about on account of the dirt, and also because it is on the hillside. It is also difficult to go out in the markets and the streets even during the summer, for you must always be climbing up or down. However, the land is good and health-giving and the waters are quite good. . . . Around Safed there are many caves in which great and pious men have been buried. . . . About six miles from Safed is a certain village called Meron, where very great and pious saints . . . are buried. We entered a certain cave nearby in which twenty-two scholars lie, and they said that these were the disciples of Rabbi Shimon bar Yohai of saintly and blessed memory; and near the spot on the hillside there is an extremely fine monument, which can be seen as far as Safed.

Shimon bar Yohai was believed to be the author of the *Zohar*, the central work of Jewish mysticism (Kabbalah), and his grave in Meron was an important destination for Jewish pilgrims since the fourteenth century. In reality compiled in the late thirteenth century in Spain, the *Zohar* had become the most authoritative work of Kabbalah and was the basis for the kabbalistic imagination of all subsequent generations. The belief that its presumed author was buried close to Safed, along with numerous other holy figures of Jewish history, contributed to the reputation of the city as a highly spiritual place.

Many of the scholars attracted to sixteenth-century Safed were Sephardim, often of converso origin, and Moses di Trani later even declared, "In Galilee [i.e., in Safed] people would say: Let us be grateful to the kings of Spain for having expelled our sages and judges, so that they came here and re-established the Torah to all its pristine glory." One of these luminaries of rabbinic learning, born in either Spain or Portugal and making his way to Safed, was Joseph Karo (1488–1575). While also a mystic, Karo is most famous for his compendium of Jewish law, the *Shulhan Arukh* (first printed in Venice in 1565), which, for Orthodox Jews, remains the main code of Jewish law even today (more on the *Shulhan Arukh* and its impact in Chapter 9).

A second figure leaving his imprint not only on the Judaism of his generation but also on Jewish beliefs and practices to this day was Isaac Luria (known as *ha-Ari*; 1534–1572). Luria was born to an Ashkenazi father and a Sephardi mother in Jerusalem. When his father died while Luria was still a small child, his mother took him to live in Egypt, where he grew up and resided until immigrating to Safed in 1570. Though he lived in Safed for less than three years before his untimely death at the age of 38, Luria's teachings and the religious practices ascribed to him and his disciples transformed Jewish religious life in subsequent generations.

Safed had been a center of Kabbalah before Luria's arrival there—presumably, this was what attracted him to the city in the first place. Scholars such as Joseph Karo, Moses Cordovero (1522–1570), and others had created a culture of ascetic mystical practice and study. One Safed kabbalist, Abraham Berukhim, described the common midnight study vigil, noting that "most scholars of Torah, when they rise in the middle of the night in order to study, sit upon the ground, wrap themselves in black, mourn, and weep on account of the destruction of the Temple." The community included several individuals—for example, Joseph Karo—who claimed to have mystical visions in which they received secret divine knowledge, preparing for such visions through ascetic practices and self-mortification.

It was in this climate that Luria began to teach his own insights into Jewish mysticism. He did not put any of his highly imaginative teachings into writing, however, and what we know about Lurianic Kabbalah is from the accounts of various of his disciples, in particular Haim Vital (1543–1620), who saw himself as Luria's preeminent student.

It is impossible to introduce Luria's elaborate, imaginative, yet unsystematic teachings in the limited space available here. To give a taste of Lurianic Kabbalah—illustrating how influential it was on later Judaism, but also how "foreign" it might seem to modern readers—we present briefly two key concepts of Lurianic mysticism (*tikkun* and *gilgul*) and a religious practice invented by the Safed kabbalists (*Kabbalat Shabbat*).

Historian Lawrence Fine has described the main theme of Lurianic myth, which is the basis of the idea of *tikkun*, the "restoration" or "mending" of the world:

> Drawing on the basic themes of exile and redemption that permeated Safed even prior to Luria's activities there, he devised a complex and distinctive set of mythological doctrines. At the heart of this mythology stands the . . . notion that sparks of divine light have, in the process of God's self-disclosure or emanation [i.e., in the process of Creation], accidentally and disastrously become embedded in all material things. According to Luria, these sparks of light yearn to be liberated from their imprisoned state and return to their source within the Godhead, thus restoring the original divine unity. The human task in the face of this catastrophic situation is to bring about such liberation through proper devotional means.

This is the process of *tikkun*, or restoration, the purpose of which is not only to disentangle the sacred sparks of divine light trapped in the material world but also to restore the original unity of the "male" and "female" aspects of the godhead—often described in the kabbalistic sources employing rather explicit sexual metaphors—as it existed prior to Creation. The ultimate purpose of every religious act—whether it is prayer, a mitzvah (the performance of a religious commandment), or the study of the texts of Jewish tradition—if accompanied by the right intention, is to advance the process of *tikkun*. Lurianic Kabbalah provided a powerful rationale for accepting divine law and the performance of Jewish ritual: Nothing less than the redemption of the world depended on every single religious act as long as it was carried out with the proper intention. It thus tremendously empowered both the individual Jew and the Jewish people in general. According to Lurianic teachings, everything (and certainly everything that truly matters) depends on the religious actions of the Jewish people. In a generation facing the uprooting of the once-splendid Spanish Jewish community, this empowerment through Kabbalah proved to be attractive. It was a potent answer to the precariousness of Jewish existence.

According to Lurianic Kabbalah, it was not only the sparks of divine light that were trapped in the "shards" of the material world: As a result of Adam's sins (as reported in the famous biblical story), the "sparks" of all future souls also fell into and were trapped by the material world. Therefore, part of the process of *tikkun* is the liberation of these soul-sparks (*nitsotsot ha-neshamot*). In the understanding of the Safed Kabbalah, this happens through the transmigration of the souls, known in Hebrew as *gilgul*. The scattered soul-sparks must be "reassembled" through their various transmigrations until they are reconstituted to their original form and can be reunited with their divine root.

The idea of *gilgul* is not mentioned in the Talmud, nor was it discussed by medieval Jewish philosophers, such as Maimonides or Judah ha-Levi; others, including Saadya Gaon and Abraham ibn Daud, rejected the idea. Since the earliest Kabbalah, however, transmigration was taken for granted and can be found, for example, in the twelfth-century *Sefer ha-Bahir*. It was the Safed kabbalists who developed the idea of *gilgul* further and interpreted events in the Bible, but also the historical experience of the Jewish people or of individual Jews, as a history of transmigrations. The soul, it was taught, would return to a situation similar to the one in an earlier *gilgul* in order to mend the damage done through transgressions in a previous life.

The Lurianic kabbalists also developed elaborate theories as to the necessary reincarnations for a variety of different transgressions and sins. Eventually, this kabbalistic idea of *gilgul* proved to be highly influential in both popular and learned Jewish culture in the following centuries. In the early 1700s, Rabbi Elijah ha-Kohen of Izmir included a long list of *gilgulim* in his immensely popular work *Shevet Musar*, which was widely read by Jews in the Ottoman Empire and eastern Europe:

> I will give you many examples how the soul of the wicked returns in *gilgul*, so that the person may remember it and will not sin and will thus escape this agony. The *Kavanot ha-Ari* writes that the one who has sexual relations in candle light returns in *gilgul* of a goat. The one who is haughty against other people returns in *gilgul* of a wasp. The one who has killed a person returns in *gilgul* of water, and the proof is "[Only ye shall not eat the blood;] thou shalt pour it out upon the earth as water" [Deuteronomy 12:16]. The one who has illicit sexual relations with a woman who is married or engaged returns in *gilgul* of a water mill, and there both, man and woman, are judged. The one who speaks slander returns in *gilgul* of a stone.

Finally, a ritual developed among the Safed mystics, practiced and developed by Luria himself, is the welcoming of the Sabbath "queen," known in Hebrew as *Kabbalat Shabbat*. Described by Luria's disciple Hayim Vital, this practice involved going to the outskirts of the city on the Sabbath eve, turning one's face toward the west as the sun set, and welcoming the "Sabbath Queen." Prior to the regular evening prayer service, one would recite Psalm 29 and then the phrase "Come O Bride, Come O Bride, O Sabbath Queen," followed by Psalms 92 and 93.

Anyone familiar with synagogue services on Friday night—when the Sabbath begins at nightfall—will recognize how this tradition has survived into contemporary Jewish practice throughout all streams and traditions of Judaism, except that the ritual (turning toward the west, the recitation of the kabbalistic hymn *Lekhah dodi likrat kallah*, ending with the phrase "Come O Bride . . .") is now performed inside the synagogue rather than in the fields on the outskirts of the city, as was the practice in sixteenth-century Safed. This is by no means the only tradition common among Jews today that goes back to this moment in Jewish history—the custom of studying through the first night of the Shavuot festival is another example. It is a good illustration of how influential Lurianic Kabbalah has been for subsequent generations of Jews, regardless of whether they knew or cared about some of the more esoteric aspects of Luria's teachings.

The Jews of the Moroccan Mellah

The largest community of Jews in the Islamic world outside the Ottoman Empire was that of Morocco. Jews had lived in Northern Africa since antiquity and had been closely connected to the Jews of Muslim Spain in the Middle Ages. In the wake of the expulsion of 1492, many Spanish Jews relocated to Morocco—the city of Fez alone is said to have received 20,000 in the decades after 1492—where a sense of distinction between the exiles (known as *megorashim*) and the indigenous Moroccan Jews (*toshavim*; also called derogatively *forasteros*, or "strangers," by their Sephardi counterparts) persisted until modern times. Jewish society in Morocco was very diverse, from Spanish-speaking Jews in port cities engaging in overseas trade with Europe to Arabic-speaking Jews in the country's interior, often serving as middlemen between the urban centers and the tribal hinterlands. The Sephardi rabbinic elite (the "sages of Castile") came to dominate the religious life of Moroccan Jewry, but as in the case of the Ottoman lands, a unique blend of the Spanish Jewish heritage and local conditions developed also among the various communities of Jews in Morocco.

Jews in early modern Moroccan cities, including Fez and Marrakesh, lived in separate quarters, not unlike the Italian ghettos emerging in the same period. In 1438, the Jews in the Moroccan city of Fez were removed into a special quarter, or *mellah*—a term that denotes the Jewish quarters or ghettos that were established in various cities throughout Morocco in the early modern period. The same Moroccan ruler who moved the Jews from Old Fez into the Jewish *mellah*, Sultan Abd al-Haqq ibn Abi Sa'id (r. 1421–1465), also appointed a Jew, Aaron ben Batash, to the office of vizier (or chief minister) during the last few years of his reign. The decree moving the Jews of Fez out of mixed neighborhoods and into the Jewish *mellah* had been a response to anti-Jewish disturbances and an attempt to provide better protection. But in 1465, many of the *mellah*'s inhabitants died in the attack of Muslim rebels who rose against the ruling dynasty, partly in protest of the appointment of the Jew Aron ben Batash to the vizierate. These events illustrate the ambiguity of the Jewish experience in early modern Morocco: On the one hand, the Jews of Morocco were subject to rules and practices that were often far more restrictive than those in the Ottoman Empire. The various Moroccan rulers, through to the nineteenth century, took the Qur'anic imperative of "humiliating" or "humbling" the non-Muslim minorities quite literally, and unlike in the Ottoman lands, the Jews of Morocco lived in separate quarters, like some of their European coreligionists did. On the other hand, individual Jews, such as Aron ben Batash, could rise to prominent positions in the royal court, whereas Jews of Spanish and Portuguese origin settling in the cities of Morocco's Atlantic coast established a much-needed channel

COFFEE AND KABBALAH

In the mid-sixteenth century, a new beverage appeared on the scene in Middle Eastern cities like Cairo, Istanbul, and Damascus: coffee, imported from Yemen, where it had been popular for centuries. The adaptation of the drink was slower in Europe. When it finally caught on in the eighteenth century in Prussia, the king Frederick the Great complained:

> It is disgusting to notice the increase in the quantity of coffee used by my subjects, and the amount of money that goes out of the country in consequence. Everybody is using coffee. If possible, this must be prevented. My people must drink beer.

In the Islamic world, Muslim scholars debated whether the consumption of this stimulant was permissible, and in eighteenth-century Germany, Frederick the Great was not the only one to denounce the new drink. Mostly, however, Muslim and Christian authorities were concerned less with coffee as a commodity than with the coffeehouse as a social venue. King Charles II tried, unsuccessfully, to ban coffeehouses in England, and no more successful were successive attempts by conservative Muslims to force to closure of coffeehouses in the Ottoman Empire.

The Jewish public embraced coffee as a drink wherever it became available, whether in the sixteenth century in Ottoman Egypt and Palestine, in the late sixteenth/early seventeenth century in Italy, or by the eighteenth century in Germany. Unlike some of their Muslim or Christian counterparts, the rabbis did not question the permissibility of coffee itself; instead, they debated the proper blessing to be recited over coffee, whether it was kosher for Passover, and how one could enjoy a hot cup of coffee on the Sabbath, when cooking is not allowed. They were also wary about the social impact of the coffeehouse, which would lead to idle socializing not for the sake of the Torah and to encounters between Jews and non-Jews. Nonetheless, as Rabbi Haim Benveniste of the Ottoman city of Izmir was forced to acknowledge in the seventeenth century:

> In our city there is a bitter and bad custom that on the Sabbath, [Jews] go to coffeehouses and drink from the coffee that is prepared especially for the needs of Israel [i.e., the Jews]. . . . And there is no doubt that if it weren't for the Israelites, the proprietor of the coffeehouse would prepare only half of what he prepares. . . . And as this custom became established, there isn't a single one who wouldn't drink . . . men, women, and children, and the majority of rabbinic scholars among them. . . . And the elite are included more than the poorer people.

Drinking coffee was not only associated with secular pastimes, however. As the historian Elliott Horowitz has suggested, certain kabbalistic rituals were linked in their growing popularity during the early modern period to the spread of coffee consumption. The kabbalists of Safed, for example, emphasized nocturnal rituals. As one observer testified:

> At midnight, they sat in the darkness reciting *Tikkun Hatzot* in a lachrymose voice. After they completed the *Tikkun* they studied some Zohar, and then the drink called coffee was brought, quite hot, and given to each person. . . . Afterwards songs and hymns are recited . . . and there is celebration until the morning. At first light in the morning prayers are recited and all return home in peace.

Coffee, as a stimulant, according to Horowitz, was an important ingredient in this shift to nighttime rituals, and in his view, the spread of similar nocturnal kabbalistic practices in seventeenth-century Italy was accompanied by the simultaneous spread of the new commodity, coffee.

of trade and communication with Europe and provided crucial services to the country.

A second *mellah* was established in the city of Marrakesh, in southern Morocco, in the mid-1500s. Slowly, such separate Jewish quarters extended throughout the country, and by 1900, the Jews of most Moroccan towns lived in a *mellah*. This process was not always linked to a desire to protect the Jews or meant as a measure of oppression. In the case of Marrakesh, the creation of the Jewish quarter was part of a larger effort of the Sa'di dynasty (which ruled the country from 1511 to 1659) to transform Marrakesh, their new capital, into a royal city that could compete with the older capital, Fez. Since Fez boasted a Jewish quarter—symbolizing the sultan's direct control over his non-Muslim subjects—creating a *mellah* for the Jews of Marrakesh became part of the effort to demonstrate the legitimacy and political power of the new dynasty. While the *mellah* was designed as a separate living quarter for the Jews, it never became an exclusively Jewish space. In Marrakesh, non-Muslim foreigners—mostly European Christians—were required to take up residence in the city's *mellah*, which, by the seventeenth century, included, for example, a Franciscan church alongside the Jews' synagogues.

The ambiguity between participation in the life of the Moroccan city and physical separation of the Jewish living quarter, between cultural integration and discrimination at the hands of the majority, can be seen in the travelogues written by European travelers of the period. One Christian visitor in the late seventeenth century portrayed the Jewish community of Morocco thus:

> The Jews are very numerous in Barbary, and they are held in no more estimation than elsewhere. . . . They are subject to suffering the blows and injuries of everyone, without daring to say a word even to a child of six who throws stones at them. If they pass before a mosque, no matter what the weather or the season might be, they must remove their shoes, not even daring in the royal cities, such as Fez and Marrakesh, to wear them at all, under pain of five hundred lashes and being put into prison, from which they would be released only upon payment of a heavy fine. They dress in the Arab fashion, but their cloaks and caps are black in order to be distinguishable. In Fez and Marrakesh, they are separated from the inhabitants, having their quarters apart, surrounded by walls, the gates of which are guarded by men set by the king so that they can conduct their business in peace and sanctify their Sabbath and their other holidays. In the other cities, they are mixed with the Moors [the Muslims]. They traffic in nothing other than merchandising and their trades. There are several of them who are quite rich.

Still in the late eighteenth century, another Christian traveler described a community marked simultaneously by social isolation and cultural integration. At the same time, the author reveals his own European bias:

> The Jews in most parts of this empire [Morocco] live entirely separate from the Moors [the Muslims]; and though in other respects oppressed, are allowed the free exercise of their religion. Many of them, however, to avoid the arbitrary treatment which they constantly experience, have become converts to the Mahometan faith [i.e., to Islam]. . . . In most of the sea-port towns, and particularly in Tetuan and Tangier, the Jews have a tolerable smattering of Spanish; but at Morocco [Marrakesh] . . . and all the inland towns, they can only speak Arabic and a little Hebrew. They nearly follow the customs of the Moors [Muslims], except in their religious ceremonies; and in that particular they are by far more superstitious than the European Jews.

The image that emerges from these travelogues is distorted, to be sure, by the prejudices of their authors, who were sympathetic neither to Muslims nor to Jews. But it does give a good impression of what was a very diverse Jewish community, at once subjected to the humiliating conditions of the *dhimmi* (the Jews were the only non-Muslim minority in Morocco), but also, at the same time, thoroughly integrated into the fabric of Moroccan society and culture.

Between Ghetto and Renaissance: The Jews of Early Modern Italy

Italy served as a cultural bridge between northern Europe and the Mediterranean world, and it was a crossroads of Jewish cultures. Italy was not a unified state in the early modern period but, rather, an often-confusing mix of different principalities, duchies, republics, kingdoms, and of course, the realm of the pope, with its capital in Rome. For much of the early modern period, the Jews lived only in the northern half of the Italian peninsula. Sicily was under Spanish rule and thus expelled its Jews in 1492; when the Kingdom of Naples came under Spanish domination, its Jews were expelled in 1541. Rome had a Jewish community whose origins dated to antiquity. Other centers of Jewish life in sixteenth-century Italy were Mantua, Ferrara, Venice, and the territories of Tuscany and Savoy.

The Venetian government allowed Jews late in the fourteenth century to reside temporarily in Venice and engage in moneylending. The charter issued in 1397, however, made a stipulation that Jews could stay in Venice for no longer than 15 days at a time, and even though many Jews managed to evade the restrictions placed on their residence in the city, they still were not allowed to practice Judaism in public or to open a synagogue. It was only in 1509 that a larger number of Jews flocked into the city as war refugees. Soon after, the Venetian authorities realized that the presence of the Jews would be beneficial to the social and economic interests of the city. As moneylenders, they provided a much-needed service to the Christian poor, enabling Christians to avoid violating the Church's prohibition of lending money against interest to their coreligionists. But as in so many other parts of Christian Europe, and clearly distinct from the situation in the lands of Islam, the presence of the Jews was always controversial. As a result—in fact, a compromise between exclusion or expulsion of the Jews and granting them a right of residence—the city of Venice ordered the creation of a strictly segregated Jewish quarter. The area to which the Jews of Venice were confined was known as the *Ghetto Nuovo*. It was the term *ghetto* that came to denote the segregated Jewish quarters that were established in other Italian cities in the sixteenth and seventeenth centuries, as well as outside Italy.

The discussions in the Senate of Venice about tolerating the continued presence of Jews in the city were typical for the ways in which various Italian states and cities dealt with Jewish immigration and residence. The most powerful argument in favor of allowing the presence of Jews was one of raison d'état, or the interest of the state, balancing religious prejudice, popular resentment against Jews, and the fear of competition among the Christian "middle class." A good example of the competing attitudes was the debate in the Venetian Great Council. One Francesco Bragadin argued that "it was necessary to have Jews for the sake of the poor," as there was no other institution in place to provide loans for those in need, and "he cautioned about arguing against the Jews, for even the Pope keeps them in Rome." The next speaker supported this point:

> [A]nd he spoke well for an eighty-six-year-old man, saying that Jews are necessary to assist the poor . . . the statutes must be confirmed

> . . . and the Jews allowed to lend at interest, because they have no other livelihood.

The continued presence of Jews in Venice also met opposition, however, which was couched in religious and political language:

> Next Sier Gabriel Moro . . . got up and spoke out against the Jews, saying that they should not be kept, and that Spain drove them from her lands, then they came to Naples and King Alfonso lost his kingdom . . . and now we are going to do the same thing and stir up the wrath of God against us.

However:

> [M]any other members of the Consiglio, who were concerned for the well-being of the poor, said that when the Jews were driven out of Spain they brought with them a great quantity of gold. They went to Constantinople, and [the Ottoman sultan] Selim conquered Syria and Egypt.

The opponents of Jewish settlement then resorted to a typical medieval argument: Allowing the Jews to live in their midst would inevitably provoke God's wrath. In the face of early modern considerations of raison d'état and a secularization of European politics, this kind of argument had lost some of its persuasiveness. The party supporting continued settlement of the Jews in Venice prevailed, arguing that their services were needed (e.g., as moneylenders for the Christian poor) and greatly inflating the economic significance of the Sephardi immigration to the Ottoman Empire, which, as an Islamic state, had never seen the Jewish presence as a problem but simply as a fact of life.

In March 1516, the first ghetto in Jewish history was established in Venice. The example of Venice was later followed by many other cities throughout the Italian peninsula. In 1555, Pope Paul IV took power in Rome and issued his infamous bull referred to as *Cum nimis absurdum*, after its opening words:

> It is profoundly absurd and intolerable that the Jews, who are bound by their guilt to perpetual servitude, should show themselves ungrateful toward Christians; and, with the pretext that Christian piety welcomes them by permitting them to dwell among Christians, they repay this favor with scorn, attempting to dominate the very people whose servants they should be.

The bull of this Counter-Reformation pope initiated a new period in the history of relations between the Catholic Church and the Jews, not least for the Jews of Rome. The Church increased the pressure on the Jews in Catholic Europe. In August 1553, the Church issued a decree condemning the Talmud as blasphemous and ordered that it be burned—an order that was widely obeyed throughout Italy. The *Index* of prohibited books issued by Pope Paul IV in 1559 included the Talmud and was later extended to many other Jewish books. Jewish books that were not banned outright were subjected to censorship by the Inquisition: the *Index expurgatorius* of 1595 listed a total of 420 different Hebrew works that could be published only after certain passages that the Church considered to be offensive to Christians were taken out or revised.

Jews had lived in Rome since antiquity and had always been protected by the Roman Catholic Church. In 1555, however, the lives of the approximately 4,000 Roman Jews changed significantly when the pope decreed that they move to a small area on the northern bank of the Tiber River to be surrounded, as in the Venetian ghetto, by a wall that was to be closed at nighttime. The Jews were also ordered to wear a distinctive yellow badge (they wore a yellow head covering in Venice). A description of the crowded conditions of the Roman ghetto before it was razed to the ground (nothing of the original ghetto remains today) was provided by a traveler in the middle of the nineteenth century and probably gives a sense of what the ghetto must have looked like in the sixteenth century:

> [D]irectly ahead are the ghetto houses in a row, tower-like masses of bizarre design, with numerous flowerpots in the windows and countless household utensils hanging on the walls. The rows ascend from the river's edge, and its dismal billows wash against the walls. . . . When I first visited it, the Tiber had overflowed its banks and its yellow flood streamed through the Fiumara, the lowest of the ghetto streets, the foundations of whose houses serve as a quay to hold the river in its course. . . . What melancholy spectacle to see the wretched Jews' quarter sunk in the dreary inundation of the Tiber! Each year Israel [the Jews] in Rome has to undergo a new Deluge, and like Noah's Ark, the ghetto is tossed on the waves with man and beast. . . . Before 1847, a high wall . . . separated the Palace of the Cenci from the Jews' Square. . . . Here was the principal gate of the ghetto. If we now enter the streets of the ghetto itself we find Israel [the Jews] before its booths, buried in restless toil and distress.

Throughout the sixteenth and seventeenth centuries, most (though not all) Italian cities with a Jewish community followed the example of Venice and Rome and restricted their Jewish populations to ghettos: Florence and Siena in 1571, Verona in 1602, Padua in 1603, Mantua in 1612, Ferrara in 1624, and Modena in 1638, with the ghetto of Correggio established as late as 1779. The irony is that the era of the ghetto in Italian Jewish history was, in many ways, less violent than other periods: Almost no accusations of ritual murder were made (as had happened in the infamous blood libel of Trent in 1475, which led to the death of the entire Jewish population—some 30 persons—of the city), and in general, violence against the Jews or the threat to expel them subsided significantly.

The Jews of Rome created their own pun on the word *ghetto:* They called it their *get*, from the Hebrew word meaning "a letter of divorce." In the Roman case, the Jews were resettled in a separate part of a city in which they had lived for centuries. In Venice, the establishment of the ghetto marked the beginning of a permanent presence of the Jews in the city. In both cases, as in most other Italian cities, the establishment of the ghettos imposed a new set of restrictions on the Jews, while it created a specific space for the Jews in the urban landscape, and thus a specific slot for the Jews within Italian society. It is in this sense that the establishment of the early modern Italian ghetto was experienced with much ambivalence: The wave of expulsions from western Europe, which had begun with the expulsion from England in 1290 and reached its high point with the Spanish expulsion in 1492, was finally coming to an end.

The early modern Christian state, first in Italy and soon elsewhere in western Europe, came to terms with a continued or renewed Jewish presence. It assigned the Jews a separate space, tried to limit as much as possible and to control the interaction of Jews and Christians, and had the gates of the ghetto locked after nightfall: But in the spirit of *raison d'état*, it also came to recognize the economic utility of the Jews. Commerce began to displace religious considerations that had led to the progressive exclusion of Jews from western European Christendom at the close of the Middle Ages. This led in some instances to Jews enjoying more generous conditions than did other religious minorities. In Venice, for example, the charter of 1548 allowed the Jews to build synagogues (they previously held their religious services in private homes), whereas the Greek Orthodox Christians were allowed to build their first church in this Catholic city only in 1573, while Protestants received permission to conduct private services, but not to have their own church, the first one being erected only in 1657.

What was the impact of the ghetto on the development of Italian Jewish culture? At first, one would expect to see a growing isolation, and to a certain degree, that was the case when, in the course of the sixteenth and seventeenth centuries, Jewish mysticism, or Kabbalah, came to dominate Jewish religious practices. But at the same time, Jews continued to socialize with Christians, meeting in taverns and drinking and gambling together. Jews in Rome shared the culinary taste of their Christian neighbors, their synagogue tunes sounded much like Catholic sacred music, they routinely referred to December 25 as *Natale*, or Christmas, in their rental contracts, and they commonly used Italian names, with their Hebrew names largely employed only in the synagogue.

The autobiography of the seventeenth-century Venetian rabbi Leone Modena (1571–1648) provides ample evidence of the cultural proximity of Jews and Christians. With reference to the ancient art of alchemy (considered a serious science until the eighteenth century, a by-product of which was the belief that one could make gold or silver out of lead through chemical processes), Modena writes about his son Mordecai:

> [He] began to engage in the craft of alchemy with the priest Grillo, a very learned man. . . . Finally . . . he arranged a place in the Ghetto Vecchio and with his own hands made all the preparations needed for the craft. There he repeated an experiment that he had learned to do in the house of the priest, which was to make ten ounces of pure silver from nine ounces of lead and one of silver.

Even religious events could be shared by Jews and Christians, as the repeated reference in Modena's autobiography to a Christian audience of his sermons in Venice suggests:

> At the end of Tevet 5382 [1622], a celebration was held in the Great Synagogue at the conclusion of the study of the talmudic tractate Ketubbot. Eighteen sermons were delivered, and on the last night . . . I gave the sermon before a huge standing crowd, packed in as never before, with many Christians and noblemen among the listeners.

Even though Jews and Christians continued to socialize in this age of the ghetto and continued to partake of a shared culture, the awareness of being different persisted. As one historian of Italian Jewry has remarked, "[A]like did not mean identical." Italian Jewish culture was both Italian *and* Jewish. The subculture of the Italian Jews was, in many ways, a mirror image of the culture of their Christian neighbors. The culture of Renaissance Italy influenced them—and they adapted it to their own cultural needs—but they also defined their own Jewishness in conscious distinction from their environment. They may have shared the culinary taste of other Italians and eaten pasta, but they were also bound by the Jewish dietary laws, which set them apart from the Christians. They may have used their Italian names, but they also knew that in their synagogues they would step into a Jewish space and be identified by their Hebrew names. Thus, the Italian Jews acculturated, shaping their own culture in relation to the Christian culture that surrounded them, but they never lost their sense of difference, of "otherness." Cultural "assimilation" did not lead, and does not necessarily lead today, to a negation of Jewish identity.

An exceptional but nevertheless telling example that illustrates both inclusion and exclusion of the early modern Italian Jews is the case of Sara Coppio Sullam, born to a Venetian Jewish family around 1592. In 1618, she began a correspondence with the Italian monk Ansaldo Cebà of Genoa after reading his verse epic *L'Ester*. The two exchanged letters, pictures, and poems for many years, evidence of the cultural affinity that Jews and Christians could experience. At the same time, Cebà's unconcealed expectation that Sara would eventually convert to Christianity (which she never did) also illustrates the continuing sense of difference that always separated the members of the two groups, despite all that they might have in common.

Sara Sullam gathered a salon of learned Christian men—poets, painters, and priests—who met in her home in the Venetian ghetto for intellectual conversation and, often enough, to ask Sara for money. Some of her guests, however, later came to betray her, and one wonders whether the reason was that she was, after all, a Jew residing in the ghetto, and hence on the margins of Venetian society. One priest and poet who was a regular in Sara's salon accused her in a public treatise of having denied the immortality of the soul—considered a heretical stance by both Catholic and Jewish authorities—to which Sara Sullam responded by publishing a treatise of her own, *Manifesto di Sarra Copia Sulam hebrea*, in which she defended her own views and attacked her opponent. Sara Sullam certainly was an unusual woman, but her example demonstrates the extent to which a Jewish woman (at least one belonging to a prominent and wealthy family) living in the ghetto of Venice could participate in the culture of Renaissance Italy.

The Jewish communities of Italy were diverse and well connected to Jewish communities in both Europe and the Ottoman world. At least eight different synagogues were operational in the ghetto of Venice, where most Ashkenazi and Italian Jews were engaged in moneylending and secondhand clothes dealing; the more recent Sephardi and converso immigrants (known as Levantini and Ponentini, respectively) were mostly merchants. In the center of the ghetto in Rome, five different synagogues—called the *Cinque Scole*—were housed in the same building, each representing a different rite (Italian, Sicilian, Ashkenazi, Castilian, and Catalan). Each Italian Jewish community had its own flavor, with Ancona and Ferrara dominated by the Sephardi and converso immigrants, Verona having a strong Ashkenazi presence, and the Great Synagogue of Mantua—home to the famous Italian rabbi and philosopher Judah Messer Leon (d. c. 1526)—following the Italian rite. The Italian communities thus facilitated throughout the period the cultural exchange between Jews of different origin and their diverse traditions, a contribution greatly enhanced by Italy's emergence as the main hub of Jewish print culture in Hebrew, Yiddish, and Ladino. Its communities were much smaller than those of the Ottoman Empire (Rome about 4,000, Venice 2,500, Mantua over 2,300, and other communities numbering in the hundreds). Together, the Italian Jewish communities of the sixteenth century probably did not exceed 30,000 souls.

A distinctive feature of Italian Jewish society at that time was the proliferation of confraternities (*hevrot*), voluntary associations that were formed for a variety of purposes. The Gemilut Hasadim confraternity of Ferrara, for example, established in 1515, promised in its statutes

> to attend the sick who are poor and are in need, and to keep vigil over them at night and day, and to serve them for the honor of God until they recover. And to care for the dead when there is need, and after their death to make a coffin for them . . . and to wash their body and carry them to the cemetery and to bury them and to stand vigil over them until their burial.

Other confraternities were established for the study of the Torah (*talmud torah*)—for example, in Rome sometime before 1540—and for a host of other religious purposes. The establishment of such confraternities goes back to medieval Spain and southern France, where such pious associations are known from the thirteenth century. Imported by the Spanish Jewish émigrés after 1492, these voluntary confraternities became an important venue for socializing in the Jewish communities of early modern Italy and the Ottoman Empire. In Italy, they had their equivalent in

Christian society as well: Michel de Montaigne noted during his visit to Rome in 1581, for example, that "they have a hundred brotherhoods and more, and there is hardly a man of quality who is not attached to some one of these."

The rabbis decried any activity that did not involve performing a religious ritual or the study of the Torah. They called it *bitul torah*, literally "annulment of Torah." In the rabbinic ideal, Jewish time was guided by the rhythms of religious life—the three daily prayers, the regular study of the Torah, the weekly day of rest (Shabbat), the holidays. Jewish space, more clearly delineated in the Italian ghetto than ever before, was to be defined by a religious topography—the synagogue, the study house (*bet midrash*), the school of higher learning (*yeshiva*), and the like. The Jewish confraternities provided a new outlet for Jews to socialize without challenging the rabbinic ideals—and as mutual aid associations, they fulfilled an important function in the organization of Jewish society. They offered a setting for individuals to come together and socialize, ostensibly with a religious purpose (study, charity, etc.), but also providing a place for spending time together outside the confines of one's family and outside official communal spaces like the synagogue.

A Jewish Renaissance

In the fifteenth century, European scholars coined the term *Middle Ages*, referring to the period between the downfall of the classical world of ancient Greece and Rome and their own times, known as the period of Renaissance, which literally means "rebirth." The Renaissance was characterized by a resurging interest in the classical heritage of European civilization. Marked by a conscious break with the "medieval" past, Renaissance thought and art sought to reclaim classical learning, but it was also marked by a plethora of new discoveries: the invention of print and other technological innovations (e.g., gunpowder, which made possible the expansion of the Ottoman and Spanish Empires), the European discovery of new continents, and scientific progress, emblematic of which was the replacement of the old Ptolemaic system of astronomy with the Copernican system, questioning for the first time the centrality of earth in the known universe. Beginning in the Italian cities of Florence and Rome, the Renaissance also created a new art and architecture. Eventually, the movement spread across Europe, and hardly a European country remained untouched by the transformative force of the Renaissance.

All this did not fail to have an impact on Jews and Jewish culture. Jews in Italy were taking an interest in contemporary Italian Renaissance culture, cultivating the arts of rhetoric, music, and dance, whereas the architecture of Jewish synagogues all across Europe betrayed the influence of Renaissance art—which is evident, for example, in the extensive rebuilding in the Prague ghetto under the sponsorship of its leader, Mordechai Maisel, in the late sixteenth century.

At the same time, scientific discoveries presented new challenges to the rabbis. One case in point is Rabbi Isaac Lampronti of Ferrara in Italy (1679–1756), author of an encyclopedic work titled *Pahad Yitshaq*, which shows his interest in Jewish law and in the advances of contemporary science and medicine. A curious example is Lampronti's discussion of whether it is permitted to kill lice on the Sabbath. Traditional Jewish law forbids the killing of an animal on the Jewish day of rest, but earlier rabbis had argued that lice grew out of moisture in the ground and thus cannot be considered living creatures (e.g., in contrast to flies). Challenging this ruling, Lampronti cited contemporary scientific studies that suggested lice, like flies, reproduced themselves sexually and thus were to be considered animals, and that there was no such thing as spontaneous generation of creatures from moisture or rotten fruit. "I would say,"

Lampronti concluded, "that if the sages of Israel might have heard the proofs of the gentile sages, they might have reconsidered and acknowledged [their] opinions." Even though this conclusion may seem self-evident, others contradicted Lampronti. What was at stake, after all, was to determine what is permitted and what is prohibited on the Sabbath, and it raised the larger question of whether scientific insights could be allowed to challenge the authority of the ancient and medieval rabbis.

Scientific knowledge was spread around the Jewish world through a variety of channels. With the invention of print, the exchange of information became much easier, and knowledge became more widely accessible. The growing number of Jewish physicians who had obtained a university education and thus had become familiar with European Renaissance thought and science firsthand also contributed to the dissemination of scientific thought. Some of these Jewish physicians in the early modern period were conversos who had received their education living as Christians in the prestigious universities of Spain and Portugal at that time (e.g., Salamanca, Alcalá, Coimbra). Immigrating abroad and living there openly as Jews, these converso physicians played an important role in spreading scientific knowledge. At the same time, some Italian universities—first and foremost, the University of Padua—opened their doors to Jewish students of medicine. Providing them with a comprehensive education that included the liberal arts, Latin philology, and natural sciences, in addition to the medical curriculum, Padua attracted a growing number of Jewish students from Italy, Germany, Poland, and the Ottoman Empire.

Another example of the impact of Renaissance culture on Jewish literature is the revival of historical writing, especially in Italy, in the sixteenth century. Jews had produced works of history before, to be sure—the most prominent example was Josephus Flavius in the first century CE. In the tenth century, an anonymous author produced a Hebrew adaptation of Josephus's writings, the *Sefer Yosippon*, manuscripts of which circled from Ashkenas to Sefarad, in Italy and the Byzantine lands, and which was subsequently printed (particularly influential was the edition in Istanbul in 1510) and translated, first into Judeo-Arabic, and later into Yiddish and other languages. The generation after the expulsion from Spain saw a new wave of Jewish historical writing. Shlomo ibn Verga was a Spanish Jew living as a Christian in Portugal after the forced conversions of 1497, until he left for Italy nine years later. There, he wrote, sometime during the 1520s, his chronicle *Shevet Yehudah*, which has been described as a "proto-sociological" study of post-biblical Jewish history. Most importantly, ibn Verga was interested in finding the "natural causes" for the continuous persecution of the Jews, explaining their sufferings by means of historical analysis rather than through theology. Instead of arguing that the persecution of the Jews past and present was best understood as divine punishment for transgressing God's laws, ibn Verga suggested that social and historical reasons accounted for the violence against Jews. Samuel Usque, an Iberian Jew, wrote another historical work, *Consolaçam as Tribulaçoens de Israel* (*Consolation for the Tribulations of Israel*, in Portuguese and printed in Ferrara, 1553), likewise focusing on the long history of Jewish suffering.

Other historians of the period discovered for the first time an interest in non-Jewish history. Elijah Capsali of Crete (d. 1555), for example, had studied in Padua and wrote a history of the Venetian and the Ottoman Empires, including an extensive account of the expulsion of the Jews from Spain and their resettlement in Ottoman lands (*Seder Eliyahu Zuta*, written in the 1520s). Joseph ha-Kohen (d. 1578) wrote a chronicle of the French and Turkish kingdoms (published in 1554) and prepared a Hebrew translation of Francisco López de Gómara's Spanish *History of New India and Mexico* (1568). Beyond the Italian cultural area, it was David Gans (d. 1613), a Westphalian Jew living in Prague, who wrote a remarkable historical work titled *Tsemah David* (Prague, 1592), which was divided into two parts: One covered general history, the other Jewish history up to the date of the work's publication. The sense of parallel, rather than shared, histories of the Jews and of the world betrays a traditional outlook, to be sure, but Gans's and others' interest in general history nevertheless indicates the opening of a new horizon of knowledge.

One of the most intriguing figures in this regard, and certainly the one more imbued with the thinking of the European Renaissance than any other, was the Italian Jew Azariah de' Rossi (c. 1513/1514–1578). Born in Mantua, de' Rossi was the most accomplished representative of the Jewish Renaissance, and he was a controversial figure. Other luminaries of that time opposed his work—for example, the celebrated Rabbi Judah Loew of Prague (known as MaHaRaL), even though the latter was one of the foremost advocates of a reform of Jewish education and displayed an interest in secular and philosophical studies as long as they could be reconciled with Jewish tradition. De' Rossi's major work, *Me'or Einayim*, was banned by some of the leading rabbis of that time, and it was only with the onset of the Jewish Enlightenment in the eighteenth century that his pioneering study was rediscovered.

The third part of *Me'or Einayim* contains 60 chapters of critical historical studies, in which Rossi inquired into the ancient history of the Jews by comparing sources from the Jewish tradition—namely, the Talmud—with ancient Jewish and non-Jewish historical sources. His critical approach to the Talmud (though he did not extend it to the study of the Bible) was clearly informed by the new critical studies of the Renaissance period and was nothing short of revolutionary for Jewish literature at that time.

A typical passage from de' Rossi's work, introducing a historical problem, is the following:

> [A]nd let us return to the city of Alexandria. We are confronted with three different accounts. The wicked murderer is identified as Trajan in the Palestinian Talmud, Tarkinus in the Midrash Rabbah texts, and Alexander of Macedon in tractate Sukkah of the Babylonian Talmud, while in tractate Gittin, they change their opinion, and the name of Hadrian is proffered. Now we have undertaken to investigate the truth of all this, although we are not really concerned with the actual event, for whatever happened, happened. Rather, our aim is to ensure that our rabbis are not found to be giving contradictory accounts of well-known events.

De' Rossi acknowledges that the ancient rabbis had not had any interest in historical studies—and it is precisely this fact that serves him as a justification to call their authority on matters other than Jewish law into question. Well-known, he suggests, is the following:

> [T]he attitude of our sages toward all occurrences in the world and to events that happen over the course of time to rich and poor alike that have no connection with Torah, but are simply of a general nature and cases about which one would pronounce, "It makes no difference whichever way one looks at them." . . . We thought it worthwhile to expatiate on the truth of these [historical] matters. For since the sages of blessed memory were exclusively devoted to and immersed in the study of Torah and did not distract themselves by the conceit of idle talk or read documents about the remote past, it will not come as a surprise to us should they make some mistakes or give a shortened account of any of those stories.

Echoing the pronouncement by Maimonides, but in clear opposition to the dominant opinion of the rabbis of his own time, de' Rossi argued that the rabbis of the Talmud "proceeded on the basis of human wisdom and evaluation which was the scholarly approach prevalent in their time and in those parts of the world." To elucidate the historical past, therefore:

> [I]t has been necessary for me to seek the help of many gentile sages for the clarification and elucidation of certain issues. Of course, I would not accept their statements which hint at heresy or make light of our Torah, God forbid. But merely because they are not Jews, they are regarded as aliens whom we do not usually introduce into our community. Consequently, it might occur to some pious individual . . . to contrive against me and make me the target for his attack on the grounds that in Sanhedrin [i.e., Mishnah, tractate Sanhedrin, 10:1], our rabbis of blessed memory forbade the reading of profane literature.

Christian Humanism, the Protestant Reformation, and the Jews

Beginning in Italy, Christian scholars of the late fifteenth and sixteenth centuries began to develop an interest in the study of Hebrew. The humanists, as the Christian scholars with their renewed interest in historical and philological studies were known, directed their attention to the study of the three classical languages, including Hebrew, the language of the "Old Testament" of the Bible, in addition to Greek and Latin. The humanists emphasized the study of the classical sources in their original language—the slogan *ad fontes* ("to the sources") captures their intellectual program well—and by the middle of the sixteenth century, it was common for Hebrew to be taught formally with Greek and Latin in European universities.

Christian scholars, especially in Italy, sought the help of Jews to teach them the Hebrew language, so they could gain an understanding of rabbinic literature. Some developed a special interest in Kabbalah as they believed that they could prove the truth of Christianity from ancient Jewish traditions and, in particular, from the esoteric lore of Jewish Kabbalah. One Christian scholar, Giovanni Pico della Mirandola (d. 1494), for example, was introduced to the Hebrew language by Jewish scholars, including Elijah Delmedigo (d. 1497) and Johanan Alemanno (d. c. 1504).

Other scholars followed Pico della Mirandola's example. Though outside Italy, Christian humanists had much less direct contact with their Jewish counterparts, in Germany, humanist scholars also displayed an interest in Hebrew and in Jewish texts. Perhaps the most prominent example was Johannes Reuchlin (1455–1522), who developed a deep interest in the Hebrew language, which he considered to be the original language of humanity and the vehicle of communication between God and man. Reuchlin also showed a great curiosity for the kabbalistic tradition, which he adapted for Christian purposes. Among the books published by Reuchlin figures *De arte cabalistica* (*On the Art of Kabbalah*), published in 1517.

A few years earlier, in 1510, Reuchlin had been involved in a public controversy that came to be known as the "Reuchlin affair" and was a rallying point for scholars who defended the humanist approach to language and religious knowledge against the opposition of more conservative forces in the Church. The occasion was the anti-Jewish polemic written by a Jewish convert to Christianity, Johannes Pfefferkorn (1469–1523), who charged that what kept the Jews from recognizing Christianity was their attachment to rabbinic tradition. Pfefferkorn demanded the wholesale confiscation and destruction of all Hebrew books. The archbishop of Cologne convened a panel of scholars to evaluate Pfefferkorn's suggestion; Reuchlin turned out to be the only dissenting voice to reject the confiscation of Hebrew books. Although the Jewish community was able to bribe imperial officials to stop the confiscations, the public controversy pitting Reuchlin and other humanists against Pfefferkorn and his supporters in the Church continued for several years and preoccupied theologians well beyond Germany. Reuchlin was accused of "Judaism" by the Inquisition and was eventually fined by the papal court.

Reuchlin's vocal defense of Hebrew literature does not necessarily mean that he was free of anti-Jewish prejudice; his interest was primarily Jewish literature, not the Jews of his time. Other humanists were, in fact, openly hostile to Jews and Judaism. Erasmus of Rotterdam (c. 1466–1536), one of the most famous representatives of Christian humanism, was arguably the most prominent example of anti-Jewish attitudes within the humanist camp. Having mastered Greek and Latin, Erasmus did not attach much significance to the learning of Hebrew and was critical of Reuchlin's engagement with Jewish thought, in particular Kabbalah. In one of his books, Erasmus even declared, "I would rather, if the New Testament could remain inviolate, see the entire Old Testament done away with than see the peace of Christendom torn to ribbons for the sake of the Jewish scripture."

Humanism, with its focus on the original biblical text and its critique of Church tradition, prepared the ground for the great sixteenth-century revolution in Western Christianity, the Protestant Reformation. Creating a lasting split between Catholicism and Protestantism, the Reformation shattered the certainties of Western Christendom and produced a wide range of cultural, religious, and political transformations in European societies.

Historians have long disagreed on the Reformation's impact on the Jews and have alternatively pointed to the positive and negative ways in which the changes wrought by the Reformation affected the lives of European Jews at that time and in subsequent generations. Martin Luther (1483–1546), the German theologian who became the leading figure of the Reformation, stands for what appear to be entirely irreconcilable opinions: At first, he showed a conciliatory attitude toward the Jews that differed starkly from the traditional anti-Judaism of the late medieval Christian Church. Later, however, he adopted an increasingly intolerant and violent stance and actively lobbied for the expulsion of Jews from various German territories.

In a text Luther wrote in 1523, "That Jesus Christ Was Born a Jew," he indicted the Catholic Church for persecuting the Jews, emphasized the Jewish origins of the Christian religion, and called for tolerance toward his Jewish contemporaries. At the same time, it is clear from this pamphlet that he nevertheless anticipated the conversion of the Jews, and in fact, this was the ultimate rationale for affording them greater tolerance:

> I will therefore show by means of the Bible the causes which induce me to believe that Christ was a Jew born of a virgin. Perhaps I will attract some of the Jews to the Christian faith. For our fools—the popes, bishops, sophists, and monks—the coarse blockheads, have until this time so treated the Jews that to be a good Christian one would have to become a Jew. . . . [T]hey have dealt with the Jews as if they were dogs and not human beings. Whenever they converted them, they . . . only subjected them to papistry and monkery. When these Jews saw that Judaism had such strong scriptural basis and that Christianity [i.e., the Catholicism of the Roman Church] was pure nonsense without Biblical support, how could they quiet their hearts and become real, good Christians?

However, it soon became clear to Luther and others that the Reformation had little impact on Jewish attitudes toward Christianity. The advance of the Reformation had by no means generated larger numbers of Jewish converts, and speaking with disappointment 20 years later, Luther wrote another text, "Concerning the Jews and Their Lies" (1543), in which he reiterated his goal of Jewish conversion. Now, however, he advocated for increasing the pressure on the Jews as a means to achieve this aim. Moreover, he was increasingly concerned about what he considered to be the Jews' blasphemous rejection of Christianity—and he came to advocate the expulsion of the Jews from Christian territories, lest the Christians become complicit in such "blasphemy" committed under their eyes:

> What then shall we Christians do with this damned, rejected race of Jews? Since they live among us and we know about their lying and blasphemy and cursing, we cannot tolerate them if we wish not to share in their lies, curses, and blasphemy. . . . First, their synagogues . . . should be set on fire. . . . Secondly, their homes should likewise be broken down and destroyed. . . . Thirdly, they should be deprived of their prayer-books and Talmuds. . . . Fourthly, their rabbis must be forbidden under threat of death to teach any more. . . . Fifthly, passport and traveling privileges should be absolutely forbidden to the Jews. . . . Sixthly, they ought to be stopped from usury. . . . Seventhly, let the young and strong Jews and Jewesses be given the flail, the axe, the hoe, the spade, the distaff, the spindle, and let them earn their bread by the sweat of their noses as is enjoined upon Adam's children.

Despite what appears to be a radical shift in Luther's attitude toward Jews, he was consistently hostile to Judaism, which he never considered to be a legitimate religious option. Whether in 1523 or 20 years later, Luther's objective always was the conversion of Jews to Christianity—but as he grew increasingly frustrated with rabbinic interpretations of the Bible, which he saw as a blasphemous rejection of the Christian reading of the same text, his attitude turned more violent. "Judaism," from the outset, represented for Luther the opposite of true Christianity, and Jews shared this role of adversary with the "papists" (the Catholic Church), the Devil, and the Ottoman Turks, all of whom Luther presented as a threat to true Christendom.

Luther's diatribe against the Jews was not just theoretical talk. In 1537, for example, he actively instigated the decision to expel Jews from Saxony. The Jews developed mechanisms to defend themselves and were by no means the passive objects of Christian policymaking. Led by Josel (Joseph) of Rosheim (d. 1554), the leading representative of German Jewry who used his influence on Emperors Maximilian I (1493–1519) and Charles V (1519–1556) to advocate for the Jews, they fought back. In 1543, Josel was able to convince the city council of Strasbourg to ban the reprint of Luther's anti-Jewish writings in that city. Another case of Josel's successful lobbying on behalf of the German Jews can be found in his Hebrew memoirs:

> In the year [1537] the Elector John Frederick of Saxony was about to outlaw us and not allow the Jewish people even to set foot in his country. This was due to that priest whose name was Martin Luther—may his body and soul be bound up in hell—who wrote and issued many heretical books in which he said that whoever would help the Jews was doomed to perdition. . . . With the approval of our rabbis I was given some letters of high recommendation from certain Christian scholars. . . . I did not succeed in presenting the letters until the Elector came to Frankfurt where he met with other rulers, particularly the Margrave of Brandenburg who also intended to expel all his Jews. However, through the course of events and because of disputations which I had in the presence of Christian scholars, I succeeded in convincing the rulers, by means of our holy Torah, not to follow the views of Luther, Bucer [another Protestant reformer], and his gang, with the result that the rulers even confirmed our old privileges.

Through the sixteenth century, and into the seventeenth century, it was the more hostile attitude displayed in Luther's text of 1543 that was more influential, and the wave of expulsions that had affected Jewish communities throughout Germany before the Reformation continued, or even accelerated, in its wake. In the course of the seventeenth century, among Protestant millenarianists (those who were awaiting the imminent "Second Coming" of Christ) or among the Protestant movement of Pietism, the more tolerant attitude of Luther's earlier text on the Jews was again foregrounded. In seventeenth-century England, for example, a more tolerant attitude toward Jews developed against the exclusionary vision that persisted among Luther's followers in Germany at least until the Enlightenment and contributed to the readmission of the Jews to the British Isles.

Moreover, Protestantism challenged the established authority of the Catholic Church and set out to "demystify" Christian beliefs. One of the central aspects of the Protestant polemic against the established Catholic order was the rejection of what the reformers considered to be superstition and magic. One consequence of this "disenchantment" of the medieval Christian mindset in the wake of the Protestant Reformation was the decline of one of the oldest and vilest antisemitic accusations of the Middle Ages, the blood libel, the false accusation against Jews of committing ritual murder. After the first such blood libel had occurred in England in 1144, it was in the German-speaking lands that the number of ritual murder trials against Jews reached its height in the fifteenth and sixteenth centuries. After 1570, the number of trials declined significantly as a result of imperial protection of the Jews, Jewish self-defense, and the new thinking of the Reformation that called into question many of the old teachings of the Church. However, though ritual murder trials were suppressed from the seventeenth century on by the imperial and theological elites, the popular *belief* in the blood libel persisted well into the nineteenth century (and was revived by Nazi propaganda in the twentieth century).

The impact of humanism and the Reformation on the Jews of Central Europe was thus ambiguous. In fact, it was arguably less the Reformation than some of its unintended political consequences that led to a sea change in attitudes toward the Jews and, eventually, to the return of Jewish life to western Europe: the most important changes being the stalemate that resulted from the prolonged confrontation between Catholic and Protestant forces in the long years of the Thirty Years' War and, in its wake, the emergence of state politics that were now increasingly guided by pragmatic considerations of economic benefit rather than by religious concerns.

For Further Reading

On the period in general, see Jonathan Israel, *European Jewry in the Age of Mercantilism, 1550–1750*, 3rd ed. (Oxford, England: Littman Library of Jewish Civilization, 1998), and David Ruderman, *Early Modern Jewry: A New Cultural History* (Princeton, NJ: Princeton University Press, 2010).

On Spain and the Inquisition, see Jonathan Ray, *The Sephardic Frontier* (Ithaca, NY: Cornell University Press, 2006); Benjamin Gampel, *Anti-Jewish Riots in the Crown of Aragon and the Royal Response, 1391–1392* (Cambridge, 2016); Henry Kamen, *The Spanish Inquisition* (New Haven, CT: Yale University Press, 1999); Joseph Perez, *The Spanish Inquisition* (New Haven, CT: Yale University Press, 2006); and Haim Beinart, *The Expulsion of the Jews from Spain* (Oxford, England: Littman Library of Jewish Civilization, 2005).

On conversos, see Renée Levine Melammed, *Heretics or Daughters of Israel? The Crypto-Jewish Women of Castile* (Oxford, England: Oxford University Press, 1999); Renée Levine Melammed, *A Question of Identity: Iberian Conversos in Historical Perspective*

(Oxford, England: Oxford University Press, 2004); David Graizbord, *Souls in Dispute: Converso Identity in Iberia and the Jewish Diaspora, 1580–1700* (Philadelphia: University of Pennsylvania Press, 2003); and Ana Schaposchnik, *The Lima Inquisition: The Plight of Crypto-Jews in Seventeenth Century Peru* (Madison, WI: University of Wisconsin Press, 2015).

On the Ottoman Empire, see Esther Benbassa and Aron Rodrigue, *Sephardi Jewry* (Berkeley: University of California Press, 2000); Avigdor Levy, *The Sephardim in the Ottoman Empire* (Princeton, NJ: Darwin Press, 1993); Minna Rozen, *A History of the Jewish Community in Istanbul: The Formative Years, 1453–1566* (Leiden, The Netherlands: E. J. Brill, 2002); and Yaron Ben-Naeh, *Jews in the Realm of the Sultans* (Tübingen, Germany: Mohr Siebeck, 2008).

On Muslim lands in general, see Bernard Lewis, *The Jews of Islam* (Princeton, NJ: Princeton University Press, 1987), and Norman Stillman, *The Jews of Arab Lands* (Philadelphia, PA: Jewish Publication Society of America, 1979).

On Morocco, see Shlomo Deshen, *The Mellah Society* (Chicago: University of Chicago Press, 1989), and Emily Gottreich, *The Mellah of Marrakesh: Jewish and Muslim Space in Morocco's Red City* (Bloomington: Indiana University Press, 2006).

On Safed and Lurianic Kabbalah, see Lawrence Fine, *Physician of the Soul, Healer of the Cosmos: Isaac Luria and His Kabbalistic Fellowship* (Stanford, CA: Stanford University Press, 2003).

On Italy, see Robert Bonfil, *Jewish Life in Renaissance Italy* (Berkeley: University of California Press, 1994), and Kenneth Stow, *Theater of Acculturation: The Roman Ghetto in the Sixteenth Century* (Seattle: University of Washington Press, 2001).

On the scientific revolution, see David Ruderman, *Jewish Thought and Scientific Discovery in Early Modern Europe* (Detroit, MI: Wayne State University Press, 2001).

On the Protestant Reformation, see Dean Bell and Stephen Burnett, eds., *Jews, Judaism, and the Reformation in Sixteenth-Century Germany* (Leiden, The Netherlands: E. J. Brill, 2006).

On blood libel, see Ronnie Po-chia Hsia, *The Myth of Ritual Murder* (New Haven, CT: Yale University Press, 1988); Magda Teter, *Blood Libel: On the Trail of an Antisemitic Myth* (Cambridge, MA: Harvard University Press, 2020).

CHAPTER 9

New Worlds, East and West

In the Nobles' Republic: Jews in Early Modern Eastern Europe

The early modern period saw the exodus of Sephardi Jews from the Iberian Peninsula eastward into the Ottoman Empire, as well as a parallel migration of Ashkenazi Jews from central Europe to eastern Europe, from Germany into Poland. Like the Ottoman Empire, which became a major center of early modern Sephardi culture in the sixteenth century, Poland-Lithuania emerged as the new heartland of Ashkenazi Jewry. Continuous growth throughout the early modern period, despite the disastrous persecutions of the mid-seventeenth century, to which we shall return later in this chapter, made Polish-Lithuanian Jewry into the single largest Jewish community in the world by the end of the seventeenth century.

Also, not unlike the Jews of the Ottoman Empire, Jews in Poland-Lithuania compared their situation favorably with the conditions of Jewish life in the West. Moses Isserles (1520–1572) of Cracow (known by the Hebrew acronym of his name as the ReMA), one of the leading Polish rabbis in the sixteenth century, wrote to a former student:

> In this country [Poland] there is no fierce hatred of us [Jews] as in Germany. May it so continue until the advent of the Messiah. . . . You will be better off in this country. . . . You have here peace of mind.

Popular imagination created a pun on the Hebrew name for Poland, *Polin*. The story is that when a group of exiled Jews arrived in Poland, they heard a divine voice declare, "*Poh lin*" ("Dwell here"). This certainly does not mean that early modern Poland-Lithuania was without anti-Jewish persecutions: The historian Bernard Weinryb has counted over 50 local persecutions in Poland between the 1530s and the early 1700s, which totals 2 every three years. However, even the mass murder of Jews during the Chmielnicki massacres of 1648 and the turmoil of the Russian and Swedish invasions of Poland in the following decade, traumatic as they must have been, did not stop the demographic expansion of Polish-Lithuanian Jewry (see Map 9.1).

Jews were emigrating from Germanic lands to Poland probably no later than the eleventh century, and this pattern continued in subsequent centuries and accelerated in the sixteenth century. Only in the wake of the massacres of the seventeenth century was this trend somewhat reversed, when eastern European Jews sought refuge in Germany and elsewhere in western Europe, where the political conditions had begun to change, and a return of the Jews marked the renewed growth of Jewish communities in the west. Thanks to the massive influx of Ashkenazi Jews from Germanic

DOI: 10.4324/9781003611592-10

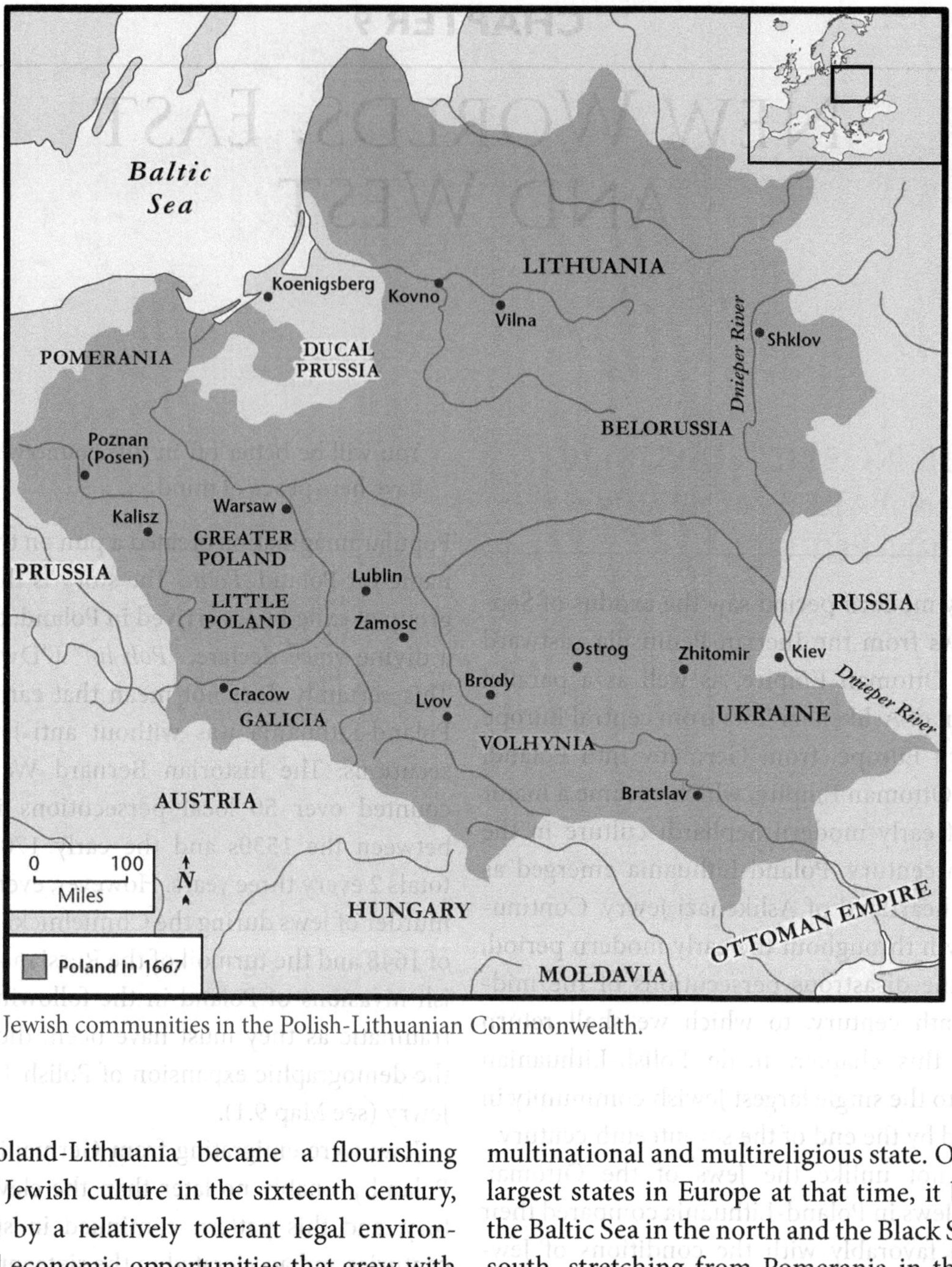

Map 9.1 Jewish communities in the Polish-Lithuanian Commonwealth.

lands, Poland-Lithuania became a flourishing center of Jewish culture in the sixteenth century, sustained by a relatively tolerant legal environment and economic opportunities that grew with the expansion of the Polish-Lithuanian Commonwealth to the east. Exact numbers are, as elsewhere during this period, difficult to establish, and estimates of the Jewish population in Poland-Lithuania vary considerably. It has been suggested that 150,000–170,000 Jews lived in Poland-Lithuania in the mid-sixteenth century.

The Polish-Lithuanian Commonwealth, created in the Union of Lublin of 1569, was a multinational and multireligious state. One of the largest states in Europe at that time, it bordered the Baltic Sea in the north and the Black Sea in the south, stretching from Pomerania in the northwest to Ukraine in the southeast. In the middle of the seventeenth century, Poles represented only about 40 percent of the country's population, with ethnic minorities including Ukrainians, Russians, and Lithuanians, but also immigrant populations, such as Germans, Italians, Scots, and—of course—the Jews. Poland-Lithuania was no less diverse religiously, with Catholics representing less than half the population and harboring Orthodox,

Protestant, Muslim, and Jewish minorities. Thus, at least a degree of religious toleration was no less imperative here than it was in the contemporary Ottoman Empire, and though the Jews hardly enjoyed "equal rights" (a foreign concept in those days), they did enjoy far-reaching religious freedom and autonomy.

Jews benefited from royal charters and the privileges granted to them by nobility and the Polish kings—for example, the privilege of Casimir III "the Great" (1310–1370), granted in 1334, which in turn confirmed the earlier charter granted by Prince Boleslav of Kalisz in 1264 for Great Poland. Such privileges were renewed and, at times, amended with each new king ascending the throne. In contrast to the Ottoman model, however, one cannot speak of a uniform legal status of all Jews in the Polish-Lithuanian Commonwealth. Jews were subject to a myriad of different authorities and different legal circumstances. A number of Polish cities—namely, Warsaw, Cracow, Gdansk, and Lublin—did not admit Jews at all, and some royal cities even extracted the privilege de non tolerandis Judaeis from the king, allowing them to exclude Jews from their midst. Warsaw, for example, obtained this right in 1527. In some cases, cities tried to restrict the Jewish population to a separate quarter or a nearby suburb, such as Kazimierz, outside Cracow, which had a Jewish population of about 4,500 in the first half of the seventeenth century (compared to a general population in Cracow of about 28,000).

With the death of the last king of the Jagiellonian dynasty, which had ruled Poland from 1386 to 1572, the country became a nobles' republic, with the landed gentry electing the king in Parliament, the *Sejm*. Earlier in the sixteenth century, the Constitution of 1505 had severely limited the power of the king, as all legislation required the unanimous approval of Parliament. The dependency of the monarchy on an often-deadlocked Sejm meant that the central authorities in the Polish-Lithuanian Commonwealth were considerably weakened at a time when other European monarchs began to consolidate their power and enhance the authority of their governments. By the seventeenth century, Poland had come to resemble a federation of territories and private estates more than one centralized state.

Especially after 1569, Polish settlement expanded eastward into Belarus and the Ukraine. Magnates and lesser noblemen acquired large estates, on which they founded numerous new villages and towns. Vast stretches of territory with thousands of little hamlets and small towns became the private domains of Polish nobility. One magnate was Jan Zamoyski, who left at his death in 1605 personal property the size of about 2,460 square miles, including 11 towns and over 200 villages. One of the towns owned by Zamoyski was the city of Zamosc, where he welcomed a number of Sephardi immigrants with the purpose of developing it into a commercial center for trade between Poland and Ottoman lands. Another magnate, Prince Konstanty Wasyl Ostrogski, owned no less than 100 towns and 1,300 villages, with an annual profit that equaled the tax revenue of the entire country. The nobles became essentially autonomous rulers over their estates, installing their own courts and maintaining their own private armies.

For the management of properties of this size, spread out geographically throughout the country, the magnates needed intermediaries and agents to oversee the thousands of peasants working for them; to administer the vast estates; to market agricultural produce, lumber, and cattle; and to provide all kinds of goods to the populations in the many villages. It was in this function as intermediaries that many Jews established themselves in ever larger numbers in the eastern parts of the country, managing the Polish nobles' estates, leasing a variety of economic monopolies, and becoming an important, often dominant part of the urban middle classes in the newly colonized territories in the east.

The lease, or *arenda*, was an arrangement of particular importance in the relation between Jews and magnates and between Jews and the general population.

A significant portion of Jews in Poland made a living as leaseholders, or *arrendators*, which came to be considered a traditionally "Jewish" economic activity. For magnates, the leasing of a monopoly on anything from the distillation and sale of alcohol to salt mining to the right to collect tolls and taxes was a convenient way of raising cash and outsourcing the exploitation of the resources in their vast estates. Liquor production (beer, vodka, etc.) and its distribution in taverns and bars were one of the hallmarks of the *arenda* system, but the *arenda* for a given town or region would likewise include monopolies on mills, salt mines, grain warehouses, tobacco sales, and collection of bridge tolls. The general *arrendator*—a wealthy individual or the entire Jewish community—would then subdivide the general *arenda* to individual leaseholders who made a living operating a distillery, running a tavern, or operating a sawmill. The Jewish *arrendator* often found himself in a conflict of interest with other sections of the population, including the peasants and townspeople, who might resent high prices, tolls, and taxes being collected by the leaseholder. Anti-Jewish hostility in this context was therefore economically motivated just as often as it was an expression of religious prejudice, and the potential for conflict between the Jewish *arrendators* and their non-Jewish (and Jewish) neighbors was real.

By 1539, King Sigismund I had granted to the nobles authority over the Jews living in the localities they owned. The decision to allow Jewish settlement or even encourage it was entirely up to each individual magnate, as was the treatment of his Jewish subjects. Some magnates, such as the founder of the town of Oleszowo, declared that "the Polish Crown flourishes with people of diverse estates, particularly in regard to their religious allegiance, on the principle that no authority shall exercise power over faith, honor, and conscience." Others took the opposite stance, such as Jan Magier, who declared in 1591, "I exclude from residence Jews, a sordid, cunning, underhanded, and anti-Christian tribe because of the principles of their faith." This situation led to many inconsistencies in the legal status of Jews in early modern Poland-Lithuania and made them subject to the whims of their noble masters. Jewish literature from the time contains examples of abuse and arbitrary treatment at the hand of Polish landowners. Generally, however, the interests of the Polish nobility and of the Jews converged, as the latter performed indispensable services for the magnates and fulfilled a crucial role in the economy of the nobles' estates, and both sides benefited from the contractual relationship between the Jewish leaseholder and landowning magnate.

A situation that was, in many ways, similar is described in the autobiography of a young Jew born in Moravia, then part of the Habsburg Empire, which was, next to the Ottoman Empire and Poland-Lithuania, the third empire in eastern/southeastern Europe with a large Jewish population. This anonymous autobiography, written in Hebrew, is a good illustration of the economic life of many Jews in eastern Europe in the seventeenth century and their dependence on the goodwill of local notables. "My mother then showed her ability in supporting the family by her own efforts," the author explains, "and [she] started to manufacture brandy out of oats. . . . This was hard labor, but she succeeded. In the meantime my father pursued his studies." Not infrequently did Jewish women play an active role in the economic life of eastern European Jews of the period, and they were by no means relegated to their homes. The arrangement described in this early part of the autobiography, a division of labor of sorts that envisioned the men as students of the Torah and women as the breadwinners, was probably more an exception in the early modern period; it became a universal ideal only later during the nineteenth century (and still informs the practice of many strictly Orthodox Jews today).

The autobiography by this Moravian Jew exemplified that a strict separation of spheres—working women and Torah-studying men—was generally not possible to sustain under the circumstances of the early modern period:

> One day a holy man, R. Loeb, the Rabbi of Trebitch . . . came to our town and stayed in our house. When he saw the troubles of my mother, . . . he had pity on her, and gave my father some gold and silver merchandise . . . to get him used to trade. . . . My father was successful and did a good business. Incidentally this brought him the acquaintance of the Count who owned the city. The latter liked him, and turned over to him the distillery in which they were working with seven great kettles, and he gave him servants to do the work and grain to prepare brandy. For this my father paid him at the end of the year a specified amount, in addition to paying a certain percentage of the income in taxes, as was customary.

As in Poland-Lithuania, the brewing and distilling of alcoholic beverages were an important economic activity of Jews elsewhere in eastern Europe.

The autobiography also testifies to the often-precarious nature of the economic alliance between Jews and the nobles. The author describes how unnamed Jewish enemies, presumably competitors, ruined his father's reputation:

> [The Count] made charges against him in connection with the distillery and other business matters, and put him into prison for two months. . . . [N]othing could be done to save my father, and he had to give up half his wealth in order to be released. On this occasion his enemies wreaked their revenge on him . . . and urged the Count to expel my father . . . from his property. The Count did so.

Thus, if the Jews fulfilled a crucial function in the magnate-dominated economy of eastern Europe, they were also dependent on the goodwill of their patrons. In fact, as the example cited here shows, at times rivalries within the Jewish community could lead individual Jews themselves to get their Christian overlords involved in internal disputes—a sign of a lack of discipline and coherence within the community that many of its lay and religious leaders were well aware of and tried to contain through ordinances that prohibited taking conflicts to non-Jewish courts.

The Jewish Community in Poland-Lithuania

The semiautonomous governing body of the Jewish community, the *kehillah*, paralleled the Christian municipality in its structure and its functions. As Gershon Hundert, a historian of early modern Polish Jewry, observed, "what divided Jews from Christians, beyond the psychological distance, was not residence but jurisdiction. . . . Jews were in the town but not of it." Though Jews tended to live in particular streets or sections of a city, they were generally not subject to the jurisdiction of the municipality and instead elected their own leadership, raised their own taxes, provided their own services—from paving streets to providing for the needs of the poor—and maintained their own courts. The leadership of the early modern Polish-Lithuanian *kehillah* was an oligarchic lay leadership that derived its legitimization from both the authority it had been endowed with by the Polish Crown and Jewish tradition and Talmudic law. The lay leaders of the community, the *tovim*, were elected annually by all taxpaying members. The rabbis were not part of the elected leadership but, rather, employees of the *kehillah*. However, the rabbi's role as representing religious authority, as teacher of rabbinic tradition, and as judge of the rabbinic courts, was crucial in providing legitimacy to the *kehillah* and its institutions.

The autonomy of the Jewish community found a clear expression in its right to grant or deny residence rights to Jews from outside the city. The prerogative over *hezqat ha-yishuv*, as the right of residence was known in Hebrew, was a common feature of Jewish autonomy in many Jewish communities in Europe since the Middle Ages (though it had not been used in Spain or in the Ottoman Empire, where, as we have seen, conditions for Jewish settlement were far less stringent and Jews generally enjoyed freedom of movement and residence throughout the empire). In Poland-Lithuania, like in many other European countries, the presence of Jewish outsiders was regulated by each community. In Kazimierz outside Cracow, for example, a nonresident Jew was not allowed to settle or do business. In general, a community's charter, usually limiting the number of residents, as well as local economic conditions, determined whether an individual received the right of residence. The purpose of such measures, as of numerous other community ordinances regulating economic and communal life, was to avoid rivalry and competition between Jews, which was seen as detrimental to the community at large. Outside Poland-Lithuania, in German-speaking lands of central Europe, government restrictions on the permissible number of Jewish settlers applied as well.

One of the most important officials of larger Jewish communities was the *shtadlan*, or intercessor, whose job it was to represent his community—and often the Jews of an entire province—to the various levels of the non-Jewish government. The communities at large were collectively responsible for the tax burden of all Jews and needed to maintain channels of communication with the royal authorities, with the city governments, and with the noble magnates. Legislation could directly or indirectly affect Jewish life in the commonwealth, and the community often had to defend itself against antisemitic accusations—namely, accusations of ritual murder and host desecration that continued to haunt Polish-Lithuanian Jewry throughout the early modern period. It fell to the *shtadlan*, always a well-connected individual with diplomatic skills and knowledge of the Polish language and of the ins and outs of politics in the commonwealth, to represent the Jewish community to the outside world.

By the sixteenth century, the desire for coordination of the collective needs of Polish Jewry led to the creation of a central body representing all Jewish communities in Poland and a similar organization in Lithuania. In Poland, the emerging institution was known as the Council of Four Lands (*va'ad arba' aratsot*), though in reality its constituent regions fluctuated between three and four until the seventeenth century and exceeded four lands in the eighteenth century. The Lithuanian Council of Provinces was an equivalent institution in that part of the commonwealth, and similar supraregional bodies existed outside Poland-Lithuania as well. Meeting on occasion of the annual commercial fairs of Lublin and other cities, when Jews from all over the region came together, the *va'ad arba' aratsot* and similar institutions did not employ a standing "national" bureaucracy but had, by 1576, established a central court, represented the Jews to the government, oversaw the distribution of the tax burden, and mediated conflicts that transcended the boundaries of individual cities and regions. Like the local communities, the central bodies of Polish-Lithuanian Jewry employed *shtadlanim*, who interceded with the central government and the Sejm. They watched the legislative process closely to head off any new measures that might be detrimental to the Jews of the realm. In 1623, for example, the Lithuanian Council of Provinces adopted a resolution that

> in any period of the *sejmiki* meeting before the Diet the heads of each community are to stand guard and carefully investigate lest any innovation be introduced which might prove to be a harmful thorn to us. The necessary expenditure should be defrayed by each community.

If the community leadership and the Council of Four Lands were dominated by lay leaders, the rabbinate continued to play a central role in the lives of early modern Polish-Lithuanian Jewry. This was a traditional society based on a shared religious tradition and Jewish religious law. Religion was not just one part of life; rather, religious beliefs and rabbinic law permeated all aspects of the individual and collective existence. The rabbis were the ones responsible for the interpretation and application of religious law in the ever-changing conditions of the rapidly expanding Polish-Lithuanian community. In doing so, they had to be mindful of the demands of Halakhah as it was represented in the Talmud and the growing body of rabbinic legal literature while also considering the requirements of social circumstances. An example is the following case described by one of the luminaries of Polish rabbinic culture in the sixteenth century, Rabbi Moses Isserles of Cracow (1520–1572):

> There was a poor man in the land who betrothed his grown daughter to her proper mate. And during the time of her engagement . . . the father died . . . and the daughter was left bereaved. She was without father and only [had] relatives who forsook her and averted their eyes from her, except for one relative . . . who brought her into his home. . . . And when the time for her wedding came . . . there was no dowry or other needs. Yet everyone told her that she should ritually immerse herself and prepare for her wedding because she would have a dowry. And this virgin did as her female neighbors told her. She listened to their voice and they covered her with the veil on Friday as is done to virgins. And when the shadows of the evening became long and the day [the Sabbath] was almost sanctified, when her relatives were to give the dowry, they tightened their hands and did not give as they were supposed to, and there was about a third missing from the dowry. Also, the groom reneged and did not want to marry her and did not pay attention to all the words of the town leaders who spoke to him saying that he should not embarrass a daughter of Israel because of contemptible money. . . . And the work of Satan succeeded until it was about an hour and one-half into the Sabbath when they reconciled themselves and the groom agreed to enter under the marriage canopy and, in order not to embarrass a worthy daughter of Israel, I arose and performed the marriage at this time.

What is remarkable here is that according to rabbinic law, as codified in the Mishnah, it was prohibited to perform a wedding on the Sabbath, yet Isserles decided to do so nonetheless "in order not to embarrass a worthy daughter of Israel" and taking into account the special circumstances of the case. One of the things illustrated by Isserles's response is the flexibility of legal practice within the confines of traditional Jewish law. Traditional society retained an unwavering commitment to Halakhah as divine law, all of which was believed to have been given to Moses at Mount Sinai along with the Ten Commandments and the remainder of the Bible. But the rabbis also retained a flexibility, a willingness to interpret and reinterpret the law, and a pragmatic approach that recognized the need to reconcile the demands of the law with the demands of particular social circumstances that could vary from case to case.

In 1648, the order of traditional Jewish society was severely shaken when a wave of violent persecution swept through Ukraine—the Chmielnicki massacres (or, in Hebrew, the *gezerot tah ve-tat*, after the years in the Jewish calendar), followed by the violence of the subsequent Russian and Swedish invasions that lasted through much of the 1650s. That year, Bogdan Chmielnicki (1595–1657), son of a minor noble, led the Cossacks of Ukraine into a major insurgency against the Polish regime. The Cossacks, as the historian Bernard Weinryb has described them, were "a by-product of the tension between the nomads of the southern Russian steppes and the inhabitants of the settled borderlands." They were independent warriors, at times in the service of the Polish Crown and at times rising in rebellion against it. In 1648, Chmielnicki forged an alliance between his Cossack forces and the Ukrainian peasantry, with which they shared their Greek Orthodox religion, pitting them against the Polish state and landowning nobility; he also ensured the support from the Crimean Tartars. The insurgency led to some of the worst massacres in Jewish history, and thousands of Jews were killed alongside many Catholic Poles.

The worst massacres occurred in the spring and summer of 1648. Many Jews fled the rural areas of the war zone to fortified cities; in many cases it was there that the Cossack forces caught and massacred them in large numbers—for example, in Nemyriv, where thousands were reported to have been killed. Numerous Jewish chronicles describe the suffering, death, and destruction of those months. One of the most famous is a book called *Yaven Metsulah* (*Abyss of Despair*), by Rabbi Nathan Neta Hanover (d. 1683). Here is what he says about some of the earliest massacres committed by Chmielnicki's followers:

> Many communities beyond the Dnieper, and close to the battlefield . . . who were unable to escape, perished for the sanctification of His Name. These persons died cruel and bitter deaths. Some were skinned alive and their flesh was thrown to the dogs; some had their hands and limbs chopped off, and their bodies thrown on the highway only to be trampled by wagons and crushed by horses; some had wounds inflicted upon them, and thrown on the street to die a slow death . . .; others were buried alive. . . . There was no cruel device of murder in the whole world that was not perpetrated by the enemies. . . . Also against the Polish people, these cruelties were perpetrated, especially against the priests and bishops. Thus, westward of the Dnieper several thousand Jewish persons perished and several hundred were forced to change their faith.

Hanover noted here and elsewhere in his chronicle that the Jews were not the only ones attacked and massacred. Modern historians have pointed out the social and political dimensions of the Chmielnicki revolt against Polish rule in the Ukraine and have suggested that perhaps Jews were not so much singled out for religious reasons as they were attacked because they were identified with the Polish regime. As we have seen, the Jews in Ukraine were playing an important role as agents of the Polish landowners and as mediators between the Polish aristocrats, often residing in faraway cities, and the local, enserfed Ukrainian peasant population. Hanover pointed to this fact in his chronicle when he wrote about a certain Jew:

> [He] was the nobleman's tax farmer, as was the customary occupation of most Jews in the kingdom of [Little] Russia [i.e., Ukraine]. For they ruled in every part of [Little] Russia, a condition which aroused the jealousy of the peasants, and which was the cause of the massacres.

Modern historians have also significantly revised the estimated number of Jews who were killed at the hands of the rebels. It is now clear that the numbers given in contemporary chronicles are unreliable and often exaggerated. Historian Shaul Stampfer has argued on the basis of archival research that perhaps 20,000 out of 40,000 Jews in the Ukraine were killed in the massacres. Even though this number, both of the total Jewish population and those killed, is significantly lower than had been assumed earlier, it still suggests that half the Jewish population of Ukraine was massacred within just a few months. What is more, Jews continued to suffer, alongside their Catholic Polish neighbors and others, from the continued violence during the Russian and Swedish invasions and the continuing Cossack rebellion in subsequent years. At that time, the massacres were seen by Ashkenazi Jewry as the "third destruction" (after the destruction of the First and Second Temples in Jerusalem), as Rabbi Shabbatai Horowitz called it.

Perhaps most surprising is the fast recovery of the Jewish communities in Poland-Lithuania from the disaster. Many Jews who had fled across the border now came back (though most of those who had fled to cities in Germany and Holland remained there). Others had survived by accepting baptism and returned to Judaism after the massacres; the Polish king authorized them to do so as early as 1649. The Chmielnicki massacres played an important role in Ashkenazi memory, and word of the horror spread throughout the Jewish world—but they did not end the continued expansion and flourishing of Polish-Lithuanian Jewry in the early modern period.

Early Modern Ashkenazi Culture

A source that is often quoted by historians of Jewish culture in early modern Poland-Lithuania is the last chapter of Rabbi Nathan Neta Hanover's chronicle of the Chmielnicki massacres. In this chapter, Hanover describes the "six pillars" of the world, all of which could be found among the Jews of Poland-Lithuania: Torah study (to the description of which he dedicated most of his chapter), prayer, charity, justice, truth, and peace. It is obvious that Hanover was drawing an idealized picture of Polish-Lithuanian Jewry, a nostalgic portrait of a world that had come under the assault of widespread violence and destruction. Yet even if we admit that Hanover idealized his community, the description in his *Yaven Metsulah* nevertheless gives an impression of the centrality of rabbinic learning in early modern Polish-Lithuanian Jewish culture:

> Throughout the dispersions of Israel there was nowhere so much learning as in the Kingdom of Poland. Each community maintained academies, and the head of each academy was given an ample salary so that . . . the study of the Torah might be his sole occupation. . . . Each community maintained young men and provided for them a weekly allowance of money that they might study with the head of the academy. And for each young man they also maintained two boys to study under his guidance. . . . If the community consisted of fifty householders it supported not less than thirty young men and boys. . . . There was scarcely a house in all the Kingdom of Poland where its members did not occupy themselves with the study of Torah.

Other contemporary sources were more critical of the shortcomings of their generation, to be sure, and admonished the public for not doing enough and for falling short of the ideal described in Hanover's chronicle. But there is other evidence of a growing reach of rabbinic learning at that time, primarily due to the impact of printing.

The Italian Sephardic Soncino family had pioneered the printing of Talmudic tractates since the 1480s, followed by a complete set of the Talmud printed by Daniel Bomberg in Venice in the 1520s. However, with the growing interference of the Catholic Church, through censorship or outright prohibition of the Talmud, Jewish printers ceased to print the Talmud in Italy after the middle of the sixteenth century. In Poland-Lithuania, however, with its more liberal religious climate, editions of the Talmud surpassed the number of all other printed works, including the Bible. Over 100 tractates of the Talmud were printed in Cracow alone in the sixteenth and seventeenth centuries, and 60 in Lublin. One historian estimated that some 48,000–80,000 copies of Talmudic tractates were thus produced in Polish printing houses at that time.

Used in the rabbinic academies throughout the commonwealth, study of the Talmud—now so widely available in print—became the main focus of Jewish learning in Poland-Lithuania and led to the rise of its peculiar method of study known as *pilpul*. *Pilpul* was a mode of study in which every single apparent inconsistency or contradiction within the Talmud, or between its medieval commentaries, was resolved and reconciled through interpretation. Inconsistencies were to be discovered and reconciled by the avid student of the Talmud without regard to either the literal meaning of the texts or the normative legal practice they established. In due course, *pilpul* came under attack from some of the leading rabbis of the period, such as Rabbi Judah Loew of Prague (the MaHaRaL, d. 1609) or Rabbi Yom-Tov Lipmann Heller (1579–1654). Their critique led eventually to a modernization of rabbinic education in subsequent generations—an educational reform that anticipated the more radical approach of the eighteenth-century Jewish Enlightenment.

In fact, rabbinic culture was by no means uniform, not without internal tensions, and underwent some significant and even radical transformations in the early modern period. We have already discussed the emergence of a new school of Jewish mysticism, Lurianic Kabbalah, in the Ottoman city of Safed in the sixteenth century. In Ashkenazi culture in the sixteenth century, Kabbalah was only one among several areas of study and, like all others, was subservient to the study of the Talmud. By the seventeenth century, however, it asserted itself as a primary source of reference and displaced other fields of study, especially philosophy. The major work of kabbalistic teaching, the *Zohar*, came to occupy a place that was second to none, not even the Talmud, and Rabbi Shabbatai Horowitz went out of his way to declare in 1647 that "surely those persons who decline to study Kabbalah do not merit a soul."

Another product of the flourishing Jewish culture of sixteenth-century Ottoman Safed had a major impact on early modern Ashkenazi rabbinic culture. The Sephardi rabbi Joseph Karo, residing in Safed, wrote in the years 1555–1563 a major new code of Jewish law. Called *Shulhan Arukh* ("the decked table"), the law code was printed for the first time in Venice in 1565. It soon gained wide acceptance and authority throughout the Sephardi Diaspora and beyond, and its growing popularity caused a major debate among the Ashkenazi rabbis of Poland-Lithuania. Eventually, the *Shulhan Arukh* became the almost universally accepted digest of Jewish law, and it remains so among Orthodox Jews to this day. At first, however, in the sixteenth and seventeenth centuries, it was highly controversial.

Jewish law had developed over many centuries and in many different places, and though its fundamental set of beliefs and practices was shared, a myriad of more or less significant differences evolved as well. Ashkenazi Jews did not allow the consumption of legumes during the Passover holiday, for example, whereas Sephardi communities did. During Passover, rice was not consumed by Ashkenazim, whereas it was permitted by some Sephardim and prohibited by others, and it actually was a typical Passover food for Syrian Jews. With the printing of a universal code of Jewish law, such differences would be challenged, as it would recognize one practice as being correct and imply that others were wrong.

Karo based his decisions in the *Shulhan Arukh* on three medieval law codes, two of which had been written by Sephardi authors and one by a German rabbi who lived in Spain. Even Moses Isserles, an Ashkenazi rabbi sympathetic in principle to the codification of Jewish law in print, could not accept an a priori primacy of Sephardi legal interpretation. What Isserles did in response was to change Ashkenazi Jewry profoundly: in the 1570s, he published in Cracow a new edition of Karo's *Shulhan Arukh* with his own commentary, called the *Mappah* ("tablecloth"), in which he clarified the Ashkenazi practice where it differed from Karo's opinion. But Isserles's version of the *Shulhan Arukh* proved to be controversial, too, because a printed and uniform code of law presented a challenge to traditional ways of learning. One rabbi, Hayim of Friedberg, argued, alluding to the title of the *Shulhan Arukh*:

> Just as a person likes only the food that he prepares for himself, in accordance with his own appetite and taste . . . thus he does not like another person's rulings unless he agrees with that person. All the more does he not wish to be dependent upon the books of other authors, just as a person likes only the food he prepares for himself, in accordance with his own appetite and taste, and does not aspire to be a guest at their decked table [*shulhan arukh*].

In the seventeenth century, individual rabbis were still opposed to the dominance of the *Shulhan Arukh*, but even Rabbi Isaiah Horowitz, who had opposed it before, admitted in 1626:

> [Isserles's] coinage has been accepted, and we must follow his opinions and render decisions in accordance with his views. . . . In the Diaspora, in the lands of the Polish Crown, in Bohemia, Moravia, and Germany, the [practice] has spread to render decisions in accordance with his views.

This quote not only testifies to the eventual widespread acceptance of the *Shulhan Arukh* with Isserles's glosses in the seventeenth century but also indicates the development of an Ashkenazi identity that found its expression here in the geographic scope within which Isserles's ruling was considered to be authoritative. This Ashkenazi cultural area included Poland-Lithuania, the Habsburg lands of Bohemia and Moravia, and the Jewish communities of Germany.

Apart from adhering to a common rabbinic tradition codified by Moses Isserles, the Ashkenazi world was characterized by its vernacular language: the use of the Yiddish language. Yiddish had developed as the spoken language of the Ashkenazi Jews in northern France and the Rhineland, and like the Spanish Jews took their Judeo-Spanish language with them when they moved eastward to the Ottoman Empire, the Ashkenazi Jews preserved their Yiddish language after they moved to Poland-Lithuania. There, the language underwent significant change, to be sure, and the Western Yiddish of Germany and the Eastern Yiddish of Poland-Lithuania are quite distinct. Perhaps surprisingly, there never emerged a Judeo-Polish language, and Yiddish—a Jewish language with a Germanic base and Hebrew-Aramaic as well as Slavic elements—remained the common language of the Ashkenazi Jews in eastern Europe.

Early modern Ashkenazi culture thus not only was rabbinic elite culture produced in Hebrew, focusing on the interpretation of the classical texts of Judaism, but also included a rich literature in the vernacular language where rabbinic and popular culture intersected. Doubtless the most popular and most well-known work of this literature was the Yiddish rendering of the Pentateuch (together with the weekly readings from the Prophets and the "five scrolls" read at certain points in the Jewish year), known as *Tsenerene* (from "*tse'enah ure'enah*"; Song of Songs 3:11) and written toward the end of the sixteenth century by Jacob ben Isaac Ashkenazi of Yanov (1550–1624/1625). Though we do not know when it was printed for the first time, the edition of 1622 declared that it had been preceded by three earlier editions that were all already out of print at that time.

Tsenerene presents the weekly portion of the reading from the Pentateuch and the prophetic readings that accompany it during the Sabbath morning service in the synagogue, using Yiddish rather than Hebrew quotations from the original throughout and providing explanations and interpretations interwoven with legends, folktales, and ethical admonishment. Avoiding philosophical or kabbalistic teachings and using an accessible language, *Tsenerene* was intended to provide a basic understanding of the tradition to uneducated readers who had no access to Hebrew education.

Tsenerene was often presented as a book for women, just as the terms *vaybertaytsh* (for Yiddish translations) and *vaybershrift* (for the typeface commonly used in Yiddish print; *vayber* means "women") suggested a gendered use of language. In reality, the title page of the earliest extant edition of *Tsenerene* states that "this work is designed to enable *men and women* . . . to understand the word of God in simple language." It is clear that Yiddish literature was not intended exclusively for women, nor was it necessarily read primarily by women. Rather, a distinction was made between those who possessed rabbinic learning and Hebrew literacy and those who did not.

It is true, however, that the traditional educational system provided only boys with a basic training in Hebrew and rabbinic literature in schools, whereas the education for girls was largely informal and done in the vernacular Yiddish. Traditional Jewish society was organized around two separate male and female cultural spheres. Men were expected to participate in public ritual in the synagogue and were, at least in theory, subject to the ideal of perpetual Torah study, whereas women were "exempt" (as rabbinic law called it, or excluded) from many rituals. Their role was, as one historian has phrased it, that of "facilitators" (enabling men to fulfill their religious duties) and of "bystanders." In the course of the early modern period, the rabbinic elite realized that it needed to provide women—and the numerous unlearned men—with a way to absorb the cultural values of the Jewish religion, and this is what led to the development of a growing Yiddish literature during early modern times.

The use of Yiddish also enabled women to develop their own, distinctly female ways of religious expression: The early modern age saw the proliferation of *tkhines*, prayers written in Yiddish for women (and, at times, *by* women, though often by male authors for a female audience). Collections of *tkhines* appeared from the late sixteenth century on and, by providing women with the possibility of religious expression independent of the male-dominated ritual of Hebrew synagogue liturgy, invested female ritual (e.g., lighting the Sabbath candles or the monthly ritual immersion in the *mikvah*) with meaning. One such *tkhine*, said upon lighting the Sabbath candles, reads like this:

> Master of the Universe, may the mitsvah of my lighting candles be accepted as equivalent to the mitsvah of the High Priest when he lit the candles in the precious Temple. As his observance was accepted so may mine be

KEEPING TIME IN EARLY MODERN EUROPE

The rhythm of time—of hours, days, weeks, and years—seems so obvious and natural to us that it is easy to forget that much of it is determined by culture no less than it is by the cycles of nature, such as the circadian and the lunar cycles or the seasons of the year. The biblical story of Creation has bequeathed upon the modern West the tradition of the seven-day week, but there are non-Western cultures that organize their lives differently, and the French revolutionaries after 1789 instituted a short-lived revolutionary calendar that replaced the seven-day with a ten-day week. The Jewish calendar differs from both its Christian and its Islamic counterparts in that it is based on a combination of the lunar and the solar cycle: As in the Islamic calendar, the months of the Jewish calendar are based on the lunar cycle. Since the lunar year is shorter than the solar year (12 lunar months are about 11 days shorter than the solar year), this means that without adjustments, festivals that occur in a specific month wander through the seasons, so that the Muslim monthlong fast, Ramadan, can occur in the summer in some years and in the winter in other years. The Bible, however, prescribes that the festival of Passover, for example, has to be observed in the spring, so the Jewish calendar needs to make up for the difference between the solar and lunar year, which is accomplished by adding an additional month 7 years out of each 19-year cycle.

Given the historical origins of Christianity, there was some overlap between the Christian and Jewish calendars. Over the centuries, however, as the Church sought to distance the Christian religion from Judaism, the Christian calendar was modified, with the explicit goal of making a clear break with the Jewish calendar. The weekly day of rest was set for Sunday, rather than the Jewish Sabbath, and it was determined that Easter was always to fall on a Sunday as well, rather than follow the date of the Jewish Passover, the time of Jesus's crucifixion and subsequent resurrection, as told in the New Testament. Emperor Constantine said at that time, "[I]t appeared an unworthy thing that in the celebration of this most holy feast [Easter] we should follow the practice of the Jews, who have impiously defiled their hands with enormous sin." The irony is that, in order to avoid the coincidence of Easter with Passover, the Christian calendar turned out to be rather complicated to calculate and had little to do with astronomical science ("Easter is a holiday, not a planet," as the late sixteenth-/early seventeenth-century astronomer Johannes Kepler reportedly quipped). Determining the correct time to observe Easter became a major issue of denominational conflict between different Christian Churches. The calendar played an important role in Catholic–Protestant conflicts in the sixteenth and seventeenth centuries, for example, and the Gregorian reform of the Christian calendar in 1582 led to differences in the calendar and the celebration of Christian holidays on different days in different parts of Europe. Protestant states resisted the adoption of the Gregorian reform until the eighteenth century, and the Orthodox churches of the East (e.g., in Russia or in Greece) celebrate Easter on a different date than Christians in the West do to this day.

The calendar also became one of the battlefields of Christian–Jewish religious polemics, and Jewish authors developed a literary genre, the *sefer evronot*, in which they discussed the Jewish calendar, laid out the rules for the intercalation of an additional month during the leap year, fixed the calculation of the new moon that determined the date of the festivals, and sought to defend its superiority over the Christian reckoning of time. Especially since the advent of printing, there also was a proliferation of calendars for popular use, everything from perpetual calendars that explained how to calculate the festivals for any given year to handy pocket diaries for a specific year. Hebrew printing houses in Italy and the Ottoman Empire

KEEPING TIME IN EARLY MODERN EUROPE (CONTINUED)

began churning out calendars from the sixteenth century, and given the ephemeral nature of the calendar, printing diaries and almanacs that had to be replaced each year was a lucrative business. Not all these calendars were always carefully produced, however, and complaints abound that faulty calendars were to blame for Jews transgressing the law. Once the production of calendars had taken off, printers customized them to make them ever more user-friendly and provide an abundance of information. The Hebrew calendars often included, for example, information on Christian holidays, which shaped the rhythm of public life and which Jews therefore needed to be aware of, as well as the dates of important trading fairs and the like. The calendars are thus emblematic of Jewish life in early modern Europe, integrating the observance of Jewish sacred time with both the rhythm of Christian sacred time and the secular calendar of trading fairs or agricultural life.

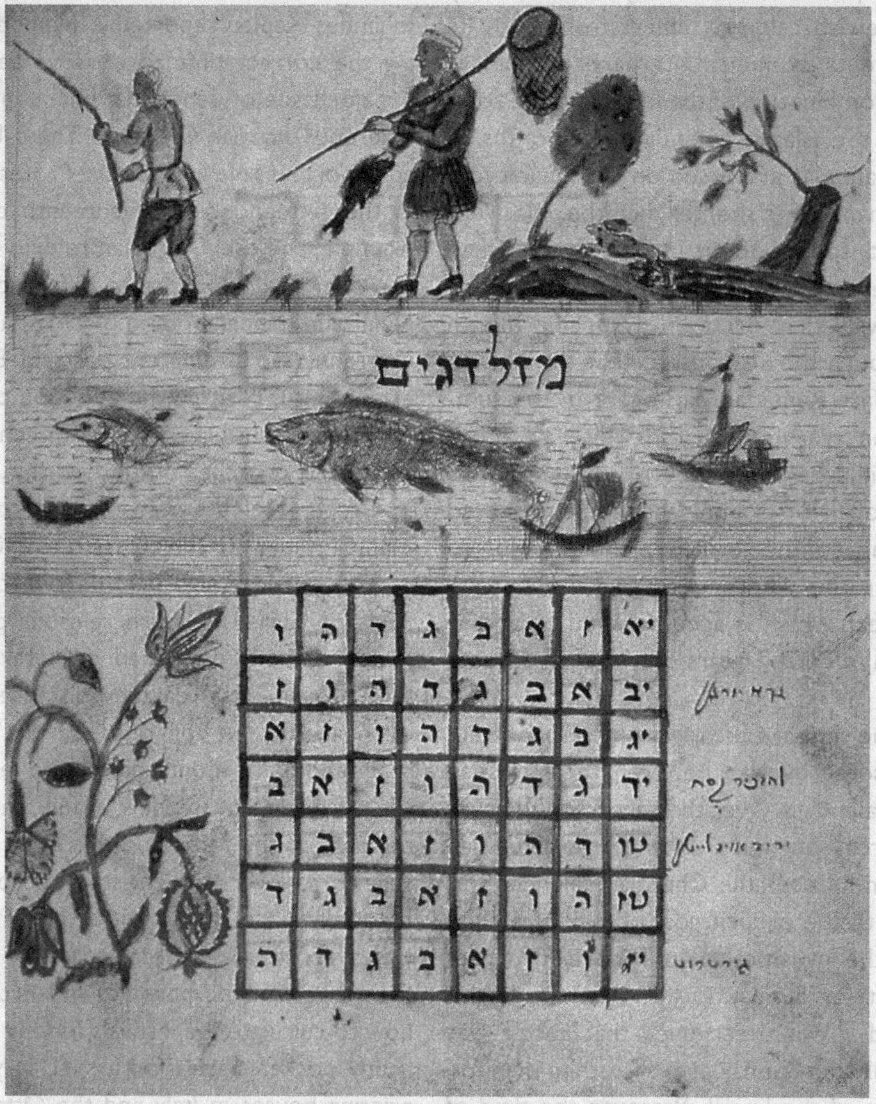

Figure 9.1 Page from a Hebrew *sefer evronot*, a book on the Jewish calendar, depicting the zodiac sign of Pisces. Halberstadt, Germany, 1716.

> accepted. . . . May the merit of the beloved Sabbath lights protect me, just as the beloved Sabbath protected Adam and kept him from premature death. So may we merit, by lighting the candles, to protect our children, that they may be enlightened by the study of Torah, and may their planets shine in the heavens so that they may be able to earn a decent living for their wives and children.

(On Jewish women in early modern Germany, *see the box* "'Glickl of Hameln' and Her *Zikhroynes*.")

The Thirty Years' War (1618–1648), Mercantilism, and the Rise of the "Court Jews"

As we discussed in Chapter 8, the impact of the Protestant Reformation, and the Catholic Counter-Reformation, on the fate of the Jews was ambiguous. No longer were the Jews the only religious minority in the Christian lands of western Europe (eastern Europe had always been more diverse, as we have seen in the case of Poland-Lithuania). The schism between Catholics and the various sects of Protestantism would, at times, divert attention from the Jews. In England or Holland, and later in colonial North America, the prime targets of religious suspicion by Protestant regimes were Catholics, whereas Jews were seen as a lesser evil or even with sympathy. On the other hand, the expulsion of Jews from territories in German-speaking lands continued in the age of Reformation, and Luther's own anti-Jewish pronouncements are notorious. The Counter-Reformation of the Catholic Church beginning in the 1550s, in turn, led to increased antisemitism as well. As we have seen, a campaign against the Talmud began in 1553, and in 1555, Pope Paul IV segregated the Jews of Rome into a ghetto and resumed the persecution of former conversos in the papal port city of Ancona.

Between 1618 and 1648, a cruel war ravaged central Europe, with the German-speaking lands of the Holy Roman Empire as the main battleground. The battles of the war and the ensuing famines and epidemics devastated entire regions, and the death toll ascended to one-half or two-thirds of the population in certain areas. The Thirty Years' War was, in part, a religious war between Catholic and Protestant forces, but it also was a war over political hegemony in Europe, pitting the Habsburgs of Austria and Spain against France, the Netherlands, Denmark, and Sweden.

The Jews of the empire generally fared better than did their Christian neighbors. One Frankfurt rabbi observed the following:

> We have seen with our own eyes and heard with our own ears that the living God dwells in our midst, even standing by us in wondrous ways. . . . The soldiers, for years now on march through the towns and villages, have often treated us more kindly than the non-Jews, so that Gentiles have sometimes brought their belongings to Jews for safekeeping.

After the crushing in 1620 of the rebellion of the Bohemian Protestants—which had triggered the initial conflagration—the city of Prague was pillaged by imperial troops, with the notable exception of the Jewish ghetto. In fact, houses owned by Protestants adjacent to the ghetto were confiscated and made available for purchase by Jews, finally alleviating the crowded conditions of the Prague Jewish quarter. This preferential treatment of the Prague Jews was no coincidence, of course: Jacob Bassevi (d. 1634), one of their leading figures, became one of the most important financiers of the war and thus rendered important services to the Habsburg war effort.

Throughout the empire, Jewish financiers and provisioners emerged as a crucial factor in the war. Jews actually benefited from their role as outsiders since they were seen as neutral in the religious confrontation between Catholics and Protestants. Most important, they were able to provide exactly the kinds of services (financing and provisioning for the armies fighting the war) that were most needed—a result, to be sure, of the economic roles into which they had been pushed in the course of the Middle Ages, such as moneylending and trade.

With the Swedish invasion of 1630 (the "Swedish war" lasted until 1635), Jews once again were able to provide essential services as financiers and provisioners, this time for the Swedish troops. It seems that the Swedes generally treated the Jews better than others—no doubt because they were relying on their services. Nonetheless, after the defeat of the Swedes, the favorable treatment of the Jews at the hands of the Habsburg emperor continued. A new Jewish elite of financiers and provisioners emerged, working on both sides of the war. Surprising as it may seem, the Jewish population appears to have remained stable, and some communities actually grew during this time.

No decisive victory having been achieved by either side, the Thirty Years' War ended with the Peace of Westphalia in 1648. Recognizing the need for religious tolerance after 30 years of bloodshed and devastation, the new order also benefited the Jews as a religious minority, albeit indirectly. Moreover, the prominent role of individual Jewish financiers and provisioners was not forgotten after the war was over. From the 1650s on, we see the rise to prominence of the so-called court Jews (*Hofjuden* in German), individuals who provided essential services to the rulers of the numerous German states in the postwar order. Arguably the most prominent one was Samuel Oppenheimer of Heidelberg (1630–1703), who organized, for example, the Austrian defense against the Ottoman siege of Vienna in 1683.

Still, the situation of European Jewry remained precarious at times. Under pressure from the local burghers, the Austrian emperor decided to expel the Jews from Vienna in 1670 (Samuel Oppenheimer was the first Jew to settle in Vienna after this last expulsion). A number of wealthy Jewish families from Vienna found a new home in Berlin, where Frederick William of Hohenzollern (1640–1688) invited them to settle. When these Viennese Jews established themselves in Berlin in 1671, they laid the foundations of what became one of the most important Jewish communities in the following two centuries. Frederick William's reasons for inviting the Jews from Vienna were mainly economic and marked a new policy vis-à-vis the Jews guided by pragmatic considerations rather than religious ideology. Recognizing their potential contribution to the reconstruction of his country after the devastation of the Thirty Years' War, the Prussian monarch encouraged the settlement of various religious minorities that would bring much-needed skills to his country. The number of Viennese Jews moving to Berlin—about 50 families—pales, to be sure, in comparison to the 20,000 or so Huguenots (French Protestants) who were taken in during the 1680s, but it did mark a new beginning.

If the previous trend of expulsion and dislocation of the Jews from west to east was reversed in the seventeenth century, it was due primarily to a new primacy of economic considerations in state politics: the rise of mercantilism. Thinking in terms of mercantilism, the wealth of a nation depends on the supply of capital and considers trade to be something of a zero-sum game in which the profit of one side means a loss for the other. As European rulers of the early modern period, in particular in the wake of the Thirty Years' War, sought to consolidate their power, the politics of mercantilism went hand in hand with a quest for expanding the role of the state. Raison d'état, the interest of the state, increasingly gained primacy over other—namely, religious—considerations.

An early example of the politics of mercantilism and the new attitude toward Jews could be

"GLICKL OF HAMELN" AND HER *ZIKHROYNES*

Glickl bas Judah Leib (often referred to as "Glickl of Hameln," after her first husband) was born in Hamburg in 1646. Following the death of her husband, Hayim, in 1689, she began to pen her memoirs (*Zikhroynes*), a unique document, written in Yiddish, that opens a window onto everyday Jewish life in the early modern period, told from a woman's perspective. Eleven years later, she moved to Metz, home of her second husband, where she died in 1724. Writing one's memoirs was in itself a new phenomenon among Jews in the seventeenth century. Memoirs suggest yet another feature of Jewish modernity emerging at that time: a sense of self and individuality, a sense that one's own experiences and sensibilities were relevant, even though they continued to be expressed, by Glickl and others, within the confines of Jewish tradition.

The passage that follows illustrates several aspects of Glickl's world: the constant presence of death; the nature of Jewish–gentile relations, showing how their respective worlds overlapped (e.g., in business transactions) but also remained apart (note the role of language); and insights into the popular culture of early modern Jews, with a dead person in this story appearing to others in their dreams, something that is simply taken as a fact.

> [My father] was already a widower when he became engaged to my mother. For fifteen years he had been married to . . . Reize, who maintained a large and fine house. . . . [A] previous marriage had blessed her with a daughter, beautiful and virtuous as the day is long. The girl knew French like water. Once this did my father a mighty good turn. My father, it seems, held a pledge against a loan of 500 Reichsthaler he had made to a nobleman. The gentleman appeared at his house one day, with two other nobles, to redeem his pledge. My father gave himself no concern, but went upstairs to fetch it, while his stepchild sat and played at the clavichord to pass away the time for his distinguished customers. The gentlemen stood about and began to confer with one another in French. "When the Jew," they agreed, "comes down with the pledge, we'll take it without paying and slip out." They never suspected, of course, that the girl understood them. However, when my father appeared, she suddenly began to sing aloud in Hebrew, "Oh, not the pledge, my soul—here today and gone tomorrow!" In her haste the poor child could blurb out nothing better. My father now turned to his gentlemen. "Sir," he said, "where is the money?" "Give me the pledge!" cried the customer. But my father said, "First the money and then the pledge." Whereupon our gentlemen spun about to his companions. "Friends," he said, "the game is up—the wench, it seems, knows French"; and hurling threats they ran from the house. . . . My father raised the child as though she were his own. And eventually he married her off. She made an excellent match . . . but she died in her first childbirth. Soon after, her body was robbed and the shroud taken from her. She revealed the outrage to someone in a dream; the body was exhumed and the robbery confirmed.
>
> (Glickl, *Zikhroynes*, Book 1, Chapter 2)

found in Italy. As we have seen in Chapter 8, the Senate of Venice acquiesced to the presence of Jews in the city because of their perceived economic benefit. Also, the Grand Duke of Tuscany, Ferdinand I, considered the potential economic benefits of Jews and new Christians if they were to settle in his territory, and in 1593, he granted a charter, known as "La Livornina," which declared that "none shall be able to make any inquisition, inquiry, examination or accusation against [Jews and new Christians] or [their] families, although living in the past outside [the Duke's] Dominion in the guise of Christians"—a hardly veiled invitation to former conversos to settle in the Tuscan cities of Livorno and Pisa without having to fear the Inquisition. Ferdinand's move proved to be a great success, and by the eighteenth century, Livorno had become not only one of the largest Sephardi communities in western Europe but also the preeminent port city of Italy and a major commercial hub.

The argument of the economic benefits derived from Jewish settlement and immigration was employed by Jewish leaders as well. Daniel Rodriga, a Jew of Portuguese converso origin, successfully lobbied the Venetian government in the 1570s and convinced it to actively invite former conversos to come and live openly as Jews in Venice, without having to fear the Inquisition. His argument was that this would help Venetian commerce with the Ottoman Empire. In the following century, in 1638, Simone Luzzatto (c. 1583–1663)—highly respected by both Christians and Jews in Venice—published his influential *Discorso circa il stato de gl'hebrei* (*Discourse on the State of the Jews*), probably the first systematic treatment of the role of the Jews in international trade, wherein he made the case for the economic usefulness of the Jews to the European states.

In central Europe, it was after the religious stalemate and disillusionment of the Thirty Years' War that a class of court Jews rose to prominence and rulers throughout western Europe began to reconsider and reverse their earlier exclusionist policy vis-à-vis the Jews. Monarchs like Frederick of Prussia encouraged the establishment of Jewish communities in cities throughout Germany, based on the perceived utility of the court Jews and the hope that these Jews, with their international connections and expertise in commerce, would attract trade to their territories (*see the box* "Rich and Poor").

Questions of Identity: Conversos and the "Port Jews" of the Atlantic World

Balthazar de Orobio, born in Portugal around 1617 to a family of conversos, was apprehended by the Inquisition in 1656. In 1662, he immigrated to the Dutch port city of Amsterdam, where he changed his name to Isaac. He explained his background:

> [In Spain] I presented a Christian appearance, since life is sweet; but I was never very good at it, and so it came out that I was in fact a Jew. If, then, whilst I was there, confronted with the risk of [loss of my] freedom, status, property, and indeed life itself, I was in reality a Jew and a Christian merely in outward appearance, common sense shows that in a domicile where Providence from above affords me a life of freedom, a true Jew is what I shall be.

Orobio was born some 120 years after the forced conversion of the Jews in Portugal in 1497. Like him, a large number of these forced converts and their descendants retained a sense of Jewishness in spite of their outward adherence to Christianity. Such a large number of conversos sought to leave Portugal that the Portuguese Crown banned emigration between 1499 and 1507, and again between 1532 and 1538, in the meantime establishing an Inquisition in 1536. The ferocious campaign of the Inquisition proved to be counterproductive. Even more than a genuine desire to return to Judaism, it was the persecution at the hands of the Inquisition that pushed an increasing number of Portuguese conversos to leave their country and establish, from the late sixteenth through the end of the seventeenth century, a diaspora of former conversos.

One of the more unlikely destinations of the Portuguese converso immigration from 1580 (when Spain annexed Portugal) until the 1640s was Spain. There, the Portuguese "new

Christians" still had to live under the guise of Catholicism, but they were safe from the Portuguese Inquisition, which had no jurisdiction over them in Spain. Especially under the Count of Olivares as head of the Spanish government, Portuguese conversos settling in Madrid assumed a leading role as bankers and tax farmers in Spain, and their connections to Portuguese conversos elsewhere in Spain, Portugal, and their colonies in the New World helped them play an important role in trade as well. In the early 1600s, a Spanish official in the province of Guipúzcoa complained that "since these people have entered this region, they have usurped the business and the profits of its natives, in the shipments made to Seville and to the Indies." Historians estimate that some 10,000 Portuguese conversos immigrated to Spain, settling in such places as Madrid, Seville, and Malaga, in those years; others established themselves in the Spanish colonies of Peru and Mexico. However, the downfall of Olivares in 1643 prompted a major backlash against the Portuguese conversos in Spain; Portugal had regained its independence from Spain three years earlier, whereas in Mexico the Inquisition renewed its persecution in the years after 1642.

RICH AND POOR

The prominence of individual court Jews in Germany or Jewish merchants in Venice and Amsterdam should not lead us to think that most early modern Jews were wealthy—they were not. Like the Christian or Muslim societies around it, Jewish society was stratified and divided into social classes, with the wealthy representing a very small percentage and the vast majority being poor. Though estimates for this period are necessarily imprecise, the image that emerges is rather consistent throughout the Jewish world: Jewish communities most everywhere were impoverished in the course of the sixteenth and seventeenth centuries, leading to social tensions within the communities and conflicts with non-Jewish neighbors. During the fifteenth century, the percentage of underprivileged Jews in German lands rose from 25 to over 50 percent; in the mid-1700s, as much as two-thirds of the Jews in Germany were poor. At the end of the eighteenth century in the city of Amsterdam, the largest and one of the wealthiest Jewish communities of western Europe, about 80 percent of the Ashkenazi Jews and 50 percent of the Sephardi Jews received public assistance. The situation was not much different in the Ottoman Empire, where poverty increased in the course of the seventeenth century and the poor made up between one-half and three-quarters of the Jewish communities.

The situation was aggravated by the arrival of large numbers of Jewish refugees from eastern Europe in the wake of the Thirty Years' War and the Chmielnicki massacres of the mid-seventeenth century. The poorest of the poor, known in German as *Betteljuden* ("beggar Jews"), were forced to move from one town to another and ask for temporary shelter and food. The Christian author Johann Buxtorf noted in his book *Synagoga Judaica* (1603):

> Where there is a man who suffers from noticeably great poverty, his rabbis, who know him, give him a begging-letter, in which they document his want and poverty; they demonstrate also that he is pious and of the Jewish faith, etc.

Equipped with such a letter of recommendation, the itinerant poor would roam the Jewish communities, which gave out tickets for a limited number of days for lodging and food in the home of a community member, after which the beggar Jew was expected to move on.

The vagrant poor were often associated in the popular imagination with crime, and indeed, Jewish

RICH AND POOR (CONTINUED)

banditry was on the rise in seventeenth-century Germany. There were all-Jewish robber bands—observing the Sabbath rest and traditional dietary laws—as well as associations between Jewish and Christian criminals. In terms of the numbers, where they are available, crime rates among Jews in early modern Germany did not differ much from those of the Christian majority, but from the 1600s on, a new anti-Jewish stereotype emerged that identified Jews (namely, the poor *Betteljuden*) with crime and gangsterism. The stereotype survived into modern antisemitic prejudice even though, in the age of emancipation, actual crime rates among Jews decreased dramatically and generally compared favorably with those of the general population.

Traditional Jewish society had long practiced charity to relieve the suffering of its poor. Codes of Jewish law, whether the writings of the medieval philosopher Maimonides or the sixteenth-century *Shulhan Arukh*, included detailed laws concerning the giving of charity (*tsedakah*). In the early modern period, Jewish communities had to deal with growing poverty that led to an expansion of the traditional modes of poor relief. Various charitable societies provided dowries for poor and orphaned girls, redeemed captives, sent money to the poor communities of the Holy Land, provided medical care, and buried the dead. Ottoman Jewry in particular developed an elaborate system of poverty relief, funded by the community taxes paid by the wealthy and the middle class. At the same time, Ottoman rabbis perpetuated the traditional belief that poverty was a divinely ordained fate and a necessary feature of human life, and that the community could only try to alleviate the suffering, not change the basic realities of social inequality.

It was first among the Sephardi communities of the West—namely, in Amsterdam—that a new—one might say, modern—approach to providing support for the poor developed. In response to the large influx of poor Ashkenazi Jews from Germany and Poland, the Sephardi leadership in Amsterdam grew anxious about the financial burden this imposed on the community—and about the negative consequences of rampant poverty for the image of the Jews in gentile society. A new approach developed there that began to consider poverty as not only an economic problem but also a moral one. This, in turn, spearheaded the emergence of a modern Jewish philanthropy that sought not just to assist the poor but also to eradicate poverty.

As the sixteenth century came to a close, the Portuguese conversos discovered new roads of emigration. Some settled in southwestern France, where they were tolerated and could even practice Judaism without being disturbed by the Inquisition, but they continued to be regarded officially as Christians until the eighteenth century. In other places—namely, in Amsterdam and Hamburg, as well as in the Italian port cities of Venice and Livorno—they found an environment that allowed them to openly return to Judaism and establish their own new Jewish communities. Converso immigration to Hamburg, Amsterdam, and Livorno began in the 1590s. By the end of the seventeenth century, the latter two communities—Amsterdam and Livorno—were the largest communities of Portuguese Jews, each exceeding 3,000 souls. Other communities were established by Portuguese Jews, as we shall see, in London, in the Caribbean, and eventually, in North America. Between 850 and 1,000 Portuguese Jews from Amsterdam were active in Dutch Brazil (in the Recife area, from 1630 until the Portuguese recaptured the region in 1654), and at the end of the seventeenth century, some 625 Portuguese Jews lived in Curaçāo, 400 in Jamaica, 300 in Barbados, and just 75 in New Amsterdam (later called New York).

The community in Amsterdam is clearly the best studied, in part because of the wealth of the archival material that is available to historians, and in part because of the importance of Amsterdam as the foremost center of world trade in the seventeenth century. In fact, it was its economic possibilities as much as the religious freedom it promised that attracted Portuguese conversos to settle in Amsterdam in the first place. Having only recently thrown off Spanish rule, the politics of the newly independent Protestant Netherlands were marked by religious tolerance that extended to the conversos who wished to return to Judaism, and obviously they were at a safe distance from the Catholic Inquisition. But the main reason the conversos were attracted to Amsterdam and similar locations in the Atlantic world, and the reason the local authorities were willing to accept the influx of this population, was the growing economic role played by the Portuguese Jewish and converso Diaspora in international commerce.

The main circuits of the Portuguese trading Diaspora linked Amsterdam with Portugal and Spain, where the former conversos continued to have extensive contacts, and across the Atlantic, linking Amsterdam, London, and Hamburg with the Spanish colonies and the non-Spanish territories of the Caribbean. When Surinam became the main source of Dutch sugar imports, Portuguese Jews from Amsterdam played a significant role in its colonization. In 1730, 115 of the 400 plantations in Surinam were owned by Jews. In 1639, Jews established the first synagogue of the Western Hemisphere in the township known as Joden Savanne ("Jews' Savannah").

The Amsterdam Jews were engaged prominently not only in the Dutch Atlantic trade and the importation of colonial goods but also in related crafts—for example, operating sugar refineries, tobacco workshops, workshops cutting and polishing diamonds, and chocolate-making facilities. They were also successful as brokers in the Amsterdam stock exchange. In 1657, a full 10 percent of the brokers at the Amsterdam stock exchange, described in colorful detail by a Sephardi author in *Confusión de confusiones* (1688), were Jewish. This book draws a picture of a gambling elite of Portuguese Jews, loving life, pleasure, and luxury—an image perpetuated by many rabbis denouncing the laxity in religious observance among the wealthy Sephardi merchants of Amsterdam and other such communities in the West.

The description of the Amsterdam Jewish quarter by a (non-Jewish) German visitor, Philipp von Zesen, in a book that reads like the early modern version of a travel guide (published in 1664), contrasts with the bleak image of the crowded Jewish quarters in other European cities and attests to the wealth of the Amsterdam Sephardim in the seventeenth century:

> [We get to] the *Breite Gasse* ["wide street"] in which there are living mostly Jews who came here from Portugal, and some from Spain, many years ago because they were persecuted. This street, adorned with beautiful buildings, is wide (as the name suggests) and leads straight to the Anthon watergate. It has two side streets on each side. . . . Between the second side street and the Mont-Albansgraft there the Portuguese Jews have their school and their Temple, or the big Jewish church [i.e., the synagogue], which was created by joining two houses and which has two entrances. . . . One goes up on a wide staircase on both sides up to the church [the synagogue] where there is always light lit in glass lamps and, during the high holidays, in precious silver chandeliers. In the middle [of the synagogue] stand the teachers [i.e., the rabbi and cantor]. . . . Around them sit or stand the other men, with Hebrew books in their hands and with a white cloth over their hat, hanging

> down their back [i.e., wrapped in the *tallit*, or prayer shawl]. The women are separate from the men, up on the balcony behind a lattice fence. Behind the wooden benches one sees a large wooden wardrobe [i.e., the ark in the front of the synagogue]. . . . In there they keep many precious objects, among others the books of Moses wrapped in artfully designed covers [i.e., the Torah scrolls].

Less than ten years after von Zesen's visit, in 1675, the Portuguese Jews of Amsterdam opened a new, magnificent synagogue, which became a popular tourist destination for both Jewish and non-Jewish visitors and which exists to this day.

Alluding to the particular setting in which these communities of former conversos found themselves, historians have called them communities of port Jews who were distinguished by their engagement in international commerce, their social integration into the surrounding society, and their sometimes rather secular orientation. The Portuguese "port Jews" of Amsterdam, Hamburg, or London are sometimes described as "the first modern Jews," for a number of reasons. To begin, this was the first Jewish community ever that had to completely "reinvent" its Jewish tradition. Unlike those Jews and conversos who had joined existing communities in Italy or the Ottoman Empire, the Portuguese community in Amsterdam, London, and Hamburg was new. When speaking of a "return" to Judaism, we need to remember that the conversos who immigrated to the port cities of northwestern Europe over the seventeenth century had been born into families that had lived as Catholics for generations. They may have had a sense of belonging to the Jewish people and may have been eager to re-embrace Judaism, but they knew little of Jewish traditions and practices and did not, of course, read Hebrew. The ex-conversos in western Europe have therefore been called "the new Jews," as they had to reinvent a tradition that they had lost generations earlier and that the Inquisition had tried to destroy.

Thus, whereas Jews elsewhere in the early modern period absorbed their knowledge of Jewish texts and rituals from their parents and grandparents, the former conversos who immigrated to Amsterdam in the seventeenth century had to learn Judaism from scratch. A rich literature was created by rabbis—many of whom were of converso origin themselves—who addressed their works to an audience of Portuguese Jews who wanted, and needed, to relearn what it meant to live according to rabbinic tradition. In 1609, Moses Altaras published an abridged version of the *Shulhan Arukh* in Spanish, printed in Venice under the title *Libro de mantenimiento de la alma* (*Book of Maintenance of the Soul*). Other such works included Isaac Athias's *Tesoro de preceptos* (*Thesaurus of Precepts*, 1627, in Spanish), *Thesouro dos Dinim* (*Thesaurus of Laws*, 1645–1647, in Portuguese) by Menasseh ben Israel, and Abraham Farrar's *Declaração das seiscentas e treze encomendanças da nossa sancta ley* (*Explanation of the 613 Commandments of Our Holy Law*, 1627, also in Portuguese). Knowledge that traditional society imparted to its children in the family home and in schools was now learned from books, often by adult immigrants, and it was learned from books written in European languages printed in Latin characters (as opposed to Yiddish and Ladino, which were written using the Hebrew alphabet). This was much more similar to the modern-day "how to run a Jewish household" type of practical guides than it was to the traditional mode of Jewish learning.

Though Amsterdam failed to produce luminaries of rabbinic learning of the caliber of the communities in eastern Europe, its educational system proved to be very successful and was showered with praise by a visiting Ashkenazi rabbi from Prague, Shabbatai Sheftel Horowitz, who expressed his admiration of the educational institutions established by the Portuguese Jewish community in Amsterdam in the seventeenth century. Another visitor from eastern Europe,

Shabbatai Bass, visited Amsterdam in 1675 and praised the curriculum of its famous academy, Ets Hayim, which introduced Jewish children gradually and in a systematic way to the teachings of Jewish tradition. The pupils were divided into six levels:

1. Learning how to read the Hebrew prayers
2. Learning how to recite the weekly portion of the biblical text according to its traditional cantillation
3. Studying of the Pentateuch with its classical commentaries
4. Studying of the Prophets and other biblical writings
5. Studying and interpreting Jewish law (Halakhah); studying grammar; studying a different law every day, based on the Talmud; and reviewing the laws of any upcoming festival according to the *Shulhan Arukh*
6. Advancing study of Jewish law, including the medieval commentaries on the Talmud and the major law codes of Maimonides and Joseph Karo

Notable is the systematic structure of the curriculum, with each level building upon the foundations of the previous one, as well as the emphasis on Hebrew grammar and the study of practical Halakhah, rather than the *pilpul* method typical of the eastern European schools that, as we have seen, was criticized for generating ever new subtleties in the interpretation of the Talmud and its commentaries without regard to the meaning of the text or its practical application. In the Amsterdam model, the influence of European humanism, with its focus on the classical languages (here Hebrew), was combined with the Spanish Jewish tradition of emphasizing grammatical studies and practical Halakhah.

In reality, this dedication to the recreation of a rabbinic tradition for the former conversos of Amsterdam represented only one part of their cultural identity. The Portuguese Sephardim of Amsterdam were eager to provide a Jewish education to their children, but their religious life was focused primarily on the synagogue and the religious calendar of Jewish life. The community tried to ensure that Jewish law—its dietary restrictions, the observance of the Sabbath—was respected and, apparently, was rather successful in its endeavor, but in contrast to other Jewish communities at that time, we find few references in rabbinic writings from Amsterdam that relate to economic life. It seems that Jewish law was not the all-encompassing point of reference that it was in traditional Jewish societies but instead was relegated to the synagogue and religious ritual. The western Sephardim in Amsterdam and elsewhere were thus also the "first modern Jews," because they distinguished between the religious and secular spheres of their individual and collective lives. Their regained Jewish religion was only part of their identity.

Though it might be surprising, given the fact that they had mostly fled Portugal and Spain to escape persecution by the Inquisition, it was precisely a continued sense of belonging to the Portuguese and Spanish culture that sustained the western Sephardim as a distinct group within European Judaism. Their Spanish and Portuguese culture was as much a factor in their self-understanding as was their Jewishness. This can be seen as yet another manifestation of their "modernity": the simultaneous identification with their Jewish origin and religion on the one hand, and general Spanish and Portuguese language, literature, and culture on the other hand.

The Sephardi Jews of Amsterdam and other communities in the west continued to use the Portuguese and Spanish languages as the community was replenished with new arrivals of converso immigrants from Spain and Portugal until the 1720s. Though most were familiar with Dutch, Portuguese remained the spoken language within the community, whereas Spanish was the language of highbrow literature, assuming an almost-sacred character as the language of biblical and liturgical translations used by the western Sephardim. What is more, the Sephardi Jews of the west, unlike their Ottoman counterparts, continued to maintain close contact with the Iberian Peninsula and were an eager audience for the literature of the early modern "golden age" (*siglo de oro*) of Spanish literature, reading the works of Góngora and Quevedo, staging Spanish plays in the Amsterdam theater, and establishing literary academies modeled after the Spanish literary circles of that time (*Academia de los sitibundos* and *Academia de los floridos*, founded in 1676 and 1685, respectively). Many Amsterdam Jews, among them leading rabbis, possessed extensive libraries containing works of European classical and Renaissance literature in the original or in Spanish translation.

Rather than being merely consumers of Spanish and Portuguese culture, Sephardi authors in Amsterdam produced their own literature in the languages of their former homeland. Miguel de Barrios (1635–1701), for example, was born in Spain and returned to Judaism in the Italian city of Livorno. Toward the end of 1662, he came to Amsterdam, though he left shortly thereafter and lived for 12 years, once again under the guise of Christianity, as a captain of the Spanish army in Brussels (part of what continued to be the Spanish Netherlands). He maintained his connection to the Jewish community of Amsterdam, however, and eventually returned there. Daniel Levi de Barrios, as he was known after reverting to Judaism, was a prolific poet and playwright. Some of his works provoked the censure of the local rabbinate. One of his supporters, Rabbi Jacob Sasportas (d. 1698)—among the leading Sephardi rabbis of that time—noted thus about de Barrios:

> [He] wrote poetry in the vernacular and . . . was called a *poeta*. He composed many works of poetry, including a Pentateuch in verse, entitled "Melody of the World," *Harmonia del mundo*, which he had divided into 12 parts each of which he dedicated to a duke, such as the Duke of Livorno, and to the princes of Holland, Portugal, Spain, and England. All of these promised to reward him and sent him their picture, their banner, their coat of arms. . . . I was among those who supported him to get permission to have the book published, while part of the Mahamad [the governing council of the Sephardi community] and most of the rabbis opposed it saying that the book contained phrases which were not in accordance with our Torah and, also, that he transformed our Torah into gentile, secular literature by copying it in verse form.

Sasportas's words testify to how much a former converso intellectual in Amsterdam like Daniel Levi de Barrios saw himself both as a Jew and as part of contemporary European culture. It was this closeness to secular European culture and the far-reaching social and cultural integration of the western Sephardim that made them more "modern" than most of their Jewish contemporaries elsewhere—and it predictably aroused the disapproval of some of their religious leaders. One of them, Rabbi Saul Levi Morteira (d. 1660) of Venice, who had become a leading rabbi in Amsterdam and a critic of its Sephardi community, admonished his listeners in one of his sermons:

> We must strive to carry out Gods will by remaining separate and recognizable and distinct from [the Gentiles] in every respect . . . [so that] whoever sees us will recognize and know and understand the difference between us and the other peoples, since in this land we have no external sign to differentiate us as is the case in all the other lands of our exile. We must therefore establish this differentiation ourselves. We must not imitate the Gentile hairstyle, we must not eat of their foods or drink of their wines. . . . When

> we travel, we must pray and bring *tefillin* [phylacteries, used during the weekday morning prayers] with us, so that all who see us will recognize us.

In another sermon, he thundered:

> What has enabled the last remnant of "the exile of Jerusalem which is in Sefarad" [Obadiah 20—that is, Iberian Jewry] to preserve its identity is their refusal to inter-marry with the Gentiles of the land. This has preserved their lineage and their identity, so that they are not lost to the community of the Eternal. Woe to the one who mixes in with them while still in a Gentile state, before conversion, for he destroys his offspring and his future remembrance.

Morteira's admonition against sexual relations between Portuguese Jews and Christian women suggests a certain religious laxity among at least some of its members. His insistence on the "pure lineage" preserved by the conversos in the Iberian lands that was then endangered through sexual licentiousness points to another issue: the concern among the western Sephardi Jews with maintaining their Iberian pedigree.

Evidently, traditional Judaism did not allow intermarriage (which, in any case, was impossible in the absence of civil marriage prior to the secularization of European law), but the preoccupation with lineage and nobility of descent was a marginal concept in Jewish law, even while it was of great importance to the Sephardim in the west. In a clear departure from Jewish law, in fact, the Sephardim tried to preserve the identity of their Spanish Portuguese Jewish "nation," as they called themselves according to the usage of that time (*natie*, in Dutch, or *nação*, in Portuguese), not only against intermarriage with non-Jews, but also against intermarriage with non-Sephardi Jews—namely, Ashkenazim.

This question became more urgent with a growing influx of Ashkenazi immigrants to western Europe, in particular to cities such as Amsterdam, Hamburg, and London, during the Thirty Years' War and in the wake of the Chmielnicki massacres of the mid-seventeenth century. The Ashkenazim of Amsterdam established their first synagogue in 1649 and maintained their own independent congregation. In 1671, the Sephardi community decided that an Ashkenazi Jewish man who married a Spanish Portuguese girl would not be able to join the Sephardi community; in 1697, they went one step further and declared that a Sephardi man who married a non-Sephardi woman would have to leave the community. Still in 1762, Isaac de Pinto, living in Amsterdam, noted in an open letter to the French philosopher Voltaire that the Portuguese Jews of western Europe

> are scrupulous not to intermingle, not by marriage, nor by covenant, nor by any other means, with the Jews of other nations. . . . The distance between them and their brethren is so great that if a Portuguese Jew dwelling in Holland or England were to marry an Ashkenazic Jewish woman, he would immediately lose all his special privileges: he would no longer be considered as a member of their synagogue, he would have no part in all sorts of ecclesiastical and lay offices, and he would be completely removed from the Nation.

Curiously, it was descent more than religion that determined one's belonging to the Spanish Portuguese Jewish "nation." As Amsterdam Rabbi Menasseh ben Israel noted in his address to Oliver Cromwell, Lord Protector of England, when he praised the advantages of the Jewish people in various countries:

> [W]e see, that not only the Jewish Nation dwelling in Holland, Italy, traffics [i.e., trades] with their own stocks but also with the riches of many others of their Nation, friends, kindsmen and acquaintance, which notwithstanding live in Spain.

That is to say, the members of the "nation" in Amsterdam continued to maintain contacts with family members who still lived in Spain—who were, in other words, still living as Christians and apparently had no intention of abandoning the Iberian Peninsula and returning to Judaism.

At the same time, one of the most well-known and influential charitable organizations maintained by the western Sephardim, the Dotar societies, which provided dowries for poor girls and orphans, established an ethnic, rather than religious, definition of who was eligible for their support. The Venetian *Dotar* society provided that the applicants had to be "poor Hebrew girls, Portuguese or Castilian on the father's or the mother's side"—a definition of ethnic descent, even though in Jewish law it was relevant only that one's *mother* be Jewish. The Amsterdam *Dotar* society founded in 1615 went even further and extended its support also to those conversos still living as Christians in Catholic lands but completely excluded non-Sephardim from its membership or as beneficiaries.

Again, what is strikingly "modern" about this is the ambiguity of Jewish identity as it developed in those ex-converso communities in western Europe. The relatively straightforward definition of *Jewishness* in rabbinic law was now becoming more complicated as cultural-ethnic distinctions irrelevant to Jewish law determined one's being part of the Spanish Portuguese Jewish "nation," while one's *religious* Jewish identity turned out to be only *part* of being a member of the "nation."

In some cases, people even changed their religious identities according to the circumstances—though, to be sure, this was a practice that was not condoned by the leadership of the community. Daniel Levi de Barrios, as we have seen, reverted to the life of a converso after having returned to Judaism for several years. Other examples are rather striking, like the case of a certain Abraham Righetto, who acted as a Christian when he was in Antwerp or Florence and as a Jew when he was in Padua or Ferrara. When he was living in Venice, it was reported that he would walk the streets of the city while alternating the yellow hat of the Jews and a black hat that he kept under his arm, depending on the circumstances.

Some more radical examples of deviation serve as counterpoint to the Jewish tradition otherwise successfully re-established by the Amsterdam Sephardim. A few intellectuals of converso origins began to question rabbinic authority and the validity of rabbinic Judaism—even of revealed religion more generally. Uriel da Costa (d. 1640), who was born in Porto and studied theology in the most prestigious Portuguese university at Coimbra, reverted to Judaism after immigrating to Amsterdam in 1615 and soon after moved to Hamburg. There he wrote a treatise challenging rabbinic law (as opposed to biblical law), and he later explained, in an account of his life written shortly before his death:

> Having finished our Voyage, and being arrived at Amsterdam, where we found the Jews professing their Religion with great freedom, as the Law directs them, we immediately fulfilled the Precept concerning Circumcision. I had not been there many Days, before I observed, that the Customs and Ordinances of the modern Jews were very different from those commanded by Moses: Now if the Law was to be strictly observed, according to the Letter, as it expressly declares, it must be very unjustifiable for the Jewish Doctors [i.e., the rabbis] to add to it Inventions of a quite contrary Nature. . . . The modern Jewish Rabbins [rabbis], like their Ancestors, are an obstinate and perverse race of Men. . . . This Situation of Affairs put me upon writing a Treatise in defense of myself, and to prove plainly out of the Law of Moses, the Vanity and Invalidity of the Traditions and Ordinances of the Pharisees [who, he claimed, were the predecessors of the rabbis], and their repugnancy to that Law. . . . Some time after this, as Age and

> Experience are apt to occasion new discoveries to the Mind of Man. . . . I began to question with myself, whether the Law of Moses ought to be accounted the Law of God, seeing there were many Arguments which seemed to persuade, or rather determine the contrary. At last I came to be fully of Opinion, that it was nothing but a human Invention, like many other Systems in the World, and that Moses was not the Writer; for it contained many Things contrary to the Law of Nature.

Da Costa sent his first treatise from Hamburg to Venice, whose rabbis urged the Hamburg community to excommunicate da Costa, which they did in 1618. Five years later, Uriel da Costa returned to Amsterdam and intended to publish a more extensive attack on rabbinic tradition, *Exame das tradições phariseas* (*Examination of Pharisaic* [i.e., rabbinic] *Traditions*). The text opens with a frontal attack on the very foundation of rabbinic Judaism, declaring that "[t]he tradition called the Oral Torah is not a truthful tradition, nor did it originate with the [written] Torah." Da Costa again ridiculed certain Jewish tenets and practices—the phylacteries, circumcision, the prohibition to consume meat and milk together—and added a lengthy argument denying the immortality of the soul. The book was banned by the Amsterdam community's leadership, and until a copy was found in the Copenhagen royal library in the 1980s, it was believed that all traces of da Costa's writing had been successfully destroyed. Excommunicated and socially isolated, da Costa reconciled with the community in a public ceremony in 1633, but seven years later, in 1640, he committed suicide, the exact circumstances of which are unclear.

It is hardly surprising that the Amsterdam community reacted as vigorously as it did to da Costa's challenge: Not only did the rabbis see their authority being challenged openly, but also the very foundations of a community established by former conversos were questioned by one of its own members. Da Costa, however, was not the last one to criticize rabbinic tradition. In 1656, the Amsterdam leadership excommunicated Barukh (Benedict) de Spinoza (1632–1677) for his heretical views (Figure 9.2). In 1670, Spinoza published in Latin his famous *Tractatus theologico politicus*, a pioneering work for modern philosophical and political thought and for modern biblical criticism. What is most relevant in terms of social history, however, is the fact that Spinoza—unlike da Costa—never sought to return to the Jewish community that had expelled him, and he never converted to Christianity either, as other critics of the Jewish tradition had done before him and would do later. Spinoza can be seen as the first-ever secular Jew, one who rejected the religious teachings of traditional Judaism without embracing another religion. Spinoza thus anticipated a form of Jewish identity that was to become a unique feature of the modern Jewish experience.

What needs to be emphasized, though, is that in spite of the ambiguous religious identity of some conversos, and in spite of individuals challenging the very foundations of rabbinic tradition, the Spanish Portuguese Jews of Amsterdam and elsewhere in western Europe integrated with surprising ease into the culture of rabbinic Judaism. Certain individuals may have been torn and struggled with their identity, but the persistence of traditionalism in these communities established by former conversos is probably more remarkable than the occasional ideological dissent or religious laxity. Though the Amsterdam Jews can be called the "first modern Jews" in the sense that their experience foreshadowed some of the dilemmas faced by modern Jews elsewhere in Europe a century or more later, they did not develop an ideology of reform and religious enlightenment. This would happen in the eighteenth century in Germany. Dissenters could be found among the Amsterdam Jews, but in general, their unique fusion of Jewish and Iberian culture was still a rather conservative one.

Figure 9.2 Barukh (Benedict) de Spinoza (1632–1677), the first modern Jewish intellectual—and one of the great philosophers and political thinkers of the seventeenth century.

In certain ways, the new Sephardi Portuguese communities in England and in the New World were a more radical example of those trends of modernity that we see in Amsterdam. Jews had been expelled from England in 1290 by Edward I. In the 1630s, a number of converso merchants established themselves in England, where they continued to live as Christians.

As radical Protestant puritans advocated for a return of Jews to England—believing that England had an important role to play in the conversion of the Jews who would be attracted finally to Christianity in its "purified" Protestant form, as opposed to Catholicism—Menasseh ben Israel, an Amsterdam rabbi, likewise began to labor for a return of Jews to England. He believed that prior to the final redemption, the prophecy had to be fulfilled that Jews would be scattered "from one end of the earth to the other" (Deuteronomy 28:64), and it was England that still had no Jewish community and

THE LOST TRIBES OF ISRAEL

When the Assyrians captured and destroyed the northern kingdom of ancient Israel in 722 BCE, they led the ten tribes making up its population into captivity. For centuries, the Jewish imagination was sparked by speculations over what had become of those "lost tribes." It was already stated in biblical prophecy (i.e., Ezekiel 37:19–24) that the "return" of the lost tribes was tied to the final redemption of the Jewish people. According to the myth that developed over time, the ten "lost tribes" lived in a mythical Israelite kingdom beyond a river called "Sambation"—a river flowing with rocks and sand that stopped running every Sabbath, and from beyond which the lost tribes would return to join their Jewish brethren in the days of the Messiah.

Throughout the centuries, Jewish and Christian writers and travelers were intrigued by the legend of the lost tribes. In the Middle Ages, the most famous case was the traveler Eldad ha-Dani (ninth century), who claimed that he hailed from the tribe of Dan, now living in Ethiopia, and who told of other tribes living in Africa, Arabia, and Asia.

The fascination with the myth of the ten tribes grew in the early modern age—the era of European discoveries. As Europeans encountered new and unknown lands and peoples to the east and west, and in particular following the European arrival in the Americas in 1492, the legend of the ten tribes became a favorite model to explain hitherto completely unknown cultures and to link foreign peoples to something familiar. The Christian Venetian traveler Marco Polo (d. 1324), for example, reported that Jewish kingdoms existed in the distant Orient. In 1644, Aaron Levi de Montezinos (d. c. 1650), a converso, returned to Amsterdam from South America and claimed that he had been greeted by a group of natives in Ecuador with the *Shema Israel* prayer. One of the most prominent Sephardi rabbis in Amsterdam at that time, Menasseh ben Israel, published a treatise, first in Spanish, and then in Latin and English translations, under the title *The Hope of Israel*. In this book, he reported on Montezinos's findings and argued that these Native Americans were descendants of the lost tribes and that their discovery hailed the dawn of messianic times. The age of discovery spawned many such accounts among both Jewish and Christian observers. Exotic lands were identified with the mythical kingdom of the ten tribes, and numerous peoples—from the English to Native Americans to the Japanese and the Pashtuns of Afghanistan—were at some point believed to be descendants of the lost tribes.

In the middle of the sixteenth century, David Reuveni (d. c. 1538) aroused messianic hopes when he claimed that he hailed from the kingdom of the lost tribes and that he had been sent to forge an alliance to fight the Ottoman Turks and hasten redemption. Reuveni was received by Pope Clement VII, and his subsequent visit to the king of Portugal (1525–1527) generated much excitement and messianic hopes among the conversos of that country. One of them, Diogo Pires (d. 1532), secretary in the council of the Portuguese king, was so taken with Reuveni's claims that he decided to return to Judaism, circumcised himself, and adopted the name Solomon Molho. He made his way to the Ottoman Empire, where he studied with several renowned kabbalists and eventually came to believe that he was the Messiah. Even though he was sought by the Inquisition as a renegade converso, Molho went to Italy, where he made a huge impression on the pope, who was awed by his prophetic predictions of a flood in Rome and an earthquake in Portugal. Reuveni and Molho met their end when they joined to visit the Holy Roman Emperor Charles V to convince him of their messianic mission and the impending intervention of the ten lost tribes in the final struggle before redemption.

The myth of the lost tribes and the emergence of prophetic-messianic figures such as Reuveni and Molho were signs of the upheavals of the early modern era as an era of discovery and acute messianic expectations among Jews and Christians alike. The myth of the lost tribes helped early modern Jews, and Christians, to understand the changing world around them—to insert the exotic features of a new world into the familiar patterns of biblical history and prophecy.

was known in medieval Jewish writings as *katseh ha-arets*, "the end of the earth" (*see the box* "The Lost Tribes of Israel").

In 1655, Menasseh ben Israel headed to London with a pamphlet he had written in praise of Jewish virtues and their beneficial impact on the economy and in refutation of several common antisemitic accusations. He wanted to convince Oliver Cromwell (d. 1658), Lord Protector of the English Commonwealth, to readmit the Jews to England. Cromwell favored this move and convened an assembly—known as the Whitehall Conference—of merchants, lawyers, and clergy to discuss the proposal. Due to the opposition of the most conservative clergy and the merchants, fearing a new rival in Jewish commercial networks, the proposal failed. However, as England went to war with Spain in 1655, a number of conversos who were still subjects of the Spanish Crown found it expedient to dissociate themselves from England's wartime foe and commercial rival and began to present themselves in public as refugees from Spanish persecution—and as Jews. Their request for permission to gather privately for Jewish worship and for a Jewish burial place was granted by the government, and thus, without much fanfare and without a formal charter allowing the Jews to return to England, the first Jewish community of modern England was born.

This London community, which attracted more former conversos and, eventually, other Jews from abroad, was among the first communities established on an entirely voluntary basis. As such, it lacked the disciplinary authority and the legal autonomy of the traditional Jewish community, which was the basis for Jewish life almost everywhere else at that time. In this sense, as in the relative lack of religious observance and the continuing ambiguity of many of these former conversos vis-à-vis rabbinic tradition, the London community, like the new communities established in the European colonies of the New World, anticipated much of what became a cornerstone of the modern Jewish experience. As historian Todd Endelman has argued, "[w]hat bound the community [of London] together in its first half century or so was less an allegiance to Jewish practice than kinship, a shared past, and a common language and cultural outlook." At the same time, it was ironic that the failure to adopt a formal charter to readmit the Jews at the Whitehall Conference opened a new and much less torturous path toward emancipation for English Jewry later, as they had never been subject to a formal set of laws defining, and restricting, their legal status.

The first Jews to establish a permanent presence in North America arrived in September 1654 in what was then the Dutch colony of New Amsterdam—a city that later, after the English took control in 1664, was renamed New York. These 23 Jewish immigrants arrived from northern Brazil, where they had settled when the area was a Dutch colony. With the Portuguese defeat of the Dutch in 1654, the Jews—many of whom were former conversos who had returned to Judaism once they were beyond the reach of the Inqui sition—had to abandon the colony. Most found a new home elsewhere in the Caribbean or went back to Holland, but a small number ventured farther north.

Most of the new arrivals were Sephardi Jews of Spanish and Portuguese descent, and throughout the seventeenth and eighteenth centuries, all American synagogues followed the Sephardi rite and traditions. However, even among the first Jewish immigrants in 1654 were a number of Ashkenazi Jews, who were joined, in the following decades, by more Ashkenazi immigrants. They eventually came to represent the majority of American Jewry, yet for a while, they continued to be integrated into the existing Sephardi congregations. The establishment of a joint

Sephardi–Ashkenazi Jewish community in New York and elsewhere in colonial North America was different from the practice in most European cities, where members of the two major Jewish groups maintained separate synagogues and avoided mingling with each other.

The initial welcome in Dutch New Amsterdam was frosty; the governor, Peter Stuyvesant, tried to have the Jews removed from his colony but had to give in to the Dutch West India Company, which had decided that the Jews were to be tolerated. The trading company did so in part under the influence of the prosperous Jewish community back in Amsterdam, but most importantly because of pragmatic considerations that guided both the Dutch and English in their policy toward the Jews: Whatever was good for the colony's wealth trumped traditional religious hostility against the Jews. Seeing as assets the Jews' family and commercial ties that spanned the Atlantic world—especially those of the Sephardim—the English chose to be more tolerant toward the Jews in their colonies than they were in England. The naturalization law for the colonies of 1740 opened naturalization to all Protestants and Jews residing at least seven years in the colonies, creating a legal status for the Jews that they would not enjoy anywhere in Europe until at least 50 years later.

By the eve of the American Revolution, five Jewish communities existed in North America, all on the Atlantic Seaboard and connected in numerous ways with communities in the Caribbean and Europe. In addition to New York, Jews had established communities and synagogues in Philadelphia, Newport, Charleston, and Savannah. The numbers throughout the colonial period remained fairly low (about 100 in New York in 1695, rising to slightly over 240 in 1771), but the Jews had created the basis for what would become, in due course, the largest Jewish community of the modern world.

Figure 9.3 Shabbatai Zvi (1626–1676), the messiah of Izmir. Zvi's appearance as the "messiah" in 1665 generated excitement throughout the Jewish world. The episode effectively ended with his conversion to Islam after the Ottoman authorities grew weary of the phenomenon.

Shabbatai Zvi: A Jewish Messiah Converts to Islam

A startling episode of messianic excitement rocked the Jewish world in the second half of the seventeenth century: In 1665, Shabbatai Zvi (1626–1676) (Figure 9.3), of the Turkish port city of Izmir, was revealed as the Messiah by a young Jewish mystic, Nathan of Gaza (1643–1680). He was not the only false messiah of the early modern age, but his movement was certainly the most successful one, his followers coming from all walks of Jewish society almost everywhere in the Jewish Diaspora.

Shabbatai Zvi, described as manic-depressive by modern scholars, reputedly engaged in a variety of "strange" and "bizarre" acts defying Jewish tradition when he was in Izmir, notably pronouncing the divine name in public (traditionally, only the high priest had been allowed to pronounce the name once a year, on the Day of Atonement, in the holiest part of the Jerusalem Temple). Zvi was married twice, but each time the union had to be annulled because he failed to consummate the marriage. Expelled from Izmir by the community in the early 1650s, he began to wander through Ottoman Greece. During periods of exaltation, Zvi continued to engage in "strange" behavior—for example, when he celebrated the three major festivals of Passover, Shavuot, and Sukkot all in one week. At times, Zvi claimed to be the Messiah and announced that the divine commandments had been abolished, introducing the ironic blessing of "[h]im [God] who permits the forbidden."

In 1662, Shabbatai Zvi settled in Jerusalem, and a year later, he was sent by the Jerusalem community on a fundraising mission to Egypt. There he was married to Sarah, an Ashkenazi girl orphaned during the massacres in the Ukraine in 1648. Raised by Christians, she had returned to Judaism and lived in Amsterdam before she moved to Livorno, Italy. Sarah—whose reputation for promiscuity only added to the scandal—had repeatedly declared that she would marry the Messiah. In 1665, Zvi visited Nathan of Gaza, a Jewish mystic of the Lurianic school, who claimed to have prophetic visions. When Nathan fell into a trance during Shavuot of that year, he publicly declared that Zvi was the Messiah, the latter now reassured in his mission.

Word that Zvi was the Messiah spread like wildfire through the Jewish communities of the Ottoman Empire, to the Sephardi communities of western Europe, and throughout Italy, North Africa, and eastern Europe. Though it was primarily the networks linking the communities of the Sephardi Diaspora that disseminated information about the Sabbatian movement, Ashkenazi Jews were likewise drawn into the excitement. Some sources claim that it had been the prophecy of Sarah, predicting her future marriage to the Messiah, that contributed to the spread of Sabbatian beliefs among Ashkenazi Jews.

Glickl of Hameln (1646–1724), in her seventeenth-century memoir, describes the response to the news about Shabbatai Zvi in Hamburg:

> About this time people began to talk of Shabbatai Zvi. . . . Our joy, when the letters arrived [bringing news about Shabbatai Zvi], is not to be told. Most of them were addressed to the Portuguese [Jews] who, as fast as they came, took them to their synagogue and read them aloud; young and old, the German [Jews] too hastened to the Portuguese synagogue. The Portuguese youth came dressed in their best finery and decked in broad green silk ribbons, the gear of Shabbatai Zvi. "With timbrels and with dances" [Exodus 15:20] they one and all trooped to the synagogue. . . . Many sold their houses and lands and all their possessions, for any day they hoped to be redeemed. My good father-in-law left his home in Hameln, abandoned his house and lands and all his goodly furniture . . . for the old man expected to sail any moment from Hamburg to the Holy Land.

On December 12, 1665, a memorable Sabbath in his hometown of Izmir, after reciting morning prayers in one synagogue, Zvi marched to the Portuguese synagogue accompanied by a large crowd. After beginning to smash the door with an axe, he was finally admitted. Historian Gershom Scholem describes the remarkable scene that followed:

> Shabbetai Zevi [*sic*] read the portion of the Torah not from the customary scroll but from

> a printed copy; ignoring the priests and levites present, he called up to the reading of the Law his brothers and many other men and women [a major innovation, of course, as women were traditionally not actively involved in the public synagogue service], distributing kingdoms to them and demanding that all of them pronounce the Ineffable Name [of God] in their blessings. In a furious speech against the unbelieving rabbis, he compared them to the unclean animals mentioned in the Bible. . . . Then he went up to the ark, took a holy scroll in his arms, and sang an ancient Castilian love song about "Meliselda, the emperor's daughter"; into this song, known as his favorite throughout his life, he read many kabbalistic mysteries. After explaining them to the congregation, he ceremonially proclaimed himself . . . the redeemer of Israel, fixing the date of redemption for the 15th of Sivan 5426 (June 18, 1666). . . . Shabbetai Zevi announced that in a short time he would seize the crown of "the great Turk" [i.e., the Ottoman sultan]. When Hayyim Benveniste, one of the dissenting rabbis present, asked him for proof of his mission, he flew into a rage and excommunicated him, at the same time calling on some of those present to testify to their faith by uttering the Ineffable Name. The dramatic scene amounted to a public messianic announcement and the substitution of a messianic Judaism for the traditional and imperfect one. . . . Besides other innovations in the law, he promised the women that he would set them free from the curse of Eve. Immediately after this Sabbath he dispatched one of his rabbinical followers to Constantinople to make preparations for his arrival.

Zvi was arrested by the Ottoman authorities on his way to the imperial capital, Istanbul, in February 1666. Though imprisoned, he was treated with leniency and transferred to the fortress of Gallipoli, which held important political prisoners. Zvi's detention by no means diminished messianic excitement throughout the Jewish Diaspora. Numerous people from near and far came as pilgrims to visit Zvi. The rabbinate, both in the Ottoman Empire and abroad, continued to be divided between supporters and opponents of the messianic movement, and news about the Messiah continued to be exchanged by both sides with great speed. The excitement reached its height in July and August, but in September the Ottoman authorities grew weary of the messianic agitation and Zvi was brought to Edirne. There, in the presence of the sultan, he was given the choice between facing death or converting to Islam. Throwing his many followers into a profound crisis, Zvi chose to embrace Islam.

Zvi's conversion spelled the end of the Sabbatian movement as a mass phenomenon. Many individuals, including some leading rabbis, however, continued to believe in his messianic mission, interpreting his apostasy as part of the process leading to redemption. Several hundred of his adherents in Salonika even followed his example and converted to Islam, forming a Muslim Sabbatian sect known as the *Dönme*, remnants of which exist in Turkey to this very day.

The success of the Sabbatian movement can be explained by a convergence of several trends of early modern Jewish history: the messianism of the former conversos in western Europe; the impact of the Chmielnicki massacres and influx of Jewish refugees from eastern Europe into western European and Ottoman communities, creating a sense of crisis and promoting messianic expectations; the consequences of print, making possible the fast exchange of information on an unprecedented scale; the impact of Lurianic Kabbalah on an elite of rabbis, many of whom supported the false messiah; and a critique of established rabbinic tradition that was pronounced elsewhere as well and found its expression in Shabbatai Zvi's open challenge of traditional rabbinic law.

Some historians point to this challenge to rabbinic authority as the beginning of "modern"

Jewish history, as if resistance to a traditional status quo was the defining trait of modernity. In truth, it is not easy to pinpoint a single point of transition between pre-modern and modern Jewish history, just as it is difficult to pinpoint a single moment of origin for the Jews. But the developments that unfolded in the seventeenth century, including the settlement of Jews in the Western hemisphere, the initiation of secular thinking in the writing of Spinoza, and the religious destabilization created by the Sabbatean movement, were transformative in their impact, so much so that we can see from our vantage point that they do indeed mark the dawn of a distinct era of Jewish history that is continuing to unfold into the present. For that part of the story of the Jewish people, we invite you to carry on with volume two of this history, an account of how modernity transformed the Jews, and how Jews helped to transform modernity in turn.

For Further Reading

On Ashkenazi Jewry of the period, see Jacob Katz, *Tradition and Crisis* (Syracuse: Syracuse University Press, 2000); on early modern Hebrew book culture, see Joshua Teplitsky, *Prince of the Press* (New Haven: Yale University Press, 2019).

On Poland-Lithuania, see Bernard Weinryb, *The Jews of Poland* (Philadelphia, PA: Jewish Publication Society of America, 1972); Gershon Hundert, *Jews in Poland-Lithuania in the Eighteenth Century* (Berkeley: University of California Press, 2006); Edward Fram, *Ideals Face Reality: Jewish Law and Life in Poland, 1550–1655* (Cincinnati: Hebrew Union College Press, 1997); and Antony Polonsky, *The Jews in Poland Russia, Vol. 1: 1350–1881* (Oxford, England: Littman Library of Jewish Civilization, 2010); on the Chmelnicki crisis, Adam Teller, *Rescue the Surviving Souls: The Great Jewish Refugee Crisis of the Seventeenth Century* (Princeton: Princeton University Press, 2020).

On early modern Germany, see Michael Meyer, ed., *German-Jewish History in Modern Times*, vol. 1 (New York: Columbia University Press, 1996), and Ronnie Po-Chia Hsia and Hartmut Lehmann, eds., *In and Out of the Ghetto* (Cambridge, England: Cambridge University Press, 1995). On the printing of Hebrew calendars and their cultural significance for early modern Jewry, see Elisheva Carlebach, *Palaces of Time: Jewish Calendar and Culture in Early Modern Europe* (Cambridge, MA: Belknap Press of Harvard University Press, 2011).

On Amsterdam and the Atlantic world, see Miriam Bodian, *Hebrews of the Portuguese Nation* (Bloomington: Indiana University Press, 1999); Yosef Kaplan, *An Alternative Path to Modernity: The Sephardi Diaspora in Western Europe* (Leiden, The Netherlands: E. J. Brill, 2000); Daniel Swetschinski, *Reluctant Cosmopolitans: The Portuguese Jews of Seventeenth-Century Amsterdam* (Oxford, England: Littman Library of Jewish Civilization, 2004); on the Dutch colonies, Aviva Ben-Ur, *Jewish Autonomy in a Slave Society: Suriname in the Atlantic World, 1651–1825* (Philadelphia: Penn University Press, 2020).

On North America, see Eli Faber, *A Time for Planting: The First Migration, 1654–1820* (Baltimore, MD: Johns Hopkins University Press, 1992).

On Shabbatai Zvi, see Gershom Scholem, *Sabbatai Sevi: The Mystical Messiah* (Princeton, NJ: Princeton University Press, 1973); Matt Goldish, *The Sabbatean Prophets* (Cambridge, MA: Harvard University Press, 2004).

INDEX

Note: Page numbers in *italics* refer to figures and boxed text.

9781041008026